GINN
Literature Series

Edward J. Gordon
SENIOR AUTHOR

Introduction to Literature
The Study of Literature
Understanding Literature
Types of Literature
American Literature
English Literature

THE STUDY OF LITERATURE

NEW EDITION

RUTH E. REEVES • WILLIAM ELLER
EDWARD J. GORDON

GINN AND COMPANY

Acknowledgments

Grateful acknowledgment is due to the following publishers, authors, and other holders of copyright material for permission to use selections from their publications.

THE ATLANTIC MONTHLY: "Turtle Eggs for Agassiz," by Dallas Lore Sharp. Copyright 1910, by The Atlantic Monthly Company, Boston, Massachusetts 02116.

BASIL BLACKWELL, PUBLISHER: "What Is the Use of Poetry?" from *Poetry for You, A Book for Boys and Girls on the Enjoyment of Poetry*, by C. Day Lewis.

BRANDT & BRANDT: "Wilbur Wright and Orville Wright," by Stephen Vincent Benét, from *A Book of Americans*, by Rosemary and Stephen Vincent Benét, Holt, Rinehart and Winston, Inc. Copyright 1933 by Rosemary and Stephen Vincent Benét. Copyright renewed 1951 by Rosemary Carr Benét. Reprinted by permission of Brandt & Brandt; "The Most Dangerous Game," by Richard Connell. Copyright 1924 by Richard Connell. Copyright renewed 1952 by Louise Fox Connell. Reprinted by permission of Brandt & Brandt.

CURTIS BROWN, LTD.: "Four Years in a Shed," from *Madame Curie* by Eve Curie. Reprinted by permission of Curtis Brown, Ltd. Copyright 1937 by Doubleday & Company, Inc.

F. R. BUCKLEY: "Gold-Mounted Guns," published in *Redbook Magazine*.

M. M. COLE PUBLISHING COMPANY: "The Strawberry Roan," from *American Ballads and Folk Songs*, compiled and collected by John A. and Alan Lomax.

COSMOPOLITAN: "Lou Gehrig—An American Hero," by Paul Gallico.

THOMAS Y. CROWELL COMPANY: "Mother Was There First," from *Belles on Their Toes*, copyright 1950 by the authors, Frank B. Gilbreth, Jr., and Ernestine Gilbreth Carey. Reprinted by permission of the publishers, Thomas Y. Crowell Company, New York.

WARING CUNEY: "Earth-Quake," by Waring Cuney.

THE DIAL PRESS, INC.: "My Dungeon Shook," by James Baldwin. Reprinted from *The Fire Next Time* by James Baldwin. Copyright © 1963, 1962 by James Baldwin and used by permission of the publisher, The Dial Press, Inc.

DODD, MEAD & COMPANY, INC.: "Ring Out, Wild Bells," reprinted by permission of Dodd, Mead & Company from *Bed of Neuroses*, by Wolcott Gibbs. Copyright 1936 by Wolcott Gibbs.

DOUBLEDAY & COMPANY, INC.: "December 2001: The Green Morning." Copyright, 1950, by Ray Bradbury. From *The Martian Chronicles* by Ray Bradbury. Reprinted by permission of Doubleday & Company, Inc.; "A Vagabond Song," by Bliss Carman, from *Golden Numbers, A Book of Verse for Youth*; "Four Years in a Shed" abridged from *Madame Curie* by Eve Curie. Copyright 1937 by Doubleday & Company, Inc. Reprinted by permission of the publisher; "How I Learned to Speak," from *The Story of My Life*, by Helen Keller. Copyright, 1902, 1903, 1905, by Helen Keller. Reprinted by permission of the publisher; "The Ransom of Red Chief." Copyright, 1907, by Doubleday & Company, Inc. From *The Complete Works of O. Henry*. Reprinted by permission of the publisher; "Sasquatch Alias 'Bigfoot'" from *Strange Monsters and Great Searches* by George Laycock. Copyright © 1973 by George Laycock. Reprinted by permission of Doubleday & Company, Inc.; "Galileo, the Stargazer Who Defied the World," from *Living Adventures in Science* by Henry and Dana Lee Thomas. Copyright, 1954, by Doubleday & Company, Inc. Reprinted by permission of the publisher.

THE DRAMATIC PUBLISHING COMPANY: *Twelve Angry Men*, by Reginald Rose, Stage Version by Sherman L. Sergel. Copyright, MCMLV, by Reginald Rose. Based upon the Television Show, *Twelve Angry Men*. All Rights Reserved.

Preface

THE STUDY OF LITERATURE may be said to have a threefold purpose: to awaken students to the traditions and beliefs of their heritage, to develop and enhance their concepts of themselves and of other people, and to increase their understanding, and thus enjoyment, of literature. This anthology is designed to accomplish these aims through guided reading. The selections have been chosen not only for their appeal to the interests and aims of student readers, but also because they illustrate the different methods by which authors achieve their literary aims. A careful reading of *The Study of Literature* will better enable even inexperienced readers to understand and appreciate the best that the world of literature has to offer.

The book is organized so that students proceed step by step to an understanding of literary works. Pages viii-xv introduce students to four of the basic themes that recur throughout the selections in the book—New Ways of Looking at the World, Justice, Courage, Exaggeration. Pages xvi-xx discuss one of the aspects of the reader-writer relationship. Within the anthology itself, there are two introductory units on the elements of fiction—plot and character. The remainder of the units are organized (a) by subject—America in Folklore and Tales, Nature, Science, Sports—and (b) by types—Biography, Drama, and Poetry. This organization provides a varied approach to literature—by theme, element, subject, and type. In addition to the unit introductions, there are notes preceding the selections to stimulate interest and to emphasize the most important literary techniques illustrated by the selection. Following the selections are discussion questions that provoke thought as well as stress comprehension. In addition to frequent vocabulary-building exercises, there are activities, closely related to the selections they follow, which emphasize composition skills. A listing of these composition activities is included on pages xxi-xxiii.

At the end of the book students will find (a) brief biographical sketches of the authors whose works appear in the text, (b) definitions and discussions of the literary terms used in the text, and (c) a glossary of unfamiliar words that students are likely to encounter more and more frequently in their reading. Difficult words that are rarely used, as well as allusions and proper names, appear as footnotes to the text.

Reading the selections in this book, with the unit introductions, the headnotes, the discussion questions, and the supplementary materials, can help students develop their own ideas and ideals, as well as increase their enjoyment of the study of literature.

New Ways of Looking at the World

Writers often compare one thing to another in order to make us see that thing in a special or new way.

Thunder blossoms gorgeously above our heads,
Great, hollow, bell-like flowers,
Rumbling in the wind . . .
> —*from* "Storm Ending"
> JEAN TOOMER

How many of your senses do you use when you see something new?

. . . I was still somewhat blinded from the sheen of tropical sunlight on the water of the bay which we had just crossed in the landing boat, leaving behind us the ship that had brought us from New York lying in the offing. Besides, being only nine years of age at the time and knowing nothing of islands I was busy attending to the alien sights and sounds of Barbados, the unfamiliar smells.
> —*from* "To Da-duh, In Memoriam"
> PAULE MARSHALL

How would your life be different if you lost one of your senses, one of your ways of looking at the world?

No deaf child who has earnestly tried to speak the words which he has never heard —to come out of the prison of silence, where no tone of love, no song of bird, no strain of music ever pierces the stillness— can forget the thrill of surprise, the joy of discovery which came over him when he uttered his first word.

—*from* "How I Learned to Speak"
HELEN KELLER

Some people devote their lives to searching for new ways of looking at the world.

To the scientist there is a nerve-tingling excitement in the chase—the compulsion to reach out for new knowledge—which is both the motivation and the reward.

—*from* "The Unending Quest"
RALPH E. LAPP

Newton saw himself as a child exploring the world with his senses:

> I do not know what I may appear to the world, but to myself I seem to have been only like a boy playing on the seashore and diverting myself in finding now and then a smoother pebble or a prettier shell than ordinary, while the great ocean of truth lay all undiscovered before me.
> —*from* "The Concentrations of Isaac Newton"
> ROBERT STROTHER

In literature you can discover innumerable ways of looking at the universe.

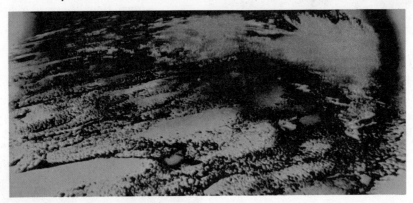

Mars was a place as unpredictable as time. He felt the baked hills simmering down into frosty night, and he thought of the rich, inky soil, a soil so black and shiny it almost crawled and stirred in your fist, a rank soil from which might sprout gigantic beanstalks from which, with boneshaking concussion, might drop screaming giants.
—from *The Martian Chronicles*
RAY BRADBURY

Selections Illustrating the Theme of *New Ways of Looking at the World*

Justice

Democratic justice is a process in which a group judges a person.

The group that judges may be a court,

"Prisoner, hear the sentence of the Court! The Court decides, subject to the approval of the President, that you shall never hear the name of the United States again."
    —from "The Man Without a Country"
    EDWARD EVERETT HALE

a community,

Poor Floyd Ireson, for his hard heart,
Tarred and feathered and carried in a cart
By the women of Marblehead!
    —from "Skipper Ireson's Ride"
    JOHN GREENLEAF WHITTIER

or a society in general.

You were born into a society which spelled out with brutal clarity, and in as many ways possible, that you were a worthless human being . . . if we had not loved each other none of us would have survived. And now you must survive because we love you.
—*from* "My Dungeon Shook"
JAMES BALDWIN

If ye do not feel the chain,
When it works a brother's pain,
Are ye not base slaves indeed,
Slaves unworthy to be freed?
—*from* "Stanzas on Freedom"
JAMES RUSSELL LOWELL

In what sense is every person a judge of self?

Selections Illustrating the Theme of *Justice*

Courage

Is a hero a person who can perform difficult tasks with ease?

Here, he told himself, was a mountain fashioned for an artist's dream: the unclimbed mountain, the unclimbable mountain. Staring up at it, he vowed that it would be his.

—*from* "A Mountain and a Man"
JAMES RAMSEY ULLMAN

Or is a hero a person who gains something by struggling for it?

As he staggered, half-blind in the dim light, to the foot of the hill, he thought of the Athenian runner finishing the first Marathon and, as he collapsed, crying, "Rejoice, we conquer!"
—*from* "Going to Run All Night"
HARRY SYLVESTER

"From the Master of Life descending,
I, the friend of man, Mondamin,
Come to warn you and instruct you,
How by struggle and by labor
You shall gain what you have prayed for.
Rise up from your bed of branches,
Rise, O youth, and wrestle with me!"
—*from* "Hiawatha's Fasting"
HENRY WADSWORTH LONGFELLOW

Does a person have to gain or accomplish something in order for a struggle to be heroic?

Well, son, I'll tell you:
Life for me ain't been no crystal stair.
. . .
But all the time
I'se been a-climbin' on . . .
    —*from* "Mother to Son"
    LANGSTON HUGHES

Is it the way a person struggles what makes him or her heroic? Or is a person heroic simply because of struggling?

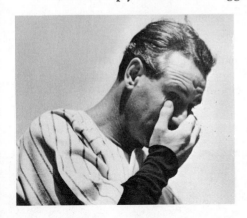

Among the elements that go to make up a hero is the capacity for quiet, uncomplaining suffering; the ability to take it and never let the world suspect that you are taking it.
    —*from* "Lou Gehrig—An American Hero"
    PAUL GALLICO

Selections Illustrating the Theme of *Courage*

Exaggeration

Many people see humor in an exaggerated situation, one which is bigger than life.

(Stabs himself.)
Thus die I, thus, thus, thus.
  Now I am dead,
  Now I am fled;
My soul is in the sky.
  Tongue, lose thy light;
  Moon, take thy flight.
Now die, die, die, die, die! *(Dies.)*
    —*from* "Pyramus and Thisbe"
    WILLIAM SHAKESPEARE

The cookstove . . . covered an acre of ground. They fastened the side of a hog on each snowshoe and four men used to skate on the griddle while the cook flipped the pancakes. The eating table was three miles long; elevators carried the cakes to the ends of the tables . . .
    —*from* "Paul Bunyan of the North Woods"
    CARL SANDBURG

Is exaggeration always funny?

Selections Illustrating *Exaggeration*

The Writer and Literature

A stern but kindly Scottish schoolmaster had been increasingly upset with his students' careless work. Rather than scold them, he decided to let them prove to themselves the error of their ways. Accordingly, the next day he opened the science lesson with "Class, you do not have the powers of observation." His remark was not popular, but he proceeded calmly with his experiment. On a table in full view of the class, he lay a single beaker of colorless fluid. "Watch what I do; then come up and repeat my actions." The teacher dipped a finger in the fluid, brought one to his mouth, tasted it, and smiled. The students thought the request simple-minded, but complied. One by one, they went up to the table, dipped a finger in the beaker, brought it to their mouths, tasted it, but could not smile. Each grimaced as though he had swallowed alum. One prune-faced student finally demanded an explanation for the teacher's smile. Still smiling, the schoolmaster repeated the experiment, this time with a commentary. "You saw what I did, but you did not do as I did. I never tasted the bitter liquid: it never touched my lips. Observe: I dip my middle finger in the liquid, but taste my index finger. Class, you must sharpen your powers of observation."

When a writer is effective, he makes it possible for his audience not only to see something clearly, but also to see that thing as he himself sees it—*his* way. Before he starts writing, then, the writer must decide not only what he is writing, but for what *purpose* and audience. If he wants to entertain, he must know what is amusing to his audience. If he wants to convince, he must know what is important to his audience. If he is writing simply to share a private thought, he must choose unusual, memorable combinations of details. An effective writer must always give common words an uncommon shape.

Notice, for instance, what effect one poet has achieved by pairing observation with imagination:

> The fog comes
> on little cat feet.
>
> It sits looking
> over harbor and city
> on silent haunches
> and then moves on.
> "Fog"
> CARL SANDBURG

Only a person who had intensively trained his powers of observation could imagine and convey such a vivid picture. Such observation rests on carefully noticing one's surroundings and on imaginatively seeing relationships and similarities between things. Sandburg's observation in "Fog" is primarily visual, but the details which help you "see" his poem are supported by other types of details. Implied details, those we fill in because we see the movement of the cat, the fog, and the city harbor, are not primarily visual. We can almost hear the silence. The absence of sound means that aural detail (sound) is important in creating the effect you feel. And aren't your senses of *touch* and *smell* involved with cats and fog? Can't you almost taste the fog? Test how important these implied senses are in this poem. Change one letter: replace the *c* of cat with *r*. . . .

Imaginative observation, then, involves *all* our senses. It may even play tricks with them and create a "sixth sense." This added sense gives us a second type of sight, insight. It helps us see and sense relationships among details. For example, how many of you have ever bothered to think about the sound of thunder? What does it sound like? What does it "look" like? Do you think of it as "just thunder" or as something unusually beautiful, as does the following poet?

> Thunder blossoms gorgeously above our heads,
> Great, hollow, bell-like flowers,
> Rumbling in the wind,
> Stretching clappers to strike our ears . . .
> —*from* "Storm Ending"
> JEAN TOOMER

Thunder is beautiful to Toomer, and because it is so beautiful, he has chosen to describe it with an image for beauty which everyone shares—flowers. His unusual use of a common visual detail to describe what is usually thought of as aural, as a sound, serves to fix his image even more sharply in the reader's mind. But how do writers of longer, more complex, forms of literature—of most prose—use details to describe effectively?

As you read the prose selections, you will notice that many of the study questions ask you to back up a feeling you get about the atmosphere or mood of a story, about a character, or about character relationships. As you become more aware of how and why you are reacting to a work, the meaning of the work—the author's purpose—will begin to emerge. At times details will add up to a simple meaning. The author's purpose may be simply to describe something vividly enough to make his subject, the things he sees or imagines, real to you, the reader. In the selection below, many details describe the central subject. Unlike the Toomer poem, no image is the sole source of descriptive detail: they are all details which contribute to a total effect. Details suggest qualities as much as central relationships.

> It is born of winter, this river, in the longest season of cold in the United States. The source mountains in the Colorado Rockies are hard and wild. The air is thin and at such altitude subject to swift, crystalline changes of condition which may bring blue darkness in midday, and yield snow during nine months of the year.
>
> * * *
>
> The river's course—here as in its whole career—widens and narrows by turns. Where it is narrow, the slopes are dark, the stream is shadowed all day but for a little while at noon, when straight fingers of sunlight reach down through the forest. The stream is clear and icy, going rapidly over polished brown speckled stones. They remind us of something. At a glance, the diamond water going over its stony bed makes the image of the fish it carries—the same speckled colors, the same watery flicker, the same half-lights of reflection and golden flecks. In and out of leaf shadow, protected by the dazzle of moving water, the trout in plain sight is safe because he and his river are so close in likeness.
>
> <div align="right">—<i>from</i> "Pages from a Rio Grande Notebook"
PAUL HORGAN</div>

If you were to add up the many qualities listed here, would your sum reveal Horgan's attitude toward his subject? Is it enough to say that the Rio Grande is "clear," "icy," and flecked with gold? The first paragraph does not directly describe the river, but lets us guess its qualities from its environment. The time of year and the place—the setting—contribute clues to the river's "personality." What qualities does it inherit from its implied parents, from the winter and the Rockies? Perhaps the final descriptive phrase rests within you, the reader. Is this also true in passages which describe people and character relationships?

In the following selection, a nine-year-old girl from New York journeys to Barbados to meet her aged grandmother for the first time. The "alien sights and sounds of Barbados, the unfamiliar smells" distract her and she temporarily forgets she is supposed to be meeting her "Da-duh."

> I did not see her, but I was alerted to her approach by my mother's hand which suddenly tightened around mine, and looking up I traced her gaze through the gloom in the shed until I finally made out the small, purposeful, painfully erect figure of the old woman headed our way.

Her face was drowned in the shadow of an ugly rolled-brim brown felt hat, but the details of her slight body and of the struggle taking place within it were clear enough—an intense, unrelenting struggle between her back which was beginning to bend ever so slightly under the weight of her eighty odd years and the rest of her which sought to deny those years and hold that back straight, keep it in line. Moving swiftly toward us (so swiftly it seemed she did not intend stopping when she reached us but would sweep past us out the doorway which opened onto the sea and like Christ walk upon the water!), she was caught between the sunlight at her end of the building and the darkness inside—and for a moment she appeared to contain them both: the light in the long severe old-fashioned white dress she wore which brought the sense of a past that was still alive into our bustling present and in the snatch of white at her eye; the darkness in her black high-top shoes and in her face which was visible now that she was closer.

—*from* "To Da-duh, In Memoriam"
Paule Marshall

Like the river, the old woman has been described as much by her surroundings as by details immediately part of her. Before we encounter specific details, we can guess general qualities. But the author of this descriptive passage has used her details to tell us not only the appearance of her subject, but also the personality. Physical details, her carriage, the look in her eye, the contrast in her clothing, seem to carry a deeper meaning. Why does the author make so much of contrasts and of activity? Why does the old woman seem to be going somewhere, somewhere "past" the narrator and her family? Perhaps the answers to these questions lie in a passage later on in the story, a passage which reveals not only the inner details, the thoughts, of the old woman of Barbados, but also those of her granddaughter from New York.

This passage not only deepens our understanding of a basic character relationship (that between two generations), but also tells us that one set of details can have several interpretations, that one plus one can equal at least three.

As soon as we left Bridgetown behind though, she relaxed, and while the others around us talked she gazed at the canes standing tall on either side of the winding marl road. "C'dear," she said softly to herself after a time. "The canes this side are pretty enough."

They were too much for me. I thought of them as giant weeds that had overrun the island, leaving scarcely any room for the small tottering houses of sunbleached pine we passed or the people, dark streaks as our lorry hurtled by. I suddenly feared that we were journeying, unaware that we were, toward some dangerous place where the canes, grown as high and thick as a forest, would close in on us and run us through with their stiletto blades. I longed then for the familiar: for the street in Brooklyn where I lived . . .

* * *

. . . She went on for some time, intoning the names of the trees as though they were those of her gods. Finally, turning to me, she said, "I know you don't have anything this nice where you come from." Then, as I hesitated: "I said I know you don't have anything this nice where you come from. . . ."

"No," I said and my world did seem suddenly lacking.

Da-duh nodded and passed on. The orchard ended and we were on the narrow cart road that led through the canepiece, the canes clashing like swords above my cowering he;.d. Again she turned and her thin muscular arms spread wide, her dim gaze embracing the small field of canes, she said— .nd her voice almost broke under the weight of her pride, "Te i me, have you got anything like these in that place where yo w، re born?"

"No."

What is beautiful to the old woman is menacing to the young girl: what are you to think? Why does the writer still include images of struggle or battle, as she did in the first description of Da-duh? To answer, you must keep reading between the lines—or rather, beyond the details of sight, sound, and action—to uncover the three of one plus one. You must even ask yourself sometimes why actions were *not* taken, as well as why certain actions occurred. Why, for instance, didn't the little girl tell the truth?

As you ask questions of what you read, you will find yourself applying to stories questions based on life outside stories. You will, in effect, be drawing on your fund of everyday observations. "Why did the little girl lie?" is really just the question form of the statement, "The truth may hurt." Details of character, setting, and plot, will—if you weigh them against your own experience— begin to add up to larger units of meaning, to a general understanding of the techniques of writing and to greater insight about the fascinating relationship between how something is said and what it means.

Composition Assignments

To the Teacher

Additional writing assignments may be found in the *Teachers' Handbook and Key* as "Additional Assignments" or "Suggested Unit Reviews." The composition assignments below are taken directly from the students' text, most often from the "Further Activities" sections. Additional information about these writing assignments is often included in the *Teachers' Handbook and Key* under the sections called "Using 'Further Activities'."

To the Student

A large number of the stories you will read this year are concerned primarily with people—how they act, think, and feel. Others are concerned primarily with the ideas that concern all people. In the composition assignments below you will have an opportunity to become a writer—to tell stories, to say how you think and feel, to react to what the writers in the book have said. In this way, you are not simply asked to read and believe what you have read. You have an opportunity to become a writer.

Assignment	Location	Page
1. Use examples from your own experience to illustrate that "a good way to learn how another feels is to put yourself in his place."	FA4[1]	25
2. Write a character sketch of Professor Van Dusen, using information from "The Problem in Cell 13."	FA	57
3. List the facts about the bombing incident in "Neighbors"; then write a newspaper article using these facts.	FA	99
4. Write down the conversation which might take place if you were a nine-year-old trying to explain a modern appliance or vehicle of transportation to the old woman in "To Da-duh, In Memoriam."	FA	125
5. Use information from the story, "The Torn Invitation," as evidence to support the statement, "When Harry decided to call his mother, I was not surprised."	FA2	144
6. Describe a place or object in such a way that you reveal the character of the person responsible for the condition of that place or object.	FA1	158
7. Describe a house you are glad to see, using words that suggest a happy mood.	FA2	158
8. Recount an incident which illustrates that a person may feel shame after hurting someone else.	FA1	166

[1]The abbreviation *FA* refers to the "Further Activities" sections of the text.

2The abbreviation UL refers to the "Understanding Literature" sections of the text.

Contents

Nature

Science

Sports

Biography

Drama

Poetry

THEMES OF POETRY

Plot

THROUGH READING, you can experience exciting and suspense-filled adventure. You can know what it is like to be hunted down as a beast, to be locked in a prison cell, to plant trees on Mars. You imaginatively experience the excitement, the danger, the intrigue, and the pleasure of such adventure. Reading stirs your imagination, arouses your curiosity, enlarges your world, and enriches your understanding.

As your reading skill improves, the adventure of reading becomes very real to you. You discover that each writer has some experience to share with you, and that your own life is more interesting because of this shared experience.

Good reading is the ability to ask the right questions. Usually the first questions you ask about a piece of literature are, What is it about? What happens in it? The plot of a story refers to what happens. However, plot is not simply action; plot refers to the arrangement of the events in the story—to what the author tells first, second, third, etc. The plot is the plan, the design, of the story. A good plot is planned so that the events at the beginning prepare the reader for future events in the story. In a good plot the conclusion is a logical and believable result of the preceding events. Here are some questions about plot which will help you to understand exactly what *does* happen in a story. The more you understand about the plot, the better you will understand what the author is saying to you.

What conflict is there in the story? What is the basis for the conflict? What does the main character want? Does he/she get it?

Short stories, dramas, and some poems contain conflict. Conflict means a struggle of some kind—a physical, or a mental, or a spiritual struggle. The basis of the conflict may be one person against another, or a person against society, or human being(s) against nature. Or it may involve a conflict of one idea against another. In most stories the conflict centers around a character who tries to win the struggle against the force or forces opposing him or her.

How does the story create suspense? When is your curiosity aroused about what is going to happen? When is this curiosity satisfied?

In the opening paragraphs of a good story, you begin to wonder what is going to happen. In stories of adventure or mystery, the suspense is particularly intense. You read eagerly to discover "What next?"

How does the story depend on a cause-and-effect relation between the scenes or incidents? How do the events in the early part of the story cause the main event?

Plot shows the cause-and-effect relationship between character and event, or between one event and another. For example, if you hear that a woman jumped from the third-floor window of an expensive, luxurious apartment, the incident may be interesting to you, but it probably does not become really meaningful to you until the incident is placed into a plot, in which you may understand how the woman's character and the previous events in her life caused the suicide. In a story, early incidents prepare you for later events; each detail is devoted to showing why the main event can happen. One incident leads to—*causes*—the next.

Out of all the possible details which make up life, what details has the author included in the story? Of more importance, what details about the subject have been left out?

In a good story, every detail—the way a character looks; what he/she does, says, or thinks; the objects around him or her—contributes to the plot of the story. The author obviously cannot include every factual or imaginary detail relating to an incident or a character. Instead, the author must choose those details which best produce the effect he/she wants and which best support or illustrate what he/she is saying in the main action of the story. Details which do not contribute to that purpose must be left out.

How many scenes are in the story? Where does the author state the transitions between them? Where does each begin and end? What is the purpose of each scene? of each incident?

Just as the author chooses details from experience which contribute most to the plot, he/she also chooses scenes which show most effectively the relationships between character and events. Each scene and each incident contributes to your understanding of what happens by preparing you for the outcome of the conflict, or by showing you what a character is like, or by explaining what has happened earlier, or by developing the story's action.

What is the high point in the action, the climax, the turning point in the action?

At the climax of the story the outcome of the conflict is decided; who (or what) will win the struggle is determined. You are usually emotionally involved in what is happening, and your suspense is greatest at this point. The conflict, the suspense, the scenes and incidents have been building to the climactic point.

The Most Dangerous Game

Richard Connell

"OFF THERE to the right—somewhere —is a large island," said Whitney. "It's rather a mystery——"

"What island is it?" Rainsford asked.

"The old charts call it 'Ship-Trap Island,'" Whitney replied. "A suggestive name, isn't it? Sailors have a curious dread of the place. I don't know why. Some superstition——"

"Can't see it," remarked Rainsford, trying to peer through the dank tropical night that was palpable[1] as it pressed its thick warm blackness in upon the yacht.

"You've good eyes," said Whitney, with a laugh, "and I've seen you pick off a moose moving in the brown fall bush at four hundred yards, but even you can't see four miles or so through a moonless Caribbean night."

"Nor four yards," admitted Rainsford. "Ugh! It's like moist velvet."

"It will be light enough in Rio," promised Whitney. "We should make it in a few days. I hope the jaguar guns have come from Purdey's. We should have some good

[1] palpable: capable of being perceived by the senses.

hunting up the Amazon. Great sport, hunting."

"The best sport in the world," agreed Rainsford.

"For the hunter," amended Whitney. "Not for the jaguar."

"Don't talk rot, Whitney," said Rainsford. "You're a big-game hunter, not a philosopher. Who cares how a jaguar feels?"

"Perhaps the jaguar does," observed Whitney.

"Bah! They've no understanding."

"Even so, I rather think they understand one thing at least—fear. The fear of pain and the fear of death."

"Nonsense," laughed Rainsford. "This hot weather is making you soft, Whitney. Be a realist. The world is made up of two classes—the hunters and the hunted. Luckily, you and I are hunters. Do you think we've passed that island yet?"

"I can't tell in the dark. I hope so."

"Why?" asked Rainsford.

"The place has a reputation—a bad one."

"Cannibals?" suggested Rainsford.

"Hardly. Even cannibals wouldn't live in such a God-forsaken place. But it's got into sailor lore, somehow. Didn't you notice that the crew's nerves seem a bit jumpy today?"

"They were a bit strange, now you mention it. Even Captain Nielsen——"

"Yes, even that tough-minded old Swede, who'd go up to the devil himself and ask him for a light. Those fishy blue eyes held a look I never saw there before. All I could get out of him was: 'This place has an evil name among seafaring men, sir.' Then he said to me, very gravely: 'Don't you feel anything?' —as if the air about us was actually poisonous. Now, you mustn't laugh when I tell you this—I did feel something like a sudden chill.

"There was no breeze. The sea was as flat as a plate-glass window. We were drawing near the island then. What I felt was a—a mental chill—a sort of sudden dread."

"Pure imagination," said Rainsford. "One superstitious sailor can taint the whole ship's company with his fear."

"Maybe. But sometimes I think sailors have an extra sense that tells them when they are in danger. Sometimes I think evil is a tangible thing—with wave lengths, just as sound and light have. An evil place can, so to speak, broadcast vibrations of evil. Anyhow, I'm glad we're getting out of this zone. Well, I think I'll turn in now, Rainsford."

"I'm not sleepy," said Rainsford. "I'm going to smoke another pipe up on the afterdeck."

"Good night, then, Rainsford. See you at breakfast."

"Right. Good night, Whitney."

There was no sound in the night as Rainsford sat there, but the muffled throb of the engine that drove the yacht swiftly through the darkness, and the swish and ripple of the wash of the propeller.

Rainsford, reclining in a steamer chair, indolently puffed on his favorite brier. The sensuous drowsiness of the night was on him. "It's so dark," he thought, "that I could sleep without closing my eyes; the night would be my eyelids——"

An abrupt sound startled him. Off to the right he heard it, and his ears, expert in such matters, could not be mistaken. Again he heard the sound, and again. Somewhere, off in the blackness, someone had fired a gun three times.

Rainsford sprang up and moved quickly to the rail, mystified. He strained his eyes in the direction from which the reports had come, but it was like trying to see through a blanket. He leaped upon the rail and balanced himself there, to get greater elevation; his pipe, striking a rope, was knocked from his mouth. He lunged for it; a short, hoarse cry came from his lips as he realized he had reached too far and had lost his balance. The cry was pinched off short as the blood-warm waters of the Caribbean Sea closed over his head.

He struggled up to the surface and tried to cry out, but the wash from the speeding yacht slapped him in the face and the salt water in his open mouth made him gag and strangle. Desperately he struck out with strong strokes after the receding lights of the yacht, but he stopped before he had swum fifty feet. A certain cool-headedness had come to him; it was not the first time he had been in a tight place. There was a chance that his cries could be heard by someone aboard the yacht, but that chance was slender, and grew more slender as the yacht raced on. He wrestled himself out of his clothes, and shouted with all his power. The lights of the yacht became faint and ever-vanishing fireflies; then they were blotted out entirely by the night.

Rainsford remembered the shots. They had come from the right, and doggedly he swam in that direction, swimming with slow, deliberate strokes, conserving his strength. For a seemingly endless time he fought the sea. He began to count his strokes desperately; he could do possibly a hundred more and then—

Rainsford heard a sound. It came out of the darkness, a high, screaming sound, the sound of an animal in an extremity of anguish and terror.

He did not recognize the animal that made the sound; he did not try to; with fresh vitality he swam toward the sound. He heard it again; then it was cut short by another noise, crisp, staccato.

"Pistol shot," muttered Rainsford, swimming on.

Ten minutes of determined effort brought another sound to his ears— the most welcome he had ever heard —the muttering and growling of the sea breaking on a rocky shore. He was almost on the rocks before he saw them; on a night less calm he would have been shattered against them. With his remaining strength he dragged himself from the swirling waters. Jagged crags appeared to jut up into the opaqueness; he forced himself upward, hand over hand. Gasping, his hands raw, he reached a flat place at the top. Dense jungle came down to the very edge of the cliffs. What perils that tangle of trees and underbrush might hold for him did not concern Rainsford just then. All he knew was that he was safe from his enemy, the sea, and that utter weariness was on him. He flung himself down at the jungle edge and tumbled headlong into the deepest sleep of his life.

When he opened his eyes he knew from the position of the sun that it was late in the afternoon. Sleep had given him new vigor; a sharp hunger was picking at him. He looked about him, almost cheerfully.

"Where there are pistol shots, there are men. Where there are men, there is food," he thought. But what kind of men, he wondered, in so forbidding a place? An unbroken front of snarled and jagged jungle fringed the shore.

He saw no sign of a trail through the closely knit web of weeds and trees; it was easier to go along the shore, and Rainsford floundered along by the water. Not far from where he had landed, he stopped.

Some wounded thing, by the evidence a large animal, had thrashed about in the underbrush; the jungle

weeds were crushed down and the moss was lacerated;[2] one patch of weeds was stained crimson. A small, glittering object not far away caught Rainsford's eye and he picked it up. It was an empty cartridge.

"A twenty-two," he remarked. "That's odd. It must have been a fairly large animal, too. The hunter had his nerve to tackle it with a light gun. It's clear that the brute put up a fight. I suppose the first three shots I heard was when the hunter flushed his quarry[3] and wounded it. The last shot was when he trailed it here and finished it."

He examined the ground closely and found what he had hoped to find —the print of hunting boots. They pointed along the cliff in the direction he had been going. Eagerly he hurried along, now slipping on a rotten log or a loose stone, but making headway; night was beginning to settle down on the island.

Bleak darkness was blacking out the sea and jungle when Rainsford sighted the lights. He came upon them as he turned a crook in the coast line, and his first thought was that he had come upon a village, for there were many lights. But as he forged along he saw to his great astonishment that all the lights were in one enormous building—a lofty structure with pointed towers plunging upward into the gloom. His eyes made out the shadowy outlines of a palatial château;[4] it was set on a

2 **lacerated** (lăs′ə rā′tĭd): torn; mangled.
3 **flushed his quarry:** caused the hunted game to come out of its hiding.
4 **palatial château** (pə lā′shəl shă tō′): magnificent castle.

PLOT

high bluff, and on three sides of it cliffs dived down to where the sea licked greedy lips in the shadows.

"Mirage," thought Rainsford. But it was no mirage, he found, when he opened the tall spiked iron gate. The stone steps were real enough; the massive door with a leering gargoyle[5] for a knocker was real enough; yet about it all hung an air of unreality.

He lifted the knocker, and it creaked up stiffly, as if it had never before been used. He let it fall, and it startled him with its booming loudness. He thought he heard footsteps within; the door remained closed. Again Rainsford lifted the heavy knocker, and let it fall. The door opened then, opened as suddenly as if it were on a spring, and Rainsford stood blinking in the river of glaring gold light that poured out. The first thing Rainsford's eyes discerned was the largest man Rainsford had ever seen—a gigantic creature, solidly made and black-bearded to the waist. In his hand the man held a long-barrel revolver, and he was pointing it straight at Rainsford's heart.

Out of the snarl of beard two small eyes regarded Rainsford.

"Don't be alarmed," said Rainsford, with a smile which he hoped was disarming. "I'm no robber. I fell off a yacht. My name is Sanger Rainsford of New York City."

The menacing look in the eyes did not change. The revolver pointed as rigidly as if the giant were a statue. He gave no sign that he understood Rainsford's words, or that he had even heard them. He was dressed in uniform, a black uniform trimmed with gray astrakhan.[6]

"I'm Sanger Rainsford of New York," Rainsford began again. "I fell off a yacht. I am hungry."

The man's only answer was to raise with his thumb the hammer of his revolver. Then Rainsford saw the man's free hand go to his forehead in a military salute, and he saw him click his heels together and stand at attention. Another man was coming down the broad marble steps, an erect, slender man in evening clothes. He advanced to Rainsford and held out his hand.

In a cultivated voice marked by a slight accent that gave it added precision and deliberateness, he said: "It is a very great pleasure and honor to welcome Mr. Sanger Rainsford, the celebrated hunter, to my home."

Automatically Rainsford shook the man's hand.

"I've read your book about hunting snow leopards in Tibet, you see," explained the man. "I am General Zaroff."

Rainsford's first impression was that the man was singularly handsome; his second was that there was an original, almost bizarre quality about the general's face. He was a tall man past middle age, for his hair was a vivid white; but his thick eyebrows and pointed military mustache were as black as the night from which Rainsford had come. His eyes, too, were black and very

---

5 gargoyle: grotesquely designed figure.   6 astrakhan: fur or skin from a lamb.

bright. He had high cheekbones, a sharp-cut nose, a spare, dark face, the face of a man used to giving orders, the face of an aristocrat. Turning to the giant in uniform, the general made a sign. The giant put away his pistol, saluted, withdrew.

"Ivan is an incredibly strong fellow," remarked the general, "but he has the misfortune to be deaf and dumb. A simple fellow, but, I'm afraid, like all his race, a bit of a savage."

"Is he Russian?"

"He is a Cossack," said the general, and his smile showed red lips and pointed teeth. "So am I."

"Come," he said, "we shouldn't be chatting here. We can talk later. Now you want clothes, food, rest. You shall have them. This is a most restful spot."

Ivan had reappeared, and the general spoke to him with lips that moved but gave forth no sound.

"Follow Ivan, if you please, Mr. Rainsford," said the general. "I was about to have my dinner when you came. I'll wait for you. You'll find that my clothes will fit you, I think."

It was to a huge, beam-ceilinged bedroom with a canopied bed big enough for six men that Rainsford followed the silent giant. Ivan laid out an evening suit, and Rainsford, as he put it on, noticed that it came from a London tailor who ordinarily cut and sewed for none below the rank of duke.

The dining room to which Ivan conducted him was in many ways remarkable. There was a medieval magnificence about it: it suggested a baronial hall of feudal times with its oaken panels, its high ceiling, its vast refectory table where twoscore men could sit down to eat. About the hall were the mounted heads of many animals—lions, tigers, elephants, moose, bears; larger or more perfect specimens Rainsford had never seen. At the great table the general was sitting, alone.

"You'll have a cocktail, Mr. Rainsford," he suggested. The cocktail was surpassingly good; and, Rainsford noted, the table appointments were of the finest, the linen, the crystal, the silver, the china.

They were eating *borsch*, the rich, red soup with sour cream so dear to Russian palates. Half apologetically General Zaroff said: "We do our best to preserve the amenities of civilization here. Please forgive any lapses. We are well off the beaten track, you know. Do you think the champagne has suffered from its long ocean trip?"

"Not in the least," declared Rainsford. He was finding the general a most thoughtful and affable host, a true cosmopolite.[7] But there was one small trait of the general's that made Rainsford uncomfortable. Whenever he looked up from his plate he found the general studying him, appraising him narrowly.

"Perhaps," said General Zaroff, "you were surprised that I recognized your name. You see, I read all books on hunting published in English, French, and Russian. I

7 **cosmopolite** (kŏz mŏp′ə lĭt′): man of the world, at home in any country.

have but one passion in my life, Mr. Rainsford, and it is the hunt."

"You have some wonderful heads here," said Rainsford as he ate a particularly well cooked filet mignon. "That Cape buffalo is the largest I ever saw."

"Oh, that fellow. Yes, he was a monster."

"Did he charge you?"

"Hurled me against a tree," said the general. "Fractured my skull. But I got the brute."

"I've always thought," said Rainsford, "that the Cape buffalo is the most dangerous of all big game."

For a moment the general did not reply; he was smiling his curious red-lipped smile. Then he said slowly: "No. You are wrong, sir. The Cape buffalo is not the most dangerous big game." He sipped his wine. "Here in my preserve on this island," he said in the same slow tone, "I hunt more dangerous game."

Rainsford expressed his surprise. "Is there big game on this island?"

The general nodded. "The biggest."

"Really?"

"Oh, it isn't here naturally, of course. I have to stock the island."

"What have you imported, General?" Rainsford asked. "Tigers?"

The general smiled. "No," he said. "Hunting tigers ceased to interest me some years ago. I exhausted their possibilities, you see. No thrill left in tigers, no real danger. I live for danger, Mr. Rainsford."

The general took from his pocket a gold cigarette case and offered his guest a long black cigarette with a silver tip; it was perfumed and gave off a smell like incense.

"We will have some capital hunting, you and I," said the general. "I shall be most glad to have your society."

"But what game——" began Rainsford.

"I'll tell you," said the general. "You will be amused, I know. I think I may say, in all modesty, that I have done a rare thing. I have invented a new sensation. May I pour you another glass of port, Mr. Rainsford?"

"Thank you, General."

The general filled both glasses, and said: "God makes some men poets. Some He makes kings, some beggars. Me He made a hunter. My hand was made for the trigger, my father said. He was a very rich man with a quarter of a million acres in the Crimea, and he was an ardent sportsman. When I was only five years old he gave me a little gun, specially made in Moscow for me, to shoot sparrows with. When I shot some of his prize turkeys with it, he did not punish me; he complimented me on my marksmanship. I killed my first bear in the Caucasus when I was ten. My whole life has been one prolonged hunt. I went into the army—it was expected of noblemen's sons—and for a time commanded a division of Cossack cavalry, but my real interest was always the hunt. I have hunted every kind of game in every land. It would be impossible for me to tell you how many animals I have killed."

The general puffed at his cigarette.

"After the debacle[8] in Russia I left the country, for it was imprudent for an officer of the Czar to stay there. Many noble Russians lost everything. I, luckily, had invested heavily in American securities, so I shall never have to open a tearoom in Monte Carlo or drive a taxi in Paris. Naturally, I continued to hunt—grizzlies in your Rockies, crocodiles in the Ganges, rhinoceroses in East Africa. It was in Africa that the Cape buffalo hit me and laid me up for six months. As soon as I recovered I started for the Amazon to hunt jaguars, for I had heard they were unusually cunning. They weren't." The Cossack sighed. "They were no match at all for a hunter with his wits about him, and a high-powered rifle. I was bitterly disappointed. I was lying in my tent with a splitting headache one night when a terrible thought pushed its way into my mind. Hunting was beginning to bore me! And hunting, remember, had been my life. I have heard that in America businessmen often go to pieces when they give up the business that has been their life."

"Yes, that's so," said Rainsford.

The general smiled. "I had no wish to go to pieces," he said. "I must do something. Now, mine is an analytical mind, Mr. Rainsford. Doubtless that is why I enjoy the problems of the chase."

"No doubt, General Zaroff."

"So," continued the general, "I

asked myself why the hunt no longer fascinated me. You are much younger than I am, Mr. Rainsford, and have not hunted as much, but you perhaps can guess the answer."

"What was it?"

"Simply this: hunting had ceased to be what you call 'a sporting proposition.' It had become too easy. I always got my quarry. Always. There is no greater bore than perfection."

The general lit a fresh cigarette.

"No animal had a chance with me any more. That is no boast; it is a mathematical certainty. The animal had nothing but his legs and his instinct. Instinct is no match for reason. When I thought of this it was a tragic moment for me, I can tell you."

Rainsford leaned across the table, absorbed in what his host was saying.

"It came to me as an inspiration what I must do," the general went on.

"And that was?"

The general smiled the quiet smile of one who has faced an obstacle and surmounted it with success. "I had to invent a new animal to hunt," he said.

"A new animal? You are joking."

"Not at all," said the general. "I never joke about hunting. I needed a new animal. I found one. So I bought this island, built this house, and here I do my hunting. The island is perfect for my purposes— there are jungles with a maze of trails in them, hills, swamps——"

"But the animal, General Zaroff?"

"Oh," said the general, "it supplies

---

8 **debacle** (dā bä′kəl): violent disruption. Zaroff is referring to the Russian revolution of 1917.

me with the most exciting hunting in the world. No other hunting compares with it for an instant. Every day I hunt, and I never grow bored now, for I have a quarry with which I can match my wits."

Rainsford's bewilderment showed in his face.

"I wanted the ideal animal to hunt," explained the general. "So I said: 'What are the attributes of an ideal quarry?' And the answer was, of course: 'It must have courage, cunning, and, above all, it must be able to reason.'"

"But no animal can reason," objected Rainsford.

"My dear fellow," said the general, "there is one that can."

"But you can't mean——" gasped Rainsford.

"And why not?"

"I can't believe you are serious, General Zaroff. This is a grisly joke."

"Why should I not be serious? I am speaking of hunting."

"Hunting? General Zaroff, what you speak of is murder."

The general laughed with entire good nature. He regarded Rainsford quizzically. "I refuse to believe that so modern and civilized a young man as you seem to be harbors romantic ideas about the value of human life. Surely your experiences in the war——" He stopped.

"Did not make me condone cold-blooded murder," finished Rainsford stiffly.

Laughter shook the general. "How extraordinarily droll you are!" he said. "One does not expect nowadays to find a young man of the educated class, even in America, with such a naïve, and, if I may say so, mid-Victorian point of view. It's like finding a snuffbox in a limousine. Ah, well, doubtless you had Puritan ancestors. So many Americans appear to have had. I'll wager you'll forget your notions when you go hunting with me. You've a genuine new thrill in store for you, Mr. Rainsford."

"Thank you, I'm a hunter, not a murderer."

"Dear me," said the general, quite unruffled, "again that unpleasant word. But I think I can show you that your scruples are quite ill founded."

"Yes?"

"Life is for the strong, to be lived by the strong, and, if needs be, taken by the strong. The weak of the world were put here to give the strong pleasure. I am strong. Why should I not use my gift? If I wish to hunt, why should I not? I hunt the scum of the earth—sailors from tramp ships—lascars, blacks, Chinese, whites, mongrels—a thoroughbred horse or hound is worth more than a score of them."

"But they are men," said Rainsford hotly.

"Precisely," said the general. "That is why I use them. It gives me pleasure. They can reason, after a fashion. So they are dangerous."

"But where do you get them?"

The general's left eyelid fluttered down in a wink. "This island is called Ship-Trap," he answered. "Sometimes an angry god of the high seas sends them to me. Sometimes, when Providence is not so kind, I help Providence a bit. Come to the window with me."

Rainsford went to the window and looked out toward the sea.

"Watch! Out there!" exclaimed the general, pointing into the night. Rainsford's eyes saw only blackness, and then, as the general pressed a button, far out to sea Rainsford saw the flash of lights.

The general chuckled. "They indicate a channel," he said, "where there's none: giant rocks with razor edges crouch like a sea monster with wide-open jaws. They can crush a ship as easily as I crush this nut." He dropped a walnut on the hardwood floor and brought his heel grinding down on it. "Oh, yes," he said casually, as if in answer to a question, "I have electricity. We try to be civilized here."

"Civilized? And you shoot down men?"

A trace of anger was in the general's black eyes, but it was there for but a second, and he said, in his most pleasant manner: "Dear me, what a righteous young man you are! I assure you I do not do the thing you suggest. That would be barbarous. I treat these visitors with every consideration. They get plenty of good food and exercise. They get into splendid physical condition. You shall see for yourself tomorrow."

"What do you mean?"

"We'll visit my training school," smiled the general. "It's in the cellar. I have about a dozen pupils down there now. They're from the Spanish bark *San Lucar* that had the bad luck to go on the rocks out there. A very inferior lot, I regret to say. Poor specimens and more accustomed to the deck than to the jungle."

He raised his hand, and Ivan, who served as waiter, brought thick Turkish coffee. Rainsford, with an effort, held his tongue in check.

"It's a game, you see," pursued the general blandly. "I suggest to one of them that we go hunting. I give him a supply of food and an excellent hunting knife. I give him three hours' start. I am to follow, armed only with a pistol of the smallest caliber and range. If my quarry eludes me for three whole days, he wins the game. If I find him"—the general smiled—"he loses."

"Suppose he refuses to be hunted."

"Oh," said the general, "I give him his option, of course. He need not play that game if he doesn't wish to. If he does not wish to hunt, I turn him over to Ivan. Ivan once had the honor of serving as official knouter to the Great White Czar, and he has his own ideas of sport. Invariably, Mr. Rainsford, invariably they choose the hunt."

"And if they win?"

The smile on the general's face widened. "To date I have not lost," he said.

Then he added, hastily: "I don't wish you to think me a braggart, Mr. Rainsford. Many of them afford only the most elementary sort of problem. Occasionally I strike a tartar.[9] One almost did win. I

9 **tartar:** person who is too strong for his attacker; a violent, savage person.

eventually had to use the dogs."

"The dogs?"

"This way, please. I'll show you."

The general steered Rainsford to a window. The lights from the windows sent a flickering illumination that made grotesque patterns on the courtyard below, and Rainsford could see moving about there a dozen or so huge black shapes; as they turned toward him, their eyes glittered greenly.

"A rather good lot, I think," observed the general. "They are let out at seven every night. If anyone should try to get into my house—or out of it—something extremely regrettable would occur to him." He hummed a snatch of song from the Folies Bergère.

"And now," said the general, "I want to show you my new collection of heads. Will you come with me to the library?"

"I hope," said Rainsford, "that you will excuse me tonight, General Zaroff. I'm really not feeling at all well."

"Ah, indeed?" the general inquired solicitously. "Well, I suppose that's only natural, after your long swim. You need a good, restful night's sleep. Tomorrow you'll feel like a new man, I'll wager. Then we'll hunt, eh? I've one rather promising prospect——"

Rainsford was hurrying from the room.

"Sorry you can't go with me tonight," called the general. "I expect rather fair sport—a big, strong black. He looks resourceful— Well, good night, Mr. Rainsford; I hope

that you have a good night's rest."

The bed was good and the pajamas of the softest silk, and he was tired in every fiber of his being, but nevertheless Rainsford could not quiet his brain with the opiate of sleep. He lay, eyes wide open. Once he thought he heard stealthy steps in the corridor outside his room. He sought to throw open the door; it would not open. He went to the window and looked out. His room was high up in one of the towers. The lights of the château were out now, and it was dark and silent, but there was a fragment of sallow moon, and by its wan light he could see, dimly, the courtyard; there, weaving in and out in the pattern of shadow, were black, noiseless forms; the hounds heard him at the window and looked up, expectantly, with their green eyes. Rainsford went back to the bed and lay down. By many methods he tried to put himself to sleep. He had achieved a doze when, just as morning began to come, he heard, far off in the jungle, the faint report of a pistol.

General Zaroff did not appear until luncheon. He was dressed faultlessly in the tweeds of a country squire. He was solicitous about the state of Rainsford's health.

"As for me," sighed the general, "I do not feel so well. I am worried, Mr. Rainsford. Last night I detected traces of my old complaint."

To Rainsford's questioning glance the general said: "Ennui. Boredom."

Then, taking a second helping of crêpes suzette, the general explained: "The hunting was not good last night. The fellow lost his head. He made a straight trail that offered no problems at all. That's the trouble with these sailors; they have dull brains to begin with, and they do not know how to get about in the woods. They do excessively stupid and obvious things. It's most annoying. Will you have another glass of Chablis, Mr. Rainsford?"

"General," said Rainsford firmly, "I wish to leave this island at once."

The general raised his thickets of eyebrows; he seemed hurt. "But, my dear fellow," the general protested, "you've only just come. You've had no hunting——"

"I wish to go today," said Rainsford. He saw the dead black eyes of the general on him, studying him. General Zaroff's face suddenly brightened.

He filled Rainsford's glass with venerable Chablis from a dusty bottle.

"Tonight," said the general, "we will hunt—you and I."

Rainsford shook his head. "No, General," he said. "I will not hunt."

The general shrugged his shoulders and delicately ate a hothouse grape. "As you wish, my friend," he said. "The choice rests entirely with you. But may I not venture to suggest that you will find my idea of sport more diverting than Ivan's?"

He nodded toward the corner to where the giant stood, scowling, his thick arms crossed on his hogshead of chest.

"You don't mean——" cried Rainsford.

"My dear fellow," said the general, "have I not told you I always mean what I say about hunting? This is really an inspiration. I drink to a foeman worthy of my steel—at last."

The general raised his glass, but Rainsford sat staring at him.

"You'll find this game worth playing," the general said enthusiastically. "Your brain against mine. Your woodcraft against mine. Your strength and stamina against mine. Outdoor chess! And the stake is not without value, eh?"

"And if I win—" began Rainsford huskily.

"I'll cheerfully acknowledge myself defeated if I do not find you by midnight of the third day," said General Zaroff. "My sloop will place you on the mainland near a town."

The general read what Rainsford was thinking.

"Oh, you can trust me," said the Cossack. "I will give you my word as a gentleman and a sportsman. Of course you, in turn, must agree to say nothing of your visit here."

"I'll agree to nothing of the kind," said Rainsford.

"Oh," said the general, "in that case— But why discuss it now? Three days hence we can discuss it over a bottle of Veuve Clicquot, unless——"

The general sipped his wine.

Then a businesslike air animated him. "Ivan," he said to Rainsford, "will supply you with hunting clothes, food, a knife. I suggest you wear moccasins; they leave a poorer trail. I suggest too that you avoid the big swamp in the southeast corner of the island. We call it Death Swamp. There's quicksand there. One foolish fellow tried it. The deplorable part of it was that Lazarus followed him. You can imagine my feelings, Mr. Rainsford. I loved Lazarus; he was the finest hound in my pack. Well, I must beg you to excuse me now. I always take a siesta after lunch. You'll hardly have time for a nap, I fear. You'll want to start, no doubt. I shall not follow till dusk. Hunting at night is so much more exciting than by day, don't you think? *Au revoir,*[10] Mr. Rainsford, *au revoir.*"

General Zaroff, with a deep, courtly bow, strolled from the room.

From another door came Ivan. Under one arm he carried khaki hunting clothes, a haversack of food, a leather sheath containing a long-bladed hunting knife; his right hand rested on a cocked revolver thrust in the crimson sash about his waist. . . .

Rainsford had fought his way through the bush for two hours. "I must keep my nerve. I must keep my nerve," he said through tight teeth.

He had not been entirely clear-headed when the château gates snapped shut behind him. His whole idea at first was to put distance between himself and General Zaroff, and, to this end, he had plunged along, spurred on by the sharp rowels[11] of something very like panic. Now he had got a grip on himself,

had stopped, and was taking stock of himself and the situation.

He saw that straight flight was futile; inevitably it would bring him face to face with the sea. He was in a picture with a frame of water, and his operations, clearly, must take place within that frame.

"I'll give him a trail to follow," muttered Rainsford, and he struck off from the rude path he had been following into the trackless wilderness. He executed a series of intricate loops; he doubled on his trail again and again, recalling all the lore of the fox hunt, and all the dodges of the fox. Night found him leg-weary, with hands and face lashed by the branches, on a thickly wooded ridge. He knew it would be insane to blunder on through the dark, even if he had the strength. His need for rest was imperative and he thought: "I have played the fox, now I must play the cat of the fable." A big tree with a thick trunk and outspread branches was near by, and, taking care to leave not the slightest mark, he climbed up into the crotch, and stretching out on one of the broad limbs, after a fashion, rested. Rest brought him new confidence and almost a feeling of security. Even so zealous a hunter as General Zaroff could not trace him there, he told himself; only the devil himself could follow that complicated trail through the jungle after dark. But, perhaps, the general was a devil——

An apprehensive night crawled slowly by like a wounded snake, and sleep did not visit Rainsford, although the silence of a dead world

10 *Au revoir* (ō rə vwàr′): Good-by until we meet again.
11 **rowels:** little wheels on spurs.

PLOT

was on the jungle. Toward morning when a dingy gray was varnishing the sky, the cry of some startled bird focused Rainsford's attention in that direction. Something was coming through the bush, coming slowly, carefully, coming by the same winding way Rainsford had come. He flattened himself down on the limb, and through a screen of leaves almost as thick as tapestry, he watched. The thing that was approaching him was a man.

It was General Zaroff. He made his way along with his eyes fixed in utmost concentration on the ground before him. He paused, almost beneath the tree, dropped to his knees and studied the ground. Rainsford's impulse was to hurl himself down like a panther, but he saw that the general's right hand held something small and metallic—an automatic pistol.

The hunter shook his head several times, as if he were puzzled. Then he straightened up and took from his case one of his black cigarettes; its pungent incenselike smoke floated up to Rainsford's nostrils. Rainsford held his breath. The general's eyes had left the ground and were traveling inch by inch up the tree. Rainsford froze there, every muscle tensed for a spring. But the sharp eyes of the hunter stopped before they reached the limb where Rainsford lay; a smile spread over his brown face. Very deliberately he blew a smoke ring into the air; then he turned his back on the tree and walked carelessly away, back along the trail he had come. The swish of the underbrush against his hunting boots grew fainter and fainter.

The pent-up air burst hotly from Rainsford's lungs. His first thought made him feel sick and numb. The general could follow a trail through the woods at night; he could follow an extremely difficult trail; he must have uncanny powers; only by the merest chance had the Cossack failed to see his quarry.

Rainsford's second thought was even more terrible. It sent a shudder of cold horror through his whole being. Why had the general smiled? Why had he turned back?

Rainsford did not want to believe what his reason told him was true, but the truth was as evident as the sun that had by now pushed through the morning mists. The general was playing with him! The general was saving him for another day's sport! The Cossack was the cat; he was the mouse. Then it was that Rainsford knew the full meaning of terror.

"I will not lose my nerve. I will not."

He slid down from the tree, and struck off again into the woods. His face was set and he forced the machinery of his mind to function. Three hundred yards from his hiding place he stopped where a huge dead tree leaned precariously on a smaller, living one. Throwing off his sack of food, Rainsford took his knife from its sheath and began to work with all his energy.

The job was finished at last, and he threw himself down behind a fallen log a hundred feet away. He did not have to wait long. The cat was coming again to play with the mouse.

Following the trail with the sureness of a bloodhound came General Zaroff. Nothing escaped those searching black eyes, no crushed blade of grass, no bent twig, no mark, no matter how faint, in the moss. So intent was the Cossack on his stalking that he was upon the thing Rainsford had made before he saw it. His foot touched the protruding bough that was the trigger. Even as he touched it, the general sensed his danger and leaped back with the agility of an ape. But he was not quite quick enough; the dead tree, delicately adjusted to rest on the cut living one, crashed down and struck the general a glancing blow on the shoulder as it fell; but for his alertness, he must have been smashed beneath it. He staggered, but he did not fall; nor did he drop his revolver. He stood there, rubbing his injured shoulder, and Rainsford, with fear again gripping his heart, heard the general's mocking laugh ring through the jungle.

"Rainsford," called the general, "if you are within sound of my voice, as I suppose you are, let me congratulate you. Not many men know how to make a Malay man catcher. Luckily for me, I too have hunted in Malacca. You are proving interesting, Mr. Rainsford. I am going now to have my wound dressed; it's only a slight one. But I shall be back. I shall be back."

When the general, nursing his bruised shoulder, had gone, Rainsford took up his flight again. It was flight now, a desperate, hopeless flight, that carried him on for some hours. Dusk came, then darkness, and still he pressed on. The ground grew softer under his moccasins; the vegetation grew ranker, denser; insects bit him savagely. Then, as he stepped forward, his foot sank into the ooze. He tried to wrench it back, but the muck sucked viciously at his foot as if it were a giant leech. With a violent effort, he tore his foot loose. He knew where he was now. Death Swamp and its quicksand.

His hands were tight closed as if his nerve were something tangible that someone in the darkness was trying to tear from his grip. The softness of the earth had given him an idea. He stepped back from the quicksand a dozen feet or so and, like some huge prehistoric beaver, he began to dig.

Rainsford had dug himself in in France when a second's delay meant death. That had been a placid pastime compared to his digging now. The pit grew deeper; when it was above his shoulders, he climbed out and from some hard saplings cut stakes and sharpened them to a fine point. These stakes he planted in the bottom of the pit with the points sticking up. With flying fingers he wove a rough carpet of weeds and branches and with it he covered the mouth of the pit. Then, wet with sweat and aching with tiredness, he crouched behind the stump of a lightning-charred tree.

He knew his pursuer was coming; he heard the paddling sound of feet on the soft earth, and the night breeze

brought him the perfume of the general's cigarette. It seemed to Rainsford that the general was coming with unusual swiftness; he was not feeling his way along, foot by foot. Rainsford, crouching there, could not see the general, nor could he see the pit. He lived a year in a minute. Then he felt an impulse to cry aloud with joy, for he heard the sharp crackle of the breaking branches as the cover of the pit gave way; he heard the sharp scream of pain as the pointed stakes found their mark. He leaped up from his place of concealment. Then he cowered back. Three feet from the pit a man was standing, with an electric torch in his hand.

"You've done well, Rainsford," the voice of the general called. "Your Burmese tiger pit has claimed one of my best dogs. Again you score. I

think, Mr. Rainsford, I'll see what you can do against my whole pack. I'm going home for a rest now. Thank you for a most amusing evening."

At daybreak Rainsford, lying near the swamp, was awakened by a sound that made him know that he had new things to learn about fear. It was a distant sound, faint and wavering, but he knew it. It was the baying of a pack of hounds.

Rainsford knew he could do one of two things. He could stay where he was and wait. That was suicide. He could flee. That was postponing the inevitable. For a moment he stood there, thinking. An idea that held a wild chance came to him, and, tightening his belt, he headed away from the swamp.

The baying of the hounds drew nearer, then still nearer, nearer, ever nearer. On a ridge Rainsford climbed a tree. Down a watercourse, not a quarter of a mile away, he could see the bush moving. Straining his eyes, he saw the lean figure of General Zaroff; just ahead of him Rainsford made out another figure whose wide shoulders surged through the tall jungle weeds; it was the giant Ivan, and he seemed pulled forward by some unseen force; Rainsford knew that Ivan must be holding the pack in leash.

They would be on him any minute now. His mind worked frantically. He thought of a native trick he had learned in Uganda. He slid down the tree. He caught hold of a springy young sapling and to it he fastened his hunting knife, with the blade pointing down the trail; with a bit of wild grapevine he tied back the sapling. Then he ran for his life. The hounds raised their voices as they hit the fresh scent. Rainsford knew now how an animal at bay[12] feels.

He had to stop to get his breath. The baying of the hounds stopped abruptly, and Rainsford's heart stopped too. They must have reached the knife.

He shinned excitedly up a tree and looked back. His pursuers had stopped. But the hope that was in Rainsford's brain when he climbed died, for he saw in the shallow valley that General Zaroff was still on his feet. But Ivan was not. The knife,

12 **at bay:** facing a pursuer, with no chance of escape.

driven by the recoil of the spring tree, had not wholly failed.

Rainsford had hardly tumbled to the ground when the pack took up the cry again.

"Nerve, nerve, nerve!" he panted, as he dashed along. A blue gap showed between the trees dead ahead. Ever nearer drew the hounds. Rainsford forced himself on toward the gap. He reached it. It was the shore of the sea. Across a cove he could see the gloomy gray stone of the château. Twenty feet below him the sea rumbled and hissed. Rainsford hesitated. He heard the hounds. Then he leaped far out into the sea. . . .

When the general and his pack reached the place by the sea, the Cossack stopped. For some minutes he stood regarding the blue-green expanse of water. He shrugged his shoulders. Then he sat down, took a drink of brandy from a silver flask, lit a perfumed cigarette, and hummed a bit from "Madame Butterfly."

General Zaroff had an exceedingly good dinner in his great paneled dining hall that evening. With it he had a bottle of Pol Roger and half a bottle of Chambertin. Two slight annoyances kept him from perfect enjoyment. One was the thought that it would be difficult to replace Ivan; the other was that his quarry had escaped him; of course, the American hadn't played the game—so thought the general as he tasted his after-dinner liqueur. In his library he read, to soothe himself, from the works of Marcus Aurelius. At ten he went up to his bedroom. He was deliciously tired, he said to himself, as he locked himself in. There was a little moonlight, so, before turning on his light, he went to the window and looked down at the courtyard. He could see the great hounds, and he called: "Better luck another time," to them. Then he switched on the light.

A man, who had been hiding in the curtains of the bed, was standing there.

"Rainsford!" screamed the general. "How did you get here?"

"Swam," said Rainsford. "I found it quicker than walking through the jungle."

The general sucked in his breath and smiled. "I congratulate you," he said. "You have won the game."

Rainsford did not smile. "I am still a beast at bay," he said, in a low, hoarse voice. "Get ready, General Zaroff."

The general made one of his deepest bows. "I see," he said. "Splendid! One of us is to furnish a repast for the hounds. The other will sleep in this very excellent bed. On guard, Rainsford." . . .

He had never slept in a better bed, Rainsford decided.

Understanding Literature

"The Most Dangerous Game" is a story of action. While you are reading, you imaginatively accompany Sanger Rainsford on his dangerous adventure to "Ship-Trap Island." Consider how the author, Richard Connell, has handled the following elements of the plot, so that the story becomes an exciting experience for you:

Conflict. The major conflict in the story is that between General Zaroff and Rainsford—between the hunter and his "most dangerous game." This conflict involves both physical and intellectual struggle: the two opponents match physical strength and, more significantly, they match wits. But even before the appearance of General Zaroff, the story contains conflict. The conversation between Rainsford and Whitney at the beginning of the story shows a conflict in ideas. What attitude toward the hunted animal does Rainsford express in this conversation? Does his attitude change later in the story?

Suspense and climax. The element of suspense is particularly strong in this story. The plot causes you to ask a series of questions about what is going to happen, and the last question is not answered until the last line of the story. The story is, in a sense, a series of questions: Why do the sailors fear "Ship-Trap Island"?

What is the mystery associated with it? Why does Whitney feel "a mental chill—a sort of sudden dread" as he passes the island? Who is firing a gun in the distance? After Rainsford falls into the sea, will he survive or drown? When he is first on the island, who or what is making the "high, screaming sound, the sound of an animal in an extremity of anguish and terror"? What kind of person lives "in so forbidding a place"? Why is Zaroff on the island, living in luxury, yet isolated from civilization? What is "the most dangerous game," the game more dangerous than Cape buffalo? In the hunt, will Rainsford elude Zaroff? If Rainsford survives, how will he? Will Zaroff see Rainsford hiding in the tree? How will Rainsford escape the dogs? Finally, in Zaroff's room, who will win the fight for life? By raising these questions as the plot progresses, the author keeps you in suspense from the opening lines until the end of the story.

The climax of the story occurs when your suspense is greatest—when Rainsford's Uganda knife trick has failed to kill Zaroff, when Zaroff and the dogs have Rainsford at bay on the edge of a cliff, when Rainsford must either jump into the sea or be killed. At the climax of the story, you learn that Rainsford "leaped far out into the sea." Although you stay in suspense until the end of the story, from the climactic point in the action, the outcome of the story is determined.

Relationship between scenes and selection of details. A scene always has some purpose in the plot of a story; if it has no purpose, the author will (or should) leave it out. In "The Most Dangerous Game," the opening conversation between Rainsford and Whitney introduces the hero, creates a sense of dread and fear with Whitney's references to the "vibrations of evil" from the mysterious island, and introduces the central idea of the hunter and the hunted. How does the later action in the story relate to the discussion of how a hunted jaguar feels? After Rainsford comes to the island and before he meets Zaroff, what clues is he given to the kind of game hunted there? During the dinner scene, how is Zaroff's attitude toward hunting "the most dangerous game" similar to Rainsford's attitude toward hunting jaguars? What does the scene at the dinner reveal about Zaroff's character? about Rainsford's? How does this scene lead to Zaroff's announcement at luncheon the next day that Rainsford is to become the hunted animal? The scenes of the hunt, then, logically grow out of—are caused by—Zaroff's challenge to Rainsford. After Rainsford's climactic leap into the sea, why does the author not include any scene or details showing what happened to Rainsford? And why does he not show what happened during the final fight between Rainsford and Zaroff?

Further Activities

1. Sounds and the interpretation of those sounds play an important part in this story. One example is this sentence: "There was no sound in the night as Rainsford sat there, but the muffled throb of the engine that drove the yacht swiftly through the darkness, and the swish and ripple of the wash of the propeller." Find other sentences or expressions in the story that cause you to hear in your imagination. Take time to imagine what the sounds described are like.
2. Listen carefully to a sound coming from a spot that you cannot see. Try to make a reader hear the sound as you describe it in one sentence.
3. Early in the story Rainsford says, "The world is made up of two classes—the hunters and the hunted." Do you agree with this statement? Discuss it in terms of your own experience.
4. How does Rainsford discover how the hunted animal feels? Write a paragraph beginning, "A good way to learn how another feels is to put yourself in his place." Give at least one example, preferably from your own experience, to illustrate this statement.

You may have heard the question, What happens when an irresistible force meets an immovable object? This story seems to ask that question, for it seems impossible to escape from Cell 13, yet Professor Van Dusen says he *will* escape.

The Problem of Cell 13

Jacques Futrelle

IMPROVING YOUR READING: The suspense in this story is based to a large extent on the questions *How?* and *Why?* When you have finished the story, you will know the how and why; then, if you trace back through what you have read, you will see that each incident is based on the one preceding it. In other words, *because* one incident takes place, the next incident happens. There is a cause-and-effect relationship between events in the plot.

PRACTICALLY ALL those letters remaining in the alphabet after Augustus S. F. X. Van Dusen was named were afterward acquired by that gentleman in the course of a brilliant scientific career, and, being honorably acquired, were tacked on to the other end. His name, therefore, taken with all that belonged to it, was a wonderfully imposing structure. He was a Ph.D., an LL.D., an F.R.S., an M.D., and an M.D.S.[1] He was also some other things—just what he himself couldn't say—through recognition of his ability by various foreign educational and scientific institutions.

In appearance he was no less striking than in nomenclature.[2] He was slender with the droop of the student in his thin shoulders and the pallor of a close, sedentary[3] life on his clean-shaven face. His eyes wore a perpetual, forbidding squint—the squint of a man who studies little things—and when they could be seen at all through his thick spectacles, were mere slits of watery blue. But above his eyes was his most striking feature. This was a tall, broad brow, almost abnormal in height and width, crowned by a heavy shock of bushy, yellow hair. All these things conspired to give him a peculiar, almost grotesque, personality.

Professor Van Dusen was remotely German. For generations his ancestors had been noted in the sciences; he was the logical result, the master mind. First and above all he was a logician. At least thirty-five years of

---

1 **Ph.D. . . . M.D.S.:** Doctor of Philosophy, Doctor of Laws, Fellow of the Royal Society, Doctor of Medicine, and Master of Dental Surgery.
2 **nomenclature** (nō′mən klā′chər): names.

3 **sedentary** (sĕd′ən tĕr′ĭ): accustomed to sitting most of the time.

PLOT

the half century or so of his existence had been devoted exclusively to proving that two and two always equal four, except in unusual cases, where they equal three or five, as the case may be. He stood broadly on the general proposition that all things that start must go somewhere, and was able to bring the concentrated mental force of his forefathers to bear on a given problem. Incidentally it may be remarked that Professor Van Dusen wore a No. 8 hat.

The world at large had heard vaguely of Professor Van Dusen as The Thinking Machine. It was a newspaper catch-phrase applied to him at the time of a remarkable exhibition at chess; he had demonstrated then that a stranger to the game might, by the force of inevitable logic, defeat a champion who had devoted a lifetime to its study. The Thinking Machine! Perhaps that more nearly described him than all his honorary initials, for he spent week after week, month after month, in the seclusion of his small laboratory from which had gone forth thoughts that staggered scientific associates and deeply stirred the world at large.

It was only occasionally that The Thinking Machine had visitors, and these were usually men who, themselves high in the sciences, dropped in to argue a point and perhaps convince themselves. Two of these men, Dr. Charles Ransome and Alfred Fielding, called one evening to discuss some theory which is not of consequence here.

"Such a thing is impossible," declared Dr. Ransome emphatically, in the course of the conversation.

"Nothing is impossible," declared The Thinking Machine with equal emphasis. He always spoke petulantly.[4] "The mind is master of all things. When science fully recognizes that fact a great advance will have been made."

"How about the airship?" asked Dr. Ransome.

"That's not impossible at all," asserted The Thinking Machine. "It will be invented some time. I'd do it myself, but I'm busy."

Dr. Ransome laughed tolerantly.

"I've heard you say such things before," he said. "But they mean nothing. Mind may be master of matter, but it hasn't yet found a way to apply itself. There are some things that can't be *thought* out of existence, or rather which would not yield to any amount of thinking."

"What, for instance?" demanded The Thinking Machine.

Dr. Ransome was thoughtful for a moment as he smoked.

"Well, say prison walls," he replied. "No man can *think* himself out of a cell. If he could, there would be no prisoners."

"A man can so apply his brain and ingenuity that he can leave a cell, which is the same thing," snapped The Thinking Machine.

Dr. Ransome was slightly amused.

"Let's suppose a case," he said, after a moment. "Take a cell where prisoners under sentence of death are confined—men who are desperate

4 **petulantly**: peevishly.

and, maddened by fear, would take any chance to escape—suppose you were locked in such a cell. Could you escape?"

"Certainly," declared The Thinking Machine.

"Of course," said Mr. Fielding, who entered the conversation for the first time, "you might wreck the cell with an explosive—but inside, a prisoner, you couldn't have that."

"There would be nothing of that kind," said The Thinking Machine. "You might treat me precisely as you treated prisoners under sentence of death, and I would leave the cell."

"Not unless you entered it with tools prepared to get out," said Dr. Ransome.

The Thinking Machine was visibly annoyed and his blue eyes snapped.

"Lock me in any cell in any prison anywhere at any time, wearing only what is necessary, and I'll escape in a week," he declared, sharply.

Dr. Ransome sat up straight in the chair, interested. Mr. Fielding lighted a new cigar.

"You mean you could actually *think* yourself out?" asked Dr. Ransome.

"I would get out," was the response.

"Are you serious?"

"Certainly I am serious."

Dr. Ransome and Mr. Fielding were silent for a long time.

"Would you be willing to try it?" asked Mr. Fielding, finally.

"Certainly," said Professor Van Dusen, and there was a trace of irony in his voice. "I have done more asinine things than that to convince other men of less important truths."

The tone was offensive and there was an undercurrent strongly resembling anger on both sides. Of course it was an absurd thing, but Professor Van Dusen reiterated his willingness to undertake the escape and it was decided upon.

"To begin now," added Dr. Ransome.

"I'd prefer that it begin tomorrow," said The Thinking Machine, "because——"

"No, now," said Mr. Fielding, flatly. "You are arrested, figuratively, of course, without any warning locked in a cell with no chance to communicate with friends, and left there with identically the same care and attention that would be given to a man under sentence of death. Are you willing?"

"All right, now, then," said The Thinking Machine, and he arose.

"Say, the death cell in Chisholm Prison."

"The death cell in Chisholm Prison."

"And what will you wear?"

"As little as possible," said The Thinking Machine. "Shoes, stockings, trousers and a shirt."

"You will permit yourself to be searched, of course?"

"I am to be treated precisely as all prisoners are treated," said The Thinking Machine. "No more attention and no less."

There were some preliminaries to be arranged in the matter of obtaining permission for the test, but all three were influential men and everything was done satisfactorily by telephone, albeit[5] the prison commissioners, to whom the experiment was explained on purely scientific grounds, were sadly bewildered. Professor Van Dusen would be the most distinguished prisoner they had ever entertained.

When The Thinking Machine had donned those things which he was to wear during his incarceration[6] he called the little old woman who was his housekeeper, cook and maidservant all in one.

"Martha," he said, "it is now twenty-seven minutes past nine o'clock. I am going away. One week from tonight, at half past nine, these gentlemen and one, possibly two, others will take supper with me here. Remember Dr. Ransome is very fond of artichokes."

The three men were driven to Chisholm Prison, where the warden was awaiting them, having been informed of the matter by telephone. He understood merely that the eminent Professor Van Dusen was to be his prisoner, if he could keep him, for one week; that he had committed no crime, but that he was to be treated as all other prisoners were treated.

"Search him," instructed Dr. Ransome.

The Thinking Machine was searched. Nothing was found on him; the pockets of the trousers were empty; the white, stiff-bosomed shirt had no pocket. The shoes and stockings were removed, examined, then replaced. As he watched all these preliminaries, and noted the pitiful, childlike physical weakness of the man—the colorless face, and the thin, white hands—Dr. Ransome almost regretted his part in the affair.

"Are you sure you want to do this?" he asked.

"Would you be convinced if I did not?" inquired The Thinking Machine in turn.

"No."

"All right. I'll do it."

What sympathy Dr. Ransome had was dissipated by the tone. It nettled him, and he resolved to see the experiment to the end; it would be a stinging reproof to egotism.[7]

"It will be impossible for him to communicate with anyone outside?" he asked.

"Absolutely impossible," replied the warden. "He will not be permitted writing materials of any sort."

"And your jailers, would they deliver a message from him?"

"Not one word, directly or indirectly," said the warden. "You may rest assured of that. They will report anything he might say or turn over to me, anything he might give them."

"That seems entirely satisfactory," said Mr. Fielding, who was frankly interested in the problem.

"Of course, in the event he fails," said Dr. Ransome, "and asks for his liberty, you understand you are to set him free?"

"I understand," replied the warden.

The Thinking Machine stood lis-

---

5 **albeit** (ôl bē′it): although.
6 **incarceration** (ĭn kär′sər ā′shən): imprisonment.

7 **egotism:** concern only with self or selfish interests.

tening, but had nothing to say until this was all ended, then:

"I should like to make three small requests. You may grant them or not, as you wish."

"No special favors, now," warned Mr. Fielding.

"I am asking none," was the stiff response. "I should like to have some tooth powder—buy it yourself to see that it is tooth powder—and I should like to have one five-dollar and two ten-dollar bills."

Dr. Ransome, Mr. Fielding and the warden exchanged astonished glances. They were not surprised at the request for tooth powder, but were at the request for money.

"Is there any man with whom our friend would come in contact that he could bribe with twenty-five dollars?"

"Not for twenty-five hundred dollars," was the positive reply.

"Well, let him have them," said Mr. Fielding. "I think they are harmless enough."

"And what is the third request?" asked Dr. Ransome.

"I should like to have my shoes polished."

Again the astonished glances were exchanged. This last request was the height of absurdity, so they agreed to it. These things all being attended to, The Thinking Machine was led back into the prison from which he had undertaken to escape.

"Here is Cell 13," said the warden, stopping three doors down the steel corridor. "This is where we keep condemned murderers. No one can leave it without my permission; and no one in it can communicate with the outside. I'll stake my reputation on that. It's only three doors back of my office and I can readily hear any unusual noise."

"Will this cell do, gentlemen?" asked The Thinking Machine. There was a touch of irony in his voice.

"Admirably," was the reply.

The heavy steel door was thrown open, there was a great scurrying and scampering of tiny feet, and The Thinking Machine passed into the gloom of the cell. Then the door was closed and double-locked by the warden.

"What is that noise in there?" asked Dr. Ransome, through the bars.

"Rats—dozens of them," replied The Thinking Machine, tersely.

The three men, with final good nights, were turning away when The Thinking Machine called:

"What time is it exactly, Warden?"

"Eleven seventeen," replied the warden.

"Thanks. I will join you gentlemen in your office at half past eight o'clock one week from tonight," said The Thinking Machine.

"And if you do not?"

"There is no 'if' about it."

Chisholm Prison was a great, spreading structure of granite, four stories in all, which stood in the center of acres of open space. It was surrounded by a wall of solid masonry eighteen feet high, and so smoothly finished inside and out as to offer no foothold to a climber, no matter how expert. Atop of this fence, as a further precaution, was a five-foot fence of steel rods, each terminating in a keen point. This fence in itself marked an absolute deadline between freedom and imprisonment, for, even if a man escaped from his cell, it would seem impossible for him to pass the wall.

The yard, which on all sides of the prison building was twenty-five feet wide, that being the distance from the building to the wall, was by day an exercise ground for those prisoners to whom was granted the boon of occasional semi-liberty. But that was not for those in Cell 13. At all times of the day there were armed guards in the yard, four of them, one patrolling each side of the prison building.

By night the yard was almost as brilliantly lighted as by day. On each of the four sides was a great arc light which rose above the prison wall and gave to the guards a clear sight. The lights, too, brightly illuminated the spiked top of the wall. The wires which fed the arc lights ran up the side of the prison building on insulators and from the top story led out to the poles supporting the arc lights.

All these things were seen and comprehended by The Thinking Machine, who was only enabled to see out his closely barred cell window by standing on his bed. This was on the morning following his incarceration. He gathered, too, that the river lay over there beyond the wall somewhere, because he heard faintly the pulsation of a motor boat and high up in the air saw a river bird. From that same direction came the shouts of boys at play and the occasional crack of a batted ball. He knew then that between the prison wall and the river was an open space, a playground.

Chisholm Prison was regarded as absolutely safe. No man had ever escaped from it. The Thinking Machine, from his perch on the bed, seeing what he saw, could readily understand why. The walls of the cell, though built he judged twenty years before, were perfectly solid, and the window bars of new iron had not a shadow of rust on them. The window itself, even with the bars out, would be a difficult mode of egress[8] because it was small.

Yet, seeing these things, The Thinking Machine was not discouraged. Instead, he thoughtfully squinted at the great arc light—there was bright sunlight now—and traced with his eyes the wire which led from it to the building. That electric wire, he reasoned, must come down the side of the building not a great distance from his cell. That might be worth knowing.

Cell 13 was on the same floor with the offices of the prison—that is, not in the basement, nor yet upstairs. There were only four steps up to the office floor, therefore the level of the floor must be only three or four feet above the ground. He couldn't see the ground directly beneath his window, but he could see it further out toward the wall. It would be an easy drop from the window. Well and good.

Then The Thinking Machine fell

8 **egress:** means of going out.

to remembering how he had come to the cell. First, there was the outside guard's booth, a part of the wall. There were two heavily barred gates there, both of steel. At this gate was one man always on guard. He admitted persons to the prison after much clanking of keys and locks, and let them out when ordered to do so. The warden's office was in the prison building, and in order to reach that official from the prison yard one had to pass a gate of solid steel with only a peephole in it. Then coming from that inner office to Cell 13, where he was now, one must pass a heavy wooden door and two steel doors into the corridors of the prison; and always there was the double-locked door of Cell 13 to reckon with.

There were then, The Thinking Machine recalled, seven doors to be overcome before one could pass from Cell 13 into the outer world, a free man. But against this was the fact that he was rarely interrupted. A jailer appeared at his cell door at six in the morning with a breakfast of prison fare; he would come again at noon, and again at six in the afternoon. At nine o'clock at night would come the inspection tour. That would be all.

"It's admirably arranged, this prison system," was the mental tribute paid by The Thinking Machine. "I'll have to study it a little when I get out. I had no idea there was such great care exercised in the prisons."

There was nothing, positively nothing, in his cell, except his iron bed, so firmly put together that no man could tear it to pieces save with sledges or a file. He had neither of these. There was not even a chair, or a small table, or a bit of tin or crockery. Nothing! The jailer stood by when he ate, then took away the wooden spoon and bowl which he had used.

One by one these things sank into the brain of The Thinking Machine. When the last possibility had been considered he began an examination of his cell. From the roof, down the walls on all sides, he examined the stones and the cement between them. He stamped over the floor carefully time after time, but it was cement, perfectly solid. After the examination he sat on the edge of the iron bed and was lost in thought for a long time. For Professor Augustus S. F. X. Van Dusen, The Thinking Machine, had something to think about.

He was disturbed by a rat, which ran across his foot, then scampered away into a dark corner of the cell, frightened at its own daring. After a while The Thinking Machine, squinting steadily into the darkness of the corner where the rat had gone, was able to make out in the gloom many little beady eyes staring at him. He counted six pair, and there were perhaps others; he didn't see very well.

Then The Thinking Machine, from his seat on the bed, noticed for the first time the bottom of his cell door. There was an opening there of two inches between the steel bar and the floor. Still looking steadily at this opening, The Thinking Machine backed suddenly into the corner where he had seen the beady eyes. There was a great scampering of tiny feet, several squeaks of frightened rodents, and then silence.

None of the rats had gone out the door, yet there were none in the cell. Therefore there must be another way out of the cell, however small. The Thinking Machine, on hands and knees, started a search for this spot, feeling in the darkness with his long, slender fingers.

At last his search was rewarded. He came upon a small opening in the floor, level with the cement. It was perfectly round and somewhat larger than a silver dollar. This was the way the rats had gone. He put his fingers deep into the opening; it seemed to be a disused drainage pipe and was dry and dusty.

Having satisfied himself on this point, he sat on the bed again for an hour, then made another inspection of his surroundings through the small cell window. One of the outside guards stood directly opposite, beside the wall, and happened to be looking at the window of Cell 13 when the head of The Thinking Machine appeared. But the scientist didn't notice the guard.

Noon came and the jailer appeared with the prison dinner of repulsively plain food. At home The Thinking Machine merely ate to live; here he took what was offered without comment. Occasionally he spoke to the jailer who stood outside the door watching him.

"Any improvements made here in the last few years?" he asked.

"Nothing particularly," replied the jailer. "New wall was built four years ago."

"Anything done to the prison proper?"

"Painted the woodwork outside, and I believe about seven years ago a new system of plumbing was put in."

"Ah!" said the prisoner. "How far is the river over there?"

"About three hundred feet. The boys have a baseball ground between the wall and the river."

The Thinking Machine had nothing further to say just then, but when the jailer was ready to go he asked for some water.

"I get very thirsty here," he explained. "Would it be possible for you to leave a little water in a bowl for me?"

"I'll ask the warden," replied the jailer, and he went away.

Half an hour later he returned with water in a small earthen bowl.

"The warden says you may keep this bowl," he informed the prisoner. "But you must show it to me when I ask for it. If it is broken, it will be the last."

"Thank you," said The Thinking Machine. "I shan't break it."

The jailer went on about his duties. For just the fraction of a second it seemed that The Thinking Machine wanted to ask a question, but he didn't.

Two hours later this same jailer, in passing the door of Cell No. 13, heard a noise inside and stopped. The Thinking Machine was down on his hands and knees in a corner of the cell, and from that same corner came several frightened squeaks. The jailer looked on interestedly.

"Ah, I've got you," he heard the prisoner say.

"Got what?" he asked, sharply.

"One of these rats," was the reply. "See?" And between the scientist's long fingers the jailer saw a small gray rat struggling. The prisoner brought it over to the light and looked at it closely.

"It's a water rat," he said.

"Ain't you got anything better to do than to catch rats?" asked the jailer.

"It's disgraceful that they should be here at all," was the irritated reply. "Take this one away and kill it. There are dozens more where it came from."

The jailer took the wriggling, squirmy rodent and flung it down on the floor violently. It gave one squeak and lay still. Later he reported the incident to the warden, who only smiled.

Still later that afternoon the outside armed guard on the Cell 13 side of the prison looked up again at the window and saw the prisoner looking out. He saw a hand raised to the barred window and then something white fluttered to the ground, directly under the window of Cell 13. It was a little roll of linen, evidently of white shirting material, and tied around it was a five-dollar bill. The guard looked up at the window again, but the face had disappeared.

With a grim smile he took the little linen roll and the five-dollar bill to the warden's office. There together they deciphered something which was written on it with a queer sort of ink, frequently blurred. On the outside was this:

"Finder of this please deliver to Dr. Charles Ransome."

"Ah," said the warden, with a chuckle. "Plan of escape number one has gone wrong." Then, as an afterthought: "But why did he address it to Dr. Ransome?"

"And where did he get the pen and ink to write with?" asked the guard.

The warden looked at the guard and the guard looked at the warden. There was no apparent solution of that mystery. The warden studied the writing carefully, then shook his head.

"Well, let's see what he was going to say to Dr. Ransome," he said at length, still puzzled, and he unrolled the inner piece of linen.

"Well, if that—what—what do you think of that?" he asked, dazed.

The guard took the bit of linen and read this:—

Epa cseot d'net niiy awe
htto n'si sih. T."

❉   ❉   ❉

The warden spent an hour wondering what sort of a cipher it was, and half an hour wondering why his prisoner should attempt to communicate with Dr. Ransome, who was the cause of his being there. After this the warden devoted some thought to the question of where the prisoner got writing materials, and what sort of writing materials he had. With the idea of illuminating this point, he examined the linen again. It was a torn part of a white shirt and had ragged edges.

Now it was possible to account for the linen, but what the prisoner had used to write with was another matter. The warden knew it would have been impossible for him to have either pen or pencil, and, besides, neither pen nor pencil had been used in this writing. What, then? The warden decided to investigate personally. The Thinking Machine was his prisoner; he had orders to hold his prisoners; if this one sought to escape by sending cipher messages to persons outside, he would stop it, as he would have stopped it in the case of any other prisoner.

The warden went back to Cell 13 and found The Thinking Machine on his hands and knees on the floor, engaged in nothing more alarming than catching rats. The prisoner heard the warden's step and turned to him quickly.

"It's disgraceful," he snapped, "these rats. There are scores of them."

"Other men have been able to stand them," said the warden. "Here is another shirt for you—let me have the one you have on."

"Why?" demanded The Thinking Machine, quickly. His tone was hardly natural, his manner suggested actual perturbation.

"You have attempted to communicate with Dr. Ransome," said the warden severely. "As my prisoner, it is my duty to put a stop to it."

The Thinking Machine was silent for a moment.

"All right," he said, finally. "Do your duty."

The warden smiled grimly. The prisoner arose from the floor and removed the white shirt, putting on instead a striped convict shirt the warden had brought. The warden took the white shirt eagerly, and then and there compared the pieces of linen on which was written the cipher with certain torn places in the shirt. The Thinking Machine looked on curiously.

"The guard brought *you* those, then?" he asked.

"He certainly did," replied the warden triumphantly. "And that ends your first attempt to escape."

The Thinking Machine watched the warden as he, by comparison, established to his own satisfaction that only two pieces of linen had been torn from the white shirt.

"What did you write this with?" demanded the warden.

"I should think it a part of your duty to find out," said The Thinking Machine, irritably.

The warden started to say some harsh things, then restrained himself and made a minute search of the cell and of the prisoner instead. He found absolutely nothing; not even a match or toothpick which might have been used for a pen. The same mystery surrounded the fluid with which the cipher had been written. Although the warden left Cell 13 visibly annoyed, he took the torn shirt in triumph.

"Well, writing notes on a shirt won't get him out, that's certain," he told himself with some complacency.

He put the linen scraps into his desk to await developments. "If that man escapes from that cell I'll—hang it— I'll resign."

On the third day of his incarceration The Thinking Machine openly attempted to bribe his way out. The jailer had brought his dinner and was leaning against the barred door, waiting, when The Thinking Machine began the conversation.

"The drainage pipes of the prison lead to the river, don't they?" he asked.

"Yes," said the jailer.

"I suppose they are very small."

"Too small to crawl through, if that's what you're thinking about," was the grinning response.

There was silence until The Thinking Machine finished his meal. Then:

"You know I'm not a criminal, don't you?"

"Yes."

"And that I've a perfect right to be freed if I demand it?"

"Yes."

"Well, I came here believing that I could make my escape," said the prisoner, and his squint eyes studied the face of the jailer. "Would you consider a financial reward for aiding me to escape?"

The jailer, who happened to be an honest man, looked at the slender, weak figure of the prisoner, at the large head with its mass of yellow hair, and was almost sorry.

"I guess prisons like these were not built for the likes of you to get out of," he said, at last.

"But would you consider a propo-sition to help me get out?" the prisoner insisted, almost beseechingly.

"No," said the jailer, shortly.

"Five hundred dollars," urged The Thinking Machine. "I am not a criminal."

"No," said the jailer.

"A thousand?"

"No," again said the jailer, and he started away hurriedly to escape further temptation. Then he turned back. "If you should give me ten thousand dollars I couldn't get you out. You'd have to pass through seven doors, and I only have the keys to two."

Then he told the warden all about it.

"Plan number two fails," said the warden, smiling grimly. "First a cipher, then bribery."

When the jailer was on his way to Cell 13 at six o'clock, again bearing food to The Thinking Machine, he paused, startled by the unmistakable scrape, scrape of steel against steel. It stopped at the sound of his steps, then craftily the jailer, who was beyond the prisoner's range of vision, resumed his tramping, the sound being apparently that of a man going away from Cell 13. As a matter of fact he was in the same spot.

After a moment there came again the steady scrape, scrape, and the jailer crept cautiously on tiptoes to the door and peered between the bars. The Thinking Machine was standing on the iron bed working at the bars of the little window. He was using a file, judging from the backward and forward swing of his arms.

Cautiously the jailer crept back to the office, summoned the warden in person, and they returned to Cell 13 on tiptoes. The steady scrape was still audible. The warden listened to satisfy himself and then suddenly appeared at the door.

"Well?" he demanded, and there was a smile on his face.

The Thinking Machine glanced back from his perch on the bed and leaped suddenly to the floor, making frantic efforts to hide something. The warden went in, with hand extended.

"Give it up," he said.

"No," said the prisoner, sharply.

"Come, give it up," urged the warden. "I don't want to have to search you again."

"No," repeated the prisoner.

"What was it—a file?" asked the warden.

The Thinking Machine was silent and stood squinting at the warden with something very nearly approaching disappointment on his face—nearly, but not quite. The warden was almost sympathetic.

"Plan number three fails, eh?" he asked, good-naturedly. "Too bad, isn't it?"

The prisoner didn't say.

"Search him," instructed the warden.

The jailer searched the prisoner carefully. At last, artfully concealed in the waistband of the trousers, he found a piece of steel about two inches long, with one side curved like a half moon.

"Ah," said the warden, as he received it from the jailer. "From your

shoe heel," and he smiled pleasantly.

The jailer continued his search and on the other side of the trousers waistband found another piece of steel identical with the first. The edges showed where they had been worn against the bars of the window.

"You couldn't saw a way through those bars with these," said the warden.

"I could have," said The Thinking Machine firmly.

"In six months, perhaps," said the warden, good-naturedly.

The warden shook his head slowly as he gazed into the slightly flushed face of his prisoner.

"Ready to give it up?" he asked.

"I haven't started yet," was the prompt reply.

Then came another exhaustive search of the cell. Carefully the two men went over it, finally turning out the bed and searching that. Nothing. The warden in person climbed upon the bed and examined the bars of the window where the prisoner had been sawing. When he looked he was amused.

"Just made it a little bright by hard rubbing," he said to the prisoner, who stood looking on with a somewhat crestfallen air. The warden grasped the iron bars in his strong hands and tried to shake them. They were immovable, set firmly in the solid granite. He examined each in turn and found them all satisfactory. Finally he climbed down from the bed.

"Give it up, Professor," he advised.

The Thinking Machine shook his head and the warden and jailer

passed on again. As they disappeared down the corridor The Thinking Machine sat on the edge of the bed with his head in his hands.

"He's crazy to try to get out of that cell," commented the jailer.

"Of course he can't get out," said the warden. "But he's clever. I would like to know what he wrote that cipher with."

It was four o'clock next morning when an awful, heart-racking shriek of terror resounded through the great prison. It came from a cell, somewhere about the center, and its tone told a tale of horror, agony, terrible fear. The warden heard and with three of his men rushed into the long corridor leading to Cell 13.

As they ran there came again that awful cry. It died away in a sort of wail. The white faces of prisoners appeared at cell doors upstairs and down, staring out wonderingly, frightened.

"It's that fool in Cell 13," grumbled the warden.

He stopped and stared in as one of the jailers flashed a lantern. "That fool in Cell 13" lay comfortably on his cot, flat on his back with his mouth open, snoring. Even as they looked there came again the piercing cry, from somewhere above. The warden's face blanched[9] a little as he started up the stairs. There on the top floor he found a man in Cell 43, directly above Cell 13, but two floors higher, cowering in a corner of his cell.

"What's the matter?" demanded the warden.

9 blanched: turned white.

"Thank God you've come," exclaimed the prisoner, and he cast himself against the bars of his cell.

"What is it?" demanded the warden again.

He threw open the door and went in. The prisoner dropped on his knees and clasped the warden about the body. His face was white with terror, his eyes were widely distended, and he was shuddering. His hands, icy cold, clutched at the warden's.

"Take me out of this cell, please take me out," he pleaded.

"What's the matter with you, anyhow?" insisted the warden, impatiently.

"I heard something—something," said the prisoner, and his eyes roved nervously around the cell.

"What did you hear?"

"I—I can't tell you," stammered the prisoner. Then, in a sudden burst of terror: "Take me out of this cell—put me anywhere—but take me out of here."

The warden and the three jailers exchanged glances.

"Who is this fellow? What's he accused of?" asked the warden.

"Joseph Ballard," said one of the jailers. "He's accused of throwing acid in a woman's face. She died from it."

"But they can't prove it," gasped the prisoner. "They can't prove it. Please put me in some other cell."

He was still clinging to the warden, and that official threw his arms off roughly. Then for a time he stood looking at the cowering wretch, who seemed possessed of all the wild, unreasoning terror of a child.

"Look here, Ballard," said the warden, finally, "if you heard anything, I want to know what it was. Now tell me."

"I can't, I can't," was the reply. He was sobbing.

"Where did it come from?"

"I don't know. Everywhere—nowhere. I just heard it."

"What was it—a voice?"

"Please don't make me answer," pleaded the prisoner.

"You must answer," said the warden, sharply.

"It was a voice—but—but it wasn't human," was the sobbing reply.

"Voice, but not human?" repeated the warden, puzzled.

"It sounded muffled and—and far away—and ghostly," explained the man.

"Did it come from inside or outside the prison?"

"It didn't seem to come from anywhere—it was just here, here, everywhere. I heard it. I heard it."

For an hour the warden tried to get the story, but Ballard had become suddenly obstinate and would say nothing—only pleaded to be placed in another cell, or to have one of the jailers remain near him until daylight. These requests were gruffly refused.

"And see here," said the warden, in conclusion, "if there's any more of this screaming I'll put you in the padded cell."

Then the warden went his way, a sadly puzzled man. Ballard sat at his cell door until daylight, his face, drawn and white with terror, pressed against the bars, and looked out into the prison with wide, staring eyes.

That day, the fourth since the incarceration of The Thinking Machine, was enlivened considerably by the volunteer prisoner, who spent most of his time at the little window of his cell. He began proceedings by throwing another piece of linen down to the guard, who picked it up dutifully and took it to the warden. On it was written:

"Only three days more."

The warden was in no way surprised at what he read; he understood that The Thinking Machine meant only three days more of his imprisonment, and he regarded the note as a boast. But how was the thing written? Where had The Thinking Machine found this new piece of linen? Where? How? He carefully examined the linen. It was white, of fine texture, shirting material. He took the shirt which he had taken and carefully fitted the two original pieces of the linen to the torn places. This third piece was entirely superfluous; it didn't fit anywhere, and yet it was unmistakably the same goods.

"And where—where does he get anything to write with?" demanded the warden of the world at large.

Still later on the fourth day The Thinking Machine, through the window of his cell, spoke to the armed guard outside.

"What day of the month is it?" he asked.

"The fifteenth," was the answer.

The Thinking Machine made a mental astronomical calculation and

satisfied himself that the moon would not rise until after nine o'clock that night. Then he asked another question:

"Who attends to those arc lights?"

"Man from the company."

"You have no electricians in the building?"

"No."

"I should think you could save money if you had your own man."

"None of my business," replied the guard.

The guard noticed The Thinking Machine at the cell window frequently during that day, but always the face seemed listless and there was a certain wistfulness in the squint eyes behind the glasses. After a while he accepted the presence of the leonine[10] head as a matter of course. He had seen other prisoners do the same thing; it was the longing for the outside world.

That afternoon, just before the day guard was relieved, the head appeared at the window again, and The Thinking Machine's hand held something out between the bars. It fluttered to the ground and the guard picked it up. It was a five-dollar bill.

"That's for you," called the prisoner.

As usual, the guard took it to the warden. That gentleman looked at it suspiciously; he looked at everything that came from Cell 13 with suspicion.

"He said it was for me," explained the guard.

10 leonine (lē′ə nīn): lionlike.

"It's a sort of a tip, I suppose," said the warden. "I see no particular reason why you shouldn't accept——"

Suddenly he stopped. He had remembered that The Thinking Machine had gone into Cell 13 with one five-dollar bill and two ten-dollar bills; twenty-five dollars in all. Now a five-dollar bill had been tied around the first pieces of linen that came from the cell. The warden still had it, and to convince himself he took it out and looked at it. It was five dollars; yet here was another five dollars, and The Thinking Machine had only had ten-dollar bills.

"Perhaps somebody changed one of the bills for him," he thought at last, with a sigh of relief.

But then and there he made up his mind. He would search Cell 13 as a cell was never before searched in this world. When a man could write at will, and change money, and do other wholly inexplicable things, there was something radically wrong with his prison. He planned to enter the cell at night—three o'clock would be an excellent time. The Thinking Machine must do all the weird things he did sometime. Night seemed the most reasonable.

Thus it happened that the warden stealthily descended upon Cell 13 that night at three o'clock. He paused at the door and listened. There was no sound save the steady, regular breathing of the prisoner. The keys unfastened the double locks with scarcely a clank, and the warden entered, locking the door behind him. Suddenly he flashed his dark lantern in the face of the recumbent[11] figure.

If the warden had planned to startle The Thinking Machine he was mistaken, for that individual merely opened his eyes quietly, reached for his glasses and inquired, in a most matter-of-fact tone:

"Who is it?"

It would be useless to describe the search that the warden made. It was minute. Not one inch of the cell or the bed was overlooked. He found the round hole in the floor, and with a flash of inspiration thrust his thick fingers into it. After a moment of fumbling there he drew up something and looked at it in the light of his lantern.

"Ugh!" he exclaimed.

The thing he had taken out was a rat—a dead rat. His inspiration fled as a mist before the sun. But he continued the search. The Thinking Machine, without a word, arose and kicked the rat out of the cell into the corridor.

The warden climbed on the bed and tried the steel bars in the tiny window. They were perfectly rigid; every bar of the door was the same.

Then the warden searched the prisoner's clothing, beginning at the shoes. Nothing hidden in them! Then the trousers waistband. Still nothing! Then the pockets of the trousers. From one side he drew out some paper money and examined it.

"Five one-dollar bills," he gasped.

"That's right," said the prisoner.

"But the—you had two tens and a five—what the—how do you do it?"

11 **recumbent:** reclining; lying down.

"That's my business," said The Thinking Machine.

"Did any of my men change this money for you—on your word of honor?"

The Thinking Machine paused just a fraction of a second.

"No," he said.

"Well, do you make it?" asked the warden. He was prepared to believe anything.

"That's my business," again said the prisoner.

The warden glared at the eminent scientist fiercely. He felt—he knew —that this man was making a fool of him, yet he didn't know how. If he were a real prisoner he would get the truth—but, then, perhaps, those inexplicable things which had happened would not have been brought before him so sharply. Neither of the men spoke for a long time, then suddenly the warden turned fiercely and left the cell, slamming the door behind him. He didn't dare to speak, then.

He glanced at the clock. It was ten minutes to four. He had hardly settled himself in bed when again came that heartbreaking shriek through the prison. With a few muttered words, which, while not elegant, were highly expressive, he relighted his lantern and rushed through the prison again to the cell on the upper floor.

Again Ballard was crushing himself against the steel door, shrieking, shrieking at the top of his voice. He stopped only when the warden flashed his lamp in the cell.

"Take me out, take me out," he

screamed. "I did it, I did it, I killed her. Take it away."

"Take what away?" asked the warden.

"I threw the acid in her face—I did it—I confess. Take me out of here."

Ballard's condition was pitiable; it was only an act of mercy to let him out into the corridor. There he crouched in a corner, like an animal at bay, and clasped his hands to his ears. It took half an hour to calm him sufficiently for him to speak. Then he told incoherently what had happened. On the night before at four o'clock he had heard a voice—a sepulchral[12] voice, muffled and wailing in tone.

"What did it say?" asked the warden, curiously.

"Acid—acid—acid!" gasped the prisoner. "It accused me. Acid! I threw the acid, and the woman died. Oh!" It was a long, shuddering wail of terror.

"Acid?" echoed the warden, puzzled. The case was beyond him.

"Acid. That's all I heard—that one word, repeated several times. There were other things, too, but I didn't hear them."

"That was last night, eh?" asked the warden. "What happened tonight—what frightened you just now?"

"It was the same thing," gasped the prisoner. "Acid—acid—acid!" He covered his face with his hands and sat shivering. "It was acid I used on her, but I didn't mean to kill

her. I just heard the words. It was something accusing me—accusing me." He mumbled, and was silent.

"Did you hear anything else?"

"Yes—but I couldn't understand—only a little bit—just a word or two."

"Well, what was it?"

"I heard 'acid' three times, then I heard a long, moaning sound, then—then—I heard 'No. 8 hat.' I heard that twice."

"No. 8 hat," repeated the warden. "What the devil—No. 8 hat? Accusing voices of conscience have never talked about No. 8 hats, so far as I ever heard."

"He's insane," said one of the jailers, with an air of finality.

"I believe you," said the warden. "He must be. He probably heard something and got frightened. He's trembling now. No. 8 hat! What the——"

When the fifth day of The Thinking Machine's imprisonment rolled around the warden was wearing a hunted look. He was anxious for the end of the thing. He could not help but feel that his distinguished prisoner had been amusing himself. And if this were so, The Thinking Machine had lost none of his sense of humor. For on this fifth day he flung down another linen note to the outside guard, bearing the words: "Only two days more." Also he flung down half a dollar.

Now the warden knew—he *knew*—that the man in Cell 13 didn't have any half dollars—he *couldn't* have any half dollars, no more than he could have pen and ink and linen, and yet he did have them. It was a condition, not a theory; that is one reason why the warden was wearing a hunted look.

That ghastly, uncanny thing, too, about "Acid" and "No. 8 hat" clung to him tenaciously. They didn't mean anything, of course, merely the ravings of an insane murderer who had been driven by fear to confess his crime, still there were so many things that "didn't mean anything" happening in the prison now since The Thinking Machine was there.

On the sixth day the warden received a postal stating that Dr. Ransome and Mr. Fielding would be at Chisholm Prison on the following evening, Thursday, and in the event Professor Van Dusen had not yet escaped—and they presumed he had not because they had not heard from him—they would meet him there.

"In the event he had not yet escaped!" The warden smiled grimly. Escaped!

The Thinking Machine enlivened this day for the warden with three notes. They were on the usual linen and bore generally on the appointment at half past eight o'clock Thursday night, which appointment the scientist had made at the time of his imprisonment.

On the afternoon of the seventh day the warden passed Cell 13 and glanced in. The Thinking Machine was lying on the iron bed, apparently sleeping lightly. The cell appeared precisely as it always did from a casual glance. The warden would swear that no man was going to

leave it between that hour—it was then four o'clock—and half past eight o'clock that evening.

On his way back past the cell the warden heard the steady breathing again, and coming close to the door looked in. He wouldn't have done so if The Thinking Machine had been looking, but now—well, it was different.

A ray of light came through the high window and fell on the face of the sleeping man. It occurred to the warden for the first time that his prisoner appeared haggard and weary. Just then The Thinking Machine stirred slightly and the warden hurried on up the corridor guiltily. That evening after six o'clock he saw the jailer.

"Everything all right in Cell 13?" he asked.

"Yes, sir," replied the jailer. "He didn't eat much, though."

It was with a feeling of having done his duty that the warden received Dr. Ransome and Mr. Fielding shortly after seven o'clock. He intended to show them the linen notes and lay before them the full story of his woes, which was a long one. But before this came to pass the guard from the river side of the prison yard entered the office.

"The arc light in my side of the yard won't light," he informed the warden.

"Confound it, that man's a hoodoo," thundered the official. "Everything has happened since he's been here."

The guard went back to his post in the darkness, and the warden phoned to the electric light company.

"This is Chisholm Prison," he said through the phone. "Send three or four men down here quick, to fix an arc light."

The reply was evidently satisfactory, for the warden hung up the receiver and passed out into the yard. While Dr. Ransome and Mr. Fielding sat waiting the guard at the outer gate came in with a special delivery letter. Dr. Ransome happened to notice the address, and, when the guard went out, looked at the letter more closely.

"By George!" he exclaimed.

"What is it?" asked Mr. Fielding.

Silently the doctor offered the letter. Mr. Fielding examined it closely.

"Coincidence," he said. "It must be."

It was nearly eight o'clock when the warden returned to his office. The electricians had arrived in a wagon, and were now at work. The warden pressed the buzz-button communicating with the man at the outer gate in the wall.

"How many electricians came in?" he asked, over the short phone. "Four? Three workmen in jumpers and overalls and the manager? Frock coat and silk hat? All right. Be certain that only four go out. That's all."

He turned to Dr. Ransome and Mr. Fielding.

"We have to be careful here—particularly," and there was broad sarcasm in his tone, "since we have scientists locked up."

The warden picked up the special delivery letter carelessly, and then began to open it.

"When I read this I want to tell you gentlemen something about how —— Great Caesar!" he ended, suddenly, as he glanced at the letter. He sat with mouth open, motionless, from astonishment.

"What is it?" asked Mr. Fielding.

"A special delivery letter from Cell 13," gasped the warden. "An invitation to supper."

"What?" and the two others arose, unanimously.

The warden sat dazed, staring at the letter for a moment, then called sharply to a guard outside in the corridor.

"Run down to Cell 13 and see if that man's in there."

The guard went as directed, while Dr. Ransome and Mr. Fielding examined the letter.

"It's Van Dusen's handwriting; there's no question of that," said Dr. Ransome. "I've seen too much of it."

Just then the buzz on the telephone from the outer gate sounded, and the warden, in a semi-trance, picked up the receiver.

"Hello! Two reporters, eh? Let 'em come in." He turned suddenly to the doctor and Mr. Fielding. "Why, the man *can't* be out. He must be in his cell."

Just at that moment the guard returned.

"He's still in his cell, sir," he reported. "I saw him. He's lying down."

"There, I told you so," said the warden, and he breathed freely

again. "But how did he mail that letter?"

There was a rap on the steel door which led from the jail yard into the warden's office.

"It's the reporters," said the warden. "Let them in," he instructed the guard; then to the two other gentleman: "Don't say anything about this before them, because I'd never hear the last of it."

The door opened, and the two men from the front gate entered.

"Good evening, gentlemen," said one. That was Hutchinson Hatch; the warden knew him well.

"Well?" demanded the other, irritably. "I'm here."

That was The Thinking Machine. He squinted belligerently[13] at the

13 belligerently: in a warlike manner.

warden, who sat with mouth agape. For the moment that official had nothing to say. Dr. Ransome and Mr. Fielding were amazed, but they didn't know what the warden knew. They were only amazed; he was paralyzed. Hutchinson Hatch, the reporter, took in the scene with greedy eyes.

"How—how—how did you do it?" gasped the warden, finally.

"Come back to the cell," said The Thinking Machine, in the irritated voice which his scientific associates knew so well.

The warden, still in a condition bordering on trance, led the way.

"Flash your light in there," directed The Thinking Machine.

The warden did so. There was nothing unusual in the appearance of the cell, and there—there on the bed lay the figure of The Thinking Machine. Certainly! There was the yellow hair! Again the warden looked at the man beside him and wondered at the strangeness of his own dreams.

With trembling hands he unlocked the cell door and The Thinking Machine passed inside.

"See here," he said.

He kicked at the steel bars in the bottom of the cell door and three of them were pushed out of place. A fourth broke off and rolled away in the corridor.

"And here, too," directed the erstwhile prisoner as he stood on the bed to reach the small window. He swept his hand across the opening and every bar came out.

"What's this in bed?" demanded the warden, who was slowly recovering.

"A wig," was the reply. "Turn down the cover."

The warden did so. Beneath it lay a large coil of strong rope, thirty feet or more, a dagger, three files, ten feet of electric wire, a thin, powerful pair of steel pliers, a small tack hammer with its handle, and—and a derringer pistol.

"How did you do it?" demanded the warden.

"You gentlemen have an engagement to supper with me at half past nine o'clock," said The Thinking Machine. "Come on, or we shall be late."

"But how did you do it?" insisted the warden.

"Don't ever think you can hold any man who can use his brain," said The Thinking Machine. "Come on; we shall be late."

It was an impatient supper party in the rooms of Professor Van Dusen and a somewhat silent one. The guests were Dr. Ransome, Alfred Fielding, the warden, and Hutchinson Hatch, reporter. The meal was served to the minute, in accordance with Professor Van Dusen's instructions of one week before; Dr. Ransome found the artichokes delicious. At last the supper was finished and The Thinking Machine turned full on Dr. Ransome and squinted at him fiercely.

"Do you believe it now?" he demanded.

"I do," replied Dr. Ransome.

"Do you admit that it was a fair test?"

"I do."

With the others, particularly the warden, he was waiting anxiously for the explanation.

"Suppose you tell us how——" began Mr. Fielding.

"Yes, tell us how," said the warden.

The Thinking Machine readjusted his glasses, took a couple of preparatory squints at his audience, and began the story. He told it from the beginning logically; and no man ever talked to more interested listeners.

"My agreement was," he began, "to go into a cell, carrying nothing except what was necessary to wear, and to leave that cell within a week. I had never seen Chisholm Prison. When I went into the cell I asked for tooth powder, two ten- and one five-dollar bills, and also to have my shoes blacked. Even if these requests had been refused it would not have mattered seriously. But you agreed to them.

"I knew there would be nothing in the cell which you thought I might use to advantage. So when the warden locked the door on me I was apparently helpless, unless I could turn three seemingly innocent things to use. They were things which would have been permitted any prisoner under sentence of death, were they not, warden?"

"Tooth powder and polished shoes, yes, but not money," replied the warden.

"Anything is dangerous in the hands of a man who knows how to use it," went on The Thinking Machine. "I did nothing that first night but sleep and chase rats." He glared at the warden. "When the matter was broached I knew I could do nothing that night, so suggested next day. You gentlemen thought I wanted time to arrange an escape with outside assistance, but this was not true. I knew I could communicate with whom I pleased, when I pleased."

The warden stared at him a moment, then went on smoking solemnly.

"I was aroused next morning at six o'clock by the jailer with my breakfast," continued the scientist. "He told me dinner was at twelve and supper at six. Between these times, I gathered, I would be pretty much to myself. So immediately after breakfast I examined my outside surroundings from my cell window. One look told me it would be useless to try to scale the wall, even should I decide to leave my cell by the window, for my purpose was to leave not only the cell, but the prison. Of course, I could have gone over the wall, but it would have taken me longer to lay my plans that way. Therefore, for the moment, I dismissed all idea of that.

"From this first observation I knew the river was on that side of the prison, and that there was also a playground there. Subsequently these surmises were verified by a keeper. I knew then one important thing— that anyone might approach the prison wall from that side if necessary without attracting any particular attention. That was well to remember. I remembered it.

"But the outside thing which most attracted my attention was the feed wire to the arc light which ran within a few feet—probably three or four— of my cell window. I knew that would be valuable in the event I found it necessary to cut off that arc light."

"Oh, you shut it off tonight, then?" asked the warden.

"Having learned all I could from that window," resumed The Thinking Machine, without heeding the interruption, "I considered the idea of escaping through the prison proper. I recalled just how I had come into the cell, which I knew would be the only way. Seven doors lay between me and the outside. So, also for the time being, I gave up the idea of escaping that way. And I couldn't go through the solid granite walls of the cell."

The Thinking Machine paused for a moment and Dr. Ransome lighted a new cigar. For several minutes there was silence, then the scientific jailbreaker went on:

"While I was thinking about these things a rat ran across my foot. It suggested a new line of thought. There were at least half a dozen rats in the cell—I could see their beady eyes. Yet I had noticed none come under the cell door. I frightened them purposely and watched the cell door to see if they went out that way. They did not, but they were gone. Obviously they went another way. Another way meant another opening.

"I searched for this opening and found it. It was an old drainpipe, long unused and partly choked with dirt and dust. But this was the way the rats had come. They came from somewhere. Where? Drainpipes usually lead outside prison grounds. This one probably led to the river, or near it. The rats must therefore come from that direction. If they came a part of the way, I reasoned that they came all the way, because it was extremely unlikely that a solid iron or lead pipe would have any hole in it except at the exit.

"When the jailer came with my luncheon he told me two important things, although he didn't know it. One was that a new system of plumbing had been put in the prison seven years before; another that the river was only three hundred feet away. Then I knew positively that the pipe was a part of an old system; I knew, too, that it slanted generally toward the river. But did the pipe end in the water or on land?

"This was the next question to be decided. I decided it by catching several of the rats in the cell. My jailer was surprised to see me engaged in this work. I examined at least a dozen of them. They were perfectly dry; they had come through the pipe, and, most important of all, they were *not house rats, but field rats*. The other end of the pipe was on land, then, outside the prison walls. So far, so good.

"Then, I knew that if I worked freely from this point I must attract the warden's attention in another direction. You see, by telling the warden that I had come there to escape you made the test more severe, because I had to trick him by false scents."

The warden looked up with a sad expression in his eyes.

"The first thing was to make him think I was trying to communicate with you, Dr. Ransome. So I wrote a note on a piece of linen I tore from my shirt, addressed it to Dr. Ransome, tied a five-dollar bill around it and threw it out the window. I knew the guard would take it to the warden, but I rather hoped the warden would send it as addressed. Have you that first linen note, warden?"

The warden produced the cipher.

"What the deuce does it mean, anyhow?" he asked.

"Read it backward, beginning with the 'T' signature and disregard the division into words," instructed The Thinking Machine.

The warden did so.

"*T-h-i-s*, this," he spelled, studied it a moment, then read it off, grinning:

"This is not the way I intend to escape."

"Well, now what do you think o' that?" he demanded, still grinning.

"I knew that would attract your attention, just as it did," said The Thinking Machine, "and if you really found out what it was it would be a sort of gentle rebuke."

"What did you write it with?" asked Dr. Ransome, after he had examined the linen and passed it to Mr. Fielding.

"This," said the erstwhile prisoner, and he extended his foot. On it was the shoe he had worn in prison, though the polish was gone—scraped off clean. "The shoe blacking, moistened with water, was my ink; the metal tip of the shoe lace made a fairly good pen."

The warden looked up and suddenly burst into a laugh, half of relief, half of amusement.

"You're a wonder," he said, admiringly. "Go on."

"That precipitated a search of my cell by the warden, as I had intended," continued The Thinking Machine. "I was anxious to get the warden into the habit of searching my cell, so that finally, constantly finding nothing, he would get disgusted and quit. This at last happened, practically."

The warden blushed.

"He then took my white shirt away and gave me a prison shirt. He was satisfied that those two pieces of the shirt were all that was missing. But while he was searching my cell I had another piece of that same shirt, about nine inches square, rolled into a small ball in my mouth."

"Nine inches of that shirt?" demanded the warden. "Where did it come from?"

"The bosoms of all stiff white shirts are of triple thickness," was the explanation. "I tore out the inside thickness, leaving the bosom only two thicknesses. I knew you wouldn't see it. So much for that."

There was a little pause, and the warden looked from one to another of the men with a sheepish grin.

"Having disposed of the warden for the time being by giving him something else to think about, I took my first serious step toward freedom," said Professor Van Dusen. "I knew, within reason, that the pipe led somewhere to the playground outside; I knew a great many boys played there; I knew that rats came into my cell from out there. Could I communicate with some one outside with these things at hand?

"First was necessary, I saw, a long and fairly reliable thread, so—but here," he pulled up his trousers legs and showed that the tops of both stockings, of fine, strong lisle, were gone. "I unraveled those—after I got them started it wasn't difficult—and I had easily a quarter of a mile of thread that I could depend on.

"Then on half of my remaining linen I wrote, laboriously enough I assure you, a letter explaining my situation to this gentleman here," and he indicated Hutchinson Hatch.

"I knew he would assist me—for the value of the newspaper story. I tied firmly to this linen letter a ten-dollar bill—there is no surer way of attracting the eye of anyone—and wrote on the linen: 'Finder of this deliver to Hutchinson Hatch, *Daily American,* who will give another ten dollars for the information.'

"The next thing was to get this note outside on that playground where a boy might find it. There were two ways, but I chose the best. I took one of the rats—I became adept in catching them—tied the linen and money firmly to one leg, fastened my lisle thread to another, and turned him loose in the drainpipe. I reasoned that the natural fright of the rodent would make him run until he was outside the pipe and then out on earth he would probably stop to gnaw off the linen and money.

"From the moment the rat disappeared into that dusty pipe I became anxious. I was taking so many chances. The rat might gnaw the string, of which I held one end; other rats might gnaw it; the rat might run out of the pipe and leave the linen and money where they would never be found; a thousand other things might have happened. So began some nervous hours, but the fact that the rat ran on until only a few feet of the string remained in my cell made me think he was outside the pipe. I had carefully instructed Mr. Hatch what to do in case the note reached him. The question was: Would it reach him?

"This done, I could only wait and make other plans in case this one failed. I openly attempted to bribe my jailer, and learned from him that he held the keys to only two of seven doors between me and freedom. Then I did something else to make the warden nervous. I took the steel supports out of the heels of my shoes and made a pretense of sawing the bars of my cell window. The warden raised a pretty row about that. He developed, too, the habit of shaking the bars of my cell window to see if they were solid. They were—then."

Again the warden grinned. He had ceased being astonished.

"With this one plan I had done all I could and could only wait to see what happened," the scientist went on. "I couldn't know whether my note had been delivered or even found, or whether the mouse had gnawed it up. And I didn't dare to draw back through the pipe that one slender thread which connected me with the outside.

"When I went to bed that night I didn't sleep, for fear there would come the slight signal twitch at the thread which was to tell me that Mr. Hatch had received the note. At half past three o'clock, I judge, I felt this twitch, and no prisoner actually under sentence of death ever welcomed a thing more heartily."

The Thinking Machine stopped and turned to the reporter.

"You'd better explain just what you did," he said.

"The linen note was brought to me by a small boy who had been playing baseball," said Mr. Hatch. "I immediately saw a big story in it, so I gave the boy another ten dollars, and got several spools of silk, some twine, and a roll of light, pliable wire. The professor's note suggested that I have the finder of the note show me just where it was picked up, and told me to make my search from there, beginning at two o'clock in the morning. If I found the other end of the thread I was to twitch it gently three times, then a fourth.

"I began the search with a small-bulb electric light. It was an hour and twenty minutes before I found the end of the drain pipe, half hidden in weeds. The pipe was very large there, say twelve inches across. Then I found the end of the lisle thread, twitched it as directed and immediately I got an answering twitch.

"Then I fastened the silk to this and Professor Van Dusen began to pull it into his cell. I nearly had heart disease for fear the string would break. To the end of the silk I fastened the twine, and when that had been pulled in I tied on the wire. Then that was drawn into the pipe and we had a substantial line, which rats couldn't gnaw, from the mouth of the drain into the cell."

The Thinking Machine raised his hand and Hatch stopped.

"All this was done in absolute silence," said the scientist. "But when the wire reached my hand I could have shouted. Then we tried another experiment, which Mr. Hatch was prepared for. We tested the pipe as a speaking tube. Neither of us could hear very clearly, but I dared not speak loud for fear of attracting attention in the prison. At last I made him understand what I wanted immediately. He seemed to have great difficulty in understanding when I asked for nitric acid, and I repeated the word 'acid' several times.

"Then I heard a shriek from a cell above me. I knew instantly that someone had overheard, and when I heard you coming, Mr. Warden, I feigned sleep. If you had entered my cell at that moment that whole plan of escape would have ended there. But you passed on. That was the nearest I ever came to being caught.

"Having established this improvised trolley it is easy to see how I got things in the cell and made them disappear at will. I merely dropped them back into the pipe. You, Mr. Warden, could not have reached the connecting wire with your fingers; they are too large. My fingers, you see, are longer and more slender. In addition I guarded the top of that pipe with a rat—you remember how."

"I remember," said the warden, with a grimace.

"I thought that if anyone were tempted to investigate that hole the rat would dampen his ardor. Mr. Hatch could not send me anything useful through the pipe until next night, although he did send me change for ten dollars as a test, so I proceeded with other parts of my plan. Then I evolved the method of escape which I finally employed.

"In order to carry this out successfully it was necessary for the guard in the yard to get accustomed to seeing me at the cell window. I arranged this by dropping linen notes to him, boastful in tone, to make the warden believe, if possible, one of his assistants was communicating with the outside for me. I would stand at my window for hours gazing out, so the guard could see, and occasionally I spoke to him. In that way I learned that the prison had no electricians of its own, but was dependent upon the lighting company if anything should go wrong.

"That cleared the way to freedom perfectly. Early in the evening of the last day of my imprisonment, when it was dark, I planned to cut the feed wire which was only a few feet from my window, reaching it with an acid-tipped wire I had. That would make that side of the prison perfectly dark while the electricians were searching for the break. That would also bring Mr. Hatch into the prison yard.

"There was only one more thing to do before I actually began the work of setting myself free. This was to arrange final details with Mr. Hatch through our speaking tube. I did this within half an hour after the warden left my cell on the fourth night of my imprisonment. Mr. Hatch again had serious difficulty in understanding me, and I repeated the word 'acid' to him several times, and later on the words: 'No. 8 hat'— that's my size—and these were the things which made a prisoner upstairs confess to murder, so one of the jailers told me next day. This prisoner heard our voices, confused of course, through the pipe, which also went to his cell. The cell directly over me was not occupied, hence no one else heard.

"Of course the actual work of cutting the steel bars out of the window and door was comparatively easy with nitric acid, which I got through the pipe in tin bottles, but it took time. Hour after hour on the fifth and sixth and seventh days the guard below was looking at me as I worked on the bars of the window with the acid on a piece of wire. I used the tooth powder to prevent the acid spreading. I looked away abstractedly as I worked and each minute the acid cut deeper into the metal. I noticed that the jailers always tried the door by shaking the upper part, never the lower bars, therefore I cut the lower bars, leaving them hanging in place by thin strips of metal. But that was a bit of daredeviltry. I could not have gone that way so easily."

The Thinking Machine sat silent for several minutes.

"I think that makes everything clear," he went on. "Whatever points I have not explained were merely to confuse the warden and jailers. These things in my bed I brought in to please Mr. Hatch, who wanted to improve the story. Of course, the wig was necessary in my plan. The special delivery letter I wrote and directed in my cell with Mr. Hatch's fountain pen, then sent it out to him and he mailed it. That's all, I think."

"But your actually leaving the prison grounds and then coming in through the outer gate to my office?" asked the warden.

"Perfectly simple," said the scientist. "I cut the electric light wire with acid, as I said, when the current was off. Therefore when the current was turned on the arc didn't light. I knew it would take some time to find out what was the matter and make repairs. When the guard went to report to you the yard was dark. I crept out the window—it was a tight fit, too—replaced the bars by standing on a narrow ledge and remained in a shadow until the force of electricians arrived. Mr. Hatch was one of them.

"When I saw him I spoke and he handed me a cap, a jumper and overalls, which I put on within ten feet of you, Mr. Warden, while you were in the yard. Later Mr. Hatch called me, presumably as a workman, and together we went out the gate to get something out of the wagon. The gate guard let us pass out readily as two workmen who had just passed in. We changed our clothing and reappeared, asking to see you. We saw you. That's all."

There was silence for several minutes. Dr. Ransome was first to speak.

"Wonderful!" he exclaimed. "Perfectly amazing."

"How did Mr. Hatch happen to come with the electricians?" asked Mr. Fielding.

"His father is manager of the company," replied The Thinking Machine.

"But what if there had been no Mr. Hatch outside to help?"

"Every prisoner has one friend outside who would help him escape if he could."

"Suppose—just suppose—there had

been no old plumbing system there?" asked the warden, curiously.

"There were two other ways out," said The Thinking Machine, enigmatically.[14]

Ten minutes later the telephone bell rang. It was a request for the warden.

"Light all right, eh?" the warden asked, through the phone. "Good.

Wire cut beside Cell 13? Yes, I know. One electrician too many? What's that? Two came out?"

The warden turned to the others with a puzzled expression.

"He only let in four electricians, he has let out two and says there are three left."

"I was the odd one," said The Thinking Machine.

"Oh," said the warden. "I see." Then through the phone: "Let the fifth man go. He's all right."

Reading Skills

1. The first several paragraphs of the story are designed to convince the reader that Professor Van Dusen is very intelligent. What are some of the details suggesting his great intelligence?
2. What circumstances lead up to the test? Explain the conditions of the test.
3. What three requests does the professor make before he enters the cell?
4. What does the professor learn about his cell, the prison, and the prison routine on the first evening and day of his imprisonment? What seem to be the possibilities of escape?
5. Why does Van Dusen drop the coded message, try to bribe a guard, and try to file his prison bars with a steel support from his shoe heel?
6. How does the professor use the elements in his surroundings to make his escape?

Understanding Literature

1. In this story the real suspense for the reader is not in the question, Does he escape? but, How does he escape? The plot is arranged so that the reader stays in great suspense to the very end of the story. In what order do the following elements of the story occur?

Presentation of a problem that seems insoluble.

Explanation of how the problem was solved.

Description of the conditions of the problem that emphasize its difficulty.

Description of the great intelligence of the main character.

Presentation of clues to the solution of the problem.

2. The first section of the story arouses the reader's suspense by posing certain questions: Will Van Dusen accept the challenge of Ransome and Fielding? Why does he make his strange requests to the warden, and how will he escape? What questions are posed in each of the other sections?

3. Where is the climax of the story? (At what point is your suspense greatest?)

4. The author has not made The Thinking Machine very likable; in fact, Van Dusen has several characteristics that usually irritate others. Why, then, does the reader want Van Dusen to succeed in escaping from the cell?

Further Activity

Write a character study of Professor Van Dusen, following this outline:

Professor Van Dusen's physical appearance.

His great abilities.

His idiosyncracies (odd traits of character).

Other qualities that make him a satisfactory hero for "The Problem of Cell 13."

Use only the information about Van Dusen that is given in the story. Use examples from the story to illustrate your general statements.

This story tells about a humorous adventure. True, kidnaping is not funny—except when the kidnapers are Bill and Sam, the "kidnapee" is Red Chief, and the story is told by O. Henry, a master of stories with a surprise ending.

The Ransom of Red Chief

O. Henry

IMPROVING YOUR READING: A good deal of the humor in this story is based on the *contrast* between what people expect and what they get. What does each character here want? What does he get?

IT LOOKED LIKE a good thing: but wait till I tell you. We were down South, in Alabama—Bill Driscoll and myself—when this kidnaping idea struck us. It was, as Bill afterward expressed it, "during a moment of temporary mental apparition";[1] but we didn't find that out till later.

There was a town down there, as flat as a flannel cake, and called Summit, of course. It contained inhabitants of as undeleterious[2] and self-satisfied a class of peasantry as ever clustered around a Maypole.

Bill and me had a joint capital of about six hundred dollars, and we needed just two thousand dollars more to pull off a fraudulent town-lot scheme in Western Illinois with. We talked it over on the front steps of the hotel. Philoprogenitoveness,[3]

says we, is strong in semirural communities; therefore, and for other reasons, a kidnaping project ought to do better there than in the radius of newspapers that send reporters out in plain clothes to stir up talk about such things. We knew that Summit couldn't get after us with anything stronger than constables and, maybe, some lackadaisical bloodhounds and a diatribe or two in the *Weekly Farmers' Budget*. So, it looked good.

We selected for our victim the only child of a prominent citizen named Ebenezer Dorset. The father was respectable and tight, a mortgage fancier and a stern, upright collection-plate passer and forecloser. The kid was a boy of ten, with bas-relief freckles, and hair the color of the cover of the magazine you buy at the newsstand when you want to catch a train. Bill and me figured that Ebenezer would melt down for a ransom of two thousand dollars to a cent. But wait till I tell you.

1 **apparition:** Bill means *aberration*, a disorder of the mind. What is an apparition?
2 **undeleterious:** not harmful.
3 **Philoprogenitoveness:** Sam means *philoprogenitiveness*, love for offspring.

About two miles from Summit was a little mountain, covered with a dense cedar brake. On the rear elevation of this mountain was a cave. There we stored provisions.

One evening after sundown, we drove in a buggy past old Dorset's house. The kid was in the street, throwing rocks at a kitten on the opposite fence.

"Hey, little boy!" says Bill, "would you like to have a bag of candy and a nice ride?"

The boy catches Bill neatly in the eye with a piece of brick.

"That will cost the old man an extra five hundred dollars," says Bill, climbing over the wheel.

That boy put up a fight like a welterweight cinnamon bear; but, at last, we got him down in the bottom of the buggy and drove away. We took him up to the cave, and I hitched the horse in the cedar brake. After dark I drove the buggy to the little village, three miles away, where we had hired it, and walked back to the mountain.

Bill was pasting court plaster over the scratches and bruises on his features. There was a fire burning behind the big rock at the entrance of the cave, and the boy was watching a pot of boiling coffee, with two buzzard tail-feathers stuck in his red hair. He points a stick at me when I come up, and says:

"Ha! cursed paleface, do you dare to enter the camp of Red Chief, the terror of the plains?"

"He's all right now," says Bill, rolling up his trousers and examining some bruises on his shins. "We're playing Indian. We're making Buffalo Bill's show look like magic-lantern views of Palestine in the town hall. I'm Old Hank, the Trapper, Red Chief's captive, and I'm to be scalped at daybreak. By Geronimo! that kid can kick hard."

Yes, sir, that boy seemed to be having the time of his life. The fun of camping out in a cave had made him forget that he was a captive himself. He immediately christened me Snake-eye, the Spy, and announced that, when his braves returned from the warpath, I was to be broiled at the stake at the rising of the sun.

Then we had supper; and he filled his mouth full of bacon and bread and gravy, and began to talk. He made a during-dinner speech something like this:

"I like this fine. I never camped out before; but I had a pet 'possum once, and I was nine last birthday. I hate to go to school. Rats ate up sixteen of Jimmy Talbot's aunt's speckled hen's eggs. Are there any real Indians in these woods? I want some more gravy. Does the trees moving make the wind blow? We had five puppies. What makes your nose so red, Hank? My father has lots of money. Are the stars hot? I whipped Ed Walker twice, Saturday. I don't like girls. You dassent catch toads unless with a string. Do oxen make any noise? Why are oranges round? Have you got beds to sleep on in this cave? Amos Murray has got six toes. A parrot can talk, but a monkey or a fish can't. How many does it take to make twelve?"

Every few minutes he would remember that he was a pesky red-skin, and pick up his stick rifle and tiptoe to the mouth of the cave to rubber for the scouts of the hated paleface. Now and then he would let out a war whoop that made Old Hank the Trapper shiver. That boy had Bill terrorized from the start.

"Red Chief," says I to the kid, "would you like to go home?"

"Aw, what for?" says he. "I don't have any fun at home. I hate to go to school. I like to camp out. You won't take me back home again, Snake-eye, will you?"

"Not right away," says I. "We'll stay here in the cave awhile."

"All right!" says he. "That'll be fine. I never had such fun in all my life."

We went to bed about eleven o'clock. We spread down some wide blankets and quilts and put Red Chief between us. We weren't afraid he'd run away. He kept us awake for three hours, jumping up and reaching for his rifle and screeching: "Hist! pard," in mine and Bill's ears, as the fancied crackle of a twig or the rustle of a leaf revealed to his young imagination the stealthy approach of the outlaw band. At last, I fell into a troubled sleep, and dreamed that I had been kidnaped and chained to a tree by a ferocious pirate with red hair.

Just at daybreak, I was awakened by a series of awful screams from Bill. They weren't yells, or howls, or shouts, or whoops, or yawps, such as you'd expect from a manly set of vocal organs—they were simply indecent, terrifying, humiliating screams, such as women emit when they see ghosts or caterpillars. It's an awful thing to hear a strong, desperate, fat man scream incontinently in a cave at daybreak.

I jumped up to see what the matter was. Red Chief was sitting on Bill's chest, with one hand twined in Bill's hair. In the other he had the sharp case knife we used for slicing bacon; and he was industriously and realistically trying to take Bill's scalp, according to the sentence that had been pronounced upon him the evening before.

I got the knife away from the kid and made him lie down again. But, from that moment, Bill's spirit was broken. He laid down on his side of the bed, but he never closed an eye again in sleep as long as that boy was with us. I dozed off for a while, but along toward sunup I remembered that Red Chief had said I was to be burned at the stake at the rising of the sun. I wasn't nervous or afraid; but I sat up and lit my pipe and leaned against a rock.

"What you getting up so soon for, Sam?" asked Bill.

"Me?" says I. "Oh, I got a kind of pain in my shoulder. I thought sitting up would rest it."

"You're a liar!" says Bill. "You're afraid. You was to be burned at sunrise, and you was afraid he'd do it. And he would, too, if he could find a match. Ain't it awful, Sam? Do you think anybody will pay out money to get a little imp like that back home?"

"Sure," said I. "A rowdy kid like that is just the kind that parents dote on. Now, you and the Chief get up and cook breakfast, while I go up on the top of this mountain and reconnoiter."

I went up on the peak of the little mountain and ran my eye over the contiguous vicinity. Over toward Summit I expected to see the sturdy yeomanry[4] of the village armed with scythes and pitchforks beating the countryside for the dastardly kid-napers. But what I saw was a peaceful landscape dotted with one man plowing with a dun mule. Nobody was dragging the creek; no couriers dashed hither and yon, bringing tidings of no news to the distracted parents. There was a sylvan attitude of somnolent sleepi-ness pervading that section of the external outward surface of Alabama that lay exposed to my view. "Per-haps," says I to myself, "it has not yet been discovered that the wolves have borne away the tender lambkin from the fold. Heaven help the wolves!" says I, and I went down the mountain to breakfast.

When I got to the cave I found Bill backed up against the side of it, breathing hard, and the boy threat-ening to smash him with a rock half as big as a coconut.

"He put a red-hot boiled potato down my back," explained Bill, "and then mashed it with his foot; and I boxed his ears. Have you got a gun about you, Sam?"

I took the rock away from the boy and kind of patched up the argu-ment. "I'll fix you," says the kid to

4 yeomanry (yō'mən rĭ): body of small land owners.

Bill. "No man ever yet struck the Red Chief but he got paid for it. You better beware!"

After breakfast the kid takes a piece of leather with strings wrapped around it out of his pocket and goes outside the cave unwinding it.

"What's he up to now?" says Bill, anxiously. "You don't think he'll run away, do you, Sam?"

"No fear of it," says I. "He don't seem to be much of a homebody. But we've got to fix up some plan about the ransom. There don't seem to be much excitement around Sum-mit on account of his disappearance; but maybe they haven't realized yet that he's gone. His folks may think he's spending the night with Aunt Jane or one of the neighbors. Any-how, he'll be missed today. Tonight we must get a message to his father demanding the two thousand dollars for his return."

Just then we heard a kind of war whoop, such as David might have emitted when he knocked out the champion Goliath. It was a sling that Red Chief had pulled out of his pocket, and he was whirling it around his head.

I dodged, and heard a heavy thud and a kind of a sigh from Bill, like a horse gives out when you take his saddle off. A rock the size of an egg had caught Bill just behind his left ear. He loosened himself all over and fell in the fire across the frying pan of hot water for washing the dishes. I dragged him out and poured cold water on his head for half an hour.

By and by, Bill sits up and feels

behind his ear and says: "Sam, do you know who my favorite Biblical character is?"

"Take it easy," says I. "You'll come to your senses presently."

"King Herod,"[5] says he. "You won't go away and leave me here alone, will you, Sam?"

I went out and caught that boy and shook him until his freckles rattled.

"If you don't behave," says I, "I'll take you straight home. Now, are you going to be good, or not?"

"I was only funning," says he, sullenly. "I didn't mean to hurt Old Hank. But what did he hit me for? I'll behave, Snake-eye, if you won't send me home, and if you'll let me play the Black Scout today."

"I don't know the game," says I. "That's for you and Mr. Bill to decide. He's your playmate for the day. I'm going away for a while, on business. Now, you come in and make friends with him and say you are sorry for hurting him, or home you go, at once."

I made him and Bill shake hands, and then I took Bill aside and told him I was going to Poplar Grove, a little village three miles from the cave, and find out what I could about how the kidnaping had been regarded in Summit. Also, I thought it best to send a peremptory letter to old man Dorset that day, demanding the ransom and dictating how it should be paid. •

"You know, Sam," says Bill, "I've stood by you without batting an eye in earthquakes, fire and flood—in poker games, dynamite outrages, police raids, train robberies, and cyclones. I never lost my nerve yet till we kidnaped that two-legged sky-rocket of a kid. He's got me going. You won't leave me long with him, will you, Sam?"

"I'll be back some time this afternoon," says I. "You must keep the boy amused and quiet till I return. And now we'll write the letter to old Dorset."

Bill and I got paper and pencil and worked on the letter while Red Chief, with a blanket wrapped around him, strutted up and down, guarding the mouth of the cave. Bill begged me tearfully to make the ransom fifteen hundred dollars instead of two thousand. "I ain't attempting," says he, "to decry the celebrated moral aspect of parental affection, but we're dealing with humans, and it ain't human for anybody to give up two thousand dollars for that forty-pound chunk of freckled wildcat. I'm willing to take a chance at fifteen hundred dollars. You can charge the difference up to me."

So, to relieve Bill, I acceded, and we collaborated a letter that ran this way:

Ebenezer Dorset, Esq.:

We have your boy concealed in a place far from Summit. It is useless for you or the most skillful detectives to attempt to find him. Absolutely, the only terms on which you can have him restored to you are these: We de-

---

5 **King Herod:** the king of Judea (40-4 B.C.) who, according to Matthew 2, ordered all the infants of Bethlehem killed.

mand fifteen hundred dollars in large bills for his return; the money to be left at midnight tonight at the same spot and in the same box as your reply—as hereinafter described. If you agree to these terms, send your answer in writing by a solitary messenger tonight at half past eight o'clock. After crossing Owl Creek on the road to Poplar Grove, there are three large trees about a hundred yards apart, close to the fence of the wheat field on the right-hand side. At the bottom of the fence post, opposite the third tree, will be found a small pasteboard box.

The messenger will place the answer in this box and return immediately to Summit.

If you attempt any treachery or fail to comply with our demand as stated, you will never see your boy again.

If you pay the money as demanded, he will be returned to you safe and well within three hours. These terms are final, and if you do not accede to them no further communication will be attempted.

Two Desperate Men

I addressed this letter to Dorset, and put it in my pocket. As I was about to start, the kid comes up to me and says:

"Aw, Snake-eye, you said I could play the Black Scout while you was gone."

"Play it, of course," says I. "Mr. Bill will play with you. What kind of a game is it?"

"I'm the Black Scout," says Red Chief, "and I have to ride to the stockade to warn the settlers that the Indians are coming. I'm tired of playing Indian myself. I want to be the Black Scout."

"All right," says I. "It sounds harmless to me. I guess Mr. Bill will

help you foil the pesky savages."

"What am I to do?" asks Bill, looking at the kid suspiciously.

"You are the hoss," says Black Scout. "Get down on your hands and knees. How can I ride to the stockade without a hoss?"

"You'd better keep him interested," said I, "till we get the scheme going. Loosen up."

Bill gets down on his all fours, and a look comes in his eye like a rabbit's when you catch it in a trap.

"How far is it to the stockade, kid?" he asks, in a husky manner of voice.

"Ninety miles," says the Black Scout. "And you have to hump yourself to get there on time. Whoa, now!"

The Black Scout jumps on Bill's back and digs his heels in his side.

"For Heaven's sake," says Bill, "hurry back, Sam, as soon as you can. I wish we hadn't made the ransom more than a thousand. Say, you quit kicking me or I'll get up and warm you good."

I walked over to Poplar Grove and sat around the post office and store, talking with the chawbacons that came in to trade. One whiskerando says that he hears Summit is all upset on account of Elder Ebenezer Dorset's boy having been lost or stolen. That was all I wanted to know. I bought some smoking tobacco, referred casually to the price of black-eyed peas, posted my letter surreptitiously, and came away. The postmaster said the mail carrier would come by in an hour to take the mail to Summit.

When I got back to the cave Bill and the boy were not to be found. I explored the vicinity of the cave, and risked a yodel or two, but there was no response.

So I lighted my pipe and sat down on a mossy bank to await developments.

In about half an hour I heard the bushes rustle, and Bill wabbled out into the little glade in front of the cave. Behind him was the kid, stepping softly like a scout, with a broad grin on his face. Bill stopped, took off his hat, and wiped his face with a red handkerchief. The kid stopped about eight feet behind him.

"Sam," says Bill, "I suppose you'll think I'm a renegade, but I couldn't help it. I'm a grown person with masculine proclivities and habits of self-defense, but there is a time when all systems of egotism and predominance fail. The boy is gone. I sent him home. All is off. There was martyrs in old times," goes on Bill, "that suffered death rather than give up the particular graft they enjoyed. None of 'em ever was subjugated to such supernatural tortures as I have been. I tried to be faithful to our articles of depredation; but there came a limit."

"What's the trouble, Bill?" I asks him.

"I was rode," says Bill, "the ninety miles to the stockade, not barring an inch. Then, when the settlers was rescued, I was given oats. Sand ain't a palatable substitute. And then, for an hour I had to try to explain to him why there was nothin' in holes, how a road can run both ways, and what makes the grass green. I tell you, Sam, a human can only stand so much. I takes him by the neck of his clothes and drags him down the mountain. On the way he kicks my legs black and blue from the knees down; and I've got to have two or three bites on my thumb and hand cauterized.

"But he's gone"—continues Bill—"gone home. I showed him the road to Summit and kicked him about eight feet nearer there at one kick. I'm sorry we lose the ransom; but it was either that or Bill Driscoll to the madhouse."

Bill is puffing and blowing, but there is a look of ineffable peace and growing content on his rose-pink features.

"Bill," says I, "there isn't any heart disease in your family, is there?"

"No," says Bill, "nothing chronic except malaria and accidents. Why?"

"Then you might turn around," says I, "and have a look behind you."

Bill turns and sees the boy, and loses his complexion and sits down plump on the ground and begins to pluck aimlessly at grass and little sticks. For an hour I was afraid of his mind. And then I told him that my scheme was to put the whole job through immediately and that we would get the ransom and be off with it by midnight if old Dorset fell in with our proposition. So Bill braced up enough to give the kid a weak sort of a smile and a promise to play the Russian in a Japanese war with him as soon as he felt a little better.

I had a scheme for collecting that ransom without danger of being caught by counterplots that ought to commend itself to professional kidnapers. The tree under which the answer was to be left—and the money later on—was close to the road fence with big, bare fields on all sides. If a gang of constables should be watching for anyone to come for the note, they could see him a long way off crossing the fields or in the road. But no, sirree! At half-past eight I was up in that tree as well hidden as a tree toad, waiting for the messenger to arrive.

Exactly on time, a half-grown boy rides up the road on a bicycle, locates the pasteboard box at the foot of the fence post, slips a folded piece of paper into it, and pedals away again back toward Summit.

I waited an hour and then concluded the thing was square. I slid down the tree, got the note, slipped along the fence till I struck the woods, and was back at the cave in another half an hour. I opened the note, got near the lantern, and read it to Bill. It was written with a pen in a crabbed hand, and the sum and substance of it was this:

Two Desperate Men.

Gentlemen: I received your letter today by post, in regard to the ransom you ask for the return of my son. I think you are a little high in your demands, and I hereby make you a counterproposition, which I am inclined to believe you will accept. You bring Johnny home and pay me two hundred and fifty dollars in cash, and I agree to take him off your hands. You had better come at night, for the neighbors believe he is lost, and I couldn't be responsible for what they would do to anybody they saw bringing him back. Very respectfully,

Ebenezer Dorset

"Great pirates of Penzance," says I; "of all the impudent——"

But I glanced at Bill, and hesitated. He had the most appealing look in his eyes I ever saw on the face of a dumb or a talking brute.

"Sam," says he, "what's two hundred and fifty dollars, after all? We've got the money. One more night of this kid will send me to a bed in Bedlam. Besides being a thorough gentleman, I think Mr. Dorset is a spendthrift for making us such a liberal offer. You ain't going to let the chance go, are you?"

"Tell you the truth, Bill," says I, "this little he ewe lamb has somewhat got on my nerves too. We'll take him home, pay the ransom, and make our getaway."

We took him home that night. We got him to go by telling him that his father had bought a silver-mounted rifle and a pair of moccasins for him, and we were to hunt bears the next day.

It was just twelve o'clock when we knocked at Ebenezer's front door. Just at the moment when I should have been abstracting the fifteen hundred dollars from the box under the tree, according to the original proposition, Bill was counting out two hundred and fifty dollars into Dorset's hand.

When the kid found out we were going to leave him at home he started up a howl like a calliope and fastened himself as tight as a leech to Bill's leg. His father peeled him away gradually, like a porous plaster.

"How long can you hold him?" asks Bill.

"I'm not as strong as I used to be," says old Dorset, "but I think I can promise you ten minutes."

"Enough," says Bill. "In ten minutes I shall cross the Central, South-ern, and Middle Western States, and be legging it trippingly for the Canadian border."

And, as dark as it was, and as fat as Bill was, and as good a runner as I am, he was a good mile and a half out of Summit before I could catch up with him.

Reading Skills

1. Why do Bill and Sam plan the kidnaping? Why do they decide to kidnap Ebenezer Dorset's child?
2. What preparations and plans do the two men make?
3. When Red Chief first appears in the story, how do his actions suggest his nature?
4. List the other actions of Red Chief that make him an increasingly difficult victim of kidnaping.
5. What hints are given rather early in the story of the attitude of the townspeople toward the kidnaping? Where is Sam when he hears that Summit is "all upset"? How might the report have been different in Summit?
6. How does the title of the story change in meaning at the end?

Understanding Literature

1. How does the amount of the ransom demanded by the kidnapers change as the plot develops? Why does the amount change?
2. With what people and forces are Sam and Bill in conflict? What is the main conflict? At what point do you know how the conflict will end?
3. Below are statements about what Sam and Bill expect from their kidnaping scheme. How does the outcome of the action contrast in each instance with their expectations?
   (a) "It [the kidnaping plot] looked like a good thing."
   (b) "Philoprogenitoveness, says we, is strong in semirural communities."
   (c) A kidnaped child will be frightened and eager to return home.
   (d) "Bill and me figured that Ebenezer would melt down for a ransom of two thousand dollars to a cent."
   (e) " 'That will cost the old man an extra five hundred dollars,' says Bill."

(f) "A rowdy kid like that is just the kind that parents dote on."

(g) "Over towards Summit I expected to see the sturdy yeomanry of the village armed with scythes and pitchforks beating the countryside for the dastardly kidnapers."

4. Stories about kidnaping would ordinarily never be humorous. However, from the beginning of the story the reader senses that the situation is not going to be serious. Find illustrations of some of the following devices that lead you to understand that the story is a humorous, not a serious, treatment of the subject:

(a) The contrast between the large words used by Bill and Sam and their poor grammar;

(b) The diminishing size of the ransom;

(c) Humorous description of a character or an action;

(d) Reactions of the kidnapers as difficulties arise;

(e) Words and phrases used in an unusual context.

Focusing on Words

Much of the humor in this story depends on the choice of words.

1. The narrator, one of the kidnapers, says that "we needed just two thousand dollars more to pull off a fraudulent town-lot scheme." What does *fraudulent* mean? Who would be more likely to use the word—the person involved in the scheme or a newspaper writer reporting it? Later, the narrator speaks of "dastardly kidnapers." Why would you not expect a kidnaper to use such an expression?

2. What are "bas-relief freckles"?

3. What does "welterweight cinnamon bear" mean?

4. Why is the following expression humorous as it is used in this story: "stealthy approach of the outlaw band"?

5. Explain what these sentences mean: "Perhaps . . . it has not yet been discovered that the wolves have borne away the tender lambkin from the fold. Heaven help the wolves!"

6. What does *renegade* mean? What does Bill mean when he says, "I suppose you'll think I'm a renegade, but I couldn't help it"?

Ray Bradbury, the author of *The Martian Chronicles*, specializes in writing science fiction and fantasy. *The Martian Chronicles* is a book of imaginative stories about future expeditions to Mars. "December 2001: The Green Morning" tells about a Johnny Appleseed of the 21st century, a space traveler who plants trees on Mars. The subject matter of the story is necessarily fantastic, because no one knows what life on Mars would really be like. But Bradbury has made the events in the story seem real by including details familiar in ordinary life.

December 2001:
The Green Morning

from The Martian Chronicles

Ray Bradbury

IMPROVING YOUR READING: Although this story begins on an evening and ends the next morning, by the end of the story you know what has happened to Benjamin Driscoll during the past month. To give you this information, the author uses a *flashback*, a scene which interrupts the major action to return to an earlier event. You are no doubt familiar with the technique of flashback in motion pictures.

WHEN THE SUN set he crouched by the path and cooked a small supper and listened to the fire crack while he put the food in his mouth and chewed thoughtfully. It had been a day not unlike thirty others, with many neat holes dug in the dawn hours, seeds dropped in, and water brought from the bright canals. Now, with an iron weariness in his slight body, he lay and watched the sky color from one darkness to another.

His name was Benjamin Driscoll, and he was thirty-one years old. And the thing that he wanted was Mars grown green and tall with trees and foliage, producing air, more air, growing larger with each season; trees to cool the towns in the boiling summer, trees to hold back the winter winds. There were so many things a tree could do: add color, provide shade, drop fruit, or become a children's playground, a whole sky universe to climb and hang from; an architecture of food and pleasure, that was a tree. But most of all the trees would distill an icy air for the lungs, and a gentle rustling for the ear when you lay nights in your snowy bed and were gentled to sleep by the sound.

He lay listening to the dark earth gather itself, waiting for the sun, for the rains that hadn't come yet. His ear to the ground, he could hear the feet of the years ahead moving at a distance, and he imagined the seeds he had placed today sprouting up with green and taking hold on the sky, pushing out branch after branch, until Mars was an afternoon forest, Mars was a shining orchard.

In the early morning, with the small sun lifting faintly among the folded hills, he would be up and finished with a smoky breakfast in a few minutes and, trodding out the fire ashes, be on his way with knapsacks, testing, digging, placing seed or sprout, tamping lightly, watering, going on, whistling, looking at the clear sky brightening toward a warm noon.

"You need the air," he told his night fire. The fire was a ruddy, lively companion that snapped back at you, that slept close by with drowsy pink eyes warm through the chilly night. "We all need the air. It's a thin air here on Mars. You get tired so soon. It's like living in the Andes, in South America, high. You inhale and don't get anything. It doesn't satisfy."

He felt his rib case. In thirty days, how it had grown. To take in more air, they would all have to build their lungs. Or plant more trees.

"That's what I'm here for," he said. The fire popped. "In school they told a story about Johnny Appleseed walking across America planting apple trees. Well, I'm doing more. I'm planting oaks, elms, and maples, every kind of tree, aspens and deodars and chestnuts. Instead of making just fruit for the stomach, I'm making air for the lungs. When those

trees grow up some year, *think* of the oxygen they'll make!"

He remembered his arrival on Mars. Like a thousand others, he had gazed out upon a still morning and thought, How do I fit here? What will I do? Is there a job for me?

Then he had fainted.

Someone pushed a vial of ammonia to his nose and, coughing, he came around.

"You'll be all right," said the doctor.

"What happened?"

"The air's pretty thin. Some can't take it. I think you'll have to go back to Earth."

"No!" He sat up and almost immediately felt his eyes darken and Mars revolve twice around under him. His nostrils dilated and he forced his lungs to drink in deep nothingnesses. "I'll be all right. I've got to stay here!"

They let him lie gasping in horrid fishlike motions. And he thought, Air, air, air. They're sending me back because of air. And he turned his head to look across the Martian fields and hills. He brought them to focus, and the first thing he noticed was that there were no trees, no trees at all, as far as you could look in any direction. The land was down upon itself, a land of black loam, but nothing on it, not even grass. Air, he thought, the thin stuff whistling in his nostrils. Air, air. And on top of hills, or in their shadows, or even by little creeks, not a tree and not a single green blade of grass. Of course! He felt the answer came not from his mind, but his lungs and his throat. And the thought was like a sudden gust of pure oxygen, raising him up. Trees and grass. He looked down at his hands and turned them over. He would plant trees and grass. That would be his job, to fight against the very thing that might prevent his staying here. He would have a private horticultural war with Mars. There lay the old soil, and the plants of it so ancient they had worn themselves out. But what if new forms were introduced? Earth trees, great mimosas and weeping willows and magnolias and magnificent eucalyptus. What then? There was no guessing what mineral wealth hid in the soil, untapped because the old ferns, flowers, bushes, and trees had tired themselves to death.

"Let me up!" he shouted. "I've got to see the Co-ordinator!"

He and the Co-ordinator had talked an entire morning about things that grew and were green. It would be months, if not years, before organized planting began. So far, frosted food was brought from Earth in flying icicles; a few community gardens were greening up in hydroponic plants.[1]

"Meanwhile," said the Co-ordinator, "it's your job. We'll get what seed we can for you, a little equipment. Space on the rockets is mighty precious now. I'm afraid, since these first towns are mining communities, there won't be much sympathy for your tree planting——"

1 **hydroponic plants:** plants grown in water instead of soil.

"But you'll let me do it?"

They let him do it. Provided with a single motorcycle, its bin full of rich seeds and sprouts, he had parked his vehicle in the valley wilderness and struck out on foot over the land.

That had been thirty days ago, and he had never glanced back. For looking back would have been sickening to the heart. The weather was excessively dry; it was doubtful if any seeds had sprouted yet. Perhaps his entire campaign, his four weeks of bending and scooping were lost. He kept his eyes only ahead of him, going on down this wide shallow valley under the sun, away from First Town, waiting for the rains to come.

Clouds were gathering over the dry mountains now as he drew his blanket over his shoulders. Mars was a place as unpredictable as time. He felt the baked hills simmering down into frosty night, and he thought of the rich, inky soil, a soil so black and shiny it almost crawled and stirred in your fist, a rank soil from which might sprout gigantic beanstalks from which, with bone-shaking concussion, might drop screaming giants.

The fire fluttered into sleepy ash. The air tremored to the distant roll of a cartwheel. Thunder. A sudden odor of water. Tonight, he thought, and put his hand out to feel for rain. Tonight.

He awoke to a tap on his brow.

Water ran down his nose into his lips. Another drop hit his eye, blurring it. Another splashed his chin.

RAY BRADBURY

71

The rain.

Raw, gentle, and easy, it mizzled out of the high air, a special elixir, tasting of spells and stars and air, carrying a peppery dust in it, and moving like a rare light sherry on his tongue.

Rain.

He sat up. He let the blanket fall and his blue denim shirt spot, while the rain took on more solid drops. The fire looked as though an invisible animal were dancing on it, crushing it, until it was angry smoke. The rain fell. The great black lid of sky cracked in six powdery blue chips, like a marvelous crackled glaze, and rushed down. He saw ten billion rain crystals, hesitating long enough to be photographed by the electrical display. Then darkness and water.

He was drenched to the skin, but he held his face up and let the water hit his eyelids, laughing. He clapped his hands together and stepped up and walked around his little camp, and it was one o'clock in the morning.

It rained steadily for two hours and then stopped. The stars came out, freshly washed and clearer than ever.

Changing into dry clothes from his cellophane pack, Mr. Benjamin Driscoll lay down and went happily to sleep.

The sun rose slowly among the hills. It broke out upon the land quietly and wakened Mr. Driscoll where he lay.

He waited a moment before aris-ing. He had worked and waited a long hot month, and now, standing up, he turned at last and faced the direction from which he had come.

It was a green morning.

As far as he could see the trees were standing up against the sky. Not one tree, not two, not a dozen, but the thousands he had planted in seed and sprout. And not little trees, no, not saplings, not little tender shoots, but great trees, huge trees, trees as tall as ten men, green and huge and round and full, trees shimmering their metallic leaves, trees whispering, trees in a line over hills, lemon trees, lime trees, redwoods and mimosas and oaks and elms and aspens, cherry, maple, ash, apple, orange, eucalyptus, stung by a tumultuous rain, nourished by alien and magical soil and, even as he watched, throwing out new branches, popping open new buds.

"Impossible!" cried Mr. Benjamin Driscoll.

But the valley and the morning were green.

And the air!

All about, like a moving current, a mountain river, came the new air, the oxygen blowing from the green trees. You could see it shimmer high in crystal billows. Oxygen, fresh, pure, green, cold oxygen turning the valley into a river delta. In a moment the town doors would flip wide, people would run out through the new miracle of oxygen, sniffing, gusting in lungfuls of it, cheeks pinking with it, noses frozen with it, lungs revivified, hearts leaping, and worn bodies lifted into a dance.

Mr. Benjamin Driscoll took one long deep drink of green water air and fainted.

Before he woke again five thousand new trees had climbed up into the yellow sun.

Reading Skills

1. What is Driscoll's principal reason for wanting trees on Mars? What are some of the other reasons?
2. Explain the reference to the enlarged rib cage; to Johnny Appleseed.
3. Relate the steps leading to Driscoll's being given the work of planting trees on Mars.
4. What do you understand to be the function of the Co-ordinator?
5. Why did Driscoll never look back as he went about his work?
6. Explain what happened as a result of the rain. What explanation earlier in the story suggests that the soil might be very productive?

Understanding Literature

1. The author makes imaginary events seem real to the reader by using many details from everyday life and by using words which appeal to the five senses. For instance, in the first paragraph he describes such ordinary activities as cooking, eating, planting, and resting. And throughout the story he tells
   (a) how things look: "watched the sky color from one darkness to another";
   (b) how things sound: "listened to the fire crack";
   (c) how things smell: "A sudden odor of water";
   (d) how things feel: "Water ran down his nose and into his lips. Another drop hit his eye, blurring it. Another splashed his chin."
   Find other illustrations of such details that help make the story seem believable.
2. How many scenes are there in the story? What is the purpose of each? Is the purpose to explain something? to reveal something about Driscoll's character? to portray action? to describe Mars? (Keep in mind that a scene may achieve more than one purpose.)
3. Where does the flashback begin and end? What is the purpose of the flashback? What specific information are you given in the flashback? Why do you think the author chose to start the story as he did rather than to start the story with the information in the flashback?

To understand the state of Jan's mind in this story, you must know that the scene of the story, Labrador, is the extreme northeastern portion of North America—cold and lonely, too cold for crops to grow, too cold for any means of transportation except sled. Fur trapping in such a spot is not for a man weak in body or will. Survival involves a grim struggle in the far North.

Without Words

Elliott Merrick

IMPROVING YOUR READING: The author of "Without Words" has included only those details which the central character, Jan, would be able to observe; in other words, he tells the story from Jan's *point of view*. Thus the reader sees what is happening through Jan's eyes. Although the author usually uses his own words to tell what Jan thinks and does, from time to time he expresses Jan's thoughts in words Jan himself would use.

HE CAME over a knoll and stopped, head back, his rifle in one mitten, his ax in the other. Below him spread the river, ice-locked between the hills. A mile across, the birch bluffs were turning blue in the twilight.

He was not given to poetic fancies, but it touched him always, coming out to the river after days and nights in the spruces to the west, following brooks and isolated chains of lakes that didn't lead anywhere, plowing through willow tangles and up and down the wooded hills. It gave him a feeling of spaciousness, like stepping out of doors to see the broad river again, sweeping out of sight between the hills.

That country behind him, his east trap line where he had been for ten days, was just a cut-up jumble of wilderness, lost, nameless, known only to himself. But the river was the river. This was the road to home, this was the known thread that joined him to other men.

This water that was flowing under the ice would slide past the village sometime, in a month maybe. "It'll get there 'fore I do, anyways," he said aloud. It was nine weeks now since the day the crowd had waved from the wharf, and the double-barrel shotguns split the air in the old-time farewell, "Boomboom" . . . and a pause to load . . . "Boom," saying "Good-by. . . . Luck"; nine weeks since the trappers fired their one answering shot, "Luck." It gave a fellow something to remember way off here where you didn't hear anything much except your own voice.

It would be pretty near three months yet before he'd be home and

maybe see Luce, he was thinking as he scrambled down the bank and legged it along the ice for the house. *This* cabin had a window, and a door with hinges, a good tight roof of birch bark, and within, such luxuries as a sleeping bag, which his tiny log tilts back in the woods had not.

It was nearly dark when he got there, but not too dark to see in the cove the print of strange snowshoes. And by the point where the current flowed fast and the ice was thin, somebody had been chopping a water hole. "Hello!" he called to the cabin.

From the ridge that rose up behind the cabin came a silvery, mocking "hello," and faintly, seconds later, a distant hello from across the river, the echo of the echo. Jan crossed the cove, bent double, studying the

tracks. There were three of them, a big pair of snowshoes and two smaller pairs. The smaller snowshoes had been dragging in a stick of firewood from alongshore—the women.

Jan threw off his bag and hurried into the cabin. Nobody made snowshoes of that pattern but Mathieu Susaka-shish, the Seven Islands Indian. Nobody but Mathieu knew this cabin was here. He and his wife and daughter had come last year and begged a little tea and sugar. Now they were here again with their Indian idea that food belongs to anybody who is hungry. The dirty dogs! Where three fifty-pound bags of flour had been hanging, only two hung now. They had dripped candle grease onto his bunk and left his big meat kettle unwashed. He dove under the bunk and pulled out his food boxes. They'd made off with some of his split peas and a few of his beans, a handful of candles too. They had sliced a big chunk of salt pork neatly down the middle.

In a frenzy of rage he ripped open his fur bag. Every skin was there, and in addition, a black and shining otter skin lay crosswise on his bundles of mink and marten, fox and ermine. He held it up and blew the hair and felt its thickness and its length, stroking its blue-black luster. It was a prize. It would bring forty dollars, perhaps. But the sight of it made him angrier than before.

"So!" he muttered. "Mathieu thinks one miserable skin of fur pays me for my grub, eh?" He lit a candle, and his hand was trembling with rage. From now on he'd be half-hungry all the time, and hunting meat when he ought to be tending the trap line. This was his whole year's earnings, these five months in the bush. And Mathieu thought he could steal the grub that made it possible, did he? He thought he could come every year and fit himself out, likely.

Jan took his rifle and emptied the magazine. It was only one bag of flour—but still, there were men way off here in the country who'd died for lack of a cupful, yes, a spoonful. Slowly he reloaded with the soft-nosed cartridges he had always kept for caribou, heretofore. Would he ever tell anybody, Luce for instance, would he ever be able to forget that somewhere back in the ridges, by some secret little lake that no one knew, he had shot three Indians and

stuffed them through the ice? Didn't the Bible say, an eye for an eye and a tooth for a tooth?

Jan had already walked twenty miles today. And he was tired with the piled-up weariness of weeks and weeks of that, traveling, traveling to cover and re-cover his two hundred miles of fur paths. With a sigh he set to work; wood to chop, water from the river, a partridge to be stewed and ten cakes of bannock bread to bake in the frying pan. While the bread was baking he skinned two mink, a marten, four weasels, humming as he did so a song that he was very fond of:

"Oh, we've sailed the seven seas from pole to pole,
And we've conquered stormy gale and stinging foam,
And we've seen the strangest sights of far-off lands,
But the best is to see the cheery lights of home."

It called up visions of a light in the window, if he should ever have a real home, if, perhaps, Luce did not go away at all.

It was too bad he couldn't just shoot Mathieu, but it would be no use to leave the women to wander around and starve. At the thought of actually squeezing the trigger and seeing them drop, he shuddered.

It was nearly midnight when he stoked up the stove and rolled in on the bunk for the last good sleep he expected to know for a while. At five o'clock, in the starlight, he was out on the river shore with a candle lantern made of a baking powder can, examining tracks. The polished, shallow trench that their two toboggans had left was so plain a child could have followed it. Mathieu was ahead, taking long steps, hurrying. The two women were behind, hauling their toboggan in double harness, tandem fashion. One of them fell and left the print of her knee going down the bank. Jan smiled as though he had seen it and heard her mutter.

He followed their track across the river to the top of a draw between two bare hills. There in the sunrise he turned and looked back at the ice, sparkling with frost in the soft golden light, spotted with long blue shadows of the hills. As he plunged downhill into the thick country to the north he had an ominous feeling that he was leaving something. Maybe Mathieu would ambush him; it would be an easy thing to do on a track like this. Would Mathieu guess that he was being tracked?

Jan studied the track, unconsciously noting every detail. Here in this book of the snow he might perhaps read Mathieu's thoughts, even a warning of an ambush. Ah, but Indians were smart in the woods. Did he really think he could outtrack an Indian hunter?

"I can have a try," he whispered to himself.

Two mornings ago, he decided it was, that they had passed through here under the firs, across that little brook. Two days were not much of a start for them. They had sleds and he had none. Mathieu had to break trail, while he had their hard frozen track to walk on. They had all their winter gear, their blankets and kettles, their tin stove and tent, traps, trout nets probably. He had nothing but the gamebag on his back, nine cakes of bread, tea and sugar, his rifle and ax, a single blanket. The chances were he could travel twice as fast as they.

He passed their first fire, where they had stopped to boil tea and thrown the leaves on the embers. The tea leaves were frozen stiff.

All day he swung on, parting the boughs where the spruces were thick, slipping through them as effortlessly as a weasel, trotting down all the hills with a tireless shuffle, trotting again where the way was level and open. Once he stopped for ten minutes to sit on a log and munch dry bread, then lit his pipe and swung on. It was frosty, and the edges of his fur cap grew white with his breathing.

Before sunset he had long passed their first night's camp. Through the semidarkness of early twilight he pressed on, following the hardness of their track more by touch than by sight. In the starlight he made his fire and boiled tea in a ravine by a brook. Here and there a tree snapped with the frost. The brook murmured under the ice. On the western hill a horn owl was hooting.

Every hour he woke with the cold, threw on more wood, turned over and slept again. Once, around three o'clock, he woke and could not sleep. He sat hunched in the blanket looking into the fire thinking what a fool he was. He should be on the trap line, not here. He had not come up the river so far away to waste time chasing Indians around the hills. Already he was hungry and wished he had brought more food.

The wind had risen and was blowing hard. That was bad. He could not feel it here, but the treetops were rocking, and branches now and then rubbed together and spoke with weird, childlike voices.

By half past four he had boiled tea and eaten, and was picking his way along the track again. He should have rested another hour, he knew. But he could not rest, though he was tired. He wanted to get it over with. Probably they would not bleed much, it was so cold.

The Indians were still heading northwest. Likely they were bound for the headwaters of streams that flowed into Hudson's Bay. Mathieu would feel safe there. And he would be too. It was much farther than Jan could track him with only three days' grub in the bag.

In the morning he passed their second night's camp. By noontime he had come to the edge of a big, oval marsh that was about six miles wide at its narrowest. On its barren floor were occasional clumps of dead sticks, juniper and fir, no higher than a man's head, the firs rotten and falling, the junipers gaunt and wind-carved. Compared to its bleak, dead savagery the greenwoods' borders seemed sociable and friendly and snug. As the merciless northwest wind had stunted and killed the trees, so it could shrivel and kill a man if it caught him out there in a blizzard.

The trail was dim and wind-scoured on the marsh. A mile out and there was nothing but the dully shining spots the sleds had polished; two miles out and Mathieu was veering off to the east, deviating for the first time from his northwest course.

The marks petered out entirely, heading at the last straight east. Jan stopped and rubbed his forehead. "Mathieu, you're a cute fox, eh?"

If Mathieu was heading northwest the blue notch was the obvious way for him. Then why, in the middle of the marsh, did he swing off for the steep ridges?

Jan trotted about in a circle, slapping his mittens together and pounding the toes that were aching in his moccasins. The drifting snow slid by like sand, rising in little eddies as the wind rose.

He stopped and stood with his back to the wind, leaning against it. "Now look. Mathieu wants to go through the blue notch, but it's too plain. He knows I'd pick up his track there first thing. So he cuts off in the middle of the marsh, thinkin' there'll be no sign of it when I gets yere, and he makes a big half a circle. When I gets to the blue draw I can't find ere a sign of him, and I don't know where he's gone.

"I don't, eh? Well, I know he's got to strike the valley of that notch-stream somewheres. Him and his women haulin' sleds can't get along in the hills no faster than a fox with a trap on his foot."

Jan picked up his gamebag and trotted off toward the now-invisible

78

notch. If he'd guessed right, all right; if he'd guessed wrong, all right too. What odds! He was hungry. In all this time he hadn't seen a partridge, though he'd seen plenty of feathers where that devil Mathieu'd shot all there was.

He began to sing a song to rival the sweep of the strong wind. In the wind it was good to sing, the wind drowned sound, sang a song of its own, saved a man from feeling that miles of quiet woods were listening. He roared in a strong baritone:

"Oh, we've sailed the seven seas from pole
   to pole,
And we've conquered stormy gale and
   stinging foam,
And we've seen the strangest sights of
   far-off lands,
But the be-e-e-est is to see the chee-eery
   lights of ho-o-me."

The drift had obscured the shores now and he was as though alone in the middle of a white sea, snow above, below and on all sides. But he did not think of it. The wind was compass enough for him and had been since boyhood.

He clasped his gun and ax in the crook of one elbow, put his curled mitts up around his mouth and imitated a mouth organ, hunching his shoulders and swinging his body, dancing on his snowshoes in the gale. When he got home and the fiddle was squeaking in the schoolhouse and old Si Willetts was callin' out the figures, oh he'd swing his girl like this—and he whirled around with his gun and ax, holding them high in the air and shaking them.

"You! you got no more sense than a porcupine," he said.

At dusk, miles beyond the blue notch he picked up the Indians' track again. He glowed with the warmth of a hunter's pride, his nostrils quivered and his jaw clenched. How they had traveled. But he had them now. They'd never get away, they were doomed, unless it snowed.

A mile farther on they had camped, and there he camped too. A few split chunks of wood that they hadn't burned he used. There was still a faint warmth in the depths of their ashes. But something in the low branches of a spruce made him pause. Lashed there, rolled up in a hairy caribouskin were a big trout net and a heavyish iron Dutch oven. So, they were lightening loads were they? They knew they were being tracked then. How did they know?

Jan sat on the fir brush of their tent site and thought about it. They didn't know, they couldn't know. Mathieu was just playing safe, that was all, announcing, if he should be followed, that he was still a-drivin' 'er for all he was worth, bluffing a pursuer, trying to say, "I know I am being followed"—just in case he should be followed. Mathieu would go on for a week, get his women set in a good camp, then circle back, hunting, setting traps in likely places, looking for beaver houses, back to this very tree. Here he'd pick up his stuff, have a look around, and mosey along westward.

"That's what you think, Mathieu."

That night he ate another half a bannock, only half when he could easily have eaten three whole ones.

What a fool he was to have traveled so light. If by some mischance he didn't catch them now, he'd be stranded off here with nothing to eat.

Rolled in his blanket and their caribou robe he had the best sleep yet. It was risky. He had his gun beside him. For why couldn't Mathieu come back tonight as well as in a week? All about was the ring of darkness. Here was the firelight. What a perfect mark to shoot at. Yes, but Mathieu wouldn't shoot him. Why, Mathieu's father used to camp on the shore at Turner's Harbor years ago. Mathieu's cousin used to wrestle with Jan by the hour, and Mathieu himself had been in the foot races they ran on the beach summer afternoons long ago by the blue cool bay. Mathieu knew him all to pieces, even if they didn't meet but once in years and years way off in the country. Mathieu'd steal a little grub, but Mathieu'd never shoot him.

He sat looking into the fire. "Mathieu wouldn't shoot you," he said, "but you'd shoot Mathieu. You wouldn't steal Mathieu's grub, but he'd steal yours." He rocked his head in his hands, bewildered and hating this mental tangle. Life was simple. You went up the river in winter, and you were home by the bay in summer. You had good luck furring, or you didn't. You were hungry once in a while, and you froze your chin, or a cheek or a toe odd times, but what was that? You fell through the thin ice, or you didn't. You lived or you died, and that was all there was to it.

Yes, but it wasn't so simple when people stole your grub. Oh, if only Mathieu hadn't taken a whole bag of flour, he would be so glad for Mathieu. He settled it this way: if Mathieu wants to come along and shoot me tonight, let him, that's good luck for Mathieu; but if Mathieu doesn't, maybe Mathieu will get shot himself tomorrow night.

The stars paled and the east grayed the same as on other mornings. Jan did not set out until there was a little light. It would be so easy for Mathieu to wait hidden by the track.

He walked with his cap on the side, exposing one ear, and when that ear began to freeze he tilted the cap and uncovered the other. Every mile he stopped and listened, mouth open, holding his breath. Late in the forenoon he came to a small valley thick with willows and boulders. As he examined it he was conscious from the corner of his eye that a tuft of snow was slipping down the face of a gray boulder on his left. Was somebody behind there? He turned and ran, dodging through the trees. Skirting the end of the willows he stealthily approached the trail farther on. No, no one had been there. It must have been a willow twig brushing the rock in the breeze. Here were the three prints, just the three prints, Mathieu's almost indistinguishable under the women's and the sled's. The women had given up hauling tandem. They took turns single, and when they changed places Mathieu didn't wait for them. They had to run a little

to catch up, poor things. Luce could never have hauled like that.

As he tramped he got to thinking of the otter skin Mathieu had left. It was funny the way Indian hunters would take food. They'd been hunters for so many ages they thought a bag of flour, like a caribou, was for anybody who needed it. But they wouldn't steal fur. It would be better if they *did* steal fur and left the grub alone. They could pack food into this height-of-land country as well as anybody else if they wanted to. They let the trappers wear themselves to skin and bone struggling up the river in canoes loaded to the gunnels, risking their lives for it in the white rapids, lugging their loads up The Great Bank, a mile long and steeper than the bridge of Satan's own nose, breaking their backs for it across twelve miles of swamps and brooks and slippery rocks on the Grand Portage where the tumplines[1] pulled their hair out by the roots and they carried till their eyes turned black and their trembling knees sagged under them. And then—then the Indians came along and helped themselves as though flour were worth no more up here than down on the bay shore.

"They won't help themselves to my grub," said Jan grimly. "Some day I'll come back to my house maybe, and find it cleaned right out. And then what about me, livin' on jays' legs and moss till I fall in the snow and die?"

1 tumpline(s): strap slung across the forehead or chest to support a load carried on the back.

The sky was growing deeper gray, darkness coming early. The air was chill with a suspicion of dampness. Come a big batch of snow to cover their track and make the walkin' back heavy, right to the knees, no food, he'd be in a fine fix, wouldn't he? He smelled the wind and it smelled like snow. Before dark it began to fall, and at dark he still had not caught them. Must be gettin' weak, he thought ruefully. He'd set some rabbit snares tonight. Or maybe he'd get a partridge. And maybe he wouldn't.

He stood on the shore of a little lake and leaned against a tree, uncertain. What with the new snow and the dark, there was only the barest sign of the track now. By morning it would be gone. What was that sharp smell?

He threw back his head and sniffed. Wood smoke! He had caught them. Let the snow pelt down. Let it snow six feet in the night, he had caught them and they couldn't get away.

Strange, though, that they should camp before the snow got thick. An hour more and they would have been safe. Well, Mathieu had made his last mistake this time.

Over a knoll in a thick clump of firs he built a small fire to boil the kettle. He was ravenous, and weary to the bone. They were camped, they would keep till he got ready for them. And they couldn't smell his smoke with the wind this way.

He ate the last of his bannock, drank four cups of tea and smoked his pipe to the last dregs. Then he left his bag and ax, took his rifle and stole out across the dark lake. It was black as ink, and the new snow was like cotton wool to muffle his steps. Just back from the far shore he saw their dome-shaped *meetch-wop* glimmering. They were burning a candle in there, one of his own probably.

He crept up closer, on his belly, foot by foot. The two sleds were stuck up against a tree, there was the chopping block, the ax, the chips. Snowshoes were hanging from a limb, the two small pairs. The women inside were baking bread. He could hear the frying pan scrape on the tin stove. They were talking in their soft musical voices, more like a brook under the ice than like human talk. But he could not bring himself to walk into the tent and shoot the women in cold blood. Better get Mathieu first. But where were the big snowshoes? Where was Mathieu? Behind that black tree there with his rifle cocked?

Jan lay silent, scarcely breathing, ears stretched for the slightest sound. But there were only the wind and the falling snow and the women's voices and the scraping pan.

Fifteen minutes, half an hour, he lay thus.

He was freezing, he couldn't lie there all night. Inch by inch he crawled away. Silent as a shadow he went back across the lake. There was danger everywhere now, every time he moved a muscle. He could feel it all around him, feel a prickling in his scalp and a supernatural certainty that as he was stalking

Mathieu, Mathieu was stalking him. Cautiously, with long waits, he approached his camp. The fire was out. His fingers touched the game-bag and drew back. Something was there, something that shouldn't be! *Something was wrong.* Chills went up and down his spine. He whirled toward a deeper patch of shadow, knowing with the certainty of panic that gunfire would belch from that shadow and blind him. His eyes roamed round in his head in the darkness and he waited, turned to stone.

There was no sound. Nothing but the soft hiss of the snowflakes drifting down.

Then he smelled it. Bread, new-baked bread, sweet as life to his nostrils. He drew off his mitten and touched the gamebag again. His

finger counted them—seven crusty bannock cakes, still warm.

"Mathieu," he whispered to the engulfing darkness. There was no answer. He struck a match and looked at the cakes. He bit one, and shook his head, ashamed. All his muscles sagged, and he slumped into the snow as though it were a bed.

Everything was different now. Noisily he crashed down a big tree for his night's fire. He was sticking up a lean-to by the fireplace, chilled by the night's cold, not by the cold horror of that other unthinkable job. He'd rather Mathieu plugged him full of holes than to take a sight on Mathieu. It was like waking up from a nightmare. He had half a mind to go across the lake now and ask Mathieu's woman to sew up the tear in his britches and have a good sleep in the Indian's warm tent. How they'd giggle and talk, with their black eyes!

But he was too ashamed. Mathieu was a better man than he was, that was all; more forgiving, smarter in the woods. "I wouldn't forgive him for taking a bag of flour, but he forgives me for tryin' to kill him. All the time the snow's comin' down and he only had to go on a little piece farther tonight to lose me altogether. He knows that and he knows I was going to shoot him. But he takes a chance and sneaks back to feed me, me that's chasin' him to kill him. Mathieu don't want I should starve goin' back to the river. Mathieu—he don't want us to part unfriendly."

It beat all. If ever he told this to Luce, she'd say he was the head liar of all the liars on the whole river.

He finished one of the fragrant, tender bread cakes and lay down with his back to the fire. It was a long time since he'd felt so happy. Wonderful strange too, how much he and Mathieu had said to each other without words, way off here, never meeting, eating each other's grub.

Toward morning the snow stopped. Just after sunrise the Indian family broke camp and climbed the hill up from the shore. Jan, watching from the opposite hill across the lake, saw them silhouetted, three dark figures on the bare ridge. He pointed his gun at a treetop and let go greeting. Boom-boom. . . . Boom. He saw the two women, startled, duck behind their sled.

But Mathieu stood erect against the brightening sky. He raised his rifle and fired one answering shot.

So they stood for a moment, on opposite hills, with upraised hand. *Good-by. Luck.*

Reading Skills

1. As Jan is introduced at the beginning of the story, what do you learn about him? What has he been doing before the story begins?
2. As he returns to his cabin, what has happened there? How does he know?
3. Why does he track the Indians? What indications do you get that his conscience is bothering him?
4. What are Jan's advantages over the Indians as he trails them? Give instances of his skill in tracking.
5. When Jan catches up to the Indians, where is Mathieu?
6. When Jan crosses the lake, he thinks that something is wrong. Why does he think so?
7. What does the author mean by saying that Jan is "chilled by the night's cold, not by the cold horror of that other unthinkable job"?

8. How does the story contrast the ideas of revenge and forgiveness? What does Jan learn in the story?

Understanding Literature

1. Why do you think that the author limited the point of view to what Jan does, sees, and thinks? (In answering, consider how the story would be different if you knew what Mathieu was doing, seeing, and thinking while Jan tracked him.)
2. What is the basic conflict in the story? What is the climax of the story?
3. Many details in the story emphasize the intense cold. Find five of the best ones.

Further Activity

This sentence comes near the end of the story: "Wonderful strange too, how much he and Mathieu had said to each other without words, way off here, never meeting, eating each other's grub." Explain what you believe was said by Jan and Mathieu not only by "eating each other's grub," but also by their other actions.

"Neighbors" is a story that is relevant to every American because it is concerned with one of the most pressing social and moral issues of recent years.

Neighbors

Diane Oliver

IMPROVING YOUR READING: You need to read this story carefully because the author does not tell you frankly what is going on. You have to figure out what is happening by collecting hints that the author gives you.

THE BUS turning the corner of Patterson and Talford Avenue was dull this time of evening. Of the four passengers standing in the rear, she did not recognize any of her friends. Most of the people tucked neatly in the double seats were women, maids and cooks on their way from work or secretaries who had worked late and were riding from the office building at the mill. The cotton mill was out from town, near the house where she worked. She noticed that a few men were riding too. They were obviously just working men, except for one gentleman dressed very neatly in a dark grey suit and carrying what she imagined was a push-button umbrella.

He looked to her as though he usually drove a car to work. She immediately decided that the car probably wouldn't start this morning so he had to catch the bus to and from work. She was standing in the rear of the bus, peering at the passengers, her arms barely reaching the over-head railing, trying not to wobble with every lurch. But every corner the bus turned pushed her head toward a window. And her hair was coming down too, wisps of black curls swung between her eyes. She looked at the people around her. Some of them were white, but most of them were her color. Looking at the passengers at least kept her from thinking of tomorrow. But really she would be glad when it came, then everything would be over.

She took a firmer grip on the green leather seat and wished she had on her glasses. The man with the umbrella was two people ahead of her on the other side of the bus, so she could see him between other people very clearly. She watched as he unfolded the evening newspaper, craning her neck to see what was on the front page. She stood, impatiently trying to read the headlines, when she realized he was staring up at her rather curiously. Biting her lips she turned her head and stared out the window until the downtown section was in sight.

She would have to wait until she was home to see if they were in the newspaper again. Sometimes she felt that if another person snapped a picture of them she would burst out screaming. Last Monday reporters were already inside the pre-school clinic when she took Tommy for his last polio shot. She didn't understand how anyone could be so heartless to a child. The flashbulb went off right when the needle went in and all the picture showed was Tommy's open mouth.

The bus pulling up to the curb jerked to a stop, startling her and confusing her thoughts. Clutching in her hand the paper bag that contained her uniform, she pushed her way toward the door. By standing in the back of the bus, she was one of the first people to step to the ground. Outside the bus, the evening air felt humid and uncomfortable and her dress kept sticking to her. She looked up and remembered that the weatherman had forecast rain. Just their luck—why, she wondered, would it have to rain on top of everything else?

As she walked along, the main street seemed unnaturally quiet but she decided her imagination was merely playing tricks. Besides, most of the stores had been closed since five o'clock.

She stopped to look at a reversible raincoat in Ivey's window, but although she had a full time job now, she couldn't keep her mind on clothes. She was about to continue walking when she heard a horn blowing. Looking around, half-scared but also curious, she saw a man beckoning to her in a grey car. He was nobody she knew but since a nicely dressed woman was with him in the front seat, she walked to the car.

"You're Jim Mitchell's girl, aren't you?" he questioned. "You Ellie or the other one?"

She nodded yes, wondering who he was and how much he had been drinking.

"Now honey," he said leaning over the woman, "you don't know me but your father does and you tell him that if anything happens to that boy of his tomorrow we're ready to set things straight." He looked her straight in the eye and she promised to take home the message.

Just as the man was about to step on the gas, the woman reached out and touched her arm. "You hurry up home, honey, it's about dark out here."

Before she could find out their names, the Chevrolet had disappeared around a corner. Ellie wished someone would magically appear and tell her everything that had happened since August. Then maybe she could figure out what was real and what she had been imagining for the past couple of days.

She walked past the main shopping district up to Tanner's where Saraline was standing in the window peeling oranges. Everything in the shop was painted orange and green and Ellie couldn't help thinking that poor Saraline looked out of place. She stopped to wave to her friend who pointed the knife to her watch and then to her boyfriend standing in the rear of the shop. Ellie nodded that she understood. She knew Sara wanted her to tell her grandfather that she had to work late again. Neither one of them could figure out why he didn't like Charlie. Saraline had finished high school three years ahead of her and it was time for her to be getting married. Ellie watched as her friend stopped peeling the orange long enough to cross her fingers. She nodded again but she was afraid all the crossed fingers in the world wouldn't stop the trouble tomorrow.

She stopped at the traffic light and spoke to a shrivelled woman hunched against the side of a building. Scuffing the bottom of her sneakers on the curb she waited for the woman to open her mouth and grin as she usually did. The kids used to bait her to talk, and since she didn't have but one tooth in her whole head they called her Doughnut Puncher. But the woman was still, the way everything else had been all week.

From where Ellie stood, across the street from the Sears and Roebuck parking lot, she could see their house, all of the houses on the single street white people called Welfare Row. Those newspaper men always made her angry. All of their articles showed how rough the people were on their street. And the reporters never said her family wasn't on welfare, the papers always said the family lived on that street. She paused to look across the street at a group of kids pouncing on one rubber ball. There were always white kids around their neighborhood mixed up in the games, but playing with them was almost an unwritten rule. When everybody started going to school nobody played together any more.

She crossed at the corner ignoring the cars at the stop light and the closer she got to her street the more she realized that the newspaper was right. The houses were ugly, there were not even any trees, just patches of scraggly bushes and grasses. As she cut across the sticky asphalt pavement covered with cars she was conscious of the parking lot floodlights casting a strange glow on her street. She stared from habit at the house on the end of the block and except for the way the paint was peeling they all looked alike to her. Now at twilight the flaking grey paint had a luminous glow and as she walked down the dirt sidewalk she noticed Mr. Paul's pipe smoke added to the hazy atmosphere. Mr. Paul would be sitting in that same spot waiting until Saraline came home. Ellie slowed her pace to speak to the elderly man sitting on the porch.

"Evening, Mr. Paul," she said. Her voice sounded clear and out of place on the vacant street.

"Eh, who's that?" Mr. Paul leaned over the rail. "What you say, girl?"

"How are you?" she hollered louder. "Sara said she'd be late tonight, she has to work." She waited for the words to sink in.

His head had dropped and his eyes were facing his lap. She could see that he was disappointed. "Couldn't help it," he said finally. "Reckon they needed her again." Then as if he suddenly remembered he turned toward her.

"You people be ready down there? Still gonna let him go tomorrow?"

She looked at Mr. Paul between the missing rails on his porch, seeing how his rolled up trousers seemed to fit exactly in the vacant banister space.

"Last I heard this morning we're still letting him go," she said.

Mr. Paul had shifted his weight back to the chair. "Don't reckon they'll hurt him," he mumbled, scratching the side of his face. "Hope he don't mind being spit on though. Spitting ain't like cutting. They can spit on him and nobody'll ever know who did it," he said, ending his words with a quiet chuckle.

Ellie stood on the sidewalk grinding her heel in the dirt waiting for the old man to finish talking. She was glad somebody found something funny to laugh at. Finally he shut up.

"Goodbye, Mr. Paul," she waved. Her voice sounded loud to her own ears. But she knew the way her head ached intensified noises. She walked home faster, hoping they had some aspirin in the house and that those men would leave earlier tonight.

From the front of her house she could tell that the men were still there. The living room light shone behind the yellow shades, coming through brighter in the patched places. She thought about moving the geranium pot from the porch to catch the rain but changed her mind. She kicked a beer can under a car parked in the street and stopped to look at her reflection on the car door. The tiny flowers of her printed dress made her look as if she had a strange tropical disease. She spotted another can and kicked it out of the way of the car, thinking that one of these days some kid was going to fall and hurt himself. What she wanted to do she knew was kick the car out of the way. Both the station wagon and the Ford had been parked in front of her house all week, waiting. Everybody was just sitting around waiting.

Suddenly she laughed aloud. Reverend Davis' car was big and black and shiny just like, but no, the smile disappeared from her face, her mother didn't like for them to say things about other people's color. She looked around to see who else came, and saw Mr. Moore's old beat up blue car. Somebody had torn away half of his NAACP[1] sign. Sometimes she really felt sorry for the man. No matter how hard he glued on his stickers somebody always yanked them off again.

Ellie didn't recognize the third car but it had an Alabama license plate. She turned around and looked up and down the street, hating to go inside. There were no lights on their street, but in the distance she could see the bright lights of the parking lot. Slowly she did an about face and climbed the steps.

She wondered when her mama was going to remember to get a yellow bulb for the porch. Although the lights hadn't been turned on, usually

1 NAACP: National Association for the Advancement of Colored People.

June bugs and mosquitoes swarmed all around the porch. By the time she was inside the house she always felt like they were crawling in her hair. She pulled on the screen and saw that Mama finally had made Hezekiah patch up the holes. The globs of white adhesive tape scattered over the screen door looked just like misshapen butterflies.

She listened to her father's voice and could tell by the tone that the men were discussing something important again. She rattled the door once more but nobody came.

"Will somebody please let me in?" Her voice carried through the screen to the knot of men sitting in the corner.

"The door's open," her father yelled. "Come on in."

"The door is not open," she said evenly. "You know we stopped leaving it open." She was feeling tired again and her voice had fallen an octave lower.

"Yeah, I forgot, I forgot," he mumbled walking to the door.

She watched her father almost stumble across a chair to let her in. He was shorter than the light bulb and the light seemed to beam down on him, emphasizing the wrinkles around his eyes. She could tell from the way he pushed open the screen that he hadn't had much sleep either. She'd overheard him telling Mama that the people down at the shop seemed to be piling on the work harder just because of this thing. And he couldn't do anything or say anything to his boss because they probably wanted to fire him.

"Where's Mama?" she whispered. He nodded toward the back.

"Good evening, everybody," she said looking at the three men who had not looked up since she entered the room. One of the men half stood, but his attention was geared back to something another man was saying. They were sitting on the sofa in their shirt sleeves and there was a pitcher of ice water on the window sill.

"Your mother probably needs some help," her father said. She looked past him trying to figure out who the white man was sitting on the end. His face looked familiar and she tried to remember where she had seen him before. The men were paying no attention to her. She bent to see what they were studying and saw a large sheet of white drawing paper. She could see blocks and lines and the man sitting in the middle was marking a trail with the eraser edge of the pencil.

The quiet stillness of the room was making her head ache more. She pushed her way through the red embroidered curtains that led to the kitchen.

"I'm home, Mama," she said, standing in front of the back door facing the big yellow sun Hezekiah and Tommy had painted on the wall above the iron stove. Immediately she felt a warmth permeating her skin. "Where is everybody?" she asked, sitting at the table where her mother was peeling potatoes.

"Mrs. McAllister is keeping Helen and Teenie," her mother said. "Your brother is staying over with Harry tonight." With each name she uttered, a slice of potato peeling tumbled to the newspaper on the table. "Tommy's in the bedroom reading that Uncle Wiggily book."

Ellie looked up at her mother but her eyes were straight ahead. She knew that Tommy only read the Uncle Wiggily book by himself when he was unhappy. She got up and walked to the kitchen cabinet.

"The other knives dirty?" she asked.

"No," her mother said, "look in the next drawer."

Ellie pulled open the drawer, flicking scraps of white paint with her fingernail. She reached for the knife and at the same time a pile of envelopes caught her eye.

"Any more come today?" she asked, pulling out the knife and slipping the envelopes under the dish towels.

"Yes, seven more came today," her mother accentuated each word carefully. "Your father has them with him in the other room."

"Same thing?" she asked picking up a potato and wishing she could think of some way to change the subject.

The white people had been threatening them for the past three weeks. Some of the letters were aimed at the family, but most of them were directed to Tommy himself. About once a week in the same handwriting somebody wrote that he'd better not eat lunch at school because they were going to poison him.

They had been getting those letters ever since the school board made Tommy's name public. She sliced the potato and dropped the pieces in the pan of cold water. Out of all those people he had been the only one the board had accepted for transfer to the elementary school. The other children, the members said, didn't live in the district. As she cut the eyes out of another potato she thought about the first letter they had received and how her father just set fire to it in the ashtray. But then Mr. Belk said they'd better save the rest, in case anything happened, they might need the evidence for court.

She peeped up again at her mother, "Who's that white man in there with Daddy?"

"One of Lawyer Belk's friends," she answered. "He's pastor of the church that's always on television Sunday morning. Mr. Belk seems to think that having him around will do some good." Ellie saw that her voice was shaking just like her hand as she reached for the last potato. Both of them could hear Tommy in the next room mumbling to himself. She was afraid to look at her mother.

Suddenly Ellie was aware that her mother's hands were trembling violently. "He's so little," she whispered and suddenly the knife slipped out of her hands and she was crying and breathing at the same time.

Ellie didn't know what to do but after a few seconds she cleared away the peelings and put the knives in the sink. "Why don't you lie down?" she suggested. "I'll clean up and get Tommy in bed." Without saying anything her mother rose and walked to her bedroom.

Ellie wiped off the table and draped the dishcloth over the sink. She stood back and looked at the rusting pipes powdered with a whitish film. One of these days they would have to paint the place. She tiptoed past her mother who looked as if she had fallen asleep from exhaustion.

"Tommy," she called softly; "come in and get ready for bed."

Tommy sitting in the middle of the floor did not answer. He was sitting the way she imagined he would be, cross-legged, pulling his ear lobe as he turned the ragged pages of *Uncle Wiggily at the Zoo.*

"What you doing, Tommy?" she said squatting on the floor beside him. He smiled and pointed at the picture of the ducks.

"School starts tomorrow," she said, turning a page with him. "Don't you think it's time to go to bed?"

"Oh Ellie, do I have to go now?" She looked down at the serious brown eyes and the closely cropped hair. For a minute she wondered if he questioned having to go to bed now or to school tomorrow.

"Well," she said, "aren't you about through with the book?" He shook his head. "Come on," she pulled him up, "you're a sleepy head." Still he shook his head.

"When Helen and Teenie coming home?"

"Tomorrow after you come home from school they'll be here."

She lifted him from the floor thinking how small he looked to be facing all those people tomorrow.

"Look," he said breaking away from her hand and pointing to a blue shirt and pair of cotton twill pants, "Mama got them for me to wear tomorrow."

While she ran water in the tub, she heard him crawl on top of the bed. He was quiet and she knew he was untying his sneakers.

"Put your shoes out," she called through the door, "and maybe Daddy will polish them."

"Is Daddy still in there with those men? Mama made me be quiet so I wouldn't bother them."

He padded into the bathroom with bare feet and crawled into the water. As she scrubbed him they played Ask Me A Question, their own version of Twenty Questions. She had just dried him and was about to have him step into his pajamas when he asked: "Are they gonna get me tomorrow?"

"Who's going to get you?" She looked into his eyes and began rubbing him furiously with the towel.

"I don't know," he answered. "Somebody I guess."

"Nobody's going to get you," she said, "who wants a little boy who gets bubblegum in his hair anyway— but us?" He grinned but as she hugged him she thought how much he looked like his father. They walked to the bed to say his prayers and while they were kneeling she heard the first drops of rain. By the time she covered him up and tucked the spread off the floor the rain had changed to a steady downpour.

When Tommy had gone to bed her mother got up again and began ironing clothes in the kitchen. Something, she said, to keep her thoughts busy. While her mother folded and sorted the clothes Ellie drew up a chair from the kitchen table. They sat in the kitchen for a while listening to the voices of the men in the next room. Her mother's quiet speech broke the stillness in the room.

"I'd rather," she said making sweeping motions with the iron, "that you stayed home from work tomorrow and went with your father to take Tommy. I don't think I'll be up to those people."

Ellie nodded. "I don't mind," she said, tracing circles on the oil cloth covered table.

"Your father's going," her mother continued. "Belk and Reverend Davis are too. I think that white man in there will probably go."

"They may not need me," Ellie answered.

"Tommy will," her mother said, folding the last dish towel and storing it in the cabinet.

"Mama, I think he's scared," the girl turned toward the woman. "He was so quiet while I was washing him."

"I know," she answered sitting down heavily. "He's been that way all day." Her brown wavy hair glowed in the dim lighting of the kitchen. "I told him he wasn't going to school with Jakie and Bob any more but I said he was going to meet some other children just as nice."

Ellie saw that her mother was twisting her wedding band around and around on her finger.

"I've already told Mrs. Ingraham that I wouldn't be able to come out tomorrow." Ellie paused. "She didn't say very much. She didn't even say anything about his pictures in the newspaper. Mr. Ingraham said we were getting right crazy but even he didn't say anything else."

She stopped to look at the clock sitting near the sink. "It's almost time for the cruise cars to begin," she said. Her mother followed Ellie's eyes to the sink. The policemen circling their block every twenty minutes was supposed to make them feel safe, but hearing the cars come so regularly and that light flashing through the shade above her bed only made her nervous.

She stopped talking to push a wrinkle out of the shiny red cloth, dragging her finger along the table edges. "How long before those men going to leave?" she asked her mother. Just as she spoke she heard one of the men say something about getting some sleep. "I didn't mean to run them away," she said smiling. Her mother half-smiled too. They listened for the sound of motors and tires and waited for her father to shut the front door.

In a few seconds her father's head pushed through the curtain. "Want me to turn down your bed now, Ellie?" She felt uncomfortable staring up at him, the whole family looked drained of all energy.

"That's all right," she answered. "I'll sleep in Helen and Teenie's bed tonight."

"How's Tommy?" he asked looking toward the bedroom. He came in and sat down at the table with them.

They were silent before he spoke. "I keep wondering if we should send him." He lit a match and watched the flame disappear into the ashtray, then he looked into his wife's eyes. "There's no telling what these fool white folks will do."

Her mother reached over and patted his hand. "We're doing what we have to do, I guess," she said. "Sometimes though I wish the others weren't so much older than him."

"But it seems so unfair," Ellie broke in, "sending him there all by himself like that. Everybody keeps asking me why the MacAdams didn't apply for their children."

"Eloise." Her father's voice sounded curt. "We aren't answering for the MacAdams, we're trying to do what's right for your brother. He's not old enough to have his own say so. You and the others could decide for yourselves, but we're the ones that have to do for him."

She didn't say anything but watched him pull a handful of envelopes out of his pocket and tuck them in the cabinet drawer. She knew that if anyone had told him in August that Tommy would be the only one going to Jefferson Davis they would not have let him go.

"Those the new ones?" she asked. "What they say?"

"Let's not talk about the letters," her father said. "Let's go to bed."

Outside they heard the rain become heavier. Since early evening she had become accustomed to the sound. Now it blended in with the rest of the noises that had accumulated in the back of her mind since the whole thing began.

As her mother folded the ironing board they heard the quiet wheels of the police car. Ellie noticed that the clock said twelve-ten and she wondered why they were early. Her mother pulled the iron cord from the switch and they stood silently waiting for the police car to turn around and pass the house again, as if the car's passing were a final blessing for the night.

Suddenly she was aware of a noise that sounded as if everything had broken loose in her head at once, a loudness that almost shook the foundation of the house. At the same time the lights went out and instinctively her father knocked them to the floor. They could hear the tinkling of glass near the front of the house and Tommy began screaming.

"Tommy, get down," her father yelled.

She hoped he would remember to roll under the bed the way they had practiced. She was aware of objects falling and breaking as she lay perfectly still. Her breath was coming in jerks and then there was a second noise, a smaller explosion but still drowning out Tommy's cries.

"Stay still," her father commanded. "I'm going to check on Tommy. They may throw another one."

She watched him crawl across the floor, pushing a broken flower vase and an iron skillet out of his way. All of the sounds, Tommy's crying, the breaking glass, everything was echoing in her ears. She felt as if they had been crouching on the floor for hours but when she heard the police car door slam, the luminous hands of the clock said only twelve-fifteen.

She heard other cars drive up and pairs of heavy feet trample on the porch. "You folks all right in there?"

She could visualize the hands pulling open the door, because she knew the voice. Sergeant Kearns had been responsible for patrolling the house during the past three weeks. She heard him click the light switch in the living room but the darkness remained intense.

Her father deposited Tommy in his wife's lap and went to what was left of the door. In the next fifteen minutes policemen were everywhere. While she rummaged around underneath the cabinet for a candle, her mother tried to hush up Tommy. His cheek was cut where he had scratched himself on the springs of the bed. Her mother motioned for her to dampen a cloth and put some petroleum jelly on it to keep him quiet. She tried to put him to bed again but he would not go, even when she promised to stay with him for the rest of the night. And so she sat in the kitchen rocking the little boy back and forth on her lap.

Ellie wandered around the kitchen but the light from the single candle put an eerie glow on the walls making her nervous. She began picking up pans, stepping over pieces of broken crockery and glassware. She did not want to go into the living room yet, but if she listened closely, snatches of the policemen's conversation came through the curtain.

She heard one man say that the bomb landed near the edge of the yard, that was why it had only gotten the front porch. She knew from

their talk that the living room window was shattered completely. Suddenly Ellie sat down. The picture of the living room window kept flashing in her mind and a wave of feeling invaded her body making her shake as if she had lost all muscular control. She slept on the couch, right under that window.

She looked at her mother to see if she too had realized, but her mother was looking down at Tommy and trying to get him to close his eyes. Ellie stood up and crept toward the living room trying to prepare herself for what she would see. Even that minute of determination could not make her control the horror that she felt. There were jagged holes all along the front of the house and the sofa was covered with glass and paint. She started to pick up the picture that had toppled from the book shelf, then she just stepped over the broken frame.

Outside her father was talking and, curious to see who else was with him, she walked across the splinters to the yard. She could see pieces of the geranium pot and the red blossoms turned face down. There were no lights in the other houses on the street. Across from their house she could see forms standing in the door and shadows being pushed back and forth. "I guess the MacAdams are glad they just didn't get involved." No one heard her speak, and no one came over to see if they could help; she knew why and did not really blame them. They were afraid their house could be next.

Most of the policemen had gone

now and only one car was left to flash the revolving red light in the rain. She heard the tall skinny man tell her father they would be parked outside for the rest of the night. As she watched the reflection of the police cars returning to the station, feeling sick on her stomach, she wondered now why they bothered.

Ellie went back inside the house and closed the curtain behind her. There was nothing anyone could do now, not even to the house. Everything was scattered all over the floor and poor Tommy still would not go to sleep. She wondered what would happen when the news spread through their section of town, and at once remembered the man in the grey Chevrolet. It would serve them right if her father's friends got one of them.

Ellie pulled up an overturned chair and sat down across from her mother who was crooning to Tommy. What Mr. Paul said was right, white people just couldn't be trusted. Her family had expected anything but even though they had practiced ducking, they didn't really expect anybody to try tearing down the house. But the funny thing was the house belonged to one of them. Maybe it was a good thing her family were just renters.

Exhausted, Ellie put her head down on the table. She didn't know what they were going to do about tomorrow, in the day time they didn't need electricity. She was too tired to think any more about Tommy, yet she could not go to sleep. So, she sat at the table trying to sit still, but

every few minutes she would involuntarily twitch. She tried to steady her hands, all the time listening to her mother's sing-songy voice and waiting for her father to come back inside the house.

She didn't know how long she lay hunched against the kitchen table, but when she looked up, her wrists bore the imprints of her hair. She unfolded her arms gingerly, feeling the blood rush to her fingertips. Her father sat in the chair opposite her, staring at the vacant space between them. She heard her mother creep away from the table, taking Tommy to his room.

Ellie looked out the window. The darkness was turning to grey and the hurt feeling was disappearing. As she sat there she could begin to look at the kitchen matter-of-factly. Although the hands of the clock were just a little past five-thirty, she knew somebody was going to have to start clearing up and cook breakfast.

She stood and tipped across the kitchen to her parents' bedroom. "Mama," she whispered, standing near the door of Tommy's room. At the sound of her voice, Tommy made a funny throaty noise in his sleep. Her mother motioned for her to go out and be quiet. Ellie knew then that Tommy had just fallen asleep. She crept back to the kitchen and began picking up the dishes that could be salvaged, being careful not to go into the living room.

She walked around her father, leaving the broken glass underneath the kitchen table. "You want some coffee?" she asked.

He nodded silently, in strange contrast she thought to the water faucet that turned with a loud gurgling noise. While she let the water run to get hot she measured out the instant coffee in one of the plastic cups. Next door she could hear people moving around in the Williams' kitchen, but they too seemed much quieter than usual.

"You reckon everybody knows by now?" she asked, stirring the coffee and putting the saucer in front of him.

"Everybody will know by the time the city paper comes out," he said. "Somebody was here last night from the *Observer*. Guess it'll make front page."

She leaned against the cabinet for support watching him trace endless circles in the brown liquid with the spoon. "Sergeant Kearns says they'll have almost the whole force out there tomorrow," he said.

"Today," she whispered.

Her father looked at the clock and then turned his head.

"When's your mother coming back in here?" he asked, finally picking up the cup and drinking the coffee.

"Tommy's just off to sleep," she answered. "I guess she'll be in here when he's asleep for good."

She looked out the window of the back door at the row of tall hedges that had separated their neighborhood from the white people for as long as she remembered. While she stood there she heard her mother walk into the room. To her ears the steps seemed much slower than usual. She heard her mother stop in front of her father's chair.

"Jim," she said, sounding very timid, "what we going to do?" Yet as Ellie turned toward her she noticed her mother's face was strangely calm as she looked down on her husband.

Ellie continued standing by the door listening to them talk. Nobody asked the question to which they all wanted an answer.

"I keep thinking," her father said finally, "that the policemen will be with him all day. They couldn't hurt him inside the school building without getting some of their own kind."

"But he'll be in there all by himself," her mother said softly. "A hundred policemen can't be a little boy's only friends."

She watched her father wrap his calloused hands, still splotched with machine oil, around the salt shaker on the table.

"I keep trying," he said to her, "to tell myself that somebody's got to be the first one and then I just think how quiet he's been all week."

Ellie listened to the quiet voices that seemed to be a room apart from her. In the back of her mind she could hear phrases of a hymn her grandmother used to sing, something about trouble, her being born for trouble.

"Jim, I cannot let my baby go." Her mother's words, although quiet, were carefully pronounced.

"Maybe," her father answered, "it's not in our hands. Reverend Davis and I were talking day before yesterday how God tested the Israelites, maybe he's just trying us."

"God expects you to take care of

your own," his wife interrupted. Ellie sensed a trace of bitterness in her mother's voice.

"Tommy's not going to understand why he can't go to school," her father replied. "He's going to wonder why, and how are we going to tell him we're afraid of them?" Her father's hand clutched the coffee cup. "He's going to be fighting them the rest of his life. He's got to start sometime."

"But he's not on their level. Tommy's too little to go around hating people. One of the others, they're bigger, they understand about things."

Ellie still leaning against the door saw that the sun covered part of the sky behind the hedges and the light slipping through the kitchen window seemed to reflect the shiny red of the table cloth.

"He's our child," she heard her mother say. "Whatever we do, we're going to be the cause." Her father had pushed the cup away from him and sat with his hands covering part of his face. Outside Ellie could hear a horn blowing.

"God knows we tried but I guess there's just no use." Her father's voice forced her attention back to the two people sitting in front of her. "Maybe when things come back to normal, we'll try again."

He covered his wife's chunky fingers with the palm of his hand and her mother seemed to be enveloped in silence. The three of them remained quiet, each involved in his own thoughts, but related, Ellie knew, to the same thing. She was the first to break the silence.

"Mama," she called after a long pause, "do you want me to start setting the table for breakfast?"

Her mother nodded.

Ellie turned the clock so she could see it from the sink while she washed the dishes that had been scattered over the floor.

"You going to wake up Tommy or you want me to?"

"No," her mother said, still holding her father's hand, "let him sleep. When you wash your face, you go up the street and call Hezekiah. Tell him to keep up with the children after school, I want to do something to this house before they come home."

She stopped talking and looked around the kitchen, finally turning to her husband. "He's probably kicked the spread off by now," she said. Ellie watched her father, who without saying anything walked toward the bedroom.

She watched her mother lift herself from the chair and automatically push in the stuffing underneath the cracked plastic cover. Her face looked set, as it always did when she was trying hard to keep her composure.

"He'll need something hot when he wakes up. Hand me the oatmeal," she commanded, reaching on top of the icebox for matches to light the kitchen stove.

Reading Skills

1. Up to the point that Ellie arrives at her home, what do you learn about her? What hints do you get about the conflict in the story?
2. By what steps does the suspense build up? By putting all the hints together, summarize the situation that the family is to face "tomorrow."
3. What is the attitude of each member of the family toward the coming crisis?
4. How does the author feel toward the family? How do you know?
5. What are the men in the living room planning?
6. Why was the house bombed? Did the author prepare you at all to expect the bombing?
7. What contrasts are built up between Ellie's family and the MacAdams's?
8. Find references to darkness and rain. What do they add to the mood and meaning of the story?
9. What did the mother mean (on page 97) by saying, "But he'll be in there all by himself"? How can Tommy be "all by himself" in school?
10. A few lines earlier, she said, "Jim, what are we going to do?" What do they decide to do? How do you know? What is the significance of each action in the final scene?
11. Why is the story called "Neighbors"? What kinds of neighbors do we learn about?

Further Activity

The story refers to the newspaper article, about the bombing, that will be on the front page of the *Observer*. List all the facts as you know them and then write the article as you think it will appear. Remember that early in a news article we find out *who*, *when*, *where*, *what* and *why*.

Character

Except for too infrequent moments of solitude, you spend most of your waking hours with people. While you are with people, you are continually discovering more about them, and they are discovering more about you. And people are fascinating, maddening, and unpredictable, aren't they? You devote a good deal of time to analyzing the characters of others and also wondering about yourself.

"What is that person *really* like?"

"I wouldn't have thought he'd *do* such a thing!"

"I don't know *why* I said that to her."

You have all heard and made similar statements. They reveal your interest in people—including yourself.

Why does anyone want to know what other people are like? One reason is that, without some understanding of others, a person cannot mature. A baby does not understand others; he/she is concerned only with his/her own little world. But in growing, the child becomes increasingly aware of the world. The mature person tries to understand as much as possible about that world and, of course, the people in it. Through an understanding of character, you become more tolerant; it is a little easier to put up with a mean person if you understand why he/she is mean. Through an understanding of character, you learn that human nature is diverse—that "it takes all kinds. . . ." Through an understanding of character, you also learn more about yourself, because, in spite of human differences, people have many attitudes and goals and ideas in common; they are remarkably alike in many ways. Finally, through an understanding of character, you satisfy your curiosity about others; your life becomes more interesting because of the people you know.

A person reveals his/her character by what he/she says and does—in even the most casual and trivial speech and action. The way he or she walks or speaks, puts on a coat, hangs up (or does not hang up) a coat show something about his or her character. In real life you never see enough of one person to understand his/her total character—and you never know for certain what he/she is thinking. In literature, you have the advantage of being able to know not only what a person says and does, but also what he/she thinks. And, as you come to understand how character is revealed in literature, you become more sensitive to the significance of your own and others' behavior.

When you read, you want to know not only, What happens? but also, To whom does it happen? More specifically, you want to know, What are the characters like? What are their attitudes, their ambitions, their abilities, their faults? Here are some questions which will help you to understand people in literature.

How does the author reveal character?

An author may reveal character
through what a person says,
through what a person does,
through what a person thinks,
through how a person looks (his/her physical appearance),
through what other characters say or think about a person,
through what the author says about him/her.

What characteristic does each speech or action of a person reveal?

Each speech or action of a person reveals something about his/her character. If a girl combs her hair every time she passes a shop window, you infer that there is some vanity in her character. If a man kicks a cat, you infer that he may have some marked dislike of animals; or that he may be angry at a person and be taking out his anger on a helpless animal; or that he may be vicious and cruel. Or possibly his character includes all these traits. How you interpret a character's action depends on what else you know about that person's character as it has been revealed to you in previous speeches and actions.

How does what you learn about a person's character traits add up to a total characterization?

Because a figure in literature is not a real person (although he or she may be *like* a real person), you can generalize about his or her character. Generalizing about a person's character in real life is sometimes dangerous, because you get only random glimpses of character. But in literature, the author chooses the speeches and actions that suggest that total character of a person; the details chosen by the author are designed to give you a general impression of the person's entire character.

Why does the person act as he or she does? Has the author suggested believable motives—reasons—for the way a person acts?

An author gives a character motivation for his/her behavior; that is, the author supplies a reason for the character's actions. This reason—or motivation—is usually suggested, not directly stated, by the author. And, if the author skillfully motivates the character, you will feel that the character's actions are true to life; they are believable, and they do not surprise you, since the character acts as you would expect him/her to.

Who is the main character? What is the function of each minor character?

A story often centers around one character. In such a story, however, the minor characters are not unimportant. What do they say and think about the main character? How do their characters compare or contrast with his/hers? How does the main character act and react toward others? How are the problems of the minor characters like the main character's? How do they solve their problems? What does their solution tell you about the wisdom or folly of the main character's solution? By answering such questions about the minor characters, you come to understand better the main character, his/her problem, and its solution.

The New Kid

Murray Heyert

BY THE TIME Marty ran up the stairs, past the dentist's office, where it smelled like the time his father was in the hospital, past the fresh paint smell, where the new kid lived, past the garlic smell, and waited for Mommer to open the door; and threw his schoolbooks on top of the old newspapers that were piled on the sewing machine in the hall; and drank his glass of milk ("How many times must I tell you not to gulp! Are you going to stop gulping like that or must I smack your face!"); and set the empty glass in the sink under the faucet; and changed into his brown keds; and put trees into his school shoes ("How many times must I talk to you! When will you learn to take care of your clothes and not make me follow you around like this!"); and ran downstairs again, past the garlic and the paint and the hospital smells; by the time he got into the street and looked breathlessly around him, it was too late. The fellows were all out there, all ready for a game, and just waiting for Eddie Deakes to finish chalking a base against the curb.

Running up the street with all his might, Marty could see that the game would start any minute now. Out in the gutter Paulie Dahler was tossing high ones to Ray-Ray Stickerling, whose father was a bus driver and sometimes gave the fellows transfers so they could ride free. The rest were sitting on the curb, waiting for Eddie to finish making the base and listening to Gelberg, who was a Jew, explain what it meant to be bar mizvah'd,[1] like he was going to be next month.

They did not look up as Marty galloped up to them all out of breath. Eddie finished making his base and after looking at it critically a moment, with his head on one side, moved down toward the sewer that was home plate and began drawing a scoreboard alongside it. With his nose running from excitement Marty trotted over to him.

"Just going to play with two bases?" he said, wiping his nose on the sleeve of his lumber jacket, and hoping with all his might that Eddie would think he had been there all the while and was waiting for a game like all the other fellows.

Eddie raised his head and saw that it was Marty. He gave Marty a

---

1 **bar mizvah'd** (bär mĭts′vəd): recognized in a ceremony celebrating a boy's reaching the age of thirteen and hence the age of religious responsibility.

shove. "Why don't you watch where you're walking?" he said. "Can't you see I'm making a scoreboard!"

He bent over again and with his chalk repaired the lines that Marty had smudged with his sneakers. Marty hopped around alongside him, taking care to keep his feet off the chalked box. "Gimme a game, Eddie?" he said.

"What are you asking me for?" Eddie said without looking up. "It ain't my game."

"Aw, come on, Eddie. I'll get even on you!" Marty said.

"Ask Gelberg. It's his game," Eddie said, straightening himself and shoving his chalk into his pants pocket. He trotted suddenly into the middle of the street and ran sideways a few feet. "Here go!" he hollered. "All the way!"

From his place up near the corner Paulie Dahler heaved the ball high into the air, higher than the telephone wires. Eddie took a step back, then a step forward, then back again, and got under it.

Marty bent his knees like a catcher, pounded his fist into his palm as though he were wearing a mitt, and held out his hands. "Here go, Eddie!" he hollered. "Here go!"

Holding the ball in his hand, and without answering him, Eddie walked toward the curb, where the rest of the fellows were gathered around Gelberg. Marty straightened his knees, put down his hands, and, sniffling his nose, trotted after Eddie.

"All right, I'll choose Gelberg for sides," Eddie said.

Gelberg heaved himself off the curb and put on his punchball glove, which was one of his mother's old kid gloves, with the fingers and thumb cut off short. "Odds, once takes it," he said.

After a couple of preparatory swings of their arms they matched fingers. Gelberg won. He chose Albie Newbauer. Eddie looked around him and took Wally Reinhard. Gelberg took Ray-Ray Stickerling. Eddie took Wally Reinhard's brother Howey.

Marty hopped around on the edge of the group. "Hey, Gelberg," he hollered in a high voice. "Gimme a game, will you?"

"I got Arnie," Gelberg said.

Eddie looked around him again. "All right, I got Paulie Dahler."

They counted their men. "Choose you for up first," Gelberg said. Feeling as though he were going to cry, Marty watched them as they swung their arms, stuck out their fingers. This time Eddie won. Gelberg gathered his men around him and they trotted into the street to take up positions on the field. They hollered, "Here go!" threw the ball from first to second, then out into the field, and back again to Gelberg in the pitcher's box.

Marty ran over to him. "Gimme a game, will you, Gelberg?"

"We're all choosed up," Gelberg said, heaving a high one to Arnie out in center field.

Marty wiped his nose on his sleeve. "Come on, gimme a game. Didn't I let you lose my Spaulding Hi-Bouncer down the sewer once?"

"Want to give the kid a game?"

Gelberg called to Eddie, who was seated on the curb, figuring out his batting order with his men.

"Aw, we got the sides all choosed up!" Eddie said.

Marty stuck out his lower lip and wished that he would not have to cry. "You give Howey Reinhard a game!" he said, pointing at Howey sitting on the curb next to Eddie. "He can't play any better than me!"

"Yeah," Howey yelled, swinging back his arm as though he were going to punch Marty in the jaw. "You couldn't hit the side of the house!"

"Yeah, I can play better than you any day!" Marty hollered.

"You can play left outside!" Howey said, looking around to see how the joke went over.

"Yeah, I'll get even on you!" Marty hollered, hoping that maybe they would get worried and give him a game after all.

With a fierce expression on his face, as if to indicate that he was through joking and now meant serious business, Howey sprang up from the curb and sent him staggering with a shove. Marty tried to duck, but Howey smacked him across the side of the head. Flinging his arms up about his ears, Marty scrambled down the street; for no reason at all Paulie Dahler booted him in the pants as he went by.

"I'll get even on you!" Marty yelled when he was out of reach. With a sudden movement of his legs Howey pretended to rush at him. Almost falling over himself in panic, Marty dashed toward the house, but stopped, feeling ashamed, when he saw that Howey had only wanted to make him run.

For a while he stood there on the curb, wary and ready to dive into the house the instant any of the fellows made a move toward him. But presently he saw that the game was beginning, and that none of them was paying any more attention to him. He crept toward them again and, seating himself on the curb a little distance away, watched the game start. For a moment he thought of breaking it up, rushing up to the scoreboard and smudging it with his sneakers before any one could stop him, and then dashing into the house before they caught him. Or grabbing the ball when it came near him and flinging it down the sewer. But he decided not to; the fellows would catch him in the end, smack him, and make another scoreboard or get another ball, and then he would never get a game.

Every minute feeling more and more like crying, he sat there on the curb, his elbow on his knee, his chin in his palm, and tried to think where he could get another fellow, so that they could give him a game and still have even sides. Then he lifted his chin from his palm and saw that the new kid was sitting out on the stoop in front of the house, chewing something and gazing toward the game; and all at once the feeling that he was going to cry disappeared. He sprang up from the curb.

"Hey, Gelberg!" he hollered. "If I get the new kid for even sides can I get a game?"

Without waiting for an answer he

dashed down the street toward the stoop where the new kid was sitting.

"Hey, fellow!" he shouted. "Want a game? Want a game of punchball?"

He could see now that what the new kid was eating was a slice of rye bread covered with applesauce. He could see too that the new kid was smaller than he was, and had a narrow face and a large nose with a few little freckles across the bridge. He was wearing Boy Scout pants and a brown woolen pullover, and on the back of his head was a skullcap made from the crown of a man's felt hat, the edge turned up and cut into sharp points that were ornamented with brass paper clips.

All out of breath, he stopped in front of the new kid. "What do you say?" he hollered. "Want a game?"

The new kid looked at him and took another bite of rye bread. "I don't know," he said, with his mouth full of bread, turning to take another look at the fellows in the street. "I guess I got to go to the store soon."

"You don't have to go to the store right away, do you?" Marty said in a high voice.

The new kid swallowed his bread and continued looking up toward the game. "I got to stay in front of the house in case my mother calls me."

"Maybe she won't call you for a while," Marty said. He could see that the inning was ending, that they would be starting a new inning in a minute, and his legs twitched with impatience.

"I don't know," the new kid said, still looking up at the game. "Anyway, I got my good shoes on."

"Aw, I bet you can't even play punchball!" cried Marty.

The new kid looked at him with his lower lip stuck out. "Yeah, I can so play! Only I got to go to the store!"

Once more he looked undecidedly up toward the game. Marty could see that the inning was over now. He turned pleadingly to the new kid.

"You can hear her if she calls you, can't you? Can't you play just till she calls you? Come on, can't you?"

Putting the last of his rye bread into his mouth, the new kid got up from the stoop. "Well, when she calls me," he said, brushing off the seat of his pants with his hand, "when she calls me I got to quit and go to the store."

As fast as he could run Marty dashed up the street with the new kid trailing after him. "Hey, I got another man for even sides!" he yelled. "Gimme a game now? I got another man!"

The fellows looked at the new kid coming up the street behind Marty.

"You new on the block?" Howey Reinhard asked, eying the Boy Scout pants, as Marty and the new kid came up to them.

"You any good?" Gelberg demanded, bouncing the ball at his feet and looking at the skullcap ornamented with brass paper clips. "Can you hit?"

"Come on!" Marty said. He wished that they would just give him a game and not start asking a lot of questions. "I got another man for even sides, didn't I?"

"Aw, we got the game started al-

ready!" Ray-Ray Stickerling hollered.

Marty sniffled his nose, which was beginning to run again, and looked at him as fiercely as he was able. "It ain't your game!" he yelled. "It's Gelberg's game! Ain't it your game, Gelberg?"

Gelberg gave him a shove. "No one said you weren't going to get a game!" With a last bounce of his ball he turned to Eddie, who was looking the new kid over carefully.

"All right, Eddie. I'll take the new kid and you can have Marty."

Eddie drew his arm back as though he were going to hit him. "Like fun! Why don't you take Marty, if you're so wise?"

"I won the choose-up!" Gelberg hollered.

"Yeah, that was before! I'm not taking Marty!"

"I won the choose-up, didn't I?"

"Well, you got to choose up again for the new kid!"

Marty watched them as they stood up to each other, each eying the other suspiciously, and swung their arms to choose. Eddie won. "Cheating shows!" he yelled, seizing the new kid by the arm and pulling him into the group on his side.

Trying to look like the ballplayers he had seen the time his father had taken him to the Polo Grounds, Marty ran into the outfield and took the position near the curb that Gelberg had selected for him. He tried not to feel bad because Eddie had taken the new kid, that no one knew anything about, how he could hit, or anything; and that he had had to go to the loser of the choose-up. As soon as he was out in the field he leaned forward, with his hands propped on his knees, and hollered: "All right, all right, these guys can't hit!" Then he straightened up and pounded his fist into his palm as though he were wearing a fielder's glove and shouted: "Serve it to them on a silver platter, Gelberg! These guys are just a bunch of fan artists!" He propped his hands on his knees again, like a big-leaguer, but all the while he felt unhappy, not nearly the way he should have felt, now that they had finally given him a game. He hoped that they would hit to him, and he would make one-handed catches over his head, run way out with his back to the ball and spear them blind, or run in with all his might and pick them right off the tops of his shoes.

A little nervous chill ran through his back as he saw Paulie Dahler get up to hit. On Gelberg's second toss Paulie stepped in and sent the ball sailing into the air. A panic seized Marty as he saw it coming at him. He took a step nervously forward, then backward, then forward again, trying as hard as he could to judge the ball. It smacked into his cupped palms, bounced out and dribbled toward the curb. He scrambled after it, hearing them shouting at him, and feeling himself getting more scared every instant. He kicked the ball with his sneaker, got his hand on it, and, straightening himself in a fever of fright, heaved it with all his strength at Ray-Ray on first. The moment the ball left his hand he knew he had done the wrong thing. Paulie was already on his way to second; and besides, the throw was wild. Ray-Ray leaped into the air, his arms flung up, but it was way over his head, bouncing beyond him on the sidewalk and almost hitting a woman who was jouncing a baby carriage at the door of the apartment house opposite.

With his heart beating the same way it did whenever anyone chased him, Marty watched Paulie gallop across the plate. He sniffled his nose, which was beginning to run again, and felt like crying.

"Holy Moses!" he heard Gelberg yell. "What do you want, a basket? Can't you hold on to them once in a while?"

"Aw, the sun was in my eyes!" Marty said.

"You wait until you want another game!" Gelberg shouted.

Breathing hard, Ray-Ray got back on first and tossed the ball to Gelberg. "Whose side are you on anyway?" he hollered.

Eddie Deakes put his hands to his mouth like a megaphone. "Attaboy, Marty!" he yelled. "Having you out there is like having another man on our side!"

The other fellows on the curb laughed, and Howey Reinhard made them laugh harder by pretending to catch a fly ball with the sun in his eyes, staggering around the street with his eyes screwed up and his hands cupped like a sissy, so that the wrists touched and the palms were widely separated.

No longer shouting or punching his fist into his palm, Marty took his place out in the field again. He stood there, feeling like crying, and wished that he hadn't dropped that ball, or thrown it over Ray-Ray's head. Then, without knowing why, he looked up to see whether the new kid was laughing at him like all the rest. But the new kid was sitting a little off by himself at one end of the row of fellows on the curb, and with a serious expression on his face gnawed at the skin at the side of his thumbnail. Marty began to wonder if the new kid was any good or not. He saw him sitting there, with the serious look on his face, his ears sticking out, not joking like the other fellows, and from nowhere the thought leaped into Marty's head that maybe the new kid was no good. He looked at the skinny legs, the Boy Scout pants, and the mama's-boy shoes, and all at once he began to hope that Eddie would send the new kid in to hit, so that he could know right away whether he was any good or not.

But Wally Reinhard was up next. He fouled out on one of Gelberg's twirls, and after him Howey popped up to Albie Newbauer and Eddie was out on first. The fellows ran in to watch Eddie chalk up Paulie's run on the scoreboard alongside the sewer. They were still beefing and hollering at Marty for dropping that ball, but he pretended he did not hear them and sat down on the curb to watch the new kid out in the field.

He was over near the curb, playing in closer than Paulie Dahler. Marty could see that he was not hollering "Here go!" or "All the way!" like the others, but merely stood

there with that serious expression on his face and watched them throw the ball around. He held one leg bent at the ankle, so that the side of his shoe rested on the pavement, his belly was stuck out, and he chewed the skin at the side of his thumbnail.

Gelberg got up to bat. Standing in the pitcher's box, Eddie turned around and motioned his men to lay out. The new kid looked around him to see what the other fellows did, took a few steps backward, and then, with his belly stuck out again, went on chewing his thumb.

Marty felt his heart begin to beat hard. He watched Gelberg stand up to the plate and contemptuously fling back the first few pitches.

"Come on, gimme one like I like!" Gelberg hollered.

"What's the matter! You afraid to reach for them?" Eddie yelled.

"Just pitch them to me, that's all!" Gelberg said.

Eddie lobbed one in that bounced shoulder high. With a little sideways skip Gelberg lammed into it.

The ball sailed down toward the new kid. Feeling his heart begin to beat harder, Marty saw him take a hurried step backward and at the same moment fling his hands before his face and duck his head. The ball landed beyond him and bounded up on the sidewalk. For an instant the new kid hesitated, then he was galloping after it, clattering across the pavement in his polished shoes.

Swinging his arms in mock haste, Gelberg breezed across the plate. "Get a basket!" he hollered over his shoulder. "Get a basket!"

Marty let his nose run without bothering to sniffle. He jumped up from the curb and curved his hands around his mouth like a megaphone. "He's scared of the ball!" he yelled at the top of his lungs. "He's scared of the ball! That's what he is, scared of the ball!"

The new kid tossed the ball back to Eddie. "I wasn't scared!" he said, moistening his lips with his tongue. "I wasn't scared! I just couldn't see it coming!"

With an expression of despair on his face Eddie shook his head. "Holy Moses! If you can't see the ball why do you try to play punchball?" He bounced the ball hard at his feet and motioned Gelberg to send in his next batter. Arnie got up from the curb and, wiping his hands on his pants, walked toward the plate.

Marty felt his heart pounding in his chest. He hopped up and down with excitement and, seizing Gelberg by the arm, pointed at the new kid. "You see him duck?" he yelled. "He's scared of the ball, that's what he is!" He hardly knew where to turn first. He rushed up to Ray-Ray, who was sitting on the curb making marks on the asphalt with the heel of his sneaker. "The new kid's scared to stop a ball! You see him duck!"

The new kid looked toward Marty and wet his lips with his tongue. "Yeah," he yelled, "didn't you muff one that was right in your hands?"

He was looking at Marty with a sore expression on his face, and his lower lip stuck out; and a sinking feeling went through Marty, a sudden sick feeling that maybe he had started something he would be sorry for. Behind him on the curb he could hear the fellows sniggering in that way they did when they picked on him. In the pitcher's box Eddie let out a loud cackling laugh.

"Yeah, the new kid's got your number!"

"The sun was in my eyes!" Marty said. He could feel his face getting red, and in the field the fellows were laughing. A wave of self-pity flowed through him.

"What are you picking on me for!" he yelled in a high voice. "The sun was so in my eyes. Anyway, I ain't no yellowbelly! I wasn't scared of the ball!"

The instant he said it he was sorry. He sniffled his nose uneasily as he saw Gelberg look at Ray-Ray. For an instant he thought of running into the house before anything happened. But instead he just stood there, sniffling his nose and feeling his heart beating, fast and heavy.

"You hear what he called you?" Paulie Dahler yelled at the new kid.

"You're not going to let him get away with calling you a yellowbelly, are you?" Eddie said, looking at the new kid.

The new kid wet his lips with his tongue and looked at Marty. "I wasn't scared!" he said. He shifted the soles of his new-looking shoes on the pavement. "I wasn't scared! I just couldn't see it coming, that's all!"

Eddie was walking toward the new kid now, bouncing the ball slowly in front of him as he walked.

In a sudden panic Marty looked back toward the house where Old Lady Kipnis lived. She always broke up fights; maybe she would break up this one; maybe she wouldn't even let it get started. But she wasn't out on her porch. He sniffled his nose, and with all his might hoped that the kid's mother would call him to go to the store.

"Any kid that lets himself be called a yellowbelly must be a yellowbelly!" Albie Newbauer said, looking around him for approval.

"Yeah," Gelberg said. "I wouldn't let anyone call me a yellowbelly."

With a sudden shove Eddie sent the new kid scrambling forward toward Marty. He tried to check himself by stiffening his body and twisting to one side, but it was no use.

Before he could recover his balance another shove made him stagger forward.

Marty sniffled his nose and looked at the kid's face close in front of him. It seemed as big as the faces he saw in the movies; and he could see that the kid's nose was beginning to run just like his own; and he could see in the corner of his mouth a crumb of the rye bread he had eaten on the stoop. For a moment the kid's eyes looked squarely into Marty's, so that he could see the little dark specks in the colored part around the pupil. Then the glance slipped away to one side; and all at once Marty had a feeling that the new kid was afraid of him.

"You gonna let him get away with calling you a yellowbelly?" he heard

Eddie say. From the way it sounded he knew that the fellows were on his side now. He stuck out his jaw and waited for the new kid to answer.

"I got to go to the store!" the new kid said. There was a scared look on his face and he took a step back from Marty.

Paulie Dahler got behind him and shoved him against Marty. Although he tried not to, Marty couldn't help flinging his arms up before his face. But the new kid only backed away and kept his arms at his sides. A fierce excitement went through Marty as he saw how scared the look on the kid's face was. He thrust his chest up against the new kid.

"Yellowbelly!" he hollered, making his voice sound tough. "Scared of the ball!"

The new kid backed nervously away, and there was a look on his face as though he wanted to cry.

"Yeah, he's scared!" Eddie yelled.

"Slam him, Marty!" Wally Reinhard hollered. "The kid's scared of you!"

"Aw, sock the yellowbelly!" Marty heard Gelberg say, and he smacked the kid as hard as he could on the shoulder. The kid screwed up his face to keep from crying and tried to back through the fellows ringed around him.

"Lemme alone!" he yelled.

Marty looked at him fiercely, with his jaw thrust forward, and felt his heart beating. He smacked the kid again, making him stagger against Arnie in back of him.

"Yeah, yellowbelly!" Marty hollered, feeling how the fellows were on his side, and how scared the new kid was. He began smacking him again and again on the shoulder.

"Three, six, nine, a bottle of wine, I can fight you any old time!" he yelled. With each word he smacked the kid on the shoulder or arm. At the last word he swung with all his strength. He meant to hit the kid on the shoulder, but at the last instant, even while his arm was swinging, something compelled him to change his aim; his fist caught the kid on the mouth with a hard, wet, socking sound. The shock of his knuckles against the kid's mouth, and that sound of it, made Marty want to hit him again and again. He put his head down and began swinging wildly, hitting the new kid without any aim on the head and shoulders and arms.

The new kid buried his head in his arms and began to cry. "Lemme alone!" he yelled. He tried to rush through the fellows crowded around him.

With all his might Marty smacked him on the side of the head. Rushing up behind him, Arnie smacked him too. Paulie Dahler shoved the skullcap, with its paper-clip ornaments, over the kid's eyes; and as he went by Gelberg booted him in the pants.

Crying and clutching his cap, the new kid scampered over to the curb out of reach.

"I'll get even on you!" he cried.

With a fierce expression on his face Marty made a sudden movement of his legs and pretended to rush at him. The kid threw his arms about his head and darted down the street toward the house. When he saw that Marty was not coming after him he sat down on the stoop; and Marty could see him rubbing his knuckles against his mouth.

Howey Reinhard was making fun of the new kid, scampering up and down the pavement with his arms wrapped around his head and hollering, "Lemme alone! Lemme alone!" The fellows laughed, and although he was breathing hard, and his hand hurt from hitting the kid, Marty had to laugh too.

"You see him duck when that ball came at him?" he panted at Paulie Dahler.

Paulie shook his head. "Boy, just wait until we get the yellowbelly in the schoolyard!"

"And on Halloween," Gelberg said. "Wait until we get him on Halloween with our flour stockings!" He gave Marty a little shove and made as though he were whirling an imaginary flour stocking round his head.

Standing there in the middle of the street, Marty suddenly thought of Halloween, of the winter and snowballs, of the schoolyard. He saw himself whirling a flour stocking around his head and rushing at the new kid, who scampered in terror before him, hollering, "Lemme alone! Lemme alone!" As clearly as if it were in the movies, he saw himself flinging snowballs and the new kid backed into a corner of the schoolyard, with his hands over his face. Before he knew what he was doing, Marty turned fiercely toward the stoop where the new kid was still sitting, rubbing his mouth and crying.

"Hey, yellowbelly!" Marty hollered; and he pretended he was going to rush at the kid.

Almost falling over himself in fright, the new kid scrambled inside the house. Marty stood in the middle of the street and sniffled his nose. He shook his fist at the empty doorway.

"You see him run?" he yelled, so loud that it made his throat hurt. "Boy, you see him run?" He stood there shaking his fist, although the new kid was no longer there to see him. He could hardly wait for the winter, for Halloween, or the very next day in the schoolyard.

Understanding Literature

The author of "The New Kid" is concerned not so much with creating a memorable character as with developing a particular character trait which the author suggests is true to human nature. The impact of the story comes in the recognition that Marty is *not* unique—that his values (what he considers important), his attitudes, and his behavior are typical of other people as well.

MURRAY HEYERT

Total characterization and how it is revealed. From what Marty says and does in the story, you know that he wants desperately to be a good ball player and to be allowed to play with the better ball players. But you also know that he is not a good player. The conflict centers around Marty's need for recognition and his inability to achieve it. His major characteristics are his desire for acceptance, his sensitivity to slights and to bullying, his frustration at being the underdog, and his failure to accept his own limitations and to pity anyone but himself. The author reveals these characteristics by telling how Marty feels and by supplying details of Marty's speech, action, or thought. For example, what characteristics do the following details show?

Of speech: "'Aw, come on, Eddie. I'll get even on you!' Marty said."

"'Aw, the sun was in my eyes!' Marty said."

"'Hey, yellowbelly!' Marty hollered."

Of action: "Marty hopped around alongside him [Eddie], taking care to keep his feet off the chalked box."

"As soon as he was out in the field he leaned forward, with his hands propped on his knees, and hollered. . . . Then he straightened up and pounded his fist into his palm as though he were wearing a fielder's glove and shouted. . . . He propped his hands on his knees again, like a big-leaguer."

"He took a step nervously forward, then backward, then forward again, trying as hard as he could to judge the ball."

"He put his head down and began swinging wildly, hitting the new kid without any aim on the head and shoulders and arms."

Of thought: "For a moment he thought of breaking it [the game] up, rushing up to the scoreboard and smudging it with his sneakers before anyone could stop him, and then dashing into the house before they caught him. Or grabbing the ball when it came near him and flinging it down the sewer."

The only detail supplied about Marty's appearance is his perpetually runny nose—a sign of his excitement and nervousness.

Function of the minor characters. By understanding the other characters in the story, you can better understand Marty, the central character. The character most like Marty is "the new kid." How do you know what "the new kid" is like? How are his character and situation similar to Marty's? Notice that another character like Marty is Howey Reinhard. Marty says, "Howey can't play any better than me." It is Howey—not Eddie or Gelberg, the leaders of the ball players—who hits Marty and drives him away from the game; it is Howey who most ridicules Marty when he fails to catch the fly ball. How is Howey's treatment of Marty like Marty's treatment of "the new kid"?

Motivation. Why does Howey abuse Marty? And why does Marty abuse "the new kid," when Marty has every reason for sympathizing with and befriending him? Is such action believable—is it true to what you know of human nature? Does an insecure person sometimes persecute others? Does intolerance breed intolerance? In the story you see that, although Marty's behavior is wrong, it is understandable, his character being what it is.

The young girl in this story recalls a trip to see her grandmother who lives in Barbados, an island in the West Indies. The old woman only half believes the girl's stories about New York City and, on their parting, reminds the child to send her a picture of the Empire State Building.

To Da-duh, In Memoriam

Paule Marshall

IMPROVING YOUR READING: As you read, pay special attention to the author's development of the character, Da-duh. Notice how the author describes her, how she places her in a setting, and how she develops the relationship between her and the "I" of the story.

I DID NOT SEE HER at first I remember. For not only was it dark inside the crowded disembarkation shed in spite of the daylight flooding in from outside, but standing there waiting for her with my mother and sister I was still somewhat blinded from the sheen of tropical sunlight on the water of the bay which we had just crossed in the landing boat, leaving behind us the ship that had brought us from New York lying in the offing. Besides, being only nine years of age at the time and knowing nothing of islands I was busy attending to the alien sights and sounds of Barbados, the unfamiliar smells.

I did not see her, but I was alerted to her approach by my mother's hand which suddenly tightened around mine, and looking up I traced her gaze through the gloom in the shed until I finally made out the small, purposeful, painfully erect figure of the old woman headed our way.

Her face was drowned in the shadow of an ugly rolled-brim brown felt hat, but the details of her slight body and of the struggle taking place within it were clear enough—an intense, unrelenting struggle between her back which was beginning to bend ever so slightly under the weight of her eighty odd years and the rest of her which sought to deny those years and hold that back straight, keep it in line. Moving swiftly toward us (so swiftly it seemed she did not intend stopping when she reached us but would sweep past us out the doorway which opened onto the sea and like Christ walk upon the water!), she was caught between the sunlight at her end of the building and the darkness inside—and for a moment she appeared to contain them both: the light in the long severe old-fashioned white dress she wore which brought the sense of a past that was still alive into our bustling present and in the snatch of white at her eye; the darkness in her black high-top shoes and in her face which was visible now that she was closer.

It was as stark and fleshless as a death mask, that face. The maggots might have already done their work, leaving only the framework of bone beneath the ruined skin and deep wells at the temple and jaw. But her eyes were alive, unnervingly so for one so old, with a sharp light that flicked out of the dim clouded depths like a lizard's tongue to snap up all in her view. Those eyes betrayed a child's curiosity about the world, and I wondered vaguely seeing them, and seeing the way the bodice of her ancient dress had collapsed in on her flat chest (what had happened to her breasts?), whether she might not be some kind of child at the same time that she was a woman, with fourteen children, my mother included, to prove it. Perhaps she was both, both child and woman, darkness and light, past and present, life and death—all the opposites contained and reconciled in her.

"My Da-duh," my mother said formally and stepped forward. The name sounded like thunder fading softly in the distance.

"Child," Da-duh said, and her tone, her quick scrutiny of my mother, the brief embrace in which they appeared to shy from each other rather than touch, wiped out the fifteen years my mother had been away and restored the old relationship. My mother, who was such a formidable figure in my eyes, had suddenly with a word been reduced to my status.

"Yes, God is good," Da-duh said with a nod that was like a tic. "He has spared me to see my child again."

We were led forward then, apologetically because not only did Da-duh prefer boys but she also liked her grandchildren to be "white," that is, fair-skinned; and we had, I was to discover, a number of cousins, the outside children of white estate managers and the like, who qualified. We, though, were as black as she.

My sister being the oldest was presented first. "This one takes after the father," my mother said and waited to be reproved.

Frowning, Da-duh tilted my sister's face toward the light. But her frown soon gave way to a grudging smile, for my sister with her large mild eyes and little broad winged nose, with our father's high-cheeked Barbadian cast to her face, was pretty.

"She's goin' be lucky," Da-duh said and patted her once on the cheek. "Any girl-child that takes after the father does be lucky."

She turned then to me. But oddly enough she did not touch me. Instead leaning close, she peered hard at me, and then quickly drew back. I thought I saw her hand start up as though to shield her eyes. It was almost as if she saw not only me, a thin truculent child who it was said took after no one but myself, but something in me which for some reason she found disturbing, even threatening. We looked silently at each other for a long time there in the noisy shed, our gaze locked. She was the first to look away.

"But Adry," she said to my mother and her laugh was cracked, thin, apprehensive. "Where did you get this one here with this fierce look?"

"We don't know where she came out of, my Da-duh," my mother said, laughing also. Even I smiled to myself. After all I had won the encounter. Da-duh had recognized my small strength—and this was all I ever asked of the adults in my life then.

"Come, soul," Da-duh said and took my hand. "You must be one of those New York terrors you hear so much about."

She led us, me at her side and my sister and mother behind, out of the shed into the sunlight that was like a bright driving summer rain and over to a group of people clustered beside a decrepit lorry. They were our relatives, most of them from St. Andrews although Da-duh herself lived in St. Thomas, the women wearing bright print dresses, the colors vivid against their darkness, the men rusty black suits that encased them like straitjackets. Da-duh, holding fast to my hand, became my anchor as they circled round us like a nervous sea, exclaiming, touching us with their calloused hands, embracing us shyly. They laughed in awed bursts: "But look Adry got big-big childen!"/ "And see the nice things they wearing, wrist watch and all!/ "I tell you, Adry has done all right for sheself in New York. . . ."

Da-duh, ashamed at their wonder, embarrassed for them, admonished them the while. "But . . . ," she said, "why you all got to get on like you

never saw people from 'Away' before? You would think New York is the only place in the world to hear wunna. That's why I don't like to go anyplace with you St. Andrews people, you know. You all ain't been colonized."

We were in the back of the lorry finally, packed in among the barrels of ham, flour, cornmeal and rice and the trunks of clothes that my mother had brought as gifts. We made our way slowly through Bridgetown's clogged streets, part of a funereal procession of cars and open-sided buses, bicycles and donkey carts. The dim little limestone shops and offices along the way marched with us, at the same mournful pace, toward the same grave ceremony—as did the people, the women balancing huge baskets on top their heads as if they were no more than hats they wore to shade them from the sun. Looking over the edge of the lorry I watched as their feet slurred the dust. I listened, and their voices, raw and loud and dissonant in the heat, seemed to be grappling with each other high overhead.

Da-duh sat on a trunk in our midst, a monarch amid her court. She still held my hand, but it was different now. I had suddenly become her anchor, for I felt her fear of the lorry with its asthmatic motor (a fear and distrust, I later learned, she held of all machines) beating like a pulse in her rough palm.

As soon as we left Bridgetown behind though, she relaxed, and while the others around us talked she gazed at the canes standing tall on

either side of the winding marl road. "C'dear," she said softly to herself after a time. "The canes this side are pretty enough."

They were too much for me. I thought of them as giant weeds that had overrun the island, leaving scarcely any room for the small tottering houses of sunbleached pine we passed or the people, dark streaks as our lorry hurtled by. I suddenly feared that we were journeying, unaware that we were, toward some dangerous place where the canes, grown as high and thick as a forest, would close in on us and run us through with their stiletto blades. I longed then for the familiar: for the street in Brooklyn where I lived, for my father who had refused to accompany us ("Blowing out good money on foolishness," he had said of the trip), for a game of tag with my friends under the chestnut tree outside our aging brownstone house.

"Yes, but wait till you see St. Thomas canes," Da-duh was saying to me. "They's canes father, bo," she gave a proud arrogant nod. "Tomorrow, God willing, I goin' take you out in the ground and show them to you."

True to her word Da-duh took me with her the following day out into the ground. It was a fairly large plot adjoining her weathered board and shingle house and consisting of a small orchard, a good-sized cane-piece and behind the canes, where the land sloped abruptly down, a gully. She had purchased it with Panama money sent her by her eldest son, my uncle Joseph, who had died

working on the canal. We entered the ground along a trail no wider than her body and as devious and complex as her reasons for showing me her land. Da-duh strode briskly ahead, her slight form filled out this morning by the layers of sacking petticoats she wore under her working dress to protect her against the damp. A fresh white cloth, elaborately arranged around her head, added to her height, and lent her a vain, almost roguish air.

Her pace slowed once we reached the orchard, and glancing back at me occasionally over her shoulder, she pointed out the various trees.

"This here is a breadfruit," she said. "That one yonder is a papaw. Here's a guava. This is a mango. I know you don't have anything like these in New York. Here's a sugar apple [the fruit looked more like artichokes than apples to me]. This one bears limes. . . ." She went on for some time, intoning the names of the trees as though they were those of her gods. Finally, turning to me, she said, "I know you don't have anything this nice where you come from." Then, as I hesitated: "I said I know you don't have anything this nice where you come from. . . ."

"No," I said and my world did seem suddenly lacking.

Da-duh nodded and passed on. The orchard ended and we were on the narrow cart road that led through the canepiece, the canes clashing like swords above my cowering head. Again she turned and her thin muscular arms spread wide, her dim gaze embracing the small field of canes, she said—and her voice almost broke under the weight of her pride, "Tell me, have you got anything like these in that place where you were born?"

"No."

"I din' think so. I bet you don't even know that these canes here and the sugar you eat is one and the same thing. That they does throw the canes into some ... machine at the factory and squeeze out all the little life in them to make sugar for you all so in New York to eat. I bet you don't know that."

"I've got two cavities and I'm not allowed to eat a lot of sugar."

But Da-duh didn't hear me. She had turned with an inexplicably angry motion and was making her way rapidly out of the canes and down the slope at the edge of the field which led to the gully below. Following her apprehensively down the incline amid a stand of banana plants whose leaves flapped like elephants ears in the wind, I found myself in the middle of a small tropical wood —a place dense and damp and gloomy and tremulous with the fitful play of light and shadow as the leaves high above moved against the sun that was almost hidden from view. It was a violent place, the tangled foliage fighting each other for a chance at the sunlight, the branches of the trees locked in what seemed an immemorial struggle, one both necessary and inevitable. But despite the violence, it was pleasant, almost peaceful in the gully, and beneath the thick undergrowth the earth smelled like spring.

This time Da-duh didn't even bother to ask her usual question, but simply turned and waited for me to speak.

"No," I said, my head bowed. "We don't have anything like this in New York."

"Ah," she cried, her triumph complete. "I din' think so. Why, I've heard that's a place where you can walk till you near drop and never see a tree."

"We've got a chestnut tree in front of our house," I said.

"Does it bear?" She waited. "I ask you, does it bear?"

"Not anymore," I muttered. "It used to, but not anymore."

She gave the nod that was like a nervous twitch. "You see," she said. "Nothing can bear there." Then, secure behind her scorn, she added, "But tell me, what's this snow like that you hear so much about?"

Looking up, I studied her closely, sensing my chance, and then I told her, describing at length and with as much drama as I could summon not only what snow in the city was like, but what it would be like here, in her perennial summer kingdom.

". . . And you see all these trees you got here," I said. "Well, they'd be bare. No leaves, no fruit, nothing. They'd be covered in snow. You see your canes. They'd be buried under tons of snow. The snow would be higher than your head, higher than your house, and you wouldn't be able to come down into this here gully because it would be snowed under. . . ."

She searched my face for the lie,

still scornful but intrigued. "What a thing, huh?" she said finally, whispering it softly to herself.

"And when it snows you couldn't dress like you are now," I said. "Oh no, you'd freeze to death. You'd have to wear a hat and gloves and galoshes and ear muffs so your ears wouldn't freeze and drop off, and a heavy coat. I've got a Shirley Temple coat with fur on the collar. I can dance. You wanna see?"

Before she could answer I began, with a dance called the Truck which was popular back then in the 1930's. My right forefinger waving, I trucked around the nearby trees and around Da-duh's awed and rigid form. After the Truck I did the Suzy-Q, my lean hips swishing, my sneakers sidling zigzag over the ground. "I can sing," I said and did so, starting with "I'm Gonna Sit Right Down and Write Myself a Letter," then without pausing, "Tea For Two," and ending with "I Found a Million Dollar Baby in a Five and Ten Cent Store."

For long moments afterwards Da-duh stared at me as if I were a creature from Mars, an emissary from some world she did not know but which intrigued her and whose power she both felt and feared. Yet something about my performance must have pleased her, because bending down she slowly lifted her long skirt and then, one by one, the layers of petticoats until she came to a drawstring purse dangling at the end of a long strip of cloth tied round her waist. Opening the purse she handed me a penny. "Here," she said half-smiling against her will. "Take this

to buy yourself a sweet at the shop up the road. There's nothing to be done with you, soul."

From then on, whenever I wasn't taken to visit relatives, I accompanied Da-duh out into the ground, and alone with her amid the canes or down in the gully I told her about New York. It always began with some slighting remark on her part: "I know they don't have anything this nice where you come from," or "Tell me, I hear those foolish people in New York does do such and such. . . ." But as I answered, re-creating my towering world of steel and concrete and machines for her, building the city out of words, I would feel her give way. I came to know the signs of her surrender: the total stillness that would come over her little hard dry form, the probing gaze that like a surgeon's knife sought to cut through my skull to get at the images there, to see if I were lying; above all, her fear, a fear nameless and profound, the same one I had felt beating in the palm of her hand that day in the lorry.

Over the weeks I told her about refrigerators, radios, gas stoves, elevators, trolley cars, wringer washing machines, movies, airplanes, the cyclone at Coney Island, subways, toasters, electric lights: "At night, see, all you have to do is flip this little switch on the wall and all the lights in the house go on. Just like that. Like magic. It's like turning on the sun at night."

"But tell me," she said to me once with a faint mocking smile, "do the white people have all these things too or it's only the people looking like us?"

I laughed. "What d'ya mean," I said. "The white people have even better." Then: "I beat up a white girl in my class last term."

"Beating up white people!" Her tone was incredulous.

"How you mean!" I said, using an expression of hers. "She called me a name."

For some reason Da-duh could not quite get over this and repeated in the same hushed, shocked voice, "Beating up white people now! Oh, the lord, the world's changing up so I can scarce recognize it anymore."

One morning toward the end of our stay, Da-duh led me into a part of the gully that we had never visited before, an area darker and more thickly overgrown than the rest, almost impenetrable. There in a small clearing amid the dense bush, she stopped before an incredibly tall royal palm which rose cleanly out of the ground, and drawing the eye up with it, soared high above the trees around it into the sky. It appeared to be touching the blue dome of sky, to be flaunting its dark crown of fronds right in the blinding white face of the late morning sun.

Da-duh watched me a long time before she spoke, and then she said very quietly, "All right, now, tell me if you've got anything this tall in that place you're from."

I almost wished, seeing her face, that I could have said no. "Yes," I said. "We've got buildings hundreds of times this tall in New York. There's one called the Empire State

building that's the tallest in the world. My class visited it last year and I went all the way to the top. It's got over a hundred floors. I can't describe how tall it is. Wait a minute. What's the name of that hill I went to visit the other day, where they have the police station?"

"You mean Bissex?"

"Yes, Bissex. Well, the Empire State Building is way taller than that."

"You're lying now!" she shouted, trembling with rage. Her hand lifted to strike me.

"No, I'm not," I said. "It really is, If you don't believe me I'll send you a picture postcard of it soon as I get back home so you can see for yourself. But it's way taller than Bissex."

All the fight went out of her at that. The hand poised to strike me fell limp to her side, and as she stared at me, seeing not me but the building that was taller than the highest hill she knew, the small stubborn light in her eyes (it was the same amber as the flame in the kerosene lamp she lit at dusk) began to fail. Finally, with a vague gesture that even in the midst of her defeat still tried to dismiss me and my world, she turned and started back through the gully, walking slowly, her steps groping and uncertain, as if she was suddenly no longer sure of the way, while I followed triumphant yet strangely saddened behind.

The next morning I found her dressed for our morning walk but stretched out on the Berbice chair in the tiny drawing room where she sometimes napped during the afternoon heat, her face turned to the window beside her. She appeared thinner and suddenly indescribably old.

"My Da-duh," I said.

"Yes, nuh," she said. Her voice was listless and the face she slowly turned my way was, now that I think back on it, like a Benin mask, the features drawn and almost distorted by an ancient abstract sorrow.

"Don't you feel well?" I asked.

"Girl, I don't know."

"My Da-duh, I goin' boil you some bush tea," my aunt, Da-duh's youngest child, who lived with her, called from the shed roof kitchen.

"Who tell you I need bush tea?" she cried, her voice assuming for a moment its old authority. "You can't even rest nowadays without some malicious person looking for you to be dead. Come girl," she motioned me to a place beside her on the old-fashioned lounge chair, "give us a tune."

I sang for her until breakfast at eleven, all my brash irreverent Tin Pan Alley songs, and then just before noon we went out into the ground. But it was a short, dispirited walk. Da-duh didn't even notice that the mangoes were beginning to ripen and would have to be picked before the village boys got to them. And when she paused occasionally and looked out across the canes or up at her trees it wasn't as if she were seeing them but something else. Some huge, monolithic shape had imposed itself, it seemed, between her and the land, obstructing her vision. Returning to the house she slept the entire afternoon on the Berbice chair.

She remained like this until we left, languishing away the mornings on the chair at the window gazing out at the land as if it were already doomed; then, at noon, taking the brief stroll with me through the ground during which she seldom spoke, and afterwards returning home to sleep till amost dusk sometimes.

On the day of our departure she put on the austere, ankle length white dress, the black shoes and brown felt hat (her town clothes she called them), but she did not go with us to town. She saw us off on the road outside her house and in the midst of my mother's tearful protracted farewell, she leaned down and whispered in my ear, "Girl, you're not to forget now to send me the picture of that building, you hear."

By the time I mailed her the large colored picture postcard of the Empire State building she was dead. She died during the famous '37 strike which began shortly after we left. On the day of her death England sent planes flying low over the island in a show of force—so low, according to my aunt's letter, that the downdraft from them shook the ripened mangoes from the trees in Da-duh's orchard. Frightened, everyone in the village fled into the canes. Except Da-duh. She remained in the house at the window so my aunt said, watching as the planes came swooping and screaming like monstrous birds down over the village, over her house, rattling her trees and flattening the young canes in her field. It must have seemed to her lying there that they did not intend pulling out of their dive, but like the hardback beetles which hurled themselves with suicidal force against the walls of the house at night, those menacing silver shapes would hurl themselves in an ecstasy of self-immolation onto the land, destroying it utterly.

When the planes finally left and the villagers returned they found her dead on the Berbice chair at the window.

She died and I lived, but always, to this day even, within the shadow of her death. For a brief period after I was grown I went to live alone, like one doing penance, in a loft above a noisy factory in downtown New York and there painted seas of sugarcane and huge swirling Van Gogh suns and palm trees striding like brightly-plumed Watusi across a tropical landscape, while the thunderous tread of the machines downstairs jarred the floor beneath my easel, mocking my efforts.

Reading Skills

1. What is the situation at the beginning of the story?
2. What does the child, the "I," see that is so different from New York? What does Da-duh learn about New York?
3. How is each of the two major characters affected by what they learn about each other?
4. What contrasts do you see in the story, between the child and Da-duh? between New York and Barbados? between old ideas and new? Where are machines used in the story? With what situations are they contrasted?
5. What is Da-duh like? What is the child like? What kind of life does each represent?

Further Activity

On page 122 the child says, "Over the weeks I told her about refrigerators, radios, gas stoves, elevators, trolley cars, wringer washing machines, movies, airplanes, the cyclone at Coney Island, subways, toasters, electric lights. . . ." Assume that *you* are trying to explain one of these things to Da-duh, and write down the conversation. Remember that you are pretending to be a nine-year-old explaining something to someone who knows nothing about it. Use only one side of one piece of composition paper.

PAULE MARSHALL

"A Prince and a Cowboy" is a chapter from *The Autobiography of Lincoln Steffens*. This selection deals with the growing world of a boy who was to become one of America's important writers. Have you ever imagined that you were living another kind of life entirely? If so, you will understand Lennie and his friends.

A Prince and a Cowboy*

from *The Autobiography of Lincoln Steffens*

Lincoln Steffens

IMPROVING YOUR READING: The *theme*, the major idea, of "A Prince and a Cowboy" concerns the question of which is real—the imaginative world or the everyday world. The story also asks which is preferable. One way Steffens emphasizes these questions is by the repetition of the word *really* in Lennie's and the cowboy's conversations. As you read, try to answer the cowboy's question, "What's really?" Who is really a prince? Who is really a cowboy?

A BOY'S LIFE is pestered with problems—hard ones, as hard as any adult's. There is the whole world to get into your head. You have to make a picture of it; that's easy, but the picture has to correspond somewhat with the world outside, which keeps changing. You have the sun going fine around the earth, and then all of a sudden you learn something more and the earth starts whirling around the sun. This means a complete readjustment. It happens often. Every time I had everything all right and working harmoniously inside so that I could leave it and mind my own business, some fact would bob up to throw it all out. I remember how, when the earth was flat, I had to put China and the Far East to the west of me, no easy task for a boy; and then when I had that done, I studied a book which made the earth round like an orange. Where was one to put China then?

I consulted some of the other boys about that, and they looked dazed for a moment; but they soon turned to the ball and bats and bade me do likewise.

"Ah, play ball," they said in effect....

And this, the construction of the universe as a whole, was only the main business of life. There were minor problems. It took me and my crowd days of exploration to discover and map in our minds the confluence of our two rivers, the American and the Sacramento. It took longer to make out how the river steamboats and the railroad trains could start

CHARACTER

from Sacramento at right angles and arrive both at the same place, San Francisco. Also there were the inhabitants of the earth to understand, the grownups who do and say such queer things. They say they love you and yet they balk you like enemies. They tell you to be good and you'll succeed, and the next thing you know they will be chuckling about how dishonest some successful man was. Nor will they explain anything, not seriously. They laugh at a fellow's questions. Or if they pretend to throw a light, they only cast a shadow that darkens and complicates the puzzle. They don't seem to realize how painful your need is to find out just where you are at in a mixed-up world. Sometimes it seemed to me almost as if they didn't know where they were at themselves.

As I was leaving the Neely farm that day I was wondering what Jim Neely meant by what he said about Mrs. Neely wanting a boy like me and what Mrs. Neely meant by being so cross with me and then so soft. If she wanted me why couldn't she take me straight as a regular fellow would? I could not make it out. I thought and thought, but the sun was hot over me and the pony was hot under me. I did what I had to do with many, many questions: I gave them up, for the present; I laid them aside and hung on to the thought that anyhow I had a feeding station seven miles out on the Stockton road. And before I reached home I had another feeding station still farther out, and another problem.

Single-footing along the flaming road, I picked up the track of cattle going my way, and pretty soon there was a cloud of dust ahead. Hurrying as much as I could on such a day, I caught up with a cowboy driving a small herd of big calves and young steers to market. I asked if I might help him.

"You betcher life," he answered. "My horse is about in."

No wonder. It was a small drove, and, as the cowboy said, it's easier to handle a big drove. If there's a mob, cattle will herd like humans. But when they're a few, and of mixed ages, they are like a bunch of shooting stars. "Maybe we can do it together," he said. "I'll drive from behind here and you'll ride along the side of the next crossroad, doing the dirty work."

It was dirty work. A calf would bleat and bolt. My pony would spring ahead and cut him off. Then a young steer, smelling water, would bellow and go, with others after him, down the road. I had to race to the front, stop short, and hold them. An open lane on one side was easy; the pony would of himself see and take and hold it, but when there was a crossroad, open both sides, we had, us two cowboys, alternately to drive and head. I would shoot up, yelling, along one side, then fall back and drive as he galloped up the other side. By good teamwork we got by. I was sweating, my pony was in a lather, and the cowboy and his horse were caked with the mud of the damp dust. He was pleased, however, and, to keep me with him, he paid me a compliment (the way grownups do).

"You know the cattle game, don't you?" he said.

"No," I answered, "but my pony does, and I'm learning it from him. How long you been on the road?"

"All day," he said. "The ranch is about twenty miles out."

Twenty miles out! Just right. I began fishing for an invitation to visit him, asking him questions. The ranch was not a big one, he said; it was mostly a wheat farm, only part hay and cattle. He was one of five or six hands that worked steady on the place.

"Why don't you ride out and see us sometime?" he invited. "You like to work cattle. We'll let you have all you want of it."

I told him about my gang, and he laughed. "Five or six! All kids? Well, you may all come. Why not? Make a week end of it." A week end? What was that? He used lots of funny words, and he spoke them very English. And he suggested a date when there would be work for us to do, cattle work.

I liked the idea, accepted it, and I liked this fellow. I stared at him approvingly till he turned away as if embarrassed, and when he looked back at me, he asked me a diverting question.

"Why no saddle?"

I explained that my father wanted me to learn bareback, and that led to the Comanches. I told him all about them, how they rode, fought,

and—I must have become so enthusiastic about those Indians that he suspected me.

"I see," he said, "you are a Comanche Indian chief."

This struck me at first as fresh. I did not like to have anybody walk right into my—my privacy, like that, sit down, and stick his feet up on the table. But my second thought was that maybe he was my kind of a fellow, like the bridge-tender. I decided to see.

"No," I said. "I used to be a Comanche chief's son, but that was long ago; several weeks back. I am— something else now. I'll tell you what I am if you'll tell me first what you are."

"Why," he said, "I am, as you see, a cowboy."

I was disappointed. He did not understand. I said as much. "Of course, I can see you're a cowpuncher, but that's only your job. I don't mean that. What I mean is, what are you really?"

"Really?" he echoed. "What's really? I'm a real cowboy."

"That's funny," I said, "I thought you'd tumble to what I meant, and you didn't."

I was about to give up, and he seemed to sense that. He looked almost ashamed, and I didn't care. If he wasn't my sort, if he didn't belong to our crowd, he didn't matter. We rode along in a silence that could be felt, like the heat, till a steer charged the fence. "Water," I called as my pony charged at the steer, and I was glad that the rest of the herd joined the attack on that fence. It kept us busy for a while. When we could fall back and ride together, the cowboy had decided to talk.

"I'll tell you about myself," he said. "My name, my cattle name, is Duke. That's what the cattlemen call me from Texas to the Pacific, only they pronounce it Dook. And they name me so, not because I am a duke. My father, as it happens, is a lord, but my older brother will inherit his title. I myself, I am nothing, as you see. I'm called by an English title because I am English, but as a matter of fact, I am a plain American cowboy."

I was thrilled. I had read about the English nobility, books on books, and here for the first time I was seeing one.

"Is that what you mean by 'really'?" he inquired.

"Maybe," I answered, and it was his turn to be disappointed. I was sorry now. It was my turn to talk. I told him about me, to explain what I meant.

I had been reading Scott's novels lately, I said, and lots of other English stories about knights and gentlemen and ladies. I knew what a younger son was and had even thought I'd like to be one.

"Really?" he said, only he said it differently from me.

"Yes-s—" I hesitated. But I decided to trust him. "Yes," I confessed. "I wouldn't have minded being the son of a lord, and, as a matter of fact, I was—not exactly that, but I've been something like that for a good while lately."

"But why?" he asked. "You are in the way of being what I wanted to be when I was a boy, and yet here you are—"

"Nothing," I interrupted, and I poured out my woes.

Here I was, a boy, just an ordinary boy. I wasn't a poor boy, like the boys I had read about in stories, the fellows that started with nothing, no father, no mother, no home. They starved in the streets, picking up now and then a crust of bread to eat, and finding here and there a dark hallway to sleep in, but they begin by selling papers and shining shoes; they are smart, industrious, honest, and brave; so they rise slowly but surely and by and by they are a success. They own the paper they sold or—whatever it is they are at.

"That's great," I summed up. "They are heroes of books. I'd like to be the hero of a book."

But, I grieved, I could not be that. My father and mother did not die when I was young. They are both still living, and they had a home for me. I didn't have a chance; I could not go out and suffer, strive, and become a success.

The Duke saw my predicament. He tried to be encouraging. There were other things I might do.

"What?" I demanded. "I can't be one of those rich men's sons or the son of a duke and do what they do." There were stories about them, too. They had boats and rivers they could row on; not like the Sacramento and the American Rivers: not swift floods or all dried up. They had snow and ice and parks. They could go sledding, and skating, and they had

places to go riding in, made on purpose for saddle horses, and grooms to follow them. Not like me. I had to ride over to the river bottom or out on the plains, always with other boys, among farmers and—and—

I halted. I had almost said something that might hurt his feelings. He saw my embarrassment, and like a duke, he bridged it gracefully (the nobility is very graceful, you know).

"And cowboys," he suggested.

"Yes," I said, and to make it easy for him, I explained gracefully that I didn't mean him. I was glad I had met him; I was certainly coming out to his ranch with my crowd to help with his cattle. I had to do something to fill up my time.

"But you can see, can't you," I said, "that working cattle on a ranch isn't what a fellow with ambition would choose to do if he had his choice."

A team was coming toward me. "I'll head 'em," I said, and I rode up and turned our cattle off to the right side of the road. After that there were two crossroads in succession; both the Duke and I were busy, and by that time, the city limit was near. There were other things to think of.

What butcher were his calves for? When he told me, I told him that all would be well. Loony Louie was that butcher's ranchman; he would be on the lookout for us, with the bars down, and there was a pond in his corral. The cattle would turn in of themselves for the water. And this happened. We had a couple of miles of very hard work. The herd split, and half of them got away up one of the many lanes. My pony brought them back, and—well, we worked the whole tired, famished drove to the butcher's place. There was Louie standing out in the middle of the road with his gate wide open. The cattle rushed in, and our horses followed—one mad rush for the pond, and there they all waded in up to their bellies and sank their heads in up to their eyes. And Louie, closing the gate and running after us to the pond, stood and danced there; he laughed and yelled like a maniac at the sight of the drinking animals.

I saw Duke looking astonished at him.

"What's the matter with that man?" he asked, as we rode up out of the water and headed for town. I saw my chance to explain what I meant by "really."

"Well," I said, "Loony Louie is called crazy, but he isn't. He is all right, only he loves stock. You saw how he was glad when your thirsty calves wallowed in the water and drank their fill? Well, he loves that; he loves to see 'em drink and feed. He'll cry if he sees them slaughtered; sure. That's why they say he's crazy: because he loves animals and goes crazy when he sees them drink when they're thirsty and eat when they're hungry; and—and when they're killed he goes crazy too."

"Poor devil!" the Duke muttered.

"No," I corrected, "Louie was in prison once for stealing cattle and once he was in the insane asylum for the same thing. But I know him, and I knew what he wanted: knew he didn't want to own cattle but only to take good care of them, so I got him a job here to take care of the butcher's cattle. It would have been better to put him on a ranch where cattle aren't killed, but no rancher would take a loco cattle-lover. Only this old German butcher could understand about Louie. He gave him the job of priming up his cattle, and he keeps him away as much as he can from the slaughterhouse."

"Really!" the cowboy exclaimed, and I answered, "Yes, really. And there you have said it yourself."

But he didn't see it even yet. We rode along the city streets, quietly; all you could hear was the flap of his chaps and the clink of his spurs.

"Come again, kid," he said at last.

"Why, don't you see?" I said. "That butcher's man, who has the job of feeding up cattle to be killed, he is really—he is playing he's the friend of those calves of yours, and he'll take 'em into the barn, feed them a lot, pet them, talk to them, and he will listen to them, and—and—"

"And?" the cowboy boosted, and I told him straight how Louie could sit up on a fence with you and tell you how a young calf feels when it is separated from its mother and what a wild steer would like to be—really.

"He does to me," I said. "He has told me stories that are—real about what the cattle tell him."

"Really?"

"Yes," I said, and I told him about the bridge-tender, whose job was to tend the American River trestle. A good job, and dangerous, and he did it up brown. But he didn't care for it. "He's really a prospector who strikes it rich and goes home where his people live, and the girl that wouldn't marry him, and—and—"

"And—" the cowboy said, and I saw he was understanding, so I went on.

"And I go out there and sit in his cabin, and him and me, we go back home rich and spend the money; he just blows it and he makes his folks proud of him, and—and—"

"And—"

I had to go back and explain that the bridge-tender's troubles all came from a certain preacher in his home town who, because the bridge-tender got to dancing and raising the dust, denounced him to his face in a sermon in the church. The bridge-tender was with his girl, and it so shamed her that she wouldn't have him 'round any more.

"See?" I said, and he saw that much; so I trusted him with the whole truth, how, when the bridge-tender and I are alone on the trestle and there is no train due, we make his pile, we go back east to his home. We walk into that church—everybody's there, the girl, too, of course—and the bridge-tender, who has been the talk of the town for a week, he walks up the middle aisle of the church, draws his gun, and makes that preacher come down out of his pulpit, kneel down, and apologize to the girl.

"And she marries the bridge-tender?" the Duke asked.

"Sometimes," I answered. "Sometimes we take her, and sometimes she begs to be took, but we scorn her."

We had come to the corner where there was a small drovers' hotel with a stable next door, the Duke's hotel. We stopped; since the Duke did not

seem to see it, I pointed it out to him: "Your hotel," I said.

"Yes, yes," he said. "But let's finish this. Your butcher's man is—really—a cattle-lover; your bridge-tender is a rich miner. Any others like that?"

"Yes," I said. "You know Hank Dobran, the gambler, that runs this hotel and bar where you are stopping tonight? Well, he—this is a secret, of course—when Hank has made enough to be independent—he tells me he is going to turn in and clear up the dirty politics of this town and make a fine, grand town that all the other cities all over the world can copy."

"Any more?" he asked after a while, and I looked at him and he wasn't joshing me. He believed. I answered him, therefore:

"Every fellow I get to really know is that way," I told him. "Every one of them is playing he is really something else besides what his job is. And that's what I mean by really," I said, "and—and that's why I asked you what you were, really."

The Duke did not answer. He just sat there on his horse in front of the hotel stable. We were so quiet that the stableman came out and looked at us—and gave us up. But his wonder brought the Duke to. He spoke.

"I was that way, kid," he said. "I was like you. I read books, as a boy; I read and I wanted to go and be what I read. Only I read stories about the far west, Indians, scouts, cowboys. I read about knights, too, and lords and ladies, kings, queens, and princesses. Yes, but I saw that sort. I knew them as—as you know

CHARACTER

cowboys. So I didn't want to be a prince or the son of a—duke. I played I was a cowboy. I could ride; I had horses, yes, and—but I hated to ride on our silly little saddles on bridle paths in our fancy parks with a groom behind me—and my sister. I wanted to go west and be a cowboy among cowboys—and really ride—really. And—well—as you see—I did. That's what I am now and have been for ten years. It isn't what I imagined it to be. It is no more what it is cracked up to be than a lord is or the son of a lord. But no matter, here I am, Dook the cowboy—really a cowpuncher."

He seemed to be sad about it, and his sadness put up a problem to me, the hardest puzzle of that day.

"Funny!" I said. "You're a cowboy really—and I—I don't know what to be now, but for a long time lately —weeks—when I rode up to you, I was a prince, the son of a lord, the Black Prince in the Middle Ages."

The Duke didn't laugh the way some men would. He thought and thought, and at last he looked as if he was going to say something. He didn't. He changed his mind, I guess. For all he did was to put out his hand, take mine, and shake it hard, once.

"Good-by, Prince," he said. "It is time to go home. It's time for both of us to go home—really."

"Good-by, Duke," I said, and I rode off home puzzling and puzzling.

Understanding Literature

1. What is Lennie's major problem? What are some of his minor problems?
2. How does Lennie find out whether a person is his "kind of fellow"? What is his "kind of fellow"? Is the cowboy such a person? Explain.
3. How is Loony Louie like Lennie and the cowboy?
4. The title of this chapter may be interpreted in more than one way. Who is the prince and who is the cowboy—really?
5. How is Lennie's conversation with the cowboy related to Lennie's major problem?
6. After he leaves the cowboy, what is Lennie "puzzling and puzzling" about as he rides home?

Further Activity

Do you know what a *self-concept is*? Psychologists—those who study the functions of the mind—say that a person's mental pic-picture of himself or herself (one's *self-concept*) has a great influence on how he or she acts. Discuss how Lennie's and the cowboy's self-concepts influence their actions. What have you observed about the self-concepts of yourself and of people you know?

Although Harry Wojick loves his mother, he does not feel that she belongs in his school life. Why, he wonders, should she be different in speech and appearance from other mothers? The invitation to the school's open house is not the only thing in the story that is torn apart.

The Torn Invitation

Norman Katkov

IMPROVING YOUR READING: In "The Torn Invitation" Harry Wojick's problem is caused by his inability to accept his mother as she is. At the beginning of the story, Harry's values—what he considers important—are based on superficial standards: he judges his mother by her speech, her appearance, and her social graces. As Harry's values change, his character changes. As you read, note how the problems of the minor characters, especially of Frankie and Chuck, help Harry to understand himself and his mother, and enable him to solve his problem.

AT FIFTEEN, in the spring of his sophomore year at Hamilton High School, Harry Wojick was as big as a college senior, a long, thin, big-boned left-hander, who could anchor a leg in first base and stretch halfway to right field for a bad throw from his shortstop.

Now, in the waning daylight, he turned into Glover Street toward his home, his arms swinging as he moved onto the unpaved road. For a few feet he ran easily, bringing his knees up high, until, without warning, he stopped short and bent low to field the imaginary ball cleanly, beating the runner by a mile. He straightened up, grinning in the half darkness, blushing a little from the applause at the brilliant play he had made.

Harry Wojick came off the street onto the opposite sidewalk. He passed the four-family flat in the middle of the block. He passed the empty lot and beyond it the condemned building with all the windows long since broken, and then he turned into the cement walk which ran the length of his house.

The windows were raised in the kitchen and he smelled the roast. He smelled the asparagus for the roast and the fried potatoes with onions that nobody made like Ma, and he was suddenly terribly hungry after the three hours of baseball practice.

When he came into the kitchen, Theresa Wojick turned from the stove, smiling at her son, rubbing her hands on her apron as she walked to meet him. She held him at the elbows, examining him carefully, her face warm and her eyes gentle, welcoming him as though he had returned from a long and perilous journey. She was a tall woman with large, capable hands and black, unkempt hair shot through with gray. She held Harry and she said, "Hello, my little son. Will you eat supper?" joking with him as always.

He put his cheek to hers, noticing again the redness of her chapped hands. She could try to do something about it, he said to himself, as she released him, remembering the mothers of his teammates who lived above the flats on Livingston Drive and Harding Boulevard and scattered through Maple Heights. They were mothers with manicures and they were thin—and their hair was always set just right.

Harry went to the sink to wash and, turning, saw the table set for three. He thought for an instant that his father was home, that Peter Wojick had not gone to his night-watchman's job in the office building downtown. But he saw the hooks on the wall near the door empty of cap and coat.

"For Frankie Thomas," his mother whispered, looking at her son. "His mother is gone again till half the night, and leaves cold cuts. Boy like Frankie to eat cold cuts," she whispered. "You call him, Harry."

"Why can't she learn to speak English?" he asked himself savagely, turning away. "She's been here long enough!"

Harry walked through the short hall and stood under the arch which led into the living room. He saw the frail, black-haired boy with whom he had grown up, sitting in the chair under the lamp. "Hey, Frankie," Harry said. "Come on and eat." Harry whistled shrilly and came back into the kitchen.

He pulled the chair out and held it suspended off the clean, bare floor, his fingers tightening on the wood. There, next to his plate, was the white, square envelope, and atop it, covered by a transparent sheet of thin paper, was the embossed invitation.

Harry looked at his mother, who had her back to him, busy at the stove. He heard Frankie coming through the house and knew it was Frankie's work, *knew* it. He moved the chair at last and sat down and, without touching it, his hands holding his knees, he read the invitation from the faculty of Hamilton High School to an open house in honor of all the students' mothers.

It was for tomorrow.

Harry knew *that*, all right. Had known it for ten days and had kept it secret. He looked up as Frankie sat down across the table.

Harry's mother was sitting between them, and as she handed her son the roast she said, "I asked Frankie maybe he has this invitation, Harry. I heard by Celusik, the grocery man, about this open house. Must be open house for junior, senior mothers." Frankie had skipped a grade.

Harry was busy with the roast. "It's for everyone," he said, watching the roast. "Didn't you get one, Ma?" He turned to his mother. "They mailed them out," Harry said, remembering now that morning when he had waited for the postman on the corner, taken the envelopes from him, searched for the square, white one, and had torn it, scattering the pieces in the empty lot before running home and dropping the rest of the mail in the black metal box beside the door.

"Maybe they make a mistake," his mother said.

She reached for a thick slice of the rye bread she baked herself and held it flat in her left hand. She buttered it completely and thickly and brought it to her mouth, taking a large bite, and Harry wanted to leave the table and this house. He remembered the homes on Maple Heights to which he had been invited, where they called it dinner and ate in a dining room with tablecloths; where George Sidley's mother sat at one end of the table and broke her bread piece by piece, buttering it lightly and eating slowly.

"Frankie's ma got this invitation," Theresa Wojick said, nodding at their guest, who lived with his mother in one of the upstairs apartments of the four-family flat. "How long she got the open house, Frankie?"

"Mother had it," Frankie said. "She—we didn't talk about it."

She turned to Harry, smiling at her son. "You eat, Harry. Big ballplayer must eat good," she said.

Harry ate. The three sat in silence.

Later, while Theresa Wojick set out the dessert plates, Frankie said, "How's practice going, Harry?"

"All right, I guess." He wanted this supper finished.

Theresa Wojick filled the dessert plates with pudding. As she sat down she said to Frankie, "Your ma goes to this open house?"

"I don't know," he answered. "She—well, you know, she's pretty busy. One of my aunts is sick and I think she's going to be with her for a few days. She packed her suitcase when she left today."

"Ma," Harry said.

She set her coffee cup down.

"I wanted to tell you, Ma," he said. "I meant to tell you about it and then I forgot, I guess."

"Easy to forget," she said.

"It wouldn't make any difference anyway, Ma," Harry lied. "We've got that game with Central next week and the coach is worried. He's been working us hard all week. He's got a game for tomorrow. You know, he picks two teams from the squad and we play each other."

"I've got to go," Frankie said. "Thanks very much for supper, Mrs. Wojick."

"You're welcome, Frankie. Here" —she reached across the table—"here is the invitation, Frankie," and she offered it to him.

He held it, shifting it from one hand to the other. "Thanks," he said, moving toward the kitchen door. "Thanks. Thanks." And he was gone.

"I won't be finished until about six o'clock, Ma," Harry said.

She nodded. Harry watched her walking to the sink. "Do you want me to miss practice, Ma?" he asked.

She had her back to him.

"We'll go next year, Ma. I'll be a regular on the team then. We can go next year," he said, but she didn't turn, nor move, nor did she answer him, and he left the kitchen quickly. He went into the living room and stood before the windows. He tried to blame Frankie and couldn't, and he tried to blame Theresa Wojick and couldn't. He was seldom a liar, but he just didn't want her there with George Sidley's mother and Eric Portland's mother.

Harry heard the water running in the sink and the clatter of dishes, and he went back into the kitchen. He opened the cabinet door, reaching for one of the dish towels his mother had cut from sugar sacks and washed white and soft. She took it from his hand.

"You rest, Harry," his mother said. "Big ball game tomorrow. You must rest up for the ball game." She turned from him to the sink.

"All right," he thought, and now he left the house, going out into the vestibule and then to the rear porch. "Let her wash her own dishes," he thought, and walked out to the sidewalk.

Frankie said, "Hi, Harry." He was leaning against the fence in front of Harry's house. He said, "I didn't want to jam you up, Harry."

"You didn't jam me up."

"That ought to be a pretty good game tomorrow, that intrasquad game," Frankie said. "Think I'll watch it."

"There isn't any intrasquad game," Harry muttered.

"You said—"

"I said. I say a lot of things." He felt the meanness in him. He started to walk away, but Frankie took his arm.

"I've got enough for a movie," Frankie said.

"I'm busy," Harry said, jerking his arm free. He left Frankie there, walking down Glover Street. He passed the corner and went on aimlessly.

When he came home he entered the house through the front door and moved through the living room in darkness, turning into his bedroom. He could see the cracks of light below the bathroom door and heard the water running; he wondered if there was ever a time in this house when the water *wasn't* running. He made it to his bedroom and undressed in the darkness, dropping his clothes on the floor and crawling into the turned-down bed.

"All right," he thought; "this time tomorrow it'll be over." He heard the bathroom door open and his mother moving around the house. He lay still, his eyes closed, his breath coming evenly as he simulated sleep, but the sound of her footsteps faded.

For a bad moment he thought of his ma, saw her again at the kitchen table, but he chased the scene from his mind and went, instead, to baseball, seeing himself leading infield practice, and thus, at last, fell asleep.

The first thing he noticed in the morning was his clothes, arranged neatly on the chair beside the bed, the shoes together on the floor and clean socks across them. He dressed quickly.

The kitchen was deserted. He saw his cornflakes and the orange juice and the milk before his chair, but he stood behind it, gulping the juice. As he set the empty glass on the table his mother came in from the rear porch.

"You didn't eat, Harry," she said.

"I'm late, Ma. I've got a test this morning. I've got to study for the test." He wanted to be out of here now as he turned from the table, saw that her hands were full.

She held the clean, freshly dried sweatshirt and the two pairs of wool socks, and he knew now why the water had been running in the bathroom last night. "For your game today, Harry," she said. "You bring me tonight your dirty stuff."

Harry watched her wrap the bundle and he wanted to kiss her, suddenly. He wanted to put his arms around her and hold her as she tied the bundle carefully with the string she always saved. But he only took the package from her and said thanks, and left.

All the way up to school he promised he'd make it up to her. He'd start tonight. He'd sit in the kitchen with Ma; she liked him there studying while she worked. He'd take her for a walk if she wanted. Saturday and Sunday he was staying home the whole time, that's all.

He came into school on the Livingston Drive side. His locker was on the first floor. He put the package inside, took his books, and slammed the locker shut. The bell sounded for first hour and Harry went to English.

Pete Overholt, the team's catcher, sat behind Harry. As they waited for the tardy bell, he nudged Harry. "Look at the women, man," he whispered. "Look at 'em, Harry!"

Harry looked. Not a girl in the class wore saddle shoes, or blue jeans, or boys' shirts with the sleeves rolled above the elbows. They were in Sunday dresses and suits, and high heels.

"The open house," Pete whispered. "All of them showing off for their mothers."

The tardy bell sounded, and Harry saw Miss Liggett look up from the desk. He wasn't called on during the hour, and afterward, on his way to study hall, he waved to George Sidley, who played third base, and to Bernie Cremmens, the right-fielder. They were both wearing sports jackets and regular shirts, and they wore ties. Harry looked down at his sweater worn over the skivvy shirt. His corduroys were clean, but they were corduroys, and around him, in the study hall, was a sea of gray flannels.

There was only one lunch period today because they had to get the cafeteria ready for the open house. Harry bought a sandwich and a glass of milk. Then he saw that half the guys on the team, sitting at the table they shared every day, were dressed up, too. He sat down in a far corner with two guys he didn't know, ate quickly, and left by the side door so he wouldn't have to pass Sidley and Cremmens and the others.

He went to his locker for his afternoon books. He had only a French class left, because, for today, school was over after fifth hour. He sat half hearing Miss Formanek, gazing out the window until his name was called sharply.

Harry turned to the teacher, his face red, feeling the eyes of the whole class on him as Miss Formanek smiled. "Let's look alive there," said Miss Formanek. "Your mother will find her way, Harry," and she told him the place in the French book.

The bell sounded at last and Harry hurried to his locker. He saw the cafeteria cleared of tables, the floor bare and chairs lining the walls. He saw the huge coffeepots steaming, and then he got his package out and threw his books into the locker and slammed it shut.

He was half running for the door when George Sidley stopped him: "Hey, where you headed for?"

Harry stared at him. "Headed for?" he asked. "Where do you think I'm headed for? Aren't you going to practice?"

"Not me," George grinned. "Coach said anybody who wanted to could be excused. Isn't your mother coming?"

"She had to go downtown," Harry said. "She had to see a doctor. She hasn't been feeling well."

"Hey, that's not good," George said, frowning. Then his face brightened. "Well, hang around anyway. Lots of fun."

Harry shook his head. He swung his left arm. "It feels like it's stiffening up," he said. "Guess I'll work out. See you."

He walked down Livingston Drive toward the baseball field. He crossed the playing area, moving toward the Quonset hut that served as dressing room for the team. There was nobody inside but Art Hughes, the student manager.

"You alone, Harry?" Art asked.

"Yup."

Art turned and opened the doors of the uniform rack. "Anybody that's coming better come quick—that's all I got to say," he announced. "My mother is over at school waiting for me. I'm not keeping her waiting too long."

Harry sat down on the bench before the lockers and unwrapped the package. He pulled his sweater off and he was in his pants and skivvy shirt, standing in his socks on the cement floor when Oscar Anderson walked in. In a few minutes they were joined by Chuck Kellerman, the shortstop, and Mr. Quint, who taught chemistry and was assistant baseball coach.

Mr. Quint came over to the bench. "Look, you fellows; my wife's outside in the car. It seems there are only three of you here. You won't mind if I go back to school, will you?"

"Go ahead, Mr. Quint," Chuck said.

"I don't want to run out on you," Mr. Quint said. "It's just—well, with only three of you here, there doesn't seem to be much we could do."

"Can I get a ride back?" Art Hughes said. "You guys can check out your own uniforms today."

"Come ahead, Art," Mr. Quint said.

When they were gone, Chuck Kellerman slammed his baseball cap down on the cement floor. "All the way over here for nothing," he said.

He looked at Oscar Anderson. "How about you?" he asked. "Aren't you going to Mamma's Day and eat cookies?"

"Listen; I've got six brothers and sisters and I'm the baby," Oscar said. "My mother's tired of this stuff. I'm going home and get the grass cut, and then I got Saturday for myself."

"How about you, Harry?" Chuck asked.

"How about *you*, wise guy?" Harry said, beginning to tie his shoelaces.

Chuck got up from the bench and reached for a bat. "My mother is dead," he said, and he swung the bat desperately, as though he were hitting a line drive. Then he dropped the bat into the wicker basket. Harry watched him pick up his books and walk to the door and leave without turning to them.

"Will you lock up, Harry?" Oscar asked.

Harry saw his mother in the kitchen, and he reached for his sweater.

"Will you, Harry?"

He remembered the light under the bathroom door and the sound of water as she washed the sweatshirt and the socks.

"HARRY!"

"It isn't too late yet," Harry said. He had his sweater on.

"Are you nuts?" Oscar asked.

He'd call her. He'd use the phone in the principal's office. "See you to-morrow," he said, and he ran out of the Quonset hut. Far off, walking in left-center field, Harry saw Chuck Kellerman, and then he began to run.

He could call her, he thought as he ran, and she could even take a taxi. Just this once a taxi; Pa wouldn't care. Harry knew that. She could get dressed and be up there in half an hour, and he was suddenly breathless with anticipation. He'd wait out in front of the school, on Hamilton Avenue, and help her from the cab and hold her arm and lead her to the front door. He didn't care about the bread any more, or how she talked. She was his ma.

Harry was out of the alley now, running across Livingston Drive. There were cars all around the school, almost like it was graduation night. He cut across the grass, toward the long flight of steps that led up to the second floor. He was gasping for breath when he reached the door.

He stood there a moment, then pulled the heavy door open and stepped into the deserted corridor. There was nobody on the second floor, but from the cafeteria below he heard the muted murmur of a hundred voices.

The principal's door was open. There was a phone in the outer office, an ancient upright that Miss Tibbetts, the principal's secretary, used. Harry took the receiver off the hook, set it on the desk and, holding the upright with his left hand, dialed his home number.

He grinned with excitement thinking of her when she answered. Ma didn't like phones and couldn't hear good on them, but she'd hear this. He could see her listening and her face lighting up, and then, afterward, ordering Pa around to help her, getting the gray dress ready and her coat. She never wore a hat, but let the wind command her hair, and Harry didn't care.

But she didn't answer.

Aloud he said, "Wrong number," but felt the first, tiny stabs of alarm in his chest. He dialed again, slowly now, holding the receiver to his ear, hearing the first ring, the second, the third, the eighth, the ninth, and finally, the operator's voice telling him there was no answer.

He felt the ache in his chest now, and his hands were wet. "Maybe Ma is sick or something," he thought, and he knew who had to take the blame. He dialed the 0 and asked the operator to check the number; maybe the phone was out of order. But all the time he knew it wasn't.

At last he thanked the operator and replaced the receiver and stood listlessly at the desk, wondering what to do. Now he remembered his ma helping him with fractions when he was at Crowley School. He remembered her at graduation, Ma and Pa sitting alone in the back row, and after he had his diploma, when the other guys were bringing their parents up to the front of the auditorium, he had led them out to the hall and home immediately. He remembered her walking over to the skating rink on Inverness Street, standing in a corner beside the fence to watch

him skate under the floodlights, careful not to be seen, but he had seen her, all right. Seen her and kept away from that corner.

It seemed to him now, alone in the principal's office, that he had been hiding his ma all his life, and he was sick inside then, with a physical distaste in his mouth. He grimaced with self-hatred, wanting, somehow, to feel a sharper pain, to hurt himself deliberately; and he left the office and almost ran into Mr. Quint and a woman.

"Hello, Harry," Mr. Quint said. "I thought you were practicing."

"I guess not, sir."

"This is my wife, Harry," Mr. Quint said. "Harry Wojick, Emma," he said. "Harry's our first baseman."

Mrs. Quint smiled and shook hands with him.

"Mrs. Quint wants to use the phone," the assistant coach said. "She's worried about our little girl. . . . I'll see you in the cafeteria, dear," he said to his wife.

She nodded, and Mr. Quint took Harry's arm. "Let's get some of those cookies, Harry."

"I can't, sir. My mother isn't there," Harry said.

"Oh, yes. One of the boys told me. She's seeing a doctor. Hasn't been feeling well, eh?"

Harry pulled his arm away. "That's a lie," he said. "I didn't want her to come today."

Mr. Quint started laughing. He put his arm around Harry's shoulders and they walked toward the stairs. "You guys," he said, shaking his head. He looked at Harry. "Do I really look that old, Harry? An old fossil whose leg you all enjoy pulling?"

"What's the difference?" Harry thought. "What difference does it make now?" And his heart leaped as he thought of next year. There'd be an open house next year, but Ma wouldn't go. If she never went anywhere with him, he'd deserve it. If she never talked with him, he had that coming, too. "Just let me get away from Mr. Quint," he thought. Get out of here without trouble and without a fuss. But now they were in the cafeteria, in the midst of mothers and daughters and sons and teachers, and Mr. Quint was pulling him through the mob.

But they got separated and Harry was alone. He wanted to get out quickly now, away from all the laughter and gaiety. He saw Miss Formanek, the French teacher. He saw her wave at him, her finger curved beckoning him. He saw Frankie Thomas standing beside her and the woman between them. He was moving sideways, pushing through the people, and he looked up for Miss Formanek again, and then felt his heart stop. For a long time he remembered his heart stopping dead as he saw the woman in the gray dress.

He thought his legs would give away. His legs were shaking and he was shaking, and he couldn't move until someone pushed him clear and he was standing there before them. He couldn't get his hands free of sweat. He rubbed his hands up and down against the corduroys and looked at his ma.

"I was telling your mother how you were watching for her, Harry. You have a devoted son, Mrs. Wojick," the French teacher said.

Harry saw his ma smile and nod. She was beautiful.

Frankie was wearing a jacket and a tie. How come *he* was dressed up?

"And you're pinch-hitting for Frankie's mother, too," Miss Formanek said. "Frankie was my best student, Mrs. Wojick."

"Frankie's a good boy," Theresa Wojick said.

"They're all good boys," Miss Formanek said, and she excused herself and left them then.

"Ma," Harry said. He had to tell her.

She had her hand in Frankie's arm. She was smiling, and her hair was pulled back neat, and she was the loveliest woman he had ever seen. "Ma, I tore up the invitation," he said, and he looked right at her.

"I know," she said. "But Frankie has an invitation. We are two orphans: mother without a son, and son without a mother."

"I'm your son, Ma," Harry said, and saw Frankie slipping away, but his mother held the black-haired boy.

She was wearing white gloves and she looked right at him, and he was more afraid than he had ever been in his life.

"Ma." He held her elbows as she had held his and he didn't drop his eyes. He said, "Please, Ma, I'm your son. Please, Ma, let's get something to eat. There's my coach there. I want to introduce you to my coach."

"Yes," she said, and she smiled at him then, and for him. "Yes," she said, and put one hand through his arm and the other through Frankie's. "Introduce, please, to this coach, my little son."

Reading Skills

1. What is happening in the second paragraph of the story? What do the details in this paragraph reveal about Harry's character?
2. Why does Harry tear up the invitation? Why does he feel guilty about tearing it up?
3. As you read, you see that Mrs. Wojick has characteristics which Harry in his anxiety is not considering. What qualities in his mother does Harry dislike? What things does she say and do that show her kindness? her generosity? her sense of humor? her dignity?
4. The climax of the story occurs when Harry's attitude toward his mother changes. At what point does his attitude change? Is this a sudden or a gradual change? (Support your answer with evidence from the story.)
5. Which of the following best describes the new feeling that Harry has for his mother at the end of the story?
   (a) Shame that he has been embarrassed by her table manners, her speech, her careless grooming.
   (b) Understanding that a bond of love exists between him and his mother and that, in spite of temporary embarrassments, it is manly and right to show her his respect and affection.
   (c) A mature tenderness for his mother that rises above embarrassment.
6. How is the actual situation at the school's open house different from the way Harry assumes it will be?
7. In what way is Harry different at the end of the story from the way he is at the beginning?

Understanding Literature

1. Why is "The Torn Invitation" a good title for this story?
2. The invitation has already been torn up when the story begins. How does the author let you know about the torn invitation? Why does the author not tell the events in the same order that they supposedly happened?
3. What characteristics of Harry are revealed in his conversations with Frank? How does Frank's family situation contrast with Harry's? How do Frank's attitudes contrast with Harry's?

4. The writer sometimes, instead of directly telling you a fact, shows a scene or an incident that allows you to infer the fact. How, for example, does the author let you know that (*a*) Harry lives in an unattractive part of town? (*b*) Harry's father is not at home? (*c*) Mrs. Wojick's table manners are not acceptable in elegant places? (*d*) Mrs. Wojick knows that Harry is lying to her about the invitation?

Further Activities

1. Discussion Topic: Parents can embarrass teen-age sons and daughters without realizing they are doing so. Teen-age sons and daughters can also embarrass their parents. Have you or any cne of ycur friends had such an experience? How can sensitiveness to the feelings of others and respect for other people help in such situations?

2. This story deals with a change in a boy. The reader should ask whether the change is motivated; that is, when it happens, do you believe it? Have you been prepared for it?

   Write a paragraph beginning with the sentence: "When Harry decided to call his mother, I was not surprised." Then go on with evidence from the story.

One of Daisy's problems in this story is that she does not understand what she is really like, and she cannot see what others think of her or why they think that way.

A Start in Life

Ruth Suckow

IMPROVING YOUR READING: The *setting* of a story is its scene—the time and place of the action. In this story the author points to particular things in the setting to show something about the people who live in the places described. *Setting*, then, can be used as a way of characterizing people.

1

THE SWITZERS were scurrying around to get Daisy ready by the time that Elmer Kruse should get through in town. They had known all week that Elmer might be in for her any day. But they hadn't done a thing until he appeared. "Oh, it was so rainy today, the roads were so muddy, they hadn't thought he'd get in until maybe next week." It would have been the same any other day.

Mrs. Switzer was trying now at the last moment to get all of Daisy's things into the battered telescope[1] that lay open on the bed. The bed had not "got made"; and just as soon as Daisy was gone, Mrs. Switzer would have to hurry off to the Woodworths' where she was to wash today. Daisy's things were scattered over the dark brown quilt and the rumpled sheet that were dingy and

clammy in this damp weather. So was the whole bedroom, with its sloping ceiling and old-fashioned square-paned windows, the commode that they used for a dresser, littered with pin tray, curlers, broken comb, ribbons, smoky lamp, all mixed up together; the door of the closet open, showing the confusion of clothes and shabby shoes. . . . They all slept in this room—Mrs. Switzer and Dwight in the bed, the two girls in the cot against the wall.

"Mamma, I can't find the belt to that plaid dress."

"Oh, ain't it somewheres around? Well, I guess you'll have to let it go. If I come across it I can send it out to you. Someone'll be going past there."

She had meant to get Daisy all mended and "fixed up" before she went out to the country. But somehow . . . oh, there was always so much to see to when she came home. Gone all day, washing and cleaning

---

1 telescope: adjustable traveling bag consisting of two cases, the larger slipping over the other.

for other people; it didn't leave her much time for her own house.

She was late now. The Woodworths liked to have her get the washing out early so that she could do some cleaning too before she left. But she couldn't help it. She would have to get Daisy off first. She had already had on her wraps ready to go, when Elmer came—her cleaning cap, of a blue faded almost into gray, and the ancient black coat with gathered sleeves that she wore over her work dress when she went out to wash.

"What's become of all your underclothes? They ain't all dirty, are they?"

"They are, too. You didn't wash for us last week, Mamma."

"Well, you'll just have to take along what you've got. Maybe there'll be some way of getting the rest to you."

"Elmers come in every week, don't they?" Daisy demanded.

"Yes, but maybe they won't always be bringing you in."

She jammed what she could into the telescope, thinking with her helpless, anxious fatalism that it would have to do somehow.

"Daisy, you get yourself ready now."

"I am ready. Mamma, I want to put on my other ribbon."

"Oh, that's way down in the telescope somewhere. You needn't be so anxious to fix yourself up. This ain't like going visiting."

Daisy stood at the little mirror preening herself—such a homely child, "all Switzer," skinny, with pale sharp eyes set close together and thin, stringy, reddish hair. But she had never really learned yet how homely she was. She was the oldest, and she got the pick of what clothes were given to the Switzers. Goldie and Dwight envied her. She was important in her small world. She was proud of her blue coat that had belonged to Alice Brooker, the town lawyer's daughter. It hung unevenly about her bony little knees, and the buttons came down too far. Her mother had tried to make it over for her.

Mrs. Switzer looked at her, troubled, but not knowing how she could tell her all the things she ought to be told. Daisy had never been away before except to go to her Uncle Fred's at Lehigh. She seemed to think that this would be the same. She had so many things to learn. Well, she would find them out soon enough—only too soon. Working for other people—she would learn what that meant. Elmer and Edna Kruse were nice young people. They would mean well enough by Daisy. It was a good chance for her to start in. But it wasn't the same.

Daisy was so proud. She thought it was quite a thing to be "starting in to earn." She thought she could buy herself so much with that dollar and a half a week. The other children stood back watching her, round-eyed and impressed. They wished that they were going away, like Daisy.

They heard a car come splashing through the mud in low.

"There he is back! Have you got your things on? Goldie—go out and tell him she's coming."

"No, me tell him, me!" Dwight shouted jealously.

"Well—both of you tell him. Land! . . ."

She tried hastily to put on the cover of the bulging telescope and to fasten the straps. One of them broke.

"Well, you'll have to take it the way it is."

It was an old thing, hadn't been used since her husband, Mert, had "left off canvassing" before he died. And he had worn it all to pieces.

"Well, I guess you'll have to go now. He won't want to wait. I'll try and send you out what you ain't got with you." She turned to Daisy. Her face was working. There was nothing else to do, as everyone said. Daisy would have to help, and she might as well learn it now. Only, she hated to see Daisy go off, to have

her starting in. She knew what it meant. "Well—you try and work good this summer, so they'll want you to stay. I hope they'll bring you in sometimes."

Daisy's homely little face grew pale with awe, suddenly, at the sight of her mother crying, at something that she dimly sensed in the pressure of her mother's thin strong arms. Her vanity in her new importance was somehow shamed and dampened.

Elmer's big new Buick, mud-splashed but imposing, stood tilted on the uneven road. Mud was thick on the wheels. It was a bad day for driving, with the roads a yellow mass, water lying in all the wheel ruts. This little road that led past these few houses on the outskirts of town, and up over the hill, had a cold rainy loneliness. Elmer sat in the front seat of the Buick, and in the back was a big box of groceries.

"Got room to sit in there?" he asked genially. "I didn't get out, it's so muddy here."

"No, don't get out," Mrs. Switzer said hastily. "She can put this right on the floor there in the back." She added, with a timid attempt at courtesy, "Ain't the roads pretty bad out that way?"

"Yes, but farmers get so they don't think so much about the roads."

"I s'pose that's so."

He saw the signs of tears on Mrs. Switzer's face, and they made him anxious to get away. She embraced Daisy hastily again. Daisy climbed over the grocery box and scrunched herself into the seat.

"I guess you'll bring her in with you some time when you're coming," Mrs. Switzer hinted.

"Sure. We'll bring her."

He started the engine. It roared, half died down as the wheels of the car spun in the thick wet mud.

In that moment, Daisy had a startled view of home—the small house standing on a rough rise of land, weathered to a dim color that showed dark streaks from the rain; the narrow sloping front porch whose edge had a soaked, gnawed look; the chickens, grayish-black, pecking at the wet ground; their playthings, stones, a wagon, some old pail covers littered about; a soaked, discolored piece of underwear hanging on the line in the back yard. The yard was tussocky and overhung the road with shaggy long grass where the yellow bank

was caved in under it. Goldie and Dwight were gazing at her solemnly. She saw her mother's face—a thin, weak, loving face, drawn with neglected weeping, with its reddened eyes and poor teeth . . . in the old coat and heavy shoes and cleaning cap, her work-worn hand with its big knuckles clutching at her coat. She saw the playthings they had used yesterday, and the old swing that hung from one of the trees, the ropes sodden, the seat in crooked. . . .

The car went off, slipping on the wet clay. She waved frantically, suddenly understanding that she was leaving them. They waved at her.

Mrs. Switzer stood there a little while. Then came the harsh rasp of the old black iron pump that stood out under the box-elder tree. She was pumping water to leave for the children before she went off to work.

2

Daisy held on as the car skidded going down the short clay hill. Elmer didn't bother with chains. He was too used to the roads. But her eyes brightened with scared excitement. When they were down, and Elmer slowed up going along the tracks in the deep wet grass that led to the main road, she looked back, holding on her hat with her small scrawny hand.

Just down this little hill—and home was gone. The big car, the feel of her telescope under her feet, the fact that she was going out to the country, changed the looks of everything. She saw it all now.

Dunkels' house stood on one side

of the road. A closed-up white house. The windows stared blank and cold between the old shutters. There was a chair with a broken straw seat under the fruit trees. The Dunkels were old Catholic people who seldom went anywhere. In the front yard was a clump of tall pines, the rough brown trunks wet, the green branches, dark and shining, heavy with rain, the ground underneath mournfully sodden and black.

The pasture on the other side. The green grass, lush, wet and cold, and the outcroppings of limestone that held little pools of rain water in all the tiny holes. Beyond, the low hills gloomy with timber against the lowering sky.

They slid out on to the main road. They bumped over the small wooden bridge above the swollen creek that came from the pasture. Daisy looked down. She saw the little swirls of foam, the long grass that swished with the water, the old rusted tin cans lodged between the rocks.

She sat up straight and important, her thin, homely little face strained with excitement, her sharp eyes taking in everything. The watery mudholes in the road, the little thickets of plum trees, low and wet, in dark interlacings. She held on fiercely, but made no sound when the car skidded.

She felt the grandeur of having a ride. One wet Sunday, Mr. Brooker had driven them all home from church, she and Goldie and Dwight packed tightly into the back seat of the car, shut in by the side curtains against which the rain lashed, catch-ing the muddy scent of the roads. Sometimes they could plan to go to town just when Mr. Pattey was going to work in his Ford. Then they would run out and shout eagerly, "Mr. Pattey! Are you going through town?" Sometimes he didn't hear them. Sometimes he said, with curt good nature, "Well, pile in"; and they all hopped into the truck back. "He says we can go along with him."

She looked at the black wet fields through which little leaves of bright green corn grew in rows, at showery bushes of sumac along the roadside. A gasoline engine pumping water made a loud, desolate sound. There were somber-looking cattle in the wet grass, and lonely, thick-foliaged trees growing here and there in the pastures. She felt her telescope on the floor of the car, the box of groceries beside her. She eyed these with a sharp curiosity. There was a fresh pineapple—something the Switzers didn't often get at home. She wondered if Edna would have it for dinner. Maybe she could hint a little to Edna.

She was out in the country. She could no longer see her house even if she wanted to—standing dingy, streaked with rain, in its rough grass on the little hill. A lump came into her throat. She had looked forward to playing with Edna's children. But Goldie and Dwight would play all morning without her. She was still proud of her being the oldest, of going out with Elmer and Edna; but now there was a forlornness in the pride.

She wished she were in the front

seat with Elmer. She didn't see why he hadn't put her there. She would have liked to know who all the people were who lived on these farms; how old Elmer's babies were; and if he and Edna always went to the movies when they went into town on Saturday nights. Elmer must have lots of money to buy a car like this. He had a new house on his farm, too, and Mrs. Metzinger had said that it had plumbing. Maybe they would take her to the movies, too. She might hint about that.

When she had gone to visit Uncle Fred, she had had to go on the train. She liked this better. She hoped they had a long way to go. She called out to Elmer:

"Say, how much farther is your place?"

"What's that?" He turned around. "Oh, just down the road a ways. Scared to drive in the mud?"

"No, I ain't scared. I like to drive most any way."

She looked at Elmer's back, the old felt hat crammed down carelessly on his head, the back of his neck with the golden hair on the sunburned skin above the blue of his shirt collar. Strong and easy and slouched a little over the steering wheel that he handled so masterfully. Elmer and Edna were just young folks; but Mrs. Metzinger said that they had more to start with than most young farmers did, and that they were hustlers. Daisy felt that the pride of this belonged to her too, now.

"Here we are!"

"Oh, is this where you folks live?" Daisy cried eagerly.

The house stood back from the road beyond a space of bare yard with a little scattering of grass just starting—small, modern, painted a bright new white and yellow. The barn was new too, a big splendid barn of frescoed brick, with a silo of the same. There were no trees. A raw desolate wind blew across the back yard as they drove up beside the back door.

Edna had come out on the step. Elmer grinned at her as he took out the box of groceries, and she slightly raised her eyebrows. She said kindly enough:

"Well, you brought Daisy. Hello, Daisy, are you going to stay with us this summer?"

"I guess so," Daisy said importantly. But she suddenly felt a little shy and forlorn as she got out of the car and stood on the bare ground in the chilly wind.

"Yes, I brought her along," Elmer said.

"Are the roads very bad?"

"Kind of bad. Why?"

"Well, I'd like to get over to Mamma's some time today."

"Oh, I guess they aren't too bad for that."

Daisy pricked up her sharp little ears. Another ride. That cheered her.

"Look in the door," Edna said in a low fond voice, motioning with her head.

Two little round, blond heads were pressed tightly against the screen door. There was a clamor of "Daddy, Daddy!" Elmer grinned with a half bashful pride as he stood with the box of groceries, raising his eyebrows with mock surprise and demanding: "Who's this? What you shoutin' 'Daddy' for? You don't think Daddy's got anything for you, do you?" He and Edna were going into the kitchen together, until Edna remembered and called back hastily:

"Oh, come in, Daisy!"

Daisy stood, a little left out and solitary, there in the kitchen, as Billy, the older of the babies, climbed frantically over Elmer, demanding candy, and the little one toddled smilingly about. Her eyes took in all of it. She was impressed by the shining blue-and-white linoleum, the range with its nickel and enamel, the bright new woodwork. Edna was laughing and scolding at Elmer and the baby. Billy had made his father produce the candy. Daisy's sharp little eyes looked hungrily at the lemon drops until Edna remembered her.

"Give Daisy a piece of your candy," she said.

He would not go up to Daisy. She had to come forward and take one of the lemon drops herself. She saw where Edna put the sack, in a dish high in the cupboard. She hoped they would get some more before long.

"My telescope's out there in the car," she reminded them.

"Oh! Elmer, you go and get it and take it up for her," Edna said.

"What?"

"Her valise—or whatever it is—out in the car."

"Oh, sure," Elmer said with a cheerful grin.

"It's kind of an old telescope," Daisy said conversationally. "I guess it's been used a lot. My papa used to have it. The strap broke when Mamma was fastening it this morning. We ain't got any suitcase. I had to take this because it was all there was in the house, and Mamma didn't want to get me a new one."

Edna raised her eyebrows politely. She leaned over and pretended to spat the baby as he came toddling up to her, then rubbed her cheek against his round head with its funny fuzz of hair.

Daisy watched solemnly. "I didn't know both of your children was boys. I thought one of 'em was a girl. That's what there is at home now— one boy and one girl."

"Um-hm," Edna replied absently. "You can go up with Elmer and take off your things, Daisy," she said. "You can stop and unpack your valise now, I guess, if you'd like to. Then you can come down and help me in the kitchen. You know we got you to help me," she reminded.

Daisy, subdued, followed Elmer up the bright new stairs. In the upper hall, two strips of very clean rag rug were laid over the shining yellow of the floor. Elmer had put her telescope in one of the bedrooms.

"There you are!"

She heard him go clattering down the stairs, and then a kind of murmuring and laughing in the kitchen. The back door slammed. She hurried to the window in time to see Elmer go striding off toward the barn.

She looked about her room with

intense curiosity. It too had a bright varnished floor. She had a bed all of her own—a small, old-fashioned bed, left from some old furnishings, that had been put in this room that had the pipes and the hot-water tank. She had to see everything, but she had a stealthy look as she tiptoed about, started to open the drawers of the dresser, looked out of her window. She put her coat and hat on the bed. She would rather be down in the kitchen with Edna than unpack her telescope now.

She guessed she would go down where the rest of them were.

3

Elmer came into the house for dinner. He brought in a cold, muddy, outdoor breath with him. The range was going, but the bright little kitchen seemed chilly, with the white oilcloth on the table, the baby's varnished high chair and his little fat, mottled hands.

Edna made a significant little face at Elmer. Daisy did not see. She was standing back from the stove, where Edna was at work, looking at the baby.

"He can talk pretty good, can't he? Dwight couldn't say anything but 'Mamma' when he was that little."

Edna's back was turned. She said meaningly:

"Now, Elmer's come in to dinner, Daisy, we'll have to hurry. You must help me get on the dinner. You can cut bread and get things on the table. You must help, you know. That's what you are supposed to do."

Daisy looked startled, a little scared and resentful. "Well, I don't know where you keep your bread."

"Don't you remember where I told you to put it this morning? Right over in the cabinet, in that big box. You must watch, Daisy, and learn where things are."

Elmer, a little embarrassed at the look that Edna gave him, whistled as he began to wash his hands at the sink.

"How's Daddy's old boy?" he said loudly, giving a poke at the baby's chin.

As Edna passed him, she shook her head, and her lips just formed: "Been like that all morning!"

He grinned comprehendingly. Then both their faces became expressionless.

Daisy had not exactly heard, but she looked from one to the other, silent and dimly wondering. The queer ache that had kept starting all through the morning, under her interest in Edna's things and doings, came over her again. She sensed something different in the atmosphere than she had ever known before—some queer difference between the position of herself and of the two babies, a faint notion of what Mamma had meant when she had said that this would not be visiting.

"I guess I'm going to have the toothache again," she said faintly.

No one seemed to hear her.

Edna whisked off the potatoes, drained the water. . . . "You might bring me a dish, Daisy." Daisy searched a long time while Edna turned impatiently and pointed. Edna put the rest of the things on

CHARACTER

the table herself. Her young, fresh, capable mouth was tightly closed, and she was making certain resolutions.

Daisy stood hesitating in the middle of the room, a scrawny, unappealing little figure. Billy—fat, blond, in funny, dark blue union-alls —was trotting busily about the kitchen. Daisy swooped down upon him and tried to bring him to the table. He set up a howl. Edna turned, looked astonished, severe.

"I was trying to make him come to the table," Daisy explained weakly.

"You scared him. He isn't used to you. He doesn't like it. Don't cry, Billy. The girl didn't mean anything."

"Here, Daddy'll put him in his place," Elmer said hastily.

Billy looked over his father's shoulder at Daisy with suffused, resentful blue eyes. She did not understand it, and felt strangely at a loss. She had been left with Goldie and Dwight so often. She had always made Dwight go to the table. She had been the boss.

Edna said in a cool, held-in voice, "Put these things on the table, Daisy."

They sat down. Daisy and the other children had always felt it a great treat to eat away from home instead of at their own scanty, hastily set table. They had hung around Mrs. Metzinger's house at noon, hoping to be asked to stay, not offended when told that "it was time for them to run off now." Her pinched little face had a hungry look as she stared at the potatoes and fried ham and pie. But they did not watch and urge her to have more, as Mrs. Metzinger did, and Mrs. Brooker when she took pity on the Switzers and had them there. Daisy wanted more pie. But none of them seemed to be taking more, and so she said nothing. She remembered what her mother had said, with now a faint comprehension: "You must remember you're out working for other folks, and it won't be like it is at home."

After dinner, Edna said: "Now you can wash the dishes, Daisy."

She went into the next room with the children. Daisy, as she went hesitatingly about the kitchen alone, could hear Edna's low contented humming as she sat in there rocking, the baby in her lap. The bright kitchen was empty and lonely now. Through the window, Daisy could see the great barn looming up against the rainy sky. She hoped that they would drive to Edna's mother's soon.

She finished as soon as she could, and went into the dining room, where Edna was sewing on the baby's rompers. Edna went on sewing. Daisy sat down disconsolately. That queer low ache went all through her. She said in a small dismal voice:

"I guess I got the toothache again."

Edna bit off a thread.

"I had it awful hard a while ago. Mamma come pretty near taking me to the dentist."

"That's too bad," Edna murmured politely. But she offered no other condolence. She gave a secret little smile at the baby asleep on a blanket and a pillow in one corner of the shiny leather davenport.

"Is Elmer going to drive into town tomorrow?"

"Tomorrow? I don't suppose so."

"Mamma couldn't find the belt of my plaid dress and I thought if he was, maybe I could go along and get it. I'd like to have it."

Daisy's homely mouth drooped at the corners. Her toothache did not seem to matter to anyone. Edna did not seem to want to see that anything was wrong with her. She had expected Edna to be concerned, to mention remedies. But it wasn't toothache, that strange lonesome ache all over her. Maybe she was going to be terribly sick. Mamma wouldn't come home for supper to be told about it.

She saw Mamma's face as in that last glimpse of it—drawn with crying, and yet trying to smile, under the old cleaning cap, her hand holding her coat together. . . .

Edna glanced quickly at her. The child was so mortally unattractive, unappealing even in her forlornness. Edna frowned a little, but said kindly:

"Now you might take Billy into the kitchen out of my way, Daisy, and amuse him."

"Well, he cries when I pick him up," Daisy said faintly.

"He won't cry this time. Take him out and help him play with his blocks. You must help me with the children, you know."

"Well, if he'll go with me."

"He'll go with you, won't he, Billy boy? Won't you go with Daisy, sweetheart?"

Billy stared and then nodded. Daisy felt a thrill of comfort as Billy put his little fat hand in hers and trotted into the kitchen beside her. He had the fattest hands, she thought. Edna brought the blocks and put the box down on the floor beside Daisy.

"Now, see if you can amuse him so that I can get my sewing done."

"Shall you and me play blocks, Billy?" Daisy murmured.

He nodded. Then he got hold of the box with one hand, tipped out all the blocks on the floor with a bang and a rattle, and looked at her with a pleased proud smile.

"Oh, no, Billy. You mustn't spill out the blocks. Look, you're too little to play with them. No, now— now wait! Let Daisy show you. Daisy'll build something real nice— shall she?"

He gave a solemn nod of consent.

Daisy set out the blocks on the bright linoleum. She had never had such blocks as these to handle before. Dwight's were only a few old, unmatched, broken ones. Her spirit of leadership came back, and she firmly put away that fat hand of Billy's whenever he meddled with her building. She could make something really wonderful with these blocks.

"No, Billy, you mustn't. See, when Daisy's got it all done, then you can see what the lovely building is."

She put the blocks together with great interest. She knew what she was going to make—it was going to be a new house; no, a new church.

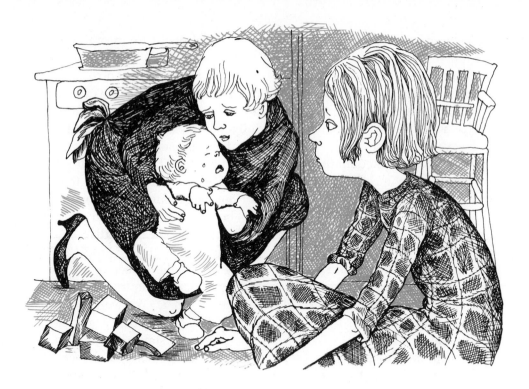

Just as she got the walls up, in came that little hand again, and then with a delighted grunt Billy swept the blocks pell-mell about the floor. At the clatter, he sat back, pursing up his mouth to give an ecstatic "Ooh!"

"Oh, Billy—you mustn't, the building wasn't done! Look, you've spoiled it. Now you've got to sit 'way off here while I try to build it over again."

Billy's look of triumph turned to surprise and then to vociferous protest as Daisy picked him up and firmly transplanted him to another corner of the room. He set up a tremendous howl. He had never been set aside like that before. Edna came hurrying out. Daisy looked at Edna for justification, but instinctively on the defensive.

"Billy knocked over the blocks. He spoiled the building."

"Wah! Wah!" Billy gave loud heartbroken sobs. The tears ran down his fat cheeks and he held out his arms piteously toward his mother.

"I didn't hurt him," Daisy said, scared.

"Never mind, lover," Edna was crooning. "Of course he can play with his blocks. They're Billy's blocks, Daisy," she said. "He doesn't like to sit and see you put up buildings. He wants to play, too. See, you've made him cry now."

"Do' wanna stay here," Billy wailed.

"Well, come in with Mother then." She picked him up, wiping his tears.

"I didn't hurt him," Daisy protested.

"Well, never mind now. You can pick up the blocks and then sweep the floor, Daisy. You didn't do that when you finished the dishes. Never mind," she was saying to Billy. "Pretty soon Daddy'll come in and we'll have a nice ride."

Daisy soberly picked up the blocks and got the broom. What had she done to Billy? He had tried to spoil her building. She always made Dwight keep back until she had finished. Of course it was Daisy, the oldest, who should lead and manage. There had been no one to hear her side. Everything was different. She winked back tears as she swept, poorly and carelessly.

Then she brightened up as Elmer came tramping up on the back porch and then through the kitchen.

"Edna!"

"She's in there," Daisy offered.

"Want to go now? What! Is the baby asleep?" he asked blankly.

Edna gave him a warning look and the door was closed.

Daisy listened hard. She swept very softly. She could catch only a little of what they said— "Kind of hate to go off . . . I know, but if we once start . . . not a thing all day . . . what we got her for . . ." She had no real comprehension of it. She hurried and put away the broom. She wanted to be sure and be ready to go.

Elmer tramped out, straight past her. She saw from the window that he was backing the car out from the shed. She could hear Edna and Billy upstairs, could hear the baby cry a little as he was wakened.

Maybe she ought to go out and get on her wraps, too.

Elmer honked the horn. A moment later Edna came hurrying downstairs, in her hat and coat, and Billy in a knitted cap and red sweater crammed over his union-alls, so that he looked like a little Brownie. The baby had his little coat, too.

Edna called out: "Come in and get this boy, Daddy." She did not look at Daisy, but said hurriedly: "We're going for a little ride, Daisy. Have you finished the sweeping? Well, then, you can pick up those pieces in the dining room. We won't be gone so very long. When it's a quarter past five, you start the fire, like I showed you this noon, and slice the potatoes that were left, and the meat. And set the table."

The horn was honked again.

"Yes! Well, we'll be back, Daisy. Come, lover, Daddy's in a hurry."

Daisy stood looking after them. Billy clamored to sit beside his daddy. Edna took the baby from Elmer and put him beside her on the back seat. There was room—half of the big back seat. There wasn't anything, really, to be done at home. That was the worst of it. They just didn't want to take her. They all belonged together. They didn't want to take anyone else along. She was an outsider. They all—even the baby—had a freshened look of expectancy.

The engine roared—they had started; slipping on the mud of the drive, then forging straight ahead, around the turn, out of sight.

4

She went forlornly into the dining room. The light from the windows was dim now in the rainy, late afternoon. The pink pieces from the baby's rompers were scattered over the gay rug. She got down on her hands and knees, slowly picking them up, sniffing a little. She heard the Big Ben clock in the kitchen ticking loudly.

That dreadful ache submerged her. No one would ask about it, no one would try to comfort her. Before, there had always been Mamma coming home, anxious, scolding sometimes, but worried over them if they didn't feel right, caring about them. Mamma and Goldie and Dwight cared about her—but she was away out in the country, and they were at home. She didn't want to stay here, where she didn't belong. But Mamma had told her that she must begin helping this summer.

Her ugly little mouth contorted into a grimace of weeping. But silent weeping, without any tears; because she already had the cold knowledge that no one would notice or comfort it.

*

Reading Skills

1. In the opening scene (up to the time the car arrives), what do you learn about Daisy and Mrs. Switzer? What is Daisy like? Point out evidence in the story for your conclusions.
2. What do you think of Edna as an employer? Find lines which show whether or not she is a desirable person to work for.
3. What sort of employee is Daisy? Explain your opinion by citing references in the story.
4. Where do you find evidence that Edna is not pleased with Daisy? What mistakes does Daisy make?
5. What is the significance of Daisy's toothache? At what points in the story does Daisy say that she has a toothache? Explain the relation of the "ache" mentioned in the last paragraph to the toothache she has been having from time to time. Describe other reactions that Daisy feels toward her new situation.
6. Will Daisy have changed when she returns home for a visit? Do you see any indication of a change in her at the end of the story?
7. What does the title of the story mean?

Understanding Literature

1. In two columns, list the specific details that describe the Switzers' and the Kruses' homes.

DESCRIPTION OF THE SWITZERS' HOME	DESCRIPTION OF THE KRUSES' HOME
Outside:	*Outside:*
—a muddy little road that has "a cold rainy loneliness"; —a "small house standing on a rough rise of land, weathered to a dim color that showed dark streaks from the rain."	—"a space of bare yard with a little scattering of grass just starting" —a house "small, modern, painted a bright new white and yellow."

   Complete this chart, listing all the details given about the outside and the inside of the two homes. What is the author telling you about the characters in these descriptions of their surroundings? One family is poor and the other is not, of course —but what else does the setting show?

2. On the way to the Kruses' farm Daisy is excited about her new life. Yet, at the same time, she is frightened and lonely. How does the reader know Daisy's feeling?

   Beginning with the description of the Dunkels' house, where "The windows stared blank and cold between the old shutters," see how many details you can find that Daisy sees (or hears or smells) that reflect her innermost fears.

Further Activities

1. Write a description of a room, a car, a desk, or some other place or object that shows the kind of person responsible for its condition. Before you begin to write, decide what the person is like. (Is he/she very neat? always in a hurry? interested in many hobbies?) Then, make the reader know what the person is like through your description of his/her room, desk, or car.

2. As Elmer drives Daisy away, she "had a startled view of home." Reread the paragraph describing her house as she sees it for the last time. Point out the words which are used to give a desolate feeling. Write a similar paragraph describing a house which you are glad to see. Make the descriptive words ones which would suggest a happy mood. For example, change the rainy day to a sunny one and put in bright colors.

Although this story is about cowboys, it is also about everybody.   One of the reasons for reading is that you can, in imagination, become someone else.   If you do that, if you know how others feel when you do unkind things to them, you become more considerate.   The ability to see how others feel is one of the major elements of maturity.

Gold-Mounted Guns

F. R. Buckley

IMPROVING YOUR READING: "Gold-Mounted Guns" could easily be converted into a short play, because in this story the author uses a dramatic method of developing plot and character.   The author sets the scene; then he shows the speech and action of the characters.   He does not explain what the characters are thinking and feeling; he does not explain their backgrounds and their motives; he does not comment on the significance of the action.   He develops the plot and reveals character—as he would in a drama—only through scene, action, and dialogue.

EVENING had fallen on Longhorn City, and already, to the south, an eager star was twinkling in the velvet sky, when a spare, hard-faced man slouched down the main street and selected a pony from the dozen hitched beside Tim Geogehan's general store.   The town, which in the daytime suffered from an excess of eye-searing light in its open spaces, confined its efforts at artificial lighting to the one store, the one saloon, and its neighbor, the Temple of Chance; so it was from a dusky void that the hard-faced man heard himself called by name.

"Tommy!" a subdued voice accosted him.

The hard-faced man made, it seemed, a very slight movement—a mere flick of the hand at his low-slung belt; but it was a movement perfectly appraised by the man in the shadows.

"Wait a minute!" the voice pleaded.

A moment later, his hands upraised, his pony's bridle reins caught in the crook of one arm, a young man moved into the zone of light that shone bravely out through Tim Geogehan's back window.

"Don't shoot," he said, trying to control his nervousness before the weapon unwaveringly trained on him.   "I'm—a friend."

For perhaps fifteen seconds the newcomer and the hard-faced man examined each other with the unwinking scrutiny of those who take chances of life and death.   The younger, with that lightning draw fresh in his mind, noted the sinister droop of a gray mustache over a hidden mouth, and shivered a little as his gaze met that of a pair of steel-blue eyes. The man with the gun saw before him a rather handsome face, marred, even in this moment of submission, by a certain desperation.

"What do you want?" he asked, tersely.

"Can I put my hands down?" countered the other.

The lean man considered.

"All things bein' equal," he said, "I think I'd rather you'd first tell me how you got round to callin' me Tommy. Been askin' people in the street?"

"No," said the boy. "I only got into town this afternoon, an' I ain't a fool anyway. I seen you ride in this afternoon, and the way folks backed away from you made me wonder who you was. Then I seen them gold-mounted guns of yourn, an' of course I knew. Nobody ever had guns like them but Pecos Tommy. I could ha' shot you while you was gettin' your horse, if I'd been that way inclined."

The lean man bit his mustache.

"Put 'em down. What do you want?"

"I want to join you."

"You want to *what?*"

"Yeah, I know it sounds foolish to you, mebbe," said the young man. "But, listen—your sidekicker's in jail down in Rosewell. I figured I could take his place—anyway, till he got out. I know I ain't got any record, but I can ride, an' I can shoot the pips out of a ten-spot at ten paces, an'—I got a little job to bring into the firm, to start with."

The lean man's gaze narrowed.

"Have, eh?" he asked, softly.

"It ain't anythin' like you go in for as a rule," said the boy, apologetically, "but it's a roll of cash an'—I guess it'll show you I'm straight. I only got on to it this afternoon. Kind of providential I should meet you right now."

The lean man chewed his mustache. His eyes did not shift.

"Yeah," he said, slowly. "What you quittin' punchin' for?"

"Sick of it."

"Figurin' robbin' trains is easier money?"

"No," said the young man, "I ain't. But I like a little spice in life. They ain't none in punchin'."

"Got a girl?" asked the lean man.

The boy shook his head. The hard-faced man nodded reflectively.

"Well, what's the job?" he asked.

The light from Geogehan's window was cut off by the body of a man who, cupping his hands about his eyes, stared out into the night, as if to locate the buzz of voices at the back of the store.

"If you're goin' to take me on," said the young man, "I can tell you while we're ridin' toward it. If you ain't—why, there's no need to go no further."

The elder slipped back into its holster the gold-mounted gun he had drawn, glanced once at the obscured window and again, piercingly, at the boy whose face now showed white in the light of the rising moon. Then he turned his pony and mounted.

"Come on," he commanded.

Five minutes later the two had passed the limits of the town, heading for the low range of hills which encircled it to the south—and Will Arblaster had given the details of his job to the unemotional man at his side.

"How do you know the old guy's got the money?" came a level question.

"I saw him come out of the bank this afternoon, grinnin' all over his face an' stuffin' it into his pants-pocket," said the boy. "An' when he was gone, I kind of inquired who he was. His name's Sanderson, an' he lives in this yer cabin right ahead a mile. Looked kind of a soft old geezer—kind that'd give up without any trouble. Must ha' been quite some cash there, judgin' by the size of the roll. But I guess when *you* ask him for it, he won't mind lettin' it go."

"I ain't goin' to ask him," said the lean man. "This is your job."

The boy hesitated.

"Well, if I do it right," he asked, with a trace of tremor in his voice, "will you take me along with you sure?"

"Yeah—I'll take you along."

The two ponies rounded a shoulder of the hill: before the riders there loomed, in the moonlight, the dark shape of a cabin, its windows unlighted. The lean man chuckled.

"He's out."

Will Arblaster swung off his horse.

"Maybe," he said, "but likely the money ain't. He started off home, an' if he's had to go out again, likely he's hid the money some place. Folks know *you're* about. I'm goin' to see."

Stealthily he crept toward the house. The moon went behind a cloud bank, and the darkness swallowed him. The lean man, sitting his horse, motionless, heard the rap of knuckles on the door—then a pause, the rattle of the latch. A moment later there came the heavy thud of a shoulder against wood—a cracking sound, and a crash as the door went down. The lean man's lips tightened. From within the cabin came the noise of one stumbling over furniture, then the fitful fire of a match illumined the windows. In the quiet, out there in the night, the man on the horse, twenty yards away, could hear the clumping of the other's boots on the rough board floor, and every rustle of the papers that he fumbled in his search. Another match scratched and sputtered, and then, with a hoarse cry of triumph, was flung down. Running feet padded across the short grass and Will Arblaster drew up, panting.

"Got it!" he gasped. "The old fool! Put it in a tea canister right on the mantelshelf. Enough to choke a horse! Feel it!"

The lean man, unemotional as ever, reached down and took the roll of money.

"Got another match?" he asked.

Willie struck one, and panting, watched while his companion, moistening a thumb, ruffled through the bills.

"Fifty tens," said the lean man. "Five hundred dollars. Guess I'll carry it."

His cold blue eyes turned downward, and focused again with pierc-

ing attention on the younger man's upturned face. The bills were stowed in a pocket of the belt right next one of those gold-mounted guns which, earlier in the evening, had covered Willie Arblaster's heart. For a moment, the lean man's hand seemed to hesitate over its butt; then, as Willie smiled and nodded, it moved away. The match burned out.

"Let's get out of here," the younger urged; whereupon the hand which had hovered over the gun butt grasped Will Arblaster's shoulder.

"No, not yet," he said quietly, "not just yet. Get on your hawss, an' set still awhile."

The young man mounted. "What's the idea?"

"Why!" said the level voice at his right. "This is a kind of novelty to me. Robbin' trains, you ain't got any chance to see results, like: this here's different. Figure this old guy'll be back pretty soon. I'd like to see what he does when he finds his wad's gone. Ought to be amusin'!"

Arblaster chuckled uncertainly.

"Ain't he liable to——"

"He can't see us," said the lean man with a certain new cheerfulness in his tone. "An' besides, he'll think we'd naturally be miles away; an' besides that, we're mounted, all ready."

"What's that?" whispered the young man, laying a hand on his companion's arm.

The other listened.

"Probably him," he said. "Now stay still."

There were two riders—by their voices, a man and a girl: they were laughing as they approached the rear of the house, where, roughly made of old boards, stood Pa Sanderson's substitute for a stable. They put up the horses; then their words came clearer to the ears of the listeners, as they turned the corner of the building, walking toward the front door.

"I feel mean about it, anyhow," said the girl's voice. "You going on living here, Daddy, while——"

"Tut-tut-tut!" said the old man. "What's five hundred to me? I ain't never had that much in a lump, an' shouldn't know what to do with it if I had. 'Sides, your Aunt Elviry didn't give it to you for nothin'. 'If she wants to go to college,' says she, 'let her prove it by workin'. I'll pay half, but she's got to pay t'other half.' Well, you worked, an'—— Where on earth did I put that key?"

There was a silence, broken by the grunts of the old man as he contorted himself in the search of his pockets; and then the girl spoke: the tone of her voice was the more terrible for the restraint she was putting on it.

"Daddy—the—the—did you leave the money in the house?"

"Yes. What is it?" cried the old man.

"Daddy—the door's broken down, and——"

There was a hoarse cry: boot heels stumbled across the boards, and again a match flared. Its pale light showed a girl standing in the doorway of the cabin, her hands clasped on her bosom—while beyond the wreckage of the door a bent figure with silver hair tottered away from the mantelshelf. In one hand Pa Sanderson held the flickering match, in the other a tin box.

"Gone!" he cried in his cracked voice. "Gone!"

Willie Arblaster drew a breath through his teeth and moved uneasily in his saddle. Instantly a lean, strong hand, with a grip like steel, fell on his wrist and grasped it. The man behind the hand chuckled.

"Listen!" he said.

"Daddy—Daddy—don't take on so —please don't," came the girl's voice, itself trembling with repressed tears. There was a scrape of chair legs on the floor as she forced the old man into his seat by the fireplace. He hunched there, his face in his hands, while she struck a match and laid the flame to the wick of the lamp on the table. As it burned up she went back to her father, knelt by him, and threw her arms about his neck.

"Now, now, now!" she pleaded. "Now, Daddy, it's all right. Don't take on so. It's all right."

But he would not be comforted.

"I can't replace it!" cried Pa Sanderson, dropping trembling hands from his face. "It's gone! Two years you've been away from me; two years you've slaved in a store; and now I've——"

"Hush, hush!" the girl begged. "Now, Daddy—it's all right. I can go on working, and——"

With a convulsive effort, the old man got to his feet. "Two years more slavery, while some skunk drinks your money, gambles it— throws it away!" he cried. "Curse him! Whoever it is, curse him! Where's God's justice? What's a man goin' to believe when years of scrapin' like your aunt done, an' years of slavin' like yours in Laredo there, an' all our happiness today can be wiped out by a . . . thief in a minute?"

The girl put her little hand over her father's mouth.

"Don't, Daddy," she choked. "It only makes it worse. Come and lie down on your bed, and I'll make you some coffee. Don't cry, Daddy darling. Please."

Gently, like a mother with a little child, she led the heartbroken old man out of the watchers' line of vision, out of the circle of lamplight. More faintly, but still with heart-rending distinctness, the listeners could hear the sounds of weeping.

The lean man sniffed, chuckled, and pulled his bridle.

"Some circus!" he said appreciatively. "C'mon, boy."

His horse moved a few paces, but Will Arblaster's did not. The lean man turned in his saddle.

"Ain't you comin'?" he asked.

For ten seconds, perhaps, the boy made no answer. Then he urged his pony forward until it stood side by side with his companion's.

"No," he said. "An'—an' I ain't goin' to take that money, neither."

"Huh?"

The voice was slow and meditative.

"Don't know as ever I figured what this game meant," he said. "Always seemed to me that all the hardships was on the stick-up man's side—

gettin' shot at an' chased and so on. Kind of fun, at that. Never thought 'bout—old men cryin'."

"That ain't my fault," said the lean man.

"No," said Will Arblaster, still very slowly. "But I'm goin' to take that money back. You didn't have no trouble gettin' it, so you don't lose nothin'."

"Suppose I say I won't let go of it?" suggested the lean man with a sneer.

"Then," snarled Arblaster, "I'll blow your . . . head off an' take it! Don't you move, you! I've got you covered. I'll take the money out myself."

His revolver muzzle under his companion's nose, he snapped open the pocket of the belt and extracted the roll of bills. Then, regardless of a possible shot in the back, he swung off his horse and shambled, with the mincing gait of the born horseman, into the lighted doorway of the cabin. The lean man, unemotional as ever, sat perfectly still, looking alternately at the cloud-dappled sky and at the cabin, from which now came a murmur of voices harmonizing with a strange effect of joy, to the half-heard bass of the night wind.

It was a full ten minutes before Will Arblaster reappeared in the doorway alone, and made, while silhouetted against the light, a quick movement of his hand across his eyes, then stumbled forward through the darkness toward his horse. Still the lean man did not move.

"I'm—sorry," said the boy as he

mounted. "But——"

"I ain't," said the lean man quietly. "What do you think I made you stay an' watch for, you young fool?"

The boy made no reply. Suddenly the hair prickled on the back of his neck and his jaw fell.

"Say," he demanded hoarsely at last. "Ain't you Pecos Tommy?"

The lean man's answer was a short laugh.

"But you got his guns, an' the people in Longhorn all kind of fell back!" the boy cried. "If you ain't him, who are you?"

The moon had drifted from behind a cloud and flung a ray of light across the face of the lean man as he turned it, narrow-eyed, toward Arblaster. The pallid light picked out with terrible distinctness the grim lines of that face—emphasized the cluster of sun-wrinkles about the corners of the piercing eyes and marked as if with underscoring black lines the long sweep of the fighting jaw.

"Why," said the lean man dryly, "I'm the sheriff that killed him yesterday. Let's be ridin' back."

Reading Skills

1. Why does Will Arblaster want to become an outlaw?
2. What kind of person is Will Arblaster? How do you know that the man with the gold-mounted guns understands Will's true nature?
3. Why does the man with the gold-mounted guns insist on staying after the robbery to watch the old man discover his loss? Why does he pretend that he is not going to allow Will to return the money?
4. At what point in the story did you guess the identity of the man with the gold-mounted guns? What details in the story seem to be describing an outlaw but actually describe a sheriff?
5. What does Will learn in the story? How does what he learns affect his life?
6. Why is the story called "Gold-Mounted Guns"? What is their importance in the story?

Understanding Literature

1. The author uses light and shadow in the scenes of this story just as a dramatist might specify stage lighting. Describe the scenes in the story which have special lighting effects.
2. In two scenes you hear, but do not see, the action. Reread these scenes. Why does the author use only sound to present the action in these scenes?

F. R. BUCKLEY

A person can be eager for something—for example, a child may be eager for candy or a working man eager for payday. But how can a *star* be eager? Explain the meaning of the following italicized words as they are used in the story:

1. ". . . an *eager* star was twinkling in a *velvet* sky."
2. ". . . a *spare, hard-faced* man *slouched* down the main street."
3. ". . . which in the daytime *suffered* from an excess of *eye-searing* light in its open spaces."
4. ". . . a mere *flick* of the hand at his low-slung belt."
5. ". . . a movement perfectly *appraised* by the man in the shadow."
6. " 'How do you know the old guy's got the money?' came a *level* question."

Further Activities

1. Write a paragraph, using an incident which illustrates the truth of the following sentence:
    "When a person treats someone else badly and then realizes how the other feels, the first person is often ashamed of what he has done."
2. Some members of your class might convert this story into a play. Stage directions would indicate setting, physical action, and off-stage sounds. The characters' speeches would become the dialogue. For instance, scene i might begin in this manner:

TIME: Evening.

SCENE: The street of a small western town. The street is dark, except for lights coming from Tim Geogehan's general store, a saloon, and the Temple of Chance. One lone star is in the sky. A spare, hard-faced man slouches down the street and pauses in front of the general store.

A VOICE (*subdued*). Tommy!

(*The hard-faced man, making only a slight movement, quickly draws his gun from his low-slung belt.*)

VOICE. Wait a minute!

(*A young man moves into the light, hands upraised.*)

YOUNG MAN (*nervously*). Don't shoot. I'm—a friend. . . .

Where would scene ii begin? How many scenes would there be?

This story begins with Sylvia's idyllic life, into which evil (as she thinks) comes as a man with a gun. After the stranger arrives, Sylvia is tempted to destroy part of her world.

A White Heron

Sarah Orne Jewett

IMPROVING YOUR READING: In "A White Heron" Sylvia has to choose between two ways of life—one represented by the heron and another represented by the stranger. As you read, consider what the heron means to Sylvia. What qualities do Sylvia and the bird have in common? What does the stranger mean to Sylvia? Why does she want to help him?

THE WOODS WERE already filled with shadows one June evening, just before eight o'clock, though a bright sunset still glimmered faintly among the trunks of the trees. A little girl was driving home her cow, a plodding, dilatory, provoking creature in her behavior, but a valued companion for all that. They were going away from whatever light there was, and striking deep into the woods, but their feet were familiar with the path, and it was no matter whether their eyes could see it or not.

There was hardly a night the summer through when the old cow could be found waiting at the pasture bars; on the contrary, it was her greatest pleasure to hide herself away among the huckleberry bushes, and though she wore a loud bell she had made the discovery that if one stood perfectly still it would not ring. So Sylvia had to hunt for her until she found her, and call "Co'! Co'!" with never an answering "Moo," until her childish patience was quite spent. If the creature had not given good milk and plenty of it, the case would have seemed very different to her owners. Besides, Sylvia had all the time there was, and very little use to make of it. Sometimes in pleasant weather it was a consolation to look upon the cow's pranks as an intelligent attempt to play hide-and-seek, and as the child had no playmates she lent herself to this amusement with a good deal of zest. Though this chase had been so long that the wary animal herself had given an unusual signal of her whereabouts, Sylvia had only laughed when she came upon Mistress Moolly at the swampside, and urged her affectionately homeward with a twig of birch leaves. The old cow was not inclined to wander farther, she even turned in the right direction for once as they left the pasture, and stepped along the road at a good pace. She was quite ready to be milked now, and seldom stopped to browse. Sylvia wondered what her grandmother would say because they were so late. It was a great while since she had left home at half past five o'clock, but everybody knew the difficulty of making this errand a short one. Mrs. Tilley had chased the horned torment too many summer evenings herself to blame any one else for lingering, and was only thankful as she waited that she had Sylvia, nowadays, to give such valuable assistance. The good woman suspected that Sylvia loitered occasionally on her own account; there never was such a child for straying about out of doors since the world was made! Everybody said that it was a good change for a little maid who had tried to grow for eight years in a crowded manufacturing town, but, as for Sylvia herself, it seemed as if she never had been alive at all before she came to live at the farm. She thought often with wistful compassion of a wretched geranium that belonged to a town neighbor.

"'Afraid of folks,'" old Mrs. Tilley said to herself, with a smile, after she had made the unlikely choice of Sylvia from her daughter's houseful of children, and was returning to the farm. "'Afraid of folks,' they said! I guess she won't be troubled no great with 'em up to the old place!" When they reached the door of the lonely house and stopped to unlock it, and the cat came to purr loudly, and rub against them, a deserted pussy, indeed, but fat with young robins, Sylvia whispered that this was a beautiful place to live in, and she never should wish to go home.

The companions followed the shady wood-road, the cow taking slow steps and the child very fast ones. The cow stopped long at the brook to drink, as if the pasture were not half a swamp, and Sylvia stood still and waited, letting her bare feet cool themselves in the shoal water, while the great twilight moths struck softly against her. She waded on through the brook as the cow moved away, and listened to the thrushes with a heart that beat fast with pleasure. There was a stirring in the great boughs overhead. They were full of little birds and beasts that seemed to be wide awake, and going about their world, or else saying good night to each other in sleepy twitters. Sylvia herself felt sleepy as she walked along. However, it was not much farther to the house, and the air was soft and sweet. She was not often in the woods so late as this, and it made her feel as if she were a part of the gray shadows and the moving leaves. She was just thinking how long it seemed since she first came to the farm a year ago, and wondering if everything went on in the noisy town just the same as when she was there; the thought of the great red-faced boy who used to chase and frighten her made her hurry along the path to escape from the shadow of the trees.

Suddenly this little woods-girl is horror-stricken to hear a clear whistle not very far away. Not a bird's whistle, which would have a sort of friendliness, but a boy's whistle, determined, and somewhat aggressive. Sylvia left the cow to whatever sad fate might await her, and stepped discreetly aside into the brushes, but she was just too late. The enemy had discovered her, and called out in a very cheerful and persuasive tone, "Halloa, little girl, how far is it to the road?" and trembling Sylvia answered almost inaudibly, "A good ways."

She did not dare to look boldly at the tall young man, who carried a gun over his shoulder, but she came out of her bush and again followed the cow, while he walked alongside.

"I have been hunting for some birds," the stranger said kindly, "and I have lost my way, and need a friend very much. Don't be afraid," he added gallantly. "Speak up and tell me what your name is, and whether you think I can spend the night at your house, and go out gunning early in the morning."

Sylvia was more alarmed than before. Would not her grandmother consider her much to blame? But who could have foreseen such an accident as this? It did not seem to be her fault, and she hung her head as if the stem of it were broken, but managed to answer "Sylvy," with much effort when her companion again asked her name.

Mrs. Tilley was standing in the doorway when the trio came into view. The cow gave a loud moo by way of explanation.

"Yes, you'd better speak up for yourself, you old trial! Where'd she tucked herself away this time, Sylvy?" But Sylvia kept an awed silence; she knew by instinct that her grandmother did not comprehend the gravity of the situation. She must be mistaking the stranger for one of the farmer-lads of the region.

The young man stood his gun beside the door, and dropped a lumpy gamebag beside it; then he bade Mrs. Tilley good evening, and repeated his wayfarer's story, and asked if he could have a night's lodging.

"Put me anywhere you like," he said. "I must be off early in the morning, before day; but I am very hungry, indeed. You can give me some milk at any rate, that's plain."

"Dear sakes, yes," responded the hostess, whose long slumbering hospitality seemed to be easily awakened. "You might fare better if you went out to the main road a mile or so, but you're welcome to what we've got. I'll milk right off, and you make yourself at home. You can sleep on husks or feathers," she proffered graciously. "I raised them all myself. There's good pasturing for geese just below here towards the ma'sh. Now step round and set a plate for the gentleman, Sylvy!" And Sylvia promptly stepped. She was glad to have something to do, and she was hungry herself.

It was a surprise to find so clean and comfortable a little dwelling in this New England wilderness. The young man had known the horrors of its most primitive housekeeping, and the dreary squalor of that level of society which does not rebel at the companionship of hens. This was the best thrift of an old-fashioned farmstead, though on such a small scale

that it seemed like a hermitage. He
listened eagerly to the old woman's
quaint talk, he watched Sylvia's pale
face and shining gray eyes with ever-
growing enthusiasm, and insisted
that this was the best supper he had
eaten for a month, and afterward the
new-made friends sat down in the
doorway together while the moon
came up.

Soon it would be berry time, and
Sylvia was a great help at picking.
The cow was a good milker, though
a plaguy thing to keep track of, the
hostess gossiped frankly, adding
presently that she had buried four
children, so Sylvia's mother, and a
son (who might be dead) in California
were all the children she had left.
"Dan, my boy, was a great hand to
go gunning," she explained sadly. "I
never wanted for pa'tridges or gray

squer'ls while he was to home. He's
been a great wand'rer, I expect, and
he's no hand to write letters. There,
I don't blame him, I'd ha' seen the
world myself if it had been so I
could.

"Sylvy takes after him," the grandmother continued affectionately,
after a minute's pause. "There ain't
a foot o' ground she don't know
her way over, and the wild crea-
turs counts her one o' themselves.
Squer'ls she'll tame to come an' feed
right out o' her hands, and all sorts o'
birds. Last winter she got the jay
birds to bangeing[1] here, and I believe
she'd 'a' scanted herself of her own
meals to have plenty to throw out
amongst 'em, if I hadn't kep' watch.
Anything but crows, I tell her, I'm

1 **bangeing:** spending their time.

170

willin' to help support—though Dan he had a tamed one o' them that did seem to have reason same as folks. It was round here a good spell after he went away. Dan an' his father they didn't hitch—but he never held up his head ag'in after Dan had dared him an' gone off."

The guest did not notice this hint of family sorrows in his eager interest in something else.

"So Sylvy knows all about birds, does she?" he exclaimed, as he looked round at the little girl who sat, very demure but increasingly sleepy, in the moonlight. "I am making a collection of birds myself. I have been at it ever since I was a boy." (Mrs. Tilley smiled.) "There are two or three very rare ones I have been hunting for these five years. I mean to get them on my own ground if they can be found."

"Do you cage 'em up?" asked Mrs. Tilley doubtfully, in response to this enthusiastic announcement.

"Oh no, they're stuffed and preserved, dozens and dozens of them," said the ornithologist, "and I have shot or snared every one myself. I caught a glimpse of a white heron a few miles from here on Saturday, and I have followed it in this direction. They have never been found in this district at all. The little white heron, it is," and he turned again to look at Sylvia with the hope of discovering that the rare bird was one of her acquaintances.

But Sylvia was watching a hoptoad in the narrow footpath.

"You would know the heron if you saw it," the stranger continued eagerly. "A queer tall white bird with soft feathers and long thin legs. And it would have a nest perhaps in the top of a high tree, made of sticks, something like a hawk's nest."

Sylvia's heart gave a wild beat; she knew that strange white bird, and had once stolen softly near where it stood in some bright green swamp grass, away over at the other side of the woods. There was an open place where the sunshine always seemed strangely yellow and hot, where tall, nodding rushes grew, and her grandmother had warned her that she might sink in the soft black mud underneath and never be heard of more. Not far beyond were the salt marshes just this side of the sea itself, which Sylvia wondered and dreamed much about, but never had seen, whose great voice could sometimes be heard above the noise of the woods on stormy nights.

"I can't think of anything I should like so much as to find that heron's nest," the handsome stranger was saying. "I would give ten dollars to anybody who could show it to me," he added desperately, "and I mean to spend my whole vacation hunting for it if need be. Perhaps it was only migrating, or had been chased out of its own region by some bird of prey."

Mrs. Tilley gave amazed attention to all this, but Sylvia still watched the toad, not divining, as she might have done at some calmer time, that the creature wished to get to its hole under the doorstep, and was much hindered by the unusual spectators at that hour of the evening. No amount of thought, that night, could decide how many wished-for treasures the ten dollars, so lightly spoken of, would buy.

The next day the young sportsman hovered about the woods, and Sylvia kept him company, having lost her first fear of the friendly lad, who proved to be most kind and sympathetic. He told her many things about the birds and what they knew and where they lived and what they did with themselves. And he gave her a jackknife, which she thought as great a treasure as if she were a desert-islander. All day long he did not once make her troubled or afraid except when he brought down some unsuspecting singing creature from its bough. Sylvia would have liked him vastly better without his gun; she could not understand why he killed the very birds he seemed to like so much. But as the day waned, Sylvia still watched the young man with loving admiration. She had never seen anybody so charming and delightful; the woman's heart, asleep in the child, was vaguely thrilled by a dream of love. Some premonition of that great power stirred and swayed these young creatures who traversed the solemn woodlands with soft-footed silent care. They stopped to listen to a bird's song; they pressed forward again eagerly, parting the branches—speaking to each other rarely and in whispers; the young man going first and Sylvia following, fascinated, a few steps behind, with her gray eyes dark with excitement. She grieved because the longed-for white heron was elusive, but she did

not lead the guest, she only followed, and there was no such thing as speaking first. The sound of her own unquestioned voice would have terrified her—it was hard enough to answer yes or no when there was need of that. At last evening began to fall, and they drove the cow home together, and Sylvia smiled with pleasure when they came to the place where she heard the whistle and was afraid only the night before.

II

Half a mile from home, at the farther edge of the woods, where the land was highest, a great pine tree stood, the last of its generation. Whether it was left for a boundary mark, or for what reason, no one could say; the woodchoppers who had felled its mates were dead and gone long ago, and a whole forest of sturdy trees, pines and oaks and maples, had grown again. But the stately head of this old pine towered above them all and made a landmark for sea and shore miles and miles away. Sylvia knew it well. She had always believed that whoever climbed to the top of it could see the ocean; and the little girl had often laid her hand on the great rough trunk and looked up wistfully at those dark boughs that the wind always stirred, no matter how hot and still the air might be below. Now she thought of the tree with a new excitement, for why, if one climbed it at break of day could not one see all the world, and easily discover from whence the white heron flew, and mark the place, and find the hidden nest?

What a spirit of adventure, what wild ambition! What fancied triumph and delight and glory for the later morning when she could make known the secret! It was almost too real and too great for the childish heart to bear.

All night the door of the little house stood open and the whippoorwills came and sang upon the very step. The young sportsman and his old hostess were sound asleep, but Sylvia's great design kept her broad awake and watching. She forgot to think of sleep. The short summer night seemed as long as the winter darkness, and at last when the whippoorwills ceased, and she was afraid the morning would after all come too soon, she stole out of the house and followed the pasture path through the woods, hastening toward the open ground beyond, listening with a sense of comfort and companionship to the drowsy twitter of a half-awakened bird, whose perch she had jarred in passing. Alas, if the great wave of human interest which flooded for the first time this dull little life should sweep away the satisfactions of an existence heart to heart with nature and the dumb life of the forest!

There was the huge tree asleep yet in the paling moonlight, and small and silly Sylvia began with utmost bravery to mount to the top of it, with tingling, eager blood coursing the channels of her whole frame, with her bare feet and fingers, that pinched and held like bird's claws to the monstrous ladder reaching up, up, almost to the sky itself. First she must mount the white oak tree that grew alongside, where she was almost lost among the dark branches and the green leaves heavy and wet with dew; a bird fluttered off its nest, and a red squirrel ran to and fro and scolded pettishly at the harmless housebreaker. Sylvia felt her way easily. She had often climbed there, and knew that higher still one of the oak's upper branches chafed against the pine trunk, just where its lower boughs were set close together. There, when she made the dangerous pass from one tree to the other, the great enterprise would really begin.

She crept out along the swaying oak limb at last, and took the daring step across into the old pine tree. The way was harder than she thought; she must reach far and hold fast, the sharp dry twigs caught and held her and scratched her like angry talons, the pitch made her thin little fingers clumsy and stiff as she went round and round the tree's great stem, higher and higher upward. The sparrows and robins in the woods below were beginning to wake and twitter to the dawn, yet it seemed much lighter there aloft in the pine tree, and the child knew she must hurry if her project were to be of any use.

The tree seemed to lengthen itself out as she went up, and to reach farther and farther upward. It was like a great mainmast to the voyaging earth; it must truly have been amazed that morning through all its

ponderous frame as it felt this determined spark of human spirit wending
its way from higher branch to branch.
Who knows how steadily the least
twigs held themselves to advantage
this light, weak creature on her way!
The old pine must have loved his
new dependent. More than all the
hawks, and bats, and moths, and
even the sweet-voiced thrushes, was
the brave, beating heart of the solitary gray-eyed child. And the tree
stood still and frowned away the
winds that June morning while the
dawn grew bright in the east.

Sylvia's face was like a pale star,
if one had seen it from the ground,
when the last thorny bough was past,
and she stood trembling and tired but
wholly triumphant, high in the treetop. Yes, there was the sea with the
dawning sun making a golden dazzle

over it, and toward that glorious east
flew two hawks with slow-moving
pinions. How low they looked in the
air from that height when one had
only seen them before far up, and
dark against the blue sky. Their
gray feathers were as soft as moths:
they seemed only a little way from
the tree, and Sylvia felt as if she too
could go flying away among the
clouds. Westward, the woodlands
and farms reached miles and miles
into the distance; here and there
were church steeples, and white villages; truly it was a vast and awe-
some world!

The birds sang louder and louder.
At last the sun came up bewilder-
ingly bright. Sylvia could see the
white sails of ships out at sea, and
the clouds that were purple and rose-
colored and yellow at first began to

fade away. Where was the white heron's nest in the sea of green branches, and was this wonderful sight and pageant of the world the only reward for having climbed to such a giddy height? Now look down again, Sylvia, where the green marsh is set among the shining birches and dark hemlocks; there where you saw the white heron once you will see him again; look, look! a white spot of him like a single floating feather comes up from the dead hemlock and grows larger, and rises, and comes close at last, and goes by the landmark pine with steady sweep of wing and outstretched slender neck and crested head. And wait! wait! do not move a foot or a finger, little girl, do not send an arrow of light and consciousness from your two eager eyes, for the heron has perched on a pine bough not far beyond yours, and cries back to his mate on the nest and plumes his feathers for the new day!

The child gives a long sigh a minute later when a company of shouting catbirds comes also to the tree, and vexed by their fluttering and lawlessness the solemn heron goes away. She knows his secret now, the wild, light, slender bird that floats and wavers, and goes back like an arrow presently to his home in the green world beneath. Then Sylvia, well satisfied, makes her perilous way down again, not daring to look far below the branch she stands on, ready to cry sometimes because her fingers ache and her lamed feet slip. Wondering over and over again what the stranger would say to her, and what he would think when she told him how to find his way straight to the heron's nest.

"Sylvy, Sylvy!" called the busy old grandmother again and again, but nobody answered, and the small husk bed was empty and Sylvia had disappeared.

The guest waked from a dream, and remembering his day's pleasure hurried to dress himself that might it sooner begin. He was sure from the way the shy little girl looked once or twice yesterday that she had at least seen the white heron, and now she must really be made to tell. Here she comes now, paler than ever, and her worn old frock is torn and tattered, and smeared with pine pitch. The grandmother and the sportsman stand in the door together and question her, and the splendid moment has come to speak of the dead hemlock tree by the green marsh.

But Sylvia does not speak after all, though the old grandmother fretfully rebukes her, and the young man's kind, appealing eyes are looking straight in her own. He can make them rich with money; he has promised it, and they are poor now. He is so well worth making happy, and he waits to hear the story she can tell.

No, she must keep silence! What is it that suddenly forbids her and makes her dumb? Has she been nine years growing and now, when the great world for the first time puts out a hand to her, must she thrust it aside for a bird's sake? The murmur of the pine's green branches is in her ears, she remembers how the white heron came flying through the golden air and how they watched the sea and the morning together, and Sylvia cannot speak; she cannot tell the heron's secret and give its life away.

Dear loyalty, that suffered a sharp pang as the guest went away disappointed later in the day, that could have served and followed him and loved him as a dog loves! Many a night Sylvia heard the echo of his whistle haunting the pasture path as she came home with the loitering cow. She forgot even her sorrow at the sharp report of his gun and the sight of thrushes and sparrows dropping silent to the ground, their songs hushed and their pretty feathers stained and wet with blood. Were the birds better friends than their hunter might have been—who can tell? Whatever treasures were lost to her, woodlands and summertime, remember! Bring your gifts and graces and tell your secrets to this lonely country child!

Reading Skills

1. What kind of life has Sylvia lived before the beginning of this story?
2. Find lines that tell what kind of girl Sylvia is. Why does the author make her this kind of person for this story?
3. Why is Sylvia afraid of the stranger? Why is she "more alarmed than before" at the thought of taking him home?
4. What is the young man looking for? Why does he think that Sylvia may be able to help him? Why does Mrs. Tilley smile when he says, "I've been at it ever since I was a boy"? Why, during the conversation after supper, does Sylvia watch the hoptoad?
5. Find as many reasons as you can for Sylvia's telling the heron's secret. Why does Sylvia not tell?
6. Explain what this statement means: "Alas, if the great wave of human interest which flooded for the first time this dull little life should sweep away the satisfactions of an existence heart to heart with nature and the dumb life of the forest!"
7. In the last paragraph, what does the author mean by "Whatever treasures were lost to her"?

Understanding Literature

1. What words and phrases in the story describe the white heron? What does the heron represent?
2. The name of the young man is never given. How does the author identify him in the story? (Once he is called the "enemy." Why? How else is he identified?) Why does the author not tell his name? What does he represent?
3. Find lines in the account of Sylvia's climb to the top of the tree in which the author (*a*) tells how things seem to Sylvia, (*b*) tells how things seem to the tree, and (*c*) speaks directly to Sylvia.
4. Sylvia's conflict involves a choice between the heron (all that it represents) and the young man (all that he represents). Why does she choose the heron? According to the story, which choice is better? (Before you answer, reread the last paragraph.)

Focusing on Words

1. Why is the cow called "the horned torment"?
2. In Mrs. Tilley's home, the young man finds none of "the dreary squalor of that level of society which does not rebel at the society of hens." In what other words might this idea have been expressed?
3. Explain what comparison is suggested in each of the following:
   - (*a*) ". . . the sharp dry twigs caught and held her and scratched her like angry talons."
   - (*b*) The tree "was like a great mainmast to the voyaging earth."
   - (*c*) "Sylvia's face was like a pale star."
   - (*d*) She "could have served and followed him and loved him as a dog loves."

Further Activities

1. Discussion topic: What happens to Sylvia when she is high in the treetop? What does she understand that she never understood before? What other stories have you read in which a character experiences a moment when he understands some truth about life that he has never seen before? Have you ever experienced such a moment?
2. Write an explanation of why Sylvia does not tell the location of the heron's nest. You might pretend to be writing a letter that Sylvia might write some years later to the young hunter or to her grandmother.

America in
Folklore and Tales

THE SELECTIONS in this unit deal with persons, places, and events in American folklore and legend. People in all times have made up stories and told them to one another. As the stories are handed down from one person to another, they often change and become more elaborate in the telling. But how do they begin?

A legend is a story which is partly true. Paul Bunyan, if he lived at all, was probably the fastest lumberman in cutting down a tree, and Hiawatha was the name of a real Indian leader. These men had characteristics that were important to the people of the time in which they lived. And so the people made up exaggerated stories about them. The stories expressed what many people wanted to be. Often the American legends were very funny; Americans have never taken themselves too seriously.

The legends and tales which a people hands on from generation to generation become its folklore. Folk stories, as they are first told, are usually not written down but are told by word of mouth for many years until they become traditional, a part of the common heritage of the people. Then, at some time in history, a writer becomes especially interested in a legend and writes it down.

Much of the legend and folklore of nations has been included in great literature. If you have not already done so, you will someday read the *Iliad*, the *Odyssey*, the *Aeneid*, the *Song of Roland*, *Beowulf*, and other great legends. In these works the writers use folklore as a basis for their literature. You will find that some American writers, such as Henry Wadsworth Longfellow in *The Song of Hiawatha*, use American folklore as a basis for their literary works.

Sometimes, however, scholars or writers simply record as accurately as possible the folk songs and stories they hear. An American who became so interested in collecting folk material of America that he made it the most important activity of his life was John A. Lomax. Before you read the stories in this section, read the excerpts from *Adventures of a Ballad Hunter*, by a man who, with his son, was responsible for recording more than ten thousand American folk songs.

Why does a man decide to devote most of his life to a search throughout America for folk ballads—a search that will take him over cattle trails, into penitentiaries, and to the backwoods, as well as into colleges and learned societies?

Adventures of a Ballad Hunter: Preface

John A. Lomax

IMPROVING YOUR READING: *Preface* means, literally, "made/done before." In his Preface to *Adventures of a Ballad Hunter*, John A. Lomax explains how he became interested in folk ballads and why he decided to write a book about his long search. He compares in detail the process of choosing materials for his book with the process of planting corn. As you read, decide why this detailed comparison is an effective one.

One for the blackbird, one for the crow,
One for the cutworm, and two to grow.

YEARS AGO I used to chant this rhyme as I dropped seed corn into a freshly turned furrow. I followed close behind a scooter, pulled by two sturdy mules, that ripped open a trench in the warm earth. Even in the early morning the soft, moist loam felt friendly to my bare feet.

One plowboy and team opened a furrow, another plowboy and team followed to cover up the corn, while I, younger and smaller than the other field hands, walking between the two teams, dropped the seed corn close behind the plow that opened the land. A tin bucket full of grains swung from my left hand, holding every color—white and yellow and speckled and red. We picked the longest ears and planted only the fully grown kernels. Plant full-grown seed from big ears, and you'll reap big ears, said my wise old father.

With my free right hand I would reach for a handful of corn from the bucket; then, as I walked along the furrow, I would let the grains slip through my fingers down alongside my bare leg, a steady trickle of color, one and one, and one and two: two kernels for the fowls of the air, one for the burrowing worm, two to fill wagonloads of corn for our log cribs. Backward and forward across the broad field went this group— two teams, two plows, and one chanting barefoot boy:

> Whistle and hoe,
> Sing as you go;
> Shorten the rows
> By the songs you know.

All through the day, though my hands grew tired (I plunged them deep into the cool, shiny grains when we stopped for a moment at the turnrow), my legs ached and my feet grew heavy, I would bolster my courage with jingles, chanting the old rhymes. For long before sundown a six-year-old boy drooped from weariness. Scattered over the field were flocks of blackbirds and crows, a line of them almost filling the freshly opened furrows, scratching busily for worms and their share of the seed; while Brother Cutworm he "lay low," waiting for the corn to sprout, for tender shoots to push upward on which he could feast.

Just as I dropped corn when I was a six-year-old boy, blindly trusting the chance of wind and rain and sunshine, openly paying tribute to the known enemies of growing corn, the blackbird, the crow, the cutworm, so in some such way have I put together *The Adventures of a Ballad Hunter*. I kept few notes during the more than thirty years wherein I was on the lookout for folk songs. I write from memory, from letters, and from some stories cut into records.

All my life I have been interested in the songs of the people—the intimate poetic and musical expression of unlettered people, from which group I am directly sprung. In my boyhood we sang songs around our fireside on winter evenings in a home where the library consisted of *Pilgrim's Progress* and the Bible. At work and at play folk songs were my mental food. I began early to set down the words; later the music also. And now the Library of Congress houses records of more than ten thousand tunes placed there by my son, Alan, and myself.

In 1934 at the close of the annual meeting of the Modern Language Association in Philadelphia, Professor S. B. Hustvedt of the University of California at Los Angeles urged me to set down the story of my experiences as a ballad collector. A day or so previously I had appeared before the Division of Popular Literature with the Negro, Lead Belly, a paroled convict from the Louisiana penitentiary. I translated the words of the Negro's songs each time before he sang. His dramatic rendition of raw folk songs shocked his hearers into attention.

Professor Hustvedt, perhaps, thought that more of my encounters had been as romantic as the finding of Lead Belly when a convict. He declared that my experiences had been unique, that the detailed story of my search might prove helpful to other collectors. He set me to thinking about what I should tell and what I should omit in case I did attempt to relive ballad-collecting journeys, half a million miles or so, that I have taken into all the states except North Dakota. The tale has turned out to be tortuous and long, quite enough to fill half a dozen volumes.

Choosing the incidents reminded me of my corn-planting days. Some of the seed that looked most promising turned out to be fit only for blackbirds, crows, and cutworms. Moreover, I have lost some of the confident hope of the barefoot boy who trusted two kernels would grow into kingly stalks burdened with hanging ears of corn.

A ballad collector meets many people, the real people, the plain people, devoid of tinsel and glamour, some base, a few suspicious and surly, many beautifully kind. And many are the stories they tell. From the thousands I may choose only a few. The reader will find herein no theories about ballad origins or parallels. That task is for others. I have merely taken some pictures from my files and rearranged them in story form. I have made another book; though not the book my friend, Professor Hustvedt, had in mind.

In Texas we call land, grubbed of stumps, freshly broken and cultivated for the first time, "new ground." On such virgin land the first crop is usually bountiful. There have been many ballad hunters. I have heard of no one who has attempted to fill a book with stories of his search. My trail has been longer than most, both in miles and in years. In so far, then, I cultivate new ground.

Understanding Literature

1. Who are the "unlettered people"?
2. At what point does the author sum up his explanation of his early interest in folk songs and begin telling why he wrote *Adventures of a Ballad Hunter*?
3. Why does the author hope for a successful book? (The reason is implied rather than stated.)
4. Why does the author begin the Preface to *Adventures of a Ballad Hunter* with a rhyme chanted by a boy planting corn? What connection does the rhyme have with the rest of the Preface? In which paragraphs is this connection explained?

Focusing on Words

What do the italicized expressions in the following phrases and clauses mean? Try to put the idea into other words.

1. "The soft, moist loam felt *friendly* to my bare feet."
2. "I would let the grains slip through my fingers down alongside my bare leg, *a steady trickle of color, one and one, and one and two.*"
3. "*Shorten the rows*
   By the songs you know."

4. ". . . when we stopped for a moment at the *turnrow*."
5. "I would *bolster* my courage."
6. ". . . *openly paying tribute* to the known enemies of growing corn."
7. ". . . the real people, the plain people, *devoid of tinsel and glamour*, some *base*, a few *suspicious* and *surly*, many *beautifully* kind."

Further Activities

1. Read the preface to one of your textbooks and determine what purpose the author had in writing the preface. Has the author, for example, told you
   (*a*) how he/she became interested in the subject?
   (*b*) where he/she got his/her information?
   (*c*) how he/she gathered and organized his/her information?
   (*d*) why he/she felt qualified to write about the subject?
   (*e*) why this subject needed to be written about?
   (*f*) how this book is different from other books on the same subject?
2. Recall from your own childhood rhymes or chants that go with playing certain games or doing certain work, folk stories that you enjoyed hearing, and folk songs about people or events in your locality. Report to the class. If enough material comes to light, the class may wish to make a folklore book for the library, a book containing beliefs, tales, songs, and sayings that have come down to you through the history of your locality.

In his Preface, John Lomax says, "A ballad collector meets many people, the real people, the plain people, devoid of tinsel and glamour, some base, a few suspicious and surly, many beautifully kind." The following excerpts from Chapter III of *Adventures of a Ballad Hunter* tell of a few of these people.

Hunting Cowboy Songs

from Adventures of a Ballad Hunter

John A. Lomax

IMPROVING YOUR READING: In "Hunting Cowboy Songs" John Lomax has collected a number of *anecdotes* about ballad hunting. An anecdote is a brief story about an interesting incident. The first paragraphs in this selection prepare the reader for the following anecdotes by explaining how Lomax came to be traveling about the country searching for ballads. Most of the anecdotes concern colorful characters he encountered in his search.

WHEN IN 1908 a check for $500 came from Harvard University for my first year as a Sheldon Fellow,[1] I was the happiest person in the world. Never before at one time had I owned so much money, money that brought me both honor and responsibility. I was entirely free to spend it in running down the words and music of cowboy songs. In a glow of anticipation I made plans to travel the following summer throughout the cattle country.

It proved a long and hard road that I started on, as I made my way, walking, on horseback, by buggy, by train and automobile, a tortuous journey that has since then wound a half-million miles into every part of the United States. Very few of my associates in the University of Texas expressed sympathy or took the project seriously. For them this crude product of the West had no interest, no value, no charm whatever. Governor Jim Ferguson quoted stanzas of my cowboy songs in political addresses to cheering crowds, and sneered at the University of Texas for having me on its faculty, just as he sneered at a teacher of zoology, asserting repeatedly that this professor was trying to make wool grow on the backs of armadillos and thus bring down the price of sheep! Both of us were sorry fools to him.

It was cowboy songs I most wished, in those early days, to round up and "close herd." These I jotted

---

[1] Fellow: a scholar who is chosen to receive a sum of money to make a special study of some subject for which he has shown special talent. In this case the money was provided from the estate of a man named Sheldon.

down on a table in a saloon back room, scrawled on an envelope while squatting about a campfire near a chuck wagon, or caught behind the scenes of a broncho-busting outfit or rodeo. To capture the cowboy music proved an almost impossible task. The cowboys would simply wave away the large horn[2] I carried and refused to sing into it! . . . Once I was invited to speak at the Texas Cattlemen's Convention in San Antonio. To advertise my undertaking, I attempted to sing some of the tunes I wished to record from the trail men. My poor efforts brought only derisive whoops. One belligerent cattleman arose and announced: "I have been singin' them songs ever since I was a kid. Everybody knows them. Only a fool would spend his time tryin' to set 'em down. I move we adjourn." And adjourn they did, to a convenient bar.

One night in the back room of the White Elephant Saloon in Fort Worth, where I had cornered a bunch of Ediphone-shy cowboy singers, a cowboy said to the crowd: "I told the professor" (that's what they jokingly called me) "that the old Chisholm Trail Song was as long as the trail from Texas to Montana. I can sing eighty-nine verses myself. Some of the verses would burn up his old horn, and anyhow, I'm not goin' to poke my face up to his blamed old horn and sing. The tune ain't much nohow." The tune wasn't much—but it suited the cowboy's work. He could sing it when he went dashing out to turn a runaway steer back to the herd, singing:

Feet in the stirrups and seat in the saddle,
And I hung and rattled with them long-
   horn cattle,
Coma-ti-yi-yippee, yippee yea, yippee yea,
Coma-ti-yi-yippee, yippee yea.

And he could sing it with a roaring chorus as the men sat about the campfire during the long winter evenings.

"Back in the Seventies," said another cowboy in the crowd, "we sang 'The Old Chisholm Trail' all the way from San Antonio to Dodge City. There was never a day that some one did not build a new verse." There is another "Chisholm Trail" tune—a quiet, jig-joggy tune—when a fellow was riding alone, scouting for drifting cattle, riding the "line" through lonely stretches of country. I finally persuaded one of the boys to sing it. But not for my recording machine. I learned the tune and later recorded it myself for the Folk Song Archive.[3]

      ✿   ✿   ✿

Out on a busy corner near the cattle pens of the Fort Worth stockyards I had come upon a blind old man twanging his guitar while he sang doleful ditties and listened for the ring of quarters in his tin cup.

"I don't know any cowboy songs," he explained to me. "But lead me home to lunch; my wife can sing you a bookful."

2 horn: for the gramophone (called an "Ediphone" and "Edison machine" in this selection) invented by Thomas A. Edison in 1877. The sound to be recorded was directed into a horn.

3 Archive (är′kīv): public records.

The old man shuffled along beside me, clasping his guitar as I guided him over the rough places in our path. We were headed for the trees that fringed the West Fork of the Trinity River near Fort Worth. Often I stumbled, for I was carrying the heavy Edison machine.

We found the blind singer's wife out behind a covered truck, a forerunner of the trailer, seated in front of a gaily colored tent. She wore a gypsy costume, richly brocaded. She had used paint and powder with skillful discretion on a face naturally comely. While I chatted with her, the old man disappeared into the tent. In a few minutes out he came. Gone were the round, humped shoulders, the white hair, the shambling gait, the tottering figure—and the colored glasses! Before me stood a young, handsome, dark-eyed man, alert and athletic. He made no explanation. He was a perfect and fascinating faker.

"We do team work here. My wife shakes down the saps who like to hold her hand while she reads their fortunes in the stars. All the self-righteous fools go away from my tin cup happy, marking down one more good deed on their passports to Heaven. We aim to please our customers, and I think we do." Thus the faker rambled on while a smiling Negro man served delicious food and a bottle of wine. Later on through the long Texas afternoon, amid the cheerful talk, the fortune teller sang the songs of the road. She and her family for generations had lived as gypsies.

"This lady," said the faker, "who has joined her fortunes with mine, travels with me now from Miami, Florida, to San Diego, California. We belong to that fringe of society which takes life the easiest way. We toil not, neither do we spin." Raising a tent flap he showed me rich purple hangings, thick Persian rugs, a divan spread with soft silken covers—amazing luxury.

"With our burros, Abednego and Sennacherib, to pull our covered wagon, we travel as we like. Our rackets roll in the money."

He lay flat on his back on the mesquite grass, puffing a cigar, as he gazed at the white patches of clouds that swept across the deep blue Texas sky. I glanced curiously at Abednego and Sennacherib as they munched their alfalfa. They seemed as old as the pyramids and as solemn as a pair of Aztec idols —which they, indeed, resembled. They seemed to talk to each other with abundant, constantly moving ears, fastened loosely to their great bony heads. And here, close by, sat the fake gypsy lady, dressed like a princess, strumming her guitar and singing the songs that she had picked up in her wanderings.

She scorned the clumsy horn fastened to my recording machine, and I caught few of the tunes. I remember that she sang me the first blues that I ever heard, moving me almost to tears, and a pathetic ballad of a factory girl who got splinters in her toes. Many and many another song she sang that unhappily are gone with the Texas wind. Then came four stanzas and the refrain:

As I was walkin', one mornin' for pleasure
I met a young cowboy all ridin' along;
His hat was throwed back and his spurs
    was a-jinglin',
As he approached me a-singin' this song:

Whoopee ti yi yo, git along, little dogies,
It's your misfortune and none of my own.
Whoopee ti yi yo, git along, little dogies,
For you know Wyoming will be your new
    home.

"To me," she said, "that's the loveliest of all cowboy songs. Like others, its rhythm comes from the movement of a horse. It is not the roisterous, ... wild gallop of 'The Old Chisholm Trail,' nor the slow easy canter of 'Goodbye, Old Paint.' You musn't frighten the dogies. They get nervous in crowds. Lope around them gently in the darkness as you sing about punching them along to their new home in Wyoming. They'll sleep the night through and never have a bad dream."

After the refrain she would give the night-herding yodel of the cowboy, born of the vast melancholy of the plains; a yodel to quiet a herd of restless cattle in the deep darkness of a rainy night, when far-off flashes of lightning and the rumble of distant thunder meant danger. While the cattle milled around and refused to lie down, close to the fringe of the circle of moving animals rode the cowboys giving this wordless cry to the cattle, like the plea of a lonesome lobo wolf calling for his mate, like the croon of a mother trying to quiet a restless babe in the long watches of the night, like the soft moo of a cow wooing her young offspring from its hiding place to come for its milk. "Quiet, cattle, quiet. Darkness is everywhere, but we, your friends, are near. Lie down, little dogies, lie down." The yodel was pervasive, far-reaching. Even in its high notes it was soothing and tender. It seemed to catch up in its lilt all the perils of the night and merge them into a paean[4] of peace.

As the gypsy woman, swayed by the beauty of her notes, yodeled on, the leaves of the overhanging cottonwood trees fluttered noiselessly, the katydids in the branches stopped their song and seemed to listen. In all our world there was no other sound save that beautiful voice imploring all little dogies to "lay still, little dogies, lay still."

*   *   *

I visited many cattle ranches, among them the widely known King Ranch, the Swenson Ranch, both in Texas, and the New Mexico Hearst ranch before it was split up. Often the men would have none of the horn. With smaller groups on remote ranches I enjoyed better fortune. Two or three Negro cowboys sang lustily when I got them away from the crowd. Students from the cattle regions, attending colleges throughout the country, brought me a lot of material when I gave talks to them on folk songs.

I read through the files of Texas newspapers that printed columns of

4 **paean** (pē′ən): song of joy, praise, or triumph.

old songs, and I bedeviled librarians for possible buried treasures in frontier chronicles. In a second-hand bookstore in San Antonio I found a battered copy of *Johnson's New Comic Songs* with a San Francisco date line of 1863. Along with the old favorites, "Gentle Annie" and "Nellie Gray," I came on the words of "Poker Jim," "The Miner's Song," "The Dying Californian," and other song products of the days of Forty-nine.

Some months afterward I asked the Librarian of the University of California at Berkeley if he knew of other pamphlets of early frontier songs. He had none catalogued. He then took me to the Bancroft Library and left me to rummage in some habitually locked-up cases. I came on a stack of dog-eared, paper-backed pamphlets tied together with an ancient cotton string. Though I lifted out the pile with care, the cotton string crumbled in my fingers. There they were—not a complete file of the "20,000 song books" advertised by D. E. Appleton & Co., San Francisco, but a choice selection of early "California Songsters": *Ben Cotton's Songster*, *The Sally Come Up Songster*, *Put's Original California Songster*, *Put's Golden Songster*, and many another. I discovered that "Old Put" and a group of men singers went from gold camp to gold camp in the early Fifties and sang to the miners. When they ran out of songs Old Put and his like made up songs describing the life of a mining town, telling how the Forty-

Niners got to California and sometimes how they got back East. They were rough and crude creations, but among them I turned up "Sweet Betsy from Pike" and the "Days of Forty-nine," and afterward also discovered the tunes to which they were sung:

Did you ever hear tell of Sweet Betsy from
    Pike,
Who crossed the wide prairies with her
    lover Ike,
With two yokes of cattle and one spotted
    hog,
A tall Shanghai rooster and an old yaller
    dog?

Betsy and her man lived—

In the days of old when they dug out the
    gold,
In the days of Forty-nine.

There's old "Lame Jess," that hard old
    cuss,
Who never would repent;
He never missed a single meal
Nor never paid a cent.
But old "Lame Jess," like all the rest,
At death he did resign,
And in his bloom went up the flume[5]
In the days of Forty-nine.

Uncovering these two songs repaid me for the long trip from Texas.

＊　　＊　　＊

Tom Hight and I spent two happy days together recording songs in an Oklahoma City hotel. . . . Tom knew more cowboy melodies than any other person I have ever found. He gave me fifty.

"Ever since I was a boy," said Tom, "I have been a singing fool. I could sing down any man in our

5 **flume:** artificial channel used by gold miners to change the direction of a stream of water.

cow-camp in the Panhandle. When the fellers backed me against the neighboring camp, I won. They challenged the whole Panhandle. The champeens of each camp met at a central point, and we lifted up our heads like a pack of coyotes, only we lifted 'em one at a time. The rules was that each man was to sing in turn, one after the other, round and round. The man that sung the last song, he won the prize. It took us mighty near all night to get sung out. The other feller couldn't sing no more, because he didn't know no more songs. But I was ready with the last one and had more roped and ready. Of course you couldn't use no books and no writing. I was mighty proud of being the champeen singer of the Texas Panhandle. My cowboy friends even gave me a pair of silver-mounted spurs for a prize with my name engraved on them."

＊　　＊　　＊

Among my students in the A. & M. College of Texas was a young fellow from Denison, Texas, by the name of Harry Stephens. Harry had worked cattle in New Mexico and Arizona for three or four years; and he brought with him to college a handsome saddle, saddle blanket, bridle, spurs, and other equipment. His saddle was ornamented with silver. He used to wear his high-top boots and ten-gallon white hat to class, whenever he could. Harry didn't like the college uniform and he wasn't much interested in English literature, but he warmed up when

I mentioned cowboy songs. He would stay after class and recite and sing songs to me. Now and then he would drift down to my home on Sunday and lean over the fence and sing a song to attract my attention. I never could get him further than the gate.

Early in the spring, when the world was turning green again, Harry called on me one morning just as the bugle was blowing for the first class period. I went out to the gate on which he leaned. "Well, Professor," he said, "grass is rising —and I got to move on. I'm lonesome. I want to hear the wolves howl and the owls hoot." Twenty years went by before I saw Harry again. Meanwhile, for years afterward, he sent me Western songs. Some I'm sure he made up. Some he "doctored"; some he had taken down from the singing of others. One day I received a letter from him. He was on a ranch in southern Idaho. Enclosed were the words of what I consider the most beautiful cowboy poem in the language. The opening stanza runs:

Oh, it was a long and a tiresome go,
Our herd rolled on to Mexico;
With music sweet of the cowboy song,
For New Mexico we rolled along.

*   *   *

One day out in Abilene, Texas, I met an old-time buffalo hunter and asked him to tell me some of his adventures. Back in the days just after the Civil War, these hunters used to go out on the plains in wagon trains and kill buffalo for their hides. The stark naked, ghastly looking bodies were left lying on the plains and down along the ravines to rot and to furnish food for wolves and buzzards. (My Uncle Charlie Cooper killed as many as seventy-five a day with his famous Needle gun.) The hides were hauled to the nearest railroad and from there shipped East where the skin side was tanned and softened, while the "warm side, fur side, outside," was left untouched. The fur was long, soft, shiny, of all shades from light brown to deep black. Big buffalo bull fur was often jet black at certain seasons of the year. The first hunters were glad to get a dollar for one undressed hide. Years later, a fine, dressed buffalo hide sold for one hundred dollars, buffalo overcoats up to $250. Buffalo hides, properly tanned, made beautiful rugs and were also often cut and fashioned into cloaks for fair ladies. Indians likewise wore them thrown over their shoulders, and also sometimes used them as floor coverings for their teepees.

The old man had been a sharpshooter in his younger days. He carried a Needle gun and killed the buffalo for the entire hunting party. The gun carried so far that the bullet "never landed till next day." While some of the gang skinned the dead animals and spread the skins out to dry, the others packed the hides and loaded them into the wagons. "Two to shoot, four to skin, one to cook," says an old chronicle.

The old hunter went on to tell the story of a group of buffalo hunters that he had led from Jacksboro, Texas, to that region of Texas far beyond the Pease River. The hunt lasted for several months. The plains were dry and parched. The party drank alkali water . . . so thick it had to be chewed; fought sandstorms, flies, mosquitoes, bedbugs, and wolves. . . . At the close of the season the manager of the outfit, who had been hauling the hides to the nearest market, announced to the men as they broke camp for the trip home that he had lost money on the enterprise and could not pay them any wages. The men argued the question with the manager.

"So," the old man told me, "we shot down old Crego, the manager, and left his ol' bones to bleach where we had left many hundreds of stinking buffalo. It took us many days to get back to Jacksboro. As we sat around the campfire at night, some one of the boys started up a song about our hunt and the hard times and old Crego. And we all set in to help him. Before we got to Jacksboro we shaped it up and our whole crowd would sing it together."

And he sang to me in nasal, monotonous tones, "The Buffalo Skinners." Professor Kittredge[6] called it his favorite American ballad. From twenty-one separate versions from all over the West, I put together the five stanzas quoted here and six others:

6 **Professor Kittredge:** a professor at Harvard University (1888-1936), famous for his scholarly work in English literature.

Come, all you jolly fellows and listen to my song,
There are not many verses, it will not detain you long;
It's concerning some young fellows who did agree to go
And spend one summer pleasantly on the range of the buffalo.

It happened in Jacksboro in the spring of '73,
A man by the name of Crego came stepping up to me,
Saying, "How do you do, young fellow, and how would you like to go,
And spend one summer pleasantly on the range of the buffalo?"

"It's me being out of employment," this to Crego did I say,
"This going out on the buffalo range depends upon the pay.
But if you will pay good wages, give transportation, too
I think, sir, I will go with you to the range of the buffalo."

The season being near over, old Crego he did say
The crowd had been extravagant, was in debt to him that day.
We coaxed him and we begged him, but still it was no go—
We left old Crego's bones to bleach on the range of the buffalo.

Oh, it's now we've crossed Pease River and homeward we are bound.
No more in that . . . country shall ever we be found.
Go home to our wives and sweethearts, tell others not to go,
For God's forsaken the buffalo range and the . . . old buffalo.

   *   *   *

[One day in 1908 a Negro saloonkeeper sang several songs into Lomax's recording machine. Among them was "Home on the Range."

From this record a blind teacher of music in the Austin State School for the Blind set down the music. This folk song has become a favorite of many well-known people.]

The story goes that on the night that Franklin D. Roosevelt was first elected to the Presidency, New York reporters gathered on his doorstep and sang "Home on the Range." At a White House press conference, the President afterward called it his favorite song and at Warm Springs, Georgia, the custom grew of using the song to welcome his visits.

Admiral Richard E. Byrd told a group of San Francisco reporters a story of his six-month vigil alone near the South Pole:

"For entertainment I took along an Edison phonograph and a few records."

"What was your favorite song?" asked the reporters.

"'Home on the Range.' During the first months of my stay I gave myself daily concerts, always playing the song that tells about the land of sunshine where 'The sky is not cloudy all day.' Later, when the cold grew more intense, my phonograph froze up and wouldn't go. Then I found myself spelling my loneliness by singing 'Home on the Range' against the cold, black darkness of the South Pole."

I like to think that my San Antonio Negro saloonkeeper friend helped to make life more tolerable for the brave explorer amid the icy solitudes of the Antarctic. The words of the song which I pieced together make the precise frame-work and order universally employed today. Moreover, the tune sung by the San Antonio Negro and printed, along with the words, remains substantially the same in all current renditions. I have preserved the original sheet on which I jotted down the words taken from several sources. Yes, I know I did wrong, but I rephrased some unmetrical lines.

❊   ❊   ❊

In the summer of 1910 Theodore Roosevelt attended the Frontier Celebration in Cheyenne, Wyoming. The year before he and Elihu Root,[7] influenced by Professor Barrett Wendell,[8] had asked a grant for me (which was denied) from the Carnegie Institution, in Washington. For me the Cheyenne visit afforded a happy chance to meet him. A letter I wrote home, just after the interview, tells the story:

"In the forenoon I sent a note asking for a moment's interview. Directly he came to where I was waiting in the hotel lobby and said: 'I should have answered the letter you wrote me [about two weeks before] if a moment's time had been left me. Now I must go to church. Can you meet me in my room at two o'clock this afternoon with a sheet of unruled paper (for a statement to be copied in the book)?' I said I could, and went my way.

"He was ready at the hour, and began by asking me just what I

7 **Elihu Root:** an American political leader. He was Theodore Roosevelt's Secretary of State from 1905 to 1909.
8 **Professor Barrett Wendell:** a professor of English at Harvard University (1880-1917).

wished him to say. Thereupon I told him of the general attitude of unappreciativeness on the part of the West toward my work, and suggested that there was little recognition of the fact that the ballads throw light on western conditions and traditions. Whereupon he interjected, 'Not only that, but they illustrate the curious reproduction of medieval conditions in the West.' I ventured to hint that such a happy phrasing of the truth might go in outright; and he said, 'I am going to put it in.'

"Then he wrote, and chatted to me between sentences. . . . As he wrote on painstakingly, he remarked: 'Well, it is a tribute to the policies I stand for if the American people can read my handwriting and still think there is any man behind it.' Meanwhile someone knocked and he shouted 'Come in!' twice without turning his head. When he had done, he introduced me to his visitor, a son of Lyman Abbott,[9] told him of my work, and then asked me to read what he had written."

Mr. Roosevelt said:

You have done a work emphatically worth doing and one which should appeal to the people of all our country, but particularly to the people of the West and Southwest. Your subject is not only exceedingly interesting to the student of literature, but also to the student of the general history of the West. There is something very curious in the reproduction here on this continent of essentially the conditions of ballad growth which obtained in medieval England, including, by the way, sympathy for the outlaw, Jesse James taking the place of Robin Hood. Under modern conditions, however, the native ballad is speedily killed by competition with the music hall songs; the cowboys becoming ashamed to sing the crude homespun ballads in view of what Owen Wister[10] calls the "ill smelling saloon cleverness" of the far less interesting compositions of the music hall singers. It is therefore a work of real importance to preserve permanently this unwritten ballad literature of the back country and the frontier.

---

9 **Lyman Abbott:** an influential American minister, editor, and author who lived from 1835 to 1922.

10 **Owen Wister:** an American author. Many of his stories are about the Western cattle country; his best-known novel is *The Virginian*. He also wrote a biography of his friend Theodore Roosevelt.

Reading Skills

1. Explain why the $500 check meant "both honor and responsibility" to Lomax. What was Lomax's regular job?
2. Why did most of the cowboys refuse to sing into the horn of the Edison machine?
3. From what specific sources did Lomax obtain folk songs?
4. In his Preface, Lomax says, "The reader will find herein no theories about ballad origins." The buffalo hunter's story, however, suggests a great deal about how some ballads originate. What event prompted the composition of "The Buffalo Skinners"? Who composed the ballad? What theory about the origin of ballads does this story suggest?
5. Why did Lomax want Theodore Roosevelt to write a note about his work? Put into your own words what Roosevelt said in his note. Which sentence in the paragraph best indicates his conception of the importance of Lomax's work?

Understanding Literature

1. Reread the first two paragraphs in the chapter. How does the author arouse the reader's interest?
2. Although the characters in this selection are very briefly sketched, they come to life as memorable people. Characterize (a) the "blind" beggar, (b) Tom Hight, (c) Harry Stephens, (d) the buffalo hunter. What techniques for revealing character does the author use with each?

Focusing on Words

1. The word *sympathy* comes from two Greek words: *syn* ("with") and *pathos* ("suffering," "passion"). In the second paragraph, does *sympathy* keep this original meaning or has the original meaning changed?
2. Explain what the italicized words in the following sentence suggest about the musical performance of the blind street singer:

   "Out on a busy corner near the cattle pens of the Fort Worth stockyards I had come upon a blind old man *twanging* his guitar while he sang *doleful ditties*. . . ."

Further Activities

1. Write a theme about an activity that caused you some effort. First, think about what you will include in this theme. Then write the first paragraph, explaining how you became involved in the activity. Try to arouse the reader's interest in your subject. In the theme use two or three anecdotes about incidents that occurred. Your subject may be one of these, or another:

   (*a*) Getting a job for the summer.
   (*b*) Learning to swim (or bowl, or dance).
   (*c*) Learning to use a microscope (or another piece of equipment).
   (*d*) Learning to cook (or to make something).
   (*e*) Doing your part in some project for a club or school activity.

2. If the class plans to make a folklore book for the school library, perhaps someone who has lived in your community for many years would be willing to write a statement about the importance of preserving the folklore of the region. A small committee might make an appointment with this person to ask for such a statement. If the person does not wish to write down any ideas, the committee may, after the interview, write down what he or she said. This statement should then be used as part of the introductory material for the book.

AMERICAN BALLADS

The Strawberry Roan

IMPROVING YOUR READING: Many ballads and folk songs originated among workers of different kinds—usually those engaged in outdoor work, such as cowboys, lumberjacks, farmers, sailors, and railroad workers. "The Strawberry Roan" concerns the efforts of a cowboy to break in an "old pony [that] has never been rode." The conflict between the two is very clear, and it produces the story interest of the ballad. Although this conflict could easily have been told about in three or four stanzas, it is built up through description of the roan and then of the cowboy's ride on him. What does this addition of detail accomplish?

I was laying around town, just spending my time,
Out of a job and not making a dime,
When a feller steps up and says, "I suppose,
That you're a bronc' rider, by the looks of your clothes."

"You guessed me right—I'm a good one," I claims,   5
"Do you happen to have any bad ones to tame?"
He says that he has, and a bad un to buck,
For throwing good riders he's had lots of luck.

He says this old pony has never been rode
And the boys that gets on him is bound to get throwed.   10
Well, I gets all excited and asks what he pays
To ride this old pony for a couple of days.

He offers a ten-spot and I says, "I'm your man,
For a bronc' never lived that I wouldn't fan;
For the bronc' never lived nor never drew breath   15
That I couldn't ride till he starved plumb to death."

"Well," he says, "get your saddle and I'll give you a
  chance."
So I gits in the buckboard and we drives to the Ranch;
I stays until mornin', and right after chuck
I steps out to see if this outlaw can buck.   20

Down in the horse corral, standing alone,
Is this old caballo,[1] a strawberry roan.
His legs is all spavined,[2] he has pigeon toes,
Two little pig-eyes, and a big Roman nose.

Little pin-ears that touched at the tips,   25
And a big .44 run on his left hip.
He's ewe-necked and old with a long lower jaw,
I could see with one eye he was a reg'lar outlaw.

I buckle on my spurs, I'm sure feelin' fine,
I picks up my hat, an' curls up my twine.   30
I piles my rope on him, an' well I know then,
That afore he gets rode, I've sure earned my ten.

I gets the blinds on him, and it sure is a fight.
Next comes my old saddle, an' I screws 'er down tight,
Then I steps onto him and raises the blinds,   35
I'm right in his middle to see him unwind.

He bowed his old neck, and I guess he's unwound,
For he seemed to quit living down there on the ground,
He went towards the east, came down towards the west,
To stay in his middle, I'm doin' my best.   40

He sure is a frog walkin', he heaves a big sigh,
He only lacks wings to be on the fly.
He turns his old belly right up to the sun,
He sure is a sunfishin' son of a gun.

He's about the worst bucker I've seen on the range,   45
He can turn on a nickel an' give you the change,
An' when he's a-bucking, he squeals like a shoat,
I tell you that pony has sure got my goat.

---

1 **caballo** (kä bäl′yō): Spanish for "horse." 2 **spavined:** marked by small bony enlargements
inside the leg, due to sprain or violent effort.

I claims that, not foolin', that outlaw can step,
But I'm still in his middle and buildin' a "rep." 50
He hits on all fours and turns up his side,
I don't see how he keeps from losin' his hide.

I loses my stirrup an' also my hat,
I'm clawin' leather and blind as a bat,
With a phenomenal jump, he goes up on high, 55
An' leaves me settin' on nothin'—up there in the sky.

Well—I turned over, an' comes back to earth,
An' I lights on to cussin' the day of his birth.
Then I knows there's old ponies I'm not able to ride;
There's some of them left—they ain't all died. 60

But I bet all my money, the man ain't alive
That can stay with old Strawberry when he makes that
    high dive.

Understanding Literature

1. What do you learn about the life and character of the bronco
   rider in this ballad? What lines support your conclusions
   about him and his life?
2. Tales of the American West are particularly apt to contain
   comparison and exaggeration. Find at least one example of
   each in this ballad. In which section are they primarily used?
   What is the purpose of using them there?
3. What is accomplished by describing in detail the roan's appearance and the cowboy's ride on him?

Starving to Death on a Government Claim*

IMPROVING YOUR READING: Many American folk songs grew out of the experiences of the pioneers as they moved westward. Because the journey west was extremely difficult and settling down to make a living at its end even harder, many of these frontier ballads express the problems and grumblings of the settlers in their new life.

The following complaint shows the feelings of many who moved west under the Homestead Act (1862), which made great areas of land available in Kansas, Iowa, and Nebraska, and, later on, in other states. For eighteen dollars, a man could buy a 160-acre parcel of land, provided he would live on it for five years. Many simply dug themselves houses in the side of a hill on their claims; others built themselves houses out of the sod (as does the bachelor of this song). There were many minor irritations, which "Starving to Death on a Government Claim" humorously describes; there were also major disasters, such as blizzards, droughts, prairie fires, and grasshopper plagues. Putting their troubles into verse was probably one way by which the settlers managed to bear up under their life.

This particular song was sung to John Lomax by Tom Hight, who is described in "Hunting Cowboy Songs" (p. 184). Although the verses complain about prairie life, their spirit is more that of the man who is proud of his ability to endure such a life than that of a man who is defeated by it.

1. My name is Tom Hight, an old bach'lor I am,
   You'll find me out west in the country of fame,
   You'll find me out west on an elegant plan,
   A-starving to death on my government claim.

CHORUS: Hurrah for Greer County! the land of the free,
   The land of the bedbug, grasshopper and flea;
   I'll sing of its praises, I'll tell of its fame,
   While starving to death on my government claim.

2. My house, it is built out of national soil,
   Its walls are erected according to Hoyle,
   Its roof has no pitch, but is level and plain,
   I always get wet if it happens to rain.

* From *Folk Song USA* by John A. and Alan Lomax, by permission of Duell, Sloan & Pearce, an affiliate of Meredith Press. Copyright, 1947, by John A. and Alan Lomax.

                       AMERICA IN FOLKLORE AND TALES

3. My clothes are all ragged, as my language is rough,
   My bread is corndodgers,[1] both solid and tough;
   But yet I am happy and live at my ease
   On sorghum molasses, bacon and cheese.

4. How happy am I when I crawl into bed,
   A rattlesnake hisses a tune at my head,
   A gay little centipede, all without fear,
   Crawls over my pillow and into my ear.

5. Now all you claim holders, I hope you will stay
   And chew your hardtack till you're toothless and gray,
   But for myself I'll no longer remain
   To starve like a dog on my government claim.

CHORUS: Good-by to Greer County where blizzards arise,
         Where the sun never sinks and the flea never dies,
         And the wind never ceases but always remains
         Till it starves us all out on our government claims.

6. Farewell to Greer County, farewell to the west,
   I'll travel back east to the girl I love best,
   I'll travel to Texas and marry me a wife
   And quit corndodgers the rest of my life.

1 **corndodgers:** corn bread.

Understanding Literature

1. In speaking, a person often uses words whose meanings seem
   quite different from what he or she actually intends. For example, on a cold and rainy day, a person may say something
   like "Beautiful weather we're having, isn't it?" or "Really great
   day!" Of course, the tone of voice and the fact that a hearer
   knows what the weather is like may show that the speaker
   means the opposite of *beautiful* or *great*. What examples of
   this use of language can you find in "Starving to Death on a
   Government Claim"?
2. This folk song (*a*) gives factual information about life on the
   prairie, (*b*) expresses the reactions of many settlers to their
   lives, and (*c*) illustrates the sense of humor which was often
   found on the frontier. Find lines that show how the song does
   each of these things.

The Boll Weevil*

IMPROVING YOUR READING: The more settled parts of the country, as well as the frontier, had their problems. "The Boll Weevil" is one of the best-known folk songs describing the farming problems of the South. In it, the singer nearly covers the history of the farmers' fight with the boll weevil, an insect which crossed the Rio Grande about 1900 and moved steadily across the South at about forty miles a year. Wherever it went, it destroyed the cotton crop, the crop on which most Southern farmers supported themselves. The Texas Legislature offered a reward of $50,000 for a method that would destroy the boll weevil, and stanzas 5-7 describe the futility of everything that was tried. The last stanzas go on to show the plight in which the farmer found himself —no money and no credit.

Desperate as the farmers' situation was, their attitude toward it in this song is a humorous one; in fact, the singer shows much of the conflict from the boll weevil's point of view. Indeed, the sadness of what actually happened is apparent in these verses only when the reader realizes that the boll weevil, in looking for and finding "a home," destroyed the homes of thousands of human beings.

1. O have you heard de lates',
   De lates' of de songs?
   It's about dem little boll weevils
   Picked up bofe feet an' gone,
   CHORUS: A-lookin' for a home,
   Jes' a-lookin' for a home,
   A-lookin' for a home,
   Jes' a-lookin' for a home.

2. De boll weevil is a little black bug
   F'um Mexico, dey say,
   He come to try dis Texas soil
   An' thought he'd better stay,

* From *Folk Song USA* by John A. and Alan Lomax, by permission of Duell, Sloan & Pearce, an affiliate of Meredith Press. Copyright, 1947, by John A. and Alan Lomax.

CHORUS: A-lookin' for a home,
Jes' a-lookin' for a home,
A-lookin' for a home,
Jes' a-lookin' for a home.

3. De fus' time I seen de boll weevil
He was settin' on de square,[1]
De nex' time I saw de boll weevil
He had all his family dere—[2]
CHORUS: Dey's lookin' for a home,
Jes' a-lookin' for a home,
Dey's lookin' for a home,
Jes' a-lookin' for a home.

4. De fus' time I seen de boll weevil
He was on the western plain,
Nex' time I seen de boll weevil,
He had hopped dat Memphis train,
CHORUS: Lookin' for a home,
Jes' a-lookin' for a home,
Lookin' for a home,
Jes' a-lookin' for a home.

5. De farmer took de boll weevil
An' buried him in hot sand;
De boll weevil say to de farmer,
"I'll stand it like a man,
CHORUS: For it is my home,
It is my home,
For it is my home,
It is my home."

6. Den de farmer took de boll weevil
An' lef' him on de ice;
De boll weevil say to de farmer,
"Dis is mighty cool an' nice.
CHORUS: O it is-a my home,
It is my home,
O it is-a my home,
It is my home."

---

1 **de square:** the cotton boll in its early stages.
2 **had all his family dere:** The boll weevil deposits its eggs in the square; a pair of boll weevils are able to produce over a million others in one season.

7. Mr. Farmer took little weevil
   An' fed him on paris green;[3]
   "Thank you, Mr. Farmer,
   It's the best I ever seen.
   CHORUS: It is my home,
            It's jes' my home,
            It is my home,
            It's jes' my home."

8. De boll weevil say to de farmer,
   "You better lemme 'lone,
   I et up all yo' cotton,
   An' now I'll begin on de co'n,
   CHORUS: I'll have a home,
            I'll have a home,
            I'll have a home,
            I'll have a home."

9. De Merchant got half de cotton,
   De boll weevil got de rest;
   Didn't leave de po' ol' farmer
   But one old cotton dress;
   CHORUS: An' it's full o' holes,
            Oh, it's full o' holes,
            An' it's full o' holes,
            Oh, it's full o' holes.

10. De farmer say to de merchant,
    "I ain't made but one bale,
    But befo' I'll give you dat one
    I'll fight an' go to jail,
    CHORUS: I'll have a home,
             I'll have a home,
             I'll have a home,
             I'll have a home."

3 **paris green:** an insecticide.

11. Ef anybody axes you
    Who wuz it write dis song,
    Tell 'em 'twas a dark-skinned farmer
    Wid a pair o' blue duckin's⁴ on,
CHORUS: A-lookin' for a home,
           Jes' a-lookin' for a home,
           A-lookin' for a home,
           Jes' a-lookin' for a home.

4 **duckin's:** lightweight trousers.

Understanding Literature

1. This folk song involves at least two conflicts. What are they?
2. In what respects are the life and character of the people who made up and sang this song like those of the people who sang "Starving to Death on a Government Claim"?
3. In these verses, the boll weevil is talked about as though it were a person. What does the poem gain from this technique? (For example, consider how the personification affects the attitude of the reader toward the conflict.)

The Wonderful Crocodile[*]

IMPROVING YOUR READING: Exaggeration is one of the most frequent characteristics of folklore. The whole purpose of "The Wonderful Crocodile" is the invention of an absurdly exaggerated tale. But as usual in folklore, the speaker assumes the role of someone recounting the absolute truth, even suggesting at the end that doubters of his tale can find proof of it in the Nile. Mixing impossible fantasy with factual-sounding detail best describes the technique of this type of literature.

Come list ye, landsmen, all to me,
To tell the truth I'm bound—
What happened to me by going to sea
And the wonders that I found.
Shipwrecked I was one sappy rouse   5
And cast all on the shore,
So I resolved to take a cruise,
The country to explore.

Oh, I had not long scurried out,
When close alongside the ocean,   10
'Twas there that I saw something move,
Like all the earth in motion.
While steering close up alongside
I saw it was a crocodile;
From the end of his nose to the tip of his tail   15
It measured five hundred mile.

This crocodile I could plainly see
Was none of the common race,
For I had to climb a very high tree
Before I could see his face.   20
And when he lifted up his jaw,
Perhaps you may think it a lie,
But his back was three miles through the clouds
And his nose near touched the sky.

Oh, up aloft the wind was high,   25
It blew a hard gale from the south;
I lost my hold and away I flew
Right into the crocodile's mouth.

[*] Collected, adapted & arranged by John A. & Alan Lomax. Copyright 1934 by John A. & Alan Lomax in the book "American Ballads and Folk Songs." Copyright assigned 1958 and renewed 1962 LUDLOW MUSIC, INC., New York, N.Y. USED BY PERMISSION.

He quickly closed his jaws on me,
He thought to nab a victim; 30
But I slipped down his throat, d'ye see,
And that's the way I tricked 'im.

I traveled on for a year or two
Till I got into his maw,
And there were rum kegs not a few 35
And a thousand bullocks in store.
Through life I banished all my care
For on grub I was not stinted;
And in this crocodile lived ten years,
Very well contented. 40

This crocodile being very old,
One day at last he died;
He was three years in catching cold,
He was so long and wide.
His skin was three miles thick, I'm sure, 45
Or very near about;
For I was full six months or more
In making a hole to get out.

So now I'm safe on earth once more,
Resolved no more to roam. 50
In a ship that passed I got a berth,
So now I'm safe at home.
But, if my story you should doubt,
Did you ever cross the Nile—
'Twas there he fell—you'll find the shell 55
Of this wonderful crocodile.

Further Activity

Try writing either a poem or short tale that imitates the technique of "The Wonderful Crocodile," combining a wildly impossible exaggeration with details that make it sound like a strictly factual account. Note that the ballad uses informal, colloquial language, such as "d'ye see" and "very near about." Try to use conversational language that is natural to you or to the characters you are writing about in your poem or tale. One last word: base your poem or tale on a simple plot. As in "The Wonderful Crocodile," the action should be uninvolved and swift.

In 1854, when Longfellow began writing *The Song of Hiawatha,* the United States had been a unified, independent nation for more than half a century. Many American writers felt that the new nation needed a sense of the past, as older nations had. Longfellow decided to write a poem about America's past, to tell a story that would lend a special glory to the days before present history began. Where should he turn but to the Indian for a story of the earliest days of his land?

For his history of the American Indian, Longfellow chose the tribe of the Ojibways, who lived in the north central part of the country. The Ojibways were part of the Algonquin tribe. The hero of Longfellow's poem is Hiawatha, who is sent by Gitche Manito, the Great Spirit, to bring peace to the warring Indian nations.

Hiawatha's Fasting

from *The Song of Hiawatha*

Henry Wadsworth Longfellow

The first two parts of *The Song of Hiawatha* tell the background of Indian prophecy and lore concerning the birth of Hiawatha. In the first part Gitche Manito promises to send a prophet who will guide and teach the Indian nations. The second part tells a legend about the origin and division of the four winds. Hiawatha's father is Mud-jekeewis, the West-Wind. The third and fourth parts tell about Hiawatha's childhood and early manhood. Part 5 is "Hiawatha's Fasting."

IMPROVING YOUR READING: In *The Song of Hiawatha* Longfellow uses the *rhythm* of the Finnish epic *Kalevala.* You will find the rhythm enjoyable if you read parts of the poem aloud. The usual pattern of rhythm consists of four heavy beats to a line. Try marking them in a few lines. If you know where the accents fall, you will pronounce the Indian names easily. But when you read aloud, do not let your voice follow this pounding rhythm. Pay attention to the meaning, and accent the key words. You will then read as the poet intended the poem to sound.

   You shall hear how Hiawatha
   Prayed and fasted in the forest,
   Not for greater skill in hunting,
   Not for greater craft in fishing,
   Not for triumphs in the battle,   5
   And renown among the warriors,
   But for profit of the people,
   For advantage of the nations.
    First he built a lodge for fasting,
   Built a wigwam in the forest,   10

By the shining Big-Sea-Water,
In the blithe and pleasant Springtime,
In the Moon of Leaves he built it,
And, with dreams and visions many,
Seven whole days and nights he fasted.   15
    On the first day of his fasting
Through the leafy woods he wandered;
Saw the deer start from the thicket,
Saw the rabbit in his burrow,
Heard the pheasant, Bena, drumming,   20
Heard the squirrel, Adjidaumo,
Rattling in his hoard of acorns,
Saw the pigeon, the Omeme,
Building nests among the pine trees,
And in flocks the wild-goose, Wawa,   25
Flying to the fenlands[1] northward,
Whirring, wailing far above him.
"Master of Life!" he cried, desponding,
"Must our lives depend on these things?"
    On the next day of his fasting   30
By the river's brink he wandered,
Through the Muskoday, the meadow,
Saw the wild rice, Mahnomonee,
Saw the blueberry, Meenahga,
And the strawberry, Odahmin,   35
And the gooseberry, Shahbomin,
And the grapevine, the Bemahgut,
Trailing o'er the alder-branches,
Filling all the air with fragrance!
"Master of Life!" he cried, desponding,   40
"Must our lives depend on these things?"
    On the third day of his fasting
By the lake he sat and pondered,
By the still, transparent water;
Saw the sturgeon, Nahma, leaping,   45
Scattering drops like beads of wampum,
Saw the yellow perch, the Sahwa,
Like a sunbeam in the water,
Saw the pike, the Maskenozha,
And the herring, Okahahwis,   50
And the Shawgashee, the crawfish!

---

1 **fenlands:** swampy or marshy areas.

HENRY WADSWORTH LONGFELLOW

"Master of Life!" he cried, desponding,
"Must our lives depend on these things?"
    On the fourth day of his fasting
In his lodge he lay exhausted;   55
From his couch of leaves and branches
Gazing with half-open eyelids,
Full of shadowy dreams and visions,
On the dizzy, swimming landscape,
On the gleaming of the water,   60
On the splendor of the sunset.
    And he saw a youth approaching,
Dressed in garments green and yellow,
Coming through the purple twilight,
Through the splendor of the sunset;   65
Plumes of green bent o'er his forehead,
And his hair was soft and golden.
    Standing at the open doorway,
Long he looked at Hiawatha,
Looked with pity and compassion   70
On his wasted form and features,
And, in accents like the sighing
Of the South-Wind in the treetops,
Said he, "O my Hiawatha!
All your prayers are heard in heaven,   75
For you pray not like the others;
Not for greater skill in hunting,
Not for greater craft in fishing,
Not for triumph in the battle,
Nor renown among the warriors,   80
But for profit of the people,
For advantage of the nations.
    "From the Master of Life descending,
I, the friend of man, Mondamin,
Come to warn you and instruct you,   85
How by struggle and by labor
You shall gain what you have prayed for.
Rise up from your bed of branches,
Rise, O youth, and wrestle with me!"
    Faint with famine, Hiawatha   90
Started from his bed of branches,
From the twilight of his wigwam
Forth into the flush of sunset
Came, and wrestled with Mondamin;

At his touch he felt new courage
Throbbing in his brain and bosom,
Felt new life and hope and vigor
Run through every nerve and fiber.
    So they wrestled there together
In the glory of the sunset,
And the more they strove and struggled,
Stronger still grew Hiawatha;
Till the darkness fell around them,
And the heron, the Shuh-shuh-gah,
From her nest among the pine trees,
Gave a cry of lamentation,
Gave a scream of pain and famine.
    " 'Tis enough!" then said Mondamin,
Smiling upon Hiawatha,
"But tomorrow, when the sun sets,
I will come again to try you."
And he vanished, and was seen not;
Whether sinking as the rain sinks,
Whether rising as the mists rise,
Hiawatha saw not, knew not,
Only saw that he had vanished,
Leaving him alone and fainting,
With the misty lake below him,
And the reeling stars above him.
    On the morrow and the next day,
When the sun through heaven descending,
Like a red and burning cinder
From the hearth of the Great Spirit,
Fell into the western waters,
Came Mondamin for the trial,
For the strife with Hiawatha;
Came as silent as the dew comes,
From the empty air appearing,
Into empty air returning,
Taking shape when earth it touches,
But invisible to all men
In its coming and its going.
    Thrice they wrestled there together
In the glory of the sunset,
Till the darkness fell around them,
Till the heron, the Shuh-shuh-gah,
From her nest among the pine trees,

Uttered her loud cry of famine,
And Mondamin paused to listen.

Tall and beautiful he stood there,   140
In his garments green and yellow;
To and fro his plumes above him
Waved and nodded with his breathing,
And the sweat of the encounter
Stood like drops of dew upon him.   145

And he cried, "O Hiawatha!
Bravely have you wrestled with me,
Thrice have wrestled stoutly with me,
And the Master of Life, who sees us,
He will give to you the triumph!"   150

Then he smiled, and said: "Tomorrow
Is the last day of your conflict,
Is the last day of your fasting.
You will conquer and o'ercome me;
Make a bed for me to lie in,   155
Where the rain may fall upon me,
Where the sun may come and warm me;
Strip these garments, green and yellow,
Strip this nodding plumage from me,
Lay me in the earth, and make it   160
Soft and loose and light above me.

"Let no hand disturb my slumber,
Let no weed nor worm molest me,
Let not Kahgahgee, the raven,
Come to haunt me and molest me,   165
Only come yourself to watch me,
Till I wake, and start, and quicken,
Till I leap into the sunshine."

And thus saying, he departed;
Peacefully slept Hiawatha,   170
But he heard the Wawonaissa,
Heard the whippoorwill complaining,
Perched upon his lonely wigwam;
Heard the rushing Sebowisha,
Heard the rivulet rippling near him,   175
Talking to the darksome forest;
Heard the sighing of the branches,
As they lifted and subsided
At the passing of the night-wind,
Heard them, as one hears in slumber   180

Far-off murmurs, dreamy whispers:
Peacefully slept Hiawatha.
On the morrow came Nokomis,[2]
On the seventh day of his fasting,
Came with food for Hiawatha,   185
Came imploring and bewailing,
Lest his hunger should o'ercome him,
Lest his fasting should be fatal.
But he tasted not, and touched not,
Only said to her, "Nokomis,   190
Wait until the sun is setting,
Till the darkness falls around us,
Till the heron, the Shuh-shuh-gah,
Crying from the desolate marshes,
Tells us that the day is ended."   195
Homeward weeping went Nokomis,
Sorrowing for her Hiawatha,
Fearing lest his strength should fail him,
Lest his fasting should be fatal.
He meanwhile sat weary waiting   200
For the coming of Mondamin,
Till the shadows, pointing eastward,
Lengthened over field and forest,
Till the sun dropped from the heaven,
Floating on the waters westward,   205
As a red leaf in the Autumn
Falls and floats upon the water,
Falls and sinks into its bosom.
And behold! the young Mondamin,
With his soft and shining tresses,   210
With his garments green and yellow,
With his long and glossy plumage,
Stood and beckoned at the doorway.
And as one in slumber walking,
Pale and haggard, but undaunted,   215
From the wigwam Hiawatha
Came and wrestled with Mondamin.
Round about him spun the landscape,
Sky and forest reeled together,
And his strong heart leaped within him,   220

2 **Nokomis:** Hiawatha's grandmother, who brought
him up after his mother died.

HENRY WADSWORTH LONGFELLOW   213

As the sturgeon leaps and struggles
In a net to break its meshes.
Like a ring of fire around him
Blazed and flared the red horizon,
And a hundred suns seemed looking   225
At the combat of the wrestlers.
   Suddenly upon the greensward[3]
All alone stood Hiawatha,
Panting with his wild exertion,
Palpitating with the struggle;   230
And before him breathless, lifeless,
Lay the youth, with hair disheveled,
Plumage torn, and garments tattered,
Dead he lay there in the sunset.
   And victorious Hiawatha   235
Made the grave as he commanded,
Stripped the garments from Mondamin,
Stripped his tattered plumage from him,
Laid him in the earth, and made it
Soft and loose and light above him;   240
And the heron, the Shuh-shuh-gah,
From the melancholy moorlands,
Gave a cry of lamentation,
Gave a cry of pain and anguish!
   Homeward then went Hiawatha   245
To the lodge of old Nokomis,
And the seven days of his fasting
Were accomplished and completed.
But the place was not forgotten,
Where he wrestled with Mondamin;   250
Nor forgotten nor neglected
Was the grave where lay Mondamin,
Sleeping in the rain and sunshine,
Where his scattered plumes and garments
Faded in the rain and sunshine.   255
   Day by day did Hiawatha
Go to wait and watch beside it;
Kept the dark mold[4] soft above it,
Kept it clean from weeds and insects,
Drove away, with scoffs and shoutings,   260
Kahgahgee, the king of ravens.

---

3 **greensward** (grēn′swôrd): grassy, green sod.　　4 **mold:** ground; earth.

Till at length a small green feather
From the earth shot slowly upward,
Then another and another,
And before the Summer ended   265
Stood the maize in all its beauty,
With its shining robes about it,
And its long, soft, yellow tresses;
And in rapture Hiawatha
Cried aloud, "It is Mondamin!   270
Yes, the friend of man, Mondamin!"
    Then he called to old Nokomis
And Iagoo, the great boaster,
Showed them where the maize was growing,
Told them of his wondrous vision,   275
Of his wrestling and his triumph,
Of this new gift to the nations,
Which should be their food forever.
    And still later, when the Autumn
Changed the long, green leaves to yellow,   280
And the soft and juicy kernels
Grew like wampum hard and yellow,
Then the ripened ears he gathered,
Stripped the withered husks from off them,
As he once had stripped the wrestler,   285
Gave the first Feast of Mondamin,
And made known unto the people
This new gift of the Great Spirit.

Reading Skills

1. How are Hiawatha's prayers different from those of other
   Indians while fasting? How do his prayers suggest that Hiawatha will be the leader of his tribe?
2. Describe Hiawatha's reactions at the end of each fast day.
3. Why does Mondamin not appear until the fourth day of the fast?
4. What growing plant does Mondamin's appearance suggest?
   What is the significance of the final directions given Hiawatha
   by Mondamin? Since Mondamin certainly resembles a kind
   of plant, what is the meaning of his being buried?
5. Most legends include happenings that cannot be explained
   naturally. Sometimes there is a miracle of some kind—in other
   words, a supernatural happening. What is supernatural in
   the story of Hiawatha's fasting?

The folklore of all countries abounds with stories of creatures that look human but are larger than human. Such monsters have been with us or in our imaginations for ages. The snow-capped Himalayas have their Abominable Snowman; the American Pacific Northwest has its "Sasquatch." One or several, real or imaginary, the creature has emerged again, this time to be known as "Bigfoot."

Sasquatch Alias "Bigfoot"

George Laycock

From northern California, through Oregon, Washington, and into British Columbia, the mountains are wild and deeply timbered. In this country there are new reported sightings every year of manlike monsters, huge, hairy, and indescribably ugly.

Indians of the Pacific Northwest knew about these giant, wild men of the forests hundreds of years ago. The Indians called them "Sasquatch." More recently, people, standing spellbound before fourteen-inch-long footprints, have called the monster "Bigfoot."

Each year more people than ever before are out there in the deeply wooded valleys hoping for a glimpse of the bigfooted Sasquatch.

Where could such monsters have come from? They could, some explain, have come from the same place the native Indians and Eskimos came from to settle North America. During the time of the Wisconsin glacial epoch the level of the oceans was lower. More of the world's supply of water was locked up in ice and snow. This exposed a wide bridge of land across the North Pacific connecting Asia and North America.

Across this land bridge came the ancestors of many wild creatures found here, deer, bear, bison, wild sheep, and others. Perhaps the people, moving a few miles at a time, followed these animals, which they hunted for food. And perhaps in those times there came as well some creatures we still know very little about.

Slipping along in the shadows of night may have been tall, hairy creatures looking more like people than like any of the other creatures around them. This could explain how the ancestors of Sasquatch first came to the forests of the Pacific Northwest; they came on their big feet. They would have come, you understand, from Asia, which is also home of the Abominable Snowman, presumably a cousin to Bigfoot.

It is likely that the creature we now know as Bigfoot was never abundant. Except for the fact that they have managed to stay out of sight of men so well, there might, by now, be none of them remaining.

Not until the 1950s did many people begin thinking seriously about the possibility that there might really be a Bigfoot. Then timber workers, in lonely logging camps of northern California, began finding strange giant tracks around their dwellings and beside the forest trails. Plaster casts of these prints were sometimes made and preserved. The story spread, and people began to ask each other if such human-shaped animals did live up there in the woods. Many believed they did.

Soon someone recalled a remarkable story that had appeared in Portland, Oregon, newspapers in 1924. On the east slope of Mount St. Helens lived a grizzled old prospector, all alone in his little cabin in the silence of the deep forest. On an August day he left his cabin and hurried off to search for a forest ranger. He told the foresters his strange tale.

"They woke me up in the middle of the night," he said, "throwin' stones at my place. Some of them stones was big ones, some even come through the roof. And all the time they was around the house, they was screaming like a bunch of apes. I didn't dare go outside. That's probably what they wanted me to do. Would you have gone outside? No sir! Instead I crawled under the bed, and I stayed there till morning come. Sometime in the night them critters quit their screamin' and slunk off in the dark. Next morning when I went outside there was the tracks, big ones, a foot or more across, and right up beside my place."

That story appeared in newspapers in Washington and Oregon. Soon the wooded slopes of Mount St. Helens were filled with nervous hunters. They were alert for the slightest noise, the big footprint, or a glimpse of a furry hide in the undergrowth. Considering the assortment of rifles, shotguns, and pistols they carried, it was a blessing nobody got shot.

They saw no sign of the Bigfoot. Gradually folks around those mountains seemed to forget the giant, hairy monsters again. Sasquatch was becoming more elusive than ever. He wanted very little to do with people and this was understandable.

But following the reports from the California logging camps, the story began growing again. In the years since, the evidence has piled up. More and more, people in the Pacific Northwest are convinced that something in human form, but not very human at all, really lives in the deepest and darkest forests. There is now a list of more than three hundred reported sightings of Bigfoot. Undoubtedly there would be more except for the elusive nature of the beast and its nocturnal habits. Still no Bigfoot has been captured or killed. Seldom has one been photographed. The most notable exception occurred in the mountains of northern California in 1967.

Roger Patterson lives with his wife and three children on the little horse ranch they operate near Yakima, Washington. For several years he had been studying the exploits of Bigfoot and figuring out the best place to go look for the creature.

On October 20, 1967, Mr. Patterson and his friend, Bob Gimlin, had been high in the mountains in northern California for almost a week. On that day Mr. Patterson says, "... when riding horseback up a creek bottom, we encountered this creature. My horse smelled it, jumped, and fell." Mr. Patterson scrambled for his saddlebag. "I got the camera out of the saddlebag," he says, "and ran across the creek and we were able to get twenty-nine feet of sixteen-millimeter colored film."

After three miles of tracking through rough country, the two men lost Bigfoot's trail in deep undergrowth. They made plaster casts of the footprints. Other people returned later and also saw and measured the 14½-inch prints.

This newly made film was sent down to Hollywood. There, experts in "special effects," men who really know how to set up a fake picture, studied and restudied Patterson's disturbing movies. Each of them decided that in no way could Patterson have faked his pictures.

Next the movies were shown to a lengthy list of scientists. Among them were noted zoologists. They arrived as doubters, but following a look at the Patterson movies, left "shaken." Of special interest to the zoologists was the movement of the muscles as the Bigfoot walked. This movement was proof enough to many that the creature was real and the Patterson movies authentic. The figure photographed, a female, walked upright like a human and measured about seven and a half feet tall, three feet across the shoulders, had arms three feet long, and weighed an estimated eight hundred pounds.

In addition to his movies, Patterson tells of other evidence that Bigfoot lives. In 1958 he interviewed Charles Cates, an aging man who had once served as mayor of North Vancouver. Cates recalled three old Indians whom he considered reliable, and all of whom told of hairy giants they had seen in their youth. Perhaps there were more of the monsters around in those times. One of the Indians had been in a tent one night with friends when a Bigfoot stuck its hairy head through the tent door and looked in upon them.

Near Yankton, Oregon, according to Mr. Patterson's records, several people sighted the hairy giants in 1926. A truck driver swore that one of them had trotted along beside his logging truck looking into the cab at him.

In 1941, according to a report given Patterson by Mrs. George Chapman, she and her children saw "an eight-foot hairy man come out of the woods." The creature went into a lean-to behind their cabin. As it went in the back door, the Chapmans went out the front door. They fled into the forest. For a long time they huddled there in the shadows. When they returned to their home, huge tracks marked the place where the giant had walked. The deputy sheriff from Blaine, Washington, came out and made casts of the footprints. This Bigfoot had the biggest feet of all. They measured sixteen inches long. The Bigfoot tramped down a patch of potatoes as it departed for the forests.

Then the next year, near Eugene, Oregon, Don Hunter and his wife spotted a "giant biped" walking, taking long strides, over the mud flats of Todd Lake.

Such reports, when coupled with Patterson's movies, are not to be taken lightly. So much interest has been aroused in these stories of Bigfoot that at least three organizations have been created to seek the creature. One is the American Resources, and Development Foundation, Inc., organized by Ron Olsen, one of the most respected of all Bigfoot hunters. His organization is programing all reports of sightings on a computer in efforts to pinpoint the best possible places to continue the search.

Another is the International Wildlife Conservation Society. This group is based in Washington, D.C. At the head of it is an explorer with experience searching the Himalayas for Bigfoot's cousin, the Abominable Snowman. Even Washington socialites have helped finance the group.

Roger Patterson has also set up the Northwest Research Association. With these groups, plus uncounted individual amateur monster hunters loose in the woods, the chances seem better than ever that Bigfoot will soon slip up, be captured, measured, photographed, and verified.

Some people have admitted they plan to shoot the first Bigfoot they find, thereby ending speculation.

But most hope only to take one of the furry beasts captive long enough to study him. With this in mind, expeditions go afield equipped with dart guns carrying drugs to put Bigfoot to sleep.

Patterson has mapped out a complete course of action. On that memorable day when Bigfoot is eventually tracked to earth, the procedure will include the following steps. Small groups of specialists will be scouring the mountain country for fresh evidence. "When a specimen is obtained," Patterson explains, "all personnel and equipment will be concentrated on it." Even after the effects of the drug-carrying dart wear off, Bigfoot will be kept under full sedation. (This seems safest.) All field forces will be rushed to the scene. A call will go out for a helicopter. Blood samples, bone marrow, body fluids, all will be collected and labeled. Plastic casts will be made of teeth, jaws, hands, feet.

Meanwhile cameras will click and whine, tape recorders will run continuously, and a stenographer will record written observations. Security measures will go into effect at once. One reason will be to protect the researchers against attack by other Bigfeet. There will also, as Patterson explains, be the need to protect the field group against ". . . interference by everybody, including the press."

Patterson welcomes new members to his association. For their dues, members receive a certificate plus a colored photograph of Bigfoot. This is enough to make adventure-minded people everywhere feel a little closer to the monsters.

One of the most recent centers of Bigfoot activity is around the county seat town of The Dalles, Oregon. According to the sheriff's office in The Dalles, five people testified they saw the creature in the neighborhood June 2, 1971, a one-day record. A month later there was an additional sighting near the same location. Visitors flocked to town. But there were no more observations reported during the summer.

Bigfoot will almost certainly appear again. No one knows where. People all the way over into Montana and Wyoming, and other states as well, talk of the Bigfoot. Many would not be at all surprised to find these shaggy giants living in their mountains too. Doubters sometimes suggest that anyone with a mountain and a forest can have his own Sasquatch.

One thing is certain, if Bigfoot is really out there in the hills, his name belongs on the government's official list of rare and endangered species.

Whatever his fortunes might have been in the past, his numbers have dwindled to a precious few.

All who seek to kill a Bigfoot should reconsider. He appears, after all, to be a harmless monster.

This is the firm belief in Skamania County, Washington. County commissioners there recently passed a law making anyone who kills a Bigfoot or Sasquatch subject to a fine of one thousand dollars and five years in jail.

To man and Bigfoot alike, this is a refreshing development. We live in an age when hundreds of wild species are becoming rare and approaching extinction. Only after the passenger pigeons were already gone did we pass laws to save them. The bison nearly became extinct for the same reason. But here is a case where we pass a law to save a wild creature even before it is found—and a monster at that.

If you should see a Bigfoot, perhaps you should tell him about that. It might help convince him that people are not such monsters after all.

Reading Skills

1. According to some people, how did Sasquatch (alias Bigfoot) come to live in the Pacific Northwest?
2. What makes some people think that Bigfoot is real and not just a legend? What "evidence has piled up"?
3. Why are the Patterson movies important to the Bigfoot story? How do they relate to other stories?
4. What do the Wildlife Conservation Society, the Northwest Research Association, and the town of The Dalles have in common?
5. Does the storyteller believe in Bigfoot? Cite details to support your conclusion.

Some legends have beginnings which are lost in history. Others grew from very real incidents and men and women whom history has recorded. Such a legend is that of Johnny Appleseed, born Jonathan Chapman, in Boston, Massachusetts, in 1775.

Johnny Appleseed: A Pioneer Hero

W. D. Haley

IMPROVING YOUR READING: This account of the legendary Johnny Appleseed, from an 1871 issue of Harper's New Monthly Magazine, does not sound like the usual legend or fairy tale. The difference in *tone* comes from the attitude of the writer toward his subject. Haley seems to have looked at his "pioneer hero" as an historian looks at his or her subject—as a matter of record. As you read, be prepared for rather formal, old-fashioned language; this piece was written over one hundred years ago.

THE "FAR WEST" is rapidly becoming only a traditional designation: railroads have destroyed the romance of frontier life, or have surrounded it with so many appliances of civilization that the pioneer character is rapidly becoming mythical. The men and women who obtain their groceries and dry-goods from New York by rail in a few hours have nothing in common with those who, fifty years ago, "packed" salt a hundred miles to make their mush palatable, and could only exchange corn and wheat for molasses and calico by making long and perilous voyages in flat-boats down the Ohio and Mississippi rivers to New Orleans.

The first reliable trace of our modest hero finds him in the Territory of Ohio, in 1801, with a horse-load of apple seeds, which he planted in various places on and about the borders of Licking Creek, the first orchard thus originated by him being on the farm of Isaac Stadden, in what is now known as Licking County, in the State of Ohio. During the five succeeding years we have no authentic account of his movements until we reach a pleasant spring day in 1806, when a pioneer settler in Jefferson County, Ohio, noticed a peculiar craft, with a remarkable occupant and a curious cargo, slowly dropping down with the current of the Ohio River. It was "Johnny Appleseed," by which name Jonathan Chapman was afterward known in every log-cabin from the Ohio River to the Northern lakes, and westward to the prairies of what is now the State of Indiana. With two canoes lashed together he was transporting a load of apple seeds to the Western frontier, for the purpose of creating orchards on the farthest verge of white settlements. A long and toilsome voyage it was, and must have occupied a great deal of time, as the lonely traveler stopped at every inviting spot to plant the seeds and make his infant nurseries. These are the first well-authenticated facts in the history of Jonathan Chapman, whose birth, there is good reason for believing, occurred in Boston, Massachusetts, in 1775. According to this, which was his own statement in one of his less modest moods, he was, at the time of his appearance on Licking Creek, twenty-six years of age. His whole after-life was devoted to the work of planting apple seeds in remote places. The seeds he gathered from the cider-presses of Western Pennsylvania; but his canoe voyage in 1806 appears to have been the only occasion upon which he adopted that method of transporting them, as all his subsequent journeys were made on foot.

In personal appearance Chapman was a small, wiry man, full of restless activity; he had long dark hair, a scanty beard that was never shaved, and keen black eyes that sparkled with a peculiar brightness. His dress was of the oddest description. Generally, even in the coldest weather, he went barefooted, but sometimes, for his long journeys, he would make himself a rude pair of sandals; at other times he would wear any cast-off foot-covering he chanced to find —a boot on one foot and an old brogan or a moccasin on the other.

It appears to have been a matter of conscience with him never to purchase shoes, although he was rarely without money enough to do so. On one occasion, in an unusually cold November, while he was traveling barefooted through mud and snow, a settler who happened to possess a pair of shoes that were too small for his own use forced their acceptance upon Johnny, declaring that it was sinful for a human being to travel with naked feet in such weather. A few days afterward the donor was in the village that has since become the thriving city of Mansfield, and met his beneficiary contentedly plodding along with his feet bare and half frozen. With some degree of anger he inquired for the cause of such foolish conduct, and received for reply that Johnny had overtaken a poor, barefooted family moving Westward, and as they appeared to be in much greater need of clothing than he was, he had given them the shoes.

Johnny's dress was generally composed of cast-off clothing, that he had taken in payment for apple-trees; and as the pioneers were far less extravagant than their descendants in such matters, the homespun and buckskin garments that they discarded would not be very elegant or serviceable. In his later years, however, he seems to have thought that even this kind of second-hand raiment was too luxurious, as his principal garment was made of a coffee sack, in which he cut holes for his head and arms to pass through, and pronounced it "a very serviceable cloak, and as good clothing as any man need wear."

In the matter of head-gear his taste was equally unique; his first experiment was with a tin vessel that served to cook his mush, but this was open to the objection that it did not protect his eyes from the beams of the sun; so he constructed a hat of pasteboard with an immense peak in front, and having thus secured an article that combined usefulness with economy, it became his permanent fashion.

Thus strangely clad, he was perpetually wandering through forests and morasses, and suddenly appearing in white settlements and Indian villages; but there must have been some rare force of gentle goodness dwelling in his looks and breathing in his words, for it is the testimony of all who knew him that, notwithstanding his ridiculous attire, he was always treated with the greatest respect by the simplest frontiersman, and, what is a better test, the boys of the settlements forbore to jeer at him. With grown-up people and boys he was usually shy, but showed great affection for little girls, always having pieces of ribbon and gay calico to give to his little favorites. When he consented to eat with any family he would never sit down to the table until he was assured that there was an ample supply for the children; and his sympathy for their youthful troubles and his kindness toward them made him friends among all the juveniles of the borders.

The Indians also treated Johnny with the greatest kindness. He was regarded as a "great medicine man," on account of his strange appearance, eccentric actions, and, especially, the fortitude with which he could endure pain, in proof of which he would often thrust pins and needles into his flesh. His nervous sensibilities really seem to have been less acute than those of ordinary people, for his method of treating the cuts and sores that were the consequences of his barefooted wanderings through briers and thorns was to sear the wound with a red-hot iron, and then cure the burn. . . .

It was his custom, when he had been welcomed to some hospitable log-house after a weary day of journeying, to lie down on the split-log floor, and, after inquiring if his auditors would hear "some news right fresh from heaven," produce his few tattered books, among which would be a New Testament, and read and expound until his uncultivated hearers would catch the spirit and glow of his enthusiasm, while they scarcely comprehended his language.

A lady who knew him in his later years writes in the following terms of one of these domiciliary readings of poor, self-sacrificing Johnny Appleseed: "We can hear him read now, just as he did that summer day, when we were busy quilting up stairs, and he lay near the door, his voice rising denunciatory and thrilling—strong and loud as the roar of wind and waves, then soft and soothing as the balmy airs that quivered the morning-glory leaves about his gray beard. His was a strange eloquence at times, and he was undoubtedly a man of genius."

Next to his advocacy of his religious ideas, his enthusiasm for the cultivation of apple-trees in what he termed "the only proper way"—that is, from the seed—was the absorbing object of his life. Upon this, as upon religion, he was eloquent in his appeals. He would describe the growing and ripening fruit as such a rare and beautiful gift of the Almighty with words that became pictures, until his hearers could almost see its manifold forms of beauty present before them. To his eloquence on this subject, as well as to his actual labors in planting nurseries, the country over which he traveled for so many years is largely indebted for its numerous orchards. But he denounced as absolute wickedness all devices of pruning and grafting, and would speak of the act of cutting a tree as if it were a cruelty inflicted upon a feeling being.

Whenever Johnny saw an animal abused, or heard of it, he would purchase it and give it to some more humane settler, on condition that it should be kindly treated and properly cared for. It frequently happened that the long journey into the wilderness would cause the new settlers to be encumbered with lame and broken-down horses, that were turned loose to die. In the autumn Johnny would make a diligent search for all such animals, and, gathering them up, he would bargain for their food and shelter until the next spring, when he would lead them away to some good pasture for the summer. If they recovered so as to be capable of working, he would never sell them, but would lend or give them away, stipulating for their good usage. His conception of the absolute sin was the inflicting of pain or death upon any creature. The only occasion on which he destroyed a venomous reptile was a source of long regret, to which he could never refer without sadness.

Johnny had elected a suitable place for planting apple seeds on a small prairie, and in order to prepare the ground he was mowing the long grass, when he was bitten by a rattlesnake. In describing the event he sighed heavily, and said, "Poor fellow, he only just touched me, when I, in the heat of my ungodly passion, put the heel of my scythe in him, and went away. Some time afterward I went back, and there lay the poor fellow dead."

In 1838—thirty-seven years after his appearance on Licking Creek—Johnny noticed that civilization, wealth, and population were pressing into the wilderness of Ohio. Hitherto he had easily kept just in advance of the wave of settlement; but now towns and churches were making their appearance, and even, at long intervals, the stage-driver's horn broke the silence of the grand old forests, and he felt that his work was done in the region in which he had labored so long. He visited every house, and took a solemn farewell of all families.

During the succeeding nine years Johnny Appleseed pursued his eccentric avocation on the western border of Ohio and in Indiana. In the summer of 1847, when his labors had literally borne fruit over a hundred thousand square miles of territory, at the close of a warm day, after traveling twenty miles, he entered the house of a settler in Allen County, Indiana, and was, as usual, warmly welcomed. He declined to eat with the family, but accepted some bread and milk, which he partook of sitting on the door-step and gazing on the setting sun.

Later in the evening he delivered his "news right fresh from heaven" by reading the Beatitudes. Declining other accommodation, he slept, as usual, on the floor, and in the early morning he was found with his features all aglow, and his body so near death that he could not talk. The physician, who was hastily summoned, pronounced him dying, but added that he had never seen a man in so placid a state at the approach of death. At seventy-two years of age, forty-six of which had been devoted to his self-imposed mission, he ripened into death as naturally and beautifully as the seeds of his own planting had grown into fiber and bud and blossom and the matured fruit.

Thus died one of the memorable men of pioneer times, who never inflicted pain or knew an enemy—a man of strange habits, in whom there dwelt a comprehensive love that reached with one hand downward to the lowest forms of life, and with the other upward to the very throne of God. A laboring, self-denying benefactor of his race, homeless, solitary, and ragged, he trod the thorny earth with bare and bleeding feet, intent only upon making the wilderness fruitful.

Reading Skills

1. What hazards faced Jonathan Chapman as he ventured into the frontier country?
2. In general, what kind of impression did Chapman make on people? How was he received by settlers in the Native American villages?
3. What was Johnny's attitude toward living things in general and animals in particular? How did this attitude get him into trouble on one occasion?
4. Describe Johnny's physical appearance. How was it in keeping with his beliefs?
5. Johnny Appleseed is known today mostly for his tree planting. According to Haley's article, for what other reasons did he gain fame as a "character"?

Further Activity

How was Jonathan Chapman very much like environmentalists of today? If he were living today, what do you think he would be doing for his living?

W. D. HALEY

The ballad of "Skipper Ireson's Ride" tells the story of a sea captain who deserts his sinking ship. After Whittier had written the ballad, he discovered that, in historical fact, Skipper Ireson was innocent and had been unjustly accused of the crime.

Skipper Ireson's Ride

John Greenleaf Whittier

Of all the rides since the birth of time,
Told in story or sung in rhyme,—
On Apuleius's Golden Ass,[1]
Or one-eyed Calender's horse of brass,[2]
Witch astride of a human back,   5
Islam's prophet on Al-Borák,[3]—
The strangest ride that ever was sped
Was Ireson's, out from Marblehead![4]
  Old Floyd Ireson, for his hard heart,
    Tarred and feathered and carried in a cart   10
  By the women of Marblehead!

Body of turkey, head of owl,
Wings a-droop like a rained-on fowl,
Feathered and ruffled in every part,
Skipper Ireson stood in the cart.   15
Scores of women, old and young,
Strong of muscle, and glib of tongue,
Pushed and pulled up the rocky lane,
Shouting and singing the shrill refrain:
  "Here's Flud Oirson, fur his horrd horrt,   20
    Torr'd an' futherr'd an' corr'd in a corrt
  By the women o' Morble'ead!"

1 **Apuleius's Golden Ass:** The book *The Golden Ass,* by Apuleius, tells the adventures of a man who was changed into an ass.
2 **Calender's horse of brass:** One of the stories in *The Arabian Nights* tells of a king disguised as a calender, a wandering Moslem priest. He enters a forbidden room in a palace; there he finds a horse which carries him to Bagdad and which then knocks his eye out with a whisk of the tail.
3 **Al-Borák:** the white, winged horse that, according to legend, carried Mohammed to the heavens.
4 **Marblehead:** a town in northeastern Massachusetts, on Massachusetts Bay; long a fishing village.

AMERICA IN FOLKLORE AND TALES

Wrinkled scolds[5] with hands on hips,
Girls in bloom of cheek and lips,
Wild-eyed, free-limbed, such as chase   25
Bacchus[6] round some antique vase,
Brief of skirt, with ankles bare,
Loose of kerchief and loose of hair,
With conch shells[7] blowing and fish-horns' twang,
Over and over the Maenads[8] sang: 30
    "Here's Flud Oirson, fur his horrd horrt,
    Torr'd an futherr'd an' corr'd in a corrt
      By the women o' Morble'ead!"

Small pity for him!—He sailed away
From a leaking ship in Chaleur Bay,[9]—
Sailed away from a sinking wreck,
With his own town's-people on her deck!
"Lay by! lay by!" they called to him.
Back he answered, "Sink or swim!
Brag of your catch of fish again!"   40
And off he sailed through the fog and rain!
    Old Floyd Ireson, for his hard heart,
    Tarred and feathered and carried in a cart
      By the women of Marblehead!

Fathoms deep in dark Chaleur   45
That wreck shall lie forevermore.
Mother and sister, wife and maid,
Looked from the rocks of Marblehead
Over the moaning and rainy sea,—
Looked for the coming that might not be!   50
What did the winds and the sea birds say
Of the cruel captain who sailed away?—
    Old Floyd Ireson, for his hard heart,
    Tarred and feathered and carried in a cart
      By the women of Marblehead!   55

---

5 scolds: people addicted to abusive speech.
6 Bacchus (băk′əs): mythological god of wine.
7 conch shells: large spiral sea shells, many of which are made into horns.
8 Maenads (mē′nădz): priestesses of Bacchus;
here, girls of Marblehead who are following the cart, as the Maenads follow Bacchus on an antique vase.
9 Chaleur (shə lŏŏr′) Bay: a bay in the Gulf of St. Lawrence.

JOHN GREENLEAF WHITTIER

Through the street, on either side,
Up flew windows, doors swung wide;
Sharp-tongued spinsters, old wives gray,
Treble lent the fish-horn's bray.[10]
Seaworn grandsires, cripple-bound,   60
Hulks of old sailors run aground,
Shook head, and fist, and hat, and cane,
And cracked with curses the hoarse refrain:
    "Here's Flud Oirson, fur his horrd horrt,
    Torr'd an' futherr'd an' corr'd in a corrt   65
        By the women o' Morble'ead!"

Sweetly along the Salem road
Bloom of orchard and lilac showed.
Little the wicked skipper knew
Of the fields so green and the sky so blue.   70
Riding there in his sorry trim,
Like an Indian idol glum and grim,
Scarcely he seemed the sound to hear
Of voices shouting, far and near:
    "Here's Flud Oirson, fur his horrd horrt,   75
    Torr'd an' futherr'd an' corr'd in a corrt
        By the women o' Morble'ead!"

"Hear me, neighbors!" at last he cried,—
"What to me is this noisy ride?
What is the shame that clothes the skin   80
To the nameless horror that lives within?
Waking or sleeping, I see a wreck,
And hear a cry from a reeling deck!
Hate me and curse me,—I only dread
The hand of God and the face of the dead!"   85
    Said old Floyd Ireson, for his hard heart,
    Tarred and feathered and carried in a cart
        By the women of Marblehead!

Then the wife of the skipper lost at sea
Said, "God has touched him! why should we!"   90

10 Treble . . . bray: added the sound of their
treble voices to the bray of the fish-horn.

Said an old wife mourning her only son,
"Cut the rogue's tether and let him run!"
So with soft relentings and rude excuse,
Half scorn, half pity, they cut him loose,
And gave him a cloak to hide him in,   95
And left him alone with his shame and sin.
    Poor Floyd Ireson, for his hard heart,
    Tarred and feathered and carried in a cart
    By the women of Marblehead!

Understanding Literature

1. Why are the Golden Ass, Calender's horse, and Al-Borák mentioned in the first stanza?
2. Describe the scene portrayed in the second stanza.
3. According to the poem, what is the legend of Floyd Ireson?
4. The fourth stanza tells the facts of the legend, as Whittier understood them. What does the fifth stanza do?
5. In what way is the description of the skipper in the seventh stanza different from that in the second stanza? In the seventh stanza, what is the author's purpose in the description of the skipper?
6. What happens in the eighth and ninth stanzas? Explain "half scorn, half pity."
7. According to the story as told by the people of Marblehead, the skipper did not really speak during his shameful ride in the cart. Why does the poet have him speak?

Further Activity

This ballad can be effectively read aloud by a group. Individuals may read lines where one person speaks. Groups of boys may read lines describing the actions of the men. Groups of girls may read lines describing the actions of the women.

Although "The Man without a Country" is about the life of a fictional character, in its background are historical events of 19th-century America. In the story a young American is supposedly influenced and ruined by Aaron Burr, who in the early 19th century was associated with a scheme to set up a Southwestern Empire. Burr's scheme itself has become a legend in American history. During the presidency of Thomas Jefferson, Burr bought some land in the Louisiana Territory, which the United States had purchased from France in 1803. Burr intended to colonize his land and perhaps to establish a new state. He also intended, should war break out between the United States and Spain, to lead an expedition into Mexico, perhaps winning it for his own. The scheme was discovered and in 1807 he and others connected with it were tried for treason at Richmond, Virginia. Burr was found not guilty. In the story Philip Nolan does not escape sentence at his trial: he becomes "The Man without a Country."

The Man without a Country

Edward Everett Hale

IMPROVING YOUR READING: "The Man without a Country" is written as if it were being told by a man who knew Philip Nolan. The *point of view* is that of the "I" who tells the story. Since the author decided to tell the story from this point of view, he could tell only what the narrator observed or heard about Nolan's behavior. He could not tell what Nolan thought or felt. As another person, he is not supposed to know. To see the importance of point of view, think, as you read, how the story would be different if Philip Nolan himself had told it.

I SUPPOSE THAT very few casual readers of the *New York Herald* of August 13, 1863, observed, in an obscure corner, among the "Deaths," the announcement—

"NOLAN. Died, on board U.S. Corvette *Levant*, Lat. 2° 11′ S., Long. 131° W., on the 11th of May, PHILIP NOLAN."

I happened to observe it, because I was stranded at the old Mission House in Mackinaw, waiting for a Lake Superior steamer which did not choose to come, and I was devouring to the very stubble all the current literature I could get hold of, even down to the deaths and marriages in the *Herald*. My memory for names and people is good, and the reader will see, as he goes on, that I had reason enough to remember Philip Nolan. There are hundreds of readers who would have paused at that announcement, if the officer of the *Levant* who reported it had chosen to make it thus: "Died, May 11, THE MAN WITHOUT A COUNTRY." For it was as "The Man without a Country" that poor Philip Nolan had generally been known by the officers who had him in charge during some fifty years, as, indeed, by all the men who sailed under them. I dare say there is many a man who has taken wine with him once a fortnight, in a three years' cruise, who never knew that his name was "Nolan," or whether the poor wretch had any name at all.

There can now be no possible harm in telling this poor creature's story. Reason enough there has been till now, ever since Madison's administration went out in 1817, for very strict secrecy, the secrecy of honor itself, among the gentlemen of the Navy who have had Nolan in successive charge. And certainly it speaks well for the *esprit de corps*[1] of the profession, and the personal honor of its members, that to the press this man's story has been wholly unknown—and, I think, to the country at large also. I have reason to think, from some investigations I made in the Naval Archives[2] when I was attached to the Bureau of Construction, that every official report relating to him was burned when Ross burned the public buildings at Washington. One of the Tuckers, or possibly one of the Watsons, had Nolan in charge at the end of the war;[3] and when, on returning from his cruise, he reported at Washington to one of the Crowninshields —who was in the Navy Department when he came home—he found that the Department ignored the whole business. Whether they really knew

nothing about it, or whether it was a "*Non mi ricordo*,"[4] determined on as a piece of policy, I do not know. But this I do know, that since 1817, and possibly before, no naval officer has mentioned Nolan in his report of a cruise.

But, as I say, there is no need for secrecy any longer. And now the poor creature is dead, it seems to me worth while to tell a little of his story, by way of showing young Americans of today what it is to be A MAN WITHOUT A COUNTRY.

PHILIP NOLAN was as fine a young officer as there was in the "Legion of the West," as the Western division of our Army was then called. When Aaron Burr made his first dashing expedition down to New Orleans in 1805, at Fort Massac, or somewhere above on the river, he met, as the devil would have it, this gay, dashing, bright young fellow; at some dinner party, I think. Burr marked him, talked to him, walked with him, took him a day or two's voyage in his flatboat, and, in short, fascinated him. For the next year, barrack-life was very tame to poor Nolan. He occasionally availed himself of the permission the great man had given him to write to him. Long, high-worded, stilted letters the poor boy wrote and rewrote and copied. But never a line did he have in reply from the gay deceiver. The other boys in the garrison sneered at him, because he sacrificed in this unrequited affection for a politician

---

1 *esprit de corps* (ĕs prē′ də kôr′): team spirit.
2 **Archives:** place for keeping records.
3 **the war:** the War of 1812, between England and the United States. During the war the British under General Robert Ross captured Washington, burning the public buildings.

4 *Non mi ricordo:* I do not remember.

the time which they devoted to Monongahela,[5] hazard,[6] and high-low-jack. Bourbon, euchre,[7] and poker were still unknown. But one day Nolan had his revenge. This time Burr came down the river, not as an attorney seeking a place for his office, but as a disguised conqueror. He had defeated I know not how many district attorneys; he had dined at I know not how many public dinners; he had been heralded in I know not how many Weekly Arguses, and it was rumored that he had an army behind him and an empire before him. It was a great day —his arrival—to poor Nolan. Burr had not been at the fort an hour before he sent for him. That evening he asked Nolan to take him out in his skiff, to show him a canebrake or a cottonwood tree, as he said— really to seduce him; and by the time the sail was over, Nolan was enlisted body and soul. From that time, though he did not yet know it, he lived as A MAN WITHOUT A COUNTRY.

What Burr meant to do I know no more than you, dear reader. It is none of our business just now. Only, when the grand catastrophe came, and Jefferson and the House of Virginia of that day undertook to break on the wheel all the possible Clarences of the then House of York [8] by the great treason trial at Richmond

some of the lesser fry in that distant Mississippi Valley, which was farther from us than Puget's Sound is today, introduced the like novelty on their provincial stage; and, to while away the monotony of the summer at Fort Adams, got up, for *spectacles,* a string of court-martials on the officers there. One and another of the colonels and majors were tried, and, to fill out the list, little Nolan, against whom, Heaven knows, there was evidence enough—that he was sick of the service, had been willing to be false to it, and would have obeyed any order to march any-whither with anyone who would follow him had the order been signed, "By command of His Exc. A. Burr." The courts dragged on. The big flies escaped— rightly, for all I know. Nolan was proved guilty enough, as I say; yet you and I would never have heard of him, reader, but that, when the president of the court asked him at the close whether he wished to say anything to show that he had always been faithful to the United States, he cried out, in a fit of frenzy—

Damn the United States! I wish I may never hear of the United States again!"

I suppose he did not know how the words shocked old Colonel Morgan, who was holding the court. Half the officers who sat in it had served through the Revolution, and their lives, not to say their necks, had been risked for the very idea which he so cavalierly cursed in his madness. He, on his part, had grown up in the West of those days, in the

5 **Monongahela:** whisky.
6 **hazard:** a dice game.
7 **euchre:** a card game.
8 **all . . . York:** all the possible traitors to their government. The Duke of Clarence, of the House of York, is associated with rebellion and treason. He joined rebel forces, 1469-1470, against his brother, King Edward IV.

AMERICA IN FOLKLORE AND TALES

midst of "Spanish plot," "Orleans plot," and all the rest. He had been educated on a plantation where the finest company was a Spanish officer or a French merchant from Orleans. His education, such as it was, had been perfected in commercial expeditions to Vera Cruz, and I think he told me his father once hired an Englishman to be a private tutor for a winter on the plantation. He had spent half his youth with an older brother, hunting horses in Texas; and, in a word, to him "United States" was scarcely a reality. Yet he had been fed by "United States" for all the years since he had been in the Army. He had sworn on his faith as a Christian to be true to "United States." It was "United States" which gave him the uniform he wore, and the sword by his side. Nay, my poor Nolan, it was only because "United States" had picked you out first as one of her own confidential men of honor that "A. Burr" cared for you a straw more than for the flatboat men who sailed his ark for him.

I do not excuse Nolan; I only explain to the reader why he damned his country, and wished he might never hear her name again.

He never did hear her name but once again. From that moment, Sept. 23, 1807, till the day he died, May 11, 1863, he never heard her name again. For that half-century and more he was a man without a country.

Old Morgan, as I said, was terribly shocked. If Nolan had compared George Washington to Benedict Arnold, or had cried, "God save King George," Morgan would not have felt worse. He called the court into his private room, and returned in fifteen minutes, with a face like a sheet, to say—

"Prisoner, hear the sentence of the Court! The Court decides, subject to the approval of the President, that you never hear the name of the United States again."

Nolan laughed. But nobody else laughed. Old Morgan was too solemn, and the whole room was hushed dead as night for a minute. Even Nolan lost his swagger in a moment. Then Morgan added—

"Mr. Marshal, take the prisoner to Orleans in an armed boat, and deliver him to the naval commander there."

The marshal gave his orders and the prisoner was taken out of court.

"Mr. Marshal," continued old Morgan, "see that no one mentions the United States to the prisoner. Mr. Marshal, make my respects to Lieutenant Mitchell at Orleans, and request him to order that no one shall mention the United States to the prisoner while he is on board ship. You will receive your written orders from the officer on duty here this evening. The court is adjourned without day."

I have always supposed that Colonel Morgan himself took the proceedings of the court to Washington city, and explained them to Mr. Jefferson. Certain it is that the President approved them—certain, that is, if I may believe the men who say they have seen his signature.

Before the *Nautilus* got round from New Orleans to the Northern Atlantic coast with the prisoner on board, the sentence had been approved, and he was a man without a country.

The plan then adopted was substantially the same which was necessarily followed ever after. Perhaps it was suggested by the necessity of sending him by water from Fort Adams and Orleans. The Secretary of the Navy—it must have been the first Crowninshield, though he is a man I do not remember—was requested to put Nolan on board a government vessel bound on a long cruise, and to direct that he should be only so far confined there as to make it certain that he never saw or heard of the country. We had few long cruises then, and the Navy was very much out of favor; and as almost all of this story is traditional, as I have explained, I do not know certainly what his first cruise was. But the commander to whom he was entrusted—perhaps it was Tingey or Shaw, though I think it was one of the younger men—we are all old enough now—regulated the etiquette and the precautions of the affair, and according to his scheme they were carried out, I suppose, till Nolan died.

When I was second officer of the *Intrepid*, some thirty years after, I saw the original paper of instructions. I have been sorry ever since that I did not copy the whole of it. It ran, however, much in this way:

WASHINGTON (with a date which must have been late in 1807).

SIR,—You will receive from Lieutenant Neale the person of Philip Nolan, late a lieutenant in the United States Army.

This person on his trial by court-martial expressed, with an oath, the wish that he might "never hear of the United States again."

The Court sentenced him to have his wish fulfilled.

For the present, the execution of the order is entrusted by the President to this Department.

You will take the prisoner on board your ship, and keep him there with such precautions as shall prevent his escape.

You will provide him with such quarters, rations, and clothing as would be proper for an officer of his late rank, if he were a passenger on your vessel on the business of his Government.

The gentlemen on board will make any arrangements agreeable to themselves regarding his society. He is to be exposed to no indignity of any kind, nor is he ever unnecessarily to be reminded that he is a prisoner.

But under no circumstances is he ever to hear of his country or to see any information regarding it; and you will especially caution all the officers under your command to take care, that, in the various indulgences which may be granted, this rule, in which his punishment is involved, shall not be broken.

It is the intention of the Government that he shall never again see the country which he has disowned. Before the end of your cruise you will receive orders which will give effect to this intention.

Respectfully yours,
W. SOUTHARD, for the
Secretary of the Navy.

If I had only preserved the whole of this paper, there would be no break in the beginning of my sketch of this story. For Captain Shaw, if

it were he, handed it to his successor in the charge, and he to his, and I suppose the commander of the *Levant* has it today as his authority for keeping this man in this mild custody.

The rule adopted on board the ships on which I have met "the man without a country" was, I think, transmitted from the beginning. No mess liked to have him permanently, because his presence cut off all talk of home or of the prospect of return, of politics or letters, of peace or of war—cut off more than half the talk men liked to have at sea. But it was always thought too hard that he should never meet the rest of us, except to touch hats, and we finally sank into one system. He was not permitted to talk with the men, un-less an officer was by. With officers he had unrestrained intercourse, as far as they and he chose. But he grew shy, though he had favorites: I was one. Then the captain always asked him to dinner on Monday. Every mess in succession took up the invitation in its turn. According to the size of the ship, you had him at your mess more or less often at dinner. His breakfast he ate in his own stateroom—he always had a stateroom—which was where a sentinel or somebody on the watch could see the door. And whatever else he ate or drank, he ate or drank alone. Sometimes, when the marines or sailors had any special jollification, they were permitted to invite "Plain-Buttons," as they called him. Then Nolan was sent with some officer, and the men were forbidden to speak of home while he was there. I believe the theory was that the sight of his punishment did them good. They called him "Plain-Buttons," because, while he always chose to wear a regulation Army uniform, he was not permitted to wear the Army button, for the reason that it bore either the initials or the insignia of the country he had disowned.

I remember, soon after I joined the Navy, I was on shore with some of the older officers from our ship and from the *Brandywine*, which we had met at Alexandria. We had leave to make a party and go up to Cairo and the Pyramids. As we jogged along (you went on donkeys then), some of the gentlemen (we boys called them "Dons," but the phrase was long since changed) fell to talking about Nolan, and someone told the system which was adopted from the first about his books and other reading. As he was almost never permitted to go on shore, even though the vessel lay in port for months, his time at the best hung heavy; and everybody was permitted to lend him books, if they were not published in America and made no allusion to it. These were common enough in the old days, when people in the other hemisphere talked of the United States as little as we do of Paraguay. He had almost all the foreign papers that came into the ship, sooner or later; only somebody must go over them first, and cut out any advertisement or stray paragraph that alluded to America. This was a little cruel

sometimes, when the back of what was cut out might be as innocent as Hesiod. Right in the midst of one of Napoleon's battles, or one of Canning's speeches, poor Nolan would find a great hole, because on the back of the page of that paper there had been an advertisement of a packet for New York, or a scrap from the President's message. I say this was the first time I ever heard of this plan, which afterwards I had enough and more than enough to do with. I remember it, because poor Phillips, who was of the party, as soon as the allusion to reading was made, told a story of something which happened at the Cape of Good Hope on Nolan's first voyage; and it is the only thing I ever knew of that voyage. They had touched at the Cape, and had done the civil thing with the English Admiral and the fleet, and then, leaving for a long cruise up the Indian Ocean, Phillips had borrowed a lot of English books from an officer, which, in those days, as indeed in these, was quite a windfall. Among them, as the devil would order, was the *Lay of the Last Minstrel*,[9] which they had all of them heard of, but which most of them had never seen. I think it could not have been published long. Well, nobody thought there could be any risk of anything national in that, though Phillips swore old Shaw had cut out *The Tempest* from Shakespeare before he let Nolan have it, be-

9 *Lay of the Last Minstrel:* a narrative by Sir Walter Scott; it is set in the Bor ntry between Scotland and England.

cause he said "the Bermudas ought to be ours, and, by Jove, should be one day." So Nolan was permitted to join the circle one afternoon when a lot of them sat on deck smoking and reading aloud. People do not do such things so often now; but when I was young we got rid of a great deal of time so. Well, so it happened that in his turn Nolan took the book and read to the others; and he read very well, as I know. Nobody in the circle knew a line of the poem, only it was all magic and Border chivalry, and was ten thousand years ago. Poor Nolan read steadily through the fifth canto,[10] stopped a minute and drank something, and then began, without a thought of what was coming—

Breathes there the man, with soul so dead,
Who never to himself hath said,—

It seems impossible to us that anybody ever heard this for the first time; but all these fellows did then, and poor Nolan himself went on, still unconsciously or mechanically—

"This is my own, my native land!"

Then they all saw something was to pay; but he expected to get through, I suppose, turned a little pale, but plunged on—

Whose heart hath ne'er within him burned,
As home his footsteps he hath turned
    From wandering on a foreign strand?—
If such there breathe, go, mark him well,—

By this time the men were all beside themselves, wishing there was any way to make him turn over two pages; but he had not quite presence of mind for that; he gagged a little, colored crimson, and staggered on—

For him no minstrel raptures swell;
High though his titles, proud his name,
Boundless his wealth as wish can claim,
Despite these titles, power, and pelf,[11]
The wretch, concentered all in self,—

and here the poor fellow choked, could not go on, but started up, swung the book into the sea, vanished into his stateroom, "And by Jove," said Phillips, "we did not see him for two months again. And when we came back to the Cape I had to make up some beggarly story to that English surgeon why I did not return his Walter Scott to him."

That story shows about the time when Nolan's braggadocio must have broken down. At first, they said, he took a very high tone, considered his imprisonment a mere farce, affected to enjoy the voyage, and all that; but Phillips said that after he came out of his stateroom he never was the same man again. He never read aloud again, unless it was the Bible or Shakespeare, or something else he was sure of. But it was not that merely. He never entered in with the other young men exactly as a companion again. He was always shy afterwards, when I knew him— very seldom spoke, unless he was spoken to, except to a very few friends. He lighted up occasionally —I remember late in his life hearing him fairly eloquent on something which had been suggested to him by one of Fléchier's sermons—but gen-

10 **canto:** one of the chief divisions of a long poem.

11 **pelf:** money; gain.

erally he had the nervous, tired look of a heart-wounded man.

When Captain Shaw was coming home—if, as I say, it was Shaw—rather to the surprise of everybody they made one of the Windward Islands, and lay off and on for nearly a week. The boys said the officers were sick of salt-junk, and meant to have turtle soup before they came home. But after several days the *Warren* came to the same rendezvous; they exchanged signals; she sent to Phillips and these homeward-bound men letters and papers, and told them she was outward-bound, perhaps to the Mediterranean, and took poor Nolan and his traps[12] on the boat back to try his second cruise. He looked very blank when he was told to get ready to join her. He had known enough of the signs of the sky to know that till that moment he was going "home." But this was a distinct evidence of something he had not thought of, perhaps—that there was no going home for him, even to a prison. And this was the first of some twenty such transfers, which brought him sooner or later into half our best vessels, but which kept him all his life at least some hundred miles from the country he had hoped he might never hear of again.

It may have been on that second cruise—it was once when he was up the Mediterranean—that Mrs. Graff, the celebrated Southern beauty of those days, danced with him. They had been lying a long time in the Bay of Naples, and the officers were very intimate in the English fleet, and there had been great festivities, and our men thought they must give a great ball on board the ship. How they ever did it on board the *Warren* I am sure I do not know. Perhaps it was not the *Warren,* or perhaps ladies did not take up so much room as they do now. They wanted to use Nolan's stateroom for something, and they hated to do it without asking him to the ball; so the captain said they might ask him, if they would be responsible that he did not talk with the wrong people, "who would give him intelligence." So the dance went on, the finest party that had ever been known, I dare say; for I never heard of a man-of-war ball that was not. For ladies they had the family of the American consul, one or two travelers who had adventured so far, and a nice bevy of English girls and matrons, perhaps Lady Hamilton herself.

Well, different officers relieved each other in standing and talking with Nolan in a friendly way, so as to be sure that nobody else spoke to him. The dancing went on with spirit, and after a while even the fellows who took this honorary guard of Nolan ceased to fear any *contretemps.*[13] Only when some English lady—Lady Hamilton, as I said, perhaps—called for a set of "American dances," an odd thing happened. Everybody then danced contradances.[14] The black band, nothing

13 *contretemps* (kôN trə täN′): embarrassing occurrence.
14 **contra-dances:** country dances.

12 **traps:** personal belongings.

AMERICA IN FOLKLORE AND TALES

EDWARD EVERETT HALE

loath, conferred as to what "American dances" were, and started off with "Virginia Reel," which they followed with "Money Musk," which, in its turn in those days, should have been followed by "The Old Thirteen." But just as Dick, the leader, tapped for his fiddles to begin, and bent forward, about to say, in true Negro state, " 'The Old Thirteen,' gentlemen and ladies!" as he had said " 'Virginny Reel,' if you please!" and " 'Money Musk,' if you please!" the captain's boy tapped him on the shoulder whispered to him, and he did not announce the name of the dance; he merely bowed, began on the air, and they all fell to—the officers teaching the English girls the figure, but not telling them why it had no name.

But that is not the story I started to tell. As the dancing went on, Nolan and our fellows all got at ease, as I said—so much so, that it seemed quite natural for him to bow to that splendid Mrs. Graff, and say—

"I hope you have not forgotten me, Miss Rutledge. Shall I have the honor of dancing?"

He did it so quickly that Fellows, who was with him, could not hinder him. She laughed, and said—

"I am not Miss Rutledge any longer, Mr. Nolan; but I will dance all the same,"—just nodded to Fellows, as if to say he must leave Mr. Nolan to her, and led him off to the place where the dance was forming.

Nolan thought he had got his chance. He had known her at Philadelphia, and at other places had met her, and this was a godsend. You could not talk in contra-dances, as you do in cotillions, or even in the pauses of waltzing; but there were chances for tongues and sounds, as well as for eyes and blushes. He began with her travels, and Europe, and Vesuvius, and the French; and then, when they had worked down, and had that long talking time at the bottom of the set, he said boldly—a little pale, she said, as she told me the story years after—

"And what do you hear from home, Mrs. Graff?"

And that splended creature looked through him. Jove! how she must have looked through him!

"Home!! Mr. Nolan!!! I thought you were the man who never wanted to hear of home again!"—and she walked directly up the deck to her husband, and left poor Nolan alone, as he always was.—He did not dance again.

I cannot give any history of him in order; nobody can now; and, indeed, I am not trying to. These are the traditions, which I sort out, as I believe them, from the myths which have been told about this man for forty years. The lies that have been told about him are legion. The fellows used to say he was the "Iron Mask"; and poor George Pons went to his grave in the belief that this was the author of "Junius," who was being punished for his celebrated libel on Thomas Jefferson. Pons was not very strong in the historical line.

A happier story than either of these I have told is of the war. That came along soon after. I have heard this affair told in three or four ways—and, indeed, it may have happened more than once. But which ship it was on I cannot tell. However, in one, at least, of the great frigate-duels with the English, in which the Navy was really baptized, it happened that a round shot from the enemy entered one of our ports square, and took right down the officer of the gun himself, and almost every man of the gun's crew. Now you may say what you choose about courage, but that is not a nice thing to see. But, as the men who were not killed picked themselves up, and as they and the surgeon's people were carrying off the bodies, there appeared Nolan, in his shirt-sleeves, with the rammer in his hand, and, just as if he had been the officer, told them off with authority—who should go to the cockpit with the wounded men, who should stay with him—perfectly cheery, and with that way which makes men feel sure all is right and is going to be right. And he finished loading the gun with his own hands, aimed it, and bade the men fire. And there he stayed, captain of that gun, keeping those fellows in spirits, till the enemy struck—sitting on the carriage while the gun was cooling, though he was exposed all the time—showing them easier ways to handle heavy shot—making the raw hands laugh at their own blunders—and when the gun cooled again, getting it loaded and fired twice as often as any other gun on the ship. The captain walked forward by way of encouraging the men, and Nolan touched his hat and said—

"I am showing them how we do this in the artillery, sir."

And this is the part of the story where all the legends agree; the commodore said—

"I see you do, and I thank you, sir; and I shall never forget this day, sir, and you never shall, sir."

And after the whole thing was over, and he had had the Englishman's sword, in the midst of the state and ceremony of the quarter-deck, he said—

"Where is Mr. Nolan? Ask Mr. Nolan to come here."

And when Nolan came, he said—

"Mr. Nolan, we are all very grateful to you today; you are one of us today; you will be named in the dispatches."

And then the old man took off his own sword of ceremony, and gave it to Nolan, and made him put it on. The man told me this who saw it. Nolan cried like a baby, and well he might. He had not worn a sword since that infernal day at Fort Adams. But always afterwards, on occasions of ceremony, he wore that quaint old French sword of the commodore's.

The captain did mention him in the dispatches. It was always said he asked that he might be pardoned. He wrote a special letter to the Secretary of War. But nothing ever came of it. As I said, that was about the time when they began to ignore the whole transaction at Washington, and when Nolan's imprisonment began to carry itself on because there was nobody to stop it without any new orders from home.

I have heard it said that he was with Porter when he took possession of the Nukahiva Islands.[15] Not this Porter, you know, but old Porter, his father, Essex Porter—that is, the old Essex Porter, not this Essex. As an artillery officer, who had seen service in the West, Nolan knew more about fortifications, embrasures, ravelins, stockades, and all that, than any of them did; and he worked with a right good will in fixing that battery all right. I have always thought it was a pity Porter did not leave him in command there with Gamble. That would have settled all the question about his punishment. We should have kept the islands, and at this moment we should have one station in the Pacific Ocean. Our French friends, too, when they wanted this little watering place, would have found it was preoccupied. But Madison and the Virginians, of course, flung all that away.

All that was near fifty years ago. If Nolan was thirty then, he must have been near eighty when he died. He looked sixty when he was forty. But he never seemed to me to change a hair afterwards. As I imagine his life, from what I have seen and heard of it, he must have been in every sea, and yet almost never on land. He must have known, in a formal way, more officers in our service than any man living knows. He told me once, with a grave smile, that no man in the world lived so methodical a life as he. "You know the boys say I am the Iron Mask, and you know how busy he was." He said it did not do for anyone to try to read all the time, more than to do anything else all the time; but that he read just five hours a day. "Then," he said, "I keep up my notebooks, writing in them at such and such hours from what I have been reading; and I include in these my scrapbooks." These were very curious indeed. He had six or eight, of different subjects. There was one of History, one of Natural Science, one which he called "Odds and Ends." But they were not merely books of extracts from newspapers. They had bits of plants and ribbons, shells tied on, and carved scraps of bone and wood, which he had taught the men to cut for him, and they were beautifully illustrated. He drew admirably. He had some of the funniest drawings there and some of the most pathetic, that I have ever seen in my life. I wonder who will have Nolan's scrapbooks.

Well, he said his reading and his notes were his profession, and that they took five hours and two hours, respectively, of each day. "Then," said he, "every man should have a diversion as well as a profession. My Natural History is my diversion." That took two hours a day more.

15 Porter . . . Islands: David Porter, commander of the *Essex*, in 1813 arranged to annex the Marquesas Islands, of which Nukahiva is the largest, to the United States; but Congress took no action. The islands were annexed to France in 1842. Porter's son, David Dixon Porter, also a naval officer, is referred to in the next sentence as "this Porter."

The men used to bring him birds and fish, but on a long cruise he had to satisfy himself with centipedes and cockroaches and such small game. He was the only naturalist I ever met who knew anything about the habits of the housefly and the mosquito. All those people can tell you whether they are *Lepidoptera* or *Steptopotera;* but as for telling how you can get rid of them, or how they get away from you when you strike them—why Linnaeus[16] knew as little of that as John Foy the idiot did. These nine hours made Nolan's regular daily "occupation." The rest of the time he talked or walked. Till he grew very old, he went aloft a great deal. He always kept up his exercise; and I never heard that he was ill. If any other man was ill, he was the kindest nurse in the world; and he knew more than half the surgeons do. Then if anybody was sick or died, or if the captain wanted him to, on any other occasion, he was always ready to read prayers. I have said that he read beautifully.

My own acquaintance with Philip Nolan began six or eight years after the English war, on my first voyage after I was appointed a midshipman. It was in the first days after our Slave Trade treaty, while the Reigning House, which was still the House of Virginia, had still a sort of sentimentalism about the suppression of the horrors of the Middle Passage,[17] and something was sometimes done

that way. We were in the South Atlantic on that business. From the time I joined, I believe I thought Nolan was a sort of lay chaplain—a chaplain with a blue coat. I never asked about him. Everything in the ship was strange to me. I knew it was green to ask questions, and I suppose I thought there was a "Plain-Buttons" on every ship. We had him to dine in our mess once a week, and the caution was given that on that day nothing was to be said about home. But if they had told us not to say anything about the planet Mars or the Book of Deuteronomy, I should not have asked why; there were a great many things which seemed to me to have as little reason. I first came to understand anything about "the man without a country" one day when we overhauled a dirty little schooner which had slaves on board. An officer was sent to take charge of her, and, after a few minutes, he sent back his boat to ask that some one might be sent him who could speak Portuguese. We were all looking over the rail when the message came, and we all wished we could interpret, when the captain asked who spoke Portuguese. But none of the officers did; and just as the captain was sending forward to ask if any of the people could, Nolan stepped out and said he should be glad to interpret, if the captain wished, as he understood the language. The captain thanked him, fitted out another boat with

---

16 **Linnaeus:** 18th-century Swedish botanist who originated the modern system of classifying plants and animals.

17 **Middle Passage:** middle part of the journey of a slave from Africa to America; the trip across the Atlantic Ocean.

him, and in this boat it was my luck to go. When we got there, it was such a scene as you seldom see, and never want to. Nastiness beyond account, and chaos run loose in the midst of the nastiness. There were not a great many of the Negroes; but by way of making what there were understand that they were free, Vaughan had had their handcuffs and ankle-cuffs knocked off, and, for convenience' sake, was putting them upon the rascals of the schooner's crew. The Negroes were, most of them, out of the hold and swarming all round the dirty deck, with a central throng surrounding Vaughan and addressing him in every dialect, and *patois*[18] of a dialect, from the Zulu click up to the Parisian of Beledeljereed.

As we came on deck, Vaughan looked down from a hogshead, on which he had mounted in desperation, and said:

"For God's love, is there anybody who can make these wretches understand something? The men gave them rum, and that did not quiet them. I knocked that big fellow down twice, and that did not soothe him. And then I talked Choctaw to all of them together; and I'll be hanged if they understood that as well as they understood the English."

Nolan said he could speak Portuguese, and one or two fine-looking Kroomen were dragged out, who, as it had been found already, had worked for the Portuguese on the coast at Fernando Po.

"Tell them they are free," said Vaughan; "and tell them that these rascals are to be hanged as soon as we can get rope enough."

Nolan "put that into Spanish"— that is, he explained it in such Portuguese as the Kroomen could understand, and they in turn to such of the Negroes as could understand them. Then there was such a yell of delight, clinching of fists, leaping and dancing, kissing of Nolan's feet, and a general rush made to the hogshead by way of spontaneous worship of Vaughan, as the *deus ex machina*[19] of the occasion.

"Tell them," said Vaughan, well pleased, "that I will take them all to Cape Palmas."

This did not answer so well. Cape Palmas was practically as far from the homes of most of them as New Orleans or Rio Janeiro was; that is, they would be eternally separated from home there. And their interpreters, as we could understand, instantly said, *"Ah, non Palmas,"* and began to propose infinite other expedients in most voluble language. Vaughan was rather disappointed at this result of his liberality, and asked Nolan eagerly what they said. The drops stood on poor Nolan's white forehead, as he hushed the men down, and said:

"He says, 'Not Palmas.' He says, 'Take us home, take us to our own country, take us to our own house, take us to our own children and our own women.' He says he has an

18 *patois* (păt′wä): peasant form of speech.

19 *deus ex machina* (dē′əs eks măk′ə nə): here, a person introduced to solve a difficulty.

old father and mother who will die if they do not see him. And this one says he left his people all sick, and paddled down to Fernando to beg the white doctor to come and help them, and that these devils caught him in the bay just in sight of home, and that he has never seen anybody from home since then. And this one says," choked out Nolan, "that he has not heard a word from his home in six months, while he has been locked up in an infernal barracoon."[20]

Vaughan always said he grew gray himself while Nolan struggled through this interpretation. I, who did not understand anything of the passion involved in it, saw that the very elements were melting with fervent heat, and that something was to pay somewhere. Even the Negroes themselves stopped howling, as they saw Nolan's agony, and Vaughan's almost equal agony of sympathy. As quick as he could get words, he said:

"Tell them yes, yes, yes; tell them they shall go to the Mountains of the Moon, if they will. If I sail the schooner through the Great White Desert, they shall go home!"

And after some fashion Nolan said so. And then they all fell to kissing him again, and wanted to rub his nose with theirs.

But he could not stand it long; and getting Vaughan to say he might go back, he beckoned me down into our boat. As we lay back in the stern sheets and the men gave way, he said to me: "Youngster, let that show you what it is to be without a family, without a home, and without a country. And if you are ever tempted to say a word or to do a thing that shall put a bar between you and your family, your home, and your country, pray God in his mercy to take you that instant home to his own heaven. Stick by your family, boy; forget you have a self, while you do everything for them. Think of your home, boy; write and send, and talk about it. Let it be nearer and nearer to your thought the farther you have to travel from it; and rush back to it when you are free, as that poor black slave is doing now. And for your country, boy," and the words rattled in his throat, "and for that flag," and he pointed to the ship, "never dream a dream but of serving her as she bids you, though the service carry you through a thousand hells. No matter what happens to you, no matter who flatters you or who abuses you, never look at another flag, never let a night pass but you pray God to bless that flag. Remember, boy, that behind all these men you have to do with, behind officers, and government, and people even, there is the Country Herself, your Country, and that you belong to Her as you belong to your own mother. Stand by Her, boy, as you would stand by your mother if those devils there had got hold of her today!"

I was frightened to death by his calm, hard passion; but I blundered out that I would, by all that was holy, and that I had never thought

20 barracoon: barrack for confining slaves.

of doing anything else. He hardly seemed to hear me; but he did, almost in a whisper, say: "O, if anybody had said so to me when I was of your age!"

I think it was this half-confidence of his, which I never abused, for I never told this story till now, which afterward made us great friends. He was very kind to me. Often he sat up, or even got up, at night, to walk the deck with me, when it was my watch. He explained to me a great deal of my mathematics, and I owe to him my taste for mathematics. He lent me books, and helped me about my reading. He never alluded so directly to his story again; but from one and another officer I have learned, in thirty years, what I am telling. When we parted from him in St. Thomas harbor, at the end of our cruise, I was more sorry than I can tell. I was very glad to meet him again in 1830; and later in life, when I thought I had some influence in Washington, I moved heaven and earth to have him discharged. But it was like getting a ghost out of prison. They pretended there was no such man, and never was such a man. They will say so at the Department now! Perhaps they do not know. It will not be the first thing in the service of which the Department appears to know nothing!

There is a story that Nolan met Burr once on one of our vessels, when a party of Americans came on board in the Mediterranean. But this I believe to be a lie; or, rather, it is a myth *ben trovato*,[21] involving a tremendous blowing-up with which he sunk Burr—asking him how he liked to be "without a country." But it is clear from Burr's life, that nothing of the sort could have happened; and I mention this only as an illustration of the stories which get a-going where there is the least mystery at bottom.

So poor Philip Nolan had his wish fulfilled. I know but one fate more dreadful; it is the fate reserved for those men who shall have one day to exile themselves from their country because they have attempted her ruin, and shall have, at the same time, to see the prosperity and honor to which she rises when she has rid herself of them and their iniquities. The wish of poor Nolan, as we all learned to call him, not because his punishment was too great, but because his repentance was so clear, was precisely the wish of every Bragg and Beauregard[22] who broke a soldier's oath two years ago, and of every Maury and Barron[23] who broke a sailor's. I do not know how often they have repented. I do know that they have done all that in them lay that they might have no country—that all the honors, associations, memories, and hopes which belong to "country" might be broken up into little shreds and distributed to the winds. I know, too,

that their punishment, as they vegetate through what is left of life to them in wretched Boulognes and Leicester Squares, where they are destined to upbraid each other till they die, will have all the agony of Nolan's, with the added pang that everyone who sees them will see them to despise and to execrate them. They will have their wish, like him.

For him, poor fellow, he repented of his folly, and then, like a man, submitted to the fate he had asked for. He never intentionally added to the difficulty or delicacy of the charge of those who had him in hold. Accidents would happen; but they never happened from his fault. Lieutenant Truxton told me that, when Texas was annexed, there was a careful discussion among the officers, whether they should get hold of Nolan's handsome set of maps and cut Texas out of it—from the map of the world and the map of Mexico. The United States had been cut out when the atlas was bought for him. But it was voted, rightly enough, that to do this would be virtually to reveal to him what had happened, or, as Harry Cole said, to make him think Old Burr had succeeded. So it was from no fault of Nolan's that a great botch happened at my own table, when, for a short time, I was in command of the George Washington corvette, on the South American

21 *ben trovato*: well conceived.
22 **Bragg and Beauregard:** Braxton Bragg and Pierre Gustave Toutant Beauregard were Confederate generals.
23 **Maury and Barron:** Matthew Fontaine Maury resigned as a commander in the United States

Navy to serve the Confederacy. James Barron, an American naval officer, was court-martialed and suspended from the Navy for five years, after an incident in 1807 in which his flagship, the *Chesapeake*, was halted and attacked by the British warship *Leopard*.

station. We were lying in the La
Plata, and some of the officers, who
had been on shore and had just
joined again, were entertaining us
with accounts of their misadventures
in riding the half-wild horses of
Buenos Aires. Nolan was at table,
and was in an unusually bright and
talkative mood. Some story of a
tumble reminded him of an adventure of his own when he was catching wild horses in Texas with his
adventurous cousin, at a time when
he must have been quite a boy.
He told the story with a good deal
of spirit—so much so, that the silence which often follows a good
story hung over the table for an
instant, to be broken by Nolan himself. For he asked perfectly unconsciously:

"Pray, what has become of Texas?
After the Mexicans got their independence, I thought that province
of Texas would come forward very
fast. It is really one of the finest
regions on earth; it is the Italy of
this continent. But I have not seen
or heard a word of Texas for near
twenty years."

There were two Texan officers at
the table. The reason he had never
heard of Texas was that Texas and
her affairs had been painfully cut
out of his newspapers since Austin
began his settlements; so that, while
he read of Honduras and Tamauli-
pas, and, till quite lately, of California—this virgin province, in which
his brother had traveled so far, and,
I believe, had died, had ceased to
be to him. Waters and Williams, the
two Texas men, looked grimly at
each other and tried not to laugh.
Edward Morris had his attention
attracted by the third link in the
chain of the captain's chandelier.
Watrous was seized with a convul-
sion of sneezing. Nolan himself saw
that something was to pay, he did
not know what. And I, as master
of the feast, had to say—

"Texas is out of the map, Mr.
Nolan. Have you seen Captain
Back's curious account of Sir Thomas
Roe's Welcome?"

After that cruise I never saw Nolan again. I wrote to him at least
twice a year, for in that voyage we
became even confidentially intimate;
but he never wrote to me. The
other men tell me that in those fifteen years he *aged* very fast, as well
he might indeed, but that he was
still the same gentle, uncomplaining,
silent sufferer that he ever was,
bearing as best he could his self-
appointed punishment—rather less
social, perhaps, with new men whom
he did not know, but more anxious,
apparently, than ever to serve and
befriend and teach the boys, some
of whom fairly seemed to worship
him. And now it seems the dear
old fellow is dead. He has found
a home at last, and a country.

Since writing this, and while considering whether or no I would print
it, as a warning to the young Nolans
and Vallandighams and Tattnalls[24]
of today of what it is to throw away

24 **Vallandighams and Tattnalls:** Clement Laird
Vallandigham, an Ohio politician, was banished
from the United States in 1863, after he was
court-martialed for treasonable statements. Josiah
Tattnall was a United States naval officer who in
1861 became a captain in the Confederate Navy.

a country, I have received from Danforth, who is on board the *Levant,* a letter which gives an account of Nolan's last hours. It removes all my doubts about telling this story.

To understand the first words of the letter, the nonprofessional reader should remember that after 1817 the position of every officer who had Nolan in charge was one of the greatest delicacy. The government had failed to renew the order of 1807 regarding him. What was a man to do? Should he let him go? What, then, if he were called to account by the Department for violating the order of 1807? Should he keep him? What, then, if Nolan should be liberated some day, and should bring an action for false imprisonment or kidnapping against every man who had had him in charge? I urged and pressed this upon Southard, and I have reason to think that other officers did the same thing. But the Secretary always said, as they so often do at Washington, that there were no special orders to give, and that we must act on our own judgment. That means, "If you succeed, you will be sustained; if you fail, you will be disavowed." Well, as Danforth says, all that is over now, though I do not know but I expose myself to a criminal prosecution on the evidence of the very revelation I am making.

Here is the letter:

"LEVANT, 2° 2′ S. @ 131° W.

"DEAR FRED:— I try to find heart and life to tell you that it is all over with dear old Nolan. I have been with him on this voyage more than I ever was, and I can understand wholly now the way in which you used to speak of the dear old fellow. I could see that he was not strong, but I had no idea the end was so near. The doctor has been watching him very carefully, and yesterday morning came to me and told me that Nolan was not so well, and had not left his stateroom—a thing I never remember before. He had let the doctor come and see him as he lay there—the first time the doctor had been in the stateroom—and he said he should like to see me. Oh, dear! do you remember the mysteries we boys used to invent about his room in the old *Intrepid* days? Well, I went in, and there, to be sure, the poor fellow lay in his berth, smiling pleasantly as he gave me his hand, but looking very frail. I could not help a glance round, which showed me what a little shrine he had made of the box he was lying in. The stars and stripes were triced up above and around a picture of Washington, and he had painted a majestic eagle, with lightnings blazing from his beak and his foot just clasping the whole globe, which his wings overshadowed. The dear old boy saw my glance, and said with a sad smile, 'Here, you see, I have a country!' And then he pointed to the foot of his bed, where I had not seen before a great map of the United States, as he had drawn it from memory, and which he had there to look upon as he lay. Quaint, queer old names were on it, in large letters: 'Indiana Territory,' 'Mississippi Territory,' and 'Louisiana Territory,' as I suppose our fathers learned such things: but the old fellow had patched in Texas, too; he had carried his western boundary all the way to the Pacific, but on that shore he had defined nothing.

" 'O Danforth,' he said, 'I know I am dying. I cannot get home. Surely you will tell me something now?—Stop! stop! Do not speak till I say what I am sure you know, that there is not in this ship, that there is not in America—God bless her!—a more loyal man than I. There cannot be a man who loves the old flag as I do, or prays for it as I do, or hopes for it as I do. There are thirty-four stars in it now, Danforth. I thank God for that, though I do not know what their names are. There has never been one taken away: I thank God for that. I know by that that there has never been any successful Burr. O Danforth, Danforth,' he sighed out, 'how like a wretched night's dream a boy's idea of personal fame or of separate sovereignty seems, when one looks back on it after such a life as mine! But tell me—tell me something—tell me everything, Danforth, before I die!'

"Ingham, I swear to you that I felt like a monster that I had not told him everything before. Danger or no danger, delicacy or no delicacy, who was I, that I should have been acting the tyrant all this time over this dear, sainted old man, who had years ago expiated, in his whole manhood's life, the madness of a boy's treason? 'Mr. Nolan,' said I,

'I will tell you everything you ask about. Only, where shall I begin?'

"Oh, the blessed smile that crept over his white face! and he pressed my hand and said, 'God bless you!' 'Tell me their names,' he said, and he pointed to the stars on the flag. 'The last I know is Ohio. My father lived in Kentucky. But I have guessed Michigan and Indiana and Mississippi—that was where Fort Adams is —they make twenty. But where are your other fourteen? You have not cut up any of the old ones, I hope?'

"Well, that was not a bad text, and I told him the names in as good order as I could, and he bade me take down his beautiful map and draw them in as I best could with my pencil. He was wild with delight about Texas, told me how his cousin died there; he had marked a gold cross near where he supposed his grave was; and he had guessed at Texas. Then he was delighted as he saw California and Oregon;—that, he said, he had suspected partly, because he had never been permitted to land on that shore, though the ships were there so much. 'And the men,' said he, laughing, 'brought off a good deal besides furs.' Then he went back—heavens, how far!— to ask about the *Chesapeake*, and what was done to Barron for surrendering her to the *Leopard*, and whether Burr ever tried again—and he ground his teeth with the only passion he showed. But in a moment that was over, and he said, 'God forgive me, for I am sure I forgive him.' Then he asked about the old war—told me the true story of his serving the gun the day we took the *Java*—asked about dear old David Porter, as he called him. Then he settled down more quietly, and very happily, to hear me tell in an hour the history of fifty years.

"How I wished it had been somebody who knew something! But I did as well as I could. I told him of the English war. I told him about Fulton and the steamboat beginning. I told him about old Scott, and Jackson; told him all I could think of about the Mississippi, and New Orleans, and Texas, and his own old Kentucky. And do you think, he asked who was in command of the 'Legion of the West.' I told him it was a very gallant officer named Grant, and that, by our last news he was about to establish his headquarters at Vicksburg. Then, 'Where was Vicksburg?' I worked that out on the map; it was about a hundred miles, more or less, above his old Fort Adams; and I thought Fort Adams must be a ruin now. 'It must be at old Vick's plantation, at Walnut Hills,' said he; 'well, that is a change!'

"I tell you, Ingham, it was a hard thing to condense the history of half a century into that talk with a sick man. And I do not know what I told him—of emigration, and the means of it—of steamboats, and railroads, and telegraphs, of inventions, and books, and literature—of the colleges and West Point, and the Naval School—but with the queerest interruptions that ever you heard. You see it was Robinson Crusoe asking all the accumulated questions of fifty-six years!

"I remember he asked all of a sudden, who was President now; and when I told him, he asked if Old Abe was General Benjamin Lincoln's son. He said he met old General Lincoln, when he was quite a boy himself, at some Indian treaty. I said no, that Old Abe was a Kentuckian like himself, but I could not tell him of what family; he had worked up from the ranks. 'Good for him!' cried Nolan; 'I am glad of that. As I have brooded and wondered, I have thought our danger was in keeping up those regular successions in the first families.' Then I got talking about my visit to Washington. I told him of meeting the Oregon Congressman, Harding; I told him about the Smithsonian, and the Exploring Expedition; I told him about the Capitol, and the statues for the pediments, and Crawford's Liberty, and Greenough's Washington: Ingham, I told him everything that I could think of that would show the grandeur of his country and its prosperity; but I could not make up my mouth to tell him a word about this infernal rebellion!

"And he drank it in and enjoyed it as I cannot tell you. He grew more and more silent, yet I never thought he was tired or faint. I gave him a glass of water, but he just wet his lips, and told me not to go away. Then he asked me to bring the Presbyterian 'Book of Public Prayer,' which lay there, and said, with a smile, that it would open at the right place—and so it did. There was his double red mark down the page; and I knelt down and read, and he repeated with me, 'For ourselves and our country, O gracious God, we thank Thee, that notwithstanding our manifold transgressions of Thy holy laws, Thou hast continued to us Thy marvelous kindness,'—and so to the end of that thanksgiving. Then he turned to the end of the same book, and I read the words more familiar to me: 'Most heartily we beseech Thee with Thy favor to behold and bless Thy servant, the President of the United States, and all others in authority'— and the rest of the Episcopal collect. 'Danforth,' said he, 'I have repeated those prayers night and morning, it is now fifty-five years.' And then he said he would go to sleep. He bent me down over him and kissed me; and he said, 'Look in my Bible, Danforth, when I am gone.' And I went away.

"But I had no thought it was the end. I thought he was tired and would sleep. I knew he was happy, and I wanted him to be alone.

"But in an hour, when the doctor went in gently, he found Nolan had breathed his life away with a smile. He had something pressed close to his lips. It was his father's badge of the Order of the Cincinnati.

"We looked in his Bible, and there was a slip of paper at the place where he had marked the text:

"'They desire a country, even a heavenly: wherefore God is not ashamed to be called their God: for He hath prepared for them a city.'

"On this slip of paper he had written:

"'Bury me in the sea; it has been my home, and I love it. But will not someone set up a stone for my memory at Fort Adams or at Orleans, that my disgrace may not be more than I ought to bear? Say on it:

'In Memory of

'PHILIP NOLAN,

'Lieutenant of the Army of the United States.

'He loved his country as no other man has loved her; but no man deserved less at her hands.'"

Reading Skills

1. According to the author, why has the story of Philip Nolan never been told before?
2. Why does Philip Nolan succumb to Aaron Burr's influence?
3. What conditions in Nolan's early years are partly responsible for his lack of loyalty to his country? Do these conditions excuse him? Explain.
4. What is Nolan's first reaction to his sentence when it is pronounced by the judge?
5. Explain the plan that carries out Nolan's expressed wish.

6. In what ways does Nolan change after his reading of the lines from Scott's poem "The Lay of the Last Minstrel"? after his rebuff by Mrs. Graff at the ball?

7. Why do Nolan's courageous acts in the war not result in his freedom?

8. What does the routine that Nolan adopts indicate about his character as he matures?

9. Explain the incident that brings to Nolan his most painful recognition of his homelessness.

10. What does the narrator, as master of the feast, mean by his answer to Nolan's question about Texas? Why does he find the answer so hard to give?

11. Describe the "country" that Nolan creates for himself in his stateroom.

12. What do Nolan's last requests reveal about his character?

Understanding Literature

1. The plot of this story falls into two major divisions: (*a*) explanation of Nolan's background, and (*b*) episodes during Nolan's exile, showing his character development. Outline the order in which the episodes are told. What does each contribute to your understanding of Nolan's character? to the plot of the story?

2. The narrator says that Nolan is known by sailors as "The Man without a Country," not as Philip Nolan. The sailors also give him two other names. What are they? What do they indicate about his character?

3. In the story are a number of facts about the narrator's life and suggestions about his character. What is his occupation? Where does he get his information about Nolan? Why does he tell Nolan's story? What traits of character has the narrator?

4. In what ways would the story have been different if the author had written it as though Nolan were telling it? What points would probably have been omitted? What could have been included that is not in the story?

5. The story begins and ends with accounts of Nolan's death. How does the tone of these two accounts differ? Why is the second an appropriate climax and ending to the story of "The Man without a Country"?

6. In his letter describing Nolan's death, Danforth writes, "I could not make up my mouth to tell him a word about this infernal rebellion." To what "rebellion" is he referring? How does the time of this story contribute to the theme of loyalty to the United States?

Further Activity

Do you think that Nolan's punishment fitted his crime? Write your answer to this question in a theme of three carefully constructed paragraphs in which you include:
(a) A description of the crime,
(b) A brief explanation of the punishment, and
(c) An explanation of why you do, or do not, think that Nolan's punishment fitted his crime. Use illustrations and proof from the story.

Exaggeration has always been characteristic of American legend. From colonial times to the present, the tall tale has had a special fascination.

Wilbur Schramm is a modern author. Oliver Wendell Holmes, who wrote "The Deacon's Masterpiece," lived more than a hundred years ago. Yet the two men seem to have found pleasure in telling a tall tale about an impossible means of transportation.

Windwagon Smith

Wilbur Schramm

IMPROVING YOUR READING: Although in "Windwagon Smith" the action, the language, and the character of Windwagon involve humorous exaggeration, the story suggests an important truth about American life and character. As you read, decide what kind of person Windwagon is. How does his character contrast with Shelby Foster's? What do the people of Westport admire in Windwagon's character? Finally, how is he representative of the American pioneer spirit?

WINDWAGON SMITH HAD a face like any other man, and two legs to walk on, but the morning he rode into Westport the quietest mule in town jumped sixteen feet. And some men would have flown like bald eagles that day, if they could.

That was when Westport was the great city of the prairie. Now it is only a far corner of Kansas City and smells like gasoline and coal smoke, but in those days it smelled of prairie grass and clean wind, and was on every road west. No matter where you were going beyond the Missouri, you started at Westport. You followed a rutted trail twenty miles from town to a meadow where Jake Shafer's Negro boy had nailed a box top to a runt cottonwood and painted on it, "Rode to Oregon." There the families for Oregon turned north, and the wagons for Sante Fe

and the Spanish cities southwest. West of the crossing, two hundred miles of grass rolled away to the sky, waist-high, blowing black and green and yellow. Your shoes got slick as lard in that grass. Then you came out into the sagebrush, and the grit chewed off your soles and left you barefoot. And about that time the Comanches would come yelling out of the sand hills. All the way across a thousand miles of empty prairie you would wish you were back in Westport, sitting in Punch Dunkelberger's Star of the West saloon, listening to Jake Shafer tell how Davy Crockett could grin the bark off a tree.

Westport could have been the greatest city in the United States. It could have been Boston and New York and Detroit pressed into one and set down in the middle of the prairie, if it hadn't made one mistake. That was about Windwagon Smith.

The morning Windwagon came, Punch Dunkelberger's hound dog woke up bristling like a hairbrush. That dog always slept until noon under his master's hat peg in the Star of the West; he had slept through a cyclone and seven street fights. But that morning he woke up about ten o'clock, waved his nose in the air, howled a long quaver, and slunk into a closet. Two Pawnees in the Star looked at the dog and blew away like smoke. Jake Shafer changed his seat and drew a bead on the door. The door opened slowly. But only Shelby Foster glided in, with his apologetic way, giving a little bow before speaking, because he was from the East and knew manners. When he tried to talk he was so excited he couldn't squeeze the words out, and stood there with his mouth mostly open, his eyes big as soap kettles, and a silly polite look on his face, waving his hands toward the street as though he were batting gnats.

"I never hoped to see the Missouri flow juleps," said Jake Shafer, "or a gopher running a coyote, or Foster without anything to say."

Foster looked behind him and croaked and skipped aside, and there was a crash, and the head and shoulders of Jake's mule Martha appeared in the doorway. The doors slammed back and caught the mule's neck in a pincers, and there she stood like a moose head on the wall, rolling her eyes.

"I can stand bugs in the beer," bellowed Jake in his big barrel voice, "but when the draft animals come in I go out."

When they went out, there was Windwagon Smith.

All they saw at first was a Conestoga wagon coming down the street between the log houses. It was like any other Conestoga wagon, sway-backed, with a horseshoe canvas top. Except for one thing: there was nothing in front of it.

No oxen, no mules, no horses. Nothing. The wagon was just coming down the street.

The Pawnees were peeking from behind trees. . . . The dogs were barking, and the ponies that hadn't run away were pulling at their hackamores.[1]

"He's got a sail," said Punch suddenly.

A pole stuck up out of the wagon like a ship's mast, and on it a square of canvas turned half sideways to catch the quartering wind.

A little man in blue denim was riding on the wagon seat. He furled the sail in quick movements, locked the wagon wheel, and came to a stop exactly where Jake's mule had been. When he hopped down from the wagon he walked with a sailor's roll and sway. The dogs quit barking and balanced on their hind legs, ready to go either way. It was so quiet you could hear the stranger's feet crunch in the dust and sand.

"Ahoy!" he said out of the silence. "Think I'll drop anchor and come ashore for a bit of refreshment."

1 hackamores: halters.

His voice was deep and rolling, with something about it that prolonged the *r*'s and clipped the consonants like axbites in an oak tree.

"My name's Smith," he explained. "I'm the master, the crew, and most of the cargo of this ship, and I aim to do a lot of sailing on the prairie." There was never so much *r* in prairie until he said it.

It was Painted Dog, a Pawnee, who really named him. Painted Dog had been behind the nearest tree when Jake's mule jumped into the saloon. "Mule be there," he explained later, "door there. Wind-wagon blow down street. Whoosh! Mule: here, there!" So they called the stranger Windwagon, for he was the kind of person who had to have a shinier name than Smith.

The whole town followed the stranger to the Star. They made a circle around his table, then circles around that circle, like winding up a ball of yarn, until the room was full. Those who were near passed word over their shoulders to those who were not, so that bulletins would slide outward like waves when you throw a stone in a pond: "He's sitting down"—"sitting down"—and finally, at farthest remove, the Pawnees would hear the news and pass it on. . . .

The stranger savored his drink like a man who had been long away from the good things. He was one of those old youngsters, anywhere between thirty and fifty. His face was burned and lined, his sandy hair had been tumbled and tousled by many a wind, and his eyes had the perpetual squint that a sailor gets from peeking all day at horizons. People looked mostly at his eyes: they burned like a tent preacher's. When he began to talk, he wasn't bashful or brash, just quiet and sure, and convincing, his big burry voice rolling like the tide. He told how the prairies were going to look to-morrow, speckled with mansions and factories and towns, wealthier than India. But he said people needed one great thing before they could have any of those things. They needed a way to move fast, a way to carry goods from town to town; to build this new prairie of tomorrow they had to have the speed of the wind! Then he talked about his wagon, how it would sail any place on the prairie ten times as fast as a draft animal, yet, without animals to buy or feed, it didn't need to follow crooked trails along rivers, and it would always have free power because the wind never stops on the prairie.

Jake Shafer nodded his head at that, and the circle behind him nodded, and two minutes later the Pawnees were nodding their heads, too; they knew that prairie wind. Then the stranger looked Jake straight in the eye and said he wanted the men of Westport to ante in some money and build a fleet of big sail wagons, like his little one, for the Santa Fe trade. For a minute everybody stared at him. Then somebody snickered, and somebody laughed, and everybody around began to laugh, and the room shook, and mirth rippled outward until the farthest Pawnee was holding his belly. . . .

When the room was quiet again, the stranger said he had thought they might feel that way. He would be back in a few days; they should think it over. Then he climbed back into his wagon, unfurled the sail, and rumbled away in a great arc toward the west.

II

For the next few days they talked of nothing except Windwagon Smith. Jake Shafer said that he didn't hand over any chips until he saw the cards on the table, and everybody agreed that was sage. Shelby Foster, who had just graduated from a New England college, said that the kind of mathematics they taught in New England colleges proved that such a big wagon couldn't run, and only a fool would invest money in it. Foster had come out to write a book like Francis Parkman's about the Oregon Trail, and went around looking at people and writing in his notebook. And as soon as Foster came out against windwagons people began to look at them more favorably. Jake's daughter Rosalie, who was as sweet as clover honey, said that maybe this was one of the things you just have to believe in—like boats, the first time you see one. Someone suggested that maybe Smith had gone to St. Joe, Westport's rival town, and St. Joe would build windwagons and take over the whole trade; and everybody spent a bad day imagining St. Joe full of mil-

lionaires. But a rider from St. Joe said Smith hadn't been up there. And when he hadn't come back in four days, Westport gave him up and thought of other things.

When Windwagon Smith had been gone six days, a trapper came to Westport with a strange story. He had been riding about ten miles from town when he saw a white streak on the prairie. The streak turned out to be an old cow, sticking its head between its legs and uncoiling with ten-foot jumps, stringing its tail out behind like a fence rail. Before he could think what to do about the cow, it sailed past him and disappeared in a funnel of dust. He pondered whether he should catch the cow and race it against all comers, but he didn't know that he *could* catch it; it was the fastest cow he ever saw.

That same day a caravan that had just started west passed back through Westport, headed *east*. The men of the caravan held tight to their guns and kept their mouths shut. One woman who was a little hysterical said they weren't afraid of the Sioux or the Mormons, but they weren't going out on the prairie among the *spirits*. They were going back to Ohio where bodies stayed in their graves!

Punch Dunkelberger and Jake Shafer talked of these events in the Star, Doctor Jackson told his patients about them while he prescribed calomel and mustard plasters, Shelby Foster discussed them with Rosalie Shafer while they looked at the moon. But the meaning was not

fully comprehended until the next morning, when the dogs waved their noses in the air again and slunk away, all the ponies that could jump leaped the corrals and started east, and the Indians began to glide around, looking for wide trees. And soon Windwagon sailed down the street, waving to everyone.

"Ahoy!" he said. "I'd have been back yesterday, but came on a caravan and maybe scared them, so I took a long swing off the trail and waited until I was sure they were out of the way."

The town followed him into the Star again, and he showed a stone that was as good as an affidavit for where he had been. It was jagged and black, and still warm from lying in a little gully beyond Council Grove where all the wind blows straight up, hot as Mexican pepper. That gully is one of the side doors to Hades, people think. The Doctor worked long division on a table top, and calculated that the windwagon had made nearly seventy miles a day. An ox team was lucky to make fifteen. When Windwagon said he thought he might go to St. Joe, Jake looked at the faces around him and then jumped up and banged the table and said, "By Gum, we'll form a company *here!*" A great whoop went up behind him, and undulated outward. . . .

That is how the Westport Prairie Clipper Company was formed. You can see it in the company's minute book. Jake Shafer was elected president; Punch Dunkelberger, vice president; the Doctor, secretary and treasurer. Windwagon could have had any office he wanted, but he wanted only to be Navigator—Navigator of the Prairies, he said with a faraway look in his eyes. He said you had to believe in the future. Columbus had to believe; Dan Boone had to believe in Kentucky before he cut the Wilderness Road; Fulton had to believe that a little engine could push a big boat. Every time progress is made it's because people believe enough in something to take a chance. He said that pretty soon the prairie would be white with sails. The clippers would cruise past the oxen like coyotes past snails. Every day a clipper would dock in Westport with its hold full of gold and spices and blankets, and every day in the Spanish cities (ports, he called them) they would shout, "Make way for the Westport Prairie Clipper!"

Punch Dunkelberger was so near to tears he made the mistake of setting up the whole crowd.

They were slow in starting to build the clippers, because Windwagon was particular. He wanted white oak and hickory for the bed, so it could be curved just right to hold the cargo on slopes; and long-seasoned ash for the spokes and the tillers and all the moving parts that weren't iron. The iron had to be beaten just enough. When Jake saw what a job it was going to be, he said they would build one clipper and try it out before building the others. Windwagon looked a little hurt, but he put the measurements on paper and sent riders to St. Joe and Independence to see what materials they

could collect. Some things had to be ordered from St. Louis and Pittsburgh.

While the clipper was building, Windwagon had plenty of time to talk. He was ever one to talk grandly—not boastfully, just grandly. As soon as he got a dozen wagons promised, he began to talk of a hundred-wagon fleet. And one evening he said, "It'll never do any good to have ships unless we have sailors. We've got to build crews at the same time we build clippers. If you are going to be the first captains in the Santa Fe voyage, you've got to learn to pilot."

So Jake climbed into Smith's little wagon one day, with his jaw set firm and his hands holding tight, and Windwagon sat beside him and explained how the sail worked. He let Jake try to steer, and they staggered over the prairie for a while. When they came back, Jake climbed out quickly with the sweat running down his face and said he'd rather drive a runaway bull team than handle a 6 x 6 sail. One by one the other members of the Company began to go out for sailing lessons. They would swell out their muscles and hold on to the tiller as though they were driving a twelve-mule span, and tug at the tiny sail like wrestling a steer. Windwagon would shake his head in despair and take the tiller from them, and make the wagon glide this way and that. When Windwagon steered it was as though the man, the wagon, and the wind were all one will. But when

Jake, or Punch, or the Doctor steered, the wagon would stagger and hesitate and groan in its joints. And when the lesson was over, the pupil would climb out as quickly as possible and go into the Star for a long drink.

Windwagon explained that a captain must also know how to navigate. Foster snorted at that; he said that to navigate you need to know the kind of elevated mathematics that is taught only in New England colleges, but Windwagon said that for a man of sense it wasn't necessary to go to college, and he began to teach Westport the common rules about the stars and directions and estimating distances.

Jake Shafer ordered a sextant [2] from Baltimore, and Windwagon nearly cried when he saw it. It reminded him of the sea, and he spent a whole afternoon telling how it feels to skid before a salt breeze, and how the mountains come to the bay at Naples, and how in a few weeks the first clipper would be sailing into Santa Fe.

One day Punch Dunkelberger appeared wearing a captain's cap he had ordered from St. Louis. It was bright blue with silver braid, and Punch looked like baked ham with birthday candles. But in a few weeks everyone had a blue cap. Each new one seemed to have more trimming than the one before, until Punch got ashamed of his and talked

of putting a red turkey feather on it. The town was no longer interested in the things it had been. A caravan could hardly buy a mule or an ox in the village. The blacksmith was working on the clipper and had no time to shoe animals or repair wheels. Most of the businessmen closed up shop, hid their leathery faces under blue caps, sighted through the sextant, and tried to walk and talk like Windwagon. It was wonderful to hear them go on about tacking and hauling, port and starb'd.

Sometimes a man would look at himself in his wife's mirror or calculate how much money the experiment was costing him. Then he would go to Windwagon, clear his throat and furrow his brow, and try to say his worries. Always Windwagon would soothe him and tell him about Tomorrow and send him away figuring how much money could be made on one trip to Santa Fe. You couldn't doubt a man who believed as hard as Windwagon.

Shelby Foster was the only man in Westport that Windwagon couldn't convince. Foster stood around and wrote in his notebook and groused. He said he had learned in college how another fool once wanted to make a machine that would fly on the wind—somebody named Darius Green, he said. That led to Foster's quarrel with Rosalie Shafer. When Foster had come to Missouri he had tried once to ride a pony and taken one look at Rosalie, and decided to write his book in Westport rather than on the Trail. Before that, Rosa-

2 **sextant:** measuring instrument, used at sea to determine latitude and longitude.

lie hadn't had any beau except on Sunday nights when Punch would come over and sit beside her and talk about the mule business with Jake. She said Punch lacked imagination. Foster would kiss her hand and tell her she was a flower. They would sit close together and he would read poetry to her, the kind they learn in the New England colleges, about skylarks. But sometimes they talked about Windwagon Smith, and Foster said sensible men would lock Windwagon up, and Rosalie called Foster a coward and said he too lacked imagination, and they would sit at opposite ends of the bench and look at the moon individually.

Windwagon had imagination, Rosalie said. And finally she teased him into giving her a sailing lesson, and after that he went out often with her late in the afternoon, when the sun would glint like a Sioux bonfire on Rosalie's hair, and Foster would sit in front of the Star, looking as though he were chewing pickled nails. Rosalie might become a good sailor, Windwagon said; she had sea sense. But that's all he said about her. Foster still went to see her six nights a week, and Punch on Sunday nights, but Punch said she didn't act so interested in the mule business any more.

III

When two caravans wanted to buy windwagons, the men of Westport began to see what kind of business they were in.

"There's no end to it," Windwagon said. "When we build our fleet of a hundred we can squeeze almost everybody else off the trail. When we build a thousand we can take over the whole trade. Then we can build a thousand more and spread out into Iowa and Illinois and maybe start a water-level route beside the Lakes as far east as New York State. Then we'll build a million little wagons and sell them to the Oregon settlers. We'll keep the Santa Fe route to ourselves. We'll have our shipyards over there in the bottom by the creek, and start branches in St. Joe and Independence. We'll train other captains, and become admirals and have fleets under us."

The Doctor calculated they could make two hundred thousand dollars the first year and six million the second. They got so tangled figuring what the income might be the fourth year that Windwagon forgot Rosalie's sailing lesson, and Foster sneaked over and read Milton to her.

One day half a dozen businessmen came up on the boat from St. Louis, looked at the wagon, and offered a thousand dollars cash for it; said they didn't know whether Windwagon was crazy or a genius, but they liked to gamble. Jake laughed at them. They talked to Windwagon a while and offered ten thousand, but Jake told them to go home and dig up some real money.

Foster said Westport contained seven kinds of fools, all bad.

A company of soldiers marched down from Leavenworth one day.

They had heard that cannons were being mounted in the wagons to conquer an empire in the Southwest, like Aaron Burr's.[3] There weren't any cannons. Some people thought Windwagon looked a little crest-fallen; it was the only thing he hadn't thought of. The soldiers poked around and talked impressively about military possibilities.

Jim Bridger[4] himself came in one day and spent a long time studying the wagon. He looked sad, as though he saw the old West changing. And Kit Carson came up, with his Indian wife, and talked a long time to Windwagon like a brother, and said he wished he were thirty years younger.

Westport was becoming a tourist town. The store stopped carrying powder and stocked little wind-wagons carved from soft wood. The print shop at St. Joe put out a souvenir booklet all about Windwagon Smith, saying that he had once been an admiral in the Scotch navy, had captured the Sandwich Isles from the cannibals, and had twice sailed around the world. Foster sneered that if the truth were known he'd bet Windwagon had a past a lot different from that. Rosalie said Foster had less imagination than Punch. Windwagon just laughed.

When the windwagon was done, it seemed that the whole population of the western territories came into Westport to see it. You could hardly shuffle your feet without stepping on a dog or baby. The windwagon was ten times as large as a Conestoga wagon, and built with two decks. Passengers could shoot buffalo from the upper deck when regular service started, Windwagon said. When the windwagon service was extended to Africa, they could shoot lions. It had a mainsail as big as a house, and the wheels were a foot wide and tired with iron. Yet, big as it was, it was so beautifully fitted and greased that it moved with hardly a push of the hand. Some were in favor of painting it red, white, and blue, like most of the wagons, but Windwagon said this must have dignity; this wasn't a wagon, it was a clipper ship. They made it blue with silver trimmings, and red spokes in the wheels.

The day before the first trip, the manager of an Eastern railroad said that he didn't think the ship would run but was willing to offer twenty-five thousand for complete rights. Jake was pretty uncertain for a while, and then talked to Windwagon, and came back and laughed and said they wouldn't take a million dollars for the clipper. He talked almost as convincingly as Windwagon.

The Westport Prairie Clipper Company invited the President of the United States to dedicate the new ship, but he regretted. However, two top-hatted men walked into the Star, and when Punch went up to them and said in the new grand manner, "I am Captain Dun-

---

3 **Aaron Burr's:** In the early 19th century Burr was suspected of planning to establish a Southwestern Empire in America.
4 **Jim Bridger:** famous American fur trapper, trader, guide, and spinner of tall tales.

kelberger. I don't believe I have the pleasure of your acquaintance," they looked at him oddly and one said he was the Secretary of the Navy and the other the Secretary of War. Then they borrowed ten dollars from him.

The prairie clipper was rolled out to the edge of town, and Rosalie Shafer broke a bottle of corn whisky right prettily over one front wheel. Everybody yelled for a speech from Windwagon, everybody except Shelby Foster. Windwagon climbed up on the upper deck, blew his nose, hawked his throat, and began to talk with that faraway shine in his eyes.

"Ladies and gents," he said, "and them of you as has came a long way to see us today. I want to welcome you to the port of the prairie. And I thank you for coming to see our little ship, the first clipper ever built for trans-prairie shipping in America. And I wish I could tell you what this is going to mean to you. I wish I could paint a picture the way this prairie is going to look in five years. This ship you see here today is only a pack rat compared to the ships you are going to see tied up in this port. There'll be passenger ships and freighters big enough to carry this one on the poop deck, big enough to carry a whole caravan or a whole army. And there'll be little windwagons. Where there's big ones, there's usually little ones, you know. (*Long laughter.*) We'll make so many they won't cost much. And every one of you'll have a little windwagon in your barn, and you can get in it and go anywhere you want on the prairie just as easy as you put a chicken in a pot. This clipper shows that all you have to do is believe in these things and they'll come true. This is just like the sunrise on a new day, only you and me are helping to pull up the sun!"

It was the best speech Windwagon ever made, but he never made a bad speech.

IV

The maiden voyage, Windwagon called it, and said that only the real charter members of the company should go—and the Secretary of War and the Secretary of the Navy, if they were sober. The President could have gone, too, if he had come. But nobody else. Not even Rosalie, who almost bawled in front of everybody when Jake told her no. The passengers boarded the ship and waved their caps. Punch had a red feather in his. Then Windwagon climbed up to the seat he called the bridge, grabbed the tiller, and yelled, "Cast off!" Jake's Negro boy took a block from under one of the wheels, and the clipper began to move.

There wasn't much jerk when they started, for Windwagon payed out the sail slowly, but in a minute Westport was a quarter mile away and the grass under wheel like a green rug. Punch said so later. In two minutes they could hardly see the ponies and the crowd, and Shelby Foster out in front in his red shirt, looking as though he were balancing the family tree on his nose.

They all said they had never felt anything like that ride. It was airy, like flying. That is the way a hawk feels, they guessed. This is the way it feels to scud in a three-master before the trade winds. The clipper swished past an ox team as though it were standing still. . . .

Under full sail, the clipper rushed across the prairie. Occasionally it struck a gully or a dry creek bed, and then the body bounced on the springs, and the passengers bounced in their seats. Sometimes it swayed sharply as it hurried down a prairie swell. But the swaying and bouncing were mostly in the body. The great wheels rolled true and straight where the tiller pointed them.

"It runs like a flagship," shouted Windwagon over the whine of the wind. "It'll run to Santa Fe in a week."

He had to give his attention immediately to steering over an acre of badlands. That was when Punch Dunkelberger bounced into the lap of the Secretary of War. Punch weighed three hundred pounds.

"I say," said the Secretary, "don't you think we are going rather fast? For a maiden voyage?" he added.

The Secretary of the Navy looked at the grass swirling past, then looked hastily away from it.

"Go up and talk to him," the Doctor said to Jake.

Jake crawled to the front.

"Don't you think we are going a bit fast?" he said in Windwagon's ear. "Confidentially, some of the passengers who aren't so used to this as we are seem to be getting a little frightened."

Windwagon laughed. He threw back his head and laughed from his toes up, as free as the wind, happy as a child.

"This is just crawling," he said. "Tomorrow we'll be going over this prairie so fast we'll hardly need to touch the ground."

Jake crawled back to his seat and closed his eyes.

"The man is mad," said the Doctor.

"Knock him over the head," said Punch.

"Then who'll steer and stop this thing?" asked Jake.

"True," said the Doctor.

Windwagon looked back over his shoulder. "Would you gentlemen from Washington like to ask any questions?" he called.

"Us? No," grunted the Secretary of War weakly.

The sail thumped like a drum in the wind, and the stench of hot axle grease rose inside the wagon.

"What if we hit something at this speed?" said Jake.

"Or turn over?" said the Secretary of War.

"Don't worry," said Windwagon.

"Can you pull the brake?" asked the Doctor.

"I think I'd better," said Jake. He crawled forward until he could reach the lever.

When the brake caught, the wagon skidded, groaned, began to turn almost at a right angle. It leaned dangerously on its springs. The sail strained and the hickory mast trem-

bled. The wagon came around, grandly, thrillingly. But it didn't stop, and it didn't come out of the turn. It shuddered, hesitated, then swung around so that it was running backwards, slowly at first, then faster and faster.

They said Windwagon gave one slow look at Jake. He didn't say anything. One slow look, more sad than angry, but Jake shriveled under it. And then Windwagon laughed again, that same free laugh from his toes to his mouth, but more rueful. He laughed and turned back and worked with the sail.

Later they knew what had happened. A brake on one wheel will stop a wagon going slow, but not a prairie clipper at full speed. The brake held just long enough to throw the clipper into a sharp turn and lock the steering gear. The sail turned on the mast and twisted its rope beyond chance of furling.

Far back, the crowd watched admiringly as the wagon bore down stern-first upon them, cutting a wide arc over the waves of prairie grass. Not until it was two hundred yards away did they stop cheering. When it was a hundred yards away, they scattered like a buffalo stampede. The prairie streamed pintos.

There were three little gullies in the path of the circle. Every twenty seconds the wagon hit a gully and the passengers bounced around like popcorn. About the tenth gully, the Secretary of War bounced out. He lit in a ball and rolled like a tumbleweed. Then he got up and ran like a jack rabbit away from the path of the wagon. "Stop the ship!" shouted Jake. "Stop the ship at once! We've lost His Honor!"

"You stop it," Punch suggested.

"Excuse me," said the Secretary of the Navy, and jumped. He yelled and sprang up and began to pick things out of his pants.

"Dwarf cactus," observed Punch.

"Gentlemen," said the Doctor, "I know the consequences of broken bones. I do not advise jumping."

Two more passengers jumped, and then another, and finally the Doctor himself. That left Windwagon and Jake and Punch.

"Father," said a sweet voice in the wagon.

Jake covered his eyes with his hands. "Did you ever hear of the voices of your beloved speaking to you just before death?" he asked Punch. Punch held tight and groaned. "Speaking to me, too," he moaned.

"Father," said someone again.

Jake looked toward the back of the wagon.

"Rosalie!" he bellowed.

Rosalie was just climbing out of the compartment Windwagon had designed to hold liquids and pottery on the Santa Fe run.

"Rosalie!" said Punch Dunkelberger, between bounces.

"Miss Shafer!" said Windwagon, looking around quickly.

"What are you doing here?" Jake thundered.

"You know this is a very great thing," yelled Windwagon above the roar of wind and wagon. "Miss Shafer is the first stowaway in the history of prairie clippers." He went back to working with the sail. They said he was just as calm as though this were a box social in the schoolhouse.

Jake said some short ugly words.

"You'd better jump," Punch advised her.

"Don't you dare jump," said Windwagon over his shoulder. "You might get killed."

"I'll take care of you," offered Punch.

"You need a spanking," said Jake.

"I don't need taking care of," Rosalie said to Punch. She looked Jake in the eye.

"You pulled the brake, didn't you?" she said, low and hard.

Jake stared at her.

"You couldn't believe in Windwagon. You couldn't put your chips down and take a chance. You got scared. You pulled the brake."

Jake made gurgling noises.

"I'm going up and sit with Windwagon," Rosalie said. Once she looked back at her father and Punch, who was staring at the nearest exit.

"Don't give up the ship, Captain Dunkelberger," she said sweetly.

The wagon whirled in its circle, the wind shrieking.

"There went Jake!" yelled Punch. Then Punch went.

He said he hit the ground unanimously, every square inch of him. He pulled himself out of the track and watched the windwagon. There was something beautiful about it even going backwards, something shiplike, birdlike, not wagonlike, with the wind filling out the sail blue-white against the blue-green grass. But he could see something from the ground he couldn't from the clipper: every circle was carrying it farther west. Already at its most distant point it was out of sight behind the swell of the prairie.

"Catch it! Catch it!" yelled Jake, limping along.

"Stop them!" yelled Shelby Foster, bouncing along on a borrowed pony, holding tight to the saddle horn.

The windwagon changed its circles into ovals, its ovals into a pattern that couldn't be made out because it was so far away. The last time anybody saw it, it was scudding backwards into the west, with Shelby Foster after it, far behind, occasionally taking one hand off the saddle horn to shake his fist. Rosalie and Windwagon were sitting close. Whenever they hit a gully they held to each other.

v

The Secretary of the Navy had to walk all the way back to town because he couldn't sit. The others rode back on borrowed ponies, each jog showing up a fresh bruise. In Westport it was like a picnic breaking up after everyone had got indigestion and poison ivy. Shelby Foster came into the Star and said politely, "Good evening, Captain Dunkelberger," and Punch chased him halfway into Independence. Punch had a bandage around his head and was pale as whitewash, but full of fight. It took the Doctor two hours to pick all the cactus spines

out of the Secretary of the Navy. Then the secretaries stole two horses and gave a sort of generalized scowl at all of Westport before they rode away.

The town went back into the mule, powder, and bacon business, trying not to hear a tide of scornful laughter that rose in St. Joe and spread and bounced back and forth between the Rockies and the Appalachians. But history seemed to be moving past Westport. The wagons began to go farther north, and when the railroads came in they chose other towns. Westport shrank and Kansas City grew, and after a while Kansas City swallowed Westport and put its street railway through the place where the Star had stood and built its municipal airport on the very land where the windwagon had begun its maiden voyage.

They never saw the windwagon again, although they searched the prairie as far as Council Grove. Of course, there were stories. Every once in a while a bullwhacker[5] would be picked up barefoot and half-dead from thirst, and tell how his draft animals had suddenly reared up at a dust cloud and run away like antelope; and the worst drinker in Independence swore off and became an elder in the Lutheran church because he saw the ghost of a Conestoga wagon floating on the wind near the Pueblo. But that man was always seeing things.

5 **bullwhacker:** driver of a team of oxen.

Many a man saw Windwagon Smith after he left Westport, though. He was in the pilothouse, he and a beautiful red-haired woman, when the first steamboat came up the Yellowstone, and they swear that nobody but Windwagon Smith held the golden spike when the two railroads came together at Promontory Point. And not long ago when the first transcontinental airplane roared out of Kansas City a little sandy-haired man closed the plane's door and waved the pilot on. The little man walked like a sailor, they said. His eyes seemed to burn, and he had the perpetual squint that comes from looking always at horizons.

Reading Skills

1. What details in the first paragraph suggest that the story will be a tall tale? How do the next few paragraphs strengthen this impression?
2. Explain the plans Windwagon Smith has for his wagon in Westport. What is the first reaction of the townspeople to his plans?
3. List the reasons that the people of Westport decide to accept Windwagon's plans.
4. How does Westport change while the first windwagon is being built?
5. What famous or wealthy people express interest in the project?
6. What kind of person is Shelby Foster?
7. Describe the first ride in the new clipper. What details are used to show the speed of the wagon? Explain exactly what happens when Jake pulls the brake.
8. How do the last two paragraphs of the story make it seem like a legend?

Understanding Literature

1. The story is full of humorous exaggeration. Some of it is direct comparison, such as "there she stood like a moose head on the wall" or "eyes bulging like hard-boiled eggs." Some of it is description of an absurd and impossible event: "he had slept through a cyclone and seven street fights." Find other examples of such humorous exaggeration. What does this exaggeration contribute to the story of Windwagon Smith and his prairie clipper?

WILBUR SCHRAMM

2. What are the character traits of Windwagon Smith? How does he differ from Shelby Foster in his goals in life? in his attitude toward education? in his courtship of Rosalie? in his faith in the windwagon? Why is Windwagon admired by the townspeople? What elements of American character does he represent?

3. Windwagon is a sailor; his wagon is a clipper; Westport is his port; and the prairie is his sea. Why is the sailing metaphor in the story a good way of suggesting the American pioneer spirit? (In answering, consider what characteristics sailors and frontiersmen have in common.)

Was Paul Bunyan, the lumberman of legend, a real lumberman whose actual deeds were exaggerated with each story about him until his reputation was exaggerated beyond all belief? Or was Paul Bunyan, as the poet Sandburg suggests, "fashioned . . . forth as an apparition"—a man who never existed in the flesh, but who lived in the imaginations of lumbermen everywhere?

Paul Bunyan of the North Woods*

Carl Sandburg

IMPROVING YOUR READING: In "Paul Bunyan of the North Woods," the poet's purpose is not to give the reader facts, even imaginary facts, about the legendary hero, but to suggest an attitude toward him, a feeling about him that includes wonder at the fantastic stories spun by the lumbermen.

Who made Paul Bunyan, who gave him birth as a myth, who joked him into life as the Master Lumberjack, who fashioned him forth as an apparition easing the hours of men amid axes and trees, saws and lumber? The people, the bookless people, they made Paul and had him alive long before he got into the books for those who read. He grew up in shanties, around the hot stoves of winter, among socks and mittens drying, in the smell of tobacco smoke and the roar of laughter mocking the outside weather. And some of Paul came overseas in wooden bunks below decks in sailing vessels. And some of Paul is old as the hills, young as the alphabet.

The Pacific Ocean froze over in the winter of the Blue Snow and Paul Bunyan had long teams of oxen hauling regular white snow over from China. This was the winter Paul gave a party to the Seven Axmen. Paul fixed a granite floor sunk two hundred feet deep for them to dance on. Still, it tipped and tilted as the dance went on. And because the Seven Axmen refused to take off their hobnailed boots, the sparks from the nails of their dancing feet lit up the place so that Paul didn't light the kerosene lamps. No women being on the Big Onion river at that time the Seven Axmen had to dance with each other, the one left over in each set taking Paul as a partner. The commotion of the dancing that night brought on an earthquake and the Big Onion river moved over three counties to the east.

One year when it rained from St. Patrick's Day till the Fourth of July, Paul Bunyan got disgusted because his celebration on the Fourth was spoiled. He dived into Lake Superior and swam to where a solid pillar of water was coming down. He dived under this pillar, swam up into it and climbed with powerful swimming strokes, was gone about an hour, came splashing down, and as the rain stopped, he explained, "I turned the dam thing off." This is told in the Big North Woods and on the Great Lakes, with many particulars.

Two mosquitoes lighted on one of Paul Bunyan's oxen, killed it, ate it, cleaned the bones, and sat on a grub shanty picking their teeth as Paul came along. Paul sent to Australia for two special bumblebees to kill these mosquitoes. But the bees and the mosquitoes intermarried; their children had stingers on both ends. And things kept getting worse till Paul brought a big boatload of sorghum up from Louisiana and while all the bee-mosquitoes were eating at the sweet sorghum he floated them down to the Gulf of Mexico. They got so fat that it was easy to drown them all between New Orleans and Galveston.

Paul logged on the Little Gimlet in Oregon one winter. The cookstove at that camp covered an acre of ground. They fastened the side of a hog on each snowshoe and four men used to skate on the griddle while the cook flipped the pancakes. The eating table was three miles long, elevators carried the cakes to the ends of the table where boys on bicycles rode back and forth on a path down the center of the table dropping the cakes where called for.

Benny, the Little Blue Ox of Paul Bunyan, grew two feet every time Paul looked at him, when a youngster. The barn was gone one morning and they found it on Benny's back; he grew out of it in one night. One night he kept pawing and bellowing for more pancakes, till there were two hundred men at the cook-shanty stove trying to keep him fed. About breakfast time Benny broke loose, tore down the cook shanty, ate all the pancakes piled up for the loggers' breakfast. And after that Benny made his mistake; he ate the red-hot stove, and that finished him. This is only one of the hot-stove stories told in the North Woods.

Understanding Literature

1. In the first section, who are "the bookless people"? How did they create Paul Bunyan?
2. Explain the last sentence in the first section. In what way is Paul as "old as the hills"? In what way is he as "young as the alphabet"? (Is the alphabet young?)
3. The poet has not tried to tell a complete story but to give you an impression of the wonderful size and strength of the legendary hero of the lumbermen. How does each section contribute to this impression?

America in Folklore and Tales: Further Activities

1. Each selection in this unit presents some special quality of character that is essentially American. Identify these qualities and discuss them. Perhaps you will think that some of the qualities, though once they may have been American, are no longer so.
2. Use the life of one of the heroes or heroines of your own section of the country—one not used in this unit—and tell some part of his life in the manner of a legend. Perhaps you will wish to exaggerate his deeds to make them more awe-inspiring, or perhaps you will consider that his actual deeds are wonderful enough to be told without any exaggeration.

Nature

NATURE IS OFTEN BEAUTIFUL, but sometimes ugly; often gentle, but sometimes violent; frequently comforting, but occasionally harshly uncomfortable; usually understandable, but now and then mysterious. Because there are so many facets of nature, writers and poets have been moved to compose thousands of tributes to its beauty, violence, and mystery.

Certain elements of nature—such as air, water, and dust—are always close at hand. However, some of the other elements of nature are not so certain to be close by—the sea, forests, mountains, and wild life. Indeed, even in the age of rapid transportation, some Americans live out their lives without a glimpse of an ocean or of a mountain. For anyone who cannot view firsthand the ocean, the mountains, wild plants and animals, or the great forests, the literature about nature provides a means of imaginative transportation to remote and fascinating settings and events seen through the writer's eyes.

In almost any story which features a rattlesnake, the rattler is a very obvious villain. Do you think it possible that a story about a rattlesnake could induce you to understand the snake's point of view at least part of the time?

The Life and Death of a Western Gladiator

Charles G. Finney

Improving Your Reading: A notable characteris'ic of this story is its *objectivity*—the impersonal, matter-of-fact manner in which the author, without emotion, tells his tale. Notice, as you read, that the writing does not indicate that the author either favors or opposes the rattlesnake.

He was born on a summer morning in the shady mouth of a cave. Three others were born with him, another male and two females. Each was about five inches long and slimmer than a lead pencil.

Their mother left them a few hours after they were born. A day after that his brother and sisters left him also. He was all alone. Nobody cared whether he lived or died. His tiny brain was very dull. He had no arms or legs. His skin was delicate. Nearly everything that walked on the ground or burrowed in it, that flew in the air or swam in the water or climbed trees was his enem͏ ͏ow that. He k͏.͏.͏.. ͏.͏.͏.͏.͏..g ͏a͏. ͏a͏... He was aware of his own existence, and that was the sum of his knowledge.

The direct rays of the sun could, in a short time, kill him. If the temperature dropped too low he would freeze. Without food he would starve. Without moisture he would die of dehydration. If a man or a horse stepped on him he would be crushed. If anything chased him he could run neither very far nor very fast.

Thus it was at the hour of his birth. Thus it would be, with modifications, all his life.

But against these drawbacks he had certain qualifications that fitted him to be a competitive creature of this world and equipped him for its warfare. He could exist a long time without food or water. His very smallness at birth protected him when he most needed protection.

Instinct provided him with what he lacked in experience. In order to eat he first had to kill; and he was eminently adapted for killing. In sacs in his jaws he secreted a virulent[1] poison. To inject that poison he had two fangs, hollow and pointed. Without that poison and those fangs he would have been among the most helpless creatures on earth. With them he was among the deadliest.

He was, of course, a baby rattlesnake, a desert diamondback, named Crotalus atrox by the herpetologists Baird and Girard and so listed in the *Catalogue of North American Reptiles* in its issue of 1853. He was grayish brown in color with a series of large dark diamond-shaped blotches on his back. His tail was white with five black crossbands. It had a button on the end of it.

Little Crotalus lay in the dust in the mouth of his cave. Some of his kinfolk lay there too. It was their home. That particular tribe of rattlers had lived there for scores of years.

The cave had never been seen by a white man.

Sometimes as many as two hundred rattlers occupied the den. Sometimes the numbers shrunk to as few as forty or fifty.

The tribe members did nothing at all for each other except breed. They hunted singly; they never shared their food. They derived some automatic degree of safety from their numbers, but their actions were never concerted toward using their numbers to any end. If an enemy attacked one of them, the others did nothing about it.

Young Crotalus's brother was the first of the litter to go out into the world and the first to die. He achieved a distance of fifty feet from the den when a Sonoran racer, four feet long and hungry, came upon him. The little rattler, despite his poison fangs, was a tidbit. The racer, long skilled in such arts, snatched him up by the head and swallowed him down. Powerful digestive juices in the racer's stomach did the rest. Then the racer, appetite whetted, prowled around until it found one of Crotalus's little sisters. She went the way of the brother.

Nemesis[2] of the second sister was a chaparral cock. This cuckoo, or road runner as it is called, found the baby amid some rocks, uttered a cry of delight, scissored it by the neck, shook it until it was almost lifeless, banged and pounded it upon a rock until life had indeed left it, and then gulped it down.

Crotalus, somnolent[3] in a cranny of the cave's mouth, neither knew nor cared. Even if he had, there was nothing he could have done about it.

On the fourth day of his life he decided to go out into the world himself. He rippled forth uncertainly, the transverse plates on his belly serving him as legs.

1 **virulent** (vĭr′yə lənt): deadly.

2 **Nemesis** (nĕm′ə sĭs): agent of fate; one who brings disaster or punishment.
3 **somnolent**: sleepy; drowsy.

He could see things well enough within his limited range, but a five-inch-long snake can command no great field of vision. He had an excellent sense of smell. But, having no ears, he was stone deaf. On the other hand, he had a pit, a deep pock mark between eye and nostril. Unique, this organ was sensitive to animal heat. In pitch blackness, Crotalus, by means of the heat messages recorded in his pit, could tell whether another animal was near and could also judge its size. That was better than an ear.

The single button on his tail could not, of course, yet rattle. Crotalus wouldn't be able to rattle until that button had grown into three segments. Then he would be able to buzz.

He had a wonderful tongue. It looked like an exposed nerve and was probably exactly that. It was forked, and Crotalus thrust it in and out as he traveled. It told him things that neither his eyes nor his nose nor his pit told him.

Snake fashion, Crotalus went forth, not knowing where he was going, for he had never been anywhere before. Hunger was probably his prime mover.[4] In order to satisfy that hunger he had to find something smaller than himself and kill it.

He came upon a baby lizard sitting in the sand. Eyes, nose, pit, and tongue told Crotalus it was there. Instinct told him what it was and what to do. Crotalus gave a

tiny one-inch strike and bit the lizard. His poison killed it. He took it by the head and swallowed it. Thus was his first meal.

During his first two years Crotalus grew rapidly. He attained a length of two feet; his tail had five rattles on it and its button. He rarely bothered with lizards any more, preferring baby rabbits, chipmunks, and round-tailed ground squirrels. Because of his slow locomotion he could not run down these agile little things. He had to contrive instead to be where they were when they would pass. Then he struck swiftly, injected his poison, and ate them after they died.

At two he was formidable. He had grown past the stage where a racer or a road runner could safely tackle him. He had grown to the size where other desert dwellers—coyotes, foxes, coatis, wildcats—knew it was better to leave him alone.

And, at two, Crotalus became a father, his life being regulated by cycles. His cycles were plantlike. The peach tree does not "know" when it is time to flower, but flower it does because its cycle orders it to do so.

In the same way, Crotalus did not "know" when it was time for young desert diamondback rattlers to pair off and breed. But his cycle knew.

He found "her" on a rainy morning. Crotalus's courtship at first was sinuous and subtle, slow and stealthy. Then suddenly it became dynamic. A period of exhaustion followed. Two metabolic machines had united to produce new metabolic machines.

---

4 **prime mover:** the original force which causes action.

Of that physical union six new rattlesnakes were born. Thus Crotalus, at two, had carried out his major primary function: he had reproduced his kind. In two years he had experienced everything that was reasonably possible for desert diamondback rattlesnakes to experience except death.

He had not experienced death for the simple reason that there had never been an opportunity for anything bigger and stronger than himself to kill him. Now, at two, because he was so formidable, that opportunity became more and more unlikely.

He grew more slowly in the years following his initial spurt. At the age of twelve he was five feet long. Few of the other rattlers in his den were older or larger than he.

He had a castanet of fourteen segments. It had been broken off occasionally in the past, but with each new molting a new segment appeared.

His first skin-shedding back in his babyhood had been a bewildering experience. He did not know what was happening. His eyes clouded over until he could not see. His skin thickened and dried until it cracked in places. His pit and his nostrils ceased to function. There was only one thing to do and that was to get out of that skin.

Crotalus managed it by nosing against the bark of a shrub until he forced the old skin down over his head, bunching it like the rolled top of a stocking around his neck. Then he pushed around among rocks and sticks and branches, literally crawling out of his skin by slow degrees. Wriggling free at last, he looked like a brand-new snake. His skin was bright and satiny, his eyes and nostrils were clear, his pit sang with sensation.

For the rest of his life he was to molt three or four times a year. Each time he did it he felt as if he had been born again.

At twelve he was a magnificent reptile. Not a single scar defaced his rippling symmetry. He was diabolically beautiful and deadly poison.

His venom was his only weapon, for he had no power of constriction. Yellowish in color, his poison was odorless and tasteless. It was a highly complex mixture of proteids, each in itself direly toxic. His venom worked on the blood. The more poison he injected with a bite, the more dangerous the wound. The pain rendered by his bite was instantaneous, and the shock accompanying it was profound. Swelling began immediately, to be followed by a ghastly oozing. Injected directly into a large vein, his poison brought death quickly, for the victim died when it reached his heart.

At the age of twenty Crotalus was the oldest and largest rattler in his den. He was six feet long and weighed thirteen pounds. His whole world was only about a mile in radius. He had fixed places where he avoided the sun when it was hot and he was away from his cave. He knew his hunting grounds thoroughly, every game trail, every animal burrow.

He was a fine old machine, perfectly adapted to his surroundings, accustomed to a life of leisure and comfort. He dominated his little world.

The mighty seasonal rhythms of the desert were as vast pulsations, and the lives of the rattlesnakes were attuned to them. Spring sun beat down, spring rains fell, and, as the plants of the desert ended their winter hibernations, so did the vipers in their lair. The plants opened forth and budded; the den "opened" too, and the snakes crawled forth. The plants fertilized each other, and new plants were born. The snakes bred, and new snakes were produced. The desert was repopulated.

In the autumn the plants began to close; in the same fashion the snake den began to close, the reptiles returned to it, lay like lingering blossoms about its entrance for a while, then disappeared within it when winter came. There they slept until summoned forth by a new spring.

Crotalus was twenty years old. He was in the golden age of his viperhood.

But men were approaching. Spilling out of their cities, men were settling in that part of the desert where Crotalus lived. They built roads and houses, set up fences, dug for water, planted crops.

They homesteaded the land. They brought new animals with them—cows, horses, dogs, cats, barnyard fowl.

The roads they built were death traps for the desert dwellers. Every morning new dead bodies lay on the roads, the bodies of the things the men had run over and crushed in their vehicles.

That summer Crotalus met his first dog. It was a German shepherd which had been reared on a farm in the Midwest and there had gained the reputation of being a snake-killer. Black snakes, garter snakes, pilots, water snakes; it delighted in killing them all. It would seize them by the middle, heedless of their tiny teeth, and shake them violently until they died.

This dog met Crotalus face to face in the desert at dusk. Crotalus had seen coyotes aplenty and feared them not. Neither did the dog fear Crotalus, although Crotalus then was six feet long, as thick in the middle as a motorcycle tire, and had a head the size of a man's clenched fist. Also this snake buzzed and buzzed and buzzed.

The dog was brave, and a snake was a snake. The German shepherd snarled and attacked. Crotalus struck him in the underjaw; his fangs sank in almost half an inch and squirted big blobs of hematoxic poison into the tissues of the dog's flesh.

The shepherd bellowed with pain, backed off, groveled with his jaws in the desert sand, and attacked again. He seized Crotalus somewhere by the middle of his body and tried to flip him in the air and shake him as, in the past, he had shaken slender black snakes to their death. In return, he received another poison-blurting stab in his flank and a third in the belly and a fourth in the eye as the terri-

ble, writhing snake bit wherever it could sink its fangs.

The German shepherd had enough. He dropped the big snake and in sick, agonizing bewilderment crawled somehow back to his master's homestead and died.

The homesteader looked at his dead dog and became alarmed. If there was a snake around big enough to kill a dog that size, it could also kill a child and probably a man. It was something that had to be eliminated.

The homesteader told his fellow farmers, and they agreed to initiate a war of extermination against the snakes.

The campaign during the summer was sporadic. The snakes were scattered over the desert, and it was only by chance that the men came upon them. Even so, at summer's end, twenty-six of the vipers had been killed.

When autumn came the men decided to look for the rattlers' den and execute mass slaughter. The homesteaders had become desert-wise and knew what to look for.

They found Crotalus's lair without too much trouble—a rock outcropping on a slope that faced the south. Castoff skins were in evidence in the bushes. Bees flew idly in and out of the den's mouth. Convenient benches and shelves of rock were at hand where the snakes might lie for a final sunning in the autumn air.

They killed the three rattlers they found at the den when they first discovered it. They made plans to return in a few more days when more of the snakes had congregated. They decided to bring along dynamite with them and blow up the mouth of the den so that the snakes within would be sealed there forever and the snakes without would have no place to find refuge.

On the day the men chose to return nearly fifty desert diamondbacks were gathered at the portals of the cave. The men shot them, clubbed them, smashed them with rocks. Some of the rattlers escaped the attack and crawled into the den.

Crotalus had not yet arrived for the autumn rendezvous.[5] He came that night. The den's mouth was a shattered mass of rock, for the men had done their dynamiting well. Dead members of his tribe lay everywhere. Crotalus nosed among them,

tongue flicking as he slid slowly along.

There was no access to the cave any more. He spent the night outside among the dead. The morning sun warmed him and awakened him. He lay there at full length. He had no place to go.

The sun grew hotter upon him and instinctively he began to slide toward some dark shade. Then his senses warned him of some animal presence near by; he stopped, half coiled, raised his head and began to rattle. He saw two upright figures. He did not know what they were because he had never seen men before.

"That's the granddaddy of them all," said one of the homesteaders. "It's a good thing we came back." He raised his shotgun.

5 **rendezvous** (rän′də vōō): a meeting which occurs at an appointed time or place.

Reading Skills

1. Approximately what chance has a baby rattler of reaching the age and size of Crotalus?
2. What factors favor the survival of a young rattlesnake? What factors threaten his survival?
3. Why do Crotalus and the dog have no fear of each other?
4. What is Crotalus's reaction when he returns to his cave and finds the entrance area littered with dead snakes? Why should you have anticipated that he would react in this way?
5. The author wants the reader to understand that the snake behaves the way he does, not because he has decided to do so, but because his snake nature directs his life pattern. Find, and read orally, sentences which leave this impression.
6. The author calls the snake a gladiator. How is Crotalus similar to a gladiator?

CHARLES G. FINNEY

Understanding Literature

1. What attitude toward rattlesnakes does the author reveal? Find and be prepared to read aloud illustrations which support your answer.
2. "In order to satisfy that hunger he had to find something smaller than himself and kill it." This bit of cold-blooded statement of fact is typical of the writing in this selection. Find other expressions of this same objectivity applied to situations toward which you would ordinarily expect an emotional reaction.
3. This story is titled "The Life and Death of a Western Gladiator." How much of the selection concerns Crotalus's life? his death? The death of the snake is not actually reported. From what is it inferred? Why does the author not describe the snake's death?

Focusing on Words

1. Charles Finney uses some action words in rather unusual contexts. State in your own words the meanings of the italicized action words:

   (a) ". . . *scissored* it by the neck."
   (b) ". . . his pit *sang* with sensation."
   (c) "*Spilling* out of their cities. . . ."

2. The author also uses some interesting phrases which give special clarity to the mental pictures he creates. You will need to restudy the context before you put these expressions into your own words.

   (a) "He was diabolically beautiful. . . ."
   (b) "He was a fine old machine. . . ."
   (c) "The mighty seasonal rhythms of the desert were as vast pulsations. . . ."
   (d) "He was in the golden age of his viperhood."
   (e) "The homesteaders had become desert-wise. . . ."

Further Activity

This story is written with very little emotion. Reread the portion about the fight between Crotalus and the dog. When you have the battle well in mind, lay the book aside and write in more emotional language an account of this duel. Take the side of either the dog or the snake, and assume that the other combatant is the malicious one—the villain.

Mark Twain, whose real name was Samuel Langhorne Clemens, is known to most American students as the author of *Tom Sawyer* and *Huckleberry Finn*. Many of Twain's literary works are based on his own experiences and travels. Among these is *Roughing It*, a book containing Twain's humorous observations on Western frontier life. "The Coyote" is a selection from this book.

The Coyote

Mark Twain

IMPROVING YOUR READING: When you have finished reading this selection, you will know how Twain feels about the coyote. This is a good example of *subjective writing*, writing in which you have no doubts of how the author feels about his subject. Twain gets his own feeling into the piece partly through the modifying words and phrases he uses.

ALONG ABOUT AN HOUR after breakfast we saw the first prairie-dog villages, the first antelope, and the first wolf. If I remember rightly, this latter was the regular *coyote* (pronounced "kī ō'tī") of the farther deserts. And if it *was*, he was not a pretty creature or respectable either, for I got well acquainted with his race afterward, and can speak with confidence. The coyote is a long, slim, sick and sorry-looking skeleton, with a gray wolfskin stretched over it, a tolerably bushy tail that forever sags down with a despairing expression of forsakenness and misery, a furtive and evil eye, and a long, sharp face, with slightly lifted lip and exposed teeth. He has a general slinking expression all over. The coyote is a living, breathing allegory of Want. He is *always* hungry. He is always poor, out of luck and friendless. The meanest creatures despise him, and even the fleas would desert him for a velocipede.[1] He is so spiritless and cowardly that even while his exposed teeth are pretending a threat, the rest of his face is apologizing for it. And he is *so* homely!—so scrawny, and ribby, and coarse-haired, and pitiful. When he sees you he lifts his lip and lets a flash of his teeth out, and then turns a little out of the course he was pursuing, depresses his head a bit, and strikes a long, soft-footed trot through the sagebrush, glancing over his shoulder at you, from time to time, till he is about out of easy pistol range, and then he stops and takes a deliberate survey of you; he

1 velocipede: early form of bicycle.

will trot fifty yards and stop again—another fifty and stop again; and finally the gray of his gliding body blends with the gray of the sagebrush, and he disappears. All this is when you make no demonstration against him; but if you do, he develops a livelier interest in his journey, and instantly electrifies his heels and puts such a deal of real estate between himself and your weapon, that by the time you have raised the hammer you see that you need a Minie rifle,[2] and by the time you have got him in line you need a rifled cannon, and by the time you have "drawn a bead" on him you see well enough that nothing but an unusually long-winded streak of lightning could reach him where he is now. But if you start a swift-footed dog after him, you will enjoy it ever so much —especially if it is a dog that has a good opinion of himself, and has been brought up to think he knows something about speed. The coyote will go swinging gently off on that deceitful trot of his, and every little while he will smile a fraudful smile over his shoulder that will fill that dog entirely full of encouragement and worldly ambition, and make him lay his head still lower to the ground, and stretch his neck further to the front, and pant more fiercely, and stick his tail out straighter behind, and move his furious legs with a yet wilder frenzy, and leave a broader and broader, and higher and denser cloud of desert sand smoking behind,

and marking his long wake across the level plain! And all this time the dog is only a short twenty feet behind the coyote, and to save the soul of him he cannot understand why it is that he cannot get perceptibly closer; and he begins to get aggravated, and it makes him madder and madder to see how gently the coyote glides along and never pants or sweats or ceases to smile; and he grows still more and more incensed to see how shamefully he has been taken in by an entire stranger, and what an ignoble swindle that long, calm, soft-footed trot is; and next he notices that he is getting fagged, and that the coyote actually has to slacken speed a little to keep from running away from him—and *then* that town-dog is mad in earnest, and he begins to strain and weep and swear, and paw the sand higher than ever, and reach for the coyote with concentrated and desperate energy. This "spurt" finds him six feet behind the gliding enemy, and two miles from his friends. And then, in the instant that a wild new hope is lighting up his face, the coyote turns and smiles blandly upon him once more, and with a something about it which seems to say: "Well, I shall have to tear myself away from you, bub—business is business, and it will not do for me to be fooling along this way all day"— and forthwith there is a rushing sound, and the sudden splitting of a long crack through the atmosphere, and behold that dog is solitary and alone in the midst of a vast solitude!

It makes his head swim. He stops,

---

2 **Minie rifle:** 19th-century French gun which used long-range bullets.

and looks all around; climbs the nearest sand-mound, and gazes into the distance; shakes his head reflectively, and then, without a word, he turns and jogs along back to his train, and takes up a humble position under the hindmost wagon, and feels unspeakably mean, and looks ashamed, and hangs his tail at half-mast for a week. And for as much as a year after that, whenever there is a great hue and cry after a coyote, that dog will merely glance in that direction without emotion, and apparently observe to himself, "I believe I do not wish any of the pie."

The coyote lives chiefly in the most desolate and forbidding deserts, along with the lizard, the jack-ass-rabbit, and the raven, and gets an uncertain and precarious living, and earns it. He seems to subsist almost wholly on the carcasses of oxen, mules and horses that have dropped out of emigrant trains and died, and upon windfalls of carrion, and occasional legacies of offal[3] bequeathed to him by white men who have been opulent[4] enough to have something better to butcher than condemned army bacon. He will eat anything in the world. . . .

The coyote of the deserts beyond the Rocky Mountains has a peculiarly hard time of it, owing to the fact that his relations, the Indians, are just as apt to be the first to detect a seductive scent on the desert breeze, and follow the fragrance to the late ox it emanated from, as he is himself; and when this occurs he has to content himself with sitting off at a little distance watching those people strip off and dig out everything edible, and walk off with it. Then he and the waiting ravens explore the skeleton and polish the bones. It is considered that the coyote, and the obscene[5] bird, and the Indian of the desert, testify their blood kinship with each other in that they live together in the waste places of the earth on terms of perfect confidence and friendship, while hating all other creatures and yearning to assist at their funerals. He does not mind going a hundred miles to breakfast, and a hundred and fifty to dinner, because he is sure to have three or four days between meals, and he can just as well be traveling and looking at the scenery as lying around doing nothing and adding to the burdens of his parents.

---

3 **offal:** garbage, especially the discarded portions of butchered animals.
4 **opulent:** plentifully supplied.

5 **obscene:** filthy; disgusting.

MARK TWAIN

Reading Skills

1. What are the characteristics of the author's coyote? Read lines which support your answer.
2. According to Twain, what are one or two sources of fun for the coyote?
3. When a self-confident dog enters into a race with a coyote, what is the long-range effect on the dog's personality?
4. Although part of this selection is about the coyote as he really exists, most of it shows Twain's reaction to the coyote or his interpretation of the coyote's actions. What passages show Twain's reaction to or interpretation of the coyote? (Do you suppose the coyote really has all those thoughts that Twain says he has?)

Understanding Literature

1. Read again Mark Twain's description of the coyote's physical appearance and habits. Then, pretending that you are writing for a scientific journal, describe the animal and its habits. Do not consult an encyclopedia until you have finished; use only the information furnished by Twain. You might begin like this: "The coyote resembles the wolf in appearance, with its long slim body, gray fur, and bushy tail." Some of your other sentences might begin "It lives in. . . . It gets its food. . . . Some of its other habits are. . . ."
2. To what is the coyote compared? Be prepared to read aloud the sentences showing these comparisons. An author's comparisons greatly influence the tone of his work. *Tone* is the author's attitude toward his subject; the tone of a work, for example, may be playful, whimsical, detached, or serious. To what else might Twain have truthfully compared the coyote? How would the comparison you substitute have changed the tone of the selection?
3. There are three principal kinds of pictures: (*a*) a painting, in which an artist shows how something appears to him—not necessarily how it appears to others; (*b*) a photograph, in which a realistic view of something from the physical world is recorded; and (*c*) a cartoon, in which the artist deliberately exaggerates a subject. If you compare the scientist's writing to a photograph, to which type of picture would you compare Twain's description to the coyote? Support your decision.

Focusing on Words

In "The Coyote" Mark Twain uses the exaggeration characteristic of the American tall tale. Explain what each of these exaggerations means:

1. "The coyote is a living, breathing allegory of Want."
2. ". . . even the fleas would desert him for a velocipede."
3. ". . . while his exposed teeth are pretending to threaten, the rest of his face is apologizing for it."
4. ". . . he develops a livelier interest in his journey, and instantly electrifies his heels."
5. ". . . and forthwith there is a rushing sound, and the sudden splitting of a long crack through the atmosphere, and behold that dog is solitary and alone in the midst of a vast solitude!"
6. ". . . hangs his tail at half-mast for a week."

Further Activity

Think of some type of animal or bird which you strongly like or dislike. Describe it, its habitat, its habits, and its actions in a manner that will give the reader factual information and will also show him your love, your sympathy, your fear, your scorn, or whatever feeling you have toward your subject. Use at least one comparison to help the reader understand your attitude toward your subject.

Jean Louis Rodolphe Agassiz, a professor at Harvard from 1848 to 1873, was a famous naturalist. In order to complete a four-volume work on the natural history of the United States, he needed some turtle eggs—some fresh turtle eggs. The problem was to get the eggs to Agassiz within three hours without modern rapid transportation.

Turtle Eggs for Agassiz

Dallas Lore Sharp

IMPROVING YOUR READING: This selection has two distinct parts. In the introduction the author establishes and explains his main point; then he illustrates his main point with an interesting tale. When you have finished reading the introduction, you should know what the author's main idea—his theme—is.

IT IS ONE of the wonders of the world that so few books are written. With every human being a possible book, and with many a human being capable of becoming more books than the world could contain, is it not amazing that the books of men are so few? And so stupid!

I took down, recently, from the shelves of a great public library, the four volumes of Agassiz's *Contributions to the Natural History of the United States.* I doubt if anybody but the charwoman, with her duster, had touched those volumes for twenty-five years. They are an excessively learned, a monumental, an epoch-making work, the fruit of vast and heroic labors, with colored plates on stone, showing the turtles of the United States, and their embryology.[1] The work was published more than half a century ago (by subscription); but it looked old beyond its years—massive, heavy, weathered, as if dug from the rocks. It was difficult to feel that Agassiz could have written it—could have built it, grown it, for the laminated[2] pile had required for its growth the patience and painstaking care of a process of nature, as if it were a kind of printed coral reef. Agassiz do this? The big, human, magnetic man at work upon these pages of capital letters, Roman figures, brackets, and parentheses in explanation of the pages of diagrams and plates! I turned away with a sigh from the weary learning, to read the preface.

When a great man writes a great book he usually flings a preface after it, and thereby saves it, sometimes, from oblivion.[3] Whether so or not,

1 **embryology** (ĕm′brĭ ŏl′ə jĭ): the biology of the development of organisms before they are born or hatched.

2 **laminated:** made or built up in layers.

3 **oblivion:** state of being forgotten by the world.

the best things in most books are their prefaces. It was not, however, the quality of the preface to these great volumes that interested me, but rather the wicked waste of durable book material that went to its making. Reading down through the catalogue of human names and of thanks for help received, I came to a sentence beginning:

"In New England I have myself collected largely; but I have also received valuable contributions from the late Rev. Zadoc Thompson of Burlington . . . from Mr. D. Henry Thoreau of Concord . . . and from Mr. J. W. P. Jenks of Middleboro." And then it hastens on with the thanks in order to get to the turtles, as if turtles were the one and only thing of real importance in all the world.

Turtles no doubt are important, extremely important, embryologically, as part of our genealogical tree;[4] but they are away down among the roots of the tree as compared with the late Rev. Zadoc Thompson of Burlington. I happen to know nothing about the Rev. Zadoc, but to me he looks very interesting. Indeed any reverend gentleman of his name and day who would catch turtles for Agassiz must have been interesting. And as for Henry Thoreau, we know he was interesting. The rarest wood turtle in the United States was not so rare a specimen as this gentleman of Walden Woods and Concord. We are glad even for this line in the preface about him;

glad to know that he tried, in this untranscendental[5] way, to serve his day and generation. If Agassiz had only put a chapter in his turtle book about it! But this is the material he wasted, this and more of the same human sort, for the Mr. "Jenks of Middleboro" (at the end of the quotation) was, years later, an old college professor of mine, who told me some of the particulars of his turtle contributions, particulars which Agassiz should have found a place for in his big book. The preface says merely that this gentleman sent turtles to Cambridge by the thousands —brief and scanty recognition. For that is not the only thing this gentleman did. On one occasion he sent, not turtles, but turtle *eggs* to Cambridge—*brought* them, I should say; and all there is to show for it, so far as I could discover, is a sectional drawing of a bit of the mesoblastic layer[6] of one of the eggs!

Of course, Agassiz wanted to make that mesoblastic drawing, or some other equally important drawing, and had to have the fresh turtle egg to draw it from. He had to have it, and he got it. A great man, when he wants a certain turtle egg, at a certain time, always gets it, for he gets someone else to get it. I am glad he got it. But what makes me sad and impatient is that he did not think it worth while to tell about the getting of it, and so made merely a learned turtle book of what might

5 untranscendental: practical; concerned with worldly affairs.
6 mesoblastic layer: middle layer of cells of an embryo (here an unhatched turtle).

4 genealogical tree: family tree.

DALLAS LORE SHARP

have been an exceedingly interesting human book.

It would seem, naturally, that there could be nothing unusual or interesting about the getting of turtle eggs when you want them. Nothing at all, if you should chance to want the eggs as you chance to find them. So with anything else —good copper stock, for instance, if you should chance to want it, and should chance to be along when they chance to be giving it away. But if you want copper stock, say of C & H quality, *when* you want it, and are bound to have it, then you must command more than a college professor's salary. And likewise, precisely, when it is turtle eggs that you are bound to have.

Agassiz wanted those turtle eggs when he wanted them—not a minute over three hours from the minute they were laid. Yet even that does not seem exacting, hardly more difficult than the getting of hen eggs only three hours old. Just so, provided the professor could have had his private turtle coop in Harvard Yard; and provided he could have made his turtles lay. But turtles will not respond, like hens, to meat scraps and the warm mash. The professor's problem was not to get from a mud turtle's nest in the back yard to the table in the laboratory; but to get from the laboratory in Cambridge to some pond when the turtles were laying, and back to the laboratory within the limited time. And this, in the days of Darius Green, might have called for nice and discriminating work—as it did.

Agassiz had been engaged for a long time upon his *Contributions*. He had brought the great work nearly to a finish. It was, indeed, finished but for one small yet very important bit of observation: he had carried the turtle egg through every stage of its development with the single exception of one—the very earliest—that stage of first cleavages, when the cell begins to segment,[7] immediately upon its being laid. That beginning stage had brought the *Contributions* to a halt. To get eggs that were fresh enough to show the incubation at this period had been impossible.

There were several ways that Agassiz might have proceeded: he might have got a leave of absence for the spring term, taken his laboratory to some pond inhabited by turtles, and there camped until he should catch the reptile digging out her nest. But there were difficulties in all of that—as those who are college professors and naturalists know. As this was quite out of the question, he did the easiest thing—asked Mr. "Jenks of Middleboro" to get him the eggs. Mr. Jenks got them. Agassiz knew all about his getting of them; and I say the strange and irritating thing is that Agassiz did not think it worth while to tell us about it, at least in the preface to his monumental work.

It was many years later that Mr. Jenks, then a gray-haired college professor, told me how he got those eggs to Agassiz.

7 **segment:** divide.

"I was principal of an academy, during my younger years," he began, "and was busy one day with my classes, when a large man suddenly filled the doorway of the room, smiled to the four corners of the room, and called out with a big, quick voice that he was Professor Agassiz.

"Of course he was. I knew it, even before he had had time to shout it to me across the room.

"Would I get him some turtle eggs? he called. Yes, I would. And would I get them to Cambridge within three hours from the time they were laid? Yes, I would. And I did. And it was worth the doing. But I did it only once.

"When I promised Agassiz those eggs I knew where I was going to get them. I had got turtle eggs there before—at a particular patch of sandy shore along a pond, a few miles distant from the academy.

"Three hours was the limit. From the railroad station to Boston was thirty-five miles; from the pond to the station was perhaps three or four miles; from Boston to Cambridge we called about three miles. Forty miles in round numbers! We figured it all out before he returned, and got the trip down to two hours—record time: driving from the pond to the station; from the station by express train to Boston; from Boston by cab to Cambridge. This left an easy hour for accidents and delays.

"Cab and car and carriage we reckoned into our timetable; but what we didn't figure on was the turtle." And he paused abruptly.

"Young man," he went on, his shaggy brows and spectacles hardly hiding the twinkle in the eyes that were bent severely upon me, "young man, when *you* go after turtle eggs, take into account the turtle. No! no! That's bad advice. Youth never reckons on the turtle—and youth seldom ought to. Only old age does that; and old age would never have got those turtle eggs to Aggassiz.

"It was in the early spring that Agassiz came to the academy, long before there was any likelihood of the turtles laying. But I was eager for the quest, and so fearful of failure that I started out to watch at the pond fully two weeks ahead of the time that the turtles might be expected to lay. I remember the date clearly: it was May 14.

"A little before dawn—along near three o'clock—I would drive over to the pond, hitch my horse near by, settle myself quietly among some thick cedars close to the sandy shore, and there I would wait, my kettle of sand ready, my eye covering the whole sleeping pond. Here among the cedars I would eat my breakfast, and then get back in good season to open the academy for the morning session.

"And so the watch began.

"I soon came to know individually the dozen or more turtles that kept to my side of the pond. Shortly after the cold mist would lift and melt away they would stick up their heads through the quiet water; and as the sun slanted down over the ragged rim of treetops the slow things would float into the warm, lighted spots, or crawl out and doze comfortably on the hummocks and snags.

"What fragrant mornings those were! How fresh and new and unbreathed! The pond odors, the woods odors, the odors of the plowed fields—of water lily, and wild grape, and the dew-laid soil! I can taste them yet, and hear them yet—the still, large sounds of the waking day —the pickerel breaking the quiet with his swirl; the kingfisher dropping anchor; the stir of feet and wings among the trees. And then the thought of the great book being held up for me! Those were rare mornings!

"But there began to be a good many of them, for the turtles showed no desire to lay. They sprawled in the sun, and never one came out upon the sand as if she intended to help on the great professor's book. The embryology of her eggs was of small concern to her; her contribution to the Natural History of the United States could wait.

"And it did wait. I began my watch on the fourteenth of May; June first found me still among the cedars, still waiting, as I had waited every morning, Sundays and rainy days alike. June first saw a perfect morning, but every turtle slid out upon her log, as if egg laying might be a matter strictly of next year.

"I began to grow uneasy—not impatient yet, for a naturalist learns his lesson of patience early, and for all his years; but I began to fear lest, by some subtle sense, my presence might somehow be known to the creatures; that they might have gone to some other place to lay, while I was away at the schoolroom.

"I watched on to the end of the first week, on to the end of the second week in June, seeing the mists rise and vanish every morning, and along with them vanish, more and more, the poetry of my early morning vigil. Poetry and rheumatism cannot long dwell together in the same clump of cedars, and I had begun to feel the rheumatism. A month of morning mists wrapping me around had at last soaked through to my bones. But Agassiz was waiting, and the world was waiting, for those turtle eggs; and I would wait. It was all I could do, for there is no use bringing a china nest egg[8] to a turtle; she is not open to any such delicate suggestion.

"Then came a mid-June Sunday morning, with dawn breaking a little after three: a warm, wide-awake dawn, with the level mist lifted from the level surface of the pond a full hour higher than I had seen it any morning before.

"This was the day: I knew it. I have heard persons say that they can hear the grass grow; that they know by some extra sense when danger is nigh. That we have these extra senses I fully believe, and I believe they can be sharpened by cultivation. For a month I had been watching, brooding over this pond, and now I knew. I felt a stirring

8 china nest egg: artificial egg left in a nest to induce hens to lay eggs there.

of the pulse of things that the cold-hearted turtles could no more escape than could the clods and I.

"Leaving my horse unhitched, as if he too understood, I slipped eagerly into my covert for a look at the pond. As I did so, a large pickerel plowed a furrow out through the spatterdocks,[9] and in his wake rose the head of an enormous turtle. Swinging slowly around, the creature headed straight for the shore, and without a pause scrambled out on the sand.

"She was about the size of a big scoop shovel; but that was not what excited me, so much as her manner, and the gait at which she moved; for there was method in it, and fixed purpose. On she came, shuffling over the sand toward the higher open fields, with a hurried, determined seesaw that was taking her somewhere in particular, and that was bound to get her there on time.

"I held my breath. Had she been a dinosaurian making Mesozoic[10] footprints, I could not have been more fearful. For footprints in the Mesozoic mud, or in the sands of time, were as nothing to me when compared with fresh turtle eggs in the sands of this pond.

"But over the strip of sand, without a stop, she paddled, and up a narrow cowpath into the high grass along a fence. Then up the narrow cowpath, on all fours, just like another turtle, I paddled, and into the high wet grass along the fence.

9 **spatterdocks:** common yellow water lilies.
10 **Mesozoic:** a period in geologic history when dinosaurs inhabited the earth.

"I kept well within sound of her, for she moved recklessly, leaving a trail of flattened grass a foot and a half wide. I wanted to stand up—and I don't believe I could have turned her back with a rail—but I was afraid if she saw me that she might return indefinitely to the pond; so on I went, flat to the ground, squeezing through the lower rails of the fence, as if the field beyond were a melon patch. It was nothing of the kind, only a wild, uncomfortable pasture, full of dewberry vines, and very discouraging. They were excessively wet vines and briery. I pulled my coat sleeves as far over my fists as I could get them, and, with the tin pail of sand swinging from between my teeth to avoid noise, I stumped fiercely, but silently, on after the turtle.

"She was laying her course, I thought, straight down the length of this dreadful pasture, when, not far from the fence, she suddenly hove to, warped herself short about, and came back, barely clearing me, at a clip that was thrilling. I warped about, too, and in her wake bore down across the corner of the pasture, across the powdery public road, and on to a fence along a field of young corn.

"I was somewhat wet by this time, but not so wet as I had been before, wallowing through the deep dry dust of the road. Hurrying up behind a large tree by the fence, I peered down the corn rows and saw the turtle stop, and begin to paw about in the loose soft soil. She was going to lay!

"I held on to the tree and watched, as she tried this place, and that place, and the other place—the eternally feminine! But *the* place, evidently, was hard to find. What could a female turtle do with a whole field of possible nests to choose from? Then at last she found it, and, whirling about, she backed quickly at it, and, tail first, began to bury herself before my staring eyes.

"Those were not the supreme moments of my life; perhaps those moments came later that day; but those certainly were among the slowest, most dreadfully mixed of moments that I ever experienced. They were hours long. There she was, her shell just showing, like some old hulk in the sand alongshore. And how long would she stay there? And

how should I know if she had laid an egg?

"I could still wait. And so I waited, when, over the freshly awakened fields, floated four mellow strokes from the distant town clock.

"Four o'clock! Why, there was no train until seven! No train for three hours! The eggs would spoil! Then with a rush it came over me that this was Sunday morning, and there was no regular seven o'clock train—none till after nine.

"I think I should have fainted had not the turtle just then begun crawling off. I was weak and dizzy; but there, there in the sand, were the eggs! And Agassiz! And the great book! And I cleared the fence, and the forty miles that lay between me and Cambridge, at a single jump. He should have them, trains or no.

Those eggs should go to Agassiz by seven o'clock, if I had to gallop every mile of the way. Forty miles! Any horse could cover it in three hours, if he had to; and, upsetting the astonished turtle, I scooped out her round white eggs.

"On a bed of sand in the bottom of the pail I laid them, with what care my trembling fingers allowed; filled in between them with more sand; so with another layer to the rim; and, covering all smoothly with more sand, I ran back for my horse.

"That horse knew, as well as I, that the turtle had laid, and that he was to get those eggs to Agassiz. He turned out of that field into the road on two wheels, a thing he had not done for twenty years, doubling me up before the dashboard, the pail of eggs miraculously lodged between my knees.

"I let him out. If only he could keep this pace all the way to Cambridge! Or even halfway there; and I should have time to finish the trip on foot. I shouted him on, holding to the dasher with one hand, the pail of eggs with the other, not daring to get off my knees, though the bang on them, as we pounded down the wood road, was terrific. But nothing must happen to the eggs; they must not be jarred, or even turned over in the sand before they came to Agassiz.

"In order to get out on the pike it was necessary to drive back away from Boston toward the town. We had nearly covered the distance, and were rounding a turn from the woods into the open fields, when, ahead of me, at the station it seemed, I heard the quick sharp whistle of a locomotive.

"What did it mean? Then followed the *puff, puff, puff* of a starting train. But what train? Which way going? And, jumping to my feet for a longer view, I pulled into a side road that paralleled the track, and headed hard for the station.

"We reeled along. The station was still out of sight, but from behind the bushes that shut it from view rose the smoke of a moving engine. It was perhaps a mile away, but we were approaching, head-on, and, topping a little hill, I swept down upon a freight train, the black smoke pouring from the stack, as the mighty creature pulled itself together for its swift run down the rails.

"My horse was on the gallop, going with the track, and straight toward the coming train. The sight of it almost maddened me—the bare thought of it, on the road to Boston! On I went; on it came, a half—a quarter of a mile between us, when suddenly my road shot out along an unfenced field with only a level stretch of sod between me and the engine.

"With a pull that lifted the horse from his feet, I swung him into the field and sent him straight as an arrow for the track. That train should carry me and my eggs to Boston!

"The engineer pulled the rope. He saw me standing up in the rig, saw my hat blow off, saw me wave my arms, saw the tin pail swing in my teeth, and he jerked out a succession of sharp halts! But it was he who should halt, not I; and on we went, the horse with a flounder landing the carriage on top of the track.

"The train was already grinding to a stop; but before it was near a standstill I had backed off the track, jumped out, and, running down the rails with the astonished engineers gaping at me, had swung aboard the cab.

"They offered no resistance; they hadn't had time. Nor did they have the disposition, for I looked strange, not to say dangerous. Hatless, dew-soaked, smeared with yellow mud, and holding, as if it were a baby or a bomb, a little tin pail of sand.

"'Crazy,' the fireman muttered, looking to the engineer for his cue.

"I had been crazy, perhaps, but I was not crazy now.

"'Throw her wide open,' I commanded. 'Wide open! These are fresh turtle eggs for Professor Agassiz of Cambridge. He must have them before breakfast.'

"Then they knew I was crazy, and, evidently thinking it best to humor me, threw the throttle wide open, and away we went.

"I kissed my hand to the horse, grazing unconcernedly in the open field, and gave a smile to my crew. That was all I could give them, and hold myself and the eggs together. But the smile was enough. And they smiled through their smut at me, though one of them held fast to his shovel, while the other kept his hand upon a big ugly wrench. Neither of them spoke to me, but above the roar of the swaying engine I caught enough of their broken talk to understand that they were driving under a full head of steam, with the intention of handing me over to the Boston police, as perhaps the easiest way of disposing of me.

"I was only afraid that they would try it at the next station. But that station whizzed past without a bit of slack, and the next, and the next; when it came over me that this was the through freight, which should have passed in the night, and was making up lost time.

"Only the fear of the shovel and the wrench kept me from shaking hands with both men at this discovery. But I beamed at them; and they at me. I was enjoying it. The unwonted jar beneath my feet was wrinkling my diaphragm with spasms of delight. And the fireman beamed at the engineer, with a look that said, 'See the lunatic grin; he likes it!'

"He did like it. How the iron wheels sang to me as they took the rails! How the rushing wind in my ears sang to me! From my stand on the fireman's side of the cab I could catch a glimpse of the track just ahead of the engine, where the ties seemed to leap into the throat of the mile-devouring monster. The joy of it! Of seeing space swallowed by the mile!

"I shifted the eggs from hand to hand and thought of my horse, of Agassiz, of the great book, of my great luck—luck—luck—until the multitudinous tongues of the thundering train were all chiming 'luck! luck! luck!' They knew! They understood! This beast of fire and tireless wheels was doing its very best to get the eggs to Agassiz!

"We swung out past the Blue Hills, and yonder flashed the morning sun from the towering dome of the State House. I might have leaped from the cab and run the rest of the way on foot, had I not caught the eye of the engineer watching me narrowly. I was not in Boston yet, nor in Cambridge either. I was an escaped lunatic, who had held up a train, and forced it to carry me to Boston.

"Perhaps I had overdone my lunacy business. Suppose these two men should take it into their heads to turn me over to the police, whether I would or no? I could never explain the case in time to get the eggs to Agassiz. I looked at my watch. There were still a few minutes left, in which I might explain to these men, who, all at once, had become my captors. But it was too late. Nothing could avail against my actions, my appearance, and my little pail of sand.

"I had not thought of my appearance before. Here I was, face and clothes caked with yellow mud, my hair wild and matted, my hat gone, and in my full-grown hands a tiny tin pail of sand, as if I had been digging all night with a tiny shovel on the shore! And thus to appear in the decent streets of Boston of a Sunday morning!

"I began to feel like a hunted criminal. The situation was serious, or might be, and rather desperately funny at its best. I must in some way have shown my new fears, for both men watched me more sharply.

"Suddenly, as we were nearing the outer freight yard, the train slowed down and came to a stop. I was ready to jump, but I had no chance. They had nothing to do, apparently, but to guard me. I looked at my watch again. What time we had made! It was only six o'clock, with a whole hour to get to Cambridge.

"But I didn't like this delay. Five minutes—ten—went by.

"'Gentlemen,' I began, but was cut short by an express train coming past. We were moving again, on—into a siding; on—on to the main track; and on with a bump and a crash and a succession of crashes, running the length of the train; on at a turtle's pace, but on, when the fireman, quickly jumping for the bell rope, left the way to the step free, and—the chance had come!

"I never touched the step, but landed in the soft sand at the side of the track, and made a line for the yard fence.

"There was no hue or cry. I glanced over my shoulder to see if they were after me. Evidently their hands were full, and they didn't know I had gone.

"But I had gone; and was ready to drop over the high board fence, when it occurred to me that I might drop into a policeman's arms. Hanging my pail in a splint on top of a post, I peered cautiously over—a very wise thing to do before you jump a high board fence. There, crossing the open square toward the station, was a big, burly fellow with a club—looking for me.

"I flattened for a moment, when someone in the yard yelled at me. I preferred the policeman, and, grabbing my pail, I slid over to the street. The policeman moved on past the corner of the station out of sight. The square was free, and yonder stood a cab!

"Time was flying now. Here was the last lap. The cabman saw me coming, and squared away. I waved a paper dollar at him, but he only stared the more. A dollar can cover a good deal, but I was too much for one dollar. I pulled out another, thrust them both at him, and dodged into the cab, calling, 'Cambridge!'

"He would have taken me straight to the police station had I not said, 'Harvard College. Professor Agassiz's house! I've got eggs for Agassiz'; and pushed another dollar up at him through the hole.

"It was nearly half past six.

"'Let him go!' I ordered. "Here's another dollar if you make Agassiz's house in twenty minutes. Let him out; never mind the police!'

"He evidently knew the police, or there were none around at that time on a Sunday morning. We went down the sleeping streets as I had gone down the wood roads from the pond two hours before, but with the rattle and crash now of a fire brigade. Whirling a corner into Cambridge Street, we took the bridge at a gallop, the driver shouting out something in Hibernian to a pair of waving arms and a belt and brass buttons.

"Across the bridge with a rattle and jolt that put the eggs in jeopardy, and on over the cobblestones, we went. Half standing, to lessen the jar, I held the pail in one hand and held myself in the other, not daring to let go even to look at my watch.

"But I was afraid to look at the watch. I was afraid to see how near to seven o'clock it might be. The sweat was dropping from my nose, so close was I running to the limit of my time.

"Suddenly there was a lurch, and I dived forward, ramming my head into the front of the cab, coming up with a rebound that landed me across the small of my back on the seat, and sent half of my pail of eggs helter-skelter over the floor.

"We had stopped. Here was Agassiz's house; and without taking time to pick up the scattered eggs I tumbled out, and pounded at the door.

"No one was astir in the house. But I would stir them. And I did. Right in the midst of the racket the door opened. It was the maid.

"'Agassiz,' I gasped, 'I want Professor Agassiz, quick!' And I pushed by her into the hall.

"'Go 'way, sir. I'll call the police. Professor Agassiz is in bed. Go 'way, sir!'

"'Call him—Agassiz—instantly, or I'll call him myself.'

"But I didn't; for just then a door overhead was flung open, a great white-robed figure appeared on the dim landing above, and a quick loud voice called excitedly:

"'Let him in! Let him in! I know him. He has my turtle eggs!'

DALLAS LORE SHARP

299

"And the apparition, slipperless, and clad in anything but an academic gown, came sailing down the stairs.

"The maid fled. The great man, his arms extended, laid hold of me with both hands, and, dragging me and my precious pail into his study, with a swift, clean stroke laid open one of the eggs, as the watch in my trembling hands ticked its way to seven—as if nothing unusual were happening to the history of the world."

"You were in time, then?" I said.

"To the tick. There stands my copy of the great book. I am proud of the humble part I had in it."

Reading Skills

1. Why were three-hour-old turtle eggs so important to Agassiz?
2. Why was the procurement of turtle eggs for Agassiz an obviously difficult task? What was the major obstacle to be overcome? What problems intervened once the egg-hunt and delivery were under way?
3. At first, Mr. Jenks advised that "when *you* go after turtle eggs, take into account the turtle." Then he withdrew that advice. Why did he withdraw it?
4. Assuming that this account is reasonably accurate, explain how it illustrates the saying that "truth is stranger than fiction." If you saw this story dramatized on television and did not know that it was true, what would be your reaction?

Understanding Literature

1. In the second paragraph, Dallas Lore Sharp calls Agassiz's *Contributions to the Natural History of the United States* "a kind of printed coral reef." How is the work like a coral reef? In this paragraph, to what else does Sharp compare the work?
2. What main idea does Sharp establish in the introduction? How does he illustrate this idea in the introduction? How does Mr. Jenks's story illustrate this idea?
3. Why does the author let Mr. Jenks tell his own story?
4. How does the author magnify the suspense in Mr. Jenks's story before the acquisition of the eggs? How does he heighten the suspense when telling about Mr. Jenks's journey to Cambridge?

This description of the Rio Grande allows you to observe the impressive "Great River" and its surroundings. The author, Paul Horgan, received the 1955 Pulitzer prize for his two-volume history of the Rio Grande, entitled *Great River;* the work was praised by critics both for its literary excellence and for its historical accuracy.

Pages from a Rio Grande Notebook

Paul Horgan

IMPROVING YOUR READING: The author's organization of this description is so obvious that you should detect it before you are halfway to the end of this selection. See how quickly you can identify the pattern of organization.

IT IS BORN of winter, this river, in the longest season of cold in the United States. The source mountains in the Colorado Rockies are hard and wild. The air is thin and at such altitude subject to swift, crystalline changes of condition which may bring blue darkness in midday, and yield snow during nine months of the year.

Past monstrous peaks of ragged lifeless rock, clouds tear and roll from wall to wall up in the sky. Wind cries there much of the time, and when the atmosphere is overcharged with electricity, the cut and flare of lightning, the trundle and bounce of thunder after its valley-sharpened crash seem to require new senses, capacities, to be wholly heard.

The river's course—here as in its whole career—widens and narrows by turns. Where it is narrow, the slopes are dark, the stream is shadowed all day but for a little while at noon, when straight fingers of sunlight reach down through the forest. The stream is clear and icy, going rapidly over polished brown speckled stones. They remind us of something. At a glance the diamond water going over its stony bed makes the image of the fish it carries—the same speckled colors, the same watery flicker, the same half-lights of reflection and golden flecks. In and out of leaf shadow, protected by the dazzle of moving water, the trout in plain sight is safe because he and his river are so close in likeness.

The Rio Grande towns in Colorado —Del Norte, Monte Vista, Alamosa —are pleasant young communities whose life in each place parallels the railroad tracks for a mile or two. About twenty miles southeast of Alamosa the first sign of Spanish adobe culture appears in a little village— Los Sauses, with houses built of earth, under grand cottonwoods, on a gentle slope above the river, en-

PAUL HORGAN

301

circled by fine hills. This scene made of slow water, bounteous tree, earthen brick and irrigated field is like a symbolic image of much that is to follow as the river goes south. It is the kind of cell of family, primal want and basic sustenance[1] made visible from which, down-river, grew clusters of kinsmen, and then of neighbors, and then of material defendants, and then of parishioners, and then of descendants, in turn, until a village became a town which became a city, all originally and even now dependent upon the Rio Grande for life.

Over the three communities of Taos—the pueblo, the middle commercial town, and the old Ranchos —there is a piercing sweet illimitable clarity of light and sky. Sounds carry, meadow larks, mocking birds, black birds have returned. Over the long plain breathes the wind, sharply sweet and already warmed, disturbing nothing but the senses. Space is so great, vision is so plain, air is so clear that human activities can be seen from afar. Small figures like humanity in Brueghel[2] go about their tasks. Earthen buildings go up. Carts travel. Winter rubble is cleared off the fields and out of the acequias.[3] Furrows are seeded. Out in the sage brush of Taos plain, where the old road winds toward the canyon, tiny newborn lambs take fright and scamper before the gusty sand devils whipped up by the dart-ing wind. Flocks move more slowly than cloud shadows. Shepherds sit on a modern culvert and watch what the road brings. The valor and pity of men and women in their renewed use of a corner of the earth is as much a part of spring as everything else.

Above Albuquerque begins the lyric grace of the river in its richest passage of the pastoral life. Where life is fed by water, the landscape here recalls the opulence and grandeur and occasional vistas of order in the image of classical country painted by Nicholas Poussin, who left so many celebrations of grove and meadow, shady leaf and column of light, reflecting stream and stepped mountain and composed bodies. There is more than a reminder here, there is a real likeness. It is a likeness of grace and plenty in the midst of dramatic nature; nourishment in the desert; bounty summoned by the most ancient of agricultural rites out of the most inscrutable of antiquities; cool for the heated, slaking for the parched, food for the hungry, rest for the weary, ease for the eye blinded in the unimpeded sun.

Up to now, going south, when you looked across the river, you knew exactly how things were on the other side—just more United States of America. But at El Paso with the new concept of a boundary between nations, things are no longer the same on the opposite bank. It is another country, with another people,

---

1 **primal . . . sustenance:** the chief needs of life (food, clothing, shelter) and the materials which satisfy these needs.
2 **Brueghel** (brœ′gəl): 16th-century Flemish painter, whose paintings show small, grotesque, humorous figures.
3 **acequias** (ə sā′kyəz): irrigation trenches.

and with other ways. Many manners and customs have remained common to both sides of the Rio Grande since the time a little over a century ago when the river was not a frontier—when in fact both its banks and all its courses were Spanish or Mexican. But in the United States, subject to a more powerful energy in a more technical society, such survivals remain as exotic,[4] quaint, or commercially glamorous; while in Mexico the same expressions are sincere and not self-conscious. From El Paso southeastward, every United States town has its Mexican counterpart across the river. Commerce, appetite and corruption draw them together. Language, national boundary and law keep them apart. The river itself is hardly an obstacle anywhere, for it can be waded for most of the year, whatever else its common uses may be.

Seventy miles below El Paso, mountains reach in on both sides of the Rio Grande and present to it another of its many obstacles; but the stream bed passes between them and continues upon its depleted way. The river is dying. The desert finally seems ready to triumph over it and drink out of sight the last crawling trickles of the flow that was born in the Colorado Rockies.

And so it would, but relief and replenishment are on their way from another mountain system lying deep in Mexico, where the Rio Conchos with its major tributary the Rio San Pedro courses northeastward to join the Rio Grande at an altitude of 2400 feet a few miles above the old Texas town of Presidio. With it comes new power for the river, to create dramatic, and even melodramatic, phases of its career, in the accomplishment of water over rock, as demonstrated by the vast implausibilities of the earth features of the Big Bend.

At Presidio the replenished river fashions another of those green and easy valleys which, as at Alamosa, Espanola, Algodones, Albuquerque, Belen and Mesilla, lie on ancient fertile flats of old river bottoms between gravel terraces and outlying mountains. After the bare and voracious[5] desert in which it nearly died, the river brings again willows and cottonwoods, lilac mountains and attendant mountains, blue sky and emerald green fields and pink sand, with a sweetness in the air made from all these together.

Summer is a long season here, after the harsh, bitter wind storms of spring, with their abrasive white dust that flies out of rocky arroyos[6] to the north, casting a steel-blue obscurity across the sun.

Previously the river has always been accompanied by mountains, near or far; but they lay generally parallel to its course. Now in the Big Bend the river encounters mountains in a new and extraordinary way; for they lie, chain after chain of them, directly across its way as though to impede and divert it and

---

4 **exotic:** foreign.

5 **voracious** (vō rā′shəs): greedy.
6 **arroyos:** gullies.

deny it passage to the sea. But the pull of the sea is stronger than rock, and the river was here before the mountains, and as they rose, in slowness beyond time, it cut its way against and through them.

Born in mountains, and cradled by them, and then opposed by them, the Rio Grande has always been within sight of them. But below the Big Bend they start to fall away. If you can say so, now as the river goes southeastward, mountains are getting lost, like beads of a string which has broken so the ones at the end rest separate without apparent connection with each other until finally there are no more.

Autumn is the seasonal analogy of age; and now in autumn, and here approaching the sea, the river shows its age most plainly. In its last phase with less than two feet a mile to drop, it flows slowly, making bend after bend of wide loops. Built by the drag of silt the river banks rise above the surrounding country. Everywhere are signs of former river beds which finally became too shallow and too elevated to retain the river in storm time. The river broke over, making new courses. The older ones grew grass and softened their contours. Everywhere is the green growth of semitropical climate.

The citrus, palm, garden aspect of the lower valley land begins to merge east of Brownsville into white sand and salt grass, through which the Rio Grande twists from side to side, mild and nearly exhausted. Dunes accompany it and migrate with the wind. Sometimes hurricanes formed in the West Indies slash inland over the delta. But it is too late for weather to create much downstream change in the Rio Grande in its last wandering miles.

There is evidence of marsh life. The river banks in places are hardly an inch or two above the flow. Water fowl attend—cranes, herons, geese, ducks, curlews, plover, sandpipers. The light of the sky continuously fades and brightens according to sea clouds that hardly form but hang low and filmy, as white as the wilderness of sand on which they make glistening shadows. Salt marshes and lagoons rest like misted mirrors among the low hollows bounded by dunes. The wasted flood plain is running out with the continent.

Isolated, depleted, heavy with suspended oil, the river widens gradually to a thousand feet and leaves the dunes between low shelves of sandy beach littered with driftwood that is polished to silver by wind and sun, or blackened by saturation. Through a waste of sand, misty air and silence, in the presence of no human concern, having come more than eighteen hundred miles from mountains nearly three miles high, the Rio Grande at last enters the Gulf of Mexico and the sea.

Reading Skills

1. Describe the different kinds of territory through which the Rio Grande flows on its way to the sea.
2. How does the nature of the river itself change as it travels to the Gulf of Mexico?
3. According to the author, what difference is there between Mexican customs in Mexico and the same customs on the Texan side of the river?
4. Why does Paul Horgan state that the mountains impede the Rio Grande and "deny it passage to the sea" in the Big Bend area? (A map of Texas should reveal the reason.)
5. With a diagram, if necessary, explain what the author means when he describes the disappearance of the mountains below Big Bend. To what does he compare the disappearance of the mountains?

Understanding Literature

1. What plan does the author follow in presenting his description of the Rio Grande?
2. The author compares the stages of the river to the four seasons; for example, the first sentence says that the river "is born of winter." What stage of the river is comparable to spring? to summer? What does "Autumn is the seasonal analogy of age" mean?
3. Paul Horgan uses the works of two artists as bases for comparisons. How does he provide for the fact that his readers may not be familiar with the paintings of Poussin?
4. This selection includes a great number of sentences with expressions in series, such as "Commerce, appetite and corruption draw them together. Language, national boundary and law keep them apart." Find other examples of words or phrases in series. What effect does this sentence pattern create?

Focusing on Words

Much of the beauty of this picture of the Rio Grande comes from Paul Horgan's choice of words. For each of the following, substitute a more direct expression, such as a newspaper reporter might use. Then explain how Horgan's words provide a more precise or colorful picture.

1. ". . . the longest season of cold in the United States."
2. ". . . clouds . . . roll from wall to wall."
3. ". . . the wind, sharply sweet and already warmed, disturbing nothing but the senses."
4. ". . . the pull of the sea is stronger than rock."
5. ". . . the river shows its age most plainly."
6. ". . . the Rio Grande twists from side to side, mild and nearly exhausted."
7. "Salt marshes and lagoons rest like misted mirrors."

Further Activity

Utilizing the type of organization illustrated by "Pages from a Rio Grande Notebook," write a description which takes your readers along a course from one point to another. Consider a topic similar to one of the following:

1. Along the turnpike.
2. My first flight.
3. A walk past the cemetery at night.
4. Across the city.

Before you begin writing, make a plan for your descriptive essay.

Perhaps you think that no creature in the ocean can defeat an eighty-foot whale in a life-and-death struggle. Maybe no single creature can, but when two or three giant cuttlefish simultaneously attack a whale, the victory can go to either side.

Battle in the Depths

Paul Annixter

IMPROVING YOUR READING: The battle between the whale and the cuttlefish furnishes the excitement in this selection, but the battle makes up only a third of the story. The author uses the remainder of the tale to portray the appearance and nature of the whale, much as he would portray the personality of a human character. Before you finish reading, you should have a distinct idea of what the whale "hero" is like.

THE DEEP CHURNED. Something was happening far down in the dim, foggy-green depths. Currents and chains of bubbles came rushing to the surface and the upflung waters whipped to foam. Gradually the surface became tinged with a brickish stain that told the story of battle in these tropic seas.

Now, as if a great fire had been lighted down there, gigantic bubbles rose and broke, the waters boiled. A maelstrom[1] of foam, all creaming and seething, burst to the surface and through it cut a black triangular fin. It disappeared but another followed, and still another.

Then *he* appeared.

At first he seemed but a pearl-wreathed ghost of enormous size, becoming a darkening shadow shape, glaucous,[2] gigantic, and growing, as if a mountain or part of the sea bed had risen from the abyss. Up and up he came, an oblong mass like some great blunt-nosed torpedo up-ended in the swells.

The torpedo shape was merely his head, gigantic, blunt, square-ended, yet mild of aspect as some stupendous pollywog. As he surfaced a burst of oily vapor spurted from an S-shaped cavity at the top of his head in an upward and forward blast like a jet of steam, that could have been seen by a ship two miles away.

After he blew, yet more head appeared, with little, deep-set eyes placed far back in it, down close to the water line. Finally, the long, narrow, saw-toothed underjaw was exposed—a flat, twenty-five-foot shaft

---

1 **maelstrom** (māl′strəm): large whirlpool.

2 **glaucous** (glô′kəs): very brilliant.

of bone, hinged like a box and set with fifty enormous, conical teeth that were still chomping on a mass of deep-sea squid, the bait royal of the cachalot[3] clan.

When the whole beast lay on the surface, rising monstrously above the lapping swells, he was a dark, breathing island of whale some eighty or so feet long, and wide in proportion. A bull sperm just reaching his prime, he was already a giant of his giant race. The bulk of him was covered with skin like glistening, dark silk. Behind the head, or "junk," as whalers call it, was a hump, but there was no dorsal fin and the flukes of his tail were set horizontally, not vertically as in fish. An eon or so ago, the cachalot's ancestors had run through the primeval forest on four short legs. Then, like certain other mammals, they had taken to the water for survival during the grim Age of Transition.

He was still chomping on the squid he had fought and vanquished down there in the depths. His nine-inch teeth caught a glint of morning light as he sheared off a few more wriggling arm-tips of the cuttle. The scraps were swiftly snapped up by the mixed company of sharks that ringed him, rushing in and out with a curl of foam. Small as compared with the cachalot, averaging from twelve to twenty feet in length, they comprised the most voracious[4] of sea scavengers, hammerheads, blues, tigers, and the twenty-foot killers known as "gray nurse" to the men of the southern waters. Not content with sharing in his feast these fed also upon their host, lancing in with a twisting turn to snatch chunks of white blubber from the whale's side and to rush off with it in their saw-toothed jaws. As the sharks well knew, the whale had been down deep and was tired and winded. Once he had swallowed his meal and recovered his breath, this would be no place for such as they, but meanwhile these sea jackals would take all possible advantage.

The monster blew again. His spouting continued at regular fourteen-second intervals while his red blood was reoxidized. All that time the sharks nagged him, chop and run. Their ferocity knew no bounds, yet the worst they could do was small in the face of the calm immensity of the giant, the mountainous reservoirs of power and energy in the ninety-odd tons of him. In places his hide alone was a foot and a half thick, with barnacles and shellfish living in the wrinkles. Beneath it were incredible layers of nerveless blubber that swathed him in warmth and protection.

Abruptly, with a rush as of cataracts, the sperm whirled upon himself, flinging his great bulk almost clear of the water. With a crash that shook the sea he struck the surface again, his great jaws clashing shut in the same moment like the dropping of an iron portcullis.[5]

---

3 **cachalot** (kăsh′ə lŏt′): sperm whale.
4 **voracious** (vō rā′shəs): greedy.

5 **portcullis**: grate, dropped over the gateway of a fortress to prevent entrance.

PAUL ANNIXTER

His tormentors scattered to all sides, some of them leaping clear of the surface in their speed, revealing their evil mouths and sulphury undersides, only to whip in again when the giant had subsided.

Again and again the twelve-foot flippers of the whale lifted and struck the sea with a smash like the report of a cannon. A hammerhead floated on the surface, broken from end to end. The flipper had caught him squarely, and he lay there, blasted like a ship that had struck a mine.

Finally the tormentors drew off in a dark flotilla[6] and did not sweep in again. For the whale had completely emptied and refilled his lungs and was ready for all comers. As they sped away the sperm swept after them, a furious missile of flesh and blood surrounded by flying white spray as he smashed through the waves, one of the fastest as well as the vastest things alive. Over five miles of sea the chase led, down to a depth of twenty fathoms and up again, twisting, turning, and corkscrewing, and another shark, a tiger this time, was chopped almost in two in the whale's jaws as in retribution for their sneak attack.

Then the wrath of the whale wore off, the emberlike gleam faded from his little eyes, and he lay still upon the waters. After a time he turned northward, swimming at a steady ten knots an hour, sounding at intervals to a depth of twelve fathoms where he could get a clearer message through the water wireless. He was answering one of those mysterious calls of sea creatures more wonderful than the migratory sense of birds, a kind of pulse in the waters that told him that others of his kind were congregated a few leagues away. At times he rose on his very tail, twenty feet and more out of the water, the better to sense the situation. About midday he came upon them—a pod[7] of young male sperms like himself, lying like ships off a small island.

There were eleven whales in the pod; and for a couple of days the young bull lay up with them, playing and lazing the time away, diving at intervals to hunt for squid in the depths. For the hunger that drove these monsters was almost beyond conception. Their throats were large enough to swallow two men— it must have been the cachalot that had given rise to the Jonah story— and their stomachs were huge caldrons of digestive juices that required endless and constant replenishment.

On the third day when the pod started southward, he, too, went along, a passage that would take them across four degrees of latitude. They traveled at an even ten knots an hour, holding their course as steadily as if a compass were in the brain of each, their flippers churning the sea, their great tails leaving miles of foam behind them.

They swam the sun out of one sky and the moon out of another, only once varying their speed when they came upon a vast school of

---

6 **flotilla:** small fleet.

7 **pod:** school.

mullet packed together for nearly a square mile, so that the face of the sea seemed effervescent. Straight through the school they plowed, chomping and gulping as they went, over a hundredweight at every swallow. The pollack were united in migration and did not scatter. When the monsters had passed, the gaps were closed, and the great school passed on into the west, followed by their attendant flock of mewing, screaming sea birds and a swarm of lesser sea jackals.

Some hours later the whale pod passed a school of porpoises. They were hungry again by that time, but left these distant relatives unmolested. The porpoises were warm-blooded mammals like themselves, and whales are not cannibals.

On the fifth day of passage the whales kept sounding several times an hour to feel out the pulse of the sea ahead. From time to time they flung themselves high in the air above the crest of the swells, revolving at the same time so as to peer over the sea with their myopic, little eyes. Each knew now what he sought, the great mother herd from which they had sprung and which roved up and down the watery bulge of the planet in rhythm with the seasons. Toward day's end the pod sighted whale birds in a cloud, and shortly afterward many white jets of spume showed ahead of them. Sweeping forward in a mist of spray, they saw the calm sea covered with their kind. This was one of the immemorial[8] stopping places of the cachalot, just where the rocks of a

submerged mountain offered rubbing places to curry their wrinkled hides, and where, in the valleys below the marine mountain and on its various ledges, octopuses crouched, or walked tip-toe like great spiders.

There were more than a hundred whales in the herd, many unattached females among them, also mothers with calves that gamboled, dived, and nursed as other mammals do ashore. There were young bulls, and aging bulls, and scarred old veterans who took their ease upon the surface swells.

Little notice was taken of the newcomers. The small pod simply hove to and came to rest in the midst of the lazing herd. With this homecoming to the parent group their heedless young bachelorhood had come to an end. They would now be drawn into the ordered life of the great, moving whale city.

The old schoolmaster of the herd was a monster whose head was covered with the scars of battle and whose great bulk was as full of iron as a blacksmith shop, harpoon shafts and heads from his many encounters with whalers in years past. Those years had brought him much experience and it was to him that they all looked for warning and guidance along the great whale highways of the sea. From the schoolmaster the young bulls learned the telegraph code of whales, by which they detected one another at great distances and how to warn each other of danger by releasing the *glip*—an acrid

8 immemorial: very old.

oil which ran through the water in long streamers. Nourished by this oil were the whale birds, ever following in the wake of the herd—a species of petrel which fed, rested, and even slept on the backs of the monsters, repaying their hosts by cleaning up the mollusks and crustaceans[9] that the whales could not rub off. They were useful also in giving alarm when whale ships appeared on the horizon, for their sight was far keener than that of the whales.

Keener than any flock of petrels though was the old schoolmaster in sensing danger from man, the greatest enemy. The young bull knew nothing of men or whalers until the day a ship hove to, half a knot downwind from where he and another young bull were feeding. Small boats put out from her and came nearer. He and his companion were curious about these and surfaced for another look, despite the sting of the *glip* that lay in the wake of the retreating herd. When he surfaced a third time, there was another sharper sting in his side as a harpoon found him. Two such harpoons stood out upon the back of his companion, with taut lines leading from each to the prow of a small boat. He breached sharply in his pain and instinctively sounded. The harpoon line tolled out behind him to its limit, and for a time in an agony of pain he was towing the small boat and its crew. At last

9 **mollusks and crustaceans** (krŭs tā′shənz): in this case, the small shelled creatures which cling to the whale.

the iron shaft tore loose, and he was free.

Later, as he surfaced he saw his dying companion surrounded by three small boats, with men moving like whale birds on his broad back. He fled with a hard lesson learned.

In the days that followed, the herd traveled slowly southward, following the great chain of whale feeding grounds that were strung from pole to pole and covered all the great ocean deeps. The young bull's wound healed swiftly in the amazing way of sea creatures, but the wariness it had left in him concerning men and ships would be a protection always. He had reached his full maturity and growth that season: eighty-seven and a half English feet, with a girth that was vast in proportion, placing him among the mightiest and most powerful of his race. He had already won the favor of three admiring young cows who now constituted his self-elected following, the beginning of a family pod, but a spirit of restlessness was still upon him and their favors meant little to him.

It was weeks later that he made a choice of his own among the young females of the herd. She was scarcely half his size, a member of a family pod of five sperms. For a day he swam and fed close to the pod and saw that she was constantly escorted. Sure as he was that she was the answer to his long wanderings, there seemed nothing to do but challenge the scarred master of the pod. But a battle of giants did not ensue. The old one was merely her sire, and willing enough that she take a mate.

She, however, seemed coy and reluctant to leave her family group, though glad of his company. He tagged along. Sometimes they joined in submarine play, diving after each other in long diagonal shafts of silvery light, sounding the ray-less depths, looping around and under each other, racing headlong in the dark, rising at last to blow and breathe and rest on the surface. Always there was an urge in him to draw her away toward some se-questered[10] coast where they might live apart for a while. But always she returned to her own pod.

Now the herd had stopped for a time above that mighty chasm known as "The Abyss" which lay to the west of Thursday Island. These great depths went down five miles to the gray-brown mud of the ocean floor, the abysmal ooze con-sisting of the remains of ages of marine plants, animals, and meteoric dust settled down through centu-ries from suspension in the sea.

Here in the lightless depths dwelt the giant devilfish or decapod, the monster kraken of Norse legend. *Architeuthis* he was called, great brother to the octopus, the coveted prey of all sperm whales and often their undoing, for victory went not always to the whales.

Here was one of the richest of all whale feeding grounds, and the whole herd became lively and spor-tive as it spread out in the old fa-miliar waters and began to dive and feed. Even the young female showed a new, venturesome spirit and when she dove to go squid hunting the young bull followed her. A sort of recklessness was upon them both and it was one of the times when they kept going, the female in the lead.

Down and down they plunged to the hundred-fathom depth where the weight of waters pressed like iron bands about them, their great bod-ies bearing a pressure of thousands of pounds. Only the fact that their brains were wonderfully cushioned in many feet of bone and liquid spermaceti[11] enabled them to func-tion at such a depth. Nothing sur-vived down here, save those crea-tures whose bodies offset the pressure by being constantly filled with water themselves.

Still farther down they ventured into a realm of deathly cold where not even a ray of green seeped through, and great caverns and gorges yawned between mid-sea mountains. At the half-mile depth the female cut short her dive and began undulating along horizontally, seeking prey, the young bull close behind her. But no squid was about at this level, and presently they sounded again toward the three-thousand-foot level beyond which no warm-blooded mammal may descend and live.

Again they tapered off their dive and went shooting horizontally along the slopes of a submarine moun-

---

10 **sequestered:** separated; secluded.

11 **spermaceti:** waxy substance in whale oil.

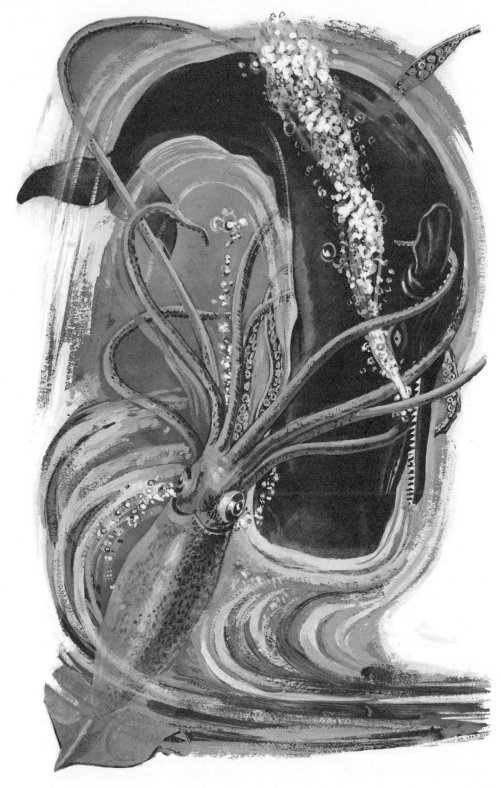

tain. Abruptly, the female, still in the lead, brought up against a forest of bleached, swinging branches. The young bull just behind had a vague impression of her struggling in the mesh of them, like a pollack in a fisherman's net. For the branches were gigantic, living tentacles, waving tree-high—the tentacles of a devilfish. The scent of musk filled the waters.

The whales had run head on into a company of the giant cuttlefish of the sea bed. The creatures were lying about everywhere on the mountain slope. The depths were not only lightless but utterly opaque now, for the cuttles had begun pumping the water and silt into a maelstrom with their siphons and squirting out clouds of sepia.[12]

Two mighty tentacles flung themselves around the young bull's head like living *reatas*[13] and pulled taut, crushing his jaw shut. Others leaped snakelike to clutch his tail. The whole underworld rocked, swayed, and tossed as in a windstorm, for all about the monsters were closing in. The very deep was on their side, for the whales had been down long already, and at this depth they were out of their element.

The bull sperm rolled completely over, spinning twice, and backed by his huge weight burst free. His jaws snapped shut, shearing off one of the pale streamers close to its base. Jetting water from the propulsion sack beneath his head, his attacker shot backward into the depths loosing ink clouds as it went. The bull plunged after, then cut his rush short and swept back at tremendous speed.

A message of dire distress had reached him. The cow sperm, despite her frantic struggles, was being borne deeper down by one of the huge cuttles. The bull sperm charged at full speed, diving beneath the female, and with his jaws slashing her free from two of the great cables that were dragging her down. But another cuttlefish, the mightiest of them all, had clutched her spiderwise. His bulk, more than twice that of the cow, pulled her irresistibly downward.

Again the bull swept in, cutting through a mighty tentacle. Two others quickly took its place, wrapping around the cow like heavy hawsers[14] from bow to stern. And wherever their sucking disks fastened the blood oozed forth. The bull sperm seized the attacking cuttle by the side of the head, and with a furious lashing of flukes and tail, strove to draw him upward. The cuttle struggled just as furiously to descend. The sounding of the creature was halted but no more. The mighty tug of war hung at an exact balance, except that the chomping jaws of the whale constantly cut into the boneless body of his foe. The curved beak of the sea devil scored deep gashes in the bull's sides, and the tigerlike claws, that fringed the suction disks on every tentacle, lashed

---

12 sepia (sē′pǐ ə): a dark brown fluid.
13 *reatas*: (Spanish) lariats.

14 hawsers: large ropes.

his flanks. But the whale's grip did not slacken and, writhing in its torment, the cuttle finally released the cow and fought for its life.

The bull sperm shook the cuttle in his jaws, dog-fashion; but the instant he ceased the offensive, the devilfish dragged him down as it had the cow. The whale could not remain at this depth much longer and live. Two hours' submersion at ordinary levels was nothing for him, but the pressure of this abyss, plus the strain of battle, had already claimed most of the oxygen in the lungs of the whale pair. Soon they must find relief in the upper waters or die. Perhaps the cuttle sensed this, for his depth pulls were cunning and unceasing.

Abruptly, the young bull gave in as if to go down with the cuttle, descending in a diagonal dive, only to break it and come up again in a long arc with the enemy now uppermost and with an added momentum against which the struggles of the cuttle were powerless. Up and up the battle went now, the devilfish writhing like a tree in a storm, the sperm chewing in and in and shaking the whole, vast bulk of him.

With all his remaining arms the cuttle strove to strangle the bull, to close shut his jaws and stop up his airhole; but a reverse process was on. With every fathom they rose the power of the cuttlefish weakened, while the whale's increased. And through it all, every instant, the sperm continued to chomp upon the pallid flesh of his foe, feeding even as he fought. The vast mollusk pulsated now with wave upon wave of evil-looking color—purple, red, mudbrown, magenta, and back to brown again.

Up in the belt of shining blue and green the finish was clear. The decapod writhed about to face the foe, but the sperm went on eating his way through the pulsing Medusa-like[15] head, tearing out chunks of flesh as large as washtubs, until it died.

After only partially filling his lungs with air, the young bull plunged into the depths once more, for she had not yet surfaced. He found her helpless once more in the grip of half a dozen strangling tentacles. Only by calling upon that last resource, the mysterious store of oxidized blood carried by whales in the dorsal arteries along their spine, could he summon the strength for further battle. Three times he dove beneath the cow in a ripping charge, his jaws working like the slash of monstrous shears among those twining, living cables, and finally he cut her free.

Together the pair shot surfaceward, racing with death itself, back to the clean, sane world of air and sky and sun. The speed of their ascent was such that their bodies shot clear into the sunlit air and fell back to the surface with a crash that shook the whole watery world. After that they rested long, panting, breathing in enormous quantities of life-giving

15 **Medusa-like:** resembling Medusa, a monster with snakes for hair (Greek mythology). The tentacles of the cuttlefish resembled the snakes.

air. And later when the red sun dipped in the sea, they were still lying there, quite close together and a long way from the herd, feeding on the remains of the king cuttle the male had conquered.

Reading Skills

1. Describe the scene as the young whale surfaces at the beginning of the story.
2. How does the whale drive off the scavenging sharks that bother him?
3. How do whales communicate and receive information from afar?
4. What strategy did the young whale employ in order to break away from the cuttlefish which was dragging him down?
5. Find sentences or expressions that "characterize" the whale. Indicate whether each describes the whale's appearance or his disposition.

Understanding Literature

1. In the battle between the sea giants, you undoubtedly found yourself hoping that the whale would win. These questions may reveal why you sympathize with the whale:

    (a) Why is the whale a natural hero and the cuttlefish a ready-made villain?
    (b) How much of the story is devoted to establishing the young bull whale as a character? How many paragraphs are devoted to the cuttlefish before the battle?
    (c) How do the bull whale's escapes from the sharks and from the harpoon affect your feeling about him? When he is harpooned, are you on the side of the men or the whale?
    (d) How does the presence of the female whale tend to keep your sympathy away from the cuttlefish?

2. Why does the author delay telling about the battle in the depths until the last third of the story? Why does he end the story so quickly after the battle?

3. How is suspense created in the first half-dozen paragraphs? What are some particularly suspense-filled moments in the story? At what point is your suspense greatest?

Science

Scientists explore the unknown in an attempt to understand and to explain natural occurrences. In this unit you will read about scientists who have explored the heavens, the Arctic wastes, and the microscopic world, from cells to atomic elements. In the following brief selection, Ralph E. Lapp, a physicist, tells about the scientist's "unending quest" for truth; he also distinguishes between science and technology, the inventions which sometimes result from scientific inquiry.

The Unending Quest

Ralph E. Lapp

If a Rip van Winkle awoke today after a sixty-year slumber, he would be confounded by the rapid changes that technology has brought about. The skyscrapers, the flood of automobiles, the immense network of roads, the fleets of jet-propelled aircraft, and the monumental works of engineering would all amaze him. And as he looked more closely into the modern household he would be equally surprised by the innovations that technology has spawned. The television set, the radio, the refrigerator, the automatic laundry, and the electronic gadgets that are judged necessities by most housewives; all these would appear as minor miracles.

But if our Rip van Winkle come to life had been a scientist, he would be even more astonished at the changes produced in six decades. He would acknowledge the technological developments and perhaps even say that they were quite predictable; but imagine what an eye-opener modern science would be for him.

Today we live in an age of science. Yet only a relatively few people know much about basic science; they are more acquainted with and impressed by technology—by things that you can see. Even a superficial appreciation of science depends upon much that you cannot see. Moreover, technology lags far behind science, even though the gap is narrowing each year. But still only a very small part of science is utilized in today's technology.

Fundamental science is pursued by overcurious men who seek after new knowledge. Scientists are exploring into the great unknown, into an infinitely small sphere deep within the atom and into measureless expanses of outer space. The true scientist has little or no thought of practical application in his research. Of course, atomic research has produced applications and even such an abstruse,[1] seemingly impractical theory as Einstein's has had world-shattering repercussions. . . .

---

1 **abstruse:** difficult to understand.

RALPH E. LAPP

319

Each time that new discoveries revealed an inner secret of nature, scientists found that they had merely sent a few rays of illumination into a great cavern of darkness. But the candlelight of new knowledge revealed glittering new possibilities for research, so the intrepid explorers plunged ahead into the unknown. Nonscientists often fail to comprehend the singleness of purpose, the utter concentration and dedication with which scientists are obsessed.

To the scientist there is a nerve-tingling excitement in the chase—the compulsion to reach out for new knowledge—which is both the motivation and the reward.

Sir Richard Gregory touched the heart of the matter when he wrote: "Science is not merely a storehouse of facts to be used for material purposes but is one of the great human endeavors to be ranked with arts and religion as the guide and expression of man's fearless quest for truth."

The conflict between supporters of established theory and a man with a new theory is a perpetually interesting one. The best-known stories about the scientist Galileo (1564-1642) tell of his experiment at the Leaning Tower of Pisa and of his reply to those who required him to deny his belief that the earth moves around the sun. Both stories emphasize the conflict which may occur when a new theory clashes with the old.

Galileo, the Stargazer Who Defied the World

Henry Thomas and Dana Lee Thomas

IMPROVING YOUR READING: In the introductory scene and in other passages of this selection, the writers emphasize the contrast between the thinking of Galileo and that of other people of his time. Watch for this contrast.

A GAY AND BOISTEROUS CROWD was gathered in front of the Leaning Tower of Pisa. It was predominantly composed of professors and students from the University of Pisa, although many townspeople were there as well. A professor of mathematics at the university was about to conduct an experiment which, as they all anticipated, was doomed to end in failure and humiliation. This young man was brash enough to challenge a theory of the august magister,[1] Aristotle, and now he was going to turn himself into the laughingstock of Pisa.

"He will make a public fool of himself," hissed one of the professors to a colleague, "and it will serve him right."

"Yes, a public demonstration of one of these absurd experiments will put an end to all this nonsense," replied the other.

"He says he will prove that a heavy object and a light object fall through the air at the same speed! Obviously this is against all logic."

"Does he defy the teachings of Aristotle?" a student asked his companion.

"He is a crackbrain," the other retorted. "He is forever diddling with pieces of string and lumps of lead. Does he believe that these will contribute more to the understanding of the world than our learned books?"

As the crowd jeeringly discussed the event, the young professor calmly mounted the steps of the Leaning

---

1 **august magister** (ô gŭst′ mə jĭs′tər): exalted master. The great Greek philosopher and scientist, Aristotle, was accepted as the scientific authority on all natural occurrences.

Tower. He carried a hundred-pound shot in one hand and a one-pound shot in the other. Undaunted by the sneers of his students and the wrath of his fellow professors, he was prepared to prove his theory that two different weights, dropped simultaneously from the same height, would fall to the ground at the same time.

He released the two balls from the tower top. A gasp of astonishment rose from the crowd. It was unbelievable! The two balls of iron had started from the top of the tower together and had reached the ground simultaneously.

The young professor was Galileo. And his triumph had a bitter taste. He had proved his theory but he had earned for himself the jealousy and hatred of his colleagues. Their minds refused to accept what their eyes had seen.

II

Galileo was born in Pisa, Italy, in the month of February, 1564. His father was an impoverished nobleman and an accomplished musician and mathematician. He was delighted to see in his son the early signs of genius. The lad was extraordinarily observant of everything about him. His senses of sight and smell and sound were unusually keen. He would construct toys for himself fashioned after boats and mills and carts he had seen. But especially, his curiosity about the world was insatiable.[2] He could not accept as authoritative the answers which the adults about him offered in response to his questions, and he was forever experimenting and devising tests to probe the mystery of things.

Galileo's father hoped to see his son choose a profession that would make him financially secure; perhaps Galileo would become a cloth merchant. But the boy, after studying for a while at the Benédictine monastery school at Vallombrosa, decided that he wanted to become a mathematician. His father argued that this would entail a lifetime of poverty. Galileo compromised by entering the University of Pisa to study medicine.

Despite his good intentions, Galileo found the study of mathematics irresistible. He paid more attention to the works of Euclid and Archimedes than he did to his medical textbooks. And he continued with his experiments.

When he was nineteen, he made his first important discovery. One day as he was saying his prayers in the cathedral at Pisa, his thoughts were interrupted by the persistent rattle of a chain. Looking about him, he discovered that the rattle came from a hanging oil lamp that was swinging back and forth. Fascinated by the rhythmic movement of the lamp, Galileo began to count its oscillations[3] by means of his own pulse beats. Suddenly he jumped to his feet and rushed out of the cathedral. A startling idea had occurred

---

2 insatiable (ĭn sā'shə bəl): not capable of being satisfied.

3 oscillations (ŏs'ə lā'shənz): movements back and forth.

to him. It seemed to him that the movements of the pendulum were regular; that whatever the range of its oscillations, they were invariably executed in equal times.

Upon reaching home Galileo put his discovery to a successful test. He attached two threads of equal length to two pieces of lead of equal weight. Then he tied the loose ends of the threads to separate nails. After enlisting the aid of his godfather, Muzio Tedaldi, for the purpose of counting the motions of one of the threads while he counted the other, he was ready to begin the experiment.

The youthful scientist pulled one of the pendulums to a distance of four hands' breadth and the other to a distance of two hands' breadth from the perpendicular, and then he let them go at the same time. After the two men had counted the movements of the two threads and compared findings, they found that the total count was 100 in each case. In spite of the difference in their starting points, both threads had reached the same point at the same time.

And so, in the rhythmic swinging of an oil lamp, Galileo discovered the principle of hydrostatic balance which is applied today in the measurement of time on the clock, the eclipses of the sun, the movement of the stars, and the counting of the human pulse.

It wasn't long before his professors found out about his secret studies and his experiments. And they expressed their disapproval in no uncertain terms. It was considered heresy for a student to think for himself, inasmuch as all scientific problems, they declared, had been conclusively settled by Aristotle. If a student was bold enough to utter a criticism of one of Aristotle's dogmatic pronouncements,[4] his professor would settle the argument with a quotation of Aristotle: *Magister dixit,* "the Master has spoken." And that was that. But Galileo went so far as to follow up his criticisms of Aristotelian dogma with tests of his own, and this was going entirely too far. For the good of the university as well as the good of his own soul, they had to curb this recklessness. They notified Galileo's father of his misdemeanors and the old musician begged his son to settle down and obey his professors.

But the plea fell on deaf ears. Galileo had dedicated his life to the examination of nature and the pursuit of scientific truths. There could be no turning back now.

As a result of his "indiscretions,"[5] the university refused to grant the incorrigible[6] experimenter his doctor's diploma. Galileo left the university, a "failure" in medicine and a "crackbrain juggler of useless figures." Nevertheless, the mathematical skill of this "juggler" had won for him an honored reputation among the foremost mathematicians of Italy —Giuseppe Moletti, Father Cristofor Clavio, and Guidubaldo del Monte.

4 **dogmatic pronouncements:** authoritative, almost dictatorial, statements.
5 **indiscretions** (ĭn′dĭs krĕsh′ənz): unwise remarks or actions.
6 **incorrigible** (ĭn kôr′ĭ jə bəl): unable to improve or to be corrected.

He had notified them of his scientific observations, and in recognition of his methods and achievements, they called him "the Archimedes of his day."

But Galileo discovered, as his father had predicted, that the mathematician's life was not an easy one financially. He tried unsuccessfully to recruit some pupils among the nobility, but no one was interested in studying abstract figures. Luckily the chair of Mathematics at the University of Pisa had become vacant, and Galileo was able to secure the position—undoubtedly because the salary that went with the job (about $65 a year) was so low, nobody else wanted it.

He tried to keep himself from starving by practicing medicine in his leisure moments. But he was so busy with his experiments now, that these leisure moments were few. Galileo's purpose was to re-evaluate the doctrines of Aristotle by investigating nature's own laws.

The students hardly attempted to conceal their smiles at his lectures, and the professors hated him. How dare he try to uproot the sacred volumes of Aristotle? If he did not stop his nonsense, they threatened to teach him a lesson he would never forget.

But Galileo could not and would not stop his "nonsense" and the professors went into action. The "lesson" with which they threatened him was their challenge to demonstrate one of his "idiotic" theories in the presence of the entire faculty and student body of the university. The scientist accepted the challenge and conducted his historic experiment regarding the laws of bodies in motion —an experiment that, as we have seen, aroused intense antagonism among the faculty.

Despite his persecution, Galileo not only continued with his unconventional studies, but disobeyed whatever other rules he considered ridiculous. He refused, for example, to wear his academic robes on the streets as well as in the classroom, as was decreed, and he was continually paying fines out of his tiny income for his steady infraction of this rule.

The authorities cast about for an excuse to dismiss him from the faculty. A suitable pretext was furnished by Prince Don Giovanni de Medici, the son of Cosimo I, who had invented a machine that he claimed could dredge the harbor of Leghorn. The prince had sent a model of his machine to Galileo for his approval, and was so outraged by the scientist's skepticism, that he demanded Galileo's dismissal from the university on the grounds of incompetence.

With the help of influential friends —mathematicians and physicists such as Moletti, Clavio, Guidubaldo— Galileo was able to obtain a much better position at the University of Padua, at what was for those days a handsome salary—$200 a year.

Here at Padua, for the first time, Galileo breathed the air of intellectual freedom.[7] The University of

---

7 **intellectual freedom:** freedom to teach whatever one believes to be true.

Padua was under the supervision of the independent Venetian Republic which had been censured by the Pope because, although devoutly Catholic, it had insisted upon the right of its scholars to pursue its scientific studies without interference by the Inquisition. No longer were his lectures greeted with sneers and catcalls, his mind fettered by restrictions. He soon became famous for his lectures. Students from all over Europe came to study under him. He wrote brilliant treatises on a variety of subjects—on mechanics, motion, sound and speech, light and color, and the system of the universe.

He was never out of debt although his salary kept increasing. In addition to his paternal obligations, the expenses of his social entertainment, and the cost of his scientific instruments, he was called upon to be the financial pillar of his family. Relatives of Galileo's in Pisa had heard about his academic success and they made unceasing demands on his purse. Time and again the scientist had to borrow money in order to meet their requests. On one occasion, his brother insisted that he advance him the money for a trip to Poland in order to enter the service of a Polish nobleman. On another, Galileo's sister, in love with a worthless young man, demanded that he supply her with a dowry. He borrowed one third of the amount she asked for and promised to send the rest later. However, immediately after the wedding ceremony, her husband sued Galileo for the unpaid balance.

Despite these burdens, he managed to enjoy himself. He attended dinners and dances in Venice, occasionally performed expertly on the lute at private musicales, and participated in carnivals and burlesques that were more famous for their wit than their delicacy, for the Venetian Republic, at that period, was a gay, boisterous city of freethinking and free living.

But underneath these surface activities of his life, Galileo's mind and heart were devoted to the pursuit of science. He organized a scientific and philosophical club—the Academy of Refugees—whose members consisted of scientists from various parts of Italy who had come to Venice to work in its freethinking atmosphere. It was at these club meetings, in a palace located near the bridge of Santa Sophia, that Galileo frequently first disclosed the results of his experiments. He told his colleagues about a new instrument he had invented—the compass; he showed them how to use another of his inventions—the thermometer; he discussed the properties of the magnet and the magnetic forces of the earth. And then he presented to them the most spectacular invention of them all—the *telescope*.

Galileo had heard of a curious instrument invented by a Dutch optician, Hans Lippershey. While working on his spectacle lenses in his shop, Lippershey had accidentally noticed that by placing a convex and concave glass together, he could make distant objects appear nearer, although inverted. This news in-

terested Galileo and he commenced to study the subject, examining the curvatures and groupings of different kinds of glasses and calculating, with exact mathematical formulas, the visual effects of these various curvatures and groupings.

Finally, he developed an instrument which could magnify objects to three times their original size and which, unlike Lippershey's telescope, did *not* invert.

On August 21, 1609, Galileo was ready publicly to demonstrate the first scientifically constructed telescope in history. Noblemen and senators followed him to the top of the Campanile[8] in Venice. One by one they peered through the magic glass, and, to their amazement, be-

held ships at sea fifty miles out of the harbor, "cattle grazing on the distant hillsides and the worshipers going in and out of their churches in the faraway towns and villages." And, at night, as they looked toward the heavens, the far-off stars came closer.

Galileo presented his instrument as a gift to the Duke of Venice. In return, the duke conferred upon Galileo a lifetime professorship at the University of Padua, at a salary of about $5000 a year.

This was the height of Galileo's prosperity and security. He had now been at Padua for eighteen years. But he was not happy. The scientist had become weary of the grind of daily teaching, and he longed to devote himself full time to the development of various scien-

8 **Campanile** (kăm′pə nē′lĭ): bell tower.

tific projects. And for years he had longed for the day when he could return in triumph to Pisa, the city which had dismissed him in disgrace years before. Numerous times he had petitioned Cosimo de' Medici, the Grand Duke of Florence and of Pisa, to hire him as his court mathematician. But his plea fell on unresponsive ears. The grand duke was even impervious to[9] the distinction of having one of Galileo's books —*Operations of the Compass*—dedicated to him.

However, after Cosimo's death, his son Cosimo II, who had once been a pupil of Galileo's, came to the throne. He offered the famous scientist the position he had so eagerly sought. Despite the warnings of his friends that he was making a tremendous mistake in exchanging an environment of freedom and security for one of medieval superstitions, Galileo broke his contract at Padua and joyously returned to Pisa.

This was the beginning of his tragedy.

In the inquisitorial atmosphere of Florence, Galileo was confronted with a book he had written in the free city of Padua—*Sidereus Nuncius* (The Messenger of the Stars). This historically significant book was the direct cause of events that were to follow.

The scientist had written his *Sidereus Nuncius*, as he declared to a friend, in order to "acquaint all the philosophers with some

observations which I have made on the celestial bodies by means of my spyglass and which infinitely amaze me . . . I give thanks to God, who has been pleased to make me the first observer of marvelous things unrevealed by bygone ages . . . I have ascertained that the moon is a body similar to the earth. . . . I have beheld a multitude of fixed stars never before seen. . . . Moreover, I have ascertained . . . the nature of the Milky Way. . . . But the greatest marvel of all is the discovery of four new planets . . . I have observed that they move around the sun."

Although he might have added, "I have observed that the earth, too, moves around the sun," he failed to declare this, either in his book or his letter. To do so would be to deliver himself into the torture chamber of the Inquisition. For years Galileo had privately doubted the orthodox Ptolemaic theory concerning the movements of the heavenly bodies. According to the Ptolemaic system, the earth was fixed and everything in the heavens—the sun, moon, and stars —revolved around it. Galileo had favored an alternative theory—one expounded by the Polish astronomer, Copernicus—which declared that the earth is a planet which revolves around a fixed sun. And Galileo's studies of the heavens through his telescope had confirmed Copernicus's ideas.

But the Grand Inquisitor, Cardinal Bellarmine, had noted the fact that although Galileo had ignored the

9 **impervious to:** here, not influenced by.

question of the earth's movements around the sun, he had nonetheless declared himself a follower of Copernicus. Therefore, on March 26, 1616, Galileo was ordered to present himself before the Inquisition.

When he arrived at the Holy Office, the cardinal "advised" him to "abandon his heretical opinions about the earth and the sun and the stars." Under the threat of persecution, he was not to think such thoughts, nor to teach them, nor to defend them either orally or in writing.

When Galileo, profoundly depressed, signed his renunciation and promised to obey, the cardinal released him. For a while, after his return to Florence, he went quietly on with his experiments, not daring to disclose the results of his work to the world. But in the end, Galileo was unable to suppress his ideas. He published another book on astronomy, and once more he fell afoul of orthodox beliefs. Again he was summoned to appear before the Inquisition. This time the charge was far more serious, for he was now accused of "recidivism"—that is, the second commission of a crime after having been punished for the first transgression. Death was the penalty for this "double crime."

Galileo was ill when he received the second summons to the Inquisition. Despite his doctors' affidavit that he ". . . is in bed, and he runs the risk of going to another world rather than to Rome," the Inquisitors were heartless. "If he is in any condition to come, let him be seized,

bound in chains and transported to Rome."

Galileo left for Rome in the frosty month of January 1633, and arrived there more dead than alive. His trial lasted six months. Although he received the support of many Catholic scholars and churchmen as well as freethinkers, the Inquisition had its way. On June 22, 1633, he was compelled to abjure his belief in the movement of the earth. "Before the Holy Sainted Gospels which I touch with my hands, I swear that . . . I reject and detest my former heresies . . . I confess that my error has been one of vain ambition and pure ignorance . . . I now declare and swear that the earth does not move around the sun. . . ."

But, as his friends led him, trembling and exhausted, away from the tribunal, Galileo is said to have remarked under his breath, *"Eppursi muove* [But the earth does move!]"

"We decree that Galileo's books be prohibited by a public edict, and we condemn their writer to the formal prison of this Holy Office for a period determinable at our pleasure."

After a while, Galileo was released from prison and permitted to return to his home at Arcetri, to live in enforced solitude.

But to the end he remained a Christian. And a scientist. Although he had been sternly forbidden to pursue his scientific pursuits, he secretly wrote another—and his greatest book—and had it smuggled out of the country for publication in Holland. This book was

The Laws of Motion, a summary of all the basic principles of mechanics.

Galileo became blind during the years of his imprisonment. In a letter to a friend he wrote, "I am . . . totally blind. These heavens, this earth . . . I had enlarged a thousand times . . . are dwindled into . . . narrow space. So it pleased God; it shall . . . please me also."

When Galileo died on January 8, 1642, he left the world he loved far better informed than it was when he entered it.

Reading Skills

1. What did Galileo do that makes him important in the history of science?
2. According to the story, how did Galileo contrast with his fellow professors at Pisa? How did his students at Pisa react to him? What other contrasts appear in the story?
3. Throughout the years, Galileo's judgment was better than that of his friends and co-workers, except for his decision to return to Pisa. Why did he return to Pisa?
4. What is the point of the story of the remark Galileo is said to have muttered to the Inquisitors? What does his remark reveal about his character?
5. In "The Unending Quest" (p. 319), scientists are defined as "overcurious men who seek after new knowledge." How does Galileo fit this definition? What specific details suggest that he was "overcurious"?

Further Activity

Write a paragraph in which the opening sentence is "A 'crack-brain' of one age often becomes a hero of another." Support your topic sentence with one or more examples. (Do not use Galileo as an example. Think of others.)

HENRY THOMAS AND DANA LEE THOMAS

The Concentrations of Isaac Newton

Robert Strother

IMPROVING YOUR READING: In this essay not only can you understand the extent of Isaac Newton's contributions to scientific knowledge, but also you can get a glimpse of the character of Newton. Notice the quotations from Newton's own comments about his scientific work. What do these comments reveal about his character? What does the essay tell you about the nature of genius?

EARLY ON CHRISTMAS DAY in 1642 a boy was born in a two-story stone farm house in the County of Lincoln in England. The baby was premature, tiny, and woefully weak. The two midwives[1] sadly predicted that he would not live through the day. If he did manage to survive, they said, he would never be strong.

And so the baby lived eighty-five years, and the "poor little weak head" that had to be supported by a special leather collar early in life proved to contain one of the finest scientific brains the world has known. Its owner was knighted, heaped with honors by poets and philosophers alike, made a fortune, and was buried in Westminster Abbey.[2] His name was Isaac Newton.

There was nothing in the ancestry of this frail little farm boy to indicate that he was the possessor of a powerful genius. His father was a ne'er-do-well who died, aged thirty-seven, a few weeks before Newton was born. His mother, whom he adored, was undistinguished in any way from

1 **midwives:** women who help with the delivery of babies.

2 **Westminster Abbey:** famous English church in which many distinguished people are buried.

her farm neighbors in the village of Woolsthorpe. Geneticists[3] in later years attempted in vain to trace his ancestry beyond three generations. The records they did find disclosed no clue to the secret of Newton's gifts.

These gifts were slow in appearing. As a schoolboy in Woolsthorpe and later in nearby Grantham, Newton was often at or near the bottom of his class—until the day he licked a larger boy in a hard fight near the school. This boy was higher in the class than he, and Newton decided to complete his triumph by proving himself the superior student.

Noting his increased studiousness, a maternal uncle suggested that he be given a higher education. Later the uncle obtained young Isaac's admission to Trinity College, Cambridge. Newton was enrolled at nineteen as a "sizar," which means he did odd jobs to earn part of his keep. The records of the College do not show where he stood in his classes, but Isaac Barrow, professor of mathematics, considered him "a man of quite exceptional ability and singular skill." In fact, when Barrow resigned his professorship, he arranged for Newton, then twenty-six, to succeed him.

The Great Plague of 1665 and 1666 interrupted Newton's education and had a remarkable effect on his career. In one ghastly three-month period one-tenth of London's population died. Cambridge University was closed and Newton, at twenty-three, returned to Woolsthorpe to "medi-tate." These meditations during eighteen months on his mother's farm laid the groundwork for all his subsequent achievements.

As a boy Newton had been regarded as a "wool-gatherer,"[4] and the neighbors said that he once walked all the way home from Grantham without noticing that the horse he was supposed to be leading was missing. The true character of this "absence of mind" became apparent during his enforced stay in the country. Plainly, the young undergraduate had an almost terrifying power of concentration, which he could bring to bear on the most complex problems for hours on end. Linked with this was another great gift—an intuitive sense for the right answer. He could penetrate to the heart of a problem with no lost motion.

From remotest times wise men had believed that the sun, stars, and planets possessed special heavenly qualities quite unlike anything on earth. To suppose otherwise was unthinkable until Newton came along. It may have been, as Voltaire later declared, that the sight of a falling apple caused Newton to ask himself if the force that drew it to the earth might not also be the force that kept the moon circling in her orbit. This seemed to Newton much more likely than the accepted theory of Descartes that the moon and planets were carried around their orbits by "vortexes" in an unseen, unfelt, and unprovable substance called "ether." He went to work on the problem, and

---

3 **Geneticists** (jĭ net′ə sĭsts): scientists who study heredity.

4 **wool-gatherer:** daydreamer; an absent-minded person

although his results were not published until twenty years later, he worked out both the laws of motion and of universal gravitation while at Woolsthorpe, before he was twenty-four years old. He also invented a new mathematical system to prove his theories. This is known today as calculus. During this productive eighteen-month period Newton plunged into an amazing variety of other studies. He worked out the orbit of a comet, discovered the laws of the tides, delved into the character of light.

By a series of brilliant experiments, conducted with prisms bought for a few pennies at a country fair, he proved that white light is composed of all the colors in the spectrum, and that each color bends in its own characteristic degree when passed through a prism. He ground lenses and mirrors, and made a new kind of telescope. He did all the mechanical work himself, and concerning this he had a complaint still heard in our own day: "Had I waited for the workmen, I'd have got nothing done."

In his old age, when praised for his great contributions to man's understanding of the Universe, Newton remarked: "I had no special sagacity,[5] only the power of patient thought." He made his discoveries, he said, "by always thinking unto them. I keep the subject constantly before me and wait until the first dawnings open little by little into the full light."

5 sagacity (sə găs'ə tĭ): wisdom.

Newton said nothing about any of his Woolsthorpe discoveries at the time, and this reticence was to involve him in angry controversies later on. Early in 1667 he returned to Cambridge and was elected a member of the faculty. Two years later he was made Professor of Mathematics, a position he was to hold for thirty years.

Not long afterward the Royal Society of London for the Promotion of Natural Knowledge saw Newton's new reflecting telescope, and immediately elected him a member. In 1703 he became president of this august assembly, a position he held until his death in 1727.

Newton expressed surprise at the enthusiasm the Royal Society showed for his telescope, which is still today its most prized possession, and offered to send in an account of the discovery in optics which led to its invention. The paper touched off a storm—not because the experiments were not accurate and the conclusions drawn from them indisputable, but because his findings did not square with certain theories then held. So many voices were raised in complaint that Newton finally exclaimed in disgust, "I see a man must either resolve to put out nothing new, or become a slave to defend it." From that time forward he was more reluctant than ever to make his discoveries known.

Although Newton had invented calculus, or "fluxions" as he called it, while an undergraduate, he had not described his method to anyone but Barrow. Some years later the great

German mathematician Gottfried Wilhelm von Leibniz, working independently, came up with much the same system. He gave it the name it bears today, the Calculus. It is an invaluable tool of modern engineering and physics.

There was great national as well as personal rivalry between scientists of the 17th century, and although Leibniz at first conceded that he and Newton were working on a similar system simultaneously, when the issue was drawn his supporters said Newton had borrowed from Leibniz. To prove the point Jean Bernoulli, a famous Swiss mathematician, published two problems, challenging anyone to solve them within a year. Leibniz solved one, and was at work on the other as the year drew to a close.

When Newton heard of the problems he promptly solved both in less than twenty-four hours, and sent the answers to the Royal Society. When the Society published them, without disclosing the author, Bernoulli read through them and said, with a rueful shake of his head, "The lion is known by his claw." The test proved beyond doubt that Newton had indeed invented calculus. He could not have solved the problems otherwise.

Publication of the *Principia*, the greatest of all Newton's work, was largely fortuitous.[6] Edmund Halley, brilliant young Astronomer Royal, was baffled in his attempt to compute the orbit of the comet which now

6 **fortuitous** (fôr tu′ə təs): by chance.

bears his name. He knew of Newton's genius in mathematics, went to him for help, and learned to his astonishment that Newton had already computed the orbit. But search of Newton's cluttered desk did not at once disclose the calculations. Newton quickly did them again.

Halley, meanwhile, had realized the great value of the unpublished research so carelessly stuffed into the pigeon-holes of the great mathematician's desk and offered to publish the work at his own expense. Newton agreed, and the *Principia*, which was to be hailed as the greatest scientific book ever printed, came into being. Not until our own day when Albert Einstein came forward with his Theory of Relativity was a single scientific treatise to have an equal impact on the development of human thought.

The *Principia* was written in about eighteen months of the most concentrated work and thought. In it Newton refined and clarified all that he had discovered about the motions of the planets and their satellites, and dealt decisively with a great variety of new subjects. During his study of these problems he would often sit motionless for hours, then dash to his desk and write for hours more, without bothering to pull up a chair. His secretary reported that he seldom went to bed before two o'clock, sometimes not until five or six. He even forgot to eat. The book was published in the summer of 1687, under the auspices of The Royal Society. Newton gave it a sort of subtitle: *The*

Frame of the System of the World. Even mathematicians found the book difficult to read, not only because the problems dealt with are difficult, but because Newton purposely made it tough so that he wouldn't be bothered by "little smatterers in mathematics." It is in Latin, the universal language of science at that time, and consists to a large extent of mathematical formulae and equations. For two centuries it was the major guide to the world's scientific thought.

The book begins with an explanation of Newton's laws of motion. All previous thinkers had held that some continuous force was required to keep the planets moving in their orbits. Newton said that a body in motion would continue to travel in a straight line forever unless some force was applied to stop it. The planets move in circular paths because the gravitational force of the sun exactly equals the centrifugal force of their motion through space. Since there is no friction in empty space, no additional power is needed to keep them circling at constant speed through countless eons of time.

Newton's second law of motion shows how force is measured by the rate of change of motion. The third —that action and reaction are equal and opposite—is the principle of jet propulsion. The book states the law of gravity which every schoolboy still learns today—that every particle in the universe has a gravitational attraction for every other particle in proportion to the product of the masses of the particles, and in in-verse proportion to the square of their distances. He showed how to determine the mass of the sun and the planets. He established rules for calculating the orbits of comets. He proved that the gravitational force of the moon and the sun causes tides in the oceans of the earth; that spring tides occur when moon and sun are pulling together, neap tides when the forces are opposed. "Such a wonderful uniformity in the planetary system," Newton said, "must be allowed the effect of choice" by a Supreme Creator.

The *Principia* was a pioneering work of such astonishing power that it was not long in winning the admiration of scholars everywhere. But the greatest of all Newton's triumphs came more than a century after his death. His Law of Gravitation was considered so thoroughly proven that when astronomers found that the planet Uranus was slightly out of its predicted position they did not suspect a flaw in the theory. Instead they concluded that Uranus must be affected by the gravitational pull of a planet still undiscovered.

Leverrier in France and Adams in England independently computed by Newtonian law the mass and position of this undiscovered planet. Leverrier sent his calculations to the astronomer Galle in Germany. Galle received them on September 23, 1846. He pointed his telescope along the line indicated, and that very night, in the exact spot indicated, he discovered the new planet, which was given the name of Neptune.

Newton never married, and if there was any romance whatever in his life no trace of it has appeared. The hostess of his comfortable house in London was his niece, Miss Catherine Barton, a beautiful and vivacious young woman whose wit and good looks were toasted by Alexander Pope, Dean Swift, and other noted writers. Through her Newton met many of the famous people of the day.

In appearance Newton was of average height, with handsome, rather sharp features, and a clear ruddy complexion. He was moderate in all his habits. Once when asked why he did not smoke he replied, "Because I do not want to acquire any new necessities." He had a talent for making money, and played the stock market so successfully that, despite some reverses late in life, he left an estate of around £32,000, a large sum in those days.

Newton was elected president of the Royal Society in 1703, and two years later, in a special ceremony at Cambridge, he was knighted by Queen Anne, the first scientist ever to be so honored. Between these two events he brought out his famous book on optics, which was largely a development of his early discoveries about the characteristics of light.

In his eighty-fifth year Newton was a venerable[7] figure, renowned wherever learning was held in honor. His last illness was brief, and was brought on by complications caused by a kidney stone. He died in peace, and in the knowledge that the fathomless wonders of the Universe he had so brilliantly explored had been given their shape and their motion by the sure hand of God. Mourned by England and the world, Newton went to his last rest in Westminster Abbey where he lies today, one of the greatest names among that company of the great.

Of his life's work he had written: "I do not know what I may appear to the world, but to myself I seem to have been only like a boy playing on the seashore and diverting myself in finding now and then a smoother pebble or a prettier shell than ordinary, while the great ocean of truth lay all undiscovered before me."

7 **venerable:** respected and admired.

Reading Skills

1. Be prepared to explain two of Newton's contributions to science and mathematics. Try to make your explanations clear enough to be understood by someone who has not read this selection.
2. How did Bernoulli prove that Newton, not Leibniz, was the master of the calculus?
3. How was Newton largely responsible for the discovery of Neptune more than a hundred years after his death?

Understanding Literature

1. Explain what character trait in Newton is revealed by each of the following details:
   (*a*) "Newton remarked: 'I had no special sagacity, only the power of patient thought.'"
   (*b*) After the complaints about his paper on optics, "he was more reluctant than ever to make his discoveries known."
   (*c*) "Newton purposely made it [the *Principia*] tough so that he wouldn't be bothered by 'little smatterers in mathematics.'"
   (*d*) ". . . he would often sit motionless for hours, then dash to his desk and write for hours more, without bothering to pull up a chair."
   (*e*) "Once when asked why he did not smoke he replied, 'Because I do not want to acquire any new necessities.'"
2. In "The Unending Quest" the discoveries of scientists are compared to "a few rays of illumination [sent] into a great cavern of darkness." What comparison quoted in this essay did Newton use to express a similar idea about his own scientific discoveries?

Further Activity

Compare and contrast, either orally or in writing, the lives of Galileo and Newton. Consider the childhood, the student life, and the scientific achievements of each of the two men; also consider their own and others' attitudes toward their work.

Exploring the invisible world can be every bit as challenging as penetrating unknown jungles or scaling uncharted mountains. The discovery of radium—the key to atomic energy—resulted from the persistence of Marie and Pierre Curie, physicists at the Sorbonne at the turn of the century.

Four Years in a Shed

Eve Curie

IMPROVING YOUR READING: The inventor Thomas Edison is credited with saying that genius is one percent inspiration and ninety-nine percent perspiration. The story of the discovery of radium supports Edison's belief. At the beginning of her account, Eve Curie lists "three agonizing questions" which faced her parents. What problems did they face? How did they solve or overcome these problems?

A MAN CHOSEN AT RANDOM from a crowd to read an account of the discovery of radium would not have doubted for one moment that radium existed. . . .

The physicist colleagues of the Curies received the news in slightly different fashion. The special properties of polonium and radium upset fundamental theories in which scientists had believed for centuries. How was one to explain the spontaneous radiation of the radioactive bodies? The discovery upset a world of acquired knowledge and contradicted the most firmly established ideas on the composition of matter. Thus the physicist kept on the reserve. He was violently interested in Pierre and Marie's work, he could perceive its infinite developments, but before being convinced he awaited the acquisition of decisive results.

The attitude of the chemist was even more downright. By definition, a chemist only believes in the existence of a new substance when he has seen the substance, touched it, weighed and examined it, confronted it with acids, bottled it, and when he has determined its "atomic weight."

Now, up to the present, nobody had "seen" radium. Nobody knew the atomic weight of radium. And the chemists, faithful to their principles, concluded: "No atomic weight, no radium. Show us some radium and we will believe you."

To show polonium and radium to the incredulous, to prove to the world the existence of their "children," and to complete their own conviction, M. and Mme.[1] Curie were now to labor for four years.

1 M. and Mme.: Monsieur and Madame.

The aim was to obtain pure radium and polonium. In the most strongly radioactive products the scientists had prepared, these substances figured only in imperceptible traces. Pierre and Marie already knew the method by which they could hope to isolate the new metals, but the separation could not be made except by treating very large quantities of crude material.

Here arose three agonizing questions:

How were they to get a sufficient quantity of ore? What premises could they use to effect their treatment? What money was there to pay the inevitable cost of the work?

Pitchblende, in which polonium and radium were hidden, was a costly ore, treated at the St. Joachimstahl mines in Bohemia for the extraction of uranium salts used in the manufacture of glass. Tons of pitchblende would cost a great deal: a great deal too much for the Curie household.

Ingenuity was to make up for wealth. According to the expectation of the two scientists, the extraction of uranium should leave, intact in the ore, such traces of polonium and radium as the ore contains. There was no reason why these traces should not be found in the residue. And, whereas crude pitchblende was costly, its residue after treatment had very slight value. By asking an Austrian colleague for a recommendation to the directors of the mine of St. Joachimsthal would it not be possible to obtain a considerable quantity of such residue for a reasonable price?

It was simple enough: but somebody had to think about it.

It was necessary, of course, to buy this crude material and pay for its transportation to Paris. Pierre and Marie appropriated the required sum from their very slight savings. They were not so foolish as to ask for official credits. . . .

But at least could there not be found, in the numerous buildings attached to the Sorbonne, some kind of suitable workroom to lend to the Curie couple? Apparently not. After vain attempts, Pierre and Marie staggered back to their point of departure, which is to say to the School of Physics where Pierre taught, to the little room where Marie had done her first experiments. The room gave on a courtyard, and on the other side of the yard there was a wooden shack, an abandoned shed, with a skylight roof in such bad condition that it admitted the rain. The Faculty of Medicine had formerly used the place as a dissecting room, but for a long time now it had not even been considered fit to house the cadavers. No floor: an uncertain layer of bitumen covered the earth. It was furnished with some worn kitchen tables, a blackboard which had landed there for no known reason, and an old cast-iron stove with a rusty pipe.

A workman would not willingly have worked in such a place: Marie and Pierre, nevertheless, resigned themselves to it. The shed had one advantage: it was so untempting, so miserable, that nobody thought of refusing them the use of it. Schutzenberger, the director of the school, had always been very kind to Pierre Curie and no doubt regretted that he had nothing better to offer. However that may be, he offered nothing else; and the couple, very pleased at not being put out into the street with their material, thanked him, saying that "this would do" and that they would "make the best of it."

As they were taking possession of the shed, a reply arrived from Austria. Good news! By extraordinary luck, the residue of recent extractions of uranium had not been scattered. The useless material had been piled up in a no-man's-land planted with pine trees, near the mine of St. Joachimsthal. Thanks to the intercession of Professor Suess and the Academy of Science of Vienna, the Austrian government, which was the proprietor of the State factory there, decided to present a ton of residue to the two French lunatics who thought they needed it. If, later on, they wished to be sent a greater quantity of the material, they could obtain it at the mine on the best terms. For the moment the Curies had to pay only the transportation charges on a ton of ore.

One morning a heavy wagon, like those which deliver coal, drew up in the Rue Lhomond before the School of Physics. Pierre and Marie were notified. They hurried bareheaded into the street in their laboratory gowns. . . .

There was where radium was hidden. It was from there that Marie must extract it, even if she had to treat a mountain of this inert stuff like dust on the road.

Marya Sklodovska[2] had lived through the most intoxicating moments of her student life in a garret; Marie Curie was to know wonderful joys again in a dilapidated shed. It was a strange sort of beginning over again, in which a sharp subtle happiness (which probably no woman before Marie had ever experienced) twice elected the most miserable setting.

The shed in the Rue Lhomond surpassed the most pessimistic expectations of discomfort. In summer, because of its skylights, it was as stifling as a hothouse. In winter one did not know whether to wish for rain or frost; if it rained, the water fell drop by drop, with a soft, nerve-racking noise, on the ground or on the worktables, in places which the physicists had to mark in order to avoid putting apparatus there. If it froze, one froze. There was no recourse. The stove, even when it was stoked white, was a complete disappointment. If one went near enough to touch it, one received a little heat, but two steps away and one was back in the zone of ice.

It was almost better for Marie and Pierre to get used to the cruelty of the outside temperature, since their technical installation—hardly existent—possessed no chimneys to carry off noxious gases, and the greater part of their treatment had to be made in the open air, in the courtyard. When a shower came, the physicists hastily

2 **Marya Sklodovska:** Marie Curie's birth name.

moved their apparatus inside: to keep on working without being suffocated they set up draughts between the opened door and windows. . . .

We had no money, no laboratory and no help in the conduct of this important and difficult task [she was to write later]. It was like creating something out of nothing, and if Casimir Dluski once called my student years "the heroic years of my sister-in-law's life," I may say without exaggeration that this period was, for my husband and myself, the heroic period of our common existence.

. . . And yet it was in this miserable old shed that the best and happiest years of our life were spent, entirely consecrated to work. I sometimes passed the whole day stirring a mass in ebullition, with an iron rod nearly as big as myself. In the evening I was broken with fatigue.

In such conditions M. and Mme. Curie worked for four years—from 1898 to 1902.

During the first year they busied themselves with the chemical separation of radium and polonium and they studied the radiation of the products (more and more active) thus obtained. Before long they considered it more practical to separate their efforts. Pierre Curie tried to determine the properties of radium, and to know the new metal better. Marie continued those chemical treatments which would permit her to obtain salts of pure radium.

In this division of labor Marie had chosen the "man's job." She accomplished the toil of a day laborer. Inside the shed her husband was absorbed by delicate experiments. In the courtyard, dressed in her old dust-covered and acid-stained smock, her hair blown by the wind, sur-rounded by smoke which stung her eyes and throat, Marie was a sort of factory all by herself.

I came to treat as many as twenty kilograms of matter at a time [she writes], which had the effect of filling the shed with great jars full of precipitates and liquids. It was killing work to carry the receivers, to pour off the liquids and to stir, for hours at a stretch, the boiling matter in a smelting basin.

Radium showed no intention of allowing itself to be known by human creatures. Where were the days when Marie naïvely expected the radium content of pitchblende to be *one per cent?* The radiation of the new substance was so powerful that a tiny quantity of radium, disseminated through the ore, was the source of striking phenomena which could be easily observed and measured. The difficult, the impossible thing, was to isolate this minute quantity, to separate it from the gangue[3] in which it was so intimately mixed.

The days of work became months and years: Pierre and Marie were not discouraged. This material which resisted them, which defended its secrets, fascinated them. United by their tenderness, united by their intellectual passions, they had, in a wooden shack, the "anti-natural" existence for which they had both been made, she as well as he. . . .

Whenever Pierre and Marie, alone in this poor place, left their apparatus for a moment and quietly let their tongues run on, their talk about their beloved radium passed from the transcendent to the childish.

3 gangue: the worthless rock in which valuable metals or minerals are found.

"I wonder what *It* will be like, what *It* will look like," Marie said one day with the feverish curiosity of a child who has been promised a toy. "Pierre, what form do you imagine *It* will take?"

"I don't know," the physicist answered gently. "I should like it to have a very beautiful color...."

    ✻   ✻   ✻   ✻

Marie to Bronya,[4] 1899:

Our life is always the same. We work a lot but we sleep well, so our health does not suffer. The evenings are taken up by caring for the child. In the morning I dress her and give her her food, then I can generally go out at about nine. During the whole of this year we have not been either to the theater or a concert, and we have not paid one visit. For that matter, we feel very well.... I miss my family enormously, above all you, my dears, and Father. I often think of my isolation with grief. I cannot complain of anything else, for our health is not bad, the child is growing well, and I have the best husband one could dream of; I could never have imagined finding one like him. He is a true gift of heaven, and the more we live together the more we love each other.

Our work is progressing. I shall soon have a lecture to deliver on the subject. It should have been last Saturday but I was prevented from giving it, so it will no doubt be this Saturday, or else in a fortnight.

This work, which is so dryly mentioned in passing, was in fact progressing magnificently. In the course of the years 1899 and 1900 Pierre and Marie Curie published a report on the discovery of "induced radioactivity" due to radium, another on the effects of radioactivity, and an-

other on the electric charge carried by the rays. And at last they drew up, for the Congress of Physics of 1900, a general report on the radioactive substances, which aroused immense interest among the scientists of Europe.

The development of the new science of radioactivity was rapid, overwhelming—the Curies needed fellow workers. Up to now they had had only the intermittent help of a laboratory assistant named Petit, an honest man who came to work for them outside his hours of service—working out of personal enthusiasm, almost in secret. But they now required technicians of the first order. Their discovery had important extensions in the domain of chemistry, which demanded attentive study. They wished to associate competent research workers with them.

Our work on radioactivity began in solitude [Marie was to write]. But before the breadth of the task it became more and more evident that collaboration would be useful. Already in 1898 one of the laboratory chiefs of the school, G. Bémont, had given us some passing help. Toward 1900 Pierre Curie entered into relations with a young chemist, André Debierne, assistant in the laboratory of Professor Friedel, who esteemed him highly. André Debierne willingly accepted work on radioactivity. He undertook especially the research of a new radio element, the existence of which was suspected in the group of iron and rare clays. He discovered this element, named "actinium." Even though he worked in the physicochemical laboratory at the Sorbonne directed by Jean Perrin, he frequently came to see us in our shed and soon became a very close friend to us, to Dr. Curie, and later on to our children.

4 **Bronya:** Marie's sister, who lived in Warsaw.

Thus, even before radium and polonium were isolated, a French scientist, André Debierne, had discovered a "brother," *actinium.*

At about the same period [Marie tells us], a young physicist, Georges Sagnac, engaged in studying X rays, came frequently to talk to Pierre Curie about the analogies that might exist between these rays, their secondary rays, and the radiation of radioactive bodies. Together they performed a work on the electric charge carried by these secondary rays.

Marie continued to treat, kilogram by kilogram, the tons of pitchblende residue which were sent her on several occasions from St. Joachimsthal. With her terrible patience, she was able to be, every day for four years, a physicist, a chemist, a specialized worker, an engineer and a laboring man all at once. Thanks to her brain and muscle, the old tables in the shed held more and more concentrated products—products more and more rich in radium. . . . She was now at the stage of purification and of the "fractional crystallization" of strongly racioactive solutions. But the poverty of her haphazard equipment hindered her work more than ever. It was now that she needed a spotlessly clean workroom and apparatus perfectly protected against cold, heat, and dirt. In this shed, open to every wind, iron and coal dust was afloat which, to Marie's despair, mixed itself into the products purified with so much care. . . .

Pierre was so tired of the interminable struggle that he would have been quite ready to abandon it. Of course, he did not dream of dropping the study of radium and of radioactivity. But he would willingly have renounced, for the time being, the special operation of preparing pure radium. The obstacles seemed insurmountable. Could they not resume this work later on, under better conditions? . . .

In 1902, forty-five months after the day on which the Curies announced the probable existence of radium, Marie finally carried off the victory in this war of attrition: she succeeded in preparing a decigram of pure radium, and made a first determination of the atomic weight of the new substance, which was 225. The incredulous chemists — of whom there were still a few—could only bow before the facts, before the superhuman obstinacy of a woman.

Radium officially existed.

It was nine o'clock at night. Pierre and Marie Curie were in their little house at 108 Boulevard Kellermann, where they had been living since 1900. . . .

Old Dr. Curie, who lived with the couple, had retired to his room. Marie had bathed her child and put it to bed, and had stayed for a long time beside the cot. This was a rite. When Irène did not feel her mother near her at night, she would call out for her incessantly, with "Mé!" which was to be our substitute for "Mamma" always. And Marie, yielding to the implacability of the four-year-old baby, climbed the stairs, seated herself beside the child and stayed there in the darkness until the young voice gave way to light, regular breathing. Only then would she go down again to Pierre, who was growing impatient. In spite of his kindness, he was the most possessive and jealous of husbands. He was so used to the constant presence of his wife that her least eclipse kept him from thinking freely. If Marie delayed too long near her daughter, he received her on her return with a reproach so unjust as to be comic:

"You never think of anything but that child!"

Pierre walked slowly about the room. Marie sat down and made some stitches on the hem of Irène's new apron. One of her principles was never to buy ready-made clothes for the child: she thought them too fancy and impractical. In the days when Bronya was in Paris the two sisters cut out their children's dresses together, according to patterns of their own invention. These patterns still served for Marie.

But this evening she could not fix her attention. Nervous, she got up; then, suddenly:

"Suppose we go down there for a moment?" . . .

The day's work had been hard, and it would have been more reasonable for the couple to rest. But Pierre and Marie were not always reasonable. As soon as they had put on their coats and told Dr. Curie of their flight, they were in the street. They went on foot, arm in arm, exchanging few words. After the crowded streets of this queer district, with its factory buildings, wastelands, and poor tenements, they arrived in the Rue Lhomond and crossed the little courtyard. Pierre put the key in the lock. The door squeaked, as it had squeaked thousands of times, and admitted them to their realm, to their dream.

"Don't light the lamps!" Marie said in the darkness. Then she added with a little laugh:

"Do you remember the day when you said to me 'I should like radium to have a beautiful color'?"

The reality was more entrancing than the simple wish of long ago. Radium had something better than "a beautiful color": it was spontaneously luminous. And in the somber shed where, in the absence of cupboards, the precious particles in their tiny glass receivers were placed on tables or on shelves nailed to the walls, their phosphorescent bluish outlines gleamed, suspended in the night.

"Look . . . Look!" the young woman murmured.

She went forward cautiously, looked for and found a straw-bottomed chair. She sat down in the darkness and silence. Their two faces turned toward the pale glimmering, the mysterious sources of radiation, toward radium—their radium. Her body leaning forward, her head eager, Marie took up again the attitude which had been hers an hour earlier at the bedside of her sleeping child.

Reading Skills

1. What were the "three agonizing questions" that faced the Curies?
2. Why did the Curies not readily accept the existence of polonium and radium? How did their outlook differ from that of the population at large?
3. Eve Curie writes that her parents wanted "to prove to the world the existence of their 'children'." What does she, their daughter, mean by this statement?
4. Describe the conditions under which the Curies worked for four years. What were the attitudes of the Curies toward these conditions? Did they affect family life adversely or not?
5. The hiring of assistants was a significant moment in the Curies' research. Why?
6. Monsieur Curie is said to have complained to Madame Curie that she never thought of anything but her child. Why is this statement *ironic* (especially in the light of the last sentence in this account)?

Understanding Literature

1. What are the sources of conflict in this selection?
2. Compare and contrast Pierre and Marie Curie. What character traits did they share? How did they differ? Do you think either one of them would have been able to complete the experiments alone?
3. The narrative of this account is developed in two ways, through the words of Eve Curie, the daughter, and through material quoted from Madame Curie's writings. What types of information and insight are presented in each kind of narrative? (Hints: Which gives us more information about the Curies' private lives? Could the characterization of the Curies have been the same had no materials been quoted?)

Is there such a thing as "pure" science? Or, are "microbe hunters. . . people like the rest of us, and not stuffed shirts or sacred cows"? Read this account of two microbe hunters in search of the cause of malaria and decide for yourself.

from Microbe Hunters:
Malaria—Ross vs. Grassi

Paul de Kruif

IMPROVING YOUR READING: In this excerpt, Paul de Kruif shows a side of science unknown to many, the "not too dignified" plodding, discouragement, and politics behind some discoveries. Notice how much microbe hunters—all scientists—are like detectives trying to solve a mystery. Both need evidence to prove their cases.

In this selection, you will find many difficult words. Skim the sentences in which they occur. Ask yourself these two questions: What is the author saying about the process of solving the microbe mystery? What is the author saying about the personality of each microbe hunter?

THE LAST TEN YEARS of the nineteenth century were as unfortunate for ticks, bugs, and gnats as they were glorious for the microbe hunters. . . . Because, by the middle of 1899, two wrangling and not too dignified microbe hunters had proved that the mosquito—and only one particular kind of mosquito—was the criminal in the malaria mystery.

Two men solved that puzzle. The one, Ronald Ross, was a not particularly distinguished officer in the medical service of India. The other, Battista Grassi, was a very distinguished Italian authority on worms, white ants, and the doings of eels. You cannot put one before the other in the order of their merit—Ross would certainly have stopped short of solving the puzzle without Grassi. And Grassi might (though I am not

so sure of that!) have muddled for years if the searchings of Ross had not given him hints. So there is no doubt they helped each other, but unhappily for the Dignity of Science, before the huzzahs of the rescued populations had died away, Battista Grassi and Ronald Ross were in each other's hair on the question of who did how much. It was deplorable. To listen to these two, you would think each would rather this noble discovery had remained buried, than have the other get a mite of credit for it. Indeed, the only consolation to be got from this scientific brawl— aside from the saving of human lives —is the knowledge that microbe hunters are people like the rest of us, and not stuffed shirts or sacred cows, as certain historians would have us believe. . . .

For the first thirty-five years of his life Ronald Ross tried his best not to be a microbe hunter. He was born in the foothills of the Himalayas in India, and knowing his father (if you believe in eugenics) you might suspect that Ronald Ross would do topsy-turvy things with his life. Father Ross was a ferocious looking border-fighting English general with belligerent side-whiskers, who was fond of battles but preferred to paint landscapes. He shipped his son Ronald Ross back to England before he was ten, and presently, before he was twenty, Ronald was making a not too enthusiastic pass at studying medicine, failing to pass his examinations because he preferred composing music to the learning of Latin words and the cultivation of the bedside manner. This was in the eighteen-seventies, mind you, in the midst of the most spectacular antics of Pasteur, but from the autobiography of Ronald Ross, . . . you can only conclude that this revolution in medicine left Ronald Ross cold.

But he was, for all that, something of a chaser of moonbeams, because, finding that his symphonies didn't turn out to be anything like those of Mozart, he tried literature, in the grand manner. He neglected to write prescriptions while he nursed his natural bent for epic drama. But publishers didn't care for these masterpieces, and when Ross printed them at his own expense, the public failed to get excited about them. Father Ross became indignant at this dabbling and threatened to stop his allowance, so Ronald (he had spunk)

got a job as a ship's doctor on the Anchor Line between London and New York. On this vessel he observed the emotions and frailties of human nature in the steerage, wrote poetry on the futility of life, and got up his back medical work. Finally he passed the examination for the Indian Medical Service, found the heat of India detestable, but was glad there was little medical practice to attend to, because it left him time to compose now totally forgotten epics and sagas and blood-and-thunder romances. That was the beginning of the career of Ronald Ross!

Not that there was no chance for him to hunt microbes in India. Microbes? The very air was thick with them. The water was a soup of them. All around him in Madras were the stinking tanks breeding the Asiatic cholera; he saw men die in thousands of the black plague; he heard their teeth rattle with the ague of malaria, but he had no ears or eyes or nose for all that—for now he forgot literature to become a mathematician. He shut himself up inventing complicated equations. He devised systems of the universe of a grandeur he thought equal to Newton's. He forgot about these to write another novel. He took twenty-five-mile-a-day walking trips in spite of the heat and then cursed India bitterly because it was so hot. He was ordered off to Burma and to the Island of Moulmein, and here he did remarkable surgical operations— "which cured most of the cases"— though he had never presumed to be a surgeon. He tried everything but impressed hardly anybody. . . .

When Ross returned to London [in 1894] he met Patrick Manson, an eminent and mildly famous English doctor. Manson had got himself medically notorious by discovering that mosquitoes can suck worms out of the blood. . . . Manson had proved —this is remarkable!—that these worms can even develop in the stomachs of mosquitoes. Manson was obsessed by mosquitoes. . . . He was sneered at. And then he met Ronald Ross—whom the world had sneered at. What a pair of men these two were! Manson knew so little about mosquitoes that he believed they could suck blood only once in their lives, and Ross talked vaguely about mosquitoes and gnats not knowing that mosquitoes *were* gnats. And yet——

Manson took Ross in his office, and there he set Ross right about the malaria microbe of Laveran that Ross did not believe in. He showed Ronald Ross the pale malaria parasites, peppered with a blackish pigment. Together they watched these germs, fished out of the blood of sailors just back from the equator, turn into little squads of spheres inside the red blood cells, then burst out the blood cells. "That happens just when the man has his chill," explained Manson. Ross was amazed at the mysterious transformations and cavortings of the malaria germs in the blood. After those spheres had galloped out of the corpuscles, they turned suddenly into crescent shapes, then those crescents would shoot out

two, three, four, sometimes six long whips, which lashed and curled about and made the beast look like a microscopic octopus.

"That, Ross, is the parasite of malaria—you never find it in people without malaria—but the thing that bothers me is: How does it get from one man to another?" . . . "Do you know, Ross," he said, "I have formed the theory that mosquitoes carry malaria . . ." Ronald Ross did not sneer or laugh. Then the old doctor from Shanghai poured his fantastic theory over this young man whom he wanted to make his hands: "The mosquitoes suck the blood of people sick with malaria . . . the blood has those crescents in it . . . they get into the mosquito's stomach and shoot out those whips . . . the whips shake themselves free and get into the mosquito's carcass. . . . The whips turn into some tough form like the spore of an anthrax bacillus. . . . The mosquitoes die . . . they fall into water . . . people drink a soup of dead mosquitoes. . . ."

This, mind you, was a story, a romance, a purely trumped-up guess on the part of Patrick Manson. But it was a passionate guess, and by this time you have learned, maybe, that one guess, guessed enthusiastically enough—one guess in a billion may lead to something in this strange game of microbe hunting. . . . Mosquitoes carry malaria? That was an ancient superstition—but here was Doctor Manson, thinking about nothing else. Mosquitoes carry malaria? Well, Ross's books had not sold; his mathematics were ignored. . . . But here was a chance, a gamble! If Ronald Ross could prove mosquitoes were to blame for malaria! Why, a third of all the people in the hospitals in India were in bed with malaria. More than a million a year died, directly or indirectly, because of malaria, in India alone! But if mosquitoes were really to blame—it would be easy!—malaria could be absolutely wiped out. . . . And if he, Ronald Ross, were the man to prove that! . . .

He bungled. He was like any tyro searcher—only his innate hastiness made him worse—and he was constantly making momentous discoveries that turned out not to be discoveries at all. But his bunglings had fire in them. To read his letters to Patrick Manson, you would think he had made himself miraculously small and crawled under the lens into that blood among the objects he was learning to spy upon. And what was best, everything was a story to him, no more than a story, a melodrama. Manson had told him to watch those strange whips that grew out of the crescent malaria germs and made them look like octopuses. In vast excitement he wrote a long letter to Manson, telling of a strange fight between a whip that had shaken itself free, and a white blood cell—a phagocyte. He was a vivid man, was Ronald Ross. "He [Ross called that whip "he"] kept poking the phagocyte in the ribs(!) in different parts of his body, until the phagocyte finally turned and ran off howling . . . the fight between the whip and the phagocyte was wonderful. . . . I shall write a novel on it in the style of the 'Three Musketeers.'" That was the way he kept himself at it and got himself past the first ambushes and disappointments of his ignorance and inexperience. . . . He failed. He kept at it. He wrote to Manson: "Please send me advice. . . ." He missed important truths that lay right under his nose—that yelled to be discovered.

. . . So dragged the dreary days, the months, the years, feeding people mashed-up mosquitoes and writing to Manson: "I have a sort of feeling it will succeed—I feel a kind of religious excitement over it!" But it never succeeded. But he kept at it. He intrigued to get to places where he might find more malaria; he discovered strange new mosquitoes and from their bellies he dredged up unheard-of parasites—that had nothing to do with malaria. He tried everything. He was illogical. He was anti-scientific. He was like Edison combing the world to get proper stuff out of which to make phonograph needles. "There is only one method of solution," he wrote, "that is, by incessant trial and exclusion." He wrote that, while the simple method lay right under his hand, unfelt. . . .

So passed two years, until, in June of 1897 Ronald Ross came back to Secunderabad, to the steamy hospital of Begumpett. The monsoon bringing its cool rain should have already broken, but it had not. A fiendish wind blew gritty clouds of dust into the laboratory of Ronald Ross. He wanted to throw his microscope out of the window. Its one remaining eyepiece was cracked, and its metal work was rusted with his sweat. There was the punka, the blessed punka, but he could not start the punka going because it blew his dead mosquitoes away, and in the evening when the choking wind had died, the dust still hid the sun in a dreadful haze. Ronald Ross wrote:

> What ails the solitude?
> Is this the judgment day?
> The sky is red as blood
> The very rocks decay.

And that relieved him and released him, just as another man might escape by whiskey or by playing bottle-pool, and on the sixteenth of August he decided to begin his work all over, to start, in short, where he had begun in 1895—"only much more thoroughly this time." So he stripped his malaria patient—it was the famous Husein Khan. Under the mosquito net went Husein, for Ronald Ross had found a new kind of mosquito with which to plague this Husein Khan, and in his unscientific classification Ross called this mosquito, simply, a brown mosquito. . . .

On the nineteenth of August he had only three of the brown beasts left. He cut one of them up. Hopelessly he began to look at the walls of its stomach, with its pretty, regular cells arranged like stones in a paved road. Mechanically he peered down the tube of his microscope, when suddenly something queer forced itself up into the front of his attention. What was this? In the midst of the even pavement of the cells of the stomach wall lay a funny circular thing, about a twenty-five-hundredth of an inch its diameter was—here was another! But, curse it! It was hot—he stopped looking. . . .

The next day it was the same. Here, in the wall of the stomach of the next to the last mosquito, four days after it had sucked the blood of the unhappy malarious Husein Khan, here were those same circular outlines—clear—much more distinct than the outlines of the cells of the stomach, and in each one of these circles was "a cluster of small granules, black as jet!" Here was another of those fantastic things, and another—he counted twelve in all. He yawned. It was hot. That black pigment looked a lot like the black pigment inside of malaria microbes in the blood of human bodies—but it was hot. Ross yawned, and went home for a nap. And as he awoke—so he says in his memoirs—a thought struck him: "Those circles in the wall of the stomach of the mosquito—those circles with their dots of black pigment, they can't be anything else than the malaria parasite, growing there. . . . That black pigment is just like the specks of black pigment in the microbes in the blood of Husein Khan. . . . The longer I wait to kill my mosquitoes after they have sucked his blood, the bigger those circles should grow . . . if they are alive, they *must* grow!"

Ross fidgeted about—and how he could fidget!—waiting for the next day, that would be the fifth day after his little flock of mosquitoes had fed on Husein under the net.

That was the day for the cutting up of the last mosquito of the flock. Came the twenty-first of August. "I killed my last mosquito," Ronald Ross wrote to Manson, "and rushed at his stomach!"

Yes! Here they were again, those circle cells, one...two...six... twenty of them.... They were full of the same jet-black dots.... Sure enough! They were bigger than the circles in the mosquito of the day before.... They were really growing! They *must* be the malaria parasites growing! (Though there was no absolutely necessary reason they must be.) But they must be! Those circles with their black dots in the bellies of three measly mosquitoes now kicked Ronald Ross up to heights of exultation. He must write verses!

"I have found thy secret deeds
    Oh, million-murdering death.

I know that this little thing
    A million men will save—
Oh, death, where is thy sting?
    Thy victory, oh, grave?"

At least that is what Ronald Ross, in those memoirs of his, says he wrote on the night of the day of his first little success....

On St. Patrick's day of the year 1898, Ronald Ross let loose ten gray mosquitoes into a cage containing three larks, and the blood of those larks teemed with the germs of malaria. The ten mosquitoes bit those larks, and filled themselves with lark's blood. Three days later Ronald Ross could shout: "The microbe of the malaria of birds grows in the wall of the stomach of the gray mosquito—just as the human microbe grew in the wall of the stomach of the brown spot-winged mosquito."...

Day after day Ross killed and cut up one after another of the last set of mosquitoes. Day after day, he watched those circles swelling, growing—there was no doubt about it now; they began to look like warts sticking out of the wall of the stomach. And he watched weird things happening in those warts. Little bright colored grains multiplied in them, "like bullets in a bag." Were these young malaria microbes? Then where did they go from here? How did they get into new healthy birds? Did they, indeed, get from mosquitoes into other birds?

Excitedly Ronald Ross wrote to Patrick Manson: "Well, the theory is proved, the mosquito theory is a fact." Which of course it wasn't, but that was the way Ronald Ross encouraged himself. There was another regrettable interlude, in which the unseen hand of his incurable restless dissatisfaction took him by the throat, and dragged him away up north to Darjeeling, to the hills that make giant's steps up to the white Himalayas, but of this interlude we shall not speak, for it was lamentable, this restlessness of Ronald Ross, with the final simple experiment fairly yelling to be done.... But by the beginning of June he was back at his birds in Calcutta—it was more than 100 degrees in his laboratory— and he was asking: "Where do the malaria microbes go from the circles that grow into those big warts in the stomach wall of the mosquito?"

They went, those microbes, to the spit-gland of those mosquitoes! Squinting through his lens at a wart on the wall of the stomach of a she-mosquito, seven days after she had made a meal from the blood of a malarious bird, Ronald Ross saw that wart burst open! He saw a great regiment of weird spindle-shaped threads march out of that wart. He watched them swarm through the whole body of that she-mosquito. He pawed around in countless she-mosquitoes who had fed on malarious birds. He watched other circles grow into warts, get ripe, burst, shoot out those spindles. He pried through his lens at the "million things that go to make up a mosquito"—he hadn't the faintest notion what to call most of them—until one day, strangest of acts of malignant nature, he saw those regiments of spindle-threads, which had teemed in the body of the mosquito, march to her spit-gland. . . .

"It's by the bite mosquitoes carry malaria then," Ross whispered—he whispered it because that was contrary to the theory of his scientific father, Patrick Manson. "It is all nonsense that birds—or people either —get malaria by drinking dead mosquitoes, or by inhaling the dust of mosquitoes. . . ." "It's by the bite!" shouted Ronald Ross, so, on the twenty-fifth day of June in 1898, Mr. Mahomed Bux brought in three perfectly healthy sparrows—fine sparrows with not a single microbe of malaria in their blood. That night, and night after night after that night,

with Ronald Ross watching, Mr. Mahomed Bux let into the cage with those healthy sparrows a flock of poisonous she-mosquitoes who had fed on sick birds. . . .

On the ninth of July Ross wrote to Patrick Manson: "All three birds, perfectly healthy before, are now simply swarming with proteosoma." (Proteosoma are the malarial parasites of birds.)

Now Ronald Ross did anything but live remotely on his mountain top. He wrote this to Manson, he wired it to Manson, he wrote it to Paris to old Alphonse Laveran, the discoverer of the malaria microbe; he sent papers to one scientific journal and two medical journals about it; he told everybody in Calcutta about it; he bragged about it—in short, this Ronald Ross was like a boy who had just made his first kite finding that the kite could really fly. He went wild—and then (it is too bad!) he collapsed. Patrick Manson went to Edinburgh and told the doctors of the great medical congress about the miracle of the sojourn and the growing and the meanderings of the malaria microbes in the bodies of gray she-mosquitoes: he described how his protégé, Ronald Ross, alone, obscure, laughed at but tenacious, had tracked the germ of malaria from the blood of a bird through the belly and body of she-mosquitoes to its dangerous position in her stinger, ready to be shot into the next bird she bit.

The learned doctors gaped. . . .

But Patrick Manson was not so sure: "One can object that the facts determined for birds do not hold, necessarily, for men." He was right. There was the rub. This was what Ronald Ross seemed to forget: that nature is everlastingly full of surprises and annoying exceptions, and if there are laws and rules for the movements of the planets, there may be absolutely no apparent rime and less reason for the meanderings of the microbes of malaria. . . .

You might know Giovanni Battista Grassi would be the man to do what Ronald Ross had not quite succeeded in bringing off. He had been educated for a doctor, at Pavia where that glittering Spallanzani had held forth amid applause a hundred years before. Grassi had been educated for a doctor (Heaven knows why) because he had no sooner got his license than he set himself up in business as a searcher in zoölogy. With a certain amount of sniffishness he always insisted: "I am a zoölogo —not a medico!" Deliberate as a glacier, precise as a ship's chronometer, he started finding answers to the puzzles of nature. Correct answers! His works were pronounced classics right after he published them —but it was his habit not to publish them for years after he started to do them. He made known the secret comings and goings of the Society of the White Ants—not only this, but he discovered microbes that plagued and preyed upon these white ants. He knew more than any man in the world about eels—and you may believe it took a searcher with the insight of a Spallanzani to trace out the weird and romantic changes that eels undergo to fulfill their destiny as eels. Grassi was not strong. He had abominable eyesight. He was full of an argumentative petulance. He was a contradictory combination of a man too modest to want his picture in the papers but bawling at the same time for the last jot and title of credit for everything that he did. And he did everything. Already, when he was only twenty-nine, before Ross had dreamt of becoming a searcher, Battista Grassi was a professor, and had published his famous monograph upon the Chaetognatha (I do not know what they are!).

Before Ronald Ross knew that anybody had ever thought of mosquitoes carrying malaria, Grassi had had the idea, had taken a whirl at experiments on it, but had used the wrong mosquito, and failed. But that failure started ideas stewing in his head while he worked at other things—and how he worked! Grassi detested people who didn't work. "Mankind," he said, "is composed of those who work, those who pretend to work, and those who do neither." He was ready to admit that he belonged in the first class, and it is entirely certain that he did belong there.

In 1898, the year of the triumph of Ronald Ross, Grassi, knowing nothing of Ross, never having heard of Ross, went back at malaria again. . . . What probably finally set Grassi working at malaria—you must remember he was a very patriotic and jealous man—was the arrival of Robert Koch. Dean of the Microbe Hunters of the world, Tsar of Science (his crown was only a little battered) Koch had come to Italy to prove that mosquitoes carry malaria from man to man.

. . . And now Koch met Battista Grassi, and Grassi said to Robert Koch: "There are places in Italy where mosquitoes are absolutely pestiferous—but there is no malaria at all in those places!"

"Well—what of it?"

"Right off, that would make you think mosquitoes had nothing to do with malaria," said Battista Grassi.

"So?" . . . Koch was enough to throw cold water on any logic!

"Yes—but here is the point," persisted Grassi, "I have not found a single place where there is malaria— where there aren't mosquitoes too."

"What of that?"

"This of that!" shouted Battista Grassi. "Either malaria is carried by one special particular blood-sucking mosquito, out of the twenty or forty kinds of mosquitoes in Italy—or it isn't carried by mosquitoes at all!"

"Hrrrm-p," said Koch. So Grassi made no hit with Robert Koch, and so Koch and Grassi went their two ways, Grassi muttering to himself: "Mosquitoes—without malaria . . . but never malaria—without mosquitoes! That means one special kind of mosquito! I must discover the suspect. . . ."

That was the homely reasoning of Battista Grassi. He compared himself to a village policeman trying to discover the criminal in a village murder. "You wouldn't examine the whole population of a thousand people one by one!" muttered Grassi.

"You would try to locate the suspicious rogues first. . . ."

So it was he cleared a dozen or twenty different mosquitoes of the suspicion of the crime of malaria— he was always finding these beasts in places where there was no malaria. He ruled out two dozen different kinds of gray mosquitoes and brindled mosquitoes, that he found anywhere . . . "You are innocent!" shouted Battista Grassi at these mosquitoes. . . . He went around making a nuisance of himself. He insinuated himself into the already sufficiently annoyed families of those hot malarious towns. He snooped annoyingly into the affairs of these annoyed families: "Is there malaria in your house? . . . Has there ever been malaria in your house? . . . How many have never had malaria in your house . . . How many mosquito bites did your sick baby have last week? . . . What kind of mosquitoes bit him?" He was utterly without a sense of humor. And he was annoying. . . .

Always, where the "zan-za-ro-ne" buzzed, there Grassi found deep flushed faces on rumpled beds, or faces with chattering teeth going towards those beds. Always where that special and definite mosquito sang at twilight, Grassi found fields waiting for some one to till them, and from the houses of the little villages that sat in these fields, he saw processions emerging, and long black boxes. . . .

There was no mistaking this mosquito, zanzarone, once you had spotted her; she was a frivolous gnat that flew up from the marshes towards the lights of the towns; she was an elegant mosquito proud of four dark spots on her light brown wings; she was not a too dignified insect who sat in an odd way with the tail-end of her body sticking up in the air (that was one way he could spot her, for the Culex mosquitoes drooped their tails); she was a brave blood-sucker who thought: "The bigger they are the more blood I get out of them!" So zanzarone preferred horses to men and men to rabbits. That was zanzarone, and the naturalists had given her the name *Anopheles claviger* many years before. *Anopheles claviger!* This became the slogan of Battista Grassi. . . .

Then came an exciting autumn for Battista Grassi and an entertaining autumn for the wits of Rome, and a most important autumn for mankind. Besides all that it was a most itchy autumn for Mr. Sola, who for six years had been a patient of Dr. Bastianelli in the Hospital of the Holy Spirit, high up on the top floor of this hospital that sat on a high hill of Rome. Here zanzarone never came. Here nobody ever got malaria. Here was the place for experiments. And here was Mr. Sola, who had never had malaria, every twist and turn of whose health Dr. Bastianelli knew, who told Battista Grassi that he would not mind being shut up with three different brands of hungry she-mosquitoes every night for a month. . . .

But, one fine morning, Grassi hurried out of Rome to Moletta and came back with a couple of little bottles in which buzzed ten fine female anopheles mosquitoes. That night Mr. Sola had a particularly itchy time of it. Ten days later this stoical old gentleman shook horribly with a chill, his body temperature shot up into a high fever—and his blood swarmed with the microbes of malaria.

"The rest of the history of Sola's case has no interest for us," wrote Grassi, "but it is now certain that mosquitoes can carry malaria, to a place where there are no mosquitoes in nature, to a place where no case of malaria has ever occurred, to a man who has never had malaria— Mr. Sola!" . . .

By now Grassi had read of those experiments of Ronald Ross with birds. "Pretty crude stuff!" thought this expert Grassi, but when he came to look for those strange doings of the circles and warts and spindle-shaped threads in the stomachs and saliva-glands of his she-anopheles, he found that Ronald Ross was exactly right! The microbe of human malaria in the body of his zanzarone did exactly the same things the microbe of bird malaria had done in the bodies of those mosquitoes Ronald Ross hadn't known the names of. Grassi didn't waste too much time praising Ronald Ross, who Heaven knows, deserved praise, needed praise, and above all *wanted* praise. Not Grassi!

"By following my own way I have discovered that a special mosquito carried human malaria!" he cried, and then he set out—"It is with great regret I do this," he explained—to demolish Robert Koch. Koch had been fumbling and muddling. Koch thought malaria went from man to man just as Texas fever traveled from cow to cow. Koch believed baby mosquitoes inherited malaria from their mothers, bit people, and so infected them. And Koch had sniffed at the zanzarone.

So Grassi raised baby zanzarone. He let them hatch out in a room, and every evening in this room, for four months, sat this Battista Grassi with six or seven of his friends. What friends he must have had! For every evening they sat there in the dusk, barelegged with their trousers rolled up to their knees, bare-armed with their shirt sleeves rolled up to their elbows. Some of these friends, whom the anopheles relished particularly, were stabbed every night fifty or sixty times! So Grassi demolished Robert Koch, and so he proved his point, because, though the baby anopheles were children of mother mosquitoes who came from the most pestiferous malaria holes in Italy, not one of Grassi's friends had a sign of malaria! "It is not the mosquito's children, but only the mosquito who herself bites a malaria sufferer—it is only that mosquito who can give malaria to healthy people!" cried Grassi. . . .

In the summer of 1900 Battista Grassi went to the plain of Capaccio. The hot days were just beginning, the anopheles were on the march. In the windows and on the doors of ten little houses of station-masters and employees of the railroad Grassi put up wire screens, so fine-meshed and so perfect that the slickest and the slightest of the zanzarone could not slip through them. Then Grassi, armed with authority from the officials of the railroad, supplied with money by the Queen of Italy, became a task-master, a Pharaoh with lashes. One hundred and twelve souls—railroad men and their families —became the experimental animals of Battista Grassi and had to be careful to do as he told them. They had to stay indoors in the beautiful but dangerous twilight. Careless of death —especially unseen death—as all healthy human beings are careless, these one hundred and twelve Italians had to take precautions, to avoid the stabs of mosquitoes. Grassi had the devil of a time with them. Grassi scolded them. Grassi kept them inside those screens by giving them prizes of money. Grassi set them an indignant example by coming down to Albanella, most deadly place of all, and sleeping two nights a week behind those screens.

All around those screen-protected station houses the zanzarone swarmed in humming thousands—it was a frightful year for mosquitoes. Into the *un-screened* neighboring station houses (there were four hundred and fifteen wretches living in those houses), the zanzarone swooped and sought their prey. Almost to a man, woman, and child, those four hundred and fifteen men, women and children fell sick with the malaria.

And of those one hundred and twelve prisoners behind the screens at night? They were rained on during the day, they breathed that air that for a thousand years the wisest men were sure was the cause of malaria, they fell asleep at twilight, they did all of the things the most eminent physicians had always said it was dangerous to do, but in the dangerous evenings they stayed behind screens—and only five of them got the malaria during all that summer. Mild cases these were, too, maybe only relapses from the year before, said Grassi. "In the so-much-feared station of Albanella, from which for years so many coffins had been carried, one could live as healthily as in the healthiest spot in Italy!" cried Grassi.

Such was the fight of Ronald Ross and Battista Grassi against the assassins of the red blood corpuscles, the sappers of vigorous life, the destroyers of men, the chief scourge of the lands of the South—the microbe of malaria. There were aftermaths of this fight, some of them too long to tell, and some too painful. There were good aftermaths and bad ones. There are fertile fields now, and healthy babies, in Italy and Africa and India and America, where once the hum of the anopheles brought thin blood and chattering teeth, brought desolate land and death. There is the Panama Canal. . . .

Reading Skills

1. Why was Ronald Ross an unlikely candidate for solving the mystery of malaria?
2. Who was Patrick Manson? Why was he important to Ross?
3. What was correct about Manson's theory of malaria? What was incorrect?
4. What did the experiments with Husein Khan and the brown mosquito contribute to solving the mystery of malaria?
5. How did the experiment with birds advance Ross's research? What was Manson's first reaction to Ross's announced success with this experiment?
6. How did Giovanni Battista Grassi's personality differ from that of Ross?
7. Who was Robert Koch and how did his visit to Italy influence Grassi?
8. What discovery "cleared a dozen or twenty different mosquitoes of the suspicion of the crime of malaria"?
9. What did the Sola experiment contribute to our knowledge of malaria?
10. Describe the experiment carried out in the town of Albanella.

Further Activity

Write a brief essay summarizing the unsolved questions about malaria which faced scientists at the turn of this century. What were theories of the day and why were they insufficient?

As part of his second expedition to Antarctica, Admiral Richard E. Byrd spent four and a half months in 1934 alone on the Ross Ice Barrier. Living in a hut beneath the surface of ice and snow, Byrd was able to gather weather data and test equipment designed for cold-climate living. The expedition crew realized that certain dangers threatened Byrd's survival, and preparations had been made to reduce these dangers. Nevertheless, Byrd more than once narrowly escaped a snowy death at his Advance Base, the southernmost residence ever maintained by man up to that time.

Alone

Richard E. Byrd

IMPROVING YOUR READING: Richard Byrd writes that he wanted to winter on the Ross Ice Barrier, a region which had never before been occupied, for two reasons: for the sake of gaining scientific knowledge and "for the experience's sake." In *Alone*, he shares his experience with you. Notice that he helps you to understand that experience by his frequent *comparison* of unfamiliar with familiar things. For example, at one point he describes himself as "like a clock wound up to strike in an empty house." By such comparison, he enables you to feel as he felt.

1

THE FIRST DAYS OF May carried no hint of calamities that would overtake me at the month's end. On the contrary, they were among the most wonderful days I had ever known. The blizzards departed, the cold moved down from the South Pole, and opposite the moon in a coal-black sky the cast-up light from the departed sun burned like a bonfire. During the first six days the temperature averaged −47.03°; much of the time it was deep in the minus forties and fifties. The winds scarcely blew. And a soundlessness fell over the Barrier. I have never known such utter quiet. Sometimes it lulled and hypnotized, like a waterfall or any other steady, familiar sound. At other times it struck into the consciousness as peremptorily[1] as a sudden noise. It made me think of the fatal emptiness that comes when an airplane engine cuts out abruptly in flight. Up on the Barrier it was taut and immense; and, in spite of myself, I would be straining to listen —for nothing, really, nothing but the sheer excitement of silence. Underground, it became intense and concentrated. In the middle of a task or while reading a book, I was sometimes brought up hard with all my senses alert and suspicious, like a householder who imagines he hears

1 **peremptorily** (pĕr emp′tə rə lĭ): definitely; positively.

a burglar in the house. Then, the small sounds of the hut—the hiss of the stove, the chatter of the instruments, the overlapping beats of the chronometers—would suddenly leap out against the soundlessness, all seeming self-conscious and hurried. And after a big wind I have been startled out of a sound sleep, without understanding why, until I realized that my subconscious self, which had become attuned to the rattling of the stovepipe and the surflike pounding of the blizzard overhead, had been unsettled by the abrupt calm.

It was a queer business. I felt as though I had been plumped upon another planet or into another geologic horizon[2] of which man had no knowledge or memory. And yet, I thought at the time it was very good for me; I was learning what the philosophers have long been harping on—that a man can live profoundly without masses of things. For all my realism and skepticism there came over me, too powerfully to be denied, that exalted sense of identification—of oneness—with the outer world which is partly mystical but also uncertainty. I came to understand what Thoreau meant when he said, "My body is all sentient."[3] There were moments when I felt more *alive* than at any other time in my life. Freed from materialistic distractions, my senses sharpened in new directions, and the random or commonplace affairs of the sky and the earth and the spirit, which ordinarily I would have ignored if I had noticed them at all, became exciting and portentous.[4] Thus:

May 1

This afternoon, in the lee of the sastrugi[5] formed by the last blow, I discovered some extraordinarily fluffy snow. It was so light that my breath alone was enough to send the crystals scurrying like tumbleweed; so fragile that, when I blew hard, they fell to pieces. I have named it "snow down." Although most of the crystals were not much bigger around than a quarter, some were as small as marbles and others as big as goose eggs. Apparently they were blown in on this morning's light westerly wind. I scooped up enough to fill a box—no easy task, for even so slight a disturbance as that created by my hands caused the crystals to fly away. The box was half again as big as a shoe box (approximately 600 cubic inches), but the contents, melted in the bucket, yielded barely half a cup of water. . . .

Later, during my walk, I saw a moon halo, the first since I've been here. I had remarked inwardly that the moon seemed almost unnaturally bright, but thought no more about it until something—perhaps a subtle change in the quality of moonlight—fetched my attention back to the sky. When

---

2 **geologic horizon:** period in the history of the earth.
3 **sentient** (sĕn′shənt)**:** capable of feeling or sensation.

4 **portentous:** particularly suggestive of approaching evil.
5 **lee . . . sastrugi:** sheltered side of the ridges of hard snow.

I glanced up, a haze was spreading over the moon's face; and, as I watched, a system of luminous[6] circles formed themselves gracefully around it. Almost instantly the moon was wholly surrounded by concentric bands[7] of color, and the effect was as if a rainbow had been looped around a huge silver coin. Apple-green was the color of the wide outer band, whose diameter, I estimated, was nineteen times that of the moon itself. The effect lasted only five minutes or so. Then the colors drained from the moon, as they do from a rainbow; and almost simultaneously a dozen massive streamers of crimson-stained aurora,[8] laced together with blackish stripes, seemed to leap straight out from the moon's brow. Then they, too, vanished. . . .

May 5

This has been a beautiful day. Although the sky was almost cloudless, an impalpable[9] haze hung in the air, doubtless from falling crystals. In midafternoon it disappeared, and the Barrier to the north flooded with a rare pink light, pastel in its delicacy. The horizon line was a long slash of crimson, brighter than blood; and over this welled a straw-yellow ocean whose shores were the boundless blue of the night. I watched the sky a long time, concluding that such beauty was reserved for distant, dangerous places, and that nature has good reason for exacting her own special sacrifices from those determined to witness them. An intimation of my isolation seeped into my mood; this cold but lively afterglow was my compensation for the loss of the sun whose warmth and light were enriching the world beyond the horizon.

That afternoon, for variety's sake, I decided to direct my walk out along the radio antenna, which extended on a line about due east from the shack. The cold was not excessive—somewhere between 50° and 60° below zero—but I was astonished to find how much rime[10] had collected on the wire. It was swollen to many times its natural size; so much so, in fact, that I could just encircle it with my fingers; and the weight of the ice had caused it to sag in great loops between the poles.

A day or so before the sun had departed I had planted a bamboo stick about twenty yards beyond the last antenna pole. This was to serve as a beacon in case I ever happened to miss the pole in fog or storm. On this day I found the marker without difficulty.

I was standing there, thinking about something, when I suddenly remembered that I had left the stove going. So I turned back, making for the last antenna pole, whose shadowy pencil form I

---

6 **luminous:** bright; giving off light.
7 **concentric bands:** a series of circles, one inside another, having the same center.
8 **aurora:** curves of light in the night sky.
9 **impalpable:** too delicate to be easily noticed.

10 **rime:** frostlike ice.

RICHARD E. BYRD

could just see. Head screwed down inside the windproof hood out of the wind, I paid no attention to where I was stepping. Then I had a horrible feeling of falling, and at the same time of being hurled sideways. Afterwards I could not remember hearing any sound. When my wits returned, I was sprawled out full length on the snow with one leg dangling over the side of an open crevasse.

I lay still, not daring to make a move lest I shake down the ledge supporting me. Then, an inch at a time, I crawled away. When I had gone about two yards, I came slowly to my feet, shivering from the closeness of the escape.

I had broken through the snow bridging of a blind crevasse—a roofed-over one which you cannot tell from solid surface. I edged back with my flashlight and took a look. The hole I had made was barely two feet across; and I could see that the roof was twelve inches or so thick. Stretched out on my belly, I pounded the roof in with the marker stick for a distance of several feet; then I turned the flashlight into the crevasse. I could see no bottom. My guess was that the crevasse was at least several hundred feet deep. At the surface it was not more than three feet across; but a little way down it bellied out, making a vast cave. The walls changed from blue to an emerald green, the color of sea ice. The usual crystals, created by the condensed exhalations from the warmer depths, did not festoon[11] the walls; their absence indicated that the crevasse was of fairly recent origin.

I was glad to leave that place. Good luck had carried me across the crevasse at right angles to its length. Had I been walking in any other direction, I might well have gone to the bottom. Odd, I thought, that it hadn't let me through when I passed over it on the way out. Possibly I had hit the one weak spot. So as not to make a similar mistake, I fetched back two bamboo poles and planted them in front of the hole.

May 6

Today I broke the thermometer I keep in the hut. It is not important, really, as inside temperatures are not a part of my meteorological records; but I have been interested in finding out how cold it gets in the hut during the night when the fire is out.

Curiosity tempted me to ask Little America how the stock market was going. It was a ghastly mistake. I can in no earthly way alter the situation. Worry, therefore, is needless. Before leaving [home] I had invested my own funds—carefully, I thought—in the hope of making a little money and thus reducing the expedition's debt. This additional loss, on top of ever-mounting operating expenses, may be disastrous. Well, I don't need money here. The wisest course is to close off my mind to the bothersome details of the world.

* * *

It was one thing to instruct the mind; it was another to make the mind obey. The nature of the distinction was to be a fundamental part of my self-instruction at Advance Base, as is evidenced by a diary entry about this time: "Something—I don't know what—is getting me down," the entry goes. "I've been strangely irritable all day, and since supper have been depressed. . . . [This] would not seem important if I could only put my finger on the trouble, but I can't find any single thing to account for the mood. Yet, it has been there; and tonight, for the first time, I must admit that the problem of keeping my mind on an even keel is a serious one. . . ."

The entire entry, a longish one, is before me now. I have a clear recollection of how it came to be written. Supper was over, the dishes had been washed, the 8 P.M. "ob"[12] was out of the way, and I had settled down to read. I picked up Veblen's *Theory of the Leisure Class*, which I was halfway through, but its concerns seemed fantastically remote to the monocracy[13] of Advance Base. I went from that to *Heloïse and Abélard*, a story I have always loved; after a little while the words began

12 **ob:** abbreviation for "observation." Byrd recorded his observations of weather data at regular intervals.
13 **monocracy** (mō nŏk′rə sĭ): government by one person.

11 **festoon:** decorate.

RICHARD E. BYRD

361

to run together. Queerly, my eyes hurt, my head ached a little, though not enough to bother.

So I turned up the lamp a little, thinking that more light might help, and tried a few hands of solitaire. But this did no good. Nor did bathing my eyes in boric acid. I couldn't concentrate. My whole being was restive and unaccountably troubled. I got up and paced the room. My movements were almost automatic. Two strides—duck the light, sidestep the stove—another step—full turn at the bunk—back again—three strides from the door to the radio set—three back—and so on, tracing an endlessly repeated L. Months after I had left Advance Base, when the pain was ebbing into forgetfulness, I used to pace my room that way, my steps unconsciously regulated to the dimensions of the shack, and my head jerking away from an imaginary lantern.

That night the peace did not come that should have come. I was like a clock wound up to strike in an empty house. Everything I was doing seemed unfinished and crude, without relationship to the unfathomable desires in my mind. The futility and emptiness of my existence were symbolized by the simple act of jumping up from the chair. Nothing in the everyday habits of a man is ordinarily freighted with more purposefulness than the business of quitting a chair. The swift leverage may impel him on any one of a thousand different errands and opportunities. But with me it led only to blank walls.

I tried to be rational[14] about it. The diary testifies to that. I took my mood apart and studied it as I might have studied the register. Had anything gone wrong during the day? No, it had been a very pleasant day. Though the temperature was in the minus fifties, I had worked hard on the Escape Tunnel; I had supped well on chicken soup, beans, dehydrated potatoes, spinach, and canned peaches. Had I reason to be worried about matters in the world to the north? On the contrary, the news over the last radio schedule had been reassuring. My family was well, and nothing was wrong at Little America. The debt was a problem, but I was used to debts; I could pay off this one as I had paid off the others. My physical condition? Except for the dull ache in my eyes and head, I felt fine; the ache came only at night, anyway, and was gone before I fell asleep. Maybe the fumes from the stove accounted for it. If this was the case, I had better crack the door when the stove was going during the day, and spend more time outside. The diet might also be a contributing cause, but I doubted it. I had been careful about vitamins.

"The most likely explanation," I concluded that night in the diary, "is that the trouble lies with myself. Manifestly,[15] if I can harmonize the various things within me that may be in conflict and also fit myself more smoothly into this environment, I shall be at peace. It may be that the evenness and the darkness and the absence of life are too much for me to absorb in one chunk. I can-

14 **rational:** reasonable.
15 **Manifestly:** clearly; plainly.

not accept that as a fact, if only because I have been here but forty-three days and many months must be lived out which will be no different from the first. . . . If I am to survive —or at least keep my mental balance —I must control and direct my thoughts. This should not be difficult. Any intelligent man should be able to find means of existence within himself. . . ."

Even from this distance I maintain that the attitude was a sensible one. The only fault was its glibness. The reasoning was too pat. I can see that now, but I lacked the prescience[16] to see it then. It was true, as I reasoned that night in May, that the concerns and practices of the outer world had not intruded into my existence. That was proved by the weeks of utter tranquillity. It was also true, as I had concluded, that the way to keep them from intruding was through the censorship and control of the mind. But beyond these was a truth which that night I did not recognize; and this truth was that the whole complex nervous-muscular mechanism which is the body was waiting, as if with bated breath, for the intrusion of familiar stimuli from the outside world, and could not comprehend why they were denied.

A man can isolate himself from habits and conveniences—deliberately, as I have done; or accidentally, as a shipwrecked sailor might—and force his mind to forget. But the body is not so easily sidetracked. It keeps on remembering. Habit has set up in the core of the being a system of automatic physio-chemical actions and reactions which insist upon replenishment. That is where the conflict arises. I don't think that a man can do without sounds and smells and voices and touch, any more than he can do without phosphorus and calcium. This is, in general, what I meant by the vague term *evenness*.

So I learned at Latitude 80° 08' South. It was exhilarating to stand on the Barrier and contemplate the sky and luxuriate in a beauty I did not aspire to possess. In the presence of such beauty we are lifted above natural crassness. And it was a fine thing, too, to surrender to the illusion of intellectual disembodiment, to feel the mind go voyaging through space as smoothly and felicitously as it passes through the objects of its reflections. The body stood still, but the mind was free. It could travel the universe with the audacious mobility[17] of a Wellsian time-space machine.[18]

The senses were isolated in soundless dark; so, for that matter, was the mind; but one was stayed, while the other possessed the flight of a falcon; and the free choice and opportunity of the one everlastingly emphasized the poverty of the other. From the depth of my being would sometimes surge a fierce desire to be projected spectacularly into the living warmths

16 **prescience** (prē′shĭ əns): foresight.

17 **audacious** (ô dā′shəs) **mobility:** daring freedom of movement.
18 **Wellsian . . . machine:** H. G. Wells, a British writer, published in 1895 an early science-fiction story, *The Time Machine.*

and movements the mind revisited. Usually the desire had no special focus. It sought no single thing. Rather it darted and wavered over a panorama of human aspects—my family at dinnertime, the sound of voices in a downstairs room, the cool feeling of rain.

Small matters, all of them; not realities but only the manifestations of reality. Yet, they and a thousand other remembrances of like substance assailed me at night. Not with the calm, revivifying strength of treasured memories; but bitterly and provokingly, as if they were fragments of something vast and not wholly recognizable which I had lost forever. This was the basis of my mood that night in May. Like fingers plucking at a counterpane, my thoughts moved through the days and nights of an existence that seemed to be irrevocably[19] gone. In that mood I had walked before; I would walk like that again; and the glowing tranquillity built up in the afternoon would go out like a spent rocket.

* * *

Nevertheless, I practiced my preachments of a disciplined mind. Or perhaps discipline isn't exactly the right word; for what I did, or tried to do, was to focus my thinking on healthy, constructive images and concepts and thus crowd out the unhealthy ones. I built a wall between myself and the past in an effort to extract every ounce of diversion and creativeness inherent in my immediate surroundings. Every day I experimented with new schemes for increasing the content of the hours. "A grateful environment," according to Santayana, "is a substitute for happiness," for it can stimulate us from without just as good works can stimulate us from within. My environment was intrinsically[20] treacherous and difficult, but I saw ways to make it agreeable. I tried to cook more rapidly, take weather and auroral observations more expertly, and do routine things systematically. Full mastery of the impinging[21] moment was my goal. I lengthened my walks and did more reading, and kept my thoughts upon an impersonal plane. In other words, I tried resolutely to attend to my business.

All the while I experimented steadily with cold weather clothing. Inside the shack my usual outfit consisted of a thick woolen shirt, breeches, and underwear (medium weight); plus two pairs of woolen socks (one pair heavy, the other medium); plus a pair of homemade canvas boots, which were soled with thin strips of hairless sealskin, lined with a half-inch thickness of felt, and secured to the ankles by means of leather thongs fastened to the soles. The feet are most vulnerable to cold. They feel chilly sooner and stay that way longer than any other part of the body. This is partly because the circulation in the feet is not so good as in the rest of the body and because the cold from the snow

---

19 **irrevocably** (Ĭ rĕv′ə kə blĭ): unchangeably.

20 **intrinsically:** by its own nature.
21 **impinging** (ĭm pĭnj′ĭng): crowding in.

gets to them from conduction and causes condensation. The permeability[22] of canvas was a partial solution to the second difficulty. By making the boots two inches longer and half again as wide as ordinary shoes, I assisted the circulation. The boots were about as handsome as potato sacks, but they worked very well indeed. Whenever I had been a considerable time in the cold, I always changed my socks and inner liners and let the wet ones dry on the stove. The inner soles of my boots were coated with a layer of ice that never thawed. Cold was nothing new to me; and experience had taught me that the secret of protection is not so much the quantity or weight of the clothes as it is the size and quality and, above all, the way they are worn and cared for.

After I'd been at Advance Base a little while I could tell, from a glance at the thermograph, exactly what clothing I would need topside. If it were a matter of taking a quick observation, I'd just slip on a canvas windbreaker, mittens, and a woolen cap that pulled down over the ears. If I had shoveling to do, I'd substitute a helmet for the cap, and add windproof socks, pants, and parka. Walking, I'd wear a woolen parka under the windproofs, which are nothing more mysterious than finespun unbleached cotton blouses and pants, made of material no heavier than ordinary sheeting. I've felt wind cut through half an inch of wool as if it were nothing at all;

22 **permeability:** quality of allowing penetration, in this case by air.

whereas, paper-thin windproofs, closed at the ankles, chin, and waist with draw strings or elastics, were scarcely penetrated. The ideal material is not completely windproof, but lets enough air through to prevent moisture from collecting. At 65° below zero, I usually wore a mask. A simple thing, it consisted of a wire framework overlaid with windproof cloth. Two funnels led to the nose and mouth, and oval slits allowed me to see. I'd breathe in through the nose funnel, and out through the mouth funnel; and, when the latter clogged with ice from the breath's freezing, as it would in short order, I brushed it out with a mitten. On the very cold days, if I had to be out two hours or more, I usually wore my fur outfit (pants, parka, mittens, and mukluks), which was made of reindeer skin, the lightest and most flexible of the warm furs. Thus protected, I could walk through my own inhospitable medium as well insulated as a diver moving through his.

Thus in May, as in April, I never really lacked for something to do. For all the hush and evenness and the slow pulse of the night, my existence was anything but static. I was the inspector of snowstorms and the aurora, the night watchman, and father confessor to myself. Something was always happening, for better or worse. For example, the Tuesday radio schedule with Little America was eliminated, to save gasoline; while this left a blank spot in the hours, the remaining two schedules in turn became more animated.

There was always a message from the family in our own private code, which Dyer read with a gracious and unflagging courtesy: "A as in Arthur, L as in laughter, C as in ceiling . . ." I can still hear him going on. Sometimes there were messages from friends. One message came from my old friend Franklin D. Roosevelt in the White House, saying that he hoped that "the night was not too cold or the wind too strong for an occasional promenade in the dark." And almost always Poulter, or Rawson (now fully recovered), or Siple, or Noville, or Haines, or Innes-Taylor entered into the conversation to discuss an expedition problem or merely pass the time of day.

When I gained in one direction, I seemed to lose in another. Just when I was congratulating myself on having mastered the job of weather observer, the outside thermograph began to act up. A devilish contrivance, it occupied the instrument shelter topside, where hoarfrost settled on the trace, the pen, the drum, and even the workings. On the one occasion I brought the instrument into the shack to change the sheet and make an adjustment, the difference in temperature coated the metal with rime and stopped it dead. Thereafter I had no choice but to make the adjustments in the chill of the tunnel, with no protection for my hands except thin silk gloves; even these seemed infernally clumsy when I had to deal with the speed regulator, which must have been invented for the specific purpose of plaguing weather men.

Thus, even in the heart of the Ross Ice Barrier a solitary man had plenty to occupy him. Thus in the diary: ". . . I got Canfield twice tonight— extraordinary! The only games I played, too." And again: ". . . One of my favorite records is 'Home on the Range.' It's the second song I've ever learned to sing. (The other was 'Carry Me Back to Old Virginny,' and even that I never dared to sing except in the cockpit of an airplane, where nobody could hear me.) And tonight I sang while washing the dishes. Solitude hasn't mellowed my voice any, but I had great fun. A gala evening, in fact." The diary became more than a record; it became a means to think out loud. This was a pleasant way of filling the last hour; also, it helped to stabilize my philosophy. . . .

2

MAY WAS A round boulder sinking before a tide. Time sloughed off the last implication of urgency, and the days moved imperceptibly one into the other. The few world news items which Dyer read to me from time to time seemed almost as meaningless and blurred as they might to a Martian. My world was insulated against the shocks running through distant economies. Advance Base was geared to different laws. On getting up in the morning, it was enough for me to say to myself: Today is the day to change the barograph sheet, or, Today is the day to fill the stove tank. The night was settling down in earnest. By May 17th, one month after the sun had sunk below the horizon, the noon twilight was dwindling to a mere chink in the darkness, lit by a cold reddish glow. Days when the wind brooded in the north or east, the Barrier became a vast stagnant shadow surmounted by swollen masses of clouds, one layer of darkness piled on top of the other. This was the polar night, the morbid countenance[23] of the Ice Age. Nothing moved; nothing was visible. This was the soul of inertness. One could almost hear a distant creaking as if a great weight were settling.

Out of the deepening darkness came the cold. On May 19th, when I took the usual walk, the temperature was 65° below zero. For the first time the canvas boots failed to protect my feet. One heel was nipped, and I was forced to return to the hut and change to reindeer mukluks. That day I felt miserable; my body was racked by shooting pains—exactly as if I had been gassed. Very likely I was; in inspecting the ventilator pipes next morning I discovered that the intake pipe was completely clogged with rime and that the outlet pipe was two-thirds full. Next day—Sunday the 20th—was the coldest yet. The minimum thermometer dropped to 72° below zero; the inside thermograph, which always read a bit lower than the instruments in the shelter, stood at −74°; and the thermograph in the shelter was stopped dead—the

23 **morbid countenance:** sickly face.

ink, though well laced with glycerine, and the lubricant were both frozen. So violently did the air in the fuel tank expand after the stove was lit that oil went shooting all over the place; to insulate the tank against similar temperature spreads I wrapped around it the rubber air cushion which by some lucky error had been included among my gear. In the glow of a flashlight the vapor rising from the stovepipe and the outlet ventilator looked like the discharge from two steam engines. My fingers agonized over the thermograph, and I was hours putting it to rights. The fuel wouldn't flow from the drums; I had to take one inside and heat it near the stove. All day long I kept two primus stoves burning in the tunnel. . . .

At midnight, when I clambered topside for an auroral "ob," a wild sense of suffocation came over me the instant I pushed my shoulders through the trap door. My lungs gasped, but no air reached them. Bewildered and perhaps a little frightened, I slid down the ladder and lunged into the shack. In the warm air the feeling passed as quickly as it had come. Curious but cautious, I again made my way up the ladder. And again the same thing happened; I lost my breath, but I perceived why. A light air was moving down from eastward; and its bitter touch, when I faced into it, was constricting the breathing passages. So I turned my face away from it, breathing into my glove; and in that attitude finished the "ob." Before going below, I made an interesting experiment. I put a thermometer on the snow, let it lie there awhile, and discovered that the temperature at the surface was actually 5° colder than at the level of the instrument shelter, four feet higher. Reading in the sleeping bag afterwards, I froze one finger, although I shifted the book steadily from one hand to the other, slipping the unoccupied hand into the warmth of the bag.

* * *

Out of the cold and out of the east came the wind. It came on gradually, as if the sheer weight of the cold were almost too much to be moved. On the night of the 21st the barometer started down. The night was black as a thunderhead when I made my first trip topside; and a tension in the wind, a bulking of shadows in the night indicated that a new storm center was forming. Next morning, glad of an excuse to stay underground, I worked a long time on the Escape Tunnel by the light of a red candle standing in a snow recess. That day I pushed the emergency exit to a distance of twenty-two feet, the farthest it was ever to go. My stint done, I sat down on a box, thinking how beautiful was the red of the candle, how white the rough-hewn snow. Soon I became aware of an increasing clatter of the anemometer cups. Realizing that the wind was picking up, I went topside to make sure that everything was secured. It is a queer experience to watch a blizzard rise. First there is the wind, rising out of nowhere. Then the Barrier

unwrenches itself from quietude; and the surface, which just before had seemed as hard and polished as metal, begins to run like a making[24] sea. Sometimes, if the wind strikes hard, the drift comes across the Barrier like a hurrying white cloud, tossed hundreds of feet in the air. Other times the growth is gradual. You become conscious of a general slithering movement on all sides. The air fills with tiny scraping and sliding and rustling sounds as the first loose crystals stir. In a little while they are moving as solidly as an incoming tide, which creams over the ankles, then surges to the waist, and finally is at the throat. I have walked in drift so thick as not to be able to see a foot ahead of me; yet, when I glanced up, I could see the stars shining through the thin layer just overhead.

Smoking tendrils were creeping up the anemometer pole when I finished my inspection. I hurriedly made the trap door fast, as a sailor might batten down a hatch; and knowing that my ship was well secured, I retired to the cabin to ride out the storm. It could not reach me, hidden deep in the Barrier crust; nevertheless the sounds came down. The gale sobbed in the ventilators, shook the stovepipe until I thought it would be jerked out by the roots, pounded the roof with sledge-hammer blows. I could actually feel the suction effect through the pervious[25] snow. A breeze flickered in the

24 **making:** rising; increasing in turbulence.
25 **pervious:** able to be penetrated.

room and the tunnels. The candles wavered and went out. My only light was the feeble storm lantern.

Even so, I didn't have any idea how really bad it was until I went aloft for an observation. As I pushed back the trap door, the drift met me like a moving wall. It was only a few steps from the ladder to the instrument shelter, but it seemed more like a mile. The air came at me in snowy rushes; I breasted it as I might a heavy surf. No night had ever seemed so dark. The beam from the flashlight was choked in its throat; I could not see my hand before my face.

My windproofs were caked with drift by the time I got below. I had a vague feeling that something had changed while I was gone, but what, I couldn't tell. Presently I noticed that the shack was appreciably colder. Raising the stove lid, I was surprised to find that the fire was out, though the tank was half full. I decided that I must have turned off the valve unconsciously before going aloft; but, when I put a match to the burner, the draught down the pipe blew out the flame. The wind, then, must have killed the fire. I got it going again, and watched it carefully.

The blizzard vaulted to gale force. Above the roar the deep, taut thrumming note of the radio antenna and the anemometer guy wires reminded me of wind in a ship's rigging. The wind direction trace turned scratchy on the sheet; no doubt drift had short-circuited the electric contacts, I decided. Realizing that it was hopeless to attempt to try to keep them clear, I let the instrument be. There were other ways of getting the wind direction. I tied a handkerchief to a bamboo pole and ran it through the outlet ventilator; with a flashlight I could tell which way the cloth was whipped. I did this at hourly intervals, noting any change of direction on the sheet. But by two o'clock in the morning I had had enough of this periscope sighting. If I expected to sleep and at the same time maintain the continuity of the records, I had no choice but to clean the contact points.

The wind was blowing hard then. The Barrier shook from the concussions overhead; and the noise was as if the entire physical world were tearing itself to pieces. I could scarcely heave the trap door open. The instant it came clear I was plunged into a blinding smother. I came out crawling, clinging to the handle of the door until I made sure of my bearings. Then I let the door fall shut, not wanting the tunnel filled with drift. To see was impossible. Millions of tiny pellets exploded in my eyes, stinging like BB shot. It was even hard to breathe, because snow instantly clogged the mouth and nostrils. I made my way toward the anemometer pole on hands and knees, scared that I might be bowled off my feet if I stood erect; one false step and I should be lost forever.

I found the pole all right; but not until my head collided with a cleat. I managed to climb it, too, though ten million ghosts were tearing at me, ramming their thumbs into my eyes. But the errand was useless.

Drift as thick as this would mess up the contact points as quickly as they were cleared; besides, the wind cups were spinning so fast that I stood a good chance of losing a couple of fingers in the process. Coming down the pole, I had a sense of being whirled violently through the air, with no control over my movements. The trap door was completely buried when I found it again, after scraping around for some time with my mittens. I pulled at the handle, first with one hand, then with both. It did not give. It's a tight fit, anyway, I mumbled to myself. The drift has probably wedged the corners. Standing astride the hatch, I braced myself and heaved with all my strength. I might just as well have tried hoisting the Barrier.

Panic took me then, I must confess. Reason fled. I clawed at the three-foot square of timber like a madman. I beat on it with my fists, trying to shake the snow loose; and, when that did no good, I lay flat on my belly and pulled until my hands went weak from cold and weariness. Then I crooked my elbow, put my face down, and said over and over again, You fool, you fool. Here for weeks I had been defending myself against the danger of being penned inside the shack; instead, I was now locked out; and nothing could be worse, especially since I had only a wool parka and pants under my windproofs. Just two feet below was sanctuary—warmth, food, tools, all the means of survival. All these things were an arm's length away, but I was powerless to reach them.

There is something extravagantly insensate about an Antarctic blizzard at night. Its vindictiveness[26] cannot be measured on an anemometer sheet. It is more than just wind: it is a solid wall of snow moving at gale force, pounding like surf. The whole malevolent rush is concentrated upon you as upon a personal enemy. In the senseless explosion of sound you are reduced to a crawling thing on the margin of a disintegrating world; you can't see, you can't hear, you can hardly move. The lungs gasp after the air is sucked out of them, and the brain is shaken. Nothing in the world will so quickly isolate a man.

Half-frozen, I stabbed toward one of the ventilators, a few feet away. My mittens touched something round and cold. Cupping it in my hands, I pulled myself up. This was the outlet ventilator. Just why, I don't know—but instinct made me kneel and press my face against the opening. Nothing in the room was visible, but a dim patch of light illuminated the floor, and warmth rose up to my face. That steadied me.

Still kneeling, I turned my back to the blizzard and considered what might be done. I thought of breaking in the windows in the roof, but they lay two feet down in hard crust, and were reinforced with wire besides. If I only had something to dig with, I could break the crust and stamp the windows in with my feet. The pipe cupped between my hands supplied the first inspiration;

maybe I could use that to dig with. It, too, was wedged tight; I pulled until my arms ached, without budging it; I had lost all track of time, and the despairing thought came to me that I was lost in a task without an end. Then I remembered the shovel. A week before, after leveling drift from the last light blow, I had stabbed a shovel handle up in the crust somewhere to leeward. That shovel would save me. But how to find it in the avalanche of the blizzard?

I lay down and stretched out full length. Still holding the pipe, I thrashed around with my feet, but pummeled only empty air. Then I worked back to the hatch. The hard edges at the opening provided another grip, and again I stretched out and kicked. Again no luck. I dared not let go until I had something else familiar to cling to. My foot came up against the other ventilator pipe. I edged back to that, and from the new anchorage repeated the maneuver. This time my ankle struck something hard. When I felt it and recognized the handle, I wanted to caress it.

Embracing this thrice-blessed tool, I inched back to the trap door. The handle of the shovel was just small enough to pass under the little wooden bridge which served as a grip. I got both hands on the shovel and tried to wrench the door up; my strength was not enough, however. So I lay down flat on my belly and worked my shoulders under the shovel. Then I heaved, the door sprang open, and I rolled down the

26 **vindictiveness:** revengeful attitude.

shaft. When I tumbled into the light and warmth of the room, I kept thinking, How wonderful, how perfectly wonderful.

Reading Skills

1. What are some of the thoughts and feelings that being alone inspired in Byrd?
2. What circumstances surrounded Byrd's narrow escape on the edge of a crevasse?
3. Why was Byrd's feeling of depression puzzling to him? What reason does he give for his depression? How did he overcome his depression? How did his writing in his diary help him?
4. Describe Byrd's appearance in his indoor clothing. How did his attire change when he went outdoors for an extended period?
5. What caused Byrd to become trapped outside his shack? Describe his efforts to get into the shack and the means of his eventual success.

Understanding Literature

1. What comparisons does Byrd use to describe the polar silence? the "snow down"? Find and explain other comparisons which help to clarify Byrd's impressions.
2. Byrd uses many concrete words in his description. For example, his description of the moonlit night of May 1 contains concrete words suggesting shapes, arrangement, and colors. Find other descriptive passages which use many concrete words. What effect does the use of concrete words produce?
3. Reread the following sentence in context; then explain what it means: "The futility and emptiness of my existence were symbolized by the simple act of jumping up from the chair."

Further Activity

Write a brief essay answering the question "What is a scientist?" Include your own definition of a scientist. What are the attitudes of a true scientist? the beliefs? the goals? Use specific examples of scientists who fit your definition.

Sports

Developing athletic skill is not always simply a matter of building muscle and learning coordination. Sports activities are guided by rules and patterns; also, they usually involve other people. Therefore, becoming skilled in sports generally requires growth in character and personality as well as in muscular coordination.

In the first essay of this unit, "Lou Gehrig—An American Hero," the writer shows how one of America's greatest baseball players expressed amazing courage and determination both on the playing field and off. In other of the selections you will be able to observe that growth in character is as important as the development of physical skill.

Because the home run has great crowd appeal, many Americans consider home-run hitter Babe Ruth the greatest baseball player this country has yet seen. However, some sports experts insist that Lou Gehrig was at least as valuable a player as his more colorful teammate, the "Babe." After reading Paul Gallico's tribute, you may think so, too.

Lou Gehrig—An American Hero

Paul Gallico

IMPROVING YOUR READING: In this essay Paul Gallico tells about a sports hero whose character is the source of his greatness. What characteristics does Gallico consider important in an American hero? What is Gallico's central idea in the essay?

SUCCESS IN FULL MEASURE came to Henry Louis Gehrig, the American-born son of immigrant German parents. He had fame, money, popularity, love and companionship, and, thanks to his wife Eleanor, even a little self-assurance.

The awkward boy who could neither bat nor field as a youngster had, by his unswerving persistence, his gnawing ambition, his tenacity[1] and iron will power, made himself into the greatest first baseman in the history of organized baseball. The ballplayer whose cultural tastes seldom rose above a B movie found his interest awakened in music, books and the theater.

I remember writing years ago about Gehrig: "To my mind there is no greater inspiration to any American boy then Lou Gehrig and his career. For if the awkward, inept and downright clumsy Gehrig that I

knew and saw in the beginning could turn himself into the finest first-base-covering machine in all baseball, through sheer drive and determination, then nothing is impossible to any man or boy in this country."

Men like Connie Mack and Hughie Fullerton, baseball encyclopedias who spanned generations of players, unhesitantly placed Lou Gehrig at first base on any "All" team.

When the "All-Star" games were played each summer, there was bitter controversy about who should play many of the positions. But it was almost automatically conceded that Lou Gehrig should play first base for the American Leaguers.

In 1934 Lou won the triple batting championship of the American League, and gave it to his Eleanor as a first-anniversary present. He led his league in hitting that year, batting .363, hitting 49 home runs, and driving in 165 runs.

It is interesting to note Ruth's

1 tenacity: ability to hold fast; persistency.

waning record for the same year. He hit .288, knocked 22 out of the park, and batted in 84 runs.

In 1935, Lou Gehrig was out from beneath the shadow of Babe Ruth. The Babe was no longer with the Yankee team. Wear and tear and time had tapped Ruth. But actually, Gehrig had begun to emerge even before Ruth's retirement. For toward the end, as the figures indicate, not even the Babe could cast a shadow large enough to blanket the Iron Horse.

Gehrig's modesty and self-depreciation continued to keep him in the background, but his deeds, his amazing vitality, durability and the quality of his play refused to be submerged any longer.

Sincere tributes to the man appeared in the sports columns. From the Olympian slopes of the press box, the sports writers began to look down with honest affection at the piano legs, the broad rear porch which had earned him the name of Biscuit Pants, the powerful, smooth-swinging shoulders and the young and pleasant face of "that big dumb Dutchman."

Success! The Golden Decade was buried in the limbo[2] of beautiful dreams. There was a new era and a new team. With Lou as captain, the Bronx Bombers won the American League pennant in 1936-7-8. They won three World Series in a row, two from the Giants, 4-2 and 4-1, and one from the helpless Cubs in straight games.

2 limbo: neglected or forgotten place.

In 1936, Lou was again named the most valuable player in the American League, exactly nine years after he had first achieved this honor. His salary had been mounting steadily, and in 1938 he signed for the largest sum he ever received for playing ball, $39,000.

Toward the end of the last decade, the name, the figure, and above all, the simple engaging personality of Lou Gehrig became welded into the national scene. Came the baseball season, came Gehrig. Came Gehrig, came home runs, triples, doubles, excitement and faultless play around first base. And his consecutive-games record went on and on. Sick or well, he never missed a game.

Sick or well. I wonder whether you know what that means to a ballplayer, and particularly one who plays at first base, where the bumps are many and there is daily danger both from ball and man.

Lou played with colds. He played with fevers. He played so doubled over with lumbago that it was impossible for him to straighten up, and bent over at the plate, he still got himself a single.

In 1934, the year he won the triple crown, he fractured a toe. He played on. He was knocked unconscious by a wild pitch, suffered a concussion that would hospitalize the average man for two weeks. He was at his position the next day and collected four hits. When, late in his career, his hands were X-rayed, they found seventeen assorted fractures that had healed by themselves. He had broken every finger on both

PAUL GALLICO

377

hands and some twice, and *hadn't even mentioned it* to anyone.

The fantastic thing about all this is not that he was able to endure the pain of breaks, strains, sprains, pulled and torn tendons, muscles and ligaments, but that it failed to impair his efficiency. On the contrary, if he had something the matter with him it was the signal for him to try all the harder, so that no one, least of all his own severe conscience, could accuse him of being a handicap to his team while playing in a crippled condition.

When, in 1939, Lou Gehrig found himself slow in spring training, he began to punish his body for a failure that was unaccountable and to drive it harder than ever before.

It had begun before that, the slow tragedy of disintegration. Signs and symptoms had been mistaken. During most of 1938, Gehrig had been on a strict diet. That year had not been a good one for him. In the early winter of 1939 he had taken a $5,000 salary slash. Baseball players are paid by the records they compile. That winter, as usual, Lou and Eleanor went ice skating together. Lou was a fine skater. But, strangely, he kept falling all the time.

The teams went South for the 1939 training season and the sports writers went along with them. And the boys with one accord began sending back stories that must have saddened them to write. I know sports writers. When you grow to love an athlete the way they loved Lou Gehrig, it isn't fun to oil your typewriter with his blood and be the first to write

the story of the passing from the sports scene of a once-great figure.

What they saw was not unfamiliar to them. The useful playing lifetime of a top-flight professional athlete is on the average shockingly short. A sports writer is quick to notice the first symptoms of slowing up. They were obvious with Gehrig at St. Petersburg. He was slow afoot, afield and at bat. And while he fought like a rookie to hold his position, no improvement was evident. Sadly the sports writers wrote that the old Iron Horse was running down.

But the players on the Yankee ball club were saying something else. They were close to Gehrig—close enough to touch. They noticed things that worried and depressed them. And they had knowledge of their craft and of themselves. One of the things they knew was that a ballplayer slows up only gradually. His legs go, imperceptibly at first, then noticeably as he no longer covers the ground in the field that he used to cover. But he doesn't come apart all at one time, and in chunks.

I talked to Tony Lazzeri at his neat little home in San Francisco. Tony watched Lou in practice in Florida in 1939. Once Lou was up at the plate and ducked back from a close one. And he couldn't stop himself. He just kept on staggering backwards, unable to regain his balance, until he crashed into one of the other players, who righted him again.

The ballplayers knew that wasn't right.

378

Bill Dickey, Lou's closest friend, was worried sick. He began to watch over Lou the way a father watches over a child. And nobody would say anything to Gehrig, because, rough and tough though the ballplayer may be, he is a sensitive fellow and a respecter of private feelings.

There are grim tales of things that happened in the locker room, and one is macabre[3] with overtones of manly nobility. It tells of Gehrig dressing, leaning over to lace his spikes and falling forward to the floor, to lie momentarily helpless. And it tells further of tough men with the fine instincts to look away and not to hurt his already tortured soul the more by offering to help. Quickly they left the locker room, leaving him to struggle to his feet alone with no eyes to see his weakness.

Few men can have gone through what Gehrig did during those days.

Among the elements that go to make up a hero is the capacity for quiet, uncomplaining suffering; the ability to take it and never let the world suspect that you are taking it. This was Lou Gehrig. Not even his wife knew wholly, though she must have suspected, how terribly Gehrig suffered during those days when his speed and skill were deserting him.

Picture the fear, the worry, the helpless bewilderment that must have filled Lou's soul as he found that he could not bat, could not run, could not field. Life for him took on

nightmare aspects. All the fear-dreams to which humans are prone, dreams of shameful failure, dreams of not being able to run when pursued, dreams of performing some well-remembered daily office with grotesque results, now haunted his waking hours.

The strain and terror of it lined his face in a few short months and brought gray to his hair. But it could not force a complaint from his lips.

Gehrig's most powerful reaction when it became apparent that there was something wrong with him was to drive himself still harder, to punish his flagging muscles and sick body relentlessly. He was certain it was work he needed. It never occurred to him to blame for his apparent lack of condition something quite outside his own power to control.

His performance during the early part of 1939 was pitiful. And yet, so great was the spell cast by his integrity, his honest attempts to please and his service over the long years, that that worst-mannered, worst-tempered and most boorish individual in the world, the baseball fan, forebore to heckle him.

On Sunday, April 30, 1939, the Yankees played the Senators in Washington. Lou Gehrig came to bat four times with runners on base. He failed even to meet the ball, and the Yankees lost.

Something else happened on that day. There was a toss ball at first. The pitcher fielded a one-hop grounder, ran over toward first and

3 **macabre** (mə kä′bər): gruesome.

tossed the ball underhand to Lou, as pitchers frequently do when there is time.

Lou muffed the throw.

Monday was an off day. Lou went to Larchmont. He did a lot of thinking, but he did it to himself. He had the toughest decision of his life to make. But he had to make it alone.

Tuesday, May second, the team met in Detroit to open a series against the Tigers. Joe McCarthy flew in from Buffalo. Lou met him in the dugout and said the fateful words:

"Joe, I always said that when I felt I couldn't help the team any more I would take myself out of the line-up. I guess that time has come."

"When do you want to quit, Lou?" asked McCarthy.

Gehrig looked at him steadily and said, "Now. Put Babe Dahlgren in."

Later, alone in the dugout, he wept.

The record ended at 2,130 games.

The newspapers and the sports world buzzed with the sensation of Lou Gehrig's departure from the Yankee line-up.

At the urging of Eleanor, Lou went to the Mayo Clinic at Rochester, Minnesota, for a checkup.

There was a lull in the news. Then out of a clear sky the storm burst again. Black headlines tore across the page tops like clouds and lightninged their messages: "GEHRIG HAS INFANTILE PARALYSIS." "GEHRIG FIGHTS PARALYZING ILLNESS."

The New York Yankees released the report of the doctors at the clinic.

It was a disease diagnosed as amyotrophic lateral sclerosis, interpreted for the layman as a form of infantile paralysis, and the mystery of the too-sudden decline and passing of Henry Louis Gehrig, perennial Yankee first baseman, was solved.

Before Gehrig came home from the Mayo Clinic, Eleanor went to their family physician, gave him the name of the disease and asked to be told the truth about it. The doctor knew her well. He said quietly, "I think you can take it. And I think you should know."

Then he told her that her husband could not live more than two years.

Eleanor went home. She closed her door upon herself, shutting out the world. But before she could give in to grief and shock for the first and last time, she telephoned to the Mayo Clinic. She had but one question to ask of the doctors there: "Have you told my husband?"

Gehrig had so captivated the staff that they had not yet had the heart to tell him the truth, and they so advised Eleanor.

She begged, "Please promise me that you never will. Don't ever let him know. I don't want him to find out."

They promised. Only then did Eleanor permit herself to weep.

The time of weeping was short. Lou came home. He came home full of smiles and jokes, and the girl who met him was smiling and laughing too, though neither noticed that in the laughter of the other there was something feverish. They were too busy to notice. Too busy with their magnificent deception of each other.

Lou's cheer was based outwardly on the fact that he hadn't been just an aging ballplayer; that his sudden disintegration had been caused by disease—a disease of which he promised Eleanor he would be cured before he learned to pronounce its name.

Eleanor fought a constant fight to keep the truth from Lou. She had to be on the spot always to answer the telephone; to watch over him so that people did not get to him; to look after the mail before he saw it. Ever present was the menace of the one crackpot who might slip through the shields of love she placed about her husband and tell him that his case was hopeless.

As to what Lou knew—he never told anybody.

To all intents and purposes, Gehrig went into the battle with his chin up and his determination blazing. If the knowledge was clear within him that the cards were stacked against him and he could not win, he fought, nevertheless. He would have fought if only to keep up Eleanor's courage, to prevent her from realizing the hopelessness of his situation.

On July 4, 1939, there took place the most tragic and touching scene ever enacted on a baseball diamond —the funeral services for Henry Louis Gehrig.

Lou Gehrig attended them in person.

Lou Gehrig Appreciation Day, as it was called, was a gesture of love and appreciation on the part of everyone concerned, a spontaneous reaching out to a man who had been good and kind and decent, to thank him for having been so.

The suggestion that there be a Gehrig Day began in the sports column of Bill Corum of the *Journal-American*. Other columnists concurred, and the event was set between the games of a Fourth of July double-header.

The most touching demonstration of what the day meant was the coming from the ends of the country of Gehrig's former teammates, the famous Murderers' Row, the powerful Yankees of 1927.

Bob Meusel, balding Benny Bengough, Gehrig's first pal; gray-eyed Mark Koenig and dead-panned Poosh-'em-up Tony Lazzeri, the clown of the team; tall, skinny Joe Dugan, and even taller and skinnier Pipp the Pickler, the Yankee first baseman whose place Gehrig had taken so many years ago, all came.

Little Everett Scott turned up, the man whose endurance record Gehrig had conquered so decisively, and the great pitching staff of other days: Herb Pennock, from his Pennsylvania fox farm, Waite Hoyt from the broadcasting booths. George Pipgras was there too, but wearing the blue uniform of an umpire. Earle Combs and Art Fletcher still were in Yankee uniforms as coaches.

And finally there was George Herman Ruth. The Babe and Lou hadn't got along very well the last years they played together, and after Babe retired he had criticized Lou's long playing record in a newspaper interview. The original feud was a childish affair which gains nothing in dignity or sense in the retelling. Suffice it to say that the Babe was there on that Requiem Day, with an arm around Lou and a whispered pleasantry that came at a time when Gehrig was very near to collapse from the emotions that turmoiled within him. It needed Babe's Rabelaisian[4] nonsense to make him smile.

Present too were Lou's more recent teammates, the Bronx Bombers under Joe McCarthy, and the Washington Senators, who were the opponents of the Yankees for the double-header.

Sid Mercer, president of the Baseball Writers' Association, was the master of ceremonies. The principal speakers were Jim Farley, Postmaster General, and Mayor Fiorello LaGuardia. Sixty-one thousand, eight hundred and eight were in the stands. It was what was known as a Great Day.

To Lou Gehrig, it was good-by to everything that he had known and loved.

It was good-by to baseball; to the big steel-and-concrete stadium where he had served so long; to the neat green diamond with the smooth dirt paths cut by the sharp steel baseball cleats; to the towering stands with the waving pennons, the crowds, their roar and color.

Good-by, too, to the men with whom he had played for fourteen

years, the happy, friendly men who had been his shipmates through life.

In the stands was all that he held dear: his mother and father seated in a box, unaware of his doom; his wife seated in another. Lifelong friends were in the boxes, cheering and applauding. And as Lou observed them gathered there in his honor, he knew he was seeing them thus for the last time.

For he was the living dead, and this was his funeral.

Gifts piled up for him: a silver service, smoking sets, writing sets, fishing tackle. They were from the Yankees; from their great rivals the Giants; from the baseball writers and even from the ushers in the stadium and the peanut boys. The objects were a mockery, because Lou could no longer possess them. But the warmth of the feeling that prompted their presentation melted the iron reserve in him and broke him down.

It was so human and so heroic that Gehrig should have wept there in public before the sixty-one thousand, not for pity of himself, nor yet for the beauty and sweetness of the world he would soon leave, but because the boy who all his life had convinced himself that he had no worth, that he did not matter and never would, understood on this day, for the first time perhaps, how much people loved him.

Not only his immediate family, his adored wife, his personal friends were broadcasting their warmth to him, but huge masses of plain, simple people with whom he felt a deep

4 **Rabelaisian** (răb′ə lā′zĭ ən): Rabelais (1494?-1553), a French author, wrote *Gargantua* and *Pantagruel*. Rabelaisian humor is earthy, robust, and extravagant.

kinship. He was the lone receiving station. To tune in suddenly upon so much love was nearly too much for him.

The speeches were ended at last, the gifts given, and the stadium rocked as wave after wave of cheers rolled down from the stands and broke over him. For a little while, as he stood at the microphones, it seemed as if the huge combers of sound might engulf him. He stood with his head bowed to the tumult and pressed a handkerchief to his eyes.

But when at last, encouraged by his friend Ed Barrow, a burly bear of a man with the kindest of hearts, he faced the instruments and the people behind them, the noise stopped abruptly. Everyone waited for what he would say. With a curled finger he dashed away the tears that would not stay back, lifted his head and brought his obsequies[5] to their heartbreaking, never-to-be-forgotten finish when he spoke his epitaph:

"For the past two weeks you have been reading about a bad break I got. Yet today I consider myself the luckiest man on the face of the earth . . ."

The clangy, iron echo of the Yankee Stadium picked up the sentence that poured from the loud-speakers and hurled it forth into the world. "The luckiest man on the face of the earth . . . the luckiest man on the face of the earth . . . luckiest man . . ."

5 **obsequies** (ŏb′sə kwĭz): funeral services.

EPILOGUE

There is an epilogue, because although the tale of Lou Gehrig—an American Hero really ends above, he lived for quite a while longer, and perhaps in the simple story of how he lived what time was left to him is to be found his greatest gallantry.

For life is not the work of a master dramatist. The hero does not vanish in a cloud of fire at the supreme moment. No, life must be lived on until the curtain falls of its own accord, and that calls for the greatest heroism of all—the heroism of little things: of the breaking smile, the cheery word, the laugh that covers pain, the light phrase that denies hopelessness and a sinking heart.

Almost two more years had to pass before the end came to Henry Louis Gehrig, and Eleanor says that during that time he was always laughing, cheerful, interested in everything, impatient only of unasked-for sympathy. In short, he lived his daily life.

But he did more. And here we come to the final bit of heroism. With his doom sealed and his parting inevitable from the woman who had given him the only real happiness he had ever known, he chose to spend his last days, not in one final feverish attempt to suck from life in two years all that he might have had in forty, but in work and service.

Mayor LaGuardia appointed him a city parole commissioner. And so for the next months, as long as he was able to walk even with the assistance of others, Gehrig went daily to his office and did his work. He listened to cases, studied them; he brought to the job his thoroughness and his innate kindness and understanding.

He sat at his desk even when no longer able to move his arms. When he wanted a cigaret, his wife or his secretary lit it for him and put it between his lips, removed it to shake the ash, replaced it.

He listened to thief, vagabond, and narcotic addict. When there was help to be given, he gave it unstintingly from what strength there was left to him. He would not give in. He would not give up. He did not give up.

On June 2, 1941, Lou Gehrig died in the arms of his wife in their home in Riverdale, N.Y.

But the final beauty of his story is that, in a way, the tenacious man who had overcome every obstacle that ever faced him overcame that last one too.

Gehrig achieved the life everlasting in that he left behind a vital part of himself in the hearts and minds of men. They have tried to express it in the perpetuating of his playing number "4" and his locker in the Yankee Stadium; in the naming of the intersection at Grand Concourse and East 161st Street Gehrig Plaza; in the dedication of a World Series to him; in the screening by Samuel Goldwyn of a picture patterned after his life.

But the light that really shines like a friendly, beckoning beacon in the darkness of a disillusioned world is that of the spirit of a clean, honest, decent, kindly fellow. It is not so much the man whom our weary souls have canonized as the things by which he lived and died. And for the seeing of those we must all of us be very grateful.

Reading Skills

1. According to Gallico, what characteristics does an American hero have? How did Lou Gehrig exemplify these characteristics? Must one be a good ballplayer in order to fit Gallico's concept of a hero?
2. Why was Gehrig called the "Iron Horse"?
3. When Mayor LaGuardia appointed Gehrig to the parole commission, he could be sure that Gehrig would apply himself seriously to the job. Why?

Understanding Literature

1. What is Gallico's central idea about Gehrig? What details illustrate or support this central idea?
2. In what passages does Gallico "fictionalize" his account of the thoughts and private conversations of Gehrig and others?

Further Activities

1. In two or three paragraphs, write a summary of Paul Gallico's appraisal of Lou Gehrig.
2. Write a biographical account of some other American hero in the sports world, emphasizing outstanding character traits.

"Ol' King Solomon is a bass," said the game warden. "We call him thet because he's so smart nobody can't catch him." But even the smartest fish is no match for a clever Ozark mountain boy.

The Big Buffalo Bass

Weldon Stone

IMPROVING YOUR READING: Although this story is mainly about fishing, the author manages to give, a piece at a time, a glimpse at the character of some of the people who live in the Ozark Mountains of Arkansas. Keep mental notes about these people of the mountains as you read, so that you can name some of their major characteristics when you have completed your reading.

ACCORDING TO THE OLD SAYING, "Where there is smoke there is fire"; and likewise, where there are tales of big fish there is bound to be one. That's what I say now, but a week ago I wouldn't have believed it.

My third consecutive summer in the Arkansas Ozarks was about to end, and I was still hearing stories of a big bass that had never been caught. I had first heard of him two years before, when I had only begun to fall in love with the Big Buffalo River, particularly that part of it just above the forks in Newton County, Arkansas. That day I had been working slowly downstream, doing more exploring than fishing, when I came to a spring shaded by a giant chinquapin. I drank my fill, rolled a cigarette, and lay down in the shade to rest.

While I was wondering how many bushels of chinquapins such a tree would bear I heard a squirrel scold-ing something on the rocky bluff across the river. I spotted the squirrel in a scrubby pine, and then, lower down, I saw a man sitting in a niche of rock. He had a gun held ready and then he was still as the cliff itself.

The only sure sign that the fellow was not dead or sleeping was the peering attitude of his head. He was leaning forward and staring into the river below him. Apparently he had not heard the squirrel, though it was only about ten steps behind him.

I whistled. The man looked at me, and I pointed to the squirrel. He turned his head toward where I pointed; then he casually lifted the gun and shot the squirrel. The report of the gun, rebounding from the bluff, was deafening. The squirrel came tumbling down so near the man that he had only to get to his feet to pick it up.

Then he climbed easily up the

bluff and entered the thick, scrubby growth of cedar and pine on the top. A few minutes later he appeared on the spring path and dropped the squirrel at my feet.

"Hit's yourn," he said and, leaning his rifle against the chinquapin, kneeled down and drank from the spring.

"But you shot it," I protested, "so it's really yours."

"I don't hanker after squirrel meat," he replied, wiping his mouth with the back of a lean brown hand. His face was like his hand—lean and hard, unsmiling, but not unfriendly.

"But why—?"

Then I stopped. I had already learned not to ask too many questions of these mountain folk. Glancing at the man's rifle, I saw that it was a .30-30, old but well-kept.

I pulled out my sack of tobacco and offered it. He rolled a cigarette and handed it back to me without a word. He stood and smoked in a silence that was embarrassing to me but not, apparently, to him. I couldn't think of anything to say.

"Well," he said finally, "I reckon I jest as well to git on home," and, picking up his rifle, he was gone before I could thank him for the squirrel.

He had scarcely disappeared when I heard a rustling of leaves behind me and a man stepped out of the undergrowth in back of the spring. He was the same man I had met as a fly fisherman a few days before, but now there were two revolvers strapped to his hips. Intuitively I knew he was the game warden. I glanced at the squirrel involuntarily; I knew the season was closed. But the man was grinning.

"That's all right. I seen it all," he said.

"That's lucky for me," I said, "but I really caused him to shoot it. I thought he was hunting squirrels for food."

"No, he wa'nt huntin' nothin' thet lives in trees or wears fur. He was huntin' ol' King Solomon."

"I see," I said, though I didn't see at all. A triangle affair possibly, or a mountain feud. I waited while the warden cut a chew from his plug.

"Ol' King Solomon is a bass," he said. "We call him thet because he's so smart nobody can't catch him. Thet feller with the gun hooked 'im once, but couldn't hold 'im. Ever since, he's been tryin' off an' on to shoot 'im. Well, thet's agin' the law; an' besides, I'm acquainted with King Solomon myself, an' they ain't nobody agoin' to shoot 'im if I can help it. I had my hand on 'im once."

"How big was he?" I couldn't keep from asking that one.

"I don't choose fer strangers to think I'm a-lyin'," he said, "even when I'm a-tellin' the truth."

And that was all I could get out of him about the size of King Solomon, but that was enough. I determined then and there to keep a sharp lookout for this monarch of Big Buffalo bass.

"Where does King Solomon hold court most of the time?" I asked with a studied effort to be casual.

"Up an' down," he replied; "first one hole, then t'other."

"It seems that our friend with the gun expects to find him in this hole. Has he ever been seen here?"

"Once. 'Bout a year ago. Might be a mile or two up or down by now. Bass is like folks; they travel some when the vittles is scarce. Well, I reckon I jest as well to get on back to town. See ye agin."

"I'll look out for you," I said. And I would look out for him, especially when he had his fly rod along. King Solomon would likely be not far away.

All of this took place two years ago, during my first summer in the Ozarks. I did see the warden several times after that; and when I saw him, I usually saw the man with the gun. The game they played is a popular one with boys and girls; it's called tag. The man with the gun was trying to tag King Solomon; the warden was bent on tagging the man with the gun. I liked to see them at their game, for as long as they played it I knew the big bass had not been caught.

The rest of that summer and all during the next two summers I looked for King Solomon and mentioned his name to all the natives I chanced to meet. They all knew of him, and most of them had stories to tell about the time they had seen him or hooked him; but no one was able or willing to tell me just where and when he might be found. So I never met King Solomon till quite recently, and then it was through Dee Thompson, a boy of twelve.

The few times I tried to talk with Dee it seemed that he was little different from the many lean and taciturn[1] boys of all ages whom I came across on Big Buffalo River. All were hard to talk to; few seemed to have any interest in fishing. I probably never would have got to know Dee any better than the others if I had not mentioned King Solomon. He was a different boy then.

"Hev ye seen 'im?" he asked.

"No, I haven't seen him—just heard about him. But I guess you have," I suggested.

"I seen a big bass one day," he answered, and that was as far as I got with him then.

Another time, however, when Dee saw me with a good day's catch, he opened up and told me about the time King Solomon had broken his line after he had lifted him out of the water by the line. Dee is a tough, hickory-fibered boy, pure mountain stock, a natural stoic; yet it seemed to me that his voice quavered a bit just there, and I remember that his head was turned away.

"But I'm a-goin' to git 'im some day," he added. "It won't be with one o' them fine pretty-things like yourn, but I'm a-goin' to ketch 'im. I know somethin' thet'll git 'im."

I knew it would be futile as well as ill-mannered to ask Dee just what bait he intended to use to bring about King Solomon's downfall, but I thought he might tell me when he hoped to accomplish it.

"Hit won't be too long," he told

1 **taciturn**: silent; not talkative.

me. "When the signs is right agin."

"When do you reckon that will be?" I asked and then wished I hadn't. Dee was looking me too steadily in the eye.

"Do ye want to go with me?" he asked.

"I sure do. You know I've spent a lot of time looking for King Solomon, and even if I can't catch him I'd like to see him—just so I can tell the folks back in Texas how big these Ozark bass really get to be."

"I'll let ye know when I'm a-goin' atter 'im agin," Dee promised and left me to wonder when that would be.

Three or four days later, while I was having a second cup of coffee and trying to decide whether to go upstream or downstream that day or to try Little Buffalo for a change, Dee walked into my camp.

"I'm a-goin'," he announced.

"And may I trail along?" I asked, too hopefully, I feared.

"Thet's whut I said t'other day," he replied.

In five minutes we were on our way, downstream. I hurried after the tough bare feet ahead of me, over sharp rocks that made me cringe in spite of my thick rubber soles. Dee led me straight to the hole by the chinquapin spring, where just two years before I had heard of King Solomon from the game warden. We had a good drink of water, and I rolled a cigarette.

Dee took from his pocket a ball of stout cotton cord and tied the free end to the middle of the 12-foot cane pole he had brought with him. He measured off twice the length of his pole and cut the cord. Then he bent to the line a three-foot piece of copper wire and to that a new bronzed "catfish hook" of a murderous size.

"I'm about ready," he said.

"Go to it, boy," I said. "I hope you get him."

"Ain't ye a-goin' to fish any?" he asked.

"No," I answered, but not very firmly, "King Solomon is your fish. I'll watch. I just want to see him."

"I can show 'im to ye if ye'll climb the bluff."

He looked across the river. The sun was just topping the ridge.

"Hit's the right time," he said.

With Dee leading, we crossed below the spring and followed a goat trail up to a ledge of the bluff. There we sat down. The river was about ten feet below us. It was still and shaded by the ridge behind us—all but a narrow strip along the opposite bank.

"Do ye see thet there sycamore log, catty-cornered down the crick?" Dee asked, pointing toward the sunny strip of water.

"Yes, I caught a good one there last summer," I replied. I had tried it many times since without a single strike.

"Thet's where King Solomon lives," Dee said. "He stays under thet old log, and he won't let no other bass come around it. I seen 'im drive 'em away. Watch."

Dee broke off a piece of limestone the size of a dime and thumbed it into the middle of the narrow stream.

I wasn't prepared for what happened. An underlying limb detached itself from the log and shot like a torpedo to the spot where the piece of rock had struck the water. There it stopped dead-still a couple of feet beneath the surface. I saw fins parrying, a bulldog jaw champing, and two bulging eyes glaring upward at the widening ripples above them. At last I was looking upon King Solomon in all of his glory!

"Thet's him," Dee said quietly—and that's the only time I ever knew Dee to waste a word.

"I believe you, Dee," I said reverently.

Then he looked at me with the same expression that I had seen on his face when he asked me if I wanted to come with him to meet King Solomon.

"Do ye want to try fer 'im with one o' yer fine pretty-things?" he asked.

"Do I?" I almost shouted. "No, Dee. No. Of course not. I'd rather just watch. You go ahead. Go ahead, Dee. But where's your bait? What are you going to use for bait?"

"Hit's in a good place. But you go ahead and try 'im. I ain't in no hurry."

I did try him. But I was in a hurry. Afraid of casting over him, I thumbed the reel, and the plug fell short by several feet of my intended mark. King Solomon rose slowly till he was only a few inches below the surface. There he stood, champing his jaws like a bulldog waiting in the pit for somebody's pet poodle. I retrieved in a sweat. Then,

shaking with bass-ague, I tried again, this time miraculously placing the lure where I aimed it—three feet to the rear of King Solomon. Action exploded. King Solomon turned and struck with a fury and speed that made him invisible, but I saw my plug. It shot upward out of the water and then dropped back with a listless splash and a slack line.

Then, as the froth cleared from the water, I saw King Solomon. He was slowly heading for his sycamore log. I sat on the ledge as limp as my line and looked at the spot where I had seen his broad tail wave me farewell.

Just then I heard Dee walking away, down the trail to the crossing. I felt pretty sick. I reeled in and stood up to go back to camp, back home, back to Texas where a bungler like me belonged, where there was more room to bungle in and fewer folks per square mile to know about it.

As I started down I met Dee coming up the trail. He had something dangling from his hook—something so monstrous that I failed, at the first glance, to recognize it. The thing was a crawfish—a rough, gnarled, clawing red crawfish with pincers that might have dared a lobster to a pinch-as-pinch-can combat.

Dee had run the hook through the third joint of the crawfish's tail. I looked at it incredulously and then at Dee.

"Thet's a craw-dad," he stated. "I got five more in a live-box at the end of the hole. Watch."

Between the thumb and middle

finger of his left hand, which also held the pole, Dee coiled a part of his line; then, whirling in his right hand the lobster-sized crawfish, he let it fly. The crawfish dropped like a horseshoe beside the sunken sycamore log, at the particular spot where King Solomon had given me the Shanghai gesture.

Upon striking the water, the crawfish began gyrating in crazy downward spirals, instinctively tailing for dark water, a hiding place under a rock, a ledge, a log—any sanctuary away from deep, open water. He disappeared in the dark shadow under the log.

Dee jerked his line sharply twice, and then let it go slack again. Suddenly there was a jerk from the other end of the line and several feet of it were snaked under the log as he lowered the tip of his pole.

"Hook 'im! Hook 'im!" I yelled.

But Dee waited. The line twitched, and Dee struck. The long cane pole bent; and though Dee had both hands on it, with the butt of it braced in his groin, the tip jerked down and pointed to the darkness under the log. There were three savage lunges that I thought would tear the pole from the boy's hands or strip the line from it; then King Solomon came out to fight in the open.

He broke water first midway of the stream, and as he did so he shot the crawfish out of his jaws so savagely that it was forced up the copper wire to the line. But the hook held, and King Solomon felt it as he burrowed deep to the bed of the river; up he came again, shaking his head and shooting his jaw. We could see that the hook had gone through the toughest part of his lower lip.

Giving up his surface tactics, he went down again to stay, not under the log this time, but under the ledge directly beneath us. Dee tried to pull him out. The stout cane pole bent perilously, cracked, then splintered and broke a third of its length below the tip. But the line was tied below the break; so King Solomon was still fast, though far from landed. I didn't believe he could be landed from where we were—on a ledge ten feet above the water. But Dee had his own idea about it.

"You jest hold this yere pole a spell," he said.

Slipping off his overalls and shirt, he dived in. He came up, caught hold of the line, and dived again. I could tell by the jerking of the line that he was following it under the ledge. He was gone a long time, so long that I caught myself holding my breath; then the line went slack, and he popped up. He was paddling with his right hand and holding onto the line with his left. I knew by the way his left arm was darting about that he still had King Solomon.

"Jest drop the pole in," he spluttered. "I'm a-goin' to swim across with 'im."

Dubiously I obeyed. The boy swam on his side with a strong scissors kick. Occasionally I could see a flash of white beside him. That was King Solomon showing his belly —all tired out.

Barring a last-minute accident, I knew that Dee had won—and he did win.

I watched him scramble up the shallow bank, with his fingers through King Solomon's gill-flap, and go to the spring, where he deposited his catch and threw himself down for a well-earned rest. I picked up my rod and Dee's clothes, followed the trail down from the ledge to the rocky riffle, and crossed over to him.

This took several minutes, but he was still breathing hard when I came up. He was lying on his side, with his head propped up on one hand, while he stared in the spring pool. There was King Solomon, also lying on his side and breathing hard but regularly. He was beaten so far as the score was concerned, but not by any means in spirit. He glared at us out of one amber-rimmed defiant eye.

"Well," I remarked inanely, "you caught him."

"I reckon I did," Dee said, "but I wouldn't hev if you hadn't made 'im hungry with thet there fine pretty-thing o' yourn."

I looked at the boy closely, but could detect not the slightest sign of a smile on his face. He was watching King Solomon again. The big fish was now upright, fanning water and champing his jaw.

Just then I heard a rustling sound behind me. Turning, I saw the warden with his two guns strapped to his hips.

"Thet fine pretty-thing didn't have nary a thing to do with it," he stated definitely. "I seen it all," and the warden went down on his hands and knees to inspect King Solomon closely.

"Thet's him," he said. "There's the scar on his upper lip where I hooked 'im. Thet's him, all right. How much do ye reckon he'll weigh?"

"I wouldn't want an old friend to think I was lying," I told him, "even if I was telling the truth."

He looked at me sharply, and then grinned.

"No," he said, pulling out his plug of chewing, "I don't reckon ye would, no more'n me."

"He's got another scar, too," Dee said. "Look at his shoulder." I leaned over the spring pool. There was a deep livid furrow down the side of King Solomon's right shoulder. I looked at the warden.

"What do you think might have caused that?" I asked.

"I wouldn't want an old friend to think I was lyin'," he said, and looked across the river to the bluff.

I followed the direction of his glance. There, in the niche of rock below the scrubby pine where I had seen the squirrel, and just one ledge above that one from which Dee had hooked King Solomon, sat the man with the gun.

"I wouldn't," I said.

"Well," said the warden, "I reckon I jest as well to git on back to town. Better watch ol' Solomon, boy. Ye may lose him yet."

With that parting advice the warden went back the way he had come.

"I'm ready to call it a day, too," I said.

"I'm willin'," Dee said. "You can go on ahead. I'll ketch ye."

Presuming that he wanted to salvage his line and the remains of his pole, I followed his suggestion and started back to camp. A few minutes later I heard him running along the trail behind me. Turning to wait for him, I saw that his hands were empty. So—the warden had spoken a prophecy. King Solomon, wily King Solomon, had, after all, got away.

But the boy's face was serene—not the face of a boy who had just lost the biggest fish he ever saw. If Dee had ever smiled, he would have been smiling then. I supposed I would have to resort to cross-examination to get the truth—and I might fail to get it all then. But I got far more than I expected.

"Where's King Solomon?"

"Back yanner under thet ol' sycamore log," he answered.

"You staked him out? Won't somebody find him?" I wondered.

"Twouldn't do 'em no good. I turned 'im loose."

Here was something I had hardly dared to hope for. Here was a boy of twelve—a mountain boy —who had done the thing I had wished I might have the courage to do if I ever caught King Solomon. Then I thought of the man on the ledge with the gun. He must have seen the boy put the fish back. I remembered his deadly aim.

"But he'll get killed. That man on the bluff will shoot him," I groaned.

"Won't neither," Dee said. "Since I worked on the sights o' thet gun t'other day Pa couldn't hit a hawg with it."

Reading Skills

1. How does each of the characters—Dee, the game warden, the man with the gun, the Texan—feel about King Solomon?
2. Why is the man from Texas pleased when he learns that Dee has turned King Solomon loose? (It is not only because he might have done the same thing if he had caught the fish.)
3. Why is it such a surprise to learn in the final sentence that the man with the gun is Dee's father?

Understanding Literature

1. The author does not devote several paragraphs to a description of Dee; yet he gives many bits of information about the boy. Put these pieces together and construct as complete a picture of the Ozark lad as you can.
2. What evidence is there in this story that the mountain folk of the Ozarks waste very few words?
3. You may have expected Dee to catch King Solomon, but you probably did not think the boy would turn the fish loose again. In Dee's earlier behavior and remarks can you detect any hints that he will put the fish back in the river?
4. In "The Big Buffalo Bass" the conversations contain a great deal of substandard grammar and regional usage. Why is this kind of language used in the story?

Further Activity

The language used by Ozark residents in this fish story is different from the speech of most Americans. Notice how it differs from (or is like) the speech patterns of your own community. Find examples of words which are pronounced in an unusual way—such as *a-lyin'*, *agin'*. Find some examples of incorrect grammar, such as "Bass is like folks" and "I seen it all." Find, also, some expressions which are not used at all in much of this country, such as "hanker after squirrel meat" and "fine pretty-thing." Using standard English grammar and standard dictionary words, rewrite the paragraph spoken by the warden, beginning with "Ol' King Solomon is a bass." Then have one of your classmates read the original speech. Next, let another student read the "corrected" speech. What does this comparison illustrate concerning the value of the language used in this story?

In this story, although Corporal Nilson is not running the marathon, he needs all the skills he has learned as a distance runner. And he must win this race, not to gain a trophy, but to save human lives.

Going to Run All Night

Harry Sylvester

IMPROVING YOUR READING: Part of the *conflict* in "Going to Run All Night" involves Corporal Nilson's struggle against physical and mental fatigue. But as you read, pay particular attention to the more important conflict between doubts and ideals in Nilson's mind.

THEY BROUGHT him in before the commanding officer, a lieutenant colonel, and stood him there, almost as though he were a prisoner, a slight man, whose face, they now remembered, had been curiously harassed and marked by strain before this campaign had begun. He noticed that they walked on either side as if guarding him, as if, indeed, he were a prisoner or someone valued. And since he could think of nothing he had done or left undone for which they should make him a prisoner, he was driven to the incredible conclusion that at last he had come to be of value.

He looked at the lieutenant colonel, seeing that the officer's face was hardly less harassed than his own. All day, in the midst of the danger which constantly encircled them and intermittently killed some of them, the new legend of the lieutenant colonel's irascibility[1] had grown, so that now, standing before the man,

the corporal could wonder he was not ripped up and down with words as scores of men had been that day.

The lieutenant colonel looked at him, blinking and staring, as though making some kind of adjustment from rage to calm. Which it was, perhaps, for to Nilson's amazement he said rather mildly, "They tell me that you used to be a runner, Corporal?"

"Why, yes," Nilson said. "Yes, sir, I mean."

"You used to run distances? I mean road races and such?"

"Yes, sir."

"Ever run in Marathon races or anything like that?"

"Yes, sir," the corporal said. He was thinking: There is nothing "like" the Marathon. Just the figures alone mean something: 26 miles, 385 yards. "I run seventh one year in the Boston Marathon." Right after he said it,

1 irascibility (ĭ răs′ə bĭl′ə tĭ): bad humor; crankiness.

HARRY SYLVESTER

395

he could see that the lieutenant colonel was not impressed, that he did not know running seventh in the Boston Marathon was not the same as running seventh in another foot race.

"Well," the officer said, as though making the best of a bad bargain, rubbing his eyes tiredly and slowly with the heels of his hands. "Well, as you know, they've sort of got us over a barrel here. The one radio we still have that is working has been damaged so that we cannot vary the frequency enough to keep the enemy from picking it up rather often."

He went on like that, rubbing his eyes, explaining to the corporal as if the corporal were a general—someone who ought to be told of what the situation was. "We think we can break out at dawn, if we can synchronize our attack with some sort of aid coming from our main forces opposite the point of our own attack. Break through the ring," he said vaguely. Then: "Look! You think you could run across the hills by dark and carry them a message?"

Nilson began to think, for some reason, about how his grandmother used to talk about lightning and how you never knew where or when it was going to strike. Fear was not in him, although for a little while he would think it was fear. His gasp was silent, so that his mouth was open before he began to speak. He said, "Why, I guess so. I mean, I'm not in very good shape. I—"

"But in no worse shape than anyone else here," the lieutenant colonel said. "And you used to be a runner. How long since you stopped active competition?"

"Oh, I was running all the time. Right up until my induction, and even then, when I was still in the States and could get leave, I was competing some."

The officer nodded. "Well, that's about all. There'll be no written message . . . in case you might be taken. You'll be picked up by one of our own patrols probably. Just tell them we can't last another day here and that we're going to try to come through at dawn. It's possible they won't believe you. But that's a chance we'll have to take. If they have time, they can send a plane over with a message, to let us know that they understand, although it hasn't been very healthy here for planes. There won't be much trouble getting you through their lines at night. I'll send a guard with you until you're beyond their lines and then you'll be on your own. Just follow the road. The main idea is to get there before dawn. I figure it's thirty-five or forty miles before they'll pick you up. We won't attack for six hours. You think you could make it in, say, five hours?"

"Why, if I was in shape," Nilson said, "I could, maybe, easy."

"Still," the officer said, "you're the best we have. Good luck."

"Yes, sir," Nilson said, and saluted and turned.

Outside, the two sergeants stood on either side of him, and the tall one said, "Well, what are you gonna need?"

"I dunno," Nilson said. "I guess I won't need anything. Maybe I'll take a canteen, maybe not." He knew that thirst for water and the actual need for water were not necessarily the same thing; he was already weighing in his mind the weight of the canteen against the necessity for water.

"Well, let's get going, then," the other sergeant said.

The tall sergeant got Nilson a canteen filled with water, and they moved out into the darkness beyond where the tanks and cars stood in a shallow arc like great animals huddled in the dark.

They were more than halfway across the three-mile plain that separated them from the hills holding the enemy, when Nilson said, "Look, this isn't any good for you two, is it? I mean, if they see us, three isn't going to be much better than one?"

"Stop being noble," the tall sergeant said. "Someone's got to show you through the hills."

"I see what you mean," Nilson said.

It was simpler than he had thought it would be. You could neither hear nor see the enemy, who needed no pickets to hear tanks approaching, or a plane.

The three moved upward over the dry hills, the soil crumbling under foot as they climbed, so that at the crest the sergeants were bushed, panting in the heat and the altitude like animals, and even Nilson was sweating. In the moonlight, below them and to the west and right, they could see the road.

"I guess this is where we get off," the tall sergeant said. "You better get going."

"All right," Nilson said. "I gotta get ready, though."

He undressed in the cloud-broken dark, until he sat there in his underwear, his socks and shoes and his dog tag. The other sergeant handed him the canteen.

"I'll take a drink now," Nilson said, "and that'll have to hold me. The canteen's too heavy—"

"You take that canteen," the tall sergeant said. "You're gonna need it."

"Look," Nilson said, then stopped. He saw that they did not know about water and running or any violent exercise. You could be thirsty for an awfully long time without actually needing water, but this was no time to start explaining that to them. "Well," he said, "I'll go along then."

"Good luck," they said. They watched him move, still walking down the slope toward the road a half-mile away. They thought it was because he couldn't run down a slope that steep, but Nilson was walking until the water was out of his stomach and he could be sure he wouldn't get a stitch[2] when he started to run.

Watching him, the tall sergeant said, "You think he's gonna do any good?"

"No, I don't," the other sergeant said. "Even if he gets through their patrols, he'll drop before he gets to our people—or quit and go hide."

2 stitch: sharp pain in the side or back.

"What do you say that for?" the tall sergeant said.

"Because you're probably thinking the same thing I am!"

In the darkness, the tall sergeant nodded. "We both know we could go along, too, now and hide until this is over, because they're not going to get through tomorrow morning."

"But we go back, instead," the other sergeant said. "And I don't know why."

"I don't know why, either," the tall sergeant said.

Then they turned and began to go back the way they had come.

Nearing the road, the feeling of great adventure began to leave Nilson. Not fear but a sense of futility took him—of his own littleness in the night and the desert that was also the enemy's country. At the edge of the road he paused, although he could not tell why and attributed it to fear. It was not fear so much as an unwillingness to undergo one more futility.

He had not been a very good runner, and he was now thirty-one. Like many of the young men of the Scandinavian colonies in Brooklyn, he had run more because it was a tradition among their people. He had liked it, although after almost fifteen years of little or no glory, he had begun to feel that he was too old to keep losing that often, had begun to realize that, after a while, it did something to a man. Not that it was any fault of his; after all, you'd have to be pretty special to run well Saturdays or Sundays after being on your feet all day as a post-office clerk.

He still hesitated on the edge of the road; there was in his hesitation a quality of sullenness, a vague, shadowy resentment against some large amorphous[3] body or group that somehow had become identified with the long years of defeat.

Without quite knowing what the resentment was, he knew it to be, if not wrong, at least inappropriate now and here. He sighed and at the edge of the road did a curious little exercise that relatives of his also had done three hundred years before in Norway. He bent over, touching his toes five or six times and each time straightening up and flinging his arms wide. The idea was to open his lungs quickly and limber the muscles of his chest and arms. Although he was not a very good runner, he knew all about running; he knew that a man ran as much with his arms as with his legs.

He stepped onto the road and in a reflexive gesture pawed at the crude paving as though it were hard-packed cinders, and the heavy G.I. shoes were the short-spiked ones of the distance runner. He felt sheepish, and in the darkness his mouth twisted into a grin. He began to run.

Almost immediately he felt easier; felt confidence flow through him as though it were his blood; felt that now, at last, he was in his own country, or, more accurately, in his own medium. There are mediums of ac-

3 amorphous (ə môr′fəs): shapeless.

tion that vary with the individual; some feel best moving in an automobile, others on a horse, some walking, a few running or flying.

As he ran, he felt with his feet for the part of the tar-and-gravel road that was best suited to him. The road was slightly crowned in the center and in places pocked lightly by machine-gun bullets from the planes that had gone over it. As on most roads, he found that the shoulder was best for running. It was softer, the spikeless shoes slipped less, and its resilience would save him from shin-splints tomorrow. He thought with irony that it was of no importance whether he got the little pains along the shin from bruising or pulling the tendons that held the muscle to the bone. Certainly he would run no more tomorrow, come

what might; indeed, there might not be a tomorrow.

This started him thinking of what he called fear—but what was really an ennui,[4] a saturation in himself of having for so many years done things to no purpose. He wondered if this, too, would be to no purpose; if some burial detail, an indefinite number of days from now, would find his twisted body some place along this road.

Then he began to think that it would be worse to get to where he was going and not be believed. There was nothing he could think of to do about that, so he stopped thinking of it. Like many Scandinavians, he was a fatalist,[5] and the

4 **ennui** (än′wē): weary boredom.
5 **fatalist:** one who believes that all events are caused by necessity; that whatever happens has to happen.

war had not helped overcome that.

The night—soft, warm and windless—was all around him. In its blackness, there was a quality of brown; or perhaps he imagined this, for all day the hills were brown, so that afterward you associated the color with thirst, with violence and with the imminence[6] of death. He had discovered, only recently and to his relief, that he was not afraid of death; after all, he had no responsibilities in life, no dependents; disablement, though, was something else.

Then suddenly he began to think of the time he had run seventh in the Boston Marathon; the cold day and the girls unexpectedly lining the road at Wellesley, and the tremendous lift they had given his spirit, just standing there, calling to the runners, the wind moving their hair and their bright skirts.

He was running faster, too fast, he thought. He was beginning to breathe hard. It was too early to be breathing so hard; but he knew that would pass soon, and the thing called second wind would come to him. He slackened his pace a little, feeling the weight of the shoes and trying to reject the thought before it took too much form; trying not to think of it.

He began to think of the enemy and where the enemy might be; all around him, surely, but probably not too near the road, because, by night, planes could see a road. Still, there might be patrols knowing a man running steadily by night was a strange and unaccountable thing. But they might never see him; only hear him and the pounding of his feet on the road. So, deviously, his mind came back to the thought which he could no longer avoid: there was only one thing to do, take the G.I. shoes off and run without them.

He slowed gradually until he was walking, and walked perhaps thirty yards before he stopped. Then he sat on the ground and took off his shoes.

When he stood up, he hesitated again. Once, he had lost a shoe and had finished the race, but the cinders had taken their toll of that foot.

The road here was bad, but principally what he feared was stepping on one of the scorpions. He wondered if they were out by night—and then he began to run again.

Now the element of strangeness about this man running in the night, this Brooklyn Norwegian in a strange land, was intensified by the silence, in which only his regular, heavy breathing made a sound.

Without knowing it, he ran at times in a kind of stupor. The nights of little or fitful sleep, the days of too little food and water, were beginning to affect him, and he began to take refuge from exhaustion and pain in something at times close to unconsciousness.

Twice he passed tanks not far from the road, their crews sleeping, he himself not knowing he passed them. Like a dun ghost, he drifted

---

6 imminence: nearness.

with the short, effortless stride he had developed over the long years of competition and training. These little spells of semi-consciousness no longer occurred; effort was too much to permit them, too sustained and by now terrible, so that his senses became acute again, his thoughts long-ranging, sharp and filled with color. It was perhaps this return to acute consciousness, induced by pain, that saved him.

He had begun to think of the long dreams of his youth, of passing through lines of people at the end of the Boston Marathon, as he strode in, tired but easily first; of the Olympic Marathon and the laurel wreath he had read of.

Some place there was sound and a hoarse shouting. He could not tell for a moment whether they were in his thoughts or in the reality of the night all around him. Then the sound, now long familiar to him, but still terrible, of an automatic rifle coughing in the night.

He glanced about him, flinching, his eyes, already strained open by the night, trying to open wider, so that the muscles near them hurt. The shouting, the firing were above him—here the road was sunken—behind and to the right.

The firing sounded again, farther away. He neither heard nor felt bullets. In one of those sudden lifts of speed—instinctive and desperate now—with which a distance runner sometimes in the middle of a race tries to break the heart of his opponents, Nilson started to sprint.

The road ran downhill here, and now through the warm, dark night, the little man let his feet shoot out ahead of him, carrying his legs out with the controlled abandon of the cross-country runner going downhill.

He ran with almost no sound, although he was not aware of this. The shouting and the sound of guns continued behind him. With a faint pleasure, he realized that it was his passing that had alarmed the enemy.

There was an eeriness about him as he moved in the night. Perhaps it was this, perhaps only the adrenalin further secreted in his body by his fear when the shots sounded—but he found a new strength. The legs, the rhythmically moving arms recovered the thing of which, in his boyhood, he and the other runners had made a fetish[7]—the thing called form.

So, going downhill now, the enemy all around him, he experienced a sense of power, as though he were invisible, as though he were fleeter and stronger than anything that could seek to kill or hinder him.

Sweat bathed him, he glistened as though oiled, and there was a slight froth at his lips. He moved with a machinelike rhythm and his eyes— if they could have been seen—might have seemed mad.

The road leveled, ran flat for perhaps a quarter-mile, then began to mount again. He became aware of this only gradually. The first change he noted was in himself, first the mind, then the body. The sense of

7 fetish: object of devotion.

power, of superhuman ability was gone, almost abruptly, his lungs began to hurt badly, and the cords in his neck. He was, he suddenly realized, nothing special; he was Pete Nilson from Brooklyn, and he was bushed; he was just about done.

He shook his head, like a trapped, bewildered animal. The desire, the need to stop was extraordinarily strong in him. He tried an old trick: he tried to analyze his pain, knowing this sometimes made it disappear. There was the pain in his lungs, in his throat, in the muscles of his eyes, but not yet where his arms went into the shoulders, not yet just above the knees where the thigh muscles overlapped.

His stride had shortened with the hill and his body leaned forward. He had not been above quitting in a few races, when he was hopelessly outdistanced, when he had not been trained right, when he had not enough rest the previous week to make him strong.

It seemed that he had never been so exhausted as now, and his mind sought excuses to stop. First, came the thought that if only he knew how long he had to run, he might endure it. Twenty-six miles, 385 yards— that was the distance of the Marathon, and in Boston, in Toronto, you always knew within a few hundred yards how far you had come, how far you had to go. But now, no one knew or had known, not within four or five miles. The enemy was in the hills, and the hills were all around the lieutenant colonel and his men, and beyond the hills that held the enemy were more of your own men, some place. So late in his life he learned that it is important to all men in their various endeavors to see an end, to know how far off that end is.

Fatigue blurred his vision and he started to deviate from a straight line, veering slightly from side to side. Although he did not know it, he was beyond the enemy, and had only to combat himself. But he had forgotten about the enemy, and his mind sought reasons to stop, old resentments that could possess the weight of argument. What had they ever done for him? He should have been a sergeant by now.

Anger formed in him: he could not tell its nature or its object. He realized it might be at himself; then, that it was at himself. He must have been crazy, he thought; he supposed that, all his life, his efforts had been directed obscurely toward achieving a sense of usefulness, corrupted sometimes into what was called a sense of glory. And now, close to it, he had almost rejected it.

When the change occurred, the sudden insight, he was on top of a hill and looking down into a plain full of great shadows; there was a paleness in the sky over the shadows. He was on top of this hill, but whether he was running or standing still, he could not tell, for it was as great an effort to stand as to run.

He began to move downhill again, still veering. He sensed, if he did not see, that there were no more hills beyond and that his own people must be somewhere near, perhaps at

the bottom of the hill he now descended.

As he staggered, half-blind in the dim light, to the foot of the hill, he thought of the Athenian runner finishing the first Marathon and, as he collapsed, crying, "Rejoice, we conquer!" Nilson realized how much that image, those words had been with him, influencing him all his life. They heartened him now, sealed the sense of meaning in him.

A sentry challenged as the road leveled out into the plain, and Nilson, not knowing the password, reasoned that this was the place for him to collapse. Pheidippides, finishing the first Marathon, had cried, "Rejoice, we conquer!" but Pete Nilson, thinking this, and finishing his own run, said in a kind of prayer,

"Buddy, don't shoot," knelt and quietly fell forward in the dust.

He didn't remember exactly what he said to them, but they took him to another lieutenant colonel. And the miracle was not over. He could not believe it then; all the rest of his life, he could hardly believe it. They believed him. They believed him, and some place near him as he sat stupefied on a canvas stool in a tent, he heard all around him, in the first light, the sound of armor beginning to move, the clatter and roar of the tanks.

A staff sergeant tried to explain. "Look," the sergeant said, "nobody comes down here in the shape you're in to lie to somebody else. You see?" Especially the feet, the sergeant thought.

But all Nilson did was sit on the canvas stool and stare.

"Look," the sergeant said again, "you'll get something big for this. Don't you catch?"

Nilson stared at him. He was beginning to catch, but it would be a long time, if ever, before he could make anyone understand. The big thing, the most important thing in his life, was that he had come down here, without credentials of any sort, and they had believed him. The citation, the medal, nothing was ever going to mean that much.

"Look," the sergeant said. "They're getting you a doctor. You want anything now, though? Coffee or something?" Don't the guy know about his feet, he thought.

The little froth still at his lips, Nilson shook his head. He looked like a madman, and the sergeant thought that maybe he was mad. But all Nilson was doing was sitting there listening to the roar and thinking that he, Pete Nilson, had set it in motion. He didn't want anything right then, only to sit there and listen.

Reading Skills

1. As soon as the words are out of his mouth, Nilson wishes that he had not told the lieutenant colonel that he had placed seventh in the Boston Marathon. Why does he want to take back these words?
2. When the two sergeants send Nilson on his way alone, they do not expect him to succeed. Why are they so doubtful? Explain what the shorter sergeant means when he says, ". . . you're probably thinking the same thing I am!"
3. What skills and judgments that Nilson has learned as a runner are useful to him during the night?
4. Corporal Nilson's biggest reward comes from the fact that the Americans to whom he has carried the message believe him. Why is their belief "the most important thing in his life"?

Understanding Literature

1. What sort of man is Corporal Nilson? Answer in terms of his physical appearance, confidence, sense of accomplishment and satisfaction before he begins his long night's run. Locate sentences in the story which support your answer.
2. The author could have pictured Nilson as a man of impressive physique and confidence, a three-time winner of the Boston Marathon. How does the author enlarge the sense of triumph or victory in the story by using the "weaker" Nilson?

3. As Nilson begins running, he feels a flow of confidence. How do his feelings change as he continues to run? As he finishes his run, what is the significance of the statement that the words of the first Marathon runner "sealed the sense of meaning" in Nilson?
4. What physical obstacles must Nilson overcome in order to succeed? What mental conflict does Nilson's successful run resolve?

Further Activities

1. Harry Sylvester describes the physical and mental feelings of Corporal Nilson specifically and clearly. Select two or three highly descriptive paragraphs and prepare to read them to your classmates.
2. As the two sergeants watch Nilson start on his night's run, they realize that they can follow him part way and then hide until the fierce combat of the next day has quieted. Furthermore, they know that if they rejoin their unit, they are certain of a horrible experience as the unit tries to break out of encirclement at dawn. Both sergeants feel some inclination not to go back to the unit, and both admit that they do not know why they are going back. Yet they return to the unit.

   (a) Prepare a written account of an instance, known to you either from direct observation or news reports, in which a person carried out his assumed duty because of a sense of responsibility, even though the duty was distasteful or dangerous, and could have been avoided somehow.

   (b) After thinking about the return of the two sergeants to their unit, discuss with your classmates the reasons for the sergeants' return; then write an explanation of this sense of responsibility to duty which directs men, even though the sense of self-preservation suggests that they should try to escape from the threats of injury and death.

The sport of mountain climbing offers to man the challenge of taming the unconquerable. In "A Mountain and a Man" you will read about one mountain climber, Edward Whymper, whose passion to conquer the Matterhorn led to personal triumph and disaster.

A Mountain and a Man

James Ramsey Ullman

IMPROVING YOUR READING: This narrative essay depicts the *conflict* between a man and a mountain. It shows Edward Whymper's determination to climb the Matterhorn, which until 1865 was "the unclimbed mountain, the unclimbable mountain." His attempts to climb the mountain are seen as "the most relentless battle ever waged between mountain and man." Notice that, throughout the essay, terms associated with battle—terms of assault and conquest—are used to suggest the central conflict. Although you know the outcome of the battle after the first paragraph of the essay, the suspense in the narrative is not destroyed: your curiosity is aroused about *how* Whymper will conquer and at what cost in energy or life.

LATE IN THE MORNING of July 15, 1865, three dazed, exhausted men stumbled down from the glaciers into the Swiss village of Zermatt. They were returning from the conquest of the most famous mountain of Europe, but there was no spring to their step, no light of victory in their eyes. Swiftly and silently the villagers gathered around them, and in the eyes of all there was but one somber question:

"Where are the other four?"

It was then that Edward Whymper told the story of the climbing of the Matterhorn. And today, almost a century later, it is still one of the great, tragic adventure stories of the world.

There are hundreds of mountains higher than the Matterhorn; there are hundreds that are harder to climb. But there is none, anywhere in the world, which has so consistently and deeply stirred the imagination of men. Rising in an immense isolated pyramid on the frontier between Switzerland and Italy, it possesses not only the dimensions, but the stark simplicity, of greatness, and its sprawling neighbor-peaks, some of which actually exceed its 14,782-foot altitude, seem to shrink into insignificance beside it. Through all the centuries that men have known the Alps their eyes have been drawn irresistibly upward to its savage, soaring pinnacle. Other mountains were—well—mountains. This mountain was beauty and magic and terror.

In the early sixties of the last century the Matterhorn was as famous as it is today—but for a different reason. The previous decade had been the great age of Alpine mountaineering, and with the first ascent of the Weisshorn by Tyndall in 1861, virtually all the great peaks of the range had fallen. All, that is, save one, for the Matterhorn still towered into the sky, untouched and unchallenged as it had been since the beginning of time. But men scarcely counted it in their reckonings. The Swiss and Italian peasants of the surrounding valleys looked up at its cloud-hung battlements with superstitious awe and spoke fearfully of a ruined city on the summit where ghosts and demons dwelt. Even the unsuperstitious—travelers, scientists, and mountaineers from all over Europe—stared at it in fascination, shook their heads, and turned away. True, there had been a half dozen or so attempts to gain the upper reaches of the peak, but all had been utterly defeated, and none who returned held out any hope for future success. The Matterhorn, men were agreed, was not only an unconquered mountain. It was unconquerable.

They did not know that in the summer of 1860 Edward Whymper had made his first visit to the Alps.

In that year Whymper was only twenty and had as yet made none of the ascents which were to make him the foremost mountaineer of his day. Indeed, he did not know that he was a mountaineer at all. An artist and illustrator by profession, he came to Switzerland from England for a few weeks of sketching and intended to do no more climbing than was necessary to find vantage points for his easel and brush. But the great peaks cast their spell upon him, and the fever to climb and conquer came into his blood. Alone and with local guides, he made many notable climbs, but, once his eyes had feasted on the fabulous Matterhorn, all else became of secondary interest to him. Here, he told himself, was a mountain fashioned for an artist's dream: the unclimbed mountain, the unclimbable mountain. Staring up at it, he vowed that it would be his.

Thus began what remains to this day the most relentless battle ever waged between a mountain and a man. Seven times in five years Whymper attacked the Matterhorn, and seven times he was beaten back. The obstacles that confronted him were enough to have broken the spirit—not to mention the neck—of a lesser man. In addition to the natural perils of precipice and glacier, storm and avalanche, he had also to contend with the stupidity, cowardice and duplicity[1] of men. But he kept on, undismayed—dreaming, planning, attacking, counterattacking; on each of his seven unsuccessful attempts he made progress and learned a little more about his mighty antagonist[2] than he had known before; and at last, on the eighth attempt, he went to the top. No

1 **duplicity:** double-dealing; deception.
2 **antagonist:** opponent; enemy.

mountaineer has ever had a greater triumph. Nor, as fate in the end decreed, a more bitter one.

On his first visit, in 1860, Whymper did not actually come to grips with the mountain, but contented himself with studying it, carefully and patiently. He saw that it was built in the shape of a colossal pyramid, with four principal faces and four well-defined corners, the whole mass thrusting skyward in precipice upon precipice to a height of some five thousand feet above its skirt of glaciers. Across this vertical mile the wind howled with unchecked fury, and down its chimneys and gullies roared endless avalanches of rock and ice. For the men who ventured into that savage, slanting world death would lurk not only in the abysses below; at every moment it would be clutching at their clothing or hanging invisible above them, poised, ready to fall.

The northern and western sides of the peak seemed to Whymper to be utterly inaccessible.[3] He therefore did most of his reconnoitering[4] from the south and east, chiefly in the region of the Theodule Pass, a great glacial bridge that connects the Swiss valley of Zermatt with the Italian Val Tournanche. Two possible routes suggested themselves: the northeast and southwest ridges, the former leading up from the direction of Zermatt, the latter from the village of Breuil in the Val Tournanche. Of the two, the northeastern seemed to

Whymper the more direct, but he judged the southwestern to be less steep, and when he returned to England in the late summer of 1860 he had already determined that this would be his route of attack.

And so it was, through six fruitless attempts during the summers of 1861, 1862 and 1863. It was not until 1865 that Whymper at last turned to the northeast ridge—and to triumph and tragedy.

On the morning of August 29, 1861, Whymper set out from Breuil on the first of his great adventures. He was accompanied by a solitary guide—the only man in all the surrounding villages he could induce to go with him. They spent the first night in a shed in the highest pasture of the Val Tournanche, where their herdsmen-hosts spoke fearfully of the demons of the Matterhorn and pleaded with them to turn back. The next day, however, they pushed upward, ascending the Glacier du Lion and skirting the cliffs of the Tête du Lion at its head, until they reached a high, narrow saddle leading to the base of the Matterhorn's southwest ridge. On the snowy summit of this saddle they pitched their tent.

They were now well within the domain of the great peak, almost a mile above Breuil. On one side of them steep slopes of glassy snow descended to the glacier they had crossed. On the other a sheer wall fell away to the Tiefenmatten Glacier, so far below that when they threw down a bottle no sound re-

3 **inaccessible:** not approachable by any way.
4 **reconnoitering** (rē′kə noi′tər ĭng): examining; making a reconnaissance (survey).

turned for more than a dozen seconds. At nightfall it grew bitterly cold; the wind howled and tugged against the canvas of their tent, and the water froze in a flask under Whymper's head. They succeeded, however, in dozing for a while, until "—about midnight there came from high aloft a tremendous explosion, followed by a second of dead quiet. A great mass of rock had split off and was descending toward us. My guide started up, wrung his hands and exclaimed, 'We are lost!' We heard it coming, mass after mass pouring over the precipices, bounding and rebounding from cliff to cliff, and the great rocks in advance smiting one another." Luckily only a few fragments fell near the tent, but there was little sleep for the two men the rest of that night. Whymper had had his first taste of the cannonading of the Matterhorn.

At dawn they began the ascent of the southwest ridge. The day was fine, the climbing was hard but in no way hazardous, and the heights above seemed very near. Pausing for a moment's rest, Whymper's heart pounded with the excitement of the artist and mountaineer.

"We overlook the Tête du Lion," he writes, "and nothing except the Dent d'Hérens stands in the way. The ranges of the Graian Alps, an ocean of mountains, are seen at a glance—how soft and yet how sharp they look in the early morning! The midday mists have not begun to rise; nothing is obscured; even the pointed Viso, all but a hundred miles away, is perfectly defined.

"Turn to the east and watch the sun's slanting rays coming across the Monte Rosa snow fields. Look at the shadowed parts and see how even they, radiant with reflected light, are more brilliant than man knows how to depict. . . . Then note the sunlight as it steals noiselessly along and reveals countless unsuspected forms—the delicate ripple-lines which mark the concealed crevasse,[5] and the waves of drifted snow, producing each minute more lights and fresh shadows, sparkling on the edges and glittering on the ends of the icicles, shining on the heights and illuminating the depths, until all is aglow and the dazzled eye returns for relief to the somber crags."

His joy and exhilaration were to be short-lived. Less than an hour after leaving the Col du Lion they came to a point now known as the Chimney—a smooth, almost vertical slab of rock fixed between two other rocks, equally smooth. Bracing himself against the sides and using several tiny cracks for holds, Whymper succeeded in scrambling up, but his guide, after several unsuccessful attempts, suddenly untied himself from the rope and announced that he would go no farther. "I told him he was a coward," said Whymper, "and *he* mentioned his opinion of me." Argument, however, was fruitless; the guide insisted on going down, and the artist, frustrated and angry, had to follow.

"The day was perfect; the wind had fallen; the way seemed clear,

5 **crevasse** (krǝ văs′): deep crack or cleavage.

no insuperable[6] obstacle was in sight; but what could one do alone?"

Thus the first assault on the Matterhorn ended at a height of 12,550 feet.

Whymper did not attempt the mountain again in 1861, but the following summer he was back in full cry and launched no less than four separate attacks. Warned by his earlier experience, he had determined that in future he would not depend on the whims of a single guide. His first venture of 1862 was therefore undertaken with four companions: his friend and fellow-mountaineer, Reginald Macdonald, two Zermatt guides, Taugwald and Kronig, and, as porter, a little hunchback from the village of Breuil, Luk Meynet. Of these, strangely enough, it was Meynet who was destined to play the most heroic role in the arduous days to come.

In spite of the strong party and elaborate plans Whymper's second try was doomed to quick and complete defeat. A nasty fall by one of the guides delayed them while crossing the Glacier du Lion and dampened the spirits of the others. Then, no sooner had they reached the Col du Lion and made camp than a strong wind blew up, freezing their hands and feet and causing them to spend a sleepless night holding their wildly flapping tent.

By morning a hurricane was howling at them from the great snowfields of Monte Rosa, to the east. Taking advantage of a brief lull they made a start up the southwest ridge, only to have the gales whip back at them with renewed frenzy. "Advance or return," wrote Whymper, "were alike impossible; the ridge was denuded of its debris, and we saw stones as big as a man's fist blown away horizontally into space. We dared not attempt to stand upright and remained stationary on all fours, glued, as it were, to the rocks."

It was all they could do, in the next lull, to make the return to the tent, and even their diehard leader had to admit defeat. Battered and chagrined,[7] they descended to Breuil.

Whymper's next attempt—his third —is noteworthy in that it marked the beginning of his association with the great guide, Jean-Antoine Carrel. Carrel was famous throughout the Alps as a climber of skill and daring, and, in addition, he was perhaps the only mountaineer in the world, outside of Whymper, who believed the Matterhorn *could* be climbed. It had been his lifelong dream that he should be the first to stand upon the summit of the peak—for the honor of Italy and his native Val Tournanche—and for years past he had explored the mountain and sought vainly to conquer it. Whymper had met him in 1860 and 1861, but until now all the artist's efforts to secure him as guide had failed. Proud and strong-willed, Carrel resented the intrusion of an outsider on what he considered his own personal pre-

---

6 **insuperable:** not capable of being overcome.   7 **chagrined** (shə grīnd′): extremely vexed.

serve, and indeed, in 1861, had not only refused to accompany Whymper on his first attempt but had made a separate attack of his own on the very same day. Now at last, however, he came to the decision that it was wiser to fight with this determined Englishman than against him. The greatest climber and the greatest guide in Europe joined forces, and a strange relationship of friendship and enmity[8] began.

Whymper wasted no time between his second and third attempts on the mountain. He met Carrel at Breuil the night of his return, won him over, and the very next day set out again for the southwest ridge. In addition to Carrel he was accompanied by his friend Macdonald and a second guide called Pession. They followed the now-familiar route up the glacier, around the cliffs of the Tête du Lion and onto the narrow snow-saddle of the col;[9] but this time they did not camp there. Instead, following Carrel's advice, they went on up the ridge to the foot of the Chimney, where they found a tiny level space among the cliffs and set up their tent.

The day being fine, they then pushed on farther and within an hour came to the foot of a crag. This huge rock battlement, one of the most distinctive features of the southwest ridge as seen from below, was known as the Great Tower and, at 12,990 feet, marked the highest point on the mountain which anyone

had ever reached before. Whymper and his companions studied the wilderness above, discovered what seemed a feasible route, and descended to their tent to rest for the great effort of the following day.

It was an effort, however, that never came off. No sooner had they left their camp at daybreak and begun the passage of the Chimney than the guide Pession complained of feeling ill and declared that he could not go on. There was a long wait, and long arguments, but the man refused to budge another step upward, and Carrel declined to go further as the only guide. Whymper and Macdonald were helpless. Instead of pushing on into the unknown world above they began the long, joyless descent to Breuil.

"Three times," wrote Whymper of this stage of his campaign, "I had essayed the ascent of this mountain, and on each occasion I failed ignominiously.[10] I had not advanced a yard beyond my predecessors. Only 1800 feet remained, but they were as yet untrodden and might present the most formidable obstacles; no man could expect to climb them by himself. It was evident that a party should consist of three men at least, but where could the other two be obtained? Want of men made the difficulty, not the mountain."

There was reason for his pessimism. Macdonald had been called back to England, Carrel and the hunchback Meynet were busy with work in their village, and not a

---

8 **enmity:** hatred.
9 **col:** mountain pass.

10 **ignominiously** (ĭg′nə mĭn′ĭ əs lĭ): disgracefully.

single other guide in either Breuil or Zermatt was willing to risk his neck and immortal soul on what had come to be known throughout the Alps as "that awful mountain."

After a week of galling inactivity Whymper returned to the southwest ridge alone. He himself declares that it was for the practical reason of looking after the tent, which had been left at the Chimney, but one suspects that by this stage of the game he simply could not stay away from the mountain of his dreams. At all events, he lingered on the heights, drinking in an artist's fill of beauty.

"The sun was setting," he relates, "and its rosy rays, blending with the snowy blue, had thrown a pale, pure violet as far as the eye could see, the valleys were drowned in purple gloom, while the summits shone with unnatural brightness; and as I sat in the door of the tent and watched the twilight change to darkness the earth seemed to become less earthly and almost sublime: the world seemed dead, and I its sole inhabitant—"

He spent the night there, wrapped in a spell of height and loneliness, and in the morning began inching his way upward alone. Soon he had reached the foot of the Great Tower, the highest point of his previous ascent. The monstrous rock mass above him "stood out like a turret at the angle of a castle, and behind it a battlemented wall led upward to the citadel." Whymper had ventured this far only to search for a possible spot for a new tent platform, but now, suddenly, temptation was too much for him.

Slowly and cautiously he worked his way up the Tower. The first step necessitated his jumping up, grasping a ledge eight feet above and pulling himself onto it by the sheer strength of his arms. Directly in front of him now was an over-hanging rock wall and immediately to his left a precipice plunging to the glacier below. He bore to the right and in a moment found himself clinging to a sheer cliff, "fixed as if crucified, pressing against the rock, and feeling each rise and fall of my chest as I breathed." Making use of the tiniest cracks and ledges, he succeeded, however, in surmounting the Tower and came out on the ridge above.

Up to this point he had been climbing on firm, living rock. Now the upper reaches of the mountain soared above him in a fearful sweep of decay and ruin. For another half hour he crept upward, threading a path between huge, rotted blocks that appeared to him like the grave-stones of giants. Then, at last, prudence returned and he started back. He was filled, nevertheless, with excitement and hope, for he had reached a height of 13,400 feet and was confident he had at last found the key to the summit.

Before that day's climbing was done Whymper was to have a painful, and almost fatal, object lesson in the perils of solitary climbing. Safely down the southwest ridge, he passed the col and began the now familiar passage of the snow slope

under the cliffs of the Tête du Lion. All the hazards of the mountain were apparently behind him, and he was descending rapidly, his thoughts on Breuil, a warm bath and bed—when suddenly he slipped and fell.

The slope beneath dropped steeply away, narrowing as it went, and came to an abrupt end in an opening between two walls of rock. Beyond this opening was a thousand-foot precipice, falling to the Glacier du Lion. Toward it—and almost certain death—Whymper now plunged as if down a funnel. He pitched first into a mass of rocks, then onto ice, flying head over heels as he gained momentum and spinning through the air in great bounds of thirty and forty feet. But the demons of the mountains were on his side that day. At the very neck of the gully he brought up against the rocks to one side of it, and his fall was stopped. Dazed and bleeding he clung there, two hundred feet below the point from which he had fallen, not ten feet from the lip of the precipice.

After several minutes he was able to creep to a place of safety, where he fainted. Night had fallen when he regained consciousness and, summoning his last reserve of strength, he continued the descent. Many of the villagers had already given him up for lost when, long past midnight, dazed and blood-soaked, he staggered into Breuil.

Another and yet another try at the Matterhorn Whymper was to have before the eventful summer of 1862 was done. No sooner had his wounds healed than he was back on the southwest ridge for his fourth campaign, accompanied this time by Carrel, little Meynet and a cousin of Carrel's called Caesar.

The four camped for a night at the base of the Chimney and the next day scaled the Great Tower and emerged on the savage upper ridge where Whymper had pioneered on his solitary climb. No sooner were they there, however, than a heavy mist descended upon them, and through it driving snow. Retracing their steps, they improvised a tiny platform among the crags at the base of the Tower and crept into their tent. Then occurred another of the bitter arguments which were constantly arising between Whymper and Carrel. The former, as usual, was hopeful and wanted to wait out the storm, which he thought would be of short duration. The latter insisted that the whole mountain would soon be coated with ice and that immediate retreat was their only salvation. In the end the guide won out. They turned back, only to discover, to Whymper's intense irritation, that he had been right after all: mist and snow soon blew away and the day shone clear and warm. But it was then too late to retrace their steps.

This was nothing, however, to the vexation that was in store for him next day. The four had agreed to set out from Breuil at dawn for yet another try, but when the time came Carrel and his cousin were off marmot-hunting. Only faithful Luk Meynet was on hand and ready, and, with him as his only companion, Whymper set forth on his fifth attempt on the Matterhorn.

The little hunchback of the Val Tournanche was as strange and lovable a man as has ever trod the high mountains. In spite of his affliction he was the sole support of his dead brother's widow and children, and to earn bread for them he gladly followed Whymper into dangers before which stronger men quailed. His loyalty and devotion were absolute, and he looked upon the great peak that towered above his native valley with an almost religious adoration. Whymper has given a touching picture of him as he stood upon the Col du Lion and for the first time stared up and out at the unclouded view:

"The poor little deformed peasant," he relates, "gazed upon it silently and reverently for a time and then unconsciously fell on one knee and clasped his hands, exclaiming in ecstasy, 'Oh, beautiful mountains!' "

Now, as the artist's sole companion, Meynet was to go higher on the Matterhorn than men had ever gone before. Together the two labored up the endless crags and precipices of the southwest ridge—past the Chimney, up and over the Great Tower and onto the desolate heights beyond. They passed Whymper's previous highest point and pushed on until they were a bare half-dozen rope lengths beneath the great shoulder of the upper mountain. Here, however, the razor-edged ridge became so steep that it was unclimbable, and when they turned to the

cliffs on the right they found themselves "both spread-eagled on the
all but perpendicular face, unable
to advance and barely able to descend." Further progress was impossible for the two men, but Whymper believed that a larger party,
aided by a ladder, would be able to
go higher. As quickly as possible
he descended to Breuil to secure the
ladder and again enlist the services
of Carrel.

His plans, however, were doomed
to frustration, for during his absence on the mountain Professor
John Tyndall and his famous guide,
Bennen, had arrived in the village.
The conqueror of the Weisshorn had
made an attempt on the Matterhorn
in 1860 and departed with the conviction that it was unclimbable.
Two years, however, had apparently
changed his mind, for Whymper
found him now prepared for an immediate attack. To make matters
even worse, he had a ladder with
him and had engaged Carrel and
Caesar to accompany him.

In an agony of disappointment
and suspense Whymper fretted about
Breuil, while his expert and well-
equipped rival set out for the mountain. At sunrise of the second day
the villagers claimed excitedly that
they had seen a flag on the summit.
Scanning the peak with his binoc-
ulars, Whymper determined that this
was not so, but what he did see gave
him little comfort: the climbers had
passed his own highest point and
even as he watched were disappearing over the great shoulder of the upper mountain. With sinking heart

he resigned himself to the belief
that his prize had been snatched from
his grasp.

But the Matterhorn played no
favorites. At sunset of that day Tyndall and his men returned to Breuil
with "no spring in their step." They
had gone to a height of almost fourteen thousand feet—less than eight
hundred from the summit—but there
they too had been turned back, defeated. Tyndall was completely discouraged. "Have nothing more to
do with this awful mountain," was
his parting word to Whymper.

As it turned out, Whymper did
not have anything more to do with
it that year, for a few days later his
work called him back to England.
But, unlike Tyndall, he was to return, and return again. For that Mat-
erhorn was still there—the unconquered Matterhorn; *his* Matterhorn.

The following year, however, he
made only one attack at the mountain—his sixth—and it met with
speedy repulse. His party, which
included Carrel, Caesar, little Meynet and two other porters, was the
strongest he had ever had, and in
addition he was supplied with a ladder and other equipment he had not
had before. The chance of success
seemed bright, but it was not to be.

The ascent of the glacier, the Col
du Lion and the lower southwest
ridge were made easily and in perfect sunny weather. At the foot of
the Great Tower, however, the
climbers felt a sudden warning rush
of cold air and in a matter of seconds the sky had blackened and a

storm descended upon them. Somehow they succeeded in pitching their tent and for twenty-six hours lay huddled under its frail protection while a gale-borne blizzard screamed against the mountain walls and thunder and lightning raged above their heads.

It was the most ferocious Alpine storm any of them had encountered, and it required all their remaining strength, when at last it blew away, to make the descent to Breuil. The weather was beautiful there, and the villagers looked skeptical when they heard the climbers' story. "We have had no snow here," said the innkeeper. "It has been fine all the time. There has been only that small cloud upon the mountain."

Small cloud or raging tempest, that night of terror put an end to Whymper's 1863 campaign. Again he returned to England, defeated and disconsolate. "But like a gambler," he said, "who loses each throw, I was only the more eager to have another try—to see if the luck would change."

A change of luck he was to have in full measure, but not only the change for which he hoped.

In 1864 Whymper, already one of the most famous mountaineers of his generation, made many notable ascents in the Alps, but it was not until a year later that he returned to his greatest struggle. This time he brought with him not only all his old skill, courage and determination, but a new, revolutionary plan.

Throughout his earlier attempts he had concurred in the general opinion that the Matterhorn could be conquered, if at all, only from the southwest. Now, however, he determined to turn his back on the great ridge, up which he had struggled so often in vain, and attack the mountain from the east. His decision was based not on mere whim, but on careful observation and reasoning. For one thing, he had noted in his many crossings of the Theodule Pass that the east face appeared much less steep when seen in profile than it did head-on from the valley of Zermatt. For another, he had observed that the rock strata of the peak sloped from northeast to southwest. This meant, he reasoned, that, whereas the rocks on the southwest sloped outward and down, those on the northeast must be tilted inward and up. As a seasoned mountaineer he knew that a narrow ledge or hold that sloped upward was easier and safer than a far wider one that sloped down; if his suppositions were correct, the east face of the mountain should be, in effect, a huge natural staircase.

A thorough reconnaissance in June of 1865 served to strengthen his new convictions, and a few days later he was ready to launch his first attack by a new route. His companions on this venture were Michel-Auguste Croz, a topflight Chamonix guide with whom he had made many difficult ascents, two other guides named Christian Almer and Franz Biener and—sole veteran of his previous attempts—faithful Meynet, the hunchback.

Following the plan which had been worked out by Whymper and Croz, these five approached the mountain from the Mont Cervin Glacier and began the ascent of a steep gully which led to the Furggen, or southeast, Ridge above. It was Whymper's theory that once they gained this ridge they could cross over onto the east face and continue up and to the right until they reached the northeast shoulder, just below the summit. The great danger, he realized, was that they might encounter avalanches in the gully, but he believed that they could minimize it by keeping well out on the gully walls and avoiding the center trough, which would be a natural chute for falling stones.

He was not long in being proved wrong. Pausing for lunch at a point about halfway to the ridge, their attention was suddenly drawn to an ominous trickle of small rocks skimming down the mountainside. An instant later there was a roaring on the heights above, and they looked up to see a huge welter of boulders and stones hurtling down upon them at projectile speed. Worse yet, they saw that the avalanche was not confined to the center of the gully, but was raking its sides as well, bounding from wall to wall in the wildest confusion. Dropping their food, the men dashed for cover, hiding under defending rocks while the cannonade of death crashed past them. Almost by a miracle none of them was struck, but, white-faced and shaken, they all agreed they had had enough of the gully. To have advanced

farther in it would have been tantamount[11] to sauntering toward the muzzle of a firing cannon.

Whymper, hoping against hope, clambered out of the gully and tried to reach the ridge by scaling the neighboring cliffs. Of his companions, only Meynet followed him, a grin on his homely face, the tent slung across his gnarled back. "Come down, come down!" shouted Croz from below. "It is useless!" Even Whymper, the eternal optimist, could see that the guide was right, and after a few minutes' fruitless struggling he turned back. His seventh assault on the mountain had, like all the others, ended in failure.

Now at last began the strange and complicated sequence of events by which fate set the stage and selected the characters for the last act of the drama of the Matterhorn. No playwright has ever devised a more triumphant and tragic final curtain.

Whymper had resolved to make his next attempt by the east face and northeast, or Zermatt, ridge, and his companions of the gully were ready to accompany him. A storm, however, delayed them, and before they could make a start the guide Croz was called back to Chamonix by a previous engagement. The artist accompanied him and, while Croz was occupied elsewhere, made a notable first ascent of the Aiguille Verte, in the Mont Blanc Range, with Almer and Biener. But the Matterhorn was in his blood. Too

11 tantamount: equal in effect.

impatient to wait longer for Croz, he returned to Breuil with the other two guides, only to have them back down on him at the last moment.

"Anything but the Matterhorn," they implored him. "*Anything* but that!"

Whymper was not unduly upset by their change of heart. Carrel was available and eager for another go at the great peak, and of all the men the Englishman had ever climbed with he respected this proud, self-confident guide the most. After considerable argument Carrel agreed to attempt the east face; Caesar and another helper enlisted for the venture, and it was agreed the assault would be made on the first fine day.

As it turned out, however, the first fine day brought no setting-out for Whymper, but only anger and frustration. A few days previously a large and well-equipped party of Italians had arrived in Breuil, with the avowed intention of scaling the Matterhorn by the southwest ridge. Now the artist was to suffer the ordeal of standing helplessly by while Carrel pleaded "a previous engagement" and joined forces with his rivals. Whymper knew that the previous engagement was a fiction and that the real reasons for the guide's act lay deep in his proud and stubborn character. An Italian himself, he felt that his first duty was to his fellow countrymen, and although he had reluctantly agreed to try the east face, his heart was set on conquering the peak from the side of his native valley. But whatever Carrel's motives, the important thing to

Whymper was that his defection was an accomplished fact. Again, as on the day of Tyndall's attempt, he saw himself about to be cheated of his great prize. He had to act and act fast.

This was easier decided than done. Carrel apparently was not the only Italian patriot in the Val Tournanche, for not a man could be found who would agree to climb with him, or even to act as his porter across the pass to Zermatt. The crowning blow came when Luk Meynet turned him down; the little hunchback claimed to be in the thick of some cheese-making operations which it was impossible for him to leave. Whymper was desperate. The Italians, he knew, were burdened with ponderous equipment and were moving on the mountain very slowly. But he could not move at all.

In that dark moment fate intervened in the persons of two young men who came swinging down into Breuil from the Theodule Pass. One of them was a strong and adventuresome Englishman, Lord Francis Douglas, who had recently distinguished himself by several difficult Alpine ascents; the other was his porter, young Peter Taugwalder, son of one of the foremost guides of Zermatt. Whymper told Douglas his plight, and Douglas, for his part, said that he would like nothing better than a try at the Matterhorn. Furthermore, he declared that the elder Taugwalder, who had heard of Whymper's plans, agreed that the eastern face might be climbed and could undoubtedly be persuaded to accompany them. With high hopes the two Englishmen, with young Taugwalder as porter, raced over the pass to Zermatt. At the zero hour the fight for the Matterhorn had become an international rivalry.

But fate had yet stranger twists in store. Who should walk into the hotel in Zermatt that same night but Michel-Auguste Croz! He explained to Whymper that his employer in Chamonix had returned home earlier than expected and that he had subsequently been engaged by another climber—the distinguished clergyman-mountaineer, Charles Hudson. Hudson, with Croz and a young traveling companion named Hadow, had now come to Zermatt for the express purpose of attempting the Matterhorn. Whymper and the clergyman met after dinner that night and promptly decided to join forces.

It was therefore a party of seven that set out for the mountain the following morning. Whymper and Hudson shared the leadership; Douglas and Hadow, both of whom were only nineteen, were what might be called the junior climbers; Croz and the elder Taugwalder were the guides; the younger Taugwalder the porter. Of the seven only Whymper and Croz had ever been on the Matterhorn before, and Croz had been there only once, on the short-lived venture in the gully. But the others were all strong, able men, and Whymper was satisfied with them— and full of optimism.

Ascending steadily, they reached the foot of the northeast ridge be-

fore noon of the first day and a few hours later made camp on a ledge at about eleven thousand feet on the east face. The route thus far had been incredibly easy. During the afternoon, while the others rested, Croz and young Taugwalder made a scouting trip high on the cliffs above and returned in a state of great excitement. "Not a difficulty," they reported. "Not a single difficulty!" It was a lighthearted group of mountaineers that huddled that night on their dizzy perch. "Long after dusk," wrote Whymper, "the cliffs above echoed with our laughter and with the songs of the guides, for we were happy and feared no evil."

Seven times in five years Edward Whymper had risked life and limb in futile battle against the Matterhorn. Now, by a supreme irony, he was to go to the top with almost ridiculous ease. The morning of July 14, 1865, dawned clear and still, and as soon as it was light enough to see, the seven adventurers began the ascent. The precipices of the east face towered above them three thousand feet into the sky, but, as Croz and young Taugwalder had reported, there were no formidable obstacles. Whymper had been right. This side of the mountain was not so steep as it appeared from the valley, and the upward tilt of the rocks made it a giant staircase.

They gained altitude rapidly. Twice they struck the northeast ridge and followed it for a little distance, but both times they soon worked back onto the face, where the rock was firmer. Hadow, the least experienced climber among them, encountered some difficulty on the steeper pitches; a helping hand, however, was all that was needed to get him over them, and for the greater part of the way it was not even necessary to take the precaution of roping up. At six-thirty they had reached the height of 12,900 feet and at ten they were at fourteen thousand.

Above the point at which they now stood the last few hundred feet of the east face shot up in an almost vertical wall. It was obviously unclimbable. Bearing to the right, they again worked over to the ridge, crossed it, and crept out and upward onto the northern face. Here, for the first time, the climbing was such as to call for all their mountaineering skill. The north wall of the mountain was less precipitous than the east, but the rocks were covered with a thin film of ice and at their backs was nothing but blue air and the Matterhorn Glacier four thousand feet below. Using the rope, they advanced one by one, Croz, Whymper and Hudson leading and bracing themselves against a possible slip by those who followed.

This difficult section was of no great extent. They bore almost horizontally across the face for some four hundred feet, ascended directly toward the summit for another sixty, then doubled back to the northeast ridge. One last obstacle remained —a shoulder of rock that jutted out into space at the uppermost ex-

tremity of the ridge. Carefully they edged around it: two or three short sidling steps—one long step over the abyss. An upward glance, and their hearts were suddenly pounding with excitement. Above them was only a gentle snow slope and beyond it an empty blue dome of sky.

Whymper and Croz raced for the top and made it together. The Matterhorn was conquered.

But one great fear was still in all their minds: Were they the first? Or had Carrel and the Italians, after all, beaten them to their prize? Whymper almost ran along the narrow snow-ridge that formed the summit of the mountain, searching for footprints. There were none. Then from the extreme southern end, staring down, he saw a cluster of tiny moving dots on the ridge far below. Up went Whymper's arms in triumph. He and his companions shouted until they were hoarse; they rolled rocks down the mountainside; and at last the defeated Italians paused and gazed upward at the victors. A few minutes later they turned and began the descent of the mountain. Whymper and his men were alone in their triumph.

Yet even in that most exalted moment of his life the conqueror of the Matterhorn felt a pang of regret. "Still," he wrote later, "I would that the leader of that party might have stood with us at that moment, for our victorious shouts conveyed to him the disappointment of the ambition of a lifetime. Carrel was *the* man, of all who attempted the

ascent of the Matterhorn, who most deserved to be the first upon its summit. It was the aim of his life to make the ascent from the side of Italy, for the honor of his native valley. For a time he had the game in his hand; he played it as he thought best; but he made a false move and he lost it."

Secure in their victory, Whymper and his companions remained on the summit for an hour. They shouted and pummeled each other and danced for joy. Croz produced a tent pole, which he had carried on his back the whole way up, set it in the snow and tied his shirt to it as a flag. It was seen in Zermatt, in the Val Tournanche, in the valleys and towns of the Alps for miles around. At Breuil it was taken as a sign that the Italians had conquered, and there was great jubilation, only to be followed by bitter disappointment when their defeated champions returned. At Zermatt the excited villagers poured into the streets, staring upward at the tiny scrap of cloth that flapped triumphantly in the sky, speaking with awe of the heroes who had done the impossible. Everywhere men knew and rejoiced that the Matterhorn had been won at last.

Even nature itself seemed to be taking part in the celebration. The sun shone brilliantly; not a cloud or wisp of mist veiled the horizon; and from their perch in the sky the seven conquerors looked out upon a vast, glittering panorama of summits, snow fields and valleys. "Not one of the principal peaks of the Alps was hidden," wrote Whymper. The gigantic shining dome of Mont Blanc loomed on the horizon to the west. The great crests of the Pennines and the Oberland tiered away endlessly to the east and north—Monte Rosa, the Mischabel, the Weisshorn, the Finsteraarhorn and hosts of others —incredibly white and vivid against the blue immensity of sky. They could even see Monte Viso, a hundred miles away, clear and gleaming in the crystal light. Their shouts stilled, they gazed out upon the gorgeous pageant, too moved for words. Long years have passed since that magic summer afternoon when they stood, the first of all men, on the summit of the Matterhorn, but it is doubtful if in the whole subsequent history of mountaineering men have ever again been granted so glorious an hour of triumph. Certainly it was the most glorious of their own lives.

For four of them it was also the last.

They had reached the summit at one-forty. At exactly two-forty they began the descent. In a moment or two they had come down the snow-slope and reached the beginning of the short "difficult section" on the north face. Here they paused to rope up, and Whymper and Hudson worked out the order of descent. Croz went first and Hadow second. Then came Hudson and after him Douglas. Old Taugwalder, Whymper and young Taugwalder brought up the rear, in that order. In such a sequence the stronger members of the party were in a position to help the weaker—Hadow and Douglas—

if they should encounter any difficulties. Or so they thought.

They rounded the jutting shoulder of rock and worked cautiously down the steep slabs on the other side. Only one man was moving at a time. A moment later—

"Croz had laid aside his ax, and in order to give Mr. Hadow greater security was absolutely taking hold of his legs and putting his feet, one by one, into their proper positions. As far as I know, no one was actually descending. The two leading men were partially hidden from my sight by an intervening mass of rock, but it is my belief, from the movements of their shoulders, that Croz, having done as I said, was in the act of turning around to go down a step or two himself. At this moment Mr. Hadow slipped, fell against him, and knocked him over."

There was a sharp, choked-off cry from Croz, and he and Hadow went flying downward. In an instant Hudson was dragged violently from his steps and Douglas after him. Whymper and the two Taugwalders braced themselves, clinging to the rocks. The rope spun out between Douglas and the elder Taugwalder, went taut with a violent jerk—

And broke.

"For a few seconds we saw our unfortunate companions sliding downwards on their backs, and spreading out their hands, endeavoring to save themselves. They passed from our sight uninjured, disappeared one by one and fell from precipice to precipice on to the Matterhorn-gletscher below,

a distance of nearly 4000 feet in height."

Thus the Matterhorn adventure ended—in victory and appalling tragedy. The last great unconquered peak in the Alps had succumbed at last to the skill and courage and perseverance of men, but in the very hour of conquest it had exacted a frightful vengeance.

Whymper's descent of the mountain with the two Taugwalders was a waking nightmare such as few men have ever been called upon to endure. Even worse was the ordeal that awaited him below. It was presently disclosed that at the time of the accident the climbers had been using an old, frayed rope, although they had plenty of sound rope with them, and the surrounding countryside resounded with recrim-inations and accusations. It was even whispered that Whymper and the Taugwalders had deliberately cut the rope, consigning their companions to death to save their own skins. An official inquest cleared them; but what, a short time before, had been a joyous triumph ended in a sordid, miserable epilogue.

Croz, Hudson and Hadow were discovered lying on the great glacier and were buried in the churchyard in Zermatt. The body of Lord Francis Douglas was never found. As for Whymper, he lived on for almost half a century, but the memory of the disaster haunted him to the end. In 1874 he went back to Zermatt and made a second ascent of the Matterhorn—perhaps in an effort to exorcise[12] its ghosts—and that was

12 **exorcise:** drive away (an evil spirit).

the only time he ever climbed again in Europe. He never married. He became a heavy drinker. Lonely and taciturn,[13] he roamed the world and scaled its mountains: in the Andes, the Canadian Rockies, even Greenland. But the spell the Alps had cast upon him was never altogether broken, and in the end, an old and dying man, he returned at last to the scene of his early adventures, to pass his last days among the great peaks he loved the best of all.

In the years since Whymper the Matterhorn has become one of the most-climbed mountains in the world. Today it has been ascended by every ridge and every face, its more frequented routes bristle with fixed ropes and ladders, and scarcely a fine summer day passes that its summit does not do service as a picnicking ground for a party of tourists. The "awful mountain" has been tamed.

Yet its magic remains. It is still, as in days gone by, the most famous peak in the Alps, and it still possesses the power to move all who look upon it with wonder and excitement. For the Matterhorn is more than a mountain. It is a monument and a legend. And as long as men raise their eyes to its heights they will remember the time when Edward Whymper and his companions set out upon their great adventure— and struggled and won and lost.

13 **taciturn** (tăs′ə tûrn′): habitually silent.

Reading Skills

1. According to the introductory paragraphs of this selection, how is the Matterhorn different from other mountains?
2. Why did Whymper begin mountain climbing?
3. After surveying the Theodule Pass, why did Whymper decide to try the southwestern ridge?
4. Why was Whymper forced to abandon his first attempt to climb the mountain? Why did each of the next six attempts fail? After his third failure, why did Whymper say, "Want of men made the difficulty, not the mountain"?
5. What was the "new, revolutionary plan" which Whymper had for making his climb in 1865 (his seventh attempt)?

Understanding Literature

1. What obstacles did Whymper have to overcome in order to win his battle with the Matterhorn?
2. Find examples of battle terms in the selection. Why is battle imagery a good way to depict Whymper's climbing the Matterhorn?
3. What characteristics of Whymper are revealed as you read of his struggle with the mountain?
4. What do you learn of the character of Carrel, the guide? How is he like Whymper? Explain this statement, made in a note to the essay, about Carrel: "Carrel reached the summit by the southwest ridge only three days later [than Whymper]. But for all the joy it gave him it might as well have been a hundred years."
5. Explain the meaning of this statement about Whymper's eighth and successful attempt: "Now, by a supreme irony, he was to go to the top with almost ridiculous ease." What is the "supreme irony"?
6. The author often uses comparisons to help you visualize how things look or what is happening; for example, he says, "Whymper now plunged as if down a funnel." Find other comparisons which help you to see what is described or narrated.

Focusing on Words

1. The author says that the Matterhorn has "cloud-hung battlements." When you look up the meaning of *battlements,* you find that the term applies to ancient fortified buildings. Why is the mountain said to have "battlements"? Later the author speaks of the "turrets" and the "citadel" of the mountain. What do these terms mean? How do they apply to a mountain?
2. After his account of the conquest of the Matterhorn, the author says, "What, a short time before, had been a joyous triumph ended in a sordid, miserable epilogue." What is an epilogue? Why was it "sordid" and "miserable"? Where earlier in the narrative do you find images associated with drama—with acting out a tragedy, with setting the stage, for example?

Perhaps you have heard or read someone's view that American schools place too much emphasis on athletic competition, or that television programing reflects an overemphasis on sports. Is it possible that Americans will continue to give increasing attention to athletic activities until they finally become tired of sports?

The Decline of Sport

(A Preposterous Parable)

E. B. White

IMPROVING YOUR READING: The subtitle of this essay suggests that the content is exaggerated and ridiculous. As you read, note how exaggeration is employed to point up the specific evils which the author feels accompany the overemphasis on sports.

IN THE THIRD DECADE of the supersonic age, sport gripped the nation in an ever-tightening grip. The horse tracks, the ball parks, the fight rings, the gridirons, all drew crowds in steadily increasing numbers. Every time a game was played, an attendance record was broken. Usually some other sort of record was broken, too—such as the record for the number of consecutive doubles hit by left-handed batters in a Series game, or some such thing as that. Records fell like ripe apples on a windy day. Customs and manners changed, and the five-day business week was reduced to four days, then to three, to give everyone a better chance to memorize the scores.

Not only did sport proliferate[1]

1 **proliferate:** grow by rapidly producing new parts.

but the demands it made on the spectator became greater. Nobody was content to take in one event at a time, and thanks to the magic of radio and television nobody had to. A Yale alumnus, class of 1962, returning to the Bowl with 197,000 others to see the Yale-Cornell football game would take along his pocket radio and pick up the Yankee Stadium, so that while his eye might be following a fumble on the Cornell twenty-two-yard line, his ear would be following a man going down to second in the top of the fifth, seventy miles away. High in the blue sky above the Bowl, skywriters would be at work writing the scores of other major and minor sporting contests, weaving an interminable record of victory and defeat, and using the new high-visibility pink news-smoke perfected by Pepsi-Cola engineers. And in the frames of the giant video sets, just behind the goalposts, this same alumnus could watch Dejected win the Futurity before a record-breaking crowd of 349,872 at Belmont, each of whom was tuned to the Yale Bowl and following the World Series game in the video and searching the sky for further news of events either under way or just completed. The effect of this vast cyclorama of sport was to divide the spectator's attention, over-subtilize his appreciation, and deaden his passion. As the fourth supersonic decade was ushered in, the picture changed and sport began to wane.

A good many factors contributed to the decline of sport. Substitutions in football had increased to such an extent that there were very few fans in the United States capable of holding the players in mind during play. Each play that was called saw two entirely new elevens lined up, and the players whose names and faces you had familiarized yourself with in the first period were seldom seen or heard of again. The spectacle became as diffuse as the main concourse in Grand Central at the commuting hour.

Express motor highways leading to the parks and stadia had become so wide, so unobstructed, so devoid of all life except automobiles and trees that sport fans had got into the habit of traveling enormous distances to attend events. The normal driving speed had been stepped up to ninety-five miles an hour, and the

distance between cars had been decreased to fifteen feet. This put an extraordinary strain on the sport lover's nervous system, and he arrived home from a Saturday game, after a road trip of three hundred and fifty miles, glassy-eyed, dazed, and spent. He hadn't really had any relaxation and he had failed to see Czlika (who had gone in for Trusky) take the pass from Bkeeo (who had gone in for Bjallo) in the third period, because at that moment a youngster named Lavagetto had been put in to pinch-hit for Art Gurlack in the bottom of the ninth with the tying run on second, and the skywriter who was attempting to write "Princeton 0–Lafayette 43" had banked the wrong way, muffed the "3," and distracted everyone's attention from the fact that Lavagetto had been whiffed.

Cheering, of course, lost its stimulating effect on players, because cheers were no longer associated necessarily with the immediate scene but might as easily apply to something that was happening somewhere else. This was enough to infuriate even the steadiest performer. A football star, hearing the stands break into a roar before the ball was snapped, would realize that their minds were not on him, and would become dispirited and grumpy. Two or three of the big coaches worried so about this that they considered equipping all players with tiny ear sets, so that they, too, could keep abreast of other sporting events while playing, but the idea was abandoned as impractical, and the coaches put it aside in tickler files, to bring up again later.

I think the event that marked the turning point in sport and started it downhill was the Midwest's classic Dust Bowl game of 1975, when Eastern Reserve's great right end, Ed Pistachio, was shot by a spectator. This man, the one who did the shooting, was seated well down in the stands near the forty-yard line on a bleak October afternoon and was so saturated with sport and with the disappointments of sport that he had clearly become deranged. With a minute and fifteen seconds to play and the score tied, the Eastern Reserve quarterback had whipped a long pass over Army's heads into Pistachio's waiting arms. There was no other player anywhere near him, and all Pistachio had to do was catch the ball and run it across the line. He dropped it. At exactly this moment, the spectator—a man named Homer T. Parkinson, of 35 Edgemere Drive, Toledo, O.—suffered at least three other major disappointments in the realm of sport. His horse, Hiccough, on which he had a five-hundred-dollar bet, fell while getting away from the starting gate at Pimlico and broke its leg (clearly visible in the video); his favorite shortstop, Lucky Frimstitch, struck out and let three men die on base in the final game of the Series (to which Parkinson was tuned); and the Governor Dummer soccer team, on which Parkinson's youngest son played goalie, lost to Kent, 4–3, as recorded in the sky overhead. Before anyone could stop him, he drew a gun and drilled Pistachio, before 954,000 persons, the largest crowd that had ever attended a football game and the *second*-largest crowd that had ever assembled for any sporting event in any month except July.

This tragedy, by itself, wouldn't have caused sport to decline, I suppose, but it set in motion a chain of other tragedies, the cumulative effect of which was terrific. Almost as soon as the shot was fired, the news flash was picked up by one of the skywriters directly above the field. He glanced down to see whether he could spot the trouble below, and in doing so failed to see another skywriter approaching. The two planes collided and fell, wings locked, leaving a confusing trail of smoke, which some observers tried to interpret as a late sports score. The planes struck in the middle of the nearby eastbound coast-to-coast Sunlight Parkway, and a motorist driving a convertible coupé stopped so short, to avoid hitting them, that he was bumped from behind. The pileup of cars that ensued involved 1,482 vehicles, a record for eastbound parkways. A total of more than three thousand persons lost their lives in the highway accident, including the two pilots, and when panic broke out in the stadium, it cost another 872 in dead and injured. News of the disaster spread quickly to other sports arenas, and started other panics among the crowds trying to get to the exits, where they could buy a paper and study a list of the dead. All in all, the afternoon of sport cost 20,003 lives, a record.

And nobody had much to show for it except one small Midwestern boy who hung around the smoking wrecks of the planes, captured some aero news-smoke in a milk bottle, and took it home as a souvenir.

From that day on, sport waned. Through long, noncompetitive Saturday afternoons, the stadia slumbered. Even the parkways fell into disuse as motorists rediscovered the charms of old, twisty roads that led through main streets and past barnyards, with their mild congestions and pleasant smells.

Understanding Literature

1. The subtitle identifies this essay as a parable, a short tale designed to teach some truth or moral lesson. What lesson does E. B. White expect his readers to learn from this parable? Why does he call it a *preposterous* parable?
2. The author's exaggerations are clues to the specific aspects of sport which he thinks are receiving too much public attention. Using these clues, identify the several trends in sports which the author feels are overemphasized.
3. Which of the author's predictions are already at least partly true?
4. Even though this essay is an exaggerated prediction of a *future* trend, it is written, not as a prediction, but from what point in time?
5. What conclusion is to be drawn from the final paragraph?

Further Activities

1. E. B. White suggests that Americans pay too much attention to sports. Write a short essay about some other activity which Americans tend to overdo. Use White's technique of exaggeration to point up the undesirable symptoms of the overdone activity. One of the following topics might be suitable:

   (a) Christmas shopping in a department store.
   (b) My sister's wardrobe is out of date already.
   (c) Fourteen new Westerns (or mystery stories) on television.
   (d) More horsepower in next year's automobiles.
   (e) The electronic computer will solve all your other problems, too.

2. In one or two paragraphs explain why you agree or disagree with E. B. White's suggestion that there is too much emphasis on sports in this country. Be sure to support your opinion with specific examples. If you wish, you may use your school as an example, or else the country as a whole.

Biography

WHILE READING A STORY or a novel, you may have looked up from a page and thought, "Yes, this is interesting—rather interesting. But things have happened to me, too, that would make good reading. Maybe I should write a book." For one reason or another, some people have done just that—written a book about themselves. Sometimes they write about themselves for business reasons: a man or woman who has developed a television or motion picture "personality" may write a book to advertise his or her colorful character. More often, though, people write about themselves for other reasons: this person may have solved a problem that seemed impossible of solution and feel that others would benefit from reading about such an experience. That person may have an idea that his or her life, or relationship with other people, is unusual and that people should know about it. A book about someone's life written by the person who is the subject of the book is called an autobiography.

An account of someone's life written by another person is called a biography. People read biography because they are impressed, even thrilled, by the achievements of others and because they are curious to know *how* and *why* others succeeded or failed in life.

As you read autobiography or biography, keep certain questions in mind. The more you know about how a biographer is presenting the subject, the greater your interest will be and the more you will learn about the person whose biography it is.

How well does the biographer know the person he/she is writing about?

To what extent does the author really know the person being written about? Does the biographer know the subject personally, as a member of the family or as a close friend? Or has the knowledge come in some other way—through reading old letters, through research in books, or through interviews with people who knew the person?

Does the author really understand the person involved? In order to show what the person was like, the author has to know about things that the subject was interested in and about the customs, attitudes, and beliefs which belonged to the subject's historical era. You will find the life of the person more meaningful if you take time to understand them, too.

What is the author's attitude toward the subject?

Does the author admire the subject so much that he/she makes that person seem almost too good, too capable to be a human being? (One of George Washington's biographers, you may remember, made up stories about him, like the one about the cherry tree, in order to present him as a model of perfection.) Does the author, on the other hand, seem most interested in showing the faults of the subject—the failures and mistakes? The best biographies are those that help the reader understand the significance of a person and his/her deeds by including all the important information about that person's life.

What character traits does the author emphasize? How are they emphasized?

From early morning until late at night any person shows many qualities of character, some more admirable than others. No author can possibly show them all; if he/she tried do so, the book would have no sense of purpose and no unity. Which qualities, then, has this writer selected as the important ones to characterize the subject—to show determination, kindness, or an intense interest in some one area of life?

What incidents from the person's life does the author include? Are there any significant sections of the person's life unaccounted for? If so, why do you think the author omitted them?

A biographer, like any other writer, chooses the details about the subject which best suit the purpose for writing; then he/she arranges those details so that they will create the desired impression. For instance, if a writer wants the reader to approve of the subject's life, he/she will include and emphasize those details which tell about the subject's noble nature; conversely, if a writer dislikes the subject of the biography, he/she will choose details which emphasize that person's evil or unpleasant nature. Or if the biographer wants to present an impartial account of the subject's life, he/she will be interested in finding details that illustrate both good and bad behavior. Note, however, that even the impartial biographer must choose what to include. Because he/she cannot possibly record every event in a person's life, he/she selects certain incidents with the purpose of presenting the human failings as well as the triumphs of that life. Thus all biography, even the most objective and unprejudiced, is to some extent "fictionalized"—that is, the writer chooses materials, arranges them into some pattern of organization, and says something ("here was a good man" or "a bad man" or "a human being, both good and bad") about that subject.

Does the person "come to life" as you read?

Has the author written the biography as though he/she were writing a history book, giving dates and places and events in order? Has the writer, on the other hand, presented the person as he or she acted and spoke, as a novelist might present a character?

If the author shows the subject in action and in conversation, you will understand that many of the small actions and many of the words spoken must be imagined by the author, for you know that the writer was probably not present at all the important scenes in the subject's life, taking notes. You may not care that some words and actions are imaginary, since they cause the person to seem real to you.

If the author has imagined such scenes, are they consistent

with the subject's character and personality? You may find it interesting to read about an event from a history book or encyclopedia and then to compare it with the biographer's version.

Is the person a good subject for a biography?

What makes a person a good subject for a biography? He or she does not become a good subject merely because of a famous name. And remember that a person does not necessarily have to be a famous person in order to be a suitable subject for a biography. The one requirement is that he or she be, for some reason, an *interesting* person. Some of the reasons why you may find a biography or an autobiography rewarding to read are these:

1. The subject's life is inspiring because he or she has achieved something worth-while in spite of difficulties.
2. The subject did something that had never been done before.
3. The subject's influence was strongly felt in the lives of others.
4. The subject's life had a kind of depth that makes you realize the depth of your own nature.

You will be able to think of other reasons why people's lives make good reading, just as you will no doubt think of other questions to consider as you read the biographical selections which follow.

At the age of fourteen William Heyliger "became captivated," as he says, by the newspaper stories of the famous journalists Richard Harding Davis and Jesse Lynch Williams. He soon began writing stories himself, and he has been writing ever since, always for boys. During the years he has spent much time camping with boys and in talking with them. He has never, he says, been particularly interested in what characters do, but always "deeply interested in why they do it." In this selection about Theodore Roosevelt as a boy, notice that Heyliger is not so much interested in the incident itself as in the boy's reaction to it.

The Fighting Soul

William Heyliger

IMPROVING YOUR READING: The writer begins "The Fighting Soul" with an incident that occurred when Theodore Roosevelt was a young boy; then he sketches Roosevelt's biography before the incident. After this, he tells what happened after the incident. Consider why he does not tell events in the order in which they happened.

THE YEAR WAS 1872. The stage-coach, running through the Maine woods to Moosehead Lake, carried few passengers. Three of them were boys. Two, riding together, were plump, red-cheeked, full of an impish mischief. The other was a lad with broomstick legs, a frail body, a timid disposition, and weak, near-sighted eyes. The two who rode together found the journey dull. Boylike, they sought diversion, and found it in the weakling who sat on the other side of the coach.

At first they confined themselves to whispers and to laughter. The frail boy flushed and fidgeted nervously. The taunting continued and became audible. Wasn't it the cute little mamma's darling? And the legs—would you look at the legs?

"You'd better stop it!" the frail boy cried suddenly and furiously.

The tormentors, having secured a rise out of the victim, were delighted. Why, it could talk, anyway, couldn't it? They laughed gleefully.

The weakling, in a rage, leaped from his seat and threw himself upon them.

"Hey!" cried the startled driver. "Stop that fighting in there. Stop it, I say."

The driver, who was probably a good man with horses, was a bad judge of fisticuffs. It didn't even remotely resemble a fight, for the tall, puny boy brought nothing to the fray but an ineffectual resentment. It was the first time, in his fourteen years, he had ever struck a blow in anger. Had his tormentors been brutal, rather than thoughtlessly cruel youngsters out for a lark, they would have punished him severely. Instead, they brushed him off and finally held his arms and rendered him helpless. What was worse, they laughed all during the proceeding.

"Go sit down," they counseled, "before you get hurt."

Young Theodore Roosevelt sat down, shamefaced and humiliated. And there was no further bantering from the two he had attacked.

The ignominy of that scene lingered in Roosevelt's mind all through his stay at Moosehead Lake. He had been sickly almost from birth, a victim of weakening, racking asthma. There was night after night of gasping, wheezing misery. In infancy, his strong, virile father had walked during these attacks with the suffering boy in his arms, hour after hour. Later the father had watched hour after hour beside his bed. There were days when he could not leave that bed. And still later the father had sat his son beside him in the family carriage and had driven through the dark stretch of the night hoping that the cool, outdoor air would lessen the seizure. Always, it seemed, there had been sickness.

But if the body of young Theodore was weak, his mind was sharp, clear, active. Too ill to go to school and hold his own in the hurly-burly of group life, he was taught by private tutors. The family was wealthy and, if it could not buy him health, it could provide the things that interested his mind. He learned to read at an early age, and for years his was a world of books. Shut out of the adventure of activity, he built adventure in his imagination. Like most sickly boys he was timid; like all timid boys, he lived a make-believe swashbuckling existence of valor. The heroes of scientific exploration, the adventurous heroes of fiction became his heroes, second only to the one great flesh-and-blood hero of his life, his father.

Within the limits of his strength, the pale, sickly boy was all boy. His home in New York City had a goodly-sized yard, and there, with his sisters and a small army of cousins, he played the games of boyhood. Summers found him in the mountains of New York, or New Jersey, or New England as the family searched in vain for a climate that would deal gently with his asthma. He had imagination. Merely playing Indians was not realistic enough; he must, of necessity, stain himself with the juice of the chokecherry. He became interested in nature study and, with the cooperation of his cousins, organized the Roosevelt Museum of Natural History. For a while it confined itself to the study of ants, and small bugs, and an occasional mouse. Then a fish-market near his home made an exhibition of a dead seal. He haunted the market until the seal reached a point of decomposition that rendered its removal imperative. In some way he became the possessor of the skeleton head. It became the chief attraction of the museum. Some years later he met a man who had been a companion of Audubon's. From this man he learned something of taxidermy. Even at that age, if Roosevelt adopted a project, he followed it with single-track purpose. For years thereafter his passion for dissecting and stuffing animals was something of a horror to the more squeamish members of his family. His body might be fragile, but his will was strong. He had not yet reached the age where illness was going to dawn upon him as a bleak handicap. He kept a diary. "I stayed in the house all day," he records with laconic[1] casualness. It was merely something to be endured.

Meanwhile, the family searched in vain for a place that would give health to the weakling. He was encouraged to live in the sunshine. At thirteen he was given his first rifle. Up to that time he had been asthmatic and debilitated. Now a new liability presented itself. In sighting the gun, targets that were plain to his cousins were invisible to him. An examination showed that his eyes were weak—very weak. Thick lenses only added to his outward appearance of futility. He was still too ill to be sent to a school.

It was the following year that he was sent to Moosehead Lake. His asthma had been a bit worse than usual, and there was a hope that the thinner, keener air of Maine would bring relief. It was on that trip, in search of health, that he pitched into the two tormentors on the stagecoach.

The experience awoke him, at last, to the realization of what a weak body meant. The encounter seemed symbolic. If you were willing to accept a puny frame with resignation, then you must expect to take the short end of things all through life. It wasn't enough to dream of doing things, to live in a mental world; you had to live in a world of actuality and to *really* do things.

He came back to New York and told his father of the fight. There was a set to the boyish chin that the elder Roosevelt had never seen before.

"What do you propose to do about it, Theodore?" he asked gently. He had a hope that he did not dare express.

"I want to take boxing lessons," the frail boy said doggedly.

The father was delighted. He recognized the turning point. The boy who had accepted ill-health passively, was now aroused to try to make strong a body that, in after years, was to be the sturdy temple of a flaming, crusading spirit.

Young Theodore, with his broomstick legs, his pinched chest, his asthma and his peering eyes, was sent for instruction to a gymnasium conducted by a prize fighter who had retired from the ring. In boxing trunks, he must have been a pathetic sight. His efforts to swing, to block, to hook, to side-step, to jab, must have been ludicrous.[2] But the one-track mind had set forth for a goal, and grimly and tenaciously he stuck to the task. If he could

---

1 **laconic** (lə kŏn′ĭk): brief.

2 **ludicrous**: ridiculous.

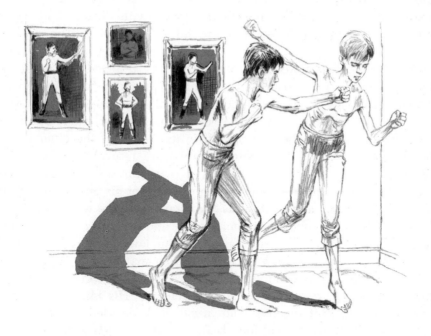

not inflict punishment, he could stand up under it with fortitude and endurance. He was what is called "game." And presently after a time —after a long time—the gymnasium held a boxing tournament for its pupils, and sickly Theodore Roosevelt won a pewter cup in the lightweight division. As a cup it was probably a cheap, tawdry affair. As a symbol of indomitable perseverance, as a heroic refusal to accept the dictates of outrageous fortune, it must have seemed to the father of Theodore Roosevelt priceless. For here was one marked as a hopeless invalid fighting that greatest of all fights, for that greatest of all rewards —a victory over self.

But victory was not won in a day, or in a year. At fifteen, despite the gymnasium work, asthma again struck him down. There was a consultation of doctors. They suggested the dry air of the African desert. The faithful father, who had stood squarely behind the boy through every discouraging up and down of illness, packed up the entire Roosevelt family and sailed for Egypt.

The Roosevelt Museum of Natural History, begun in boyhood, still existed. Starting as an amateur, Theodore had read deeply and ardently, had gone on steadily with taxidermy and had done field work in so far as his strength and opportunities admitted. He was going to Egypt as an invalid; and yet invalidism was not permitted to take possession of his thoughts. He planned for the museum. Specimens would be collected. He had shipping labels printed so that these specimens could be shipped home. His was the attitude of a boy seeking new adventure rather than a sick lad seeking solace.

One of his first purchases on reaching Africa was a book describing the birds of Egypt. Eagerly and avidly the boy devoured it. The party moved along the historic Nile. Day after day the desert wind blew over him, and day after day he explored ruins, and rode helter-skelter on a donkey, and shot birds for his collection and mounted them. Under the lash of his will there was no time to be sick. There was too much to be done, too much to be seen. His father feared that he would overdo it. But the boy who had been ailing all his life had found a new font of strength. He was tireless. He was absorbed.

And suddenly a miracle happened. The pale weakling began to take on weight. Summers out of doors, months of persistent work in an ex-prize fighter's gym, this engrossing winter in Egypt abruptly turned some delicate scale within his body. The wan cheeks began to fill out. The broomhandle legs grew imperceptibly stouter. The scrawny neck began to take on girth. The asthmatic attacks came at longer intervals and were less severe. It was an overjoyed family that returned to the United States.

But the fight was not yet won. The boy who was later to thrive on the hardships of ranch life in the Bad Lands, who was to preach the doctrine of the strenuous life, who was to lead his Rough Riders through a fever-infested tropical jungle in the war with Spain, had merely found the beginnings of a road that might lead to a splendid summit.

He was resolved to reach that summit. Back at home there was a period of discouragement. Asthma once more stormed the ramparts and flew its flag from the citadel of his body. He returned to his boxing. A gymnasium was installed on an upper floor of his father's house, and he branched into wrestling, Indian clubs, and parallel bars. If illness laid him low, he was back on the wrestling mat as soon as he had recovered. There were setbacks, but no defeats. His intent, single-track mind had decided that Theodore Roosevelt was going to be a robust man, vital and virile. He would fight for that goal until it was won.

The time came for him to prepare for college. Once more he was deemed too delicate to go off to a secondary school. Once more private tutors appeared and took him in hand. Greek and Latin; boxing gloves and wrestling; mathematics and parallel bars. So many hours a day to the kingdom of the mind; so much time each day to the empire of the body. The mind improved rapidly; the body responded very, very slowly. For it must be remembered that the body of Theodore Roosevelt had been depleted and impoverished for a great many years. It takes time to build up and make buoyantly fertile a run-down soil.

He was still asthmatic, still below par; but the doctors decided there was enough improvement to justify the end of tutors, and that Theodore could go shoulder to shoulder with other advancing men. He entered Harvard. The fight for health and stamina was transferred to Cambridge.

At that time his desire was to become a scientist. The old boyhood Roosevelt Museum of Natural History was still in his blood. He had an idea that as a scientist he would roam the world collecting specimens and studying wildlife at first hand, only to discover that, instead, he would probably be chained to a laboratory. The new vitality beginning to pour into his veins made the thought of hours cramped over a microscope intolerable. A spirit that had been chained was learning to be free, and wanted no more chains. His energy turned to literature. He became one of the editors of the *Harvard Advocate*. He began to write a naval history of the War of 1812. The thought of public service, of entering the arena of politics, had not yet dawned, though his family line was a line of service for the public's welfare.

And day by day the soul that animated the body directed a silent battle for strength and endurance. There were still distressing attacks of asthma. He wrestled and boxed regularly. Handicapped by poor eyesight, he was never a match for the college stars. However, he was striving for a laurel of more lasting value than a victorious bout. He had conquered the timidity of his early years. He had disciplined himself. He could take a stout blow without wincing, and gave one with royal will. Presently he won his way in one of the boxing tournaments to the semifinals of the lightweight division. It was the gym days of New York over again. But whereas, in New York, he had earned a pewter cup, all he took from the semifinals at Harvard was a sound, thorough drubbing. Outclassed by a stronger, faster man, punished severely, he was still trying, still fighting, at the final bell.

Not bad at all for a hollow reed that had not been strong enough to go to school.

During those four years at Harvard the battle was won. The asthmatic youth who had entered the freshman class graduated strong, vigorous, determined. Nine years before he had set out to overthrow a physical handicap. Nine years before a bitter experience on a Maine stagecoach had proved to him that he must either find ruggedness of body or be content to spend his days in a quiet, stagnant backwater of life. The way had been long and hard. Now he was the finished product of strength of will and of unshaken determination—a man fashioned and girded to do things.

The invalid had become a giant, the broken branch, an oak.

Reading Skills

1. What was young Theodore Roosevelt's first reaction to the tormenting of the two boys on the stagecoach? Why did they stop teasing him? What was his later reaction to the incident?
2. What was there about his life as a boy that shows that his mind was "sharp, clear, active"?
3. In what several ways did his parents show their devotion to him?
4. In what ways did young Roosevelt show that, before he had a body that was able to fight, he had a "fighting soul"? Why was his defeat in the boxing tournament at Harvard really a victory?

Understanding Literature

1. The author says that the encounter between young Roosevelt and the two boys in the stagecoach "seemed symbolic." What did the encounter symbolize--represent—to Roosevelt?
2. Why does the author not tell events in Roosevelt's life in chronological order?
3. How was the pewter cup which Roosevelt won in boxing "a symbol of indomitable perseverance"?
4. Reread the context in which each of the following comparisons occurs. Then tell what two things are being compared and how they are alike:
   (a) "The boy . . . was now aroused to try to make strong a body that, in after years, was to be the sturdy temple of a flaming, crusading spirit."
   (b) "The boy . . . had merely found the beginnings of a road that might lead to a splendid summit."
   (c) "It takes time to build up and make buoyantly fertile a run-down soil."
   (d) ". . . he must either find ruggedness of body or be content to spend his days in a quiet, stagnant backwater of life."
   (e) "The invalid had become a giant, the broken branch, an oak."
5. William Heyliger often uses balanced sentence construction; in many of his sentences he balances two opposites, as in "His was the attitude of a boy seeking new adventures rather than a sick lad seeking solace." Find other such balanced sentences.

Focusing on Words

You should be able to determine from context what these words mean: *ineffectual* (p. 436), *ignominy* (p. 437), *virile* (p. 437), *taxidermy* (p. 438), *debilitated* (p. 438), *tenaciously* (p. 438), *tawdry* (p. 439). Reread the passages in which the words appear; then write a brief definition of each. Check your definitions in a dictionary.

Further Activities

Think of an incident, perhaps one that happened when you were a small child, that had some effect on the way you acted or thought later. First, tell about the incident; then tell what you were like before the incident and show the effect of the incident on you. Perhaps these suggestions will help you think of such an incident:

1. A victory (or defeat) on the playground.
2. A misunderstanding (in school, or at home).
3. My worst (or best) grade.
4. An undeserved (or deserved) punishment.

You may have read books about the wonderful achievement of the Wright brothers in building the first successful airplane. Here is a poem about the brothers that is less serious than the books are.

Wilbur Wright

1867-1912
and

Orville Wright

1871-1948

Rosemary and Stephen Vincent Benét

Said Orville Wright to Wilbur Wright,
"These birds are very trying.
I'm sick of hearing them cheep-cheep
About the fun of flying.
A bird has feathers, it is true.   5
That much I freely grant.
But, must that stop us, W?"
Said Wilbur Wright, "It shan't."

And so they built a glider, first,
And then they built another.   10
—There never were two brothers more
Devoted to each other.
They ran a dusty little shop
For bicycle-repairing,
And bought each other soda-pop   15
And praised each other's daring.

They glided here, they glided there,
They sometimes skinned their noses.
—For learning how to rule the air
Was not a bed of roses—   20
But each would murmur, afterward,
While patching up his bro.
"Are we discouraged, W?"
"Of course we are not, O!"

And finally, at Kitty Hawk   25
In Nineteen-Three (let's cheer it!),
The first real airplane really flew
With Orville there to steer it!
—And kingdoms may forget their kings
And dogs forget their bites,   30
But, not till Man forgets his wings,
Will men forget the Wrights.

Further Activity

After reading this poem about two famous Americans, Wilbur
Wright and Orville Wright, you might like to read other poems
that Rosemary and Stephen Vincent Benét have written about
famous people in *A Book of Americans,* from which this poem
was taken. You may want to bring in a copy of your favorite
poem from that collection to read to your class.

Another person writing the biography of Lillian Moller Gilbreth might have emphasized her contributions to the study of motion. *Belles on Their Toes*, the book in which this selection appears, was written by her son and daughter. Here they tell about an incident that shows her as a wise and understanding mother, as well as a famous engineer. In the foreword to the book, they explain that, after their father died, leaving Mrs. Gilbreth with eleven children, she "became the family breadwinner, filled the place of two parents, guided her children individually through the growing pains of adolescence, kept the family together. In her spare time, so to speak, she became one of the foremost engineers in the world."

Mother Was There First

Frank B. Gilbreth, Jr., and Ernestine Gilbreth Carey

THOSE OF US who were away at college usually saw Mother three or four times a semester, as her lectures and business engagements took her across the country.

Sometimes she'd be delivering a speech at the college itself, and would arrange her schedule so she'd have a free day to visit. Sometimes her speech would be at a city near one of the colleges, and it was possible to cut classes, hear her lecture, and then visit with her at her hotel.

Mother knew most of the presidents and many of the professors at the various colleges we attended. Usually, too, she knew the location of all the campus buildings, their nicknames, and the geography of the town.

It was somewhat disillusioning for a wide-eyed freshman, importantly taking his female parent on a sight-seeing tour of an institution which he was sure would overwhelm her with its unique traditions and maze of modern complexities, to discover that she knew more about his university than he did.

The home economics building? The "Home Ec" building certainly was one of the most modern in the country, Mother would agree. And it would develop that she had made a speech in the building last year, and had been on the program the year before when they dedicated it.

The stadium? "Old Horseshoe" was mighty impressive, she would nod. Under cross-questioning, she might point out that she had received an honorary degree in ceremonies in the stadium a few years before.

We chose our own colleges, but in most cases Mother had preceded us in the commencement parade.

She had degrees from a dozen or more institutions, including Michigan, where Anne, Frank and Jane were graduated; Smith, Ernestine and Lillian; Rutgers, the male half of Martha's college, New Jersey State College for Women; Purdue, Bill; and Brown, Fred.

To finish calling the roll, Dan received his diploma from the University of Pennsylvania, Jack from Princeton, and Bob from the University of North Carolina.

Mother never sent tuition checks directly to our colleges. At the start of each year she'd turn over to us, in one lump sum, enough money for our tuition and all other expenses. When you took out your own checkbook and paid the college registrar your tuition, you realized you were supposed to get something for your money. All of us did all right in college.

Mother spoke most often at Purdue, in West Lafayette, Indiana, where Bill was enrolled. Purdue was opening a motion study laboratory, and Mother was going to become a professor of management there. She intended to take the new job in addition to all her old ones, and to commute from Montclair to the campus once a month, for a week or so of teaching.

On one occasion when Mother was at Purdue, she was asked unexpectedly to speak before a large lecture class in which Bill was enrolled. Bill didn't know about the invitation. It was an eight o'clock class, and he picked that particular morning to oversleep.

Bill's professor told the students they were fortunate in having a distinguished engineer in their midst. She was Dr. Lillian Gilbreth, and it was gratifying to him that one of Dr. Gilbreth's sons was a member of that very class, and doubtless intended some day to follow in his mother's footsteps.

He cleared his throat and started to call the roll. All the way from the "A's" down to the "G's," Mother's eyes roved the auditorium, searching for Bill. She was sitting on a platform, in a chair next to the professor's table.

"Gibbes," said the professor.

"Here."

"Gilbert."

"Here."

"Gilbreth."

There was an awkward pause, while Mother blushed and stopped searching. The professor looked up, cleared his throat again, this time with disapproval, and repeated loudly, "Gilbreth?"

A number of Bill's friends sensed the situation simultaneously, and thought they had better come to the rescue.

"Here," a dozen voices answered from all corners of the room.

The professor put down his roll book and looked bleakly at Mother. He didn't say so, but she gathered the look was intended to convey that he had to put up with a great deal, not the least of which was having Bill as a student.

He glared at his audience, seeking to find the offenders who had answered to Bill's name.

"There seem to be," he said sarcastically, "a good many Gilbreths here today."

"The whole family," Mother announced brightly, regaining her poise and favoring him with her warmest smile. "That's nice."

The professor, who hadn't seen as much of Bill that semester as he thought he should have, didn't think it was nice at all. He licked his pencil and made a show of marking a large zero in his grade book, opposite Bill's name.

"Goldsmith," he said precisely, continuing the roll.

Bill spent the afternoon and night with Mother, so he didn't see any members of the class during the remainder of the day. Mother didn't mention to him that she had spoken to his group, or that she knew he had cut the class. She thought he was old enough to make his own decisions, and that it wouldn't give him a sense of responsibility if she seemed to be checking up on him.

She did spend a good deal of time, though, telling him how she was studying the motions of physically disabled persons, so as to help them find jobs in industry. Bill was interested, and he and Mother looked over her notes and her photographs and diagrams of the project.

Bill was a little late, but present, for the lecture class the next morning. He slid into his seat just as the professor finished calling the "C's" in the roll book, and he was well settled by the time the professor reached the "G's" and finally Bill's name.

When the professor had run through the list, he told the class he was going to give a written quiz.

"I'm sure all of you must have learned a great deal from our visitor of yesterday," he said. "So today I'm going to ask you to write a little summary giving the high points of the talk."

Bill squirmed uncomfortably, and wished he had cut class again. He nudged the boy sitting next to him.

"Who," Bill asked out of the corner of his mouth, "did the old fool drag over here yesterday?"

"Are you kidding?"

"No, I wasn't here yesterday. I overslept."

"You overslept," the boy mimicked. "It was your own mother, you stupid jackass."

"Awk," Bill grunted, sinking down in his chair and wishing he could continue through the floor.

Everyone else in the room was writing. You could hear the pens scratching and papers rustling as pages were turned. Bill hoped no one would notice that he alone was sitting there doing nothing.

He nudged his neighbor again.

"Would you mind telling this stupid jackass," Bill apologized, "what my mother talked about?"

"Motion study of the disabled."

"Thanks," Bill grinned. He started writing, too.

Reading Skills

1. What is the meaning of the title "Mother Was There First"?
2. How would you describe Mrs. Gilbreth's attitude when Bill did not answer roll call in the class to which she was to speak? when Bill's friends tried to help by answering for him?
3. Why did she not reproach Bill for cutting class? Why did she tell him about her studies in motion for the handicapped?
4. Judging from this selection only, what do you think of Mrs. Gilbreth's method of rearing her children?

Understanding Literature

1. Why do the writers spend so much time in describing the roll call?
2. Why do the writers not describe Mrs. Gilbreth giving her speech to the class? Why do they not give part of her speech? Why do they not show the reaction of the class? In other words, how is their selection of details determined by their purpose in writing?

Certain persons make a lasting impression on us, especially when we are children. We remember these persons because they were especially kind, helpful, truthful, or exciting. Maya Angelou met one such person when she was young. Perhaps you have met someone special, too. An uncle or aunt? a grandparent? a mysterious neighbor?

from I Know Why the Caged Bird Sings

Maya Angelou

IMPROVING YOUR READING: In the writing of her autobiography, Maya Angelou (born Marguerite Johnson) used several techniques of fiction writing: conflict, dialogue, and direct action, in particular. As you read, notice what part each plays in telling the story.

WHEN I WAS THREE and Bailey four, we had arrived in the musty little town, wearing tags on our wrists which instructed—"To Whom It May Concern"—that we were Marguerite and Bailey Johnson Jr., from Long Beach, California, en route to Stamps, Arkansas, c/o Mrs. Annie Henderson.

Our parents had decided to put an end to their calamitous marriage, and Father shipped us home to his mother. A porter had been charged with our welfare—he got off the train the next day in Arizona—and our tickets were pinned to my brother's inside coat pocket.

I don't remember much of the trip, but after we reached the segregated southern part of the journey, things must have looked up. Negro passengers, who always traveled with loaded lunch boxes, felt sorry for "the poor little motherless darlings" and plied us with cold fried chicken and potato salad.

Years later I discovered that the United States had been crossed thousands of times by frightened Black children traveling alone to their newly affluent[1] parents in Northern cities, or back to grandmothers in Southern towns when the urban North reneged[2] on its economic promises.

The town reacted to us as its inhabitants had reacted to all things new before our coming. It regarded us a while without curiosity but with caution, and after we were seen to be harmless (and children) it closed in around us, as a real mother embraces a stranger's child. Warmly, but not too familiarly.

We lived with our grandmother and uncle in the rear of the Store (it was always spoken of with a capital *s*), which she had owned some twenty-five years.

Early in the century, Momma (we soon stopped calling her Grandmother) sold lunches to the sawmen

---

1 **affluent:** wealthy.
2 **reneged:** went back on a promise.

BIOGRAPHY

in the lumberyard (east Stamps) and the seedmen at the cotton gin (west Stamps). Her crisp meat pies and cool lemonade, when joined to her miraculous ability to be in two places at the same time, assured her business success. From being a mobile lunch counter, she set up a stand between the two points of fiscal interest and supplied the workers' needs for a few years. Then she had the Store built in the heart of the Negro area. Over the years it became the lay center of activities in town. On Saturdays, barbers sat their customers in the shade on the porch of the Store, and troubadours on their ceaseless crawlings through the South leaned across their benches and sang their sad songs of The Brazos while they played juice harps and cigar-box guitars.

The formal name of the Store was the Wm. Johnson General Merchandise Store. Customers could find food staples, a good variety of colored thread, mash for hogs, corn for chickens, coal oil for lamps, light bulbs for the wealthy, shoestrings, hair dressing, balloons, and flower seeds. Anything not visible had only to be ordered.

Until we became familiar enough to belong to the Store and it to us, we were locked up in a Fun House of Things where the attendant had gone home for life.

Each year I watched the field across from the Store turn caterpillar green, then gradually frosty white. I knew exactly how long it would be before the big wagons would pull into the front yard and load on the cotton pickers at daybreak to carry them to the remains of slavery's plantations.

During the picking season my grandmother would get out of bed at four o'clock (she never used an alarm clock) and creak down to her knees and chant in a sleep-filled voice, "Our Father, thank you for letting me see this New Day. Thank you that you didn't allow the bed I lay on last night to be my cooling board, nor my blanket my winding sheet. Guide my feet this day along the straight and narrow, and help me to put a bridle on my tongue. Bless this house, and everybody in it. Thank you, in the name of your Son, Jesus Christ, Amen."

Before she had quite arisen, she called our names and issued orders, and pushed her large feet into homemade slippers and across the bare lye-washed wooden floor to light the coal-oil lamp.

The lamplight in the Store gave a soft make-believe feeling to our world which made me want to whisper and walk about on tiptoe. The odors of onions and oranges and kerosene had been mixing all night and wouldn't be disturbed until the wooded slat was removed from the door and the early morning air forced its way in with the bodies of people who had walked miles to reach the pickup place.

"Sister, I'll have two cans of sardines."

"I'm gonna work so fast today I'm gonna make you look like you standing still."

"Lemme have a hunk uh cheese and some sody crackers."

"Just gimme a coupla them fat peanut paddies." That would be from a picker who was taking his lunch. The greasy brown paper sack was stuck behind the bib of his overalls. He'd use the candy as a snack before the noon sun called the workers to rest.

In those tender mornings the Store was full of laughing, joking, boasting and bragging. One man was going to pick two hundred pounds of cotton, and another three hundred. Even the children were promising to bring home fo' bits and six bits.

The champion picker of the day before was the hero of the dawn. If he prophesied that the cotton in to-day's field was going to be sparse and stick to the bolls like glue, every listener would grunt a hearty agreement.

The sound of the empty cotton sacks dragging over the floor and the murmurs of waking people were sliced by the cash register as we rang up the five-cent sales.

If the morning sounds and smells were touched with the supernatural, the late afternoon had all the features of the normal Arkansas life. In the dying sunlight the people dragged, rather than their empty cotton sacks.

Brought back to the Store, the pickers would step out of the backs of trucks and fold down, dirt-disappointed, to the ground. No matter how much they had picked, it wasn't enough. Their wages wouldn't even get them out of debt to my grand-mother, not to mention the staggering bill that waited on them at the white commissary downtown.

The sounds of the new morning had been replaced with grumbles about cheating houses, weighted scales, snakes, skimpy cotton and dusty rows. In later years I was to confront the stereotyped picture of gay song-singing cotton pickers with such inordinate rage that I was told even by fellow Blacks that my paranoia[3] was embarrassing. But I had seen the fingers cut by the mean little cotton bolls, and I had witnessed the backs and shoulders and arms and legs resisting any further demands.

Some of the workers would leave their sacks at the Store to be picked up the following morning, but a few had to take them home for repairs. I winced to picture them sewing the coarse material under a coal-oil lamp with fingers stiffening from the day's work. In too few hours they would have to walk back to Sister Henderson's Store, get vittles and load, again, onto the trucks. Then they would face another day of trying to earn enough for the whole year with the heavy knowledge that they were going to end the season as they started it. Without the money or credit necessary to sustain a family for three months. In cotton-picking time the late afternoons revealed the harshness of Black Southern life, which in the early morning had been softened by nature's blessing of

3 paranoia: feelings of extreme persecution.

grogginess, forgetfulness and the soft lamplight.

＊　　＊　　＊

Weighing the half-pounds of flour, excluding the scoop, and depositing them dust-free into the thin paper sacks held a simple kind of adventure for me. I developed an eye for measuring how full a silver-looking ladle of flour, mash, meal, sugar or corn had to be to push the scale indicator over to eight ounces or one pound. When I was absolutely accurate our appreciative customers used to admire: "Sister Henderson sure got some smart grandchildrens." If I was off in the Store's favor, the eagle-eyed women would say, "Put some more in that sack, child. Don't you try to make your profit offa me."

Then I would quietly but persistently punish myself. For every bad judgment, the fine was no silver-wrapped Kisses, the sweet chocolate drops that I loved more than anything in the world, except Bailey. And maybe canned pineapples. My obsession with pineapples nearly drove me mad. I dreamt of the days when I would be grown and able to buy a whole carton for myself alone.

Although the syrupy golden rings sat in their exotic cans on our shelves year round, we only tasted them during Christmas. Momma used the juice to make almost-black fruit cakes. Then she lined heavy soot-encrusted iron skillets with the pineapple rings for rich upside-down cakes. Bailey and I received one slice each, and I carried mine around for hours, shredding off the fruit

until nothing was left except the perfume on my fingers. I'd like to think that my desire for pineapples was so sacred that I wouldn't allow myself to steal a can (which was possible) and eat it alone out in the garden, but I'm certain that I must have weighed the possibility of the scent exposing me and didn't have the nerve to attempt it.

Until I was thirteen and left Arkansas for good, the Store was my favorite place to be. Alone and empty in the mornings, it looked like an unopened present from a stranger. Opening the front doors was pulling the ribbon off the unexpected gift. The light would come in softly (we faced north), easing itself over the shelves of mackerel, salmon, tobacco, thread. It fell flat on the big vat of lard and by noontime during the summer the grease had softened to a thick soup. Whenever I walked into the Store in the afternoon, I sensed that it was tired. I alone could hear the slow pulse of its job half done. But just before bedtime, after numerous people had walked in and out, had argued over their bills, or joked about their neighbors, or just dropped in "to give Sister Henderson a 'Hi y'all,'" the promise of magic mornings returned to the Store and spread itself over the family in washed life waves.

Momma opened boxes of crispy crackers and we sat around the meat block at the rear of the Store. I sliced onions, and Bailey opened two or even three cans of sardines and allowed their juice of oil and fishing boats to ooze down and around the sides. That was supper. In the evening, when we were alone like that, Uncle Willie didn't stutter or shake or give any indication that he had an "affliction." It seemed that the peace of a day's ending was an assurance that the covenant God made with children, Negroes and the crippled was still in effect.

Throwing scoops of corn to the chickens and mixing sour dry mash with leftover food and oily dish water for the hogs were among our evening chores. Bailey and I sloshed down twilight trails to the pig pens, and standing on the first fence rungs we poured down the unappealing concoctions to our grateful hogs. They mashed their tender pink snouts down into the slop, and rooted and grunted their satisfaction. We always grunted a reply only half in jest. We were also grateful that we had concluded the dirtiest of chores and had only gotten the evil-smelling swill on our shoes, stockings, feet and hands.

❊   ❊   ❊

"Thou shall not be dirty" and "Thou shall not be impudent"[4] were the two commandments of Grandmother Henderson upon which hung our total salvation.

Each night in the bitterest winter we were forced to wash faces, arms, necks, legs and feet before going to bed. She used to add, with a smirk that unprofane people can't control when venturing into profanity, "and wash as far as possible, then wash possible."

We would go to the well and wash in the ice-cold clear water, grease our legs with the equally cold stiff Vaseline, then tiptoe into the house. We wiped the dust from our toes and settled down for schoolwork, cornbread, clabbered milk, prayers and bed, always in that order. Momma was famous for pulling the quilts off after we had fallen asleep to examine our feet. If they weren't clean enough for her, she took the switch (she kept one behind the bedroom door for emergencies) and woke up the offender with a few aptly placed burning reminders.

The area around the well at night was dark and slick, and boys told about how snakes love water, so that anyone who had to draw water at night and then stand there alone and wash knew that moccasins and rattlers, puff adders and boa constrictors were winding their way to the well and would arrive just as the person washing got soap in her eyes. But Momma convinced us that not only was cleanliness next to Godliness, dirtiness was the inventor of misery.

The impudent child was detested by God and a shame to its parents and could bring destruction to its house and line. All adults had to be addressed as Mister, Missus, Miss, Auntie, Cousin, Unk, Uncle, Buhbah, Sister, Brother and a thousand other appellations indicating familial relationship and the lowliness of the addressor.

❊   ❊   ❊

4 **impudent:** impertinent, smart-alecky.

[Bailey and Marguerite went to live with their Mother in St. Louis. But after a brief time they returned to Stamps, Arkansas.]

For nearly a year, I sopped around the house, the Store, the school and the church, like an old biscuit, dirty and inedible. Then I met, or rather got to know, the lady who threw me my first life line.

Mrs. Bertha Flowers was the aristocrat of Black Stamps. She had the grace of control to appear warm in the coldest weather, and on the Arkansas summer days it seemed she had a private breeze which swirled around, cooling her. She was thin without the taut look of wiry people, and her printed voile dresses and flowered hats were as right for her as denim overalls for a farmer. She was our side's answer to the richest white woman in town.

Her skin was a rich black that would have peeled like a plum if snagged, but then no one would have thought of getting close enough to Mrs. Flowers to ruffle her dress, let alone snag her skin. She didn't encourage familiarity. She wore gloves too.

I don't think I ever saw Mrs. Flowers laugh, but she smiled often. A slow widening of her thin black lips to show even, small white teeth, then the slow effortless closing. When she chose to smile on me, I always wanted to thank her. The action was so graceful and inclusively benign.

She was one of the few gentlewomen I have ever known, and has remained throughout my life the measure of what a human being can be.

Momma had a strange relationship with her. Most often when she passed on the road in front of the Store, she spoke to Momma in that soft yet carrying voice, "Good day, Mrs. Henderson." Momma responded with "How you, Sister Flowers?"

Mrs. Flowers didn't belong to our church, nor was she Momma's familiar. Why on earth did she insist on calling her Sister Flowers? Shame made me want to hide my face. Mrs. Flowers deserved better than to be called Sister. Then, Momma left out the verb. Why not ask, "How *are* you, *Mrs.* Flowers?" With the unbalanced passion of the young, I hated her for showing her ignorance to Mrs. Flowers. It didn't occur to me for many years that they were as alike as sisters, separated only by formal education. . . .

She appealed to me because she was like people I had never met personally. Like women in English novels who walked the moors (whatever they were) with their loyal dogs racing at a respectful distance. Like the women who sat in front of roaring fireplaces, drinking tea incessantly from silver trays full of scones and crumpets. Women who walked over the "heath" and read moroccobound books and had two last names divided by a hyphen. It would be safe to say that she made me proud to be Negro, just by being herself.

She acted just as refined as whitefolks in the movies and books and she was more beautiful, for none of them could have come near that warm color without looking gray by comparison.

It was fortunate that I never saw her in the company of powhitefolks.[5] For since they tend to think of their whiteness as an evenizer, I'm certain that I would have had to hear her spoken to commonly as Bertha, and my image of her would have been shattered like the unmendable Humpty-Dumpty.

One summer afternoon, sweetmilk fresh in my memory, she stopped at the Store to buy provisions. Another Negro woman of her health and age would have been expected to carry the paper sacks home in one hand, but Momma said, "Sister Flowers, I'll send Bailey up to your house with these things."

She smiled that slow dragging smile, "Thank you, Mrs. Henderson. I'd prefer Marguerite, though." My name was beautiful when she said it. "I've been meaning to talk to her, anyway." They gave each other age-group looks.

Momma said, "Well, that's all right then. Sister, go and change your dress. You going to Sister Flowers's."

The chifforobe was a maze. What on earth did one put on to go to Mrs. Flowers' house? I knew I shouldn't put on a Sunday dress. It might be sacrilegious. Certainly not a house dress, since I was already wearing a fresh one. I chose a school dress, naturally. It was formal without suggesting that going to Mrs. Flowers' house was equivalent to attending church.

5 **powhitefolks:** poor whites.

I trusted myself back into the Store.

"Now, don't you look nice." I had chosen the right thing, for once.

"Mrs. Henderson, you make most of the children's clothes, don't you?"

"Yes, ma'am. Sure do. Store-bought clothes ain't hardly worth the thread it take to stitch them."

"I'll say you do a lovely job, though, so neat. That dress looks professional."

Momma was enjoying the seldom-received compliments. Since everyone we knew (except Mrs. Flowers, of course) could sew competently, praise was rarely handed out for the commonly practiced craft.

"I try, with the help of the Lord, Sister Flowers, to finish the inside just like I does the outside. Come here, Sister."

I had buttoned up the collar and tied the belt, apron-like, in back. Momma told me to turn around. With one hand she pulled the strings and the belt fell free at both sides of my waist. Then her large hands were at my neck, opening the button loops. I was terrified. What was happening?

"Take it off, Sister." She had her hands on the hem of the dress.

"I don't need to see the inside, Mrs. Henderson, I can tell . . ." But the dress was over my head and my arms were stuck in the sleeves. Momma said, "That'll do. See here, Sister Flowers, I French-seams around the armholes." Through the cloth film, I saw the shadow approach. "That makes it last longer. Children these days would bust out of sheet-metal clothes. They so rough."

"That is a very good job, Mrs. Henderson. You should be proud. You can put your dress back on, Marguerite."

"No, ma'am. Pride is a sin. And 'cording to the Good Book, it goeth before a fall."

"That's right. So the Bible says. It's a good thing to keep in mind."

I wouldn't look at either of them. Momma hadn't thought that taking off my dress in front of Mrs. Flowers would kill me stone dead. If I had refused, she would have thought I was trying to be "womanish".... Mrs. Flowers had known that I would be embarrassed and that was even worse. I picked up the groceries and went out to wait in the hot sunshine. It would be fitting if I got a sunstroke and died before they came outside. Just dropped dead on the slanting porch.

There was a little path beside the rocky road, and Mrs. Flowers walked in front swinging her arms and picking her way over the stones.

She said, without turning her head, to me, "I hear you're doing very good school work, Marguerite, but that it's all written. The teachers report that they have trouble getting you to talk in class." We passed the triangular farm on our left and the path widened to allow us to walk together. I hung back in the separate unasked and unanswerable questions.

"Come and walk along with me, Marguerite." I couldn't have refused even if I wanted to. She pronounced

my name so nicely. Or more correctly, she spoke each word with such clarity that I was certain a foreigner who didn't understand English could have understood her.

"Now no one is going to make you talk—possibly no one can. But bear in mind, language is man's way of communicating with his fellow man and it is language alone which separates him from the lower animals." That was a totally new idea to me, and I would need time to think about it.

"Your grandmother says you read a lot. Every chance you get. That's good, but not good enough. Words mean more than what is set down on paper. It takes the human voice to infuse[6] them with the shades of deeper meaning."

I memorized the part about the human voice infusing words. It seemed so valid and poetic.

She said she was going to give me some books and that I not only must read them, I must read them aloud. She suggested that I try to make a sentence sound in as many different ways as possible.

"I'll accept no excuse if you return a book to me that has been badly handled." My imagination boggled at the punishment I would deserve if in fact I did abuse a book of Mrs. Flowers'. Death would be too kind and brief.

The odors in the house surprised me. Somehow I had never connected Mrs. Flowers with food or eating or any other common experi-

6 infuse: fill with (a quality).

BIOGRAPHY

ence of common people. There must have been an outhouse, too, but my mind never recorded it.

The sweet scent of vanilla had met us as she opened the door.

"I made tea cookies this morning. You see, I had planned to invite you for cookies and lemonade so we could have this little chat. The lemonade is in the icebox."

It followed that Mrs. Flowers would have ice on an ordinary day, when most families in our town bought ice late on Saturdays only a few times during the summer to be used in the wooden ice-cream freezers.

She took the bags from me and disappeared through the kitchen door. I looked around the room that I had never in my wildest fantasies imagined I would see. Browned photographs leered or threatened from the walls and the white, freshly done curtains pushed against themselves and against the wind. I wanted to gobble up the room entire and take it to Bailey, who would help me analyze and enjoy it.

"Have a seat, Marguerite. Over there by the table." She carried a platter covered with a tea towel. Although she warned that she hadn't tried her hand at baking sweets for some time, I was certain that like everything else about her the cookies would be perfect.

They were flat round wafers, slightly browned on the edges and butter-yellow in the center. With the cold lemonade they were sufficient for childhood's lifelong diet. Remembering my manners, I took

nice little lady-like bites off the edges. She said she had made them expressly for me and that she had a few in the kitchen that I could take home to my brother. So I jammed one whole cake in my mouth and the rough crumbs scratched the insides of my jaws, and if I hadn't had to swallow, it would have been a dream come true.

As I ate she began the first of what we later called "my lessons in living." She said that I must always be intolerant of ignorance but understanding of illiteracy. That some people, unable to go to school, were more educated and even more intelligent than college professors. She encouraged me to listen carefully to what country people called mother wit. That in those homely sayings was couched the collective wisdom of generations.

When I finished the cookies she brushed off the table and brought a thick, small book from the bookcase. I had read *A Tale of Two Cities* and found it up to my standards as a romantic novel. She opened the first page and I heard poetry for the first time in my life.

"It was the best of times and the worst of times . . ." Her voice slid in and curved down through and over the words. She was nearly singing. I wanted to look at the pages. Were they the same that I had read? Or were there notes, music, lined on the pages, as in a hymn book? Her sounds began cascading gently. I knew from listening to a thousand preachers that she was nearing the end of her reading, and I hadn't really heard, heard to understand, a single word.

"How do you like that?"

It occurred to me that she expected a response. The sweet vanilla flavor was still on my tongue and her reading was a wonder in my ears. I had to speak.

I said, "Yes, ma'am." It was the least I could do, but it was the most also.

"There's one more thing. Take this book of poems and memorize one for me. Next time you pay me a visit, I want you to recite."

I have tried often to search behind the sophistication of years for the enchantment I so easily found in those gifts. The essence escapes but its aura remains. To be allowed, no, invited, into the private lives of strangers, and to share their joys and fears, was a chance to exchange the Southern bitter wormwood for a cup of mead with Beowulf or a hot cup of tea and milk with Oliver Twist. When I said aloud, "It is a far, far better thing that I do, than I have ever done . . ." tears of love filled my eyes at my selflessness.

On that first day, I ran down the hill and into the road (few cars ever came along it) and had the good sense to stop running before I reached the Store.

I was liked, and what a difference it made. I was respected not as Mrs. Henderson's grandchild or Bailey's sister but for just being Marguerite Johnson.

Reading Skills

1. How were Maya and Bailey treated on their trip south? Cite lines which support your answer.

2. How were the children received in Stamps and how did they like their new home? Account for the following statement in your answer: "Until we became familiar enough to belong to the Store and it to us, we were locked up in a Fun House of Things where the attendant had gone home for life."

3. Describe "Sister" Henderson (or "Momma," the author's grandmother), citing details from the selection to support your description of her personality. What did the children think of her? the townspeople?

4. According to the author, what was life like for her people "in cotton-picking time"?

5. What were Grandmother Henderson's two commandments? How were the children's lives affected by these two commandments?

6. Upon returning from St. Louis, Maya Angelou met "the lady who threw me my first life line." Who was this person and what does Angelou mean by describing her in such a way?

7. What were young Maya's "lessons in living"? What impact did they have on her feelings toward herself?

Understanding Literature

1. What was Uncle Willie's "affliction"? How did it affect the way he got along with people? Was the Uncle Willie the community knew the same Willie that his family saw? How do you account for the difference?

2. At the end of the Uncle Willie episode, the author writes: "It seemed that the peace of a day's ending was an assurance that the covenant God made with children, Negroes and the crippled was still in effect." Look up any unfamiliar words in this quotation; then explain what it means in the context of the story. Or, describe what the quotation means to you and then illustrate it with an incident from your life. (If it seems to fit, use dialogue in your composition.)

Helen Keller lost her sight and her hearing because of illness at the age of nineteen months. For several years, unable to communicate with other people except through touch, she lived a miserable, empty life. Then a teacher, Anne Mansfield Sullivan, so nearly blind herself that she was a graduate of a school for the blind, came to the Keller home. After her coming, life was never again meaningless for Helen Keller.

Miss Keller graduated from Radcliffe College with honors. She has made lecture tours throughout the world and has written several books. You may have seen the play or the movie, *The Miracle Worker*, written about her and Miss Sullivan. Helen Keller's life has been an inspiration to everyone who has heard about it.

How I Learned to Speak

Helen Keller

IMPROVING YOUR READING: In this selection from Helen Keller's autobiography, *The Story of My Life*, Miss Keller tells about how she learned to associate a word with a thing, then with an idea, and, finally, how she learned to speak. In order to express the feelings which these accomplishments aroused in her, she often uses comparisons. As you read, notice especially the comparisons which convey her feelings of new-found freedom and release.

THE MOST IMPORTANT DAY I remember in all my life is the one on which my teacher, Anne Mansfield Sullivan, came to me. I am filled with wonder when I consider the immeasurable contrasts between the two lives which it connects. It was the third of March, 1887, three months before I was seven years old.

On the afternoon of that eventful day, I stood on the porch, dumb, expectant. I guessed vaguely from my mother's signs and from the hurrying to and fro in the house that something unusual was about to happen, so I went to the door and waited on the steps. The afternoon sun penetrated the mass of honeysuckle that covered the porch, and fell on my upturned face. My fingers lingered almost unconsciously on the familiar leaves and blossoms which had just come forth to greet the sweet southern spring. I did not know what the future held of marvel or surprise for me. Anger and bitterness had preyed upon me continually for weeks and a deep languor had succeeded this passionate struggle.

Have you ever been at sea in a dense fog, when it seemed as if a tangible white darkness shut you in, and the great ship, tense and anxious, groped her way toward the shore with plummet and sounding-line,[1] and you waited with beating heart for something to happen? I was like that ship before my education began, only I was without compass or sounding-line, and had no way of knowing how near the harbor was. "Light! give me light!" was the wordless cry of my soul, and the light of love shone on me in that very hour.

I felt approaching footsteps. I stretched out my hand as I supposed to my mother. Someone took it, and I was caught up and held close in the arms of her who had come to reveal all things to me, and, more than all things else, to love me.

The morning after my teacher came she led me into her room and gave me a doll. The little blind children at the Perkins Institution[2] had sent it and Laura Bridgman[3] had dressed it; but I did not know this until afterward. When I had played with it a little while, Miss Sullivan slowly spelled into my hand the word "d-o-l-l." I was at once interested in this finger play and tried to imitate it. When I finally succeeded in making the letters correctly I was flushed with childish pleasure and pride. Running downstairs to my mother I held up my hand and made the letters for doll. I did not know that I was spelling a word or even that words existed; I was simply making my fingers go in monkeylike imitation. In the days that followed I learned to spell in this uncomprehending way a great many words, among them *pin, hat, cup* and a few verbs like *sit, stand,* and *walk.* But my teacher had been with me several weeks before I understood that everything has a name.

One day, while I was playing with my new doll, Miss Sullivan put my big rag doll into my lap also, spelled "d-o-l-l" and tried to make me understand that "d-o-l-l" applied to both. Earlier in the day we had had a tussle over the words "m-u-g" and "w-a-t-e-r." Miss Sullivan had tried to impress it upon me that "m-u-g" is *mug* and that "w-a-t-e-r" is *water,* but I persisted in confounding the two. In despair she had dropped the subject for the time, only to renew it at the first opportunity. I became impatient at her repeated attempts and, seizing the new doll, I dashed it upon the floor. I was keenly delighted when I felt the fragments of the broken doll at my feet. Neither sorrow nor regret followed my passionate outburst. I had not loved the doll. In the still, dark world in which I lived there was no strong sentiment or tenderness. I felt my teacher sweep the fragments to one side of the hearth, and I had a sense of satisfaction that the cause of my discomfort was removed. She brought me my hat, and I knew I was going out into the warm sunshine. This thought, if a wordless sensation may be called a

---

1 **sounding-line:** a wire or cord line with a weight (a plummet) on it, used for determining depth.
2 **Perkins Institution:** a school for the blind, near Boston, where Anne Sullivan was a pupil.
3 **Laura Bridgman:** the first blind deaf-mute to be successfully educated; she was a student at the Perkins Institution.

thought, made me hop and skip with pleasure.

We walked down the path to the well house, attracted by the fragrance of the honeysuckle with which it was covered. Someone was drawing water and my teacher placed my hand under the spout. As the cool stream gushed over one hand she spelled into the other the word *water*, first slowly, then rapidly. I stood still, my whole attention fixed upon the motions of her fingers. Suddenly I felt a misty consciousness as of something forgotten —a thrill of returning thought; and somehow the mystery of language was revealed to me. I knew then that "w-a-t-e-r" meant the wonderful cool something that was flowing over my hand. That living word awakened my soul, gave it light,

hope, joy, set it free! There were barriers still, it is true, but barriers that could in time be swept away.

I left the well house eager to learn. Everything had a name, and each name gave birth to a new thought. As we returned to the house every object which I touched seemed to quiver with life. That was because I saw everything with the strange, new sight that had come to me. On entering the door I remembered the doll I had broken. I felt my way to the hearth and picked up the pieces. I tried vainly to put them together. Then my eyes filled with tears; for I realized what I had done, and for the first time I felt repentance and sorrow.

I learned a great many new words that day. I do not remember what they all were; but I do know that *mother, father, sister, teacher* were among them—words that were to make the world blossom for me, "like Aaron's rod, with flowers." It would have been difficult to find a happier child than I was as I lay in my crib at the close of that eventful day and lived over the joys it had brought me, and for the first time longed for a new day to come. . . .

I had now the key to all language, and I was eager to learn to use it. Children who hear acquire language without any particular effort; the words that fall from others' lips they catch on the wing, as it were, delightedly, while the little deaf child must trap them by a slow and often painful process. But whatever the process, the result is wonderful. Gradually from naming an object we advance step by step until we have traversed the vast distance between our first stammered syllable and the sweep of thought in a line of Shakespeare.

At first, when my teacher told me about a new thing I asked very few questions. My ideas were vague, and my vocabulary was inadequate; but as my knowledge of things grew, and I learned more and more words, my field of inquiry broadened, and I would return again and again to the same subject, eager for further information. Sometimes a new word revived an image that some earlier experience had engraved on my brain.

I remember the morning that I first asked the meaning of the word *love*. This was before I knew many words. I had found a few early violets in the garden and brought them to my teacher. She tried to kiss me: but at that time I did not like to have anyone kiss me except my mother. Miss Sullivan put her arm gently round me and spelled into my hand, "I love Helen."

"What is love?" I asked.

She drew me closer to her and said, "It is here," pointing to my heart, whose beats I was conscious of for the first time. Her words puzzled me very much because I did not then understand anything unless I touched it.

I smelt the violets in her hand and asked, half in words, half in signs, a question which meant, "Is love the sweetness of flowers?"

"No," said my teacher.

Again I thought. The warm sun was shining on us.

"Is this not love?" I asked, pointing in the direction from which the heat came. "Is this not love?"

It seemed to me that there could be nothing more beautiful than the sun, whose warmth makes all things grow. But Miss Sullivan shook her head, and I was greatly puzzled and disappointed. I thought it strange that my teacher could not show me love.

A day or two afterward I was stringing beads of different sizes in symmetrical groups—two large beads, three small ones, and so on. I had made many mistakes, and Miss Sullivan had pointed them out again and again with gentle patience. Finally I noticed a very obvious error in the sequence and for an instant

I concentrated my attention on the lesson and tried to think how I should have arranged the beads. Miss Sullivan touched my forehead and spelled with decided emphasis, "Think."

In a flash I knew that the word was the name of the process that was going on in my head. This was my first conscious perception of an abstract idea.

For a long time I was still—I was not thinking of the beads in my lap, but trying to find a meaning for "love" in the light of this new idea. The sun had been under a cloud all day, and there had been brief showers; but suddenly the sun broke forth in all its southern splendor.

Again I asked my teacher, "Is this not love?"

"Love is something like the clouds that were in the sky before the sun came out," she replied. Then in simpler words than these, which at that time I could not have understood, she explained: "You cannot touch the clouds, you know; but you feel the rain and know how glad the flowers and the thirsty earth are to have it after a hot day. You cannot touch love either; but you feel the sweetness that it pours into everything. Without love you would not be happy or want to play."

The beautiful truth burst upon my mind—I felt that there were invisible lines stretched between my spirit and the spirits of others.

From the beginning of my education Miss Sullivan made it a practice to speak to me as she would speak to any hearing child; the only difference was that she spelled the sentences into my hand instead of speaking them. If I did not know the words and idioms necessary to express my thoughts she supplied them, even suggesting conversation when I was unable to keep up my end of the dialogue.

This process was continued for several years; for the deaf child does not learn in a month, or even in two or three years, the numberless idioms and expressions used in the simplest daily intercourse. The little hearing child learns these from constant repetition and imitation. The conversation he hears in his home stimulates his mind and suggests topics and calls forth the spontaneous expression of his own thoughts. This natural exchange of ideas is denied to the deaf child. My teacher, realizing this, determined to supply the kinds of stimulus I lacked. This she did by repeating to me as far as possible, verbatim, what she heard, and by showing me how I could take part in the conversation. But it was a long time before I ventured to take the initiative, and still longer before I could find something appropriate to say at the right time.

The deaf and the blind find it very difficult to acquire the amenities of conversation. How much more this difficulty must be augmented in the case of those who are both deaf and blind! They cannot distinguish the tone of the voice or, without assistance, go up and down the gamut of tones that give significance to words; nor can they watch the expression of the speaker's face, and a look is often the very soul of what one says. . . .

It was in the spring of 1890 that I learned to speak. The impulse to utter audible sounds had always been strong within me. I used to make noises, keeping one hand on my throat while the other hand felt the movements of my lips. I was pleased with anything that made a noise and liked to feel the cat purr and the dog bark. I also liked to keep my hand on a singer's throat, or on a piano when it was being played. Before I lost my sight and hearing, I was fast learning to talk, but after my illness it was found that I had ceased to speak because I could not hear. I used to sit in my mother's lap all day long and keep my hands on her face because it amused me to feel the motions of her lips; and I moved my lips, too, although I had forgotten what talking was. My friends say that I laughed and cried naturally, and for awhile I made many sounds and word-elements, not because they were a means of communication, but because the need of exercising my vocal organs was imperative. There was, however, one word the meaning of which I still remembered, water. I pronounced it "wa-wa." Even this became less and less intelligible until the time when Miss Sullivan began to teach me. I stopped using it only after I had learned to spell the word on my fingers.

I had known for a long time that the people about me used a method of communication different from mine; and even before I knew that a deaf child could be taught to speak, I was conscious of dissatisfaction with the means of communication I already possessed. One who is entirely dependent upon the manual alphabet has always a sense of restraint, of narrowness. This feeling began to agitate me with a vexing, forward-reaching sense of a lack that should be filled. My thoughts would often rise and beat up like birds against the wind; and I persisted in using my lips and voice. Friends tried to discourage this tendency, fearing lest it would lead to disappointment. But I persisted, and an accident soon occurred which resulted in the breaking down of this great barrier—I heard the story of Ragnhild Kaata.

In 1890 Mrs. Lamson, who had been one of Laura Bridgman's teachers, and who had just returned from a visit to Norway and Sweden, came to see me, and told me of Ragnhild Kaata, a deaf and blind girl in Norway who had actually been taught to speak. Mrs. Lamson had scarcely finished telling me about this girl's success before I was on fire with eagerness. I resolved that I, too, would learn to speak. I would not rest satisfied until my teacher took me, for advice and assistance, to Miss Sarah Fuller, principal of the Horace Mann School. This lovely, sweet-natured lady offered to teach me herself, and we began the twenty-sixth of March, 1890.

Miss Fuller's method was this: she passed my hand lightly over her face, and let me feel the position of her tongue and lips when she made a sound. I was eager to imitate every motion and in an hour had learned six elements of speech: M, P, A, S, T, I. Miss Fuller gave me eleven lessons in all. I shall never forget the surprise and delight I felt when I uttered my first connected sentence, "It is warm." True, they were broken and stammering syllables; but they were human speech. My soul, conscious of new strength, came out of bondage, and was reaching through those broken symbols of speech to all knowledge and all faith.

No deaf child who has earnestly tried to speak the words which he has never heard—to come out of the prison of silence, where no tone of love, no song of bird, no strain of music ever pierces the stillness—can forget the thrill of surprise, the joy of discovery which came over him when he uttered his first word. Only such a one can appreciate the eagerness with which I talked to my toys, to stones, trees, birds and dumb animals, or the delight I felt when at my call Mildred[4] ran to me or my dogs obeyed my commands. It is an unspeakable boon to me to be able to speak in winged words that need no interpretation. As I talked, happy thoughts fluttered up out of my words that might perhaps have struggled in vain to escape my fingers.

But it must not be supposed that I could really talk in this short time. I had learned only the elements of

4 Mildred: Helen Keller's younger sister.

speech. Miss Fuller and Miss Sullivan could understand me, but most people would not have understood one word in a hundred. Nor is it true that, after I had learned these elements, I did the rest of the work myself. But for Miss Sullivan's genius, untiring perseverance and devotion, I could not have progressed as far as I have toward natural speech. In the first place, I labored night and day before I could be understood even by my most intimate friends; in the second place, I needed Miss Sullivan's assistance constantly in my efforts to articulate each sound clearly and to combine all sounds in a thousand ways. Even now she calls my attention every day to mispronounced words.

All teachers of the deaf know what this means, and only they can at all appreciate the peculiar difficulties with which I had to contend. In reading my teacher's lips I was wholly dependent on my fingers: I had to use the sense of touch in catching the vibrations of the throat, the movements of the mouth and the expression of the face; and often this sense was at fault. In such cases I was forced to repeat the words or sentences, sometimes for hours, until I felt the proper ring in my own voice. My work was practice, practice, practice. Discouragement and weariness cast me down frequently; but the next moment the thought that I should soon be at home and show my loved ones what I had accomplished, spurred me on, and I eagerly looked forward to their pleasure in my achievement.

"My little sister will understand

me now," was a thought stronger than all obstacles. I used to repeat ecstatically, "I am not dumb now." I could not be despondent while I anticipated the delight of talking to my mother and reading her responses from her lips. It astonished me to find how much easier it is to talk than to spell with the fingers, and I discarded the manual alphabet as a medium of communication on my part; but Miss Sullivan and a few friends still use it in speaking to me, for it is more convenient and more rapid than lip reading.

Just here, perhaps, I had better explain our use of the manual alphabet, which seems to puzzle people who do not know us. One who reads or talks to me spells with his hand, using the single-hand manual alphabet generally employed by the deaf. I place my hand on the hand of the speaker so lightly as not to impede its movements. The position of the hand is as easy to feel as it is to see. I do not feel each letter any more than you see each letter separately when you read. Constant practice makes the fingers very flexible, and

some of my friends spell rapidly— about as fast as an expert writes on a typewriter. The mere spelling is, of course, no more a conscious act than it is in writing.

When I had made speech my own, I could not wait to go home. At last the happiest of happy moments arrived. I had made my homeward journey, talking constantly to Miss Sullivan, not for the sake of talking, but determined to improve to the last minute. Almost before I knew it, the train stopped at the Tuscumbia station, and there on the platform stood the whole family. My eyes fill with tears now as I think how my mother pressed me close to her, speechless and trembling with delight, taking in every syllable that I spoke, while little Mildred seized my free hand and kissed it and danced, and my father expressed his pride and affection in a big silence. It was as if Isaiah's prophecy had been fulfilled in me, "The mountains and the hills shall break forth before you into singing, and all the trees of the field shall clap their hands!"

1. How did the small Helen, unable to see or hear, know that something unusual was about to happen in her house?
2. After Helen learned the first word that Miss Sullivan spelled out in her hand, how long was it before she understood that the word was the name of the article she held and that all things had names? What change in Helen's attitude did this understanding bring about?
3. Why was the word *love* a difficult one to understand?
4. How did Helen learn to speak? What new kinds of experience did the ability to speak bring her?
5. Find illustrations of Miss Sullivan's patience and wisdom.
6. How does this selection prove the relationship between language and the ability to think?

Understanding Literature

In each of the following comparisons, what things are compared? How are they alike?

1. "Children who hear acquire language without any particular effort; the words that fall from others' lips they catch on the wing, as it were, delightedly, while the little deaf child must trap them by a slow and painful process."
2. "My thoughts would often rise and beat up like birds against the wind."
3. "My soul, conscious of new strength, came out of bondage."
4. "As I talked, happy thoughts fluttered up out of my words."

Further Activity

Write a description using only one sense—hearing, smell, sight, or touch. Make the description as vivid as you can. If you wish to use hearing, smell, or touch, you might close your eyes and concentrate on listening, smelling, or touching things; then describe your sensations, using comparisons whenever possible.

Wolcott Gibbs was for many years on the staff of *The New Yorker* magazine. He had so many talents that he could do almost everything required of anyone on the staff, and do it well; he wrote hundreds of different kinds of pieces and provided ideas for cartoons. During his later years he was one of the best drama critics of his time.

In "Ring Out, Wild Bells" he recalls some of his own acting experience—a memorable production of *A Midsummer Night's Dream*. As Puck, "the incarnation of mischief," he gave a performance at once perplexing to the actors and hilarious to the audience.

Ring Out, Wild Bells

Wolcott Gibbs

WHEN I FINALLY GOT around to seeing Max Reinhardt's cinema version of *A Midsummer Night's Dream*, and saw a child called Mickey Rooney playing Puck, I remembered suddenly that long ago I had taken the same part.

Our production was given on the open-air stage at the Riverdale Country School, shortly before the war. The scenery was only the natural scenery of that suburban dell, and the cast was exclusively male, ranging in age from eleven to perhaps seventeen. While we had thus preserved the pure, Elizabethan note[1] of the original, it must be ad-

mitted that our version had its drawbacks. The costumes were probably the worst things we had to bear, and even Penrod,[2] tragically arrayed as Lancelot in his sister's stockings and his father's drawers, might have been embarrassed for us. Like Penrod, we were costumed by our parents, and like the Schofields, they seemed on the whole a little weak historically. Half of the ladies were inclined to favor the Elizabethan, and clined to favor the Elizabethan, and

1 the pure, Elizabethan note: Women did not perform in plays in Elizabethan England; boys played women's parts.
2 Penrod: Penrod Schofield is the child hero of the novel *Penrod* by Booth Tarkington.

BIOGRAPHY

they had constructed rather bunchy ruffs and farthingales[3] for their offspring; others, who had read as far as the stage directions and learned that the action took place in an Athenian wood, had produced something vaguely Athenian, usually beginning with a sheet. Only the fairies had a certain uniformity. For some reason their parents had all decided on cheesecloth, with here and there a little ill-advised trimming with tinsel.

My own costume was mysterious, but spectacular. As nearly as I have ever been able to figure things out, my mother found her inspiration for it in a Maxfield Parrish picture of a court jester. Beginning at the top, there was a cap with three stuffed horns; then, for the main part, a pair of tights that covered me to my wrists and ankles; and finally slippers with stuffed toes that curled up at the ends. The whole thing was made out of silk in alternate green and red stripes, and (unquestionably my poor mother's most demented stroke) it was covered from head to foot with a thousand tiny bells. Because all our costumes were obviously perishable, we never wore them in rehearsal, and naturally nobody knew that I was invested with these peculiar sound effects until I made my entrance at the beginning of the second act.

Our director was a man who had strong opinions about how Shakespeare should be played, and Puck was one of his favorite characters.

It was his theory that Puck, being "the incarnation of mischief," never ought to be still a minute, so I had been coached to bound onto the stage, and once there to dance up and down, cocking my head and waving my arms.

"I want you to be a little whirlwind," this man said.

Even as I prepared to bound onto the stage, I had my own misgivings about those dangerously abundant gestures, and their probable effect on my bells. It was too late, however, to invent another technique for playing Puck, even if there had been room for anything but horror in my mind. I bounded onto the stage.

The effect, in its way, must have been superb. With every leap I rang like a thousand children's sleighs, my melodies foretelling who knows what worlds of merriment to the enchanted spectators. It was even worse when I came to the middle of the stage and went into my gestures. The other ringing had been loud but sporadic.[4] This was persistent, varying only slightly in volume and pitch with the vehemence of my gestures. To a blind man, it must have sounded as though I had recklessly decided to accompany myself on a xylophone. A maturer actor would probably have made up his mind that an emergency existed, and abandoned his gestures as impracticable under the circumstances. I was thirteen, and incapable of innovations.[5] I had

---

3 **farthingales:** hooped skirts.

4 **sporadic** (spō răd/ĭk): occurring only occasionally.
5 **innovations** (ĭn'ə vā shənz): acts introducing new techniques or customs.

been told by responsible authorities that gestures went with this part, and I continued to make them. I also continued to ring—a silvery music, festive and horrible.

If the bells were hard on my nerves, they were even worse for the rest of the cast, who were totally unprepared for my new interpretation. Puck's first remark is addressed to one of the fairies, and it is mercifully brief.

I said, "How now, spirit! Whither wander you?"

This unhappy child, already embarrassed by a public appearance in cheesecloth and tinsel, was also burdened with an opening speech of sixteen lines in verse. He began bravely:

> Over hill, over dale,
>   Through brush, through brier,
> Over park, over pale,
>   Through flood, through fire . . .

At the word *fire,* my instructions were to bring my hands up from the ground in a long, wavery sweep, intended to represent fire. The bells pealed. To my startled ears, it sounded more as if they exploded. The fairy stopped in his lines and looked at me sharply. The jingling, however, had diminished; it was no more than as if a faint wind stirred my bells, and he went on:

> I do wander everywhere,
> Swifter than the moone's sphere . . .

Here again I had another cue, for a sort of swoop and dip indicating the swiftness of the moone's sphere. Again the bells rang out, and again

the performance stopped in its tracks. The fairy was clearly troubled by these interruptions. He had, however, a child's strange acceptance of the inscrutable,[6] and was even able to regard my bells as a last-minute adult addition to the program, nerve-racking but not to be questioned. I'm sure it was only this that got him through that first speech.

My turn, when it came, was even worse. By this time the audience had succumbed to a helpless gaiety. Every time my bells rang, laughter swept the spectators, and this mounted and mingled with the bells until everything else was practically inaudible. I began my speech, another long one, and full of incomprehensible references to Titania's changeling.[7]

"Louder!" said somebody in the wings. "You'll have to talk louder."

It was the director, and he seemed to be in a dangerous state.

"And for heaven's sake, stop that jingling!" he said.

I talked louder, and I tried to stop the jingling, but it was no use. By the time I got to the end of my speech, I was shouting and so was the audience. It appeared that I had very little control over the bells, which continued to jingle in spite of my passionate efforts to keep them quiet.

All this had a very bad effect on the fairy, who by this time had many

---

6 inscrutable (ĭn skrōō'tə bəl): what cannot be understood.

7 changeling: one substituted for another. (In the play, Titania falls in love with a rustic who has been changed into an ass.)

symptoms of a complete nervous collapse. However, he began his next speech:

> Either I mistake your shape and mak-
> ing quite,
> Or else you are that shrewd and knav-
> ish sprite
> Called Robin Goodfellow: are you
> not he
> That . . .

At this point I forgot that the rules had been changed and I was supposed to leave out the gestures. There was a furious jingling, and the fairy gulped.

"Are you not he that, that . . ."

He looked miserably at the wings, and the director supplied the next line, but the tumult was too much for him. The unhappy child simply shook his head.

"Say anything!" shouted the director desperately. "Anything at all!"

The fairy only shut his eyes and shuddered.

"All right!" shouted the director. "All right, Puck. *You* begin *your* next speech."

By some miracle, I actually did remember my next lines, and had opened my mouth to begin on them when suddenly the fairy spoke. His voice was a high, thin monotone, and there seemed to be madness in it, but it was perfectly clear.

"Fourscore and seven years ago," he began, "our fathers brought forth on this continent a new nation, conceived . . ."

He said it right through to the end, and it was certainly the most successful speech ever made on that stage, and probably one of the most successful speeches ever made on any stage. I don't remember, if I ever knew, how the rest of us ever picked up the dull, normal thread of the play after that extraordinary performance, but we must have, because I know it went on. I only remember that in the next intermission the director cut off my bells with his penknife, and after that things quieted down and got dull.

WOLCOTT GIBBS

475

Reading Skills

1. Describe Puck's costume as the narrator's mother made it.
2. What instructions had the director made about acting the character of Puck? Why do you need this information?
3. What happened to different actors when the bells began to jingle? Why did Wolcott Gibbs not stop the bells when the director told him to?
4. Why did the fairy recite Lincoln's "Gettysburg Address"? Why does Gibbs say that "it was certainly the most successful speech ever made on that stage, and probably one of the most successful speeches ever made on any stage"?
5. Notice the abruptness of the ending. Would you like more description of what happened after the bells were cut off? Why or why not?

Further Activity

Write about an embarrassing childhood experience of your own. First, decide what effect you want to have on your readers. Do you want them to laugh in sympathy with you, or to feel sorry for you, or to feel that you deserved every minute of your trouble? Then decide what your climax will be. What was the moment when things were at their very worst?

Plan what information you must give your readers so that they will be prepared for the climax. Make a simple outline of your paper. After you have written the first two paragraphs, read them to friends before you continue. Ask these questions: Have I included enough details? Have I made the reader *see* the situation? Have I arranged details in the best order? Does this part of my narrative have a consistent tone, or have I started humorously and then become serious, or vice versa?

When you have finished the narration, read it to someone for suggestions before you make a final copy.

The following letter might be considered a portion of the biography of a race. James Baldwin directed the letter to his nephew, and published it in his book, *The Fire Next Time*. In it we learn something about Baldwin, his family, and his people. Many of his statements to his nephew are really comments on the position of many Negroes in American society.

My Dungeon Shook

LETTER TO MY NEPHEW ON THE ONE HUNDREDTH ANNIVERSARY OF THE EMANCIPATION

James Baldwin

Dear James:

I have begun this letter five times and torn it up five times. I keep seeing your face, which is also the face of your father and my brother. Like him, you are tough, dark, vulnerable,[1] moody—with a very definite tendency to sound truculent[2] because you want no one to think you are soft. You may be like your grandfather in this, I don't know, but certainly both you and your father resemble him very much physically. Well, he is dead, he never saw you, and he had a terrible life; he was defeated long before he died because, at the bottom of his heart, he really believed what white people said about him. This is one of the reasons that he became so holy. I am sure that your father has told you something about all that. Neither you nor your father exhibit any tendency towards holiness: you really

are of another era, part of what happened when the Negro left the land and came into what the late E. Franklin Frazier called "the cities of destruction." You can only be destroyed by believing that you really are what the white world calls a *nigger*. I tell you this because I love you, and please don't you ever forget it.

I have known both of you all your lives, have carried your Daddy in my arms and on my shoulders, kissed and spanked him and watched him learn to walk. I don't know if you've known anybody from that far back; if you've loved anybody that long, first as an infant, then as a child, then as a man, you gain a strange perspective on time and human pain and effort. Other people cannot see what I see whenever I look into your father's face, for behind your father's face as it is today are all those other faces which were his. Let him laugh and I see a cellar your father does not remember and a house he does not

1 **vulnerable:** able to be wounded.
2 **truculent:** fierce, cruel.

remember and I hear in his present laughter his laughter as a child. Let him curse and I remember him falling down the cellar steps, and howling, and I remember, with pain, his tears, which my hand or your grandmother's so easily wiped away. But no one's hand can wipe away those tears he sheds invisibly today, which one hears in his laughter and in his speech and in his songs. I know what the world has done to my brother and how narrowly he has survived it. And I know, which is much worse, and this is the crime of which I accuse my country and my countrymen, and for which neither I nor time nor history will ever forgive them, that they have destroyed and are destroying hundreds of thousands of lives and do not know it and do not want to know it. One can be, indeed one must strive to become, tough and philosophical concerning destruction and death, for this is what most of mankind has been best at since we have heard of man. (But remember: *most* of mankind is not *all* of mankind.) But it is not permissible that the authors of devastation should also be innocent. It is the innocence which constitutes the crime.

Now, my dear namesake, these innocent and well-meaning people, your countrymen, have caused you to be born under conditions not very far removed from those described for us by Charles Dickens in the London of more than a hundred years ago. (I hear the chorus of the innocents screaming, "No! This is not true! How *bitter* you are!"—but I am writing this letter to *you,* to try to tell you something about how to handle *them,* for most of them do not yet really know that you exist. I *know* the conditions under which you were born, for I was there. Your countrymen were *not* there, and haven't made it yet. Your grandmother was also there, and no one has ever accused her of being bitter. I suggest that the innocents check with her. She isn't hard to find. Your countrymen don't know that *she* exists, either, though she has been working for them all their lives.)

Well, you were born, here you came, something like fifteen years ago; and though your father and mother and grandmother, looking about the streets through which they were carrying you, staring at the walls into which they brought you, had every reason to be heavyhearted, yet they were not. For here you were, Big James, named for me—you were a big baby, I was not—here you were: to be loved. To be loved, baby, hard, at once, and forever, to strengthen you against the loveless world. Remember that: I know how black it looks today, for you. It looked bad that day, too, yes, we were trembling. We have not stopped trembling yet, but if we had not loved each other none of us would have survived. And now you must survive because we love you, and for the sake of your children and your children's children.

This innocent country set you down in a ghetto in which, in fact, it intended that you should perish. Let me spell out precisely what I mean by that, for the heart of the matter is here, and the root of my dispute with my country. You were born where you were born and faced the future that you faced because you were black and *for no other reason*. The limits of your ambition were, thus, expected to be set forever. You were born into a society which spelled out with brutal clarity, and in as many ways as possible, that you were a worthless human being. You were not expected to aspire to excellence: you were expected to make peace with mediocrity. Wherever you have turned, James, in your short time on this earth, you have been told where you could go and what you could do (and *how* you could do it) and where you could live and whom you could marry. I know your countrymen do not agree with me about this, and I hear them saying, "You exaggerate." They do not know Harlem, and I do. So do you. Take no one's word for anything, including mine—but trust your experience. Know whence you came. If you know whence you came, there is really no limit to where you can go. The details and symbols of your life have been deliberately constructed to make you believe what white people say about you. Please try to remember that what they believe, as well as what they do and cause you to endure, does not testify to your inferiority but to their inhumanity and fear. Please try to be clear, dear James, through the storm which rages about your youthful head today, about the reality which lies behind the words *acceptance* and *integration*. There is no reason for you to try to become like white people and there is no basis whatever for their impertinent[3] assumption that *they* must accept *you*. The really terrible thing, old buddy, is that *you* must accept *them*. And I mean that very seriously. You must accept them and accept them with love. For these innocent people have no other hope. They are, in effect, still trapped in a history which they do not understand; and until they understand it, they cannot be released from it. They have had to believe for many years, and for innumerable reasons, that black men are inferior to white men. Many of them, indeed, know better, but, as you will discover, people find it very difficult to act on what they know. To act is to be committed, and to be committed is to be in danger. In this case, the danger, in the minds of most white Americans, is the loss of their identity. Try to imagine how you would feel if you woke up one morning to find the sun shining and all the stars aflame. You would be frightened because it is out of the order of nature. Any upheaval in the universe is terrifying because it so profoundly attacks one's sense of one's own reality. Well, the black man has functioned in the white man's world as a fixed star, as an immovable pillar: and as he moves out of his place, heaven and earth are shaken to their foundations. You, don't be afraid. I said that it was intended that you should perish in the ghetto, perish by never being allowed to go behind the white man's

3 **impertinent:** not appropriate, absurd.

definitions, by never being allowed to spell your proper name. You have, and many of us have, defeated this intention; and, by a terrible law, a terrible paradox,[4] those innocents who believed that your imprisonment made them safe are losing their grasp of reality. But these men are your brothers—your lost, younger brothers. And if the word *integration* means anything, this is what it means: that we, with love, shall force our brothers to see themselves as they are, to cease fleeing from reality and begin to change it. For this is your home, my friend, do not be driven from it; great men have done great things here, and will again, and we can make America what America must become. It will be hard, James,

4 **paradox:** contradiction.

but you come from sturdy, peasant stock, men who picked cotton and dammed rivers and built railroads, and, in the teeth of the most terrifying odds, achieved an unassailable[5] and monumental dignity. You come from a long line of great poets, some of the greatest poets since Homer. One of them said, *The very time I thought I was lost, My dungeon shook and my chains fell off.*

You know, and I know, that the country is celebrating one hundred years of freedom one hundred years too soon. We cannot be free until they are free. God bless you, James, and Godspeed.

Your uncle,
James

5 **unassailable:** not liable to attack or question.

Focusing On Words

What words in the following sentence stand for personal qualities: "Like him, you are tough, dark, vulnerable, moody—with a very definite tendency to sound truculent because you want no one to think you are soft"? Match each of the following definitions with the personal quality it describes:

(*a*) rude of manner, harsh
(*b*) hard to influence, hard to discourage
(*c*) gentle to the point of weakness
(*d*) capable of feeling hurt
(*e*) subject to fits of gloominess

BIOGRAPHY

Understanding Literature

1. How is it possible for the boy, James, or for anyone to be both tough and vulnerable?
2. What parts of this selection are directed to the nephew as a member of the Negro race living at a certain time in history?
3. One characteristic of this selection is that it is general; it includes few specific examples. Can you, then, supply examples that will support the truth or falsity of the following general statements?
    (a) "But it is not permissible that the authors of devastation should also be innocent. It is the innocence which constitutes the crime."
    (b) "Please try to remember that what they believe, as well as what they do and cause you to endure, does not testify to your inferiority but to their inhumanity and fear."
    (c) "You were born where you were born and faced the future that you faced because you were black and for no other reason . . . You were born into a society which spelled out with brutal clarity . . . that you were a worthless human being."
4. Why, according to Baldwin, did his father become "so holy"?
5. What do you think Baldwin meant when he wrote, ". . . behind your father's face as it is today are all those other faces that were his"?
6. Where did the words of the title, "My Dungeon Shook", come from? Why do you think Baldwin chose these words for the title of this letter to his nephew?

Further Activity

Write a letter to James Baldwin in which you reply to one of the following statements. If you prefer, choose another statement from his letter.
   (a) "One can be, indeed one must strive to become, tough and philosophical concerning destruction and death, for this is what most of mankind has been best at since we have heard of man."
   (b) "And if the word integration means anything, this is what it means: that we, with love, shall force our brothers to see themselves as they are, to cease fleeing from reality and begin to change it."

Drama

For CENTURIES the make-believe world created by actors has made audiences laugh and weep. Never has there been a time or a place—as now, in America—that plays have been seen by so many people. Never before has a generation of teen-agers seen so many plays: television has brought the theater into millions of American homes. The quality of the plays may not be as high as many people would wish; but there are few young people today who have not been entertained (between commercials) by westerns, comedies, and, occasionally, by superior plays that are shown on the television screen. In addition, most teen-agers have seen motion pictures and amateur play productions, and many have seen Broadway plays.

When you read a play, you are like an actor who has been handed a script. The actor (you) must read the script carefully, imagining how to speak the lines, what gestures to use, and what stage movements to make. With the help of a director, the actor (you) and the other actors must learn the lines that have been written for them, and they must pretend that they are the characters in the play. If the actors are successful, they will convince the audience that they *are* the people about whom the playwright has written.

Reading a play can be a pleasurable experience, if you use your imagination. As you read, you must remember that the play was written to be performed by a company of actors (whether amateur or professional) before an audience. If you can be both actor and audience, at one and the same time, you will derive great satisfaction from reading the plays in this section.

Knowing something about how a play is put together can also increase your appreciation of a play. A playwright, like the writer of any other form of literature, has a major idea, or theme, to be expressed. But having chosen to express that idea in a play, the writer must cope with problems which do not occur in other forms of literature. Because a play is meant to be performed on a stage and viewed by a playgoer, the playwright can present action and reveal character only through dialogue—what the characters say to each other—or through brief directions indicating the scene, the characters' physical appearance, their physical actions, or the manner of their speech.

As you read the plays in this section, consider how the playwright deals with the following aspects of drama:

Conflict and Plot. Conflict is essential to drama, and the plot in a drama, as in a short story, refers to the plan by which the conflict is introduced, developed, and resolved. A dramatic plot usually follows this pattern—(1) Exposition: explains who the characters are and why they are there; (2) Introduction of Conflict: introduces the problem; (3) Complication (or Rising Action): develops the conflict; (4) Climax (or Crisis): reveals a decision, an action, or an event which determines the outcome of the conflict; (5) Resolution (or Falling Action): resolves the conflict, answers the questions asked by the play, solves the problem. The conflict, of course, must be developed primarily by the speeches of the characters. The action, except for occasional directions for limited physical movement (such as *sits, stands, stabs, kisses*), must be revealed through the dialogue. The playwright cannot narrate events; he or she must dramatize them.

Setting. A playwright indicates the setting through stage directions specifying the time and the place of the action. "Right" and "Left" in stage directions refer to the actor's right and left as he or she faces the audience. "Upstage" is the rear of the stage, that section farthest from the audience. "Downstage" is the front of the stage, that section nearest the audience. (These directions are frequently abbreviated as R, L, U, D, and combinations of these letters.) As you read a play, you should pay particular attention to the stage directions, which will enable you to visualize the scene of the play. Is the scene supposed to be indoors or outdoors? How is the stage furnished to suggest the scene? Are there lighting directions? If so, is the scene shadowy or bright?

Costumes and Acting. The stage directions also may indicate how a character looks and what he or she wears. The appearance of the character helps to show you what kind of person he or she is. Costume is sometimes equally important in revealing character. The stage directions in many plays let you know *how* a speech is to be delivered. Sometimes directions such as *irritably* or *admiringly* or *sarcastically*, because they tell you *how* the speech is said, are essential to your understanding of *what* is said. Be sure that you know the meaning of all the "how" words in the stage directions.

Character. Though physical appearance and costume help to reveal character, the playwright is limited for the most part to revealing character through what the characters say, through what they do (their actions and reactions), and through what others say about them. The playwright cannot tell the viewer directly what a character is like; if some other character in the play does so, remember that you are getting only that character's—not the author's—point of view. In a good drama, details about a character's attitude and beliefs are revealed only through dialogue and action—that is, they are revealed dramatically.

When you read a play, let your imagination go: visualize the scene; observe the movement of the characters; listen to their voices. Then you can imaginatively experience the drama.

Almost everyone likes a ghost story. In "The Giants' Stair," a stormy night, a possible murder, and the ravings of a madwoman about ghosts roaming the countryside will cause you to shiver along with Sheriff Bane as you witness the events unfold.

The Giants' Stair[*]

Wilbur Daniel Steele

IMPROVING YOUR READING: The conflict in "The Giants' Stair" consists of the tension between characters, particularly between Til and Sheriff Bane. Notice the way the author develops this *conflict* in the plot of the play: How does he let you know who the characters are and why they are there? How does he make one event in the plot lead to the next? How does he prepare you for the outcome of the play?

You will also notice that the author creates an air of mystery and terror in the play. He does this primarily through the *setting*—the time and the place of the action. To understand how the setting can create particular feelings in you, consider how different your feelings would be if the play took place on a sunny spring day, when the trees were just beginning to bud, and the Weatherburns' kitchen, small and cozy, was lighted by sunlight streaming through a brightly curtained window.

FOCUSING ON WORDS: Understanding the meaning of the following "how" words in the stage directions will increase your understanding of the play. Be sure that you know what these and all the stage directions mean, so that you will know how speeches are to be delivered and how actions are to be performed: *with furtive care, with an expression of malignance, apprehensively, doggedly, in a resolute undertone, with a vehemence almost of ecstasy, recoiling, with a kind of bewildered docility, with the same appearance of apathy, in a distrait monotone, sullenly, blanching, in the same eerie note, with a trancelike deliberation, with a sudden malignant fury.*

WILBUR DANIEL STEELE

MRS. WEATHERBURN
TIL, *her sister*
BANE, *the Sheriff*
THE ONE AT THE DOOR

PLACE: *A farm at the upper end of a mountain valley, "The Giants' Stair," which descends by easy alluvial benches[1] from amongst the high southern buttresses[2] of The Footstool.*

TIME: *Late November of the present: an evening when, the false autumnal summer having come to a close, winter gathers its forces for the initial assault. A storm of wind and rain invests the shell of the farmhouse with a note insistent, mournful, and menacing, and from moment to moment, in a wilder onslaught, rocks the edifice on its foundations as if with its next to tear it from its granite bed and hurl it bounding and crashing down the terraced floor of the gorge.*

SCENE: *The farmhouse kitchen, a gaunt, high-studded, white-plastered room, modified by forlorn attempts at cheer in touches of colored muslin at the windows, one on either side of the central door, and by a pink crepe-paper shade which warms the light of the kerosene lamp on the table at the left. A door at the right leads into the woodshed; above it, on pegs, rests a double-barreled shotgun.*

1 **alluvial benches:** raised level surfaces of ground, composed of soil deposited by running water (alluvium).
2 **buttresses:** projecting parts of hills.

The kitchen range, flanked by cupboards, is at the extreme right; at the extreme left an ordinary wall telephone, the kind with a crank.

At the rising of the curtain there are discovered MRS. WEATHERBURN and her sister, TIL. MRS. WEATHERBURN, a large-formed, soft-footed woman, has been manipulating the dampers of the range. When she lifts one of the lids the new wood, kindling with a pent roar, as if some of the outer gale had got down the chimney and into the stillness of the house, casts up a ruddy light and reveals the face bent over it, a face fleshy and unlined, the lips set together solidly but without strain, the eyes widely placed and so serene of expression as almost to beget a doubt of them—as if their very bovine[3] tranquility might be suspected to hide depths of ardor or passion or bitterness which would seem too silly in the scheme of existence of a mountain farm. Brooding into the heat, her hand, still holding the stove lid, poised as if it has forgotten what it is about, she remains standing so for a moment, her back to her sister, seated by the table across the room.

TIL is physically almost the counterpart of the other, large, putty-fleshed, and colorless. Beyond this outer aspect the likeness fails. TIL is what would be called in Oriental countries "inspired." She sits motionless under the pink glow,

3 **bovine** (bō′vīn): oxlike; i.e., patient, slow-moving, and dull.

her hands, pallid, puffy, inert-looking, folded loosely in her lap; her eyes staring fixedly ahead of her at nothing at all. She speaks in a high-pitched, unaccented tone.

TIL. This is another of them nights, Abbie. Hark, Abbie! Hark to that tempest! It's one of them nights again.

MRS. WEATHERBURN (*idly*). What nights, Til?

TIL. One of them nights when the giants comes up the stairs to go on the mountain. Makin' a noise on the stairs.

MRS. WEATHERBURN. Goin' *down*, I should say, Til. The wind's from *up*.

TIL. No, giants goes against the wind. Don't you know that?

MRS. WEATHERBURN (*replacing the stove lid noisily, as if to put an end to that sort of talk, and glancing at the clock above the door*). Mercy livin', Til, look the time it is. Past seven, and supper not yet gettin', say nothing of laid. (*Taking down a saucepan from behind the stove and peering into it for dust.*) It's a queer, funny thing. When John was here—

TIL. When John was alive—

MRS. WEATHERBURN. When John was here, I'd have give him a piece of my mind for bein' ten minutes late of six for supper; and yet now here it's *me* that's dawdlin'—lazin' and dawdlin' till all hours—now't John's away—

TIL. Now't John's dead—now't he's dead and gone for a ghost—ghost in the trees—'long with the dead giants' ghosts—troopin' through the trees!

Hark to that wind, Abbie! (*In the instant of silence following, the telephone bell begins to ring. With each prolonged, shrill iteration*[4] **TIL** *pronounces a name, like a child repeating in sing-song rote the rule of three. Ring!*) Banes'! (*Ring!*) Tolleys'! (*Ring!*) Jetherses'! (*Ring!*) Whites'! Mis' White's, Abbie. Somebody wantin' Mis' White's. Who could it be wantin' Mis' White's?

> (*Rising suddenly and softly, she steps to the instrument, lifts the receiver from the hook with furtive care, and puts it to her ear.*)

MRS. WEATHERBURN. Don't, Til! (*More hopelessly.*) Don't do that, Til!

> (**TIL,** *on whose face the blankness has given way to a look of animation at once eager, willful, and sly, only puts her hand over the mouthpiece for answer, and continues listening.*)

TIL. It's Mis' Jethers, talkin' with Mis' White. Mis' Jethers says Jethers is havin' trouble with his growth again. She says the Pros'-cutor was by today, and what can the Pros'cutor be snoopin' 'round this neighborhood for—unless it's about— Oh! (*She jerks the receiver from her ear.*) Oh!

> (*She looks at it with an expression of malignance, wounded, bewildered.*)

MRS. WEATHERBURN. For Heaven

4 **iteration:** repetition.

sake, Til! What—

(TIL *replaces the receiver with a vicious click, and as abruptly goes droopy and appealing, tears in her eyes.*)

TIL. They says I was *list'nin'.* They says that. Says somebody was snoopin' in, and they'd warrant the somebody wa'n't a million miles from the Weatherburn place. Abbie!

MRS. WEATHERBURN (*crossing to put an arm about her sister's shoulders*). There! Don't you take on! Come, Til, you set down in your chair again. That's a good girl! (*Having pushed and petted* TIL *into place, she turns to the phone, takes the receiver, and after a moment's listening speaks into it.*) Yes, here's "somebody" again, May White. Yes, "snoopin'," Clara Jethers. Only 'tain't the same "somebody," happens. Yes, it was Til. My Til. And all I wanted to say was, I think two *ladies,* such as you, would consider 'emselves in pretty business, mindin' *Til!* Mindin' and mockin' such a one as *Til!* That's all. Oh, no, no, I didn't mean to be snappy, Clara. No, nor to you either, May. Only— No, I don't want you should think— How? Yes, 'tis. Blowin' furies up here. Yes, perfect cats and dogs. How? The *road* bridge! (*To* TIL.) Clara Jethers says the brook's so swole down her way that their hay bridge has gone out and the road bridge like to any minute. (*To phone.*) Don't tell me! Yes, I knew 'twas swellin', even up this far. When I was out to the chickens I hear it roarin' down to the meadow bottom. Dear—dear! I guess we sha'n't look to have many callers tonight, 't any rate. More likely to be callin' ourselves down your ways, house and all. (*Hastily, to the agitated* TIL.) No, Til, no; that was only jokin'. No danger of *that,* I guess. (*To phone.*) I was speakin' to Til. Yes, good night to both of you; good night. (*Replacing the receiver, she moves away toward the range, but halts before reaching it, and stands with her head lifted, harkening to the stream of the elements without. After a moment she speaks to herself.*) I wish John was here tonight.

TIL (*apprehensively*). Don't say that! Not with *this—these!* They might hear you—and send him.

(MRS. WEATHERBURN *makes no rejoinder. As if taking herself in hand, she glances at the clock, tidies her apron, and is continuing toward the stove when a knock on the door brings her again to a halt, wheeling, startled.* TIL, *rising, open-mouthed, wide-eyed, stares from her sister to the door and to her sister again. As* MRS. WEATHERBURN, *shaking off her momentary irresolution, starts forward,* TIL *brings her up again with a whispering "Abbie!" The knock is repeated, and immediately then the door opens and* BANE *comes in.* BANE *is a stocky, hard-fleshed, red-complexioned fellow in middle age, a farmer out of a line of farmers; a man, one would say, without imagination. His cowhide boots are muddy and his short overcoat sodden with water, as is the hostler's cap which he takes off as he closes the door behind him and blinks into the unaccustomed light.*)

TIL (*with almost a sob of relief*). Why, it's—it's only Sheriff Bane!

BANE (*peering from one to the other, noting their attitudes*). So, Til! And who'd ye 'magine I would be? (*Turning to* MRS. WEATHERBURN.) And you! You're not still hopin', Mis' Weatherburn! Or—*mistrustin'!*

MRS. WEATHERBURN (*controlling a gesture of impatience*). It was only you give us a start—to think of any livin' mortal being out tonight—

TIL. Along with *them as ain't.*

BANE (*ignoring her; to* MRS. WEATHERBURN). Make certain I shouldn't've been if I'd know. It wa'n't anything like so bad when I start. I been up the mountain all afternoon on the lookout for them two young steers of mine, the red ones, that's been strayed since Tuesday night. You ain't see 'em, I suppose? Well, then, when it come on so all-creation bad, and I see the light in your window—

MRS. WEATHERBURN. And quite right you was, Bane. Look at you— drownded! Take off that overcoat and draw up to the stove.

BANE (*looking down at himself*). No, thank ye; my boots are too messed. I'll just take a chair by the door here a spell if ye don't mind.

(*Removing his coat, he hangs it over the chair back; then seats himself, his boots planted*

solidly apart, his cap hanging between his knees.)

TIL (*gazing into space*). What did them red steers of yourn die of?

BANE. *Die* of! They ain't died of anything I know of. Why?

TIL. I only thought 'twas queer a body'd be searchin' anything *livin'*—up this mountain here—tonight. Did you hear any of 'em round about you?

BANE. Any what? The steers?

TIL. The giants. Comin' up the stairs.

BANE. Giants! I *declare* for the woman! Th' ain't no such things as giants *alive!*

TIL. No, they're all dead now—long ago, long ago. And then them other dead things—passin' up through the trees and the long grass and the bushes—troopin' up—

BANE (*furiously, to* MRS. WEATHERBURN). What's she about? What's all this darnation foolishness about, anyhow?

MRS. WEATHERBURN. Nothin', Bane. Don't mind Til. It's like she's got it into her mind it'd be hard for anything mortal to get up the road tonight. We had a phone the bridge to Jetherses' is like to go out any minute. You'll hardly get home tonight, I'm afraid, will you?

BANE. Don't look it. I'll set here, if ye don't mind.

MRS. WEATHERBURN. Land, no! But you ain't et! No more've we. I'll put some eggs on directly—

BANE. I've et. Before I start—

MRS. WEATHERBURN. But I thought you was on the mountain all after—

BANE (*hastily*). I—that's what I was

goin' to say—only—only ye wouldn't leave me finish. Before I start *down,* I was goin' to say, havin' take a snack along in a paper. See?

Mrs. Weatherburn. Oh! (*And after a perceptible pause.*) Well, you don't mind if we have ourn, Til and me? I was just gettin' at it—

Bane (*doggedly*). No. But *I've* et.

(**Mrs. Weatherburn** *takes up the saucepan from the stove and, again peering into it, again falls into reverie.*)

Til (*reseated, her eyes blank*). The first step in the stairs is Banes'. The next step is Tolleys'. Big, huge steps in the dark. It's feelin' for 'em with their feet in the dark makes the din. (**Mrs. Weatherburn,** *still brooding into the saucepan, has shifted nearer to* **Bane.** **Til** *continues.*) The next step after Tolleys' is Jetherses'. That's a higher one. Some stumbles there.

Mrs. Weatherburn (*in a resolute undertone*). Bane, there's one thing I'd like if you'd make clear. When you come in you says to me: "Still hopin'?" and by that I take it you mean still hopin' it might be my husband come back. But it's what you says next I want explained. "Or *mistrustin'!*" Why'd you say, "Or *mistrustin'*"?

Bane (*confused*). What'd I mean? Land! I never meant—it was more like a—a joke. Only—

Mrs. Weatherburn. Only *what,* Bane?

Bane. Nothin'! Only— (*Straightening his shoulders and looking significantly about him.*) You been bright'nin' things up a bit since John was—was gone—eh? Them window curtains makes a difference now, don't they? John Weatherburn was never much on decoration, was he? And that there pink lamp shade. Makes the room a sight cheerier, don't it, though? And then the telephone. A telephone's a comfort, 'specially to the women folks, what with their gossipin' and egg prices and howdy-do's. I'm glad for you you got the phone in at last, after all these years it's been up the valley clean to your next door neighbor's. John was never much for contraptions, was he? 'Specially when they cut into the money. John was insured, wa'n't he?

Mrs. Weatherburn (*in a level tone, facing him squarely*). Is there anything in this valley, stick, stone, or strawstack, *ain't* insured, and insured as high's ever the agent'll let you?

Bane (*keenly*). Why'd you say "strawstack"?

Mrs. Weatherburn. Why shouldn't I say "strawstack"?

Til. And then the next step is Whites', where the walls comes closer t'gether. And there's the brook to crost again, the roarin' brook, tumblin' and roarin' and takin' the bridges out in the dark—

Mrs. Weatherburn. Bane, you never come here tonight *about steers!*

Bane (*rubbing a hand down over his face*). Well, as a matter of fact— (*Blowing out his lips.*) Set down, Mis' Weatherburn.

Mrs. Weatherburn. Thank you, I'll stand.

BANE (*blowing out his lips again*). Was a Mr. Cantpole by today?

MRS. WEATHERBURN. That's the Pros'cutor from Twinshead way, ain't it?

BANE. Yes, Cantpole happens to be Pros'cutin' Attorney; that's him.

MRS. WEATHERBURN. Yes, he was by. What's more, you know well enough he was by. Look here, Bane, speak out! Is it about—John?

BANE. About John—I'm 'fraid. About John's—vanishin'.

TIL (*in the same dreaming tone*). About John's dyin'. About John's dyin' o' murder in the dark.

BANE (*wheeling in his chair*). And how'd *you* know he was murdered, Til Jessup? *How'd you come to know?*

TIL (*shaken out of her reverie; dismayed*). How'd I know? Why—why —I'll tell you how—I hear Mis' Jethers sayin' 's much—day before yesterday, 'twas—to Mis' Tolley—or leastways to Mame Tolley—Mis' Tolley bein' to Twinshead. Mis' Tolley's always to Twinshead Thursdays, ain't she? That's her day to Twins— (*The phone rings.* TIL *counts.*) Banes'! Tolleys'! There's for Mis' Tolley's now. Wonder who could be—

(*She half rises with a yearning glance toward the instrument; then, remembering herself, casts an abashed eye in the direction of the visitor and relapses. The* SHERIFF *passes his hand again over his face and returns his attention to* MRS. WEATHERBURN.)

BANE. I trust you'll believe me, Mis' Weatherburn, when I tell ye 'tain't of my own wish I'm here tonight.

MRS. WEATHERBURN. No, I s'pose not. But hark'nin' to all the gossip that's round—

BANE. No, 'tain't no question of gossip sent me. It's Cantpole. I shouldn't've moved of myself, same as I *ain't* moved before—

MRS. WEATHERBURN. Yes, I've give you credit for a deal of sense—till now. I says to myself, there's one man in this valley's got sense enough to know John must've just gone away a spell, somewheres—

BANE. No, Mis' Weatherburn, 'twa'n't that. For that wouldn't be *sense*. Don't think I blind myself. What manner of sense would there be tryin' to believe a man like John Weatherburn, a solid church-goin' man with a good farm and a bank account, and a fam'ly—that a man like that'd be changin' all of a sudden, one special night, and skippin' for it, no word to nobody and never heard of again? That's too much!

MRS. WEATHERBURN. There's queer things happens in the world.

TIL. There's queer things happens in the world.

BANE. No, no, 'tain't that. (*He looks down at his cap, which he wrings between his fingers.*) 'Tain't that. It's something— (*Putting the palm of his hand on the crown of his head*)—something here. Something settin' heavy, and sorrowful, like a weight. Mr. Cantpole never lived in this valley. I have. I've lived neighbors with you folks; you've been to dinner to my house, and me to yourn.

I've known John Weatherburn since him and I was boys. Boy and man I've known him. Why, I was the last person to see him alive—the last that'll *confess* to it, anyhow. When he leave me that night, there at the bars of my top pasture—when I see him walkin' away in the dusk of that ev'nin'—if I had think—if I'd been able to know what was in store— Oh, dear! It sets heavy, Mis' Weatherburn. It's set so heavy on me I ain't been myself. The farm work's suffered; nothin' tended, nothin' done. And here's the Pros'cutor all the while: "When ye goin' to act, Sheriff?" And me settin' there to home, thinkin', thinkin': "Sorrow has come on that fam'ly up there. If I, Edwin Bane, was willin'ly to set out to add to that sorrow—" But today, when Cantpole was by, there wa'n't no "When ye goin' to act?" This time 'twas: "*Act!*"

MRS. WEATHERBURN. So you acted! (*Holding up the saucepan, she peers into it for the last time. She takes it to the stove, fills it from the tea-kettle, and sets it on. She glances toward* TIL. *Then, picking up the wood basket:*) Til, would you mind gettin' me in some wood? That's a good girl! And wait! Take along this candle— (*Lighting a candle end for* TIL *as she takes the basket.*) For I want some good sticks this awful night. Good, medium-small, square sticks. Mind! Pick 'em careful, won't you, Til? That's a good girl! (*Ushering her out and closing the door behind her, she stands with her back against it, facing the* SHERIFF *in his chair.*) So, Bane, you acted!

You come to accuse me of murderin' John!

BANE (*reddening*). Not so fast! Not so fast!

MRS. WEATHERBURN. You come here to accuse me of murderin' John!

BANE. Not so fast! (*Rising and casting his eyes about.*) I come here, at Cantpole's orders, simply to—to have a look around. That's all. That John's gun up there? (*Taking down the weapon and balancing it thoughtfully across his palms.*) H'm'm'm! Good gun. (*Sniffing at the muzzle.*) D'you ever try shootin' this gun, Mis' Weatherburn?

MRS. WEATHERBURN. No, I never shot that gun.

BANE. Sure o' that, ain't ye?

(*The door is attempted from the other side.* MRS. WEATHERBURN *props her back more desperately against it, calling over her shoulder.*)

MRS. WEATHERBURN. Better wood'n that, Til! Better wood'n that! (*To* BANE.) What do you mean, Bane?

BANE. I just mean—I was just wonderin'—if 'twa'n't you— (*With a quick movement he "breaks" the breech, pulls out one of the shells, notes that it is empty, and, lifting the weapon to point to the light, squints through the barrel.*) Just wonderin', Mis' Weatherburn, if 'twa'n't you, who 'twas.

MRS. WEATHERBURN (*after a moment's hesitation*). I'll tell you who 'twas. It was my husband himself. I rec'lect now. 'Twas the day before he—left. I rec'lect him comin' in with that gun, sayin' as how he'd had a shot at some quail up in the stone pasture. But he'd missed.

BANE. I don't doubt your word, Mis' Weatherburn, nor your rec'lection. Your husband may've shot this gun that day. All I want to say is (*holding up the shell*) he never shot *this load!*

MRS. WEATHERBURN. Why?

BANE. If your husband—or any other man—was to've shot this load, he'd've cleaned the gun after him. No man that'd shot his gun would leave it grimed and pittin' up like this. No, sir! He'd go to work and have his rod and rag out; that's what he'd do. (*His voice lifting.*) He'd give it a thorough cleanin', he would! (*Still higher.*) He'd set up all night cleanin' of it! (*With a vehemence almost of ecstasy.*) Cleanin' of it and cleanin' of it till it shine like the Gates of Heaven, he would!

MRS. WEATHERBURN (*abandoning the door to advance upon him*). Bane, you gi'me that ca'tridge and that gun. They're my prop'ty, not yourn.

BANE (*thrusting the shell into a pocket*). No, sir! Sorry, but I guess I'll want to hang onto these articles a spell. Sorry!

MRS. WEATHERBURN (*deliberately*). Bane, what would you do if I was to tell you 'twas me shot that gun?

BANE. Shouldn't b'lieve ye.

MRS. WEATHERBURN. Bane, what are you *at?*

BANE ("*hefting*" *the weapon thoughtfully*). H'm'm. You and John been gettin' on well together these past few months? I don't know's I take much stock in gossip, but they do say John wa'n't always the easiest

man on earth to get on with—to home. Good man—savin' man—but temp'ry—they say. And of course there's women with tempers, too—

MRS. WEATHERBURN. I sha'n't stand here hark'nin' to you—

BANE. Women with tempers, too. 'Specially out on lonesome farms—'thout telephones nor gossip nor sociability nor nothin'—tryin' to the temper that is. 'Specially after it's been goin' on some years—draggin' on—always the same—workin' on the mind and temper. 'Specially with a man to do with—a sober man—a savin' man—but—

MRS. WEATHERBURN. Bane, them ain't your words! Them ain't your ideas!

BANE. Grant it. They ain't mine. They're the Pros'cutor's.

MRS. WEATHERBURN (*starting forward again*). *You gi'me—that—gun!*

BANE (*warding her off with his free hand*). Sha'n't! (*The door to the woodshed opens.* TIL *enters and stands regarding them stupidly, the candle in one hand, in the other the basket of wood.* BANE, *with an inspiration.*) Look here, don't let's bicker over the gun. Let's leave Til decide. Here, Til, take it! (*As he extends the weapon toward her* TIL *recoils, letting the candle and basket go. A screech of repugnance escapes her lips.*) What's wrong, Til? It's a good gun, ain't it?

TIL. Don't want it! (*Recoiling another step.*)

BANE. Why?

TIL. Kills things! Murders things! All manner o' livin' things it murders and kills!

BANE. *Then why'd you shoot it that time?*

TIL (*falling into the trap*). I—I don' know. I—I feel like I wanted to—to *horrify* myself! Want to hear it *bang!* To—*horrify* myself!

BANE. And what did you shoot *at*, Til?

TIL. Nothin'. Leastways nothin' but giants and ghosts and the like.

BANE. In the dark?

TIL. In the dark.

(**BANE,** *appearing satisfied, returns to his seat, and, propping the weapon beside him, rubs his hand over his face.*)

MRS. WEATHERBURN. Ed Bane, if you pretend to think Til knows what she's sayin'—

BANE (*blowing his lips*). I don't pretend to think, one way nor t'other.

That's other folks' business. All I say is, don't be s'prized! When John's body comes to be found one of these days, hid in the bushes somewheres or 'nunder somebody's strawstack—I say—don't be s'prized if his head's found half blow off in the back with a charge of bird shot. Mark what I say, and don't be s'prized. That's all.

MRS. WEATHERBURN. Set down, Til. (**TIL** *obeys with a kind of bewildered docility.* **MRS. WEATHERBURN** *picks up the wood basket, deposits it by the stove, takes two or three sticks, and lays them in the fire. All her movements have grown* lethargic.[5] *She recovers the candle from the floor and restores it to the*

5 **lethargic** (lĭ thär′jĭk): very slow; sluggish.

shelf, and afterward stands staring dully at it. She starts to speak.) Bane! (The telephone rings.)

TIL (as before). Banes'—Tolleys'—Jetherses'—Whites'—Us! Us, Abbie! Should I—? (Half rising.)

MRS. WEATHERBURN. Set down, Til. (She crosses the floor, still moving with the same appearance of apathy, and takes the receiver.) Yes, hullo! Yes, it's Abbie. Yes, what's wantin', Marion? (To BANE.) It's to your house, Bane! your sister speakin'. Would you want to— (Back to the phone again, with a queer, new, tight note.) How? How? (She listens, standing curiously rigid, her face empty, almost stupid. After a space she takes the receiver from her ear, studies the rubber contrivance for a blank moment, replaces it on its hook, and drifts back to the stove. She starts to take up the saucepan, but desists in the act. She turns slowly to face the others.) It's him.

BANE. Not—John!

MRS. WEATHERBURN. John.

TIL. Not—livin'!

MRS. WEATHERBURN. In the flesh.

TIL. No. (Shaking her head solemnly.) No, no, no.

BANE. John! Well, of all things! And me here, then, all for nothin'! But how come? Where's he to? Not to my house? Did Marion—

MRS. WEATHERBURN (speaking in a distrait monotone). 'Twas your hired man, Eggar, see him, Marion says. She says Eggar was up to the pasture just now, lookin' to get the gray colt in out of all this storm. He had a lantern with him, lookin' every-

wheres for the colt. He think he see somethin' movin' along the road, and, thinkin' mebby 'twas the colt had got out, he climb the fence there near Tolley's strawstacks—

BANE. Where?

MRS. WEATHERBURN. —by Tolley's turn where his strawstacks are—

TIL. Mebby he's been 'nunder Tolley's strawstacks. Seems I've hear somebody sayin' he might be 'nunder somebody's strawstack—

BANE. Nothin'. Go on!

MRS. WEATHERBURN. —where his strawstacks are, and then he see 'twa'n't the colt after all. 'Twas a man. Walkin' along, Eggar says, matter o' fact, his hat pull down and his shoulders hunched and his hands in his pockets, in the rain. Eggar give him good ev'nin', Marion says, and when the man give him no answer, Eggar throw the light in his face, and he couldn't b'lieve his eyes first, when he see 'twas John. Marion says he speak to him again—ast him where he come from, and then ast him if he hadn't best stop in a spell till the rain let up, but John never says a word, 'cordin' to Eggar, but come on up along the road like a—a deaf man—

TIL (musing). —dead man—

MRS. WEATHERBURN. He look wore out, Eggar says.

TIL. Wore out. No wonder. Wore out.

BANE. Well, I vow! Of all things!

MRS. WEATHERBURN (glancing around her with a numbed air). I s'pose I better put on somethin' hot to eat, if he's comin'.

BANE. I shouldn't worry. He may

be *comin'*, all right, but I doubt he'll *reach,* a night like this. It's too much for mortal man, the way the brook's swole, and the wind—

TIL (*absorbed*). He'll reach. John'll reach. But he won't want for nothin' to eat. John won't.

MRS. WEATHERBURN. I s'pose I better put on somethin' hot. Le'me see, le'me see.

(*Wandering to the cupboard by the stove, she prods amongst its contents with aimless fingers. She examines the state of the fire. She takes three plates from a shelf and carries them to the table. Depositing them under the pink lamp shade, she suddenly relapses into a chair. After a moment she drops her arms on the table, buries her face in them, and begins to weep without sound.* TIL *remains oblivious to all this, her head lifted, attentive to the outer gale.*)

TIL. Hark to 'em! Hark to 'em come, makin' a moan and a drone and a racket on the stairs o' the mountain! All the things that's dead! The old things that's dead, like the giants! And the new things that's dead! Comin' against the wind! Hark!

BANE. Pester the woman! (*Turning his uncomfortable attention.*) Come, come, Mis' Weatherburn!

TIL. Hark to 'em troopin' through the long wet grass. Hark to 'em swishin' through the trees.

BANE (*jumping up with an exasperated clatter*). Pester the crazy— (*Moving toward* MRS. WEATHERBURN,

laying a hand on her shoulder.) Come now, Mis' Weatherburn! Come! I know it's a good deal of a shock to ye—happy shock, of course —but a shock, all the same. But you've had your cry now, ain't ye? Now's the time to smile. Ain't ye glad John's turned out alive, after all? Eh? Ain't ye glad?

MRS. WEATHERBURN (*lifting her head and speaking with a curious vehemence*). Am I glad? If you was to know *how glad!*

BANE. There! That's better! It's but natural a woman should be glad havin' her husband back again, safe and sound.

MRS. WEATHERBURN. 'Tain't that, Bane. (*With a quick glance at* TIL.) Til, I know what I'll put on for supper. You rec'lect that fowl I got hung for Sunday out in the shed? You go bring it in for me.

TIL. He won't want it.

MRS. WEATHERBURN (*sharply*). Til, you do as I say!

TIL (*sullenly, rising*). Don't like the dark. There's things.

MRS. WEATHERBURN. Don't be a scared cat. Here! (*Getting up and lighting the candle for her.*) Take this, then the dark won't be there. That's a good girl.

(*She stands facing* BANE, *as* TIL *goes out and the door closes behind her. After a moment he speaks.*)

BANE. What you mean, " 'Tain't that!"? Ain't you glad to have John back?

MRS. WEATHERBURN. John's comin' or goin'—'specially after he's laid *this* on us to bear through—his comin' or goin' ain't apt to affect my happiness one way or t'other. That's what I mean, Bane.

BANE. You do speak out, don't ye? But you says you was glad he was—

MRS. WEATHERBURN. Alive! To *know* it. More glad and relieved than I can—

BANE. I see now! Then after all 'twas about—

MRS. WEATHERBURN. Yes.

BANE. —about Til! You wa'n't so sure's you made out, about Til. About that gun, and shootin' at ghosts, and all that.

MRS. WEATHERBURN (*giving way to the revulsion of relief; wringing her hands*). I tell you true I didn't know *what* to think. Oh, if you'd had the bringin' up of that poor creature! If you'd had the worry of her and the shieldin' of her! and knowin' every minute you never know an atom of what was next in her poor wild brain! Oh, if you had! And then I was away that night, too; most an hour I was away, down to Mis' Jethers's. And then there's another thing. Til's fond of me. She's like a dog. I b'lieve she'd do *anything*—

BANE. Yes, go on. And mebby there was some special reason— mebby you and John'd had words or somethin'—

MRS. WEATHERBURN. We'd had words that day. John was his worst that day. Over my wantin' the phone. John lay a hand on me for the first time.

BANE. And Til see him?

MRS. WEATHERBURN. Til see him. Oh, if you'd had that thought weighin' on your brain, week after week!

Oh, you'd know why I was glad!

BANE (*blowing out his lips, thoughtfully*). I'm glad you been frank, Mis' Weatherburn. I'm glad you've tell me these things. I sha'n't forget—and I hope *you* won't forget—

MRS. WEATHERBURN. Ssssh! (*The woodshed door bursts open;* TIL *enters in haste, glancing nervously over her shoulder, the extinguished candle in her hand.*) What's wrong, Til? Where's the fowl?

TIL. There's things. They blow my candle out.

MRS. WEATHERBURN. *Til!* Where's that fowl?

TIL (*sulkily, still peering behind*). He won't want it. Where's the use o' spoilin' earthly victuals— (*The telephone rings. Her facile attention runs to it.*) Banes'—Tolleys' —Jetherses'—Whites'—Us! Abbie! They've see him again.

> (*She starts sidling toward the instrument, half scared, half furtive, as if hoping she may reach it first.* MRS. WEATHER- BURN *passes her and takes the receiver.*)

MRS. WEATHERBURN. Yes, it's me, Mattie. How? Speak louder. Yes, I hear now. Yes, I tell you I hear. (*She continues attentive. The hush in the room grows long.*) Yes, I'm list'nin'. He wa'n't himself, you say.

TIL. Abbie!

BANE. Be quiet, Til!

MRS. WEATHERBURN. Yes, Mattie, yes, I've hear it all. Much obliged, Mattie. (*Replacing the receiver, she half turns and stands staring at the door.*)

TIL. *Abbie!*

MRS. WEATHERBURN (*as to herself*). What's ailin' of him? There's something queer.

TIL. Abbie, for *mercy* sake, say somethin'! Where was it—to Tolleys' this time?

MRS. WEATHERBURN. Yes, to Tolleys'. He's been by. 'Twas Tolley himself see him. He was comin' back from havin' a last look at the road bridge—that's gone and carry out now after all—Tolley was, when he met him. Mis' Tolley says Tolley got home in a sweat, as if he'd see a ghost.

TIL. Yes. See a ghost.

MRS. WEATHERBURN. Seems Tolley speak to him before he see who he was. He says to him: "Best stop back, mister; the bridge is gone out above." Then, gettin' no answer, Tolley look closer and see who 'twas he was speakin' to. Tolley was so laid out for a minute he didn't know which end up. Then he think of the bridge again, and "John," he says, "if you *are* John Weatherburn, 's you seem to be, you best come back to my house along with me." But by that John was gone on up the road and disappeared.

BANE. And the bridge out, ahead of him!

MRS. WEATHERBURN (*with the new thought*). Mercy angels! he'll walk straight in—

BANE. No, but he'll see—

MRS. WEATHERBURN. —and be drownded!

TIL. Ha-ha-ha-ha— (*Her laugh rises shrill, tenuous,[6] ironic, queer.*)

6 **tenuous**: lacking force; not hearty.

BANE. Pester you! Quit!

MRS. WEATHERBURN (*staring into the pink light*). What's ailin' of him? Where's his senses gone? Where's he been to? What's he done? What makes him come on, come on, keep comin' on, never sayin' a word to no one, just comin' on, comin' on through the soakin' night? What is it—*drivin'* him?

TIL. Ha-ha-ha-ha-ha—

BANE (*in a fury*). *Goll* pester you! If you don't quit that! What makes ye keep laughin' that crazy way?

TIL. It's the horror! It's the horror gettin' into my throat!

BANE. Horror? Horror o' what?

TIL. Him! Comin'! Comin' up the wind! Drove! Comin' up the road, comin' up the field, up the cowyard, up the steps, comin' in the door there, takin' off his hat there, settin' down in his chair there 'thout a word with his back to us all, so's we'll have to see the back of his head there, half blow off, and straws stickin' into it—

BANE (*shouting*). Straws? Where from?

TIL. From Tolley's stacks. Didn't you say he come from Tolley's strawstacks? I hear you say a while back—

BANE. Mis' Weatherburn, mark that! I call on ye to make note of that! I'll ast ye to rec'lect that!

MRS. WEATHERBURN. What on earth you talkin' of— (*The phone rings. TIL's voice drones in a note of fascination.*)

TIL. —Banes'—Tolleys'—Jetherses'—Whites'—Us!

MRS. WEATHERBURN (*who has the receiver with the last signal*). Yes, me! (*After an instant she puts out a hand to the wall to steady her. She turns to the others, still holding the receiver to her ear.*) They've found his—body.

BANE. *Where?* (*Blanching.*) I—I demand you tell me *where?*

MRS. WEATHERBURN (*in the phone*). Where? In the brook? No? (*Turning again.*) No, not in the brook. This side. This is to Jetherses' now. Joe Jethers see the body lyin' on its back in the mud down by their gate. He come back for Ed. (*At a signaling flutter in the receiver.*) Yes, Clara? How? Gone! You didn't say—gone? (*She hangs up the receiver and slowly turns.*) When Joe and Ed get back to the gate, 'twas gone. So it couldn't've been his bod—he couldn't've been *dead.* He must've just swounded there a minute—like's not—

TIL (*in the same eerie note*). Ha-ha-ha-ha—

BANE (*choking*). I'll kill ye, Til Jessup! I'll strangle ye 'f you don't leave off that— Here! Where ye goin' *now?* (*As TIL moves, or, rather, seems to be pulled toward the door.*) Til, if you open that door, I vow— Quit it! Mis' Weatherburn, make her quit it, the crazy, ravin' thing! (*TIL lifts the latch with a trancelike deliberation, pulls open the door, and stands on the sill, framed by the darkness, cringing and hugging her body with her fleshy arms.*) I vow! That's the end!

MRS. WEATHERBURN. What you carryin' on so for, Til?

TIL (*peering into the night*). To horrify myself. I got to look. To horrify me. I see him! (*Crouching a little.*) Black as pitch it is, and yet I see him. 'Nunder the trees he is; 'nunder the meadow rise he is, and yet I see him—comin' on—comin' on up the road toward Whites'. (*She crouches yet a little lower. The backwash of the wind in the house's lee lifts the strings of her unkempt hair.*)

BANE (*almost in a whisper*). That's the end! That's enough!

TIL. Comin' on, comin' on. He's up the hill to Whites' now. He's under the aspen trees, up by the lower gate to Whites' now. Comin' on under the aspen trees. In the black dark there, inunder the aspen trees at the bend; inunder the drippin' aspen trees. The dead eyes shinin' pale in his head, pale as ashes in his blowed-out head—shinin' pale in the drippin' dark inunder the aspen trees. You'd think he'd drag his feet, but he don't drag his feet. His feet's not on the ground. Inches above the ground his feet is, and he comes on floatin' against the wind, sailin' against the black wind and rain. Not against the wind! Betwixt the wind! Betwixt the flakes of the wind! Comin' on out—out from inunder the aspen trees—

BANE (*who has been closing on her, step by rigid step*). That's the end! (*Grasping her arm roughly, he drags her within the room and slams the door. He stands with his right hand spread against it; with his left he shakes an ecstatic finger in her face.*) Just for that, Til Jessup—to learn ye, Til Jessup—for that—I—here *and* now—I arrest ye, Til Jessup, in the name of the law—I arrest ye for

the murder of John Partley Weatherburn on the night of—

MRS. WEATHERBURN. Edwin *Bane,*
you crazy? What you sayin'? And
him comin' there in the flesh!

BANE (*flinging around on her*).
'Tain't so! All a trick! What'd ye
think the Pros'cutor'd been by to
every house in the valley today for?
All a trick o' Cantpole's doin'! *Pre-*
'ranged, every mite of it! *R*ehearsed,
every word of it! The whole livin'
thing's a big goll-danged *trick!*
There! Don't ye b'lieve me? Me?
That was with him when he 'ranged
it? (*Still receiving no answer of
word or gesture from the suddenly
quiet woman, he returns his attention to his prisoner, whose wrist he
shakes.*) You hear me, Til? I arrest ye for the murder. Moreover, I
arrest ye for goin' to work and con-
cealin' the corpse—by your own con-
fession, mind ye—in some one or
'nother of Tolley's strawstacks—
where I and the Pros'cutor'll have a
look in the mornin'—

MRS. WEATHERBURN (*bewildered,
appealing*). Bane, that ain't right!
'Tain't true! You're just—just twistin'
the poor child's words about—that's
what you're doin'—to your own ends.

BANE (*wheeling*). Own ends?
Own ends, ye say? I'll ask ye to
weigh your words, Mis' Weatherburn. I vow! Next thing you'll be
accusin' *me* of—of—most anything!
Accusin' *me,* the Sheriff o' Twinskill
County! Of—most anything!

(TIL *stands as though untouched
by all this, inert, entranced,
staring at the door as if its*

panels were no barrier to her
occult[7] vision.)

TIL. Comin' on swifter now, he is.
Comin' on, comin' on. He's been
by Whites' now, and they've see him.
Mis' White's see him; in the light
from the porch she see him. Now
she's goin' back through the hall,
white's a sheet. Now she's goin'
acrost the dinin' room. Now she's
to the telephone— (TIL's *head
swings irresistibly in the direction of
the phone. As irresistibly the others'
gazes follow. The bell begins to
ring.*) Banes'— (*She glances at*
MRS. WEATHERBURN, *who does
not move.*) Tolleys'—Jetherses'—
(*Throwing off the* SHERIFF's *hand,
she runs to the instrument and puts
the receiver to her ear.*) Yes?
Yes? Quick, Mis' White! Yes?
Quick—

(BANE *is upon her. Wresting
the receiver from her hand,
he thrusts her aside.*)

BANE (*in the phone*). Who's there?
Hullo! Hullo! Who's there? It's
me, Bane—Sheriff Bane—me speakin'.
What? Yes, I hear! What? Hullo!
Hullo! Dang it, they're gone again!
(*Rattling the hook.*) Hullo! *Goll*
dang the thing! (*With a sudden
malignant fury he strikes the instrument from the wall, so that it hangs
swaying from one screw, the wires
broken.*) There now, dang ye!
Ring, will ye! Go on and ring!
Ring! (*Turning around with a hand
to his head, his eyes fall on* TIL, *back*

7 occult (ə kŭlt′): mysterious.

at the door again, holding it wide, staring out.) Goll dang ye, Til!

Til. He's on the farm now. I hear the gate just now. In the roar and moan of the wind I hear the gate. (*Lifting her voice to a nerve-struck scream.*) John! John!

Mrs. Weatherburn. Oh, *Til!*

Bane (*advancing*). Oh, *"Til"?* I'll *"Til"* her! I'll *"Til"* the crazy!

(*Dragging her back, he casts her violently on the floor. He slams the door with a force sufficient to carry away the latch, which falls in a clatter of bits about his feet.*)

Mrs. Weatherburn. You broke the latch!

Til (*from the floor*). You broke the latch. Now you *can't* keep it shut.

Bane (*deep in his throat*). I guess I can! *I* guess I can!

(*He stands facing it, his two hands spread against it, his feet propped out solidly behind. Silence follows, the clock-tick silence of the room enclosed in the outer shell of storm. Bane remains propped and motionless, breathing heavily. Mrs. Weatherburn sinks into a chair and holds her hands crossed on her breast. Til, still on the floor to one side of the door, holds her head erect and attentive.*)

Til (*after a time*). That's the other gate. The near one.

Bane (*his breath rasping*). I never hear a thing! (*The hush runs on again for seconds.*)

Til. You hear that, then? On the gravel? He's come out of the wind now. He's got his feet on the ground now. Hear that?

Bane. No! No! No! (*Another moment.*)

Til. On the step. There. Standin'. Standin' still.

(*The hush returns. After a space of it a voice becomes audible, racked, thin, almost falsetto.[8] It is the voice of* **Bane,** *to the door.*)

Bane. Go 'way! Go 'way, I tell ye! (*Beating the panel.*) Go 'way!

Til. He ain't gone. Still standin'.

Bane (*after a moment, putting his lips nearer the wood*). I'll tell ye somethin' there! Ye listenin'? I'll tell ye somethin'. I got a gun here. It's your own gun, John, and it's loaded with bird shot. Right here to my hand I got it. (*Removing one hand cautiously from the door, he gropes out blindly to the right, where the shotgun rests against the wall beside the chair.*) Right here I got it, John! (*Finding he cannot reach it, he takes his other hand from the door, and is about to take the furtive, necessary step, when the door begins to swing inward, slowly. A cackle emerges from* **Til**'s *open mouth; a kind of high, tight, tittering of the palate.* **Bane** *flings himself against the door again, slamming it tight.*) No, ye don't! No, ye don't!

8 falsetto: unnaturally high in pitch.

(*A summons sounds on the panels, a muffled knock as of a soft glove.*)

BANE (*screeching in his throat.*) No, ye won't! Ye can't! Ye can't touch me, John Weatherburn! No, sir! 'Twa'n't my fault! 'Twa'n't! Ye oughtn't've called me a liar, there by the gate! Not with a gun in my hand! Ye oughtn't've dare strike me! Not when I had a gun in my hand! Ye ought've know me better'n that, John! Your own fault, John! Twa'n't m-i-n-e—

VOICE FROM WITHOUT. Open the door, Bane! Open, I tell you!

MRS. WEATHERBURN (*wondering*). That's never the voice of John.

(BANE, *wilting and letting go the door, relapses into the chair and claps both his hands over his eyes.*)

BANE. It's Cantpole. Thank goodness it's only Cantpole, after all.

TIL (*from the floor*). John's went and bring the Pros'cutor along.

(*The door swings open.* MR. CANTPOLE *enters, removing his soft hat and shaking out the wet. He looks at* MRS. WEATHERBURN *still seated in her chair.*)

CANTPOLE. Good evening, Mrs. Weatherburn. I just dropped up from Mr. White's place—as by *arrangement* with Mr. Bane. (*He peers around the door at the figure huddled in the chair there.*) So, Sheriff? Just as well I came, eh? What's all this I hear? What's *that*?

(*As from the tail of his eye he perceives something scuttling past him on the floor and out of the door.*)

MRS. WEATHERBURN. That's only Til. Til, where you goin' to?

TIL (*lost in the darkness without*). To—*horrify* myself! (*And fainter, still further off.*) John! John!

CURTAIN

Understanding Literature

1. What specific elements in the setting produce feelings of horror and mystery? How is the setting appropriate to the action of the play?
2. What effect does the ringing of the telephone produce in the play? (Before answering, ask yourself, At what moments does the telephone ring? What pieces of information are received on the telephone? In what other way is the telephone related to the action of the play?
3. List several ways that the playwright creates or heightens the suspense in the play.
4. What information are you given in the opening exposition between Til and Mrs. Weatherburn?
5. What kind of person was John Weatherburn? What motive would Mrs. Weatherburn or Til have for murdering him?
6. Why does Mrs. Weatherburn weep when she learns that John is not dead but on his way home?
7. The conflict between Til and Bane becomes more and more intense until the climax of the play. Where is the climax? What specific action leads to the climax?
8. At what point did you suspect who the real murderer was?
9. If the author had been writing a short story instead of a play, what techniques for revealing character and developing a plot could he have used that he could not use in writing a play?

A group of cowboys complain bitterly about their hard life: no pay, bad food, cold weather, and no romance. Their lives are dreary and uninteresting. What they need is a change of scenery, a different outlook on life, a breath of summer. How they get their change, as summer comes to the Diamond O, may surprise you.

Summer Comes to the Diamond O*

Robert Finch

IMPROVING YOUR READING: The theme of this play is revealed by a number of contrasts. First, life on the Diamond O is in contrast with life as depicted in *Tender Wild West Romances*. Then the mysterious Stranger appears. How does the Stranger contrast with the cowboys? How does the cookshack change after the Stranger's arrival? And, most importantly, how do the attitudes of the cowboys change?

The cookshack is an old log cabin. The weather-beaten logs are indifferently chinked with mud. Upstage, near C, is a large, crude table, with a white oilcloth cover tacked onto it. There is a long bench behind the table, an upended apple box at one end, and a nail keg at the other. The cook's cot stands in the corner UR. It is spread with wrinkled horse blankets, and everything eventually finds its way onto it; though at present only a small guitar lies there. Above the cot is a small window, with a wooden box nailed to the wall under it and which contains the cook's possessions: a Wild West magazine, an old pipe, some letters, a razor, pencil, and a tablet of paper. His other shirt, a wild plaid one, hangs from a nail next to the box.

In the center of the wall R is a door which leads outside. Another door, upstage in wall L, leads to the kitchen, the opening to which is partly concealed by a ragged, burlap curtain. Downstage against this wall is a rickety wash bench, with a bucket of water, a tin dipper, and two washbasins. Next to it hangs a grimy flour-sack towel. A broken old comb hangs on a string, next to a cracked mirror. A lighted kerosene lamp, with a dark tin shade, hangs over the table. At R, downstage of *the door, is a battered heating stove, with a long length of black stovepipe. The stove is glowing, and casts flickers of light about the room, which is in semidarkness except for the pool of light on the table, the light cast by the stove, and the warm glow of another lamp which gleams through the curtains of the kitchen door.*

A saddle, bridle, and chaps hang from pegs driven into the walls. The polished leather and the steel catch the rays of the yellow lamplight. It is an evening in late October; and through the little window, the distant peaks of the Ruby Mountains glow with a purple light in the nearly darkened sky. The table is partly set for supper.

AT RISE: **COOKY**, *a short, grizzled fellow of indeterminate age, wearing a pair of dirty denim pants and a shirt, with a dirty flour sack tied about his waist for an apron, is finishing a mad dash across the room by tripping and sliding to door at R. He stoops, stretches his arm outside the door, rises, and is seen clutching a long, raw, dust-sprinkled steak. He shakes his fist at an unseen fleeing dog.*

COOKY. Danged ol' dog! (*Throws a cup out after the dog.*) Git out and stay out! (*Tries to spank dust from steak, gives up, mumbles.*) Have to sprinkle extra pepper on it. Grit ain't goin' to be noticed then. (*He throws it through doorway at L. Then he steps outside the door at R and beats vigorously on the dinner gong hanging outside. He crosses*

room and goes off at L. A gentle, sad, monotonous singing rises above the clatter of the dishes.) "Come and sit by my side if you love me. Do not hasten to bid me adieu." (*He returns, singing, with a handful of "silverware."*) "But remember the Red River Valley, and the cowboy that's waitin' for you." (*He polishes a knife, fork, and spoon on his dirty apron, then sets one place very carefully and repeats on the next place. Suddenly, realizing the futility of it all, he throws the whole batch on the table with a great clatter. He strides to door at R and yells.*) Come and git it before I throw it out!

CURLY (*in the distance*). Coming-g-g! (**COOKY** *hurries off UL, returning immediately with a huge platter of meat, a bowl of potatoes, and a pot of coffee. He has difficulty balancing these.*) Here I come, Cooky! (**CURLY** *rushes in, skims his hat onto the cot, crosses DL, and proceeds to wash, with great sputterings.*)

COOKY. Hope thet water's hot enough for that pretty face o' yours, Curly.

CURLY. You're shore a good judge of horseflesh, Cooky. (**STUB** *enters from R. He carries a short branding iron, which he places on the cot. He throws his hat and coat onto the cot.*) Ain't he, Stub?

STUB. Shore.

(*He crosses DL and washes his hands.*)

CURLY. Let's have another towel. The dog's been sleepin' on this one.

COOKY (*arranging food on table*). No clean towel till Saturday. (*Con-*

temptuously, as CURLY *gingerly dries his face.*) Dude!

> (CURLY *takes basin to door R, opens it, and flings out the water.*)

TEX'S VOICE (*just outside, howls*). Yo-o-o-ow! (CURLY *stares outside in consternation, backs away to C, as* TEX *enters, holding his dripping hat at arm's length.*) What are you coyotes tryin' to do? Drown me?

> (*He throws his wet hat onto cot, as* CURLY *turns and crosses to washstand.*)

CURLY. Don't get ornery, Tex. (*Slicking his hair down with the broken comb.*) Your face is all washed now. All you got to do is dry it.

STUB (*handing* TEX *the towel at C, as he crosses to bench above table, and glances at the table*). Fried cow for supper again.

> (TEX *dries his face, then throws the towel in the general direction of the washstand, as he crosses and sits on apple box at R end of table.*)

TEX. We been eatin' on that steer six weeks now. We ought to be right down to his backbone.

CURLY (*as he comes to apple box at L end of table and sits*). Boiled potatoes again!

STUB. Fried beef and boiled potatoes three times a day for six weeks!

> (*They push their plates away.*)

COOKY (*plaintively*). I can't hardly choke it down, myself. But that's all the Boss hands me to cook. And —we got stewed prunes for dessert tonight . . . again.

TEX. Why don't we all quit?

STUB. Where'd we go? Winter's comin' on. Most ranches are layin' off their cowpunchers now.

COOKY. Boss is lookin' for a chance to lay off you fellers too.

CURLY. Goin' to be a hard winter. The coyotes look lean and hungry. The deer left the ranges long ago. *They* know.

STUB. I don't like winter. Snow and cold and nothin' to do but think.

> (*Sad and thoughtful, they start perfunctorily to eat.* GRANNY, *a grizzled, weather-beaten cowhand of forty, comes in lugging a saddle which he throws onto the cot, adding his hat and coat. By now the cot is well piled up.*)

GRANNY. You fellers think I got lost? Was you cryin'?

TEX. We was goin' to flip a coin for your prunes. If we had a coin.

GRANNY (*sits L of* STUB *on bench, without bothering to wash*). I aim to eat everything in sight. No matter how bad it tastes. (COOKY *gives him a withering look and goes into the kitchen.*) Ridin' fences shore gives a man a real appetite.

TEX (*takes a drink of coffee, sputters and spews it out*). Phooey! Chicory in it again, so's the Boss can save on coffee.

STUB. I wish it was summer again. I like ridin' in the sun and sleepin' out nights under the sky.

GRANNY (*shivers and pulls up his coat collar*). Mighty cold in here. Boss should have chinked up the logs against the winter.

COOKY (*enters with plate of bis-*

cuits and a bowl of prunes, which he passes around as he talks). Boss ain't goin' to buy you no stove for your bunkhouse. He says you're a bunch of dudes wantin' a stove, and dessert with your meals, and all them frills and high-falutin' fandangles.

STUB. Ain't nothing wrong with wantin' something fancy now and then.

COOKY. Well, I'll put paper pants on the next batch of pork chops.

GRANNY *(dreamily).* You might not believe it to look at me, but I knew a gal once that baked angel food cakes with big gobs of whipped cream drippin' off 'em. Her name was Genevieve. *(Looks at his spoonful of prunes.)* Doggone it, I should have married 'er.

CURLY *(leaps up, yelling, takes something from his mouth, throws the biscuit down, and stamps on it).* That done settled it! That biscuit broke off the finest gold tooth I ever had!

> *(He holds the tooth between his fingers and examines it ruefully.)*

COOKY *(crossing to opening UL).* I couldn't help it. We're fresh out of bakin' powder and there wasn't hardly no lard for shortenin'.

> *(He exits.)*

CURLY *(dramatically).* I'm leavin'!

GRANNY *(as everyone looks up, startled).* Where you headin' for?

CURLY. Anywheres but here. I'll draw my pay and light out. We got two months' back pay comin', and eighty dollars will take me a long way.

GRANNY. If you leave without warnin', the Boss don't have to pay you off. It's different if he fires you, though.

CURLY. Could ask for my pay first and *then* leave.

> *(He sits on apple box again. The door R opens quietly. Unobserved by the* **COWBOYS**, **MR. HOUSTON**, *the Boss, stands in the doorway.)*

TEX. I'll go with you. Shore would teach the Boss a lesson. *(CURLY looks up and sees the Boss. Frantically he signals* **TEX**. **TEX** *pays no heed. The other* **COWBOYS** *turn and see the* **BOSS**. **ALL** *try to warn* **TEX**. *But* **TEX**, *his back to the door, talks loudly and belligerently.)* The old rattlesnake is making our life miserable, so's we'll pull out before our time's up, and he won't have to pay us. Say! Next time I see him, I'll spit right in his eye. I'll shore tell him where to head in at. *(Noticing the tension, he turns slowly and sees the* **BOSS**. *He rises. His tone changes suddenly to one of polite greeting.)* Why, howdy, Boss. Come right on in.

HOUSTON *(coming into the room at RC).* You're fired! And the rest of you can go with him.

> *(TEX sits again.)*

CURLY. How about the back pay you owe us?

HOUSTON. Well, I'll mail it to you. Send me your address when you get located.

GRANNY *(evenly).* Might take you some time to get around to it. No. We better stay on fer a spell.

HOUSTON. I can't pay you off till I sell them steers. (COWBOYS *exchange dubious looks.*) Don't you believe me? (*They stare at him.*)

STUB. Shore wish you could pay us, Boss.

HOUSTON (*after a moment's hesitation*). I didn't come over here to argue. I'm fair and square with my cowhands. Always was. (*Takes a billfold from his pocket. The* COWBOYS *look hopeful.*) Tell you what I'll do. I'll give you ten dollars apiece out of what you got comin'. (*As he gives each one a bill.*) Use it for travelin' if you want to leave the Diamond O. Or you can buy you a bunch of stoves and canned peaches and lacy curtains so's you'll be satisfied here. You'll get the rest when I sell them steers. (*Replacing his billfold and going to door R.*) And not a day sooner! I hope you all

quit! I'll be glad to get you off my place. Lazy, complainin' dudes!

(*He goes out, slamming the door.*)

CURLY. Ten measly dollars! Well, it's enough to get me out of here, anyways.

STUB. Where you goin'?

CURLY. I'm goin' to throw a saddle on old Buck and head him south and keep ridin'. Ridin' along, steady, cookin' my own grub, and campin' out nights. (*Dreamily.*) And then a day'll come when it's fine and warm, and I'll ask the first stranger I see, "Where 'bouts am I, pardner?" And he'll say, "Californy, cowboy."

GRANNY. It ain't that easy. You can travel for weeks and spend all of that ten dollars and still be in Montana. Montana's a mighty big spread.

STUB. Ain't got nothin' 'gainst the

Diamond O . . . in summer. But in winter . . .

(*He shudders, crosses to cot and sits.*)

TEX. Nothin' to do but see that a herd of white-faced cattle get through the winter.

STUB (*has rummaged under all the stuff on the cot, now pulls out his guitar*). Anyways, I got my music.

(*He sits, tunes up and tries out a few chords.*)

CURLY (*clasping hands behind his head. Dreamily*). Next to Californy, I'd like to find one of them places where the ranch is owned by a pretty young gal. Cowpuncher rides by, and she gives him a job. And she needs him to help her, 'cause her foreman is rustlin' her cattle. (*In his enthusiasm he gets himself identified as the noble cowboy.*) And I show him up and save the cattle, and the gal makes me foreman and ups and marries me, and I get to own the ranch. All in ninety days' time. Just imagine it.

TEX (*interested*). Where does all this happen?

CURLY. I don't know. (*Rises, crosses, and takes magazine from box over the cot.*) I read about it in here. *Tender Wild West Romances.*

(*He comes back to apple box, L of table.*)

STUB. Must be mighty pretty country round there.

GRANNY. You danged idiot, they're writin' about out here!

CURLY (*astonished, reseats himself*). Who'd ever believe that!

TEX. Must be somewheres the other side of the Ruby Mountains.

Never heard of such doin's hereabouts.

STUB (*striking a louder chord*). Say, fellers, I can play it! That tune we heard over in Elkhorn last summer. (*Strikes another chord and sings in a sad tenor voice.*)

"I'm a poor, lonesome cowboy,
  I'm a poor, lonesome cowboy,
  I'm a poor, lonesome cowboy,
  And a long ways from home."

(*He pauses and chords. In the distance is heard the doleful wail of a coyote.*)

TEX. Quit it! You're makin' some poor coyote lonesome, too.

STUB.

"I ain't got no sweetheart,
  I ain't got no sweetheart,
  I ain't got no sweetheart,
  To sit and talk with me."

CURLY (*over the singing*). They might maybe make me eat Cooky's grub, but you bet nobody can make me listen to that.

(*Goes to door R, followed by TEX.*)

STUB (*ignoring them*).

"I'm a poor, lonesome cowboy,
  I'm a poor, lonesome cowboy."

(CURLY, *opening door, steps back as he sees a* STRANGER *framed in the doorway.* CURLY *remains near door R.* TEX, *in surprise, backs up to R end of cot.* COOKY *reappears in opening UL.*

(*The* STRANGER *is a gaudily dressed young cowboy. He wears shining white chaps, a fine white sombrero with a snakeskin band, doeskin gloves, and an embroidered doeskin vest, also a white silk shirt, sky-blue neckerchief, and highly ornamental boots. The boys stare as he steps in.* STUB's *song trails off.*)

STRANGER. Don't stop. Keep a-playin'.

STUB (*startled*). Huh?

STRANGER. Where'd you get that there guitar? (*He smiles—a bright smile touched with happiness, enthusiasm, and friendliness. The* COWBOYS *continue to stare at this resplendent figure.*) I shore admire that instrument. Shore has a wonderful tone. (*He stares admiringly at the guitar, as he crosses to* STUB's *L and lays his hat on the cot.*) Musta cost a small fortune.

STUB (*embarrassed, but greatly pleased*). Naw. I give a feller two dollars for it. Said he got it from Sears, Roebuck.

STRANGER. He must have been loco, sure enough. (*Runs his finger over the grain of the woods.*) Look at the shine she's got.

GRANNY. Cheap shellac, and you know it.

STRANGER. Oh, no! It's patina . . . a shine that comes on fine old things. Like them guitars they have in old Spain. (STUB *tries a chord. The* STRANGER *sighs in ecstasy.*) Listen at that! (*Another chord or two.*) Ain't it beautiful?

CURLY (*surprised*). 'Tain't bad at that.

GRANNY. He's just playin' it more careful-like.

STUB. Set down, Stranger. (*Looks at the* STRANGER's *fine clothes and then wipes the box off with his sleeve. Remains standing near R end of table, holding guitar.*) But don't get them pants dirty.

STRANGER (*as he sits on box R of table*). Don't care even if I do. Got eight more pairs just like 'em.

COOKY. If you're aimin' to borrow money, we ain't got none. (*He moves to UL end of table.*)

STRANGER. That food shore looks good.

GRANNY. Don't let 'im work on you, Cooky.

(GRANNY *rises, crosses to cot and sits. Suspiciously* COOKY *moves the platter away from the* STRANGER. TEX, *drawn by the* STRANGER's *magnetic personality, moves toward bench above table.*)

STRANGER (*seeming not to hear*). Say! Don't tell me these are real, old-fashioned, bakin' powder biscuits! (*Picks one up and examines it.*) They are! Just like they make down in old New England. Didn't think anybody in Montana knew the secret of makin' 'em. (*He samples one, looks pleased.*) They're wonderful! Nice and firm! Not mushy like some.

TEX (*at UL corner of table, takes one and bites into it with an effort*). They sure ain't mushy. I can tell you that.

(*But the* STRANGER's *manner is so infectious that when he smiles delightedly at* TEX, TEX *smiles back.* STUB *lays his guitar under the R end of the bench.* TEX *and* STUB *kneel on bench.* CURLY *crosses to DL corner of table and stands with one knee on the L box. They all try the biscuits, even* COOKY.)

COOKY (*standing between* TEX *and* CURLY). I'll be dog-goned. They *are* good! (*Hurriedly pouring a cup of coffee.*) Try this coffee.

STRANGER (*drinks, looks pleased, takes another drink*). You fellers don't get coffee like this every day, do you?

GRANNY. No! Some days it's even worse!

STRANGER. It has that rich, dark taste like the coffee I used to get when I was livin' on a plantation down in old Virginia.

GRANNY (*drily*). I'll bet.

COOKY. Have a piece of meat.

STRANGER (*in awe*). Do you fellers have meat every day?

TEX. Three times.

STRANGER. Gosh! (*He eats a piece, chewing thoughtfully. Then he turns to them.*) Last time I et steak like that . . .

GRANNY (*breaking in cynically*). We know. In a swell hotel in Chicago.

STRANGER. No. It was at the Ritz Waldorf in New York City. Cost me fifteen dollars and wasn't half as good as this.

COOKY (*pleased*). Are you fellers listenin'?

STRANGER. You shore are lucky, havin' a cook like him.

STUB. He ain't so bad, I guess.

COOKY (*carried away*). I got a dab of cake out in the kitchen.

CURLY (*suspiciously*). Cake? And you handed *us* prunes?

COOKY (*furtively*). I was savin' it for a Christmas surprise. But set in, boys. There's enough for all.

(*He goes into the kitchen.* TEX *and* STUB *sit on bench,* CURLY *on the L box.* GRANNY *remains disapprovingly on the cot.*)

TEX. Stranger, I reckon you can lie as fast as a cowboy can rope a steer. But I don't hold it against you if it makes Cooky loosen up.

CURLY. Ain't no harm in his braggin'. Makes the time pass.

STRANGER (*puzzled*). Lyin'? Braggin'? *Who?*

STUB (*with an angry look at the others, changes topic*). Where you from, Stranger?

GRANNY. Yeah. That's what we'd like to know.

STRANGER. Oh, I'm from all over. Just now I'm fixed up good on the Ruby River. Got a nice little spread over there.

(COOKY *enters with a plate of sliced cake which he passes around.*)

COOKY. This is on me.

STRANGER (*as they eat*). Eatin' where he cooks is just like a party.

CURLY. How do you like it over on the Ruby . . . where you *said* you come from?

STRANGER. Fine! Fine! But I like it better down in Mexico. *Old* Mexico. This feller's guitar reminded me.

COOKY. He's Stub, and this here's Tex and Curly, and that's Granny over there.

STRANGER. I'm mighty proud to meet up with you all.

Stub. Is it nice and warm down there? (*A little bashfully.*) In old Mexico?

Stranger. It's always warm there. Even in winter. It's downright beautiful!

Granny (*sarcastically*). I better see the door's shut good. You might catch cold bein' so used to them warm climates. (*He goes to the door which is open a crack. He pulls it wide open in order to slam it. Something catches his eye.*) Well, string me up for a rustler! Whose horse is that? (*Tex, Curly, and Stub rush to the door.*) Biggest black horse I ever did see.

Stub. Them stirrups and that fancy bridle shine like silver.

Curly. That saddle horse yours, Stranger?

Stranger. Shore is. He comes clear from old Araby. Ever been there?

Tex. Nope. We don't get around much.

Curly. I don't know much about you, Stranger, but any man ownin' a horse like that must be all right.

> (**Granny** *closes the door. The* **Cowboys** *drift back to the places they left at the table.* **Granny** *remains near the door R.*)

Stranger. I'm pretty fond of him. Old Charley-mane, I call him. After that king . . . a long time ago. Mighty brave *hombre*.

Stub (*admiringly*). You must have got a good schoolin', knowin' such things.

Stranger. No, it's just I done a lot of travelin'.

GRANNY (*drily*). I can just imagine.

CURLY. Granny, why don't you just set a while and think of the gal who used to bake them pies, and leave us alone?

(GRANNY *remains standing R.*)

COOKY. He must have been all over. That's why he knows good cookin'.

(*He crosses to cot and sits.*)

STUB. Yeah. (*To* STRANGER.) What was you sayin'?

STRANGER. I was thinkin' of Charley-mane. Mighty sorry to leave him behind again.

TEX. Whatta you mean leave him behind?

STRANGER. Oh, I got to get back to old Mexico where it's warm. You fellers would like it. Sun always shinin'. Lots of good trout fishin'. All the land you want for the askin'. And them *senoritas!*

CURLY (*smoothing down his hair*). Are they pretty, like they say?

STRANGER. They're so beautiful you can't imagine it. (*Tolerantly.*) 'Course, the ladies are pretty in old Argentine, too. And they shore admire us *gauchos.*

TEX and CURLY. Us *what?*

STRANGER. Up here we're cowboys, but down there we're *gauchos.*

CURLY (*thrilled*). That's somethin' fine to know, all right.

GRANNY. What ranch do you ride for down in (*sneeringly*)—old Mexico? (*Holds up his hand as the* STRANGER *is about to answer.*) Don't tell me! I know! The biggest one in the world!

STRANGER (*pleasantly*). Oh, I don't ride for nobody. Don't have to. I got me a little gold mine down there. All I do is hire a feller to shovel the gold out for me. He's down there now. He sends me the money once a month.

TEX (*laughs loudly*). You shore overplayed your hand that time, pardner. We know that cain't be true.

CURLY. I ain't so shore of that, Tex. A lot of things go on in this world that a feller never knows about.

STUB. That must be some country down there. I'd admire to see it.

CURLY. Me too.

STRANGER. Ain't no law to stop you. (*The* COWBOYS *exchange startled glances at the idea of their ever going to such a wonderful place. The* STRANGER *continues dreamily.*) Summer all year round. Great big flowers—red and blue and yeller ones, big round as yer hat. Pretty as anythin'. Everybody plays the guitar, and all the fellers have to dress up in velvet pants with silver buttons on 'em.

GRANNY (*sarcastically*). Ain't it a pity you got to throw away that fine outfit you're wearin'?

STRANGER (*sincerely*). Yeah. But you can have it, seein' you admire it so much.

GRANNY (*embarrassed at this generosity*). Aw now . . .

STRANGER (*inspired*). Say! Why don't you fellers pack your duds and come along with me? I got a car big enough for all of us.

STUB (*eagerly*). I could pay ten dollars toward gas and oil.

STRANGER (*grandly*). Your money's

no good. I got enough for all of us.

TEX. It sounds fine. But you know things ain't that easy we could just up and rip off to Mexico.

STRANGER. Why not? It's all in the way you look at it. You stay on this here ranch because you don't know *how* to do anythin' else. Well, it's mighty simple. You just make up your mind you want to go to old Mexico with me, and tomorrow mornin' I'll drive by, and you just step in my car, and that's all there is to it. Nothin' hard about *that*.

TEX. I can't believe it'd be so easy.

STRANGER. I do it all the time. Go here, go there . . . anywheres.

CURLY (*suddenly*). I'll go with you tomorrow.

STUB. I'm all set.

COOKY. Could you, maybe, use a cook down in old Mexico?

STRANGER. Shore could.

TEX. Stranger, I ain't believin' a word you say. But if you got a car and if you come around tomorrow mornin', I'll go along with you—for the ride.

STRANGER. Good! I'll come and get you.

GRANNY (*bursting out irritably*). Have you fellers gone plumb loco? A stranger comes along and does a lot of fancy talkin', and you're all willin' to give up a good job and string along with him.

TEX (*incredulously*). A good job?

GRANNY. Well, it's a place to stay, and you got somethin' to eat anyways. And you all want to light out to Mexico with him—give up what little you got for somethin' that might never be.

STRANGER (*rises, admiringly*). You fellers shore are lucky havin' a fine feller like him around.

CURLY. You mean him? *Granny?*

STRANGER. Yeah. Everythin' he said is right, and you fellers should listen to him.

TEX. But you been tellin' us . . .

STRANGER. Once I was like you fellers. I had a good job and everythin'. But I got this restless feelin' and set off. Now if I'd a had a sensible friend like him, I might a kept on workin' and by now owned all the ranches in Prairie County and been a big boss instead of just a wanderin' feller. (*Holding out his hand.*) Shake, Granny. You shore got fine sense.

(*He crosses to* GRANNY *and they shake hands.* GRANNY *is flattered.*)

STUB. But . . . but . . . that gold mine . . .

TEX. And them *senoritas?*

STRANGER. Shore! Shore! They're wonderful! But nothin' ain't as wonderful as havin' a friend like him (*puts his hand on* GRANNY'S *shoulder*) who's watchin' out for your best interests.

GRANNY (*very flattered*). Now, Stranger, I ain't sayin' that you're wrong. I'm only sayin' the boys better go a little slow about pullin' up stakes. As for myself (*he beams*) . . . well, Stranger, I guess you can count me in on that trip.

(*They shake hands again. Everybody is happy.*)

TEX. I'm goin', but I don't expect we'll ever hit Mexico or any of them places.

STUB. Shore we will. And *I'm* all set. I know how to play the guitar already. You fellers would have to learn.

STRANGER. Say! (*As he goes to* STUB's R, GRANNY *goes to cot and sits.*) What're we all so quiet here for, when we could have music? (*Clapping* STUB *on the back.*) Give us a tune, Stub.

STUB (*as he starts to chord*). Aw, the fellers are tired of the one song I know.

STRANGER (*as* STUB *chords*). I know one! Heard it down in Wyoming, time I was bringin' cattle up to Montana. Let's see . . . (*He hums, taps his foot until* STUB *catches the rhythm in his chording. Then he sings out in a clear, joyous voice.*)
"With my foot in the stirrup and my
　hand on my thigh,
I'm the best danged cowboy that
　ever rode by."

THE OTHER COWBOYS.
"Coma ti yi yippi yippi yi yippi yay!
Coma ti yi yippi yippi yay!"

STRANGER.
"My seat's in the saddle, and my
　rope's on the side,
Show me a horse that I can't ride."

THE COWBOYS.
"Coma ti yi yippi yippi yi yippi yay!
Coma ti yi yippi yippi yay!"

STRANGER.
"On a ten-dollar horse and a forty-
　dollar saddle,
I'm the best danged cowboy ever
　punched cattle."

THE COWBOYS.
"Coma ti yi yippi yippi yi yippi yay!
Coma ti yi yippi yippi yay."

STRANGER.
"I went up to the Boss, and we had
　a little chat,
I slapped him in the face with my
　Stetson hat."
　　(*The* COWBOYS *laugh so much at
　　this verse, which strikes home,
　　that* GRANNY *and* COOKY
　　carry the next chorus alone.
　　GRANNY *sings loud and un-
　　waveringly, and* COOKY *loudly
　　and off-key.*)

COOKY *and* GRANNY.
"Coma ti yi yippi yippi yi yippi yay!
Coma ti yi yippi yippi yay!"

STRANGER (*slowing down to a sad
rhythm*).
"With my knees in the saddle and
　my seat toward the sky,
I'll quit punchin' cattle in the sweet
　by-and-by."

OTHER COWBOYS.
"Coma ti yi yippi yippi yi yippi yay!
Coma ti yi . . ."
　　(*There is a loud pounding on
　　the door soon after the chorus
　　begins. The singing dies
　　away.*)

COOKY. Come in!
　　(SHERIFF LASH *steps into the
　　room. He leans against the
　　door.*)

LASH. Howdy, Windy!
　　(*Consternation registers on the
　　COWBOYS' faces.*)

CURLY (*horrified*). Windy!
　　(*The* COWBOYS *stare at each
　　other as the full meaning of
　　the nickname sinks in.*)

LASH. Havin' yourself a time,
Windy?

WINDY (*no longer the* STRANGER,

crosses to SHERIFF). Why, howdy, Mr. Lash. Yeah! Havin' a fine time. Meet the boys. Fellers, this is Sheriff Lash.

LASH. Proud to meet you all. (*They merely stare at him.* STUB *lays his guitar under the bench.*) Well, Windy, 'bout time we was gettin' back, ain't it?

WINDY (*getting his hat off cot*). Shore is. (*Beaming.*) Say, it'll be wonderful ridin' back, with the wind blowin' and the moon shinin' like it does over the old Caribbees.

> (*He is just as friendly with* LASH *as he is with the others.* COOKY *and* GRANNY *rise and move UC.*)

LASH. That's right. You lope on ahead. I'll catch up with you.

WINDY (*putting his hat on*). Yeah.

(*At the door, he waves gaily.*) So long, fellers.

STUB. Hey! What about Mexico?

WINDY. Old Mexico?

STUB. Yeah!

WINDY (*dreamily*). It's a mighty fine country.

> (*He goes, closing the door after him. The* COWBOYS *stare at the closed door numbly.* STUB *goes to the cot, sweeps the stuff which is on it to the floor, and throws himself on the cot, with his face to the wall.* TEX *goes to the door, opens it, and looks after the retreating horse and rider.*)

TEX (*softly*). Charley-mane! After a king in olden times!

> (*He stares a second longer and then slams the door angrily.*

He stands DR, below door.)

GRANNY (*righteously*). I told you and I told you!

COWBOYS (*together, angrily*). Shut up!

(**CURLY** *rises, stands at L end of table.*)

LASH. I hope Windy ain't caused you no trouble.

COOKY. No trouble a-tall.

(*He goes to bench above table, and sits.*)

CURLY. We was talkin' 'bout goin' to Mexico with him.

LASH. Poor old Windy!

CURLY. I don't like the way you talk about him. (*But he backs away with an eye on* **LASH**'s *pistol holster.*) Sheriff or no sheriff.

LASH. Don't get on your high horse, son. I like to hear Windy talk, too. I like to hear him fine. Everybody does. But it's just talk.

(**GRANNY** *comes down to box R of table and sits, facing* **SHERIFF LASH.**)

GRANNY. I tried to tell you fellers he's never been to any of them places.

LASH. He's an awful convincin' talker, and he's nice to have around. But he ain't never been out of Montana. (*Judiciously.*) 'Course it's a mighty big state. Pretty near as big as (*shyly*)—Old Spain. Windy's from Prairie County. So'm I.

GRANNY. How come we ain't never heard of this feller? Is Prairie County far away?

LASH. 'Way the other side of the Rubies. Three-day ride from here. That is, if you know where the pass is. Otherwise, it's a week's ride.

Had a lot of trouble trailin' Windy. He shore does get around. (*Pause.*) From county to county.

GRANNY. How come?

LASH. It all started a few years back when Windy fell off his horse onto his head. (*They exchange understanding looks while* **LASH** *talks.* **STUB** *sits up on cot.*) Used to work for the Lazy K. Mr. Bland, the boss, sort of felt at fault about the accident and took good care of Windy . . . bought him the kind of fancy clothes he likes and all. But Windy always kept goin' away.

STUB. Seein' you're the Law, is Windy in trouble?

LASH. Yeah. He swiped that big black horse he's ridin', and Mr. Bland had to turn him over to us. Mr. Bland likes Windy fine, but (*he takes off his hat, and sighs*) . . . Windy swiped this horse, name of Bud, from the Apex Ranch. He gives him a new name, Charley-mane. Danged if the horse don't like it. He won't go back no more to the Apex.

CURLY. Just sort of hangs around Windy, eh?

(*He moves to L end of cot.*)

LASH. So the feller wants a hundred dollars for the horse, and Mr. Bland ain't goin' to pay it. So Windy's got to stay in jail. (*Preparing to leave.*) I should have watched Windy more careful-like. (*The* **COWBOYS** *sit silent.* **LASH** *looks at them sorrowfully, then turns to go as there seems nothing more to say.*) Well, so long, fellers.

(*They say nothing. He goes out door at R.*)

CURLY (*angry and heartbroken*).

And it all seemed so real! The gold and the senoritas and the velvet pants.

(*Angrily, he kicks the saddle which* Stub *has thrown on the floor.*)

GRANNY. Hey. (*Stands.*) Leave my saddle alone!

(*He stamps over hats and coats on floor to pick up saddle.*)

CURLY. What's the idea stampedin' all over my hat?

(*He pulls the hat from under* GRANNY's *feet.*)

TEX (*crosses C to pull on his coat, on which* CURLY *is standing*). Try usin' your own coat for a door mat.

(STUB *rises, grabs his guitar from under the bench, and holds it high over his head to protect it from the jostling* COWBOYS.)

CURLY. We ought to take that two-dollar guitar and break it over his head. His playin' started all this.

(STUB, *his guitar over his head, runs to L of* COOKY, *who is sitting on the bench, very much depressed.*)

COOKY. If you fellers want to fight, do it in your own bunkhouse. (*Standing up.*) I'm the one that's got a good mind to leave now. (TEX, CURLY, *and* GRANNY *quiet down, as they throw their hats, coats, saddle, etc. back on cot in a heap.* COOKY *resumes mournfully.*) Windy was the only cowpuncher that ever liked my cookin'.

GRANNY (*scornfully*). You and that cake you was holdin' out on us! For Chris'mas!

(COOKY *shrinks.*)

TEX (*crosses to DR corner of table, takes a drink of coffee. Spews it out.*) Worse than before.

CURLY (*crosses to DL corner of table, tries a bite of biscuit*). Harder than ever.

GRANNY (*stands UC, shivers*). It's cold in here. I wish Genevieve would write.

STUB. I wish summer would come.

TEX (*blazing out*). I'm plumb sick of hearin' talk about summertime and listenin' to that whiny music of yours.

STUB (*hurt*). 'Course, it's only a two-dollar guitar.

(*He tries a chord.*)

TEX. If you play any more on it, I'll chop it up for firewood.

STUB. Nothin's any good. I'll bust it myself.

(*He takes it by the neck and is about to break it over his knee when* GRANNY *takes it from him.*)

GRANNY. Take it easy, son.

(*He puts the guitar on cot and sits.* STUB *goes to UL corner of table.*)

STUB. But while Windy was here, the grub tasted good, the cookshack was warm, and my guitar made fine music. He shore had a way of lookin' at things.

CURLY (*picking up the magazine*). He's like the cowpunchers that ride for these magazine ranches.

TEX. Think of it! That Bland feller could have him back if he just paid the hundred dollars for that Charley-mane horse.

STUB (*sighs*). I don't see how Mr. Bland could stand to leave Windy go.

(*A pause.* CURLY *starts walking up and down the room, in the DL area, deep in thought. He starts banging his fist against his other hand as though an idea were coming to him.* TEX *and* STUB *follow him with their eyes.* COOKY *and* GRANNY *exchange puzzled headshakes and then stare at* CURLY.)

TEX. Well?

CURLY. Shut up. I'm gettin' an idea.

TEX (*puzzled*). But look. How do we know Lash was tellin' the truth?

STUB. Windy *said* he was the sheriff.

COOKY. And Windy don't lie! (*The* COWBOYS *jump in surprise.*) Well, not *really* lie.

TEX (*vaguely disappointed*). I guess he was a sheriff, all right. But gosh! Seems like we got as much right to Windy as that feller has.

STUB. We did let him go mighty easy-like.

CURLY. We should of put up an argument.

TEX. That's right.

COOKY (*very seriously*). Fellers . . . it ain't too late.

CURLY. For what?

COOKY. To argue with the sheriff. Somebody's got to go and bring them back.

TEX. Maybe we could get Windy out on bail. Curly! You go get 'em.

CURLY (*grabbing his hat*). Boys, I'm on my way.

TEX (*warningly*). And you better not come back without 'em.

STUB. Maybe we *all* ought to go.

GRANNY. Some of us ought to stay and fix the place up, so's Windy will want to stay here.

CURLY (*opening door*). I'll take the short cut through the corral and head 'em off.

GRANNY. They'll be ridin' slow on account of Windy enjoyin' the moon and all.

(*He rises.*)

CURLY. Yeah!

(*He goes.*)

GRANNY. Seems a little warmer in here already.

COOKY. I'm goin' to cook somethin' good. I got some cocoa (*his eyes shift*) . . . that . . . er . . . I forgot about. I'll make hot chocolate with it. (*At the kitchen door.*) And I'll make a puddin'. I got two cans of condensed milk. (*He ducks a biscuit thrown by* TEX.) Well, I was only savin' 'em in case somebody got sick.

(*He exits UL.*)

TEX. You clear off them dishes, Granny. (*As* GRANNY *starts to do so.*) I'll sweep up a little. (*As he goes into the kitchen for the broom.*) And look at that there cot, Stub. It's a disgrace.

STUB. All right! All right!

(*He begins to clean up the area, hanging up coats and standing the branding iron in the corner.* TEX *re-enters, starts sweeping.*)

COOKY (*reappearing in doorway UL*). Say! Maybe it won't be the same now that we know he ain't been to any of them places.

(GRANNY *pauses on his way to the kitchen with an armful of dishes.* **Tex** *holds the broom suspended.* **Stub** *pauses in the act of hanging the saddle on a peg. Finally,* **Stub** *speaks.)*

Stub *(slowly).* What a feller makes up is sometimes better than what really *is.*

> *(He finishes hanging up the saddle.)*

Cooky. Yeah.

> *(He goes back into the kitchen. The others resume their work.)*

Tex. Funny thing. When I thought it was all real, and he was braggin' on it, I called him a liar. But now that I know he's a liar, it seems kind of true. I can't figure it out.

Granny. I don't care if a feller lies . . . just so he's sincere.

Tex. Yeah!

> *(He sweeps harder, raising a great cloud of dust.* **Houston** *enters, slamming the door. He sidesteps a cloud of dust. The* **Cowboys** *glance at him briefly and then ignore him.* **Houston** *stands with his hands on his hips and sniffs in the direction of the kitchen.)*

Houston. What in time's goin' on in here?

Tex. Move your foot, Boss. I want to sweep here. *(Astonished,* **Houston** *steps aside.* **Tex** *follows him up, sweeping.)* Boss, go over and stand there *(his thumb points UC)* out of the way.

> *(Surprised,* **Houston** *follows instructions.)*

Houston. Look, fellers. *(They pay no attention to him. They are concentrating on their tasks.)* Look here! *(He speaks sharply and comes C. Mildly surprised, they look at him.)* I just come over to tell you boys that I'm goin' to have to borrow those ten-dollar bills back. I been goin' over the books, and things look mighty dark.

Tex *(with finality).* Like to help you out, Boss. But the money's all spoke for.

Houston. You might's well let me have it. You ain't got nothin' to spend it on here.

Stub. We need the money for bail money . . . for our company.

Tex. I hope the sheriff listens to reason.

> *(He is sweeping the dirt out the door.)*

Granny. If he don't, we can raise a rumpus and maybe he'll throw us in jail 'longside of Windy.

Stub. Say! Why didn't we think of that?

Houston *(angrily).* Everybody shut up a minute! I'm the boss of the Diamond O, and I got a right to know what's goin' on round here.

Tex *(calmly).* All right, Boss.

Houston. I'm sick of your complainin' all the time.

Tex. Won't be no more complainin' if our plans work out.

Stub *(shaking the cot blanket thoroughly, and speaking through cloud of dust that comes from it).* *(**Houston** sneezes.)* We don't mind the grub and the cold no more. 'Cause we're goin' to have somethin' that'll make this place beautiful!

(Tex *props the broom in the UR corner of the room, then helps* Stub *spread the blanket smoothly on the cleared cot.* Houston *takes off his hat and scratches his head in surprise.*)

Houston. I think you've all went loco.

(*The door opens.* Curly *stands there with* Sheriff Lash. *The* Cowboys *look startled.*)

Granny (*near door UL*). Where's Windy?

Lash. He's waitin' for me down by Red Rock Creek. He's showin' Charley-mane his head in the water by the light of the moon. And the danged horse is plumb crazy about it.

Tex (*standing with* Stub *below cot.*) Curly tell you our idea?

Lash. Boys, I don't think it'll work out.

Granny. Ain't no law against you rentin' him out to us.

(*He moves to DL corner of table.*)

Houston. Who?

Lash. You'd have to go over to Prairie County to bail him out. I ain't authorized to rent him.

Houston. Where? Who? What did you say?

Lash (*as though it explained all*). We're talkin' 'bout Windy. (*Back to the* Cowboys.) Only way I can see is to pay the Apex the hundred dollars for the horse and buy Windy outright.

Houston (*enlightened*). A horse!

Granny (*slapping his thigh*). Shore! We'll buy him!

(TEX, *followed by* CURLY *and* STUB, *crosses above* HOUSTON *to the bench where* TEX *and* CURLY *sit.* STUB *stands at UR end of table.*)

TEX. Why didn't we think of that before? (*Slaps his ten-dollar bill on table.*) Here's my money.

CURLY (*throws it onto table*). And mine.

(STUB *adds his money.*)

GRANNY (*sits on box L of table*). And mine.

HOUSTON. You mean mine.

TEX. But gosh! That's only forty dollars.

LASH (*turning to door*). Too bad, boys.

STUB. Wait! Mr. Houston . . .
(*But he loses his nerve.*)

HOUSTON. Just *what* are you fellers buyin' with my money?

LASH. He's a cowboy. Fell off a horse, and he's a bit loco.

GRANNY. But, Boss, he shore talks pretty.

HOUSTON (*violently throwing his hat onto floor*). Well, I'll be roped, tied, and branded if that ain't the last straw! Takin' in a loco cowpuncher to cheer you up! (*Shouting.*) I won't have it!

(WINDY *enters at R, and stands calmly listening, unseen by others.*)

CURLY. But, Boss . . .

HOUSTON. If I catch him around here, I'll herd him off the ranch so fast, it'll make his head swim.

WINDY. Howdy, fellers!
(*He is standing in kitchen door, eating a biscuit.* COOKY, *beaming, is just behind him.*)

TEX. Windy! (*The* COWBOYS *crowd around* WINDY *and shake his hand violently, as if he had returned after a year's absence.* TEX, *shaking* WINDY'S *hand:*) Windy, ol' boy, ol' boy!

GRANNY. Shore good t' see yuh.

STUB. We're real glad yer back!

CURLY. Sure got t' missin' yuh.
(*The* COWBOYS *resume their positions around the table.*)

WINDY. Wal now, I'm right pleased t' be here. (*Pointing at* HOUSTON.) An' who is that handsome-lookin' feller?

(HOUSTON *looks in back of him to see whom* WINDY *is referring to.*)

STUB (*delighted*). Why, that's our Boss. (*He introduces* WINDY *as the important personage.*) Boss, meet up with Windy.

HOUSTON (*flabbergasted*). Windy!

WINDY (*crossing C to* HOUSTON). You the feller who owns this great big beautiful ranch?

HOUSTON. Well, yeah! I own this place. Why?

WINDY. Makes me kind of homesick for old Australia. Reminds me of the big, rich ranches they have down there. Only this one is kept up better. (*He shakes* HOUSTON'S *hand in a friendly way.*) Mighty proud to know you. (*To* COWBOYS.) Don't know what you fellers are thinkin' of, wantin' to go and leave a fine boss like him.

HOUSTON (*somewhat pleased*). Oh, I guess there's something to be said on both sides.

WINDY (*looking at him more closely*). You remind me of an admiral I used to know. Big, hand-some feller. Boss of the biggest ship in the British navy.

Houston (*simpers modestly*). Is that so?

Windy. This feller's name was Henry.

Houston (*pleased*). Say! That's my name too.

Windy (*amazed*). What a coincidence! Two good-lookin' men with the same name!

Houston. My! My!

(*They shake hands delightedly.*)

Windy. Shore is remarkable. (*Sadly.*) Only thing different between you two is the other feller was a good friend of mine.

Houston. Give me time, Windy. Give me time. (*To* **Lash.**) What about this feller?

Lash (*DR*). They's a hundred dollars due on him on account his takin' a horse from the Apex Ranch.

Houston. You mean if these boys pay up the hundred dollars, they can have him *and* the horse?

Lash. That's right.

Houston (*turning on* **Cowboys**). Well, what are you idiots waitin' for?

Curly (*sadly*). We only got forty dollars.

(*The* **Cowboys** *look hopefully at the* **Boss.**)

Houston (*turns, walks to cot slowly, sits*). Shore is too bad. Sixty dollars more and you could of had him.

Tex (*sternly*). Cooky, you got any money you been savin' up for Labor Day or whatever?

(*Without a word,* **Cooky** *goes to*

the L end of cot and takes a filled tobacco sack from under mattress.)

Cooky. Here's every last cent I got . . . twenty-seven dollars.

(*He puts it on the table, then goes to UL opening.*)

Tex. That makes sixty-seven dollars. (*Tentatively.*) You wouldn't take our note for the rest, would you?

Lash. *I* would. But the Apex wouldn't. (*Moving toward door R.*) Well, Windy . . .

Windy. Shore hate to go. Charley-mane feels right to home in your corral, Mr. Houston.

(**Houston** *seems affected, but he won't give in.*)

Granny (*after a bit of inner struggle*). I got three dollars more. I was savin' it to buy Genevieve a Christmas present.

(*He tosses it on table.*)

Windy. No, fellers. We can't take a gal's present money.

Stub. That's right.

Granny. Aw, take it. I don't know about the Christmas present. Genevieve might be dead or married by this time. I ain't seen her in twenty years.

Lash. Even if she's single, it only makes seventy dollars. (*Opening door.*) Time's a-gettin' on, Windy.

Windy (*following him to door*). Yeah. Shore hate to leave your fine ranch, Mr. Houston.

(*They are almost out.*)

Houston. Wait! (**Windy** *pops back in.*) Well . . . (*He clears his throat, embarrassed.*) I . . . uh . . . (*He takes out his wallet.* **Lash**

comes back in and shuts the door, as HOUSTON *crosses to R end of table and counts out money.*)

STUB. Why, Boss!

> (*He puts an arm around* HOUSTON's *shoulder and gives him a slap.*)

HOUSTON (*avoiding everyone's eye*). Twenty-eight dollars. All I got.

LASH. Still two dollars short.

> (STUB *picks up the money, crosses DR to* LASH, *and speaks up in* HOUSTON's *manner.*)

STUB. We'll send you the rest when we sell them steers. (*Timidly.*) Eh, Boss?

HOUSTON (*sitting on apple box R of table*). Shore!

LASH (*counting it*). Well, I guess it's close enough.

STUB (*anxious to get rid of* LASH). Yeah. Well, good-by, Sheriff.

> (*He helps the* SHERIFF *stuff the money into his pockets.*)

LASH (*surprised*). Huh? Oh. Good-by. So long, Windy.

WINDY. So long, Mr. Lash. Shore had a fine time, didn't we?

> (CURLY *almost shoves* LASH *out of door R and closes it after him.*)

GRANNY (*rising*). Set down over here, Windy. (*He indicates L nail keg.* STUB *goes to cot and sits.*) We'll talk awhile. Then we'll eat, and then we'll have some more music.

> (WINDY *sits on box.* GRANNY *sits beside* TEX *on bench.*)

WINDY. Reminds me of the old days in the Foreign Legion, eh, Mr. Houston?

HOUSTON (*pleased*). Yeah.

GRANNY. 'Fore I forget it, tomorrow we got to build Windy a bed.

HOUSTON. I got one up to the house that'll just about fit 'im.

WINDY. That's mighty nice of you, but I can sleep anywheres. Why, many's the time I slept in a ship's hammock on an old square-rigged sailin' ship, plowin' through a nor'-easter. (*The* COWBOYS *look at each other, pleased, and sigh ecstatically. A faraway, excited look comes over* WINDY's *face.*) Like the time we was sailin' round the Cape. Old Cape Horn. One day . . .

> (*The door opens, and* SHERIFF LASH, *looking guilty, walks in.*)

LASH. Fellers . . . (*They look up, alarmed.*) I'm afraid it ain't right. I got to take Windy back. It ain't legal.

> (*He remains standing near door, DR.*)

HOUSTON (*rising*). You can't do that. He's bought and paid for.

LASH. I got nothin' to show for him . . . there's nothin' to prove he belongs to you. I'm liable to lose my office.

> (CURLY *gets the branding iron from the corner and starts toward kitchen with it, holding it aloft.*)

GRANNY. Curly Jackson, you put down that there brandin' iron. That ain't the way to prove he belongs here.

> (CURLY *replaces branding iron in corner and sits beside* STUB *on cot.*)

WINDY. What we need is a *doc*-u-ment.

> (*He gives the word an important sound.*)

HOUSTON. Like the bill of sale when you sell steers.

WINDY. It's got to be more legal than that. Like this. (*He thinks.*) Here! Where's some paper?

> (COOKY *gets the tablet and pencil stub from box over his bed, gives them to* HOUSTON, *then stands above bench.*)

HOUSTON. I'll take it down.

> (*He takes off a glove and sits again, pencil in hand.* WINDY *puts one foot up on L end of bench, leans his elbow on his knee, and a faraway, dreamy look comes over his face as he dictates.*)

WINDY. When in the course of human events it becomes necessary for the undersigned cowpuncher, Windy, to transfer his field of labor from the Lazy K to the Diamond O Ranch . . .

GRANNY (*sighs*). Ain't that beautiful?

WINDY. And whereas and wherefore it has been solemnly declared among the cowpunchers of the aforesaid Diamond O in solemn conclave herein assembled: (*The* COWBOYS *are happy, sigh in delight at the long words.*) That on the payment of the sum of one hundred dollars, that the undersigned Windy shall have the inalienable right to dwell here in green pastures hereafter and forever. And forsaking all others to cleave unto Mr. Houston and the cowboys and cook of the Diamond O.

HOUSTON. Better get in about the horse.

WINDY. Furthermore, he shall dwell in the aforesaid green pastures; to wit, the Diamond O (*he looks around; they all nod at him, pleased*) . . . with his beloved Arabian thoroughbred horse, Charley-mane, formerly Bud, in Powder River County wherein aforesaid ranch is located. Signed with our hand and sealed with our heart this twenty-ninth day of October. (*In his ordinary voice.*) Date it, and we'll sign it.

> (*He accepts the stub of pencil from* HOUSTON *and signs it with a great flourish.*)

HOUSTON. That'll hold 'em, all right.

> (CURLY *and* STUB *crowd around to sign after* GRANNY, TEX, *and* COOKY. CURLY *and* STUB *then return to the cot and sit.* HOUSTON *folds the document and hands it to* COOKY.)

COOKY (*as he gives the document to* LASH). Well, so long again, Sheriff. (*Turns and hurries into kitchen.*) Puddin' must be near done.

LASH. So long, all. I shore do hate to go and miss the talkin'.

ALL. Good-by. Come again.

> (LASH *leaves reluctantly, going out door at R.*)

HOUSTON (*sitting on the cot with the* COWBOYS). Now! What were you sayin' 'bout the time you sailed round Cape Horn, Windy?

> (WINDY *sits again on the apple box.* COOKY *starts setting the table lavishly with food, listening avidly all the while.*)

WINDY. Yeah. Well, sir, we was sailin' around like I said, under full sail, royal topgallants and all. One day we met up with this scary-lookin' schooner. It was a pirate ship. Ever see a pirate ship? (*They shake their heads, hanging on each word.*) Well, sir, she had white sails patched up with blue and yeller and red patches. (*The door opens quietly, and* LASH *appears, closes the door softly behind him. He takes off his hat and stands listening to* WINDY.) And she had a big black flag. A white skull and crossbones was painted on it. (COWBOYS *exchange glances and shiver happily.* COOKY *pokes his head out of the kitchen, mixing spoon in hand, to listen.* SHERIFF LASH *draws closer to the cot.*) The Captain had a red rag round his head, and one of his eyes was punched out, but he wore a black patch over it. He carried a knife between his teeth. A dirk, we call it. (*Fascinated,* LASH *draws closer. Without taking their eyes off* WINDY, *without a pause in the story, the* COWBOYS *move over to make room for* LASH. *He sits on the edge of the cot. The* CURTAINS *begin to close.*) "Ship ahoy," he hollers at us. "Ship ahoy, yourself," I yell back to him.

(*But the* CURTAINS *are closed.*)

Understanding Literature

1. How does Windy contrast with the other cowboys in appearance? in attitude? in language?

2. Windy's attitude transforms the shabby and familiar into the rich and romantic. When Granny says that the shine on the guitar is "Cheap shellac," Windy responds, "Oh, no! It's patina . . . a shine that comes on fine old things. Like them guitars they have in old Spain." Find other examples of objects or situations that are transformed by Windy.

3. Exaggeration is characteristic of most comedies. In "Summer Comes to the Diamond O," even an animal is bewitched by Windy: "He's showin' Charley-mane his head in the water by the light of the moon. And the danged horse is plumb crazy about it." In what other instances does the author make use of exaggeration for a comic effect?

4. What is the theme of the play? Explain how the following statements relate to the theme:

   (a) "**Cooky.** And Windy don't lie! . . . Well, not *really* lie."

   (b) "**Stub.** What a feller makes up is sometimes better than what really is."

   (c) "**Tex.** Funny thing. When I thought it was all real, and he was braggin' on it, I called him a liar. But now that I know he's a liar, it seems kind of true. I can't figure it out. **Granny.** I don't care if a feller lies . . . just so he's sincere."

5. The play opens at suppertime in late October and ends that same evening. Yet the title says that "Summer Comes to the Diamond O." How do you explain this title?

Further Activity

Lash says of Windy, "He's a cowboy. Fell off a horse, and he's a bit loco." Write an essay on how people would all be better off if they were all loco. Show how the school day would be different if the students had all fallen off horses and landed on their heads—and looked at life the way Windy does. Cite at least four examples of how students might think about things such as getting up in the morning, having breakfast, or going to class. Find a good title for your essay.

ROBERT FINCH

Today, in the court systems of most of the fifty American States, both men and women serve on juries in criminal, as well as in civil, trials. But such was not always the case. In fact, it is only within the last 20 years that the laws of many states have been liberalized to permit women to serve as jurors.

In 1950, when "Twelve Angry Men" was written, juries in the courts of the State of New York were made up solely of men.

Thus it is that in a stiflingly hot room, behind locked doors, twelve men must decide whether the young defendant (in the murder trial just ended) is to die. Impatient irritation gives way to explosions of temper as those twelve angry men argue the defendant's guilt or innocence.

Twelve Angry Men*

Reginald Rose
Stage Version by Sherman L. Sergel

IMPROVING YOUR READING: The cast of characters does not give names to the persons in this drama. But the individual character traits of each nameless juror will become clear to you if you pay particular attention to the ideas each juror expresses and ask yourself what kind of person would hold these ideas. By the end of Act I, you should feel that all the characters are distinct and recognizable human types. In almost any group involved in making a serious decision, you might expect to find people reacting as some of these characters do.

Since each juror is a certain kind of person and has a certain set of ideas about the way justice is done, this play is more than a conflict among people. It is a conflict of ideas, too. Through the conflict of ideas the theme of the play emerges. You will observe, as the drama unfolds, that it takes courage to refuse to go along with the crowd. And you will also observe the dangers of making a decision before weighing evidence and of holding a bias when an impartial attitude is essential.

CHARACTERS

FOREMAN OF THE JURY

JUROR NO. TWO

JUROR NO. THREE

JUROR NO. FOUR

JUROR NO. FIVE

JUROR NO. SIX

JUROR NO. SEVEN

JUROR NO. EIGHT

JUROR NO. NINE

JUROR NO. TEN

JUROR NO. ELEVEN

JUROR NO. TWELVE

GUARD

JUDGE
CLERK } *offstage voices*

PLACE: *A jury room.*
TIME: *The present. Summer.*

SYNOPSIS

ACT I: *Late afternoon.*
ACT II: *A second or two later.*
ACT III: *Immediately following Act II.*

FOREMAN: He is a small, petty man who is impressed with the authority he has and handles himself quite formally. He is not overly bright, but dogged.

JUROR No. TWO: He is a meek, hesitant man who finds it difficult to maintain any opinions of his own. He is easily swayed and usually adopts the opinion of the last person to whom he has spoken.

JUROR No. THREE: He is a very strong, very forceful, extremely opinionated man within whom can be detected a streak of sadism. Also, he is a humorless man who is intolerant of opinions other than his own, and accustomed to forcing his wishes and views upon others.

JUROR No. FOUR: He seems to be a man of wealth and position, and a practiced speaker who presents himself well at all times. He seems to feel a little bit above the rest of the jurors. His only concern is with the facts in this case and he is appalled with the behavior of the others.

JUROR No. FIVE: He is a naïve, very frightened young man who takes his obligations in this case very seriously but who finds it difficult to speak up when his elders have the floor.

JUROR No. SIX: He is an honest but dull-witted man who comes upon his decisions slowly and carefully. He is a man who finds it difficult to create positive opinions, but who must listen to and digest and accept those opinions offered by others which appeal to him most.

Juror No. Seven: He is a loud, flashy, glad-handed salesman type who has more important things to do than to sit on a jury. He is quick to show temper and equally quick to form opinions on things about which he knows nothing. He is a bully, and, of course, a coward.

Juror No. Eight: He is a quiet, thoughtful, gentle man—a man who sees all sides of every question and constantly seeks the truth. He is a man of strength tempered with compassion. Above all, he is a man who wants justice to be done, and will fight to see that it is.

Juror No. Nine: He is a mild, gentle old man, long since defeated by life, and now merely waiting to die. He recognizes himself for what he is, and mourns the days when it would have been possible to be courageous without shielding himself behind his many years.

Juror No. Ten: He is an angry, bitter man—a man who antagonizes almost at sight. He is also a bigot who places no values on any human life save his own. Here is a man who has been nowhere and is going nowhere and knows it deep within him.

Juror No. Eleven: He is a refugee from Europe. He speaks with an accent and is ashamed, humble, almost subservient to the people around him. He will honestly seek justice because he has suffered through so much injustice.

Juror No. Twelve: He is a slick, bright advertising man who thinks of human beings in terms of percentages, graphs and polls, and has no real understanding of people. He is a superficial snob, but trying to be a good fellow.

REGINALD ROSE AND SHERMAN L. SERGEL

ACT I

(AT RISE OF CURTAIN: *The curtain comes up on a dark stage; then as the lights start to come up on the scene we hear the voice of the* JUDGE, *off stage.*)

JUDGE (*off stage*). Murder in the first degree . . . premeditated homicide . . . is the most serious charge tried in our criminal courts. You have heard a long and complex case, gentlemen, and it is now your duty to sit down to try and separate the facts from the fancy. One man is dead. The life of another is at stake. If there is a reasonable doubt in your minds as to the guilt of the accused —then you must declare him not guilty. If—however—there is no reasonable doubt, then he must be found guilty. Whichever way you decide, the verdict must be unanimous. I urge you to deliberate honestly and thoughtfully. You are faced with a grave responsibility. Thank you, gentlemen.

(*There is a long pause. The lights are now up full in the jury room. There is a door* L *and a window in the* R *wall of the room. Over the door* L *is an electric clock. A water cooler is* DR, *with a wastebasket beside it. A container with paper cups is attached to the wall nearby. A long conference table is slightly upstage of* C *stage. About it are twelve uncomfortable-looking straight chairs. There is a chair at either end of the table, seven at the upstage side and three at the downstage side of the table.* [NOTE: *This arrangement of the chairs about the table will enable most of the action to be directed toward the audience, with a minority of the characters placed with their backs toward the audience.*] *There are two more straight chairs against the wall* DL *and one in the* UR *corner of the room. It is a bare, unpleasant room. After the pause the door* L *opens and the* GUARD *walks in. As he opens the door the lettering "Jury Room" can be seen on the outside of the door. The* GUARD *walks across the room and opens the window* R *as a clerk drones out, offstage* L.)

CLERK (*offstage* L). The jury will retire.

GUARD (*surveying room, shaking his head*). He doesn't stand a chance. (*Moves* L *again.*)

(*The* JURORS *file in* L. *The* GUARD *stands upstage of the door and counts them. Four or five of the jurors light cigarettes as they enter the room.* JUROR FIVE *lights a pipe which he smokes constantly.* JURORS TWO, NINE, *and* TWELVE *go to the water cooler for a drink.* JUROR SEVEN *goes to the window and opens it wider. The rest of the* JURORS *begin to take seats around the table, though some of them stand and lean forward, with both hands on the back of the chair.* JUROR SEVEN *produces a pack of gum and offers a piece to the men by the water cooler.*)

SEVEN. Chewing gum? Gum? Gum?

NINE. Thank you, but no. (JU-RORS Two *and* TWELVE *shake their heads.*)

SEVEN. Y'know something?

TWELVE. I know lots of things. I'm in advertising.

SEVEN (*tugging at collar*). Y'know, it's hot.

TWELVE (*to* TWO, *mildly sarcastic*). I never would have known that if he hadn't told me. Would you?

TWO (*missing sarcasm*). I suppose not. I'd kind of forgotten.

TWELVE. All I've done all day is sweat.

THREE (*calling out*). I bet you aren't sweating like that kid who was tried.

SEVEN. You'd think they'd at least air-condition the place. I almost dropped dead in court.

TWELVE. My taxes are high enough.

SEVEN. This should go fast, any-way. (*Moves to table, as* EIGHT *goes to window.*)

NINE (*nodding to himself, then, as he throws his paper water cup into wastebasket*). Yes, it's hot.

GUARD. Okay, gentlemen. Every-body's here. If there's anything you want, I'm right outside. Just knock. (*Goes out* L, *closing door. They all look at door, silently. The lock is turned.*)

THREE. Did he lock that door?

FOUR. Yes, he did.

THREE. What do they think we are, crooks?

FOREMAN (*seated at left end of table*). They lock us up for a little while. . . .

THREE (*breaking in*). And then they lock that kid up forever and that's okay by me.

FIVE (*motioning toward door*). I never knew they did that.

TEN (*blowing his nose*). Sure, they lock the door. What did you think?

FIVE (*a bit irritated*). I just didn't know. It never occurred to me.

FOUR. Shall we all admit right now that it is hot and humid and our tempers are short?

EIGHT (*turning from window*). It's been a pretty hard week. (*Turns back and continues looking out.*)

THREE. I feel just fine.

TWELVE. I wonder what's been go-ing on down at the office. You know how it is in advertising. In six days my job could be gone, and the whole company, too. They aren't going to like this. (JURORS *start to take off their suit coats and hang them over backs of chairs.*)

FOREMAN. Well, figure this is our duty.

TWELVE. I didn't object to doing my duty. I just mentioned that I might not have a job by the time I get back. (*He and* NINE *move to table and take their places.* NINE *sits near right end of table.*)

THREE (*motioning to* FOUR). Ask him to hire you. He's rich. Look at the suit!

FOREMAN (*to* FOUR, *as he tears off slips of paper for a ballot*). Is it cus-tom-tailored?

FOUR. Yes, it is.

FOREMAN. I have an uncle who's a tailor. (FOUR *takes his jacket off, places it carefully over back of chair and sits.*)

FOUR. How does he do?

FOREMAN (*shaking his head*). Not too well. Y'know, a friend of his, that's a friend of my uncle, the tailor —well—this friend wanted to be on this jury in my place.

SEVEN. Why didn't you let him? I would have done anything to miss this.

FOREMAN. And get caught, or something? Y'know what kind of a fine you could pay for anything like that? Anyway, this friend of my uncle's was on a jury once, about ten years ago—a case just about like this one.

TWELVE. So what happened?

FOREMAN. They let him off. Reasonable doubt. And do y'know, about eight years later they found out that he'd actually done it, anyway. A guilty man—a murderer— was turned loose in the streets.

THREE. Did they get him?

FOUR. They couldn't.

THREE. Why not?

FOUR. A man can't be held in double jeopardy. Unless it's a hung jury, they can't try a man twice for the same crime.

SEVEN. That isn't going to happen here.

THREE. Six days. They should have finished it in two. (*Slapping back of one hand into palm of other.*) Talk! Talk! Talk! (*Gets up and starts for water cooler.*) Did you ever hear so much talk about nothing?

TWO (*laughing nervously*). Well— I guess—they're entitled . . .

THREE. Everybody gets a fair trial. . . . (*Shakes his head.*) That's the system. (*Downs his drink.*) Well, I suppose you can't say anything against it. (*Tosses his water cup toward wastebasket and misses.* TWO *picks cup up and puts it in wastebasket as* THREE *returns to his seat.*)

SEVEN (*to* TEN). How did you like that business about the knife? Did you ever hear a phonier story?

TEN (*wisely*). Well, look, you've gotta expect that. You know what you're dealing with. . . .

SEVEN. He bought a switch knife that night. . . .

TEN (*with a sneer*). And then he lost it.

SEVEN. A hole in his pocket.

TEN. A hole in his father.

TWO. An awful way to kill your father—a knife in his chest. (*Crosses to table.*)

TEN. Look at the kind of people they are—you know them. (*Gets handkerchief out again.*)

SEVEN. What's the matter? You got a cold?

TEN (*blowing*). A lulu! These hot weather colds can kill you.

SEVEN. I had one last year, while I was on vacation, too.

FOREMAN (*briskly*). All right, gentlemen. Let's take seats.

SEVEN. Right. This better be fast. I've got tickets to—(*insert name of any current Broadway hit*)—for tonight. I must be the only guy in the world who hasn't seen it yet. (*Laughs and sits down, as do others still not seated.*) Okay, your honor, start the show.

FOREMAN (*to* EIGHT, *who is still looking out window*). How about sitting down? (EIGHT *doesn't hear him.*) The gentleman at the window. (**EIGHT** *turns, startled.*) How about sitting down?

EIGHT. Oh, I'm sorry. (*Sits at right end of table, opposite* **FORE-MAN.**)

TEN. It's tough to figure, isn't it? A kid kills his father. Bing! Just like that. Well, it's the element. They let the kids run wild. Maybe it serves 'em right.

FOUR. There are better proofs than some emotion you may have—perhaps a dislike for some group.

SEVEN. We all agreed that it was hot.

NINE. And that our tempers will get short.

THREE. That's if we disagree—but this is open and shut. Let's get it done.

FOREMAN. All right. Now—you gentlemen can handle this any way you want to. I mean, I'm not going to make any rules. If we want to discuss it first and then vote, that's one way. Or we can vote right now and see how we stand.

SEVEN. Let's vote now. Who knows, maybe we can all go home.

TEN. Yeah. Let's see who's where.

THREE. Right. Let's vote now.

EIGHT. All right. Let us vote.

FOREMAN. Anybody doesn't want to vote? (*Looks around table. There is a pause as* **ALL** *look at each other.*)

SEVEN. That was easy.

FOREMAN. Okay. All those voting guilty raise your hands. (**JURORS THREE, SEVEN, TEN** *and* **TWELVE** *put their hands up instantly. The* **FORE-MAN** *and* **TWO, FOUR, FIVE** *and* **SIX** *follow a second later. Then* **ELEVEN** *raises his hand and a moment later*

NINE *puts his hand up.*) Eight—nine—ten—eleven—that's eleven for guilty. Okay. Not guilty? (**EIGHT's** *hand goes up.* **ALL** *turn to look at him.*)

THREE. Hey, you're in left field!

FOREMAN. Okay. Eleven to one. Eleven guilty, one not guilty. Now we know where we stand.

THREE (*rising, to* **EIGHT**). Do you really believe he's not guilty?

EIGHT (*quietly*). I don't know.

SEVEN (*to* **FOREMAN**). After six days, he doesn't know.

TWELVE. In six days I could learn calculus. This is A, B, C.

EIGHT. I don't believe that it is as simple as A, B, C.

THREE. I never saw a guiltier man in my life. (*Sits again.*)

EIGHT. What does a guilty man look like? He is not guilty until we say he is guilty. Are we to vote on his face?

THREE. You sat right in court and heard the same things I did. The man's a dangerous killer. You could see it.

EIGHT. Where do you look to see if a man is a killer?

THREE (*irritated by him*). Oh, well! . . .

EIGHT (*with quiet insistence*). I would like to know. Tell me what the facial characteristics of a killer are. Maybe you know something I don't know.

FOUR. Look! What is there about the case that makes you think the boy is innocent?

EIGHT. He's nineteen years old.

THREE. That's old enough. He knifed his own father. Four inches into the chest. An innocent little nineteen-year-old kid.

FOUR (*to* THREE). I agree with you that the boy is guilty but I think we should try to avoid emotionally colored arguments.

THREE. All right. They proved it a dozen different ways. Do you want me to list them?

EIGHT. No.

TEN (*rising, putting his feet on seat of chair and sitting on back of it, then, to* EIGHT). Well, do you believe that stupid story he told?

FOUR (*to* TEN). Now, now.

TEN. Do you believe the kid's story?

EIGHT. I don't know whether I believe it or not. Maybe I don't.

SEVEN. So what'd you vote not guilty for?

EIGHT. There were eleven votes for guilty—it's not so easy for me to raise my hand and send a boy off to die without talking about it first.

SEVEN. Who says it's easy for me?

FOUR. Or me?

EIGHT. No one.

FOREMAN. He's still just as guilty, whether it's an easy vote or a hard vote.

SEVEN (*belligerently*). Is there something wrong because I voted fast?

EIGHT. Not necessarily.

SEVEN. I think the guy's guilty. You couldn't change my mind if you talked for a hundred years.

EIGHT. I don't want to change your mind.

THREE. Just what are you thinking of?

EIGHT. I want to talk for a while.

Look—this boy's been kicked around all his life. You know—living in a slum—his mother dead since he was nine. That's not a very good head start. He's a tough, angry kid. You know why slum kids get that way? Because we knock 'em over the head once a day, every day. I think maybe we owe him a few words. That's all. (*Looks around table. He is met by cold looks.* NINE *nods slowly while* FOUR *begins to comb his hair.*)

FOUR. All right, it's hard, sure—it was hard for me. Everything I've got I fought for. I worked my way through college. That was a long time ago, and perhaps you do forget. I fought, yes, but I never killed.

THREE. I know what it's like. I never killed nobody.

TWELVE. I've been kicked around, too. Wait until you've worked in an ad agency and the big boy that buys the advertising walks in. We all know.

ELEVEN (*who speaks with an accent*). In my country, in Europe, kicking was a science, but let's try to find something better than that.

TEN (*to* EIGHT). I don't mind telling you this, mister. We don't owe the kid a thing. He got a fair trial, didn't he? You know what that trial cost? He's lucky he got it. Look, we're all grownups here. You're not going to tell us that we're supposed to believe him, knowing what he is. I've lived among 'em all my life. You can't believe a word they say. You know that.

NINE (*to* TEN, *very slowly*). I don't know that. What a terrible thing for a man to believe! Since when is dishonesty a group characteristic? You have no monopoly on the truth!

THREE (*interrupting*). All right. It's not Sunday. We don't need a sermon.

NINE (*not heeding*). What this man says is very dangerous.

> (**EIGHT** *puts his hand on* **NINE'S** *arm and stops him.* **NINE** *draws a deep breath and relaxes.*)

FOUR. I don't see any need for arguing like this. I think we ought to be able to behave like gentlemen.

SEVEN. Right!

TWELVE (*smiling up at* **FOUR**). Oh, all right, if you insist.

FOUR (*to* **TWELVE**). Thank you.

TWELVE. Sure.

FOUR. If we're going to discuss this case, why, let's discuss the facts.

FOREMAN. I think that's a good point. We have a job to do. Let's do it.

ELEVEN. If you gentlemen don't mind, I'm going to close the window. (*Gets up and does so, then, apologetically as he moves back to table.*) It was blowing on my neck. (**TEN** *blows his nose fiercely as he gets down from back of chair and sits again.*)

SEVEN. If you don't mind, I'd like to have the window open.

ELEVEN. But it was blowing on me.

SEVEN. Don't you want a little air? It's summer—it's hot.

ELEVEN. I was very uncomfortable.

SEVEN. There are twelve of us in this room; it's the only window. If you don't mind!

ELEVEN. I have some rights, too.

SEVEN. So do the rest of us.

FOUR (*to* **ELEVEN**). Couldn't you trade chairs with someone at the other end of the table?

ELEVEN. All right, I will open the window, if someone would trade. (*Goes to window and opens it.* **TWO** *gets up and goes to* **ELEVEN'S** *chair, near right end of table.*)

TWO (*motioning*). Take my chair.

ELEVEN. Thank you. (*Goes to* **TWO'S** *chair, near left end of table.*)

FOREMAN. Shall we get back to the case?

THREE. Yeah, let's.

TWELVE. I may have an idea here. I'm just thinking out loud now, but it seems to me that it's up to us to convince this gentleman—(*motioning toward* **EIGHT**)—that we're right and he's wrong. Maybe if we each talk for a minute or two. You know—try it on for size.

FOREMAN. That sounds fair enough.

FOUR. Very fair.

FOREMAN. Supposing we go once around the table.

SEVEN. Okay—let's start it off.

FOREMAN. Right. (*To* **TWO**.) We'll start with you.

TWO (*timidly*). Oh. Well . . . (*There is a long pause.*) I just think he's guilty. I thought it was obvious.

EIGHT. In what way was it obvious?

TWO. I mean that nobody proved otherwise.

EIGHT (*quietly*). Nobody has to prove otherwise; innocent until proven guilty. The burden of proof is on the prosecution. The defendant doesn't have to open his mouth. That's in the Constitution. The Fifth Amendment. You've heard of it.

Four. Everyone has.

Two (*flustered*). Well, sure—I've heard of it. I know what it is . . . I . . . what I meant . . . well, anyway . . . I think he's guilty!

Eight (*looking at* **Two,** *shaking his head slowly*). No reasons—just guilty. There is a life at stake here.

Three. Okay, let's get to the facts. Number one: let's take the old man who lived on the second floor right underneath the room where the murder took place. At ten minutes after twelve on the night of the killing he heard loud noises in the upstairs apartment. He said it sounded like a fight. Then he heard the kid say to his father, "I'm gonna kill you." A second later he heard a body falling, and he ran to the door of his apartment, looked out and saw the kid running downstairs and out of the house. Then he called the police. They found the father with a knife in his chest.

Foreman. And the coroner fixed the time of death at around midnight.

Three. Right. Now what else do you want?

Eight. It doesn't seem to fit.

Four. The boy's entire story is flimsy. He claimed he was at the movies. That's a little ridiculous, isn't it? He couldn't even remember what picture he saw.

Three. That's right. Did you hear that? (*To* **Four.**) You're absolutely right.

Five. He didn't have any ticket stub.

Eight. Who keeps a ticket stub at the movies?

Four (*to* **Five**). That's true enough.

Five. I suppose, but the cashier didn't remember him.

Three. And the ticket taker didn't, either.

Ten. Look—what about the woman across the street? If her testimony don't prove it, then nothing does.

Twelve. That's right. She saw the killing, didn't she?

Foreman (*rapping on table*). Let's go in order.

Ten (*loudly*). Just a minute. Here's a woman who's lying in bed and can't sleep. It's hot, you know. (*Gets up and begins to walk around at* L *stage, blowing his nose and talking.*) Anyway, she wakes up and she looks out the window, and right across the street she sees the kid stick the knife into his father.

Eight. How can she really be sure it was the kid when she saw it through the windows of a passing elevated train?

Ten (*pausing* DL). She's known the kid all his life. His window is right opposite hers—across the el tracks—and she swore she saw him do it.

Eight. I heard her swear to it.

Ten. Okay. And they proved in court that you can look through the windows of a passing el train at night, and see what's happening on the other side. They proved it.

Eight. Weren't you telling us just a minute or two ago that you can't trust *them?* That you can't believe *them.*

TEN (*coldly*). So?

EIGHT. Then I'd like to ask you something. How come you believed her? She's one of *them,* too, isn't she? (TEN *crosses up to* EIGHT.)

TEN. You're a pretty smart fellow, aren't you?

FOREMAN (*rising*). Now take it easy. (THREE *gets up and goes to* TEN.)

THREE. Come on. Sit down. (*Leads* TEN *back to his seat.*) What're you letting him get you all upset for? Relax. (TEN *and* THREE *sit down.*)

FOUR. Gentlemen, they did take us out to the woman's room and we looked through the windows of a passing el train—(*to* EIGHT)—didn't we?

EIGHT. Yes. (*Nods.*) We did.

FOUR. And weren't you able to see what happened on the other side?

EIGHT. I didn't see as well as they told me I would see, but I did see what happened on the other side.

TEN (*snapping at* EIGHT). You see —do you see?

FOREMAN (*sitting again*). Let's calm down now. (*To* FIVE.) It's your turn.

FIVE. I'll pass it.

FOREMAN. That's your privilege. (*To* SIX.) How about you?

SIX (*slowly*). I don't know. I started to be convinced, you know, with the testimony from those people across the hall. Didn't they say something about an argument between the father and the boy around seven o'clock that night? I mean, I can be wrong.

ELEVEN. I think it was eight o'clock. Not seven.

EIGHT. That's right. Eight o'clock.

FOUR. They heard the father hit the boy twice and then saw the boy walk angrily out of the house.

SIX. Right.

EIGHT. What does that prove?

SIX. Well, it doesn't exactly prove anything. It's just part of the picture. I didn't say it proved anything.

FOREMAN. Anything else?

SIX. No. (*Rises, goes to water cooler for a drink and then sits again.*)

SEVEN. I don't know—most of it's been said already. We can talk all day about this thing, but I think we're wasting our time.

EIGHT. I don't.

FOUR. Neither do I. Go on.

SEVEN. Look at the kid's record. He stole a car. He's been arrested for mugging. I think they said he stabbed somebody in the arm.

FOUR. They did.

SEVEN. He was picked up for knife fighting. At fifteen he was in reform school.

THREE. And they sent him to reform school for stabbing someone!

SEVEN (*with sarcasm*). This is a very fine boy.

EIGHT. Ever since he was five years old his father beat him up regularly. He used his fists.

SEVEN. So would I! On a kid like that.

THREE. You're right. It's the kids. The way they are—you know? They don't listen. (*Bitterly.*) I've. got a kid. When he was eight years old he ran away from a fight. I saw him. I was *so* ashamed. I told him right out, "I'm gonna make a man out of you or I'm gonna bust you up into little pieces trying." When he was fifteen he hit me in the face. He's big, you know? I haven't seen him in three years. Rotten kid! I hate tough kids! You work your heart out. . . . (*Pauses.*) All right. Let's get on with it. . . . (*Gets up and goes to window, very embarrassed.*)

FOUR. We're missing the point here. This boy—let's say he's a product of a filthy neighborhood and a broken home. We can't help that. We're not here to go into the reasons why slums are breeding grounds for criminals; they are. I know it. So do you. The children who come out of slum backgrounds are potential menaces to society.

TEN. You said it there. I don't want any part of them, believe me. (*There is a dead silence for a moment, and then* **FIVE** *speaks haltingly.*)

FIVE. I've lived in a slum all my life. . . .

TEN. Now wait a second!

FIVE. I used to play in a back yard that was filled with garbage. Maybe it still smells on me.

FOREMAN. Now, let's be reasonable. There's nothing personal——

FIVE (*rising, slamming his hand down on table*). There is something personal! (*Then he catches himself, and, seeing* **EVERYONE** *looking at him, sits down, fists clenched.*)

THREE (*turning from window*). Come on, now. He didn't mean you,

feller. Let's not be so sensitive. (*There is a long pause.*)

EIGHT (*breaking silence*). Who did he mean?

ELEVEN. I can understand this sensitivity.

FOREMAN. Now let's stop the bickering.

TWELVE. We're wasting time.

FOREMAN (*to* **EIGHT**). It's your turn.

EIGHT. All right. I had a peculiar feeling about this trial. Somehow I felt that the defense counsel never really conducted a thorough cross-examination. Too many questions were left unasked.

FOUR. While it doesn't change my opinion about the guilt of the kid, still, I agree with you that the defense counsel was bad.

THREE. So-o-o-o? (*Crosses back to table and sits.*)

EIGHT. This is a point.

THREE. What about facts?

EIGHT. So many questions were never answered.

THREE (*annoyed*). What about the questions that were answered? For instance, let's talk about that cute little switch knife. You know, the one that fine upright kid admitted buying.

EIGHT. All right, let's talk about it. Let's get it in here and look at it. I'd like to see it again, Mr. Foreman. (**FOREMAN** *looks at him questioningly and then gets up and goes to door* L.)

(*During the following dialogue the* **FOREMAN** *knocks. The* **GUARD** *unlocks the door and comes in* L *and the* **FOREMAN** *whispers to him. The* **GUARD** *nods and leaves, locking the door. The* FOREMAN *returns to his seat.*)

THREE. We all know what it looks like. I don't see why we have to look at it again. (*To* FOUR.) What do you think?

FOUR. The gentleman has a right to see exhibits in evidence.

THREE (*shrugging*). Okay with me.

FOUR (*to* EIGHT). This knife is a pretty strong piece of evidence, don't you agree?

EIGHT. I do.

FOUR. Now let's get the sequence of events right as they relate to the switch knife.

TWELVE. The boy admits going out of his house at eight o'clock, after being slapped by his father.

EIGHT. Or punched.

FOUR. Or punched. (*Gets up and begins to pace at* R *stage, moving* DR *to* UR *and back again.*) He went to a neighborhood store and bought a switch knife. The storekeeper was arrested the following day when he admitted selling it to the boy.

THREE. I think everyone agrees that it's an unusual knife. Pretty hard to forget something like that.

FOUR. The storekeeper identified the knife and said it was the only one of its kind he had in stock. Why did the boy get it?

SEVEN (*sarcastically*). As a present for a friend of his, he says.

FOUR (*pausing in his pacing*). Am I right so far?

EIGHT. Right.

THREE. You bet he's right. (*To* ALL.) Now listen to this man. He knows what he's talking about.

FOUR (*standing at* R *stage*). Next, the boy claims that on the way home the knife must have fallen through a hole in his coat pocket, that he never saw it again. Now there's a story, gentlemen. You know what actually happened. The boy took the knife home, and a few hours later stabbed his father with it and even remembered to wipe off the fingerprints.

(*The door* L *opens and the* GUARD *walks in with an oddly designed knife with a tag on it.* FOUR *crosses* L *and takes the knife from him. The* GUARD *goes out* L, *closing and locking the door.*)

FOUR (*at* LC, *holding up knife*). Everyone connected with the case identified this knife. Now are you trying to tell me that someone picked it up off the street and went up to the boy's house and stabbed his father with it just to be amusing?

EIGHT. No. I'm saying that it's possible that the boy lost the knife, and that someone else stabbed his father with a similar knife. It's possible. (FOUR *flips knife open and jams it into wall just downstage of door* L.)

FOUR (*standing back to allow others to see*). Take a look at that knife. It's a very strange knife. I've never seen one like it before in my life. Neither had the storekeeper who sold it to him. (EIGHT *reaches casually into his pocket and withdraws an object. No one notices him. He stands up.*) Aren't you trying to make us accept a pretty incredible coincidence?

EIGHT (*moving toward* FOUR). I'm

not trying to make anyone accept it. I'm just saying it's possible.

THREE (*rising, shouting*). And I'm saying it's not possible! (EIGHT *swiftly flicks open blade of a switch knife, jams it into wall next to first knife and steps back. They are exactly alike. There are several gasps and* EVERYONE *stares at knife. There is a long silence.* THREE *continues, slowly, amazed.*) What are you trying to do?

TEN (*loudly*). Yeah, what is this? Who do you think you are? (*A flow of ad lib conversation bursts forth.*)

FIVE. Look at it! It's the same knife!

FOREMAN. Quiet! Let's be quiet. (JURORS *quiet down.* THREE *sits again.*)

FOUR. Where did you get it?

EIGHT. I got it in a little junk shop around the corner from the boy's house. It cost two dollars.

THREE. Now listen to me!

EIGHT (*turning to him*). I'm listening.

THREE. You pulled a real smart trick here, but you proved absolutely zero. Maybe there are ten knives like that, so what?

EIGHT. Maybe there are.

THREE. The boy lied and you know it.

EIGHT (*crossing back to his seat, sitting*). And maybe he didn't lie. Maybe he did lose the knife and maybe he did go to the movies. Maybe the reason the cashier didn't see him was because he sneaked into the movies, and maybe he was ashamed to say so. (*Looks around.*) Is there anybody here who didn't sneak into the movies once or twice when they were young? (*There is a long silence.*)

ELEVEN. I didn't.

FOUR. Really, not even once?

ELEVEN. We didn't have movies.

FOUR. Oh. (*Crosses back to his place and sits.*)

EIGHT. Maybe he did go to the movies—maybe he didn't. And—he may have lied. (*To* TEN.) Do you think he lied?

TEN (*violently*). Now that's a stupid question. Sure, he lied!

EIGHT (*to* FOUR). Do you?

FOUR. You don't have to ask me that. You know my answer. He lied.

EIGHT (*to* FIVE). Do you think he lied? (FIVE *can't answer immediately. He looks around nervously.*)

FIVE. I—I don't know.

SEVEN. Now wait a second. What are you—the guy's lawyer? Listen—there are still eleven of us who think he's guilty. You're alone. What do you think you're going to accomplish? If you want to be stubborn and hang this jury he'll be tried again, and found guilty sure as he's born.

EIGHT. You're probably right.

SEVEN. So what are you going to do about it? We can be here all night.

NINE. It's only one night. A man may die.

SEVEN. Oh, now. Come on.

EIGHT (*to* NINE). Well, yes, that's true.

FOREMAN. I think we ought to get on with it now.

THREE. Right. Let's get going here.

TEN (*to* THREE). How do you like this guy? (THREE *shrugs and turns to* EIGHT.)

THREE. Well, what do you say? You're the one holding up the show.

FOUR (*to* EIGHT). Obviously you don't think the boy is guilty.

EIGHT. I have a doubt in my mind.

FOUR. But you haven't really presented anything to us that makes it possible for us to understand your doubt. There's the old man downstairs. He heard it. He heard the kid shriek it out. . . .

THREE. The woman across the el tracks—she saw it!

SEVEN. We know he bought a switch knife that night and we don't know where he really was. At the movies?

FOREMAN. Earlier that night the kid and his father did have a fight.

FOUR. He's been a violent kid all the way, and while that doesn't prove anything . . .

TEN. Still, you know . . .

EIGHT (*standing*). I've got a proposition to make. (FIVE *stands and puts his hands on back of his chair. Several jurors glare at him. He sinks his head down a bit, then sits down.*) I want to call for a vote. I want you eleven men to vote by secret ballot. I'll abstain. If there are still eleven votes for guilty, I won't stand alone. We'll take in a guilty verdict right now.

SEVEN. Okay. Let's do it.

FOREMAN. That sounds fair. Is everyone agreed?

FOUR. I certainly am.

TWELVE. Let's roll it.

ELEVEN (*slowly*). Perhaps this is

best. (EIGHT *walks over to window and stands there for a moment looking out, then turns as* FOREMAN *passes ballot slips down table to all of them.* EIGHT *tenses as* JURORS *begin to write. Then folded ballots are passed back to* FOREMAN. *He flips through folded ballots, counts them to be sure he has eleven and then he begins to open them, reading verdict each time.*)

FOREMAN. Guilty. Guilty. Guilty. Guilty. Guilty. Guilty.

THREE. That's six.

FOREMAN. Please. (*Fumbles with one ballot.*) Six guilty. Guilty. Guilty. Guilty. (*Pauses for a moment at tenth ballot and then reads.*) Not guilty. (THREE *slams his hand down hard on table.* EIGHT *starts for table, as* FOREMAN *reads final ballot.*) Guilty.

TEN (*angrily*). How do you like that!

SEVEN (*standing, snarling*). Who was it? I think we have a right to know. (*Looks about. No one moves.*)

CURTAIN

Understanding Literature—Act I

1. If you were playing the part of the judge, what tone of voice would you use to give his first speech? What important information is given in this speech? In what way does it set the tone of the play?
2. Find several speeches in the early part of Act I showing that the minds of the jurors are not really concentrating on the extremely serious decision they are to make.
3. What "reason" does each juror have for his vote? One juror never really suggests a reason for his vote. Which juror is it?
4. As Eight questions the other jurors, is he quarrelsome? logical? prejudiced? Prove your answer.
5. When Eight promises to change his vote if he is still the only person voting "Not Guilty," he is taking a risk. Why does he take it?
6. Seven is the first juror to speak and the last to speak in this act. How does the difference in these two speeches illustrate the difference that has taken place in the group?

Act II

(AT RISE OF CURTAIN: *It is only a second or two later. The* JURORS *are in the same positions as they were at the end of Act I.*)

THREE (*after brief pause*). All right! Who did it? What idiot changed his vote?

EIGHT. Is that the way to talk about a man's life? (*Sits at his place again.*)

THREE. Whose life are you talking about? The life of the dead man or the life of a murderer?

SEVEN. I want to know. Who?

THREE. So do I.

ELEVEN. Excuse me. This was a secret ballot.

THREE. No one looked while we did it, but now I want to know.

ELEVEN. A secret ballot; we agreed on that point, no? If the gentleman wants it to remain a secret——

THREE (*standing up angrily*). What do you mean? There are no secrets in here! I know who it was. (*Turns to* FIVE.) What's the matter with you? You come in here and you vote guilty and then this—(*nods toward* EIGHT)—slick preacher starts to tear your heart out with stories about a poor little kid who just couldn't help becoming a murderer. So you change your vote. If that isn't the most sickening—— (FIVE *edges away in his chair.*)

FOREMAN. Now hold it. (SEVEN *sits again slowly.*)

FOUR (*to* THREE). I agree with you that the man is guilty, but let's be fair.

THREE. Hold it? Be fair? That's just what I'm saying. We're trying to put a guilty man into the chair where he belongs—and all of a sudden we're paying attention to fairy tales.

FIVE. Now, just a minute——

THREE (*bending toward* FIVE, *wagging finger at him*). Now, you listen to me——

FOREMAN (*rapping on table*). Let's try to keep this organized, gentlemen.

FOUR. It isn't organized, but let's try to be civilized.

ELEVEN. Please. I would like to say something here. I have always thought that a man was entitled to have unpopular opinions in this country. This is the reason I came here. I wanted to have the right to disagree.

THREE. Do you disagree with us?

ELEVEN. Usually, I would. In this one case I agree with you, but the point I wish to make is that in my own country, I am ashamed to say——

TEN. Oh, now-w-w, what do we have to listen to—the whole history of your country? (THREE *sits again in disgust.*)

FOUR. It's always wise to bear in mind what has happened in other countries, when people aren't allowed to disagree; but we are, so let's stick to the subject.

SEVEN. Yeah, let's stick to the subject. (*To* FIVE.) I want to ask you, what made you change your vote?

THREE. I want to know, too. You haven't told us yet.

FIVE. Why do you think I did change my vote?

SEVEN. Because I do. Now get on with it.

NINE (*quietly*). There's nothing for him to tell you. He didn't change his vote. I did. (ALL *look at* NINE.)

FIVE (*to* THREE). I was going to tell you, but you were so sure of yourself.

THREE. Sorry. (*To* NINE.) Okay, now. . . .

NINE. Maybe you'd like to know why.

THREE (*not giving him a chance*). Let me tell you why that kid's a——

FOREMAN. The man wants to talk. (THREE *subsides*.)

NINE (*to* FOREMAN). Thank you. (*Points at* EIGHT.) This gentleman chose not to stand alone against us. That's his right. It takes a great deal of courage to stand alone even if you believe in something very strongly. He left the verdict up to us. He gambled for support and I gave it to him. I want to hear more. The vote is ten to two. (JURORS TWO *and* FOUR *get up at about same instant and walk to water cooler as* TEN *speaks*.)

TEN. That's fine. If the speech is over, let's go on. (FOREMAN *gets up, goes to door* L, *pulls tagged knife from wall and then knocks on door*.)

(*The door is opened by the* GUARD. *The* FOREMAN *hands the* GUARD *the tagged switch knife. The* GUARD *goes out and the* FOREMAN *takes the other switch knife, closes it and puts it in the middle of the table. He sits again. The*

other JURORS *talk on, in pantomime, as* TWO *and* FOUR *stand by the water cooler*.)

FOUR (*filling cup*). If there was anything in the kid's favor I'd vote not guilty.

TWO. I don't see what it is.

FOUR (*handing cup to* TWO, *then drawing drink for himself*). Neither do I. They're clutching at straws.

TWO. As guilty as they get—that's the kid, I suppose.

FOUR. It's that one juror that's holding out, but he'll come around. He's got to and, fundamentally, he's a very reasonable man.

TWO. I guess so.

FOUR. They haven't come up with one real fact yet to back up a not guilty verdict.

TWO. It's hard, you know.

FOUR. Yes, it is. And what does "guilty beyond a reasonable doubt" really mean?

TWO. What's a reasonable doubt?

FOUR. Exactly. When a life is at stake, what is a reasonable doubt? You've got to have law and order; you've got to draw the line somewhere; if you don't, everyone would start knifing people.

TWO. Not much doubt here.

FOUR. Two men think so. I wonder why. I really wonder why.

TWO. You do hear stories about innocent men who have gone to jail —or death, sometimes—then years later things turn up.

FOUR. And then on the other hand some killers get turned loose and they go and do it again. They squeeze out on some technicality and kill again. (*Throws his cup into wastebasket, walks back and sits. We then hear* THREE *say to* FIVE:)

THREE. Look, buddy, now that we've kind of cooled off, why—ah— I was a little excited a minute ago. Well, you know how it is—I didn't mean to get nasty. Nothing personal. (TWO *trails back to his place and sits again.*)

FIVE (*after staring at* THREE *for a moment*). Okay.

SEVEN (*to* EIGHT). Look. Supposing you answer me this. If the kid didn't kill him, who did?

EIGHT. As far as I know, we're supposed to decide whether or not the boy on trial is guilty. We're not concerned with anyone else's motives here.

SEVEN. I suppose, but who else had a motive?

EIGHT. The kid's father was along in years; maybe an old grudge.

NINE. Remember, it is "guilty beyond a reasonable doubt." This is an important thing to remember.

THREE (*to* TEN). Everyone's a lawyer. (*To* NINE.) Supposing you explain to us what your reasonable doubts are.

NINE. This is not easy. So far, it's only a feeling I have. A feeling. Perhaps you don't understand.

THREE (*abruptly*). No. I don't.

TEN. A feeling! What are we gonna do, spend the night talking about your feelings? What about the facts?

THREE. You said a mouthful. (*To* NINE.) Look, the old man heard the kid yell, "I'm gonna kill you." A second later he heard the father's body falling, and he saw the boy running out of the house fifteen seconds after that.

SEVEN. Where's the reasonable doubt in that?

TWELVE. That's right. And let's not forget the woman across the street. She looked into the open window and saw the boy stab his father. She saw it!

THREE. Now, if that's not enough for you——

EIGHT (*quietly firm*). It's not enough for me.

FOUR. What is enough for you? I'd like to know.

SEVEN. How do you like him? It's like talking into a dead phone.

FOUR. The woman saw the killing through the windows of a moving elevated train. The train had five cars and she saw it through the windows of the last two cars. She remembers the most insignificant details.

THREE. Well, what have you got to say about that?

EIGHT. I don't know. It doesn't sound right to me.

THREE. Well, supposing you think about it. (*To* TWELVE.) Lend me your pencil. (TWELVE *hands him a pencil.*) Let's play some tic-tac-toe. (*Draws an X on a piece of paper, then hands pencil and paper to* TWELVE.) We might as well pass the time.

EIGHT. This isn't a game. (*Rises and snatches paper away.* THREE *jumps up.*)

THREE. Now, wait a minute!

EIGHT. This is a man's life.

THREE (*angrily*). Who do you think you are?

SEVEN (*rising*). All right, let's take it easy. (EIGHT *sits again.*)

THREE. I've got a good mind to walk around this table and belt him one!

FOREMAN. Now, please. I don't want any fights in here.

THREE. Did you see him? The nerve! The absolute nerve!

TEN. All right. Forget it. It don't mean anything.

SIX. How about sitting down?

THREE. "This isn't a game." Who does he think he is? (SIX *and* TEN *urge* THREE *back into his seat.* SEVEN *sits again, and* ALL *are seated once more.*)

FOUR (*when quiet is restored*). Weren't we talking about elevated trains?

EIGHT. Yes, we were.

FOUR. So?

EIGHT. All right. How long does it take an elevated train going at top speed to pass a given point?

FOUR. What has that got to do with anything?

EIGHT. How long would it take? Guess.

FOUR. I wouldn't have the slightest idea.

SEVEN. Neither would I.

NINE. I don't think they mentioned it.

EIGHT (*to* FIVE). What do you think?

FIVE. About ten or twelve seconds —maybe.

EIGHT. I'd say that was a fair guess. (*Looks about.*) Anyone else?

ELEVEN. I would think about ten seconds, perhaps. . . .

TWO (*reflectively*). About ten seconds, yes.

FOUR. All right, we're agreed. Ten seconds. (*To* EIGHT.) What are you getting at?

EIGHT. This. An el train passes a given point in ten seconds. That given point is the window of the room in which the killing took place. You can almost reach out of the window of that room and touch the el. Right?

FOREMAN. That's right. I tried it.

FOUR. So?

EIGHT. All right. Now let me ask you this. Did anyone here ever live right next to the el tracks?

FIVE. I've lived close to them.

EIGHT. They make a lot of noise, don't they? (FIVE *nods*.) I've lived right by the el tracks. When your window is open, and the train goes by, the noise is almost unbearable. You can't hear yourself think.

TEN (*impatiently*). Okay. You can't hear yourself think. Get to the point.

EIGHT. The old man who lived downstairs heard the boy say——

THREE (*interrupting*). He didn't *say it,* he screamed it.

EIGHT. The old man heard the boy scream, "I'm going to kill you," and one second later he heard a body fall. (*Slight pause.*) One second. That's the testimony. Right?

TWO. Right.

EIGHT. The woman across the street looked through the windows of the last two cars of the el and saw the body fall. Right?

FOUR. Right.

TWELVE. So?

EIGHT (*slowly*). The last two cars.

(*Slight pause, then repeats.*) The last two cars.

TEN. What are you giving us here?

EIGHT. An el train takes ten seconds to pass a given point, or two seconds per car. That el had been going by the old man's window for at least six seconds and maybe more *before the body fell,* according to the woman. The old man would have had to hear the boy say, "I'm going to kill you," while the front of the el was roaring past his nose. It's not possible that he could have heard it.

THREE. What do you mean! Sure, he could have heard it.

EIGHT. With an el train going by?

THREE. He said the boy yelled it out.

EIGHT. An el train makes a lot of noise.

THREE. It's enough for me.

FOUR. It's enough for me, too.

NINE. I don't think he could have heard it.

TWO. Maybe the old man didn't hear it. I mean with the el noise. . . .

THREE. What are you people talking about? Are you calling the old man a liar?

EIGHT (*shaking his head*). Something doesn't fit.

FIVE. Well, it stands to reason——

THREE. You're crazy! Why would he lie? What's he got to gain?

NINE. Attention . . . maybe.

THREE. You keep coming up with these bright sayings. Why don't you send one in to a newspaper? They pay two dollars.

EIGHT (*hard, to* THREE). What does that have to do with a man's life?

(*Then, to* NINE.) Why might the old man have lied? You have a right to be heard.

NINE (*after moment's hesitation*). It's just that I looked at him for a very long time. The seam of his jacket was split under his arm. Did you notice that? He was a very old man with a torn jacket, and he carried two canes. (*Gets up, moves* R *and leans against wall.*) I think I know him better than anyone here. This is a quiet, frightened, insignificant man who has been nothing all his life—who has never had recognition—his name in the newspapers. Nobody knows him after seventy-five years. This is a very sad thing. A man like this needs to be recognized—to be questioned, and listened to, and quoted just once. This is very important. . . .

TWELVE. And you're trying to tell us he lied about a thing like this just so he could be important?

NINE. No, he wouldn't really lie. But perhaps he'd make himself believe that he heard those words and recognized the boy's face.

THREE. Well—(*loud and brassy*) —that's the most fantastic story I've ever heard. How can you make up a thing like that?

NINE (*doggedly*). I'm not making it up.

THREE. You must be making it up. People don't lie about things like that.

NINE. He made himself believe he told the truth.

THREE. What do you know about it?

NINE (*low but firm*). I speak from experience.

SEVEN. What!

NINE. I am the same man.

FOUR. I think we all understand now. Thank you. (NINE *moves slowly back to table and sits.*)

THREE (*as* NINE *sits*). If you want to admit you're a liar, it's all right by me.

EIGHT. Now, that is too much!

THREE. He's a liar. He just told us so.

EIGHT. He did not say he was a liar; he was explaining.

THREE (*to* NINE). Didn't you admit that you're a liar?

EIGHT (*to* THREE). Please—he was explaining the circumstances so that we could understand why the old man might have lied. There is a difference.

THREE. A liar is a liar, that's all there is to it.

EIGHT. Please—have some compassion.

FOREMAN. Gentlemen, please, we have our job and our duty here.

FOUR. I think they've covered it.

EIGHT. I hope we have.

FOREMAN (*to* EIGHT). All right. Is there anything else? (**Two** *holds up a box of cough drops and speaks to* FOREMAN.)

TWO. Cough drop?

FOREMAN (*waving it aside*). No, thank you.

TWO (*hesitantly*). Anybody—want a cough—drop? (*Offers box around.*)

FOREMAN (*sharply*). Come on. Let's get on with it.

EIGHT. I'll take one. (**Two** *hands him box.*) Thank you. (*Takes one and returns box.*) Now—there's something else I'd like to point out here. I think we proved that the old man couldn't have heard the boy say, "I'm going to kill you."

THREE. Well, I disagree.

FOUR (*to* **THREE**). Let's hear him through, anyway.

EIGHT. But supposing the old man really did hear the boy say "I'm going to kill you." This phrase—how many times has each of you used it? Probably hundreds. "If you do that once more, Junior, I'm going to murder you." "Come on, Rocky, kill him!" We say it every day. This doesn't mean that we're really going to kill someone.

FOUR. Don't the circumstances alter that somewhat?

TWELVE. The old man was murdered.

THREE. One thing more. The phrase was "I'm going to kill you." And the kid screamed it out at the top of his lungs.

FOUR. That's the way I understand it.

THREE. Now don't try and tell me he didn't mean it. Anybody says a thing like that the way he said it—they mean it.

TEN. And how they mean it!

EIGHT. Well, let me ask you this. Do you really think the boy would shout out a thing like that so the whole neighborhood would hear it? I don't think so. He's much too bright for that.

TEN (*exploding*). Bright! He's a common ignorant slob. He don't even speak good English!

ELEVEN (*slowly*). He *doesn't* even speak good English.

FOUR. The boy is clever enough. (**FOUR'S** *line is spoken as* **TEN** *rises and glowers at* **ELEVEN**. *There is a momentary pause.* **TEN** *sits again as* **FIVE** *gets up and looks around. He is nervous.*)

FIVE. I'd like to change my vote to not guilty. (**THREE** *slams his fist into his hand, then walks to window and does it again.*)

FOREMAN. Are you sure?

FIVE. Yes. I'm sure.

FOREMAN. The vote is nine to three in favor of guilty.

FOUR (*to* **FIVE**). I'd like to know why you've changed your vote.

FIVE. I think there's a doubt.

THREE (*turning abruptly from window, snarling*). Where? What is the doubt?

FIVE. There's the knife. . . .

SEVEN (*slamming his hand down on table*). Oh, fine!

TEN. He—(*motioning at* **EIGHT**) —he talked you into believing a fairy tale.

FOUR (*to* **FIVE**). Go on. Give us the reasons.

FIVE. The old man, too. Maybe he didn't lie, but then just *maybe* he did. Maybe the old man doesn't like the kid.

SEVEN. Well, if that isn't the end.

FIVE. I believe that there is reasonable doubt. (*Sits again.*)

SEVEN. What are you basing it on? Stories that this guy—(*indicates* **EIGHT**)—made up! He ought to write for Amazing Detective Monthly. He'd make a fortune. Listen, the kid had a lawyer, didn't he? Why didn't his lawyer bring up all these points?

FIVE. Lawyers can't think of everything.

SEVEN. Oh, brother! (*To* EIGHT.) You sit in here and pull stories out of thin air. Now we're supposed to believe that the old man didn't get out of bed, run to the door and see the kid beat it downstairs fifteen seconds after the killing.

FOUR. That's the testimony, I believe.

SEVEN. And the old man swore to this—yes—he swore to this only so he could be important. (*Looks over at* NINE.)

FIVE. Did the old man say he *ran* to the door?

SEVEN. Ran. Walked. What's the difference? He got there.

FIVE. I don't remember what he said. But I don't see how he could run.

FOUR. He said he *went.* I remember it now. He *went* from his bedroom to the front door. That's enough, isn't it?

EIGHT. Where was his bedroom, again?

TEN (*disinterested*). Down the hall somewhere.

EIGHT (*mad*). Down the hall! Are we to send a man off to die because it's down the hall *somewhere?*

TEN. I thought you remembered everything. Don't you remember that?

EIGHT. No, I don't.

NINE. I don't remember, either.

EIGHT. Mr. Foreman, I'd like to take a look at the diagram of the apartment.

SEVEN. Why don't we have them

run the trial over just so you can get everything straight?

EIGHT. The bedroom is down the hall somewhere. Do you *know*—do you know exactly where it is? Please. A man's life is at stake. Do you *know?*

SEVEN. Well, ah . . .

EIGHT. Mr. Foreman.

FOREMAN (*rising*). I heard you. (*Goes to door* L *and knocks on door.*)

> (*During the ensuing dialogue the* GUARD *opens the door* L. *The* FOREMAN *whispers to him. The* GUARD *nods and then closes the door.*)

THREE (*stepping away from window, moving a few steps toward* EIGHT). All right. What's this one for? How come you're the only one in the room who wants to see exhibits all the time?

FIVE. I want to see this one, too.

NINE. So do I.

THREE. And I want to stop wasting time.

FOUR. Are we going to start wading through all that nonsense about where the body was found?

EIGHT. We're not. We're going to find out how a man who's had two strokes in the past three years and who walks with a pair of canes could get to his front door in fifteen seconds.

THREE. He said twenty seconds.

TWO. He said fifteen.

THREE. How does he know how long fifteen seconds is? You can't judge that kind of thing.

NINE. He said fifteen. He was very positive about it.

THREE (*angrily*). He's an old man.

You saw that. Half the time he was confused. How could he be positive about—anything? (*Looks around sheepishly, unable to cover his blunder.*) Well, ah—you know.

EIGHT. No, I don't know. Maybe you know.

(*The door* L *opens and the* GUARD *walks in carrying a large pen-and-ink diagram of the apartment done on heavy drawing board stock. It is a railroad flat. A bedroom faces the el tracks. Behind it is a series of rooms off a long hall. In the front bedroom there is a mark where the body was found. At the back of the apartment we see the entrance into the apartment hall from the building hall. We see a flight of stairs in the building hall. The diagram is clearly labeled, and included in the information on it are the various dimensions of the various rooms. The* GUARD *gives the diagram to the* FOREMAN, *who has remained by the door* L.)

GUARD. Is this what you wanted?

FOREMAN. That's right. Thank you.

GUARD. Sure, that's my job. (*Nods and goes out* L, *closing and locking door as he goes.* EIGHT *rises and starts toward* FOREMAN.)

FOREMAN. You want this?

EIGHT. Yes, please. (FOREMAN *nods.* EIGHT *takes diagram and crosses* UR. *He takes chair from* UR *corner and brings it* RC, *half*

facing table. He sets diagram up on chair so that all can see it. EIGHT looks it over. Several JURORS get up to see it better. FOREMAN comes over to look. THREE, TEN and SEVEN, however, barely bother to look at it. THREE sits abruptly again at table.)

SEVEN (*to* TEN). Do me a favor. (*Slumps in chair.*) Wake me up when this is over.

TEN. I looked at that diagram for two hours; enough is enough.

FOUR. Some of us are interested. Go ahead.

EIGHT. All right. This is the apartment in which the killing took place. The old man's apartment is directly beneath it, and exactly the same. (*Pointing.*) Here are the el tracks. The bedroom. Another bedroom. Living room. Bathroom. Kitchen. And this is the hall. Here's the front door to the apartment, and here are the steps. (*Points to front bedroom and then to front door.*) Now, the old man was in bed in this room. He says he got up, went out into the hall, down the hall to the front door and opened it and looked out just in time to see the boy racing down the stairs. Am I right?

FOUR. That's the story.

SEVEN. That's what happened!

EIGHT. Fifteen seconds after he heard the body fall.

ELEVEN. Correct. (FOREMAN *and other* JURORS *who have come over to look at diagram now drift back to table and sit again.*)

EIGHT (*still by diagram at* RC). His bed was at the window. (*Looking closer.*) It's twelve feet from his bed to the bedroom door. The length of the hall is forty-three feet six inches. He had to get up out of bed, get his canes, walk twelve feet, open the bedroom door, walk forty-three feet and open the front door—all in fifteen seconds. Do you think this possible?

TEN. You know it's possible.

FOUR. I don't see why not.

THREE. He would have been in a hurry. He did hear the scream.

ELEVEN. He can only walk very slowly. They had to help him into the witness chair.

THREE. You make it sound like a long walk. It's not. (EIGHT *goes* DL *and takes two chairs. He crosses* DR, *near water cooler, and puts them together to indicate a bed.*)

NINE. For an old man who uses canes it's a long walk.

THREE (*to* EIGHT). What are you doing?

EIGHT. I want to try this thing. Let's see how long it took him. I'm going to pace off twelve feet—the length of the bedroom. (*Begins to do so, pacing from* DR, *across stage, toward* DC.)

THREE. You're crazy! You can't re-create a thing like that.

ELEVEN. Perhaps if we could see it —this is an important point.

THREE (*angrily*). It's a ridiculous waste of time!

SIX. Let him do it.

FOUR. I can't see any harm in it. Foolish, but go ahead.

EIGHT. Hand me a chair, please. (NINE *pushes chair from right end of table to* EIGHT *and then sits again.*) All right. (*Places chair at point he has paced off.*) This is the bedroom door. How far would you say it is from here to the door of this room?

SIX (*as* ALL *look*). I'd say it was twenty feet. (*Several* JURORS, *excluding* THREE, SEVEN *and* TEN, *rise and stand near their places, watching.*)

TWO. Just about.

EIGHT. Twenty feet is close enough. All right, from here to the door and back is about forty feet. It's shorter than the length of the hall the old man had to move through. Wouldn't you say that?

NINE. A few feet, maybe.

TEN. Look, this is absolutely insane. What makes you think you can do this?

FOREMAN. We can't stop him.

EIGHT. Do you mind if I try it? According to you, it'll only take fifteen seconds. We can spare that. (*Walks over to two chairs and lies down on them.*) Who's got a watch with a second hand?

TWO. I have. (*Indicates wrist watch.*)

EIGHT. When you want me to start, stamp your foot. That'll be the body falling.

TWO. We'll time you from there.

EIGHT (*lying down on two chairs*). Let's say he keeps his canes right at his bedside. Right?

FOUR. Right!

EIGHT. Okay. I'm ready.

TWO (*explaining*). I'm waiting for the hand to get to sixty. (ALL *watch carefully; then* TWO *stamps his foot, loudly.* EIGHT *begins to get up. Slowly, he swings his legs over edges of chairs, reaches for imaginary canes and struggles to his feet.* **Two** *stares at his watch.* **Eight** *walks as a crippled old man would walk now. He goes toward chair which is serving as bedroom door. He gets to it and pretends to open it.*)

Ten (*shouting*). Speed it up. He walked twice as fast as that.

    (**Eight,** *not having stopped for this outburst, begins to walk simulated forty-foot hallway, to door* L *and back to chair.*)

Eleven. This is, I think, even more quickly than the old man walked in the courtroom.

Three. No, it isn't.

Eight. If you think I should go faster, I will.

Four. Speed it up a little. (**Eight** *speeds up his pace slightly. He reaches door* L *and turns now, heading back, hobbling as an old man would hobble, bent over his imaginary canes.* **All** *watch him tensely. He hobbles back to chair, which also serves as front door. He stops there and pretends to unlock door. Then he pretends to push it open.*)

Eight (*loudly*). Stop.

Two (*his eyes glued to watch*). Right.

Eight. What's the time?

Two. Fifteen—twenty—thirty—thirty-five—thirty-nine seconds, exactly. (*Moves toward* **Eight.** *Other* **Jurors** *now move in toward* **Eight,** *also.*)

Three. That can't be!

Eleven. Thirty-nine seconds!

Four. Now, that's interesting.

Seven (*looking at* **Jurors**). Hey, now—you know. . . .

Nine. What do you think of that!

Eleven (*nodding*). Thirty-nine seconds. Thirty-nine.

Four. And the old cripple swore, on his oath, that it was fifteen.

Eleven (*pointing to* **Eight**). He may have been a little bit off on the speed that the old cripple moved at —but twenty-four seconds off . . . well, now, you know . . .

Foreman. Far be it from me to call anyone a liar, and even allowing for quite a difference in speed between the old man and you . . . (*motions at* **Eight**). Why, still, there's quite a——

Four. Quite a discrepancy.

Eight. It's my guess that the old man was trying to get to the door, heard someone racing down the stairs and *assumed* that it was the boy.

Six. I think that's possible.

Three (*infuriated*). Assumed? Now, listen to me, you people. I've seen all kinds of dishonesty in my day—but this little display takes the cake.

Eight. What dishonesty?

Three (*to* **Four**). Tell him! (**Four** *turns away* DR *and sits silently in one of the two chairs there.* **Three** *looks at him and then he strides to* **Eight.**) You come in here with your heart bleeding all over the floor about slum kids and injustice and you make up these wild stories, and you've got some soft-hearted old ladies listening to you. Well, I'm not. I'm getting real sick of you. (*To* **All.**) What's the matter with you people? This kid is guilty! He's got to burn!

We're letting him slip through our fingers.

EIGHT (*calmly*). Our fingers. Are you his executioner?

THREE (*raging*). I'm one of 'em!

EIGHT. Perhaps you'd like to pull the switch.

THREE (*shouting*). For this kid? You bet I'd like to pull the switch!

EIGHT (*shaking his head sadly*). I'm sorry for you.

THREE (*shouting*). Don't start with me!

EIGHT. What it must feel like to want to pull the switch!

THREE. Shut up!

EIGHT. You're a sadist. . . .

THREE (*louder*). Shut up!

EIGHT (*his voice strong*). You want to see this boy die because you personally want it—not because of the facts. (*Spits out words.*) You are a beast. You disgust me.

THREE (*shouting*). Shut up! (*Lunges at* EIGHT, *but is caught by two of the* JURORS *and is held. He struggles as* EIGHT *watches calmly. Then he screams.*) Let me go! I'll kill him! I'll kill him!

EIGHT (*softly*). You don't really mean you'll kill me, do you?

(THREE *stops struggling now and stares at* EIGHT, *and all the* JURORS *watch in silence, as:*)

CURTAIN

Understanding Literature—Act II

1. What word or words of another juror cause Eight to say, "Is that the way to talk about a man's life?"
2. Why does Three assume that it was Five who changed his vote? Why has Nine changed?
3. Even though the jurors seem to be merely resentful of Nine's explanation of why he changed his vote, the reader can see that they are really affected by it, since they begin to defend their positions. Find some of these defensive speeches.
4. How do the jurors test parts of the evidence? What is the result of the testing?
5. Eight has been calm throughout. Why does he eventually become angry? How is the cause of his anger different from that of the anger of the other jurors?
6. What is the real significance of the climax of the second act?

AT RISE OF CURTAIN: *We see the same scene as at the end of Act II. There has been no time lapse.* THREE *glares angrily at* EIGHT. *He is still held by two* JURORS. *After a long pause* THREE *shakes himself loose and turns away. He walks to the window. The other* JURORS *move away and stand around the room now; they are shocked by this display of anger. There is silence. Then the door* L *opens and the* GUARD *enters. He looks around the room.*)

GUARD. Is there anything wrong, gentlemen? I heard some noise.

FOREMAN. No. There's nothing wrong. (*Points to large diagram of apartment.*) You can take that back. We're finished with it. (GUARD *nods and takes diagram. He looks curiously at some of* JURORS *and then goes out.* JURORS *still are silent; some of them begin to sit down slowly at table.* FOUR *is still seated* DR. THREE *still stands at window. He turns around now.* JURORS *look at him.*)

THREE (*loudly*). Well, what are you looking at? (*They turn away. He goes back to his seat now.* EIGHT *puts his chair back at right end of table. Silently, rest of* JURORS, *including* FOUR *but excluding* ELEVEN, *take their seats.* TWELVE *begins to doodle on a piece of paper.* ELEVEN *moves* DL *and leans reflectively against wall.* TEN *blows his nose but no one speaks. Then, finally:*)

FOUR. I don't see why we have to behave like children here.

ELEVEN. Nor do I. We have a responsibility. This is a remarkable thing about democracy. That we are—what is the word? . . . ah, notified! That we are notified by mail to come down to this place—and decide on the guilt or innocence of a man; of a man we have not known before. We have nothing to gain or lose by our verdict. This is one of the reasons why we are strong. We should not make it a personal thing. . . .

NINE (*slowly*). Thank you, very much.

ELEVEN (*slight surprise*). Why do you thank me?

NINE. We forget. It's good to be reminded. (ELEVEN *nods and leans against wall again.*)

FOUR. I'm glad that we're going to be civilized about this.

TWELVE. Well, we're still nowhere.

EIGHT. No, we're somewhere, or getting there—maybe.

FOUR. Maybe.

TWELVE. Who's got an idea?

SIX. I think maybe we should try another vote. (*Turns to* FOREMAN.) Mr. Foreman?

FOREMAN. It's all right with me. Anybody doesn't want to vote? (*Looks around table. Most of them shake their heads.* ELEVEN *has moved to table and takes his seat.*)

FOUR. Let's vote.

TWELVE. Yes, vote.

SEVEN. So all right, let's do it.

THREE. I want an open ballot.

Let's call out our votes. I want to know who stands where.

FOREMAN. That sounds fair. Anyone object? (*Looks around. There is a general shaking of heads.*) All right. I'll call off your jury numbers. (*Takes a pencil and paper and makes marks in one of two columns after each vote.*) I vote guilty. Number two?

TWO. Not guilty.

FOREMAN. Three?

THREE. Guilty.

FOREMAN. Four?

FOUR. Guilty.

FOREMAN. Five?

FIVE. Not guilty.

FOREMAN. Six?

SIX. Not guilty.

FOREMAN. Seven?

SEVEN. Guilty.

FOREMAN. Eight?

EIGHT. Not guilty.

FOREMAN. Nine?

NINE. Not guilty.

FOREMAN. Ten?

TEN. Guilty.

FOREMAN. Eleven?

ELEVEN. Not guilty.

FOREMAN. Twelve?

TWELVE. Guilty.

FOUR. That's six to six.

TEN (*mad*). I'll tell you something. The crime is being committed right in this room.

FOREMAN. The vote is six to six.

THREE. I'm ready to walk into court right now and declare a hung jury. There's no point in this going on any more.

FOUR (*to* ELEVEN). I'd like to know why you changed your mind. (*To* TWO.) And why you changed your mind. (*To* SIX.) And why you did. There are six men here who think that we may be turning a murderer loose in the streets. Emotion won't do. Why? (**TWO, ELEVEN** *and* **SIX** *look at each other.*)

SIX. It would seem that the old man did not see the boy run downstairs. I do not think it likely that the old man heard someone scream, "I'm going to kill you." Old men dream. And if the boy did scream that he was going to kill, then we have the authority of this man—(*motions at* THREE)—to prove that it might not really mean he's going to kill.

SEVEN. Why don't we take it in to the judge and let the kid take his chances with twelve other guys?

FOREMAN. Six to six. I don't think we'll ever agree—on anything.

THREE. It's got to be unanimous—(*motioning at* EIGHT)—and we're never going to convince him.

EIGHT. At first I was alone. Now five others agree; there is a doubt.

THREE. You can't ever convince me that there's a doubt, because I know there isn't no doubt.

TWELVE. I tell you what, maybe we are a hung jury. It happens sometimes.

EIGHT. We are not going to be a hung jury.

SEVEN. But we are, right now, a perfect balance. Let's take it in to the judge.

FOUR (*to* EIGHT). If there is a reasonable doubt I don't see it.

NINE. The doubt is there, in my mind.

FOREMAN. Maybe we should vote.

TWELVE. What do you mean—vote?

THREE. Not again!

TEN. I still want to know. Vote on what?

FOREMAN. Are we or aren't we a hung jury?

EIGHT. You mean that we vote yes, we are a hung jury, or no, we are not a hung jury?

FOREMAN. That's just what I was thinking of.

ELEVEN (*bitterly*). We can't even agree about whether or not the window should be open.

FOREMAN. Let's make it a majority vote. The majority wins.

FOUR. If seven or more of us vote yes, that we are a hung jury, then we take it in to the judge and tell him that we are a hung jury.

FOREMAN. Right. And if seven or more vote no, that means that we aren't a hung jury, and we go on discussing it.

FOUR. It doesn't seem quite right to me.

THREE. It's the only solution.

SEVEN. I agree, it's the only way.

TWELVE. Anything to end this.

FOREMAN (*looking around table*). Are we agreed then? Seven or more vote yes and we take it in to the judge. (ALL *nod*.)

THREE. Let's call our votes out.

FOREMAN. I vote yes, we're a hung jury. (*Makes a mark on a sheet of paper.*) Two?

TWO. No.

FOREMAN. Three?

THREE. Yes.

FOREMAN. Four?

FOUR. Yes.

FOREMAN. Five?

FIVE. No.

FOREMAN. Six?

SIX. No.

FOREMAN. Seven?

SEVEN. Yes.

FOREMAN. Eight?

EIGHT. No.

FOREMAN. Nine?

NINE. No.

FOREMAN. Ten?

TEN. Yes.

FOREMAN. Eleven?

ELEVEN. No.

FOREMAN. Twelve?

TWELVE. Yes.

THREE (*with a groan*). Oh, no!

FOREMAN. It's six to six.

NINE. We can't even get a majority to decide whether or not we're a hung jury.

FOUR (*rising*). I went along with the majority vote on this question. And I didn't agree with voting that way, not really, and I still don't. So I'm changing my vote. I say no, we are not a hung jury. I believe that the boy is guilty beyond a reasonable doubt. There are some things I want to find out from those gentlemen that changed their minds. (*Sits again.*)

FOREMAN. Then we aren't a hung jury—so we go on.

EIGHT. Good! We go on.

FOUR (*to* TWO). Why did you change your mind?

TWO (*hesitating a moment*). He—(*points to* EIGHT)—he seems so sure. And he has made a number of good points. While he—(*points to* THREE)—only gets mad and insults everybody.

Four. Does the anger and the insult change the guilt of the boy? He did do it. Are you going to turn a murderer loose because one of the jurors gets angry when he thinks a murderer is being turned loose?

Two. That's true.

Five. There is a doubt.

Four. I don't think so. The track is straight in front of the window. Let's take that point. So the el train would have made a low rumbling noise. El trains screech when they go around curves. So the old man could have heard a scream, which is high-pitched. And it is a tenement and they have thin walls.

Three. Good. Good. That's it. That's it.

Four. And what if the old man was wrong about the time it took him to get to the door but right about whom he saw? Please remember that there weren't any fingerprints on the knife, and it is summer, so gloves seem unlikely.

Three (to Eight). Now I want you to listen to this man. (Motions at Four.) He's got the goods.

Four. And it might have taken a few seconds to get a handkerchief out and wipe the fingerprints away.

Eight. This is a point.

Three. Why don't we just time this one, to see?

Five. Just what are we timing?

Eight. Yes, let's be exact, please.

Four. I am saying that the old man downstairs might have been wrong about how long it took him to get to the door but that he was right about whom he saw running down the stairs. Now it may have

taken the murderer about thirty-nine seconds to wipe away all the fingerprints and get down the stairs to the place where the old man saw him— the boy, that is.

Three. This is right.

Foreman. We reconstructed the old man getting out of bed and going to the door, and we timed that; now let's reconstruct the actual crime.

Nine. As well as we can reconstruct it.

Seven. I think a murderer could use up thirty or forty seconds pretty easily at that point.

Four. Let's reconstruct the killing.

Seven. Yes, let's.

Three (taking knife from table, giving it to Eight). Here, you do the stabbing.

Four (taking knife). No, I'll do it.

Three (to Seven). Why don't you be the one that gets stabbed? You're younger than I am. And don't forget, you take one second to fall.

Four (rising, moving toward R, turning). And he was found on his side—his right side—so fall and roll onto your right side. (To Eight.) If someone hates another person enough to kill them, don't you think that it's reasonable to suppose that the murderer would look at his victim for a second or two?

Twelve (to Eight). Divorce yourself from this particular case—just human nature.

Eight. Yes, it seems reasonable.

Three. Hey, wait a minute! (ALL look at Three.) He falls and he ends up on his right side, the father did, but stabbing someone isn't like shooting them, even when it's right in the heart. The father would have worked around for a few seconds—lying there on the floor—writhing, maybe.

Four. That's quite possible. There would have been enough oxygen in his system to carry him for two or three seconds, I should think.

Eleven. Wouldn't the father have cried out?

Three. Maybe the kid held his mouth.

Eight. That also seems possible.

Four. Also, there's another point we might bring out. Anyone who is clear enough mentally to wipe the fingerprints away after murdering someone, well, that person is also clear enough mentally to look around the apartment, or the room in this case, to see if there are any other clues. It would just be for a second or two, I should think, but still he would look around.

Three. This gets better and better.

Four. We're trying to make it clear. One doesn't talk about quality when murder is involved. Well, let's do it.

Foreman. About this on the fingerprints—the kid wiped the fingerprints off the knife. Well, what about the doorknob? If I saw a man coming into my home, a man that hated me, and if he was wiping the doorknob with a handkerchief as he came in, it would give me an uneasy feeling. (**All** smile.) So the doorknobs must have been wiped after the killing, and this, too, would take some time.

Four (to **Two**). You timed the last

one. Why don't you time this one, too?

Two. All right.

Four (as **Seven** takes his position in front of **Four** at R stage; **Four** has knife in his hand). Stamp your foot when you want me to start.

Two (waiting a few seconds). I want the hand to be at sixty. (Waits another second, then stamps foot.)

Four (not screaming, but still loud). I'm going to kill you. (Brings knife down, overhand. Blade is collapsed. **Seven** catches knife in his hands and falls to floor a second after shout. He writhes a bit, then rolls onto his right side. **Four** stares at him for a few moments, then digs into his pocket and produces a handkerchief. It takes him a moment or two to unfold handkerchief; then he bends down and wipes handle of knife. He looks about, as though checking to be sure that he has done everything. Then he rushes to door L that leads out of jury room and wipes doorknob. Then he turns around a full circle and wipes knob again.) He would have wiped both knobs. (Then he rushes R and goes back to door of jury room and repeats double process on doorknob. Then he stamps his foot and cries out.) Stop!

Two (checking watch). Twenty—yeah, twenty, twenty-five—twenty-nine—about twenty-nine and a half seconds, I'd say.

Four (moving to behind **Foreman's** chair at left end of table). And whoever did murder the old man, and I think it was the kid, he still had to run down the hall and down the stairs—at least one flight of stairs.

THREE. You see! You see! (**SEVEN** *rises from floor and dusts himself off.*)

FOUR. The old man downstairs may have been wrong on the time, but in view of this I think it's quite reasonable to assume that he did see the kid run downstairs.

TWELVE (*to* **EIGHT**). So now both time sequences check—the one you did and the one we did; what with running downstairs and everything, it does pretty much check out on times.

SEVEN. Sure—he's an old man who wants attention. . . . (*Motions at* **NINE.**) He's probably right, but the old man feels the way everyone does —a life is at stake. (*Sits again at table, placing knife back on table.*)

FOUR. So the story of the old man may well be true.

EIGHT. Except for the fact that he absolutely swore, under oath, that it was only fifteen seconds.

NINE. We seem to all agree that it was twenty-five to forty seconds later.

EIGHT. You are now admitting that the old man lied in one case and told the truth in the other. I admit that this does tend to confirm the story of the old man, but in part he is now a proven liar—and this is by your own admission.

TWO (*to* **EIGHT**). That may be true, that the old man lies in part, but I think it will change my vote once more. (*To* **FOREMAN.**) Guilty.

THREE (*to* **SIX**). What about you? What do you think now?

SIX (*getting up, crossing to water cooler*). I'm not just sure what I think. I want to talk some more. At first I thought guilty, then I changed. Now—I'm sort of swinging back to guilty. (*Takes a drink.*)

THREE (*to* **ELEVEN**). And what about you?

ELEVEN. No. (*Shakes his head.*) I am now in real doubt—real doubt. . . .

FIVE. I say guilty. I was right the first time.

THREE. Now we're beginning to make sense in here.

FOREMAN. It seems to be about nine guilty to three not guilty. (**FOUR** *sits again.*)

EIGHT. One more question about the old man downstairs. How many of you live in apartment buildings? (*Eight hands go up, including his own.*)

ELEVEN (*to* **EIGHT**). I don't know what you're thinking but I know what I'm thinking.

FOUR (*to* **ELEVEN**). What's that?

ELEVEN. I do not live in a tenement, but it is close and there is just enough light in the hall so you can see the steps, no more—the light bulbs are so small—and this murder took place in a tenement. Remember how we stumbled on the steps?

EIGHT. The police officers were using big bulbs and one even had a flashlight. Remember?

ELEVEN. An old man who misjudged the time by twenty seconds, on this we all agree, this old man looked down the dark hallway of a tenement and recognized a running figure?

EIGHT. He was one hundred per

cent wrong about the time; it took twice as long as he thought.

ELEVEN. Then could not the old man be one hundred per cent wrong about who he saw?

THREE. That's the most idiotic thing I've ever heard of. You're making that up out of thin air.

TWELVE. We're a hung jury. Let's be honest about it.

ELEVEN (*to* **SEVEN**). Do you truly feel that there is no room for reasonable doubt?

SEVEN. Yes, I do.

ELEVEN. I beg your pardon, but maybe you don't understand the term, "reasonable doubt."

SEVEN (*angrily*). What do you mean, I don't understand it? Who do you think you are to talk to me like that? (*To* **ALL.**) How do you like this guy? He comes over here running for his life, and before he can even take a big breath he's telling us how to run the show. The arrogance of him!

FOUR. No one here is asking where anyone came from.

SEVEN. I was born right here.

FOUR. Or where your father came from. (*Looks at* **SEVEN,** *who looks away.*)

EIGHT. Maybe it wouldn't hurt us to take a few tips from people who come running here! Maybe they learned something we don't know. We're not so perfect.

ELEVEN. Please. . . . I am used to this. . . . It's all right. Thank you.

EIGHT. It's not all right.

SEVEN. Okay—okay—I apologize. Is that what you want?

EIGHT (*grimly*). That's what I want.

FOREMAN. All right. Let's stop the arguing. Who's got something constructive to say?

TWO (*hesitantly*). Well, something's been bothering me a little. This whole business about the stab wound, and how it was made—the downward angle of it, you know?

THREE. Don't tell me we're going to start that. They went over it and over it in court.

TWO. I know they did—but I don't go along with it. The boy is five feet eight inches tall. His father was six feet two inches tall. That's a difference of six inches. It's a very awkward thing to stab *down* into the chest of someone who's half a foot taller than you are. (**THREE** *grabs knife from table and jumps up.*)

THREE (*moving* LC). Look, you're not going to be satisfied till you see it again. I'm going to give you a demonstration. Somebody get up. (*Looks toward table.* **EIGHT** *stands up and walks toward him.* **THREE** *closes knife and puts it in his pocket. They stand face to face and look at each other for a moment.*) Okay. (*To* **TWO.**) Now watch this. I don't want to have to do it again. (*Crouches down until he is quite a bit shorter than* **EIGHT.**) Is that six inches?

TWELVE. That's more than six inches.

THREE. Okay, let it be more. (*Reaches into his pocket and takes out knife. He flicks it open, changes its position in his hand and holds knife aloft, ready to stab. He and* **EIGHT** *look steadily into each other's*

eyes. Then he stabs downward, hard.)

Two (*shouting*). Look out! (*Reaches short just as blade reaches* **Eight**'s *chest.* **Three** *laughs.*)

Six. That's not funny. (*Crosses back to table and sits.*)

Five. What's the matter with you?

Three. Now just calm down. Nobody's hurt, are they?

Eight (*low*). No. Nobody's hurt. (*Turns, crosses back to his place but does not sit.*)

Three. All right. There's your angle. Take a look at it. (*Illustrates.*) Down and in. That's how I'd stab a taller man in the chest, and that's how it was done. (*Crosses back to his place at table.*) Take a look at it, and tell me I'm wrong. (**Two** *doesn't answer.* **Three** *looks at him for a moment, then jams*

knife into table and sits down. **All** *look at knife.*)

Six. Down and in. I guess there's no argument. (**Eight** *picks knife out of table and closes it. He flicks it open and, changing its position in his hand, stabs downward with it.*)

Eight (*to* **Six**). Did you ever stab a man?

Six. Of course not.

Eight (*to* **Three**). Did you?

Three. All right, let's not be silly.

Eight (*insistently*). Did you?

Three (*loudly*). No. I didn't!

Eight. Where do you get all your information about how it's done?

Three. What do you mean? It's just common sense.

Eight. Have you ever seen a man stabbed?

Three (*pausing, looking around rather nervously, finally*). No.

Eight. All right. I want to ask you something. The boy was an experienced knife-fighter. He was even sent to reform school for knifing someone. Isn't that so?

Twelve. That's right.

Eight. Look at this. (*Closes knife, flicks it open and changes position of knife so that he can stab overhand.*) Doesn't it seem like an awkward way to handle a knife?

Three. What are you asking me for? (**Eight** *closes blade and flicks it open, holding knife ready to slash underhanded.*)

Five. Wait a minute! What's the matter with me? Give me that knife. (*Reaches out for knife.*)

Eight. Have you ever seen a knife fight?

Five. Yes, I have.

Eight. In the movies? (*Passes knife to* **Five.**)

Five. In my back yard. On my stoop. In the vacant lot across the street. Too many of them. Switch knives came with the neighborhood where I lived. Funny that I didn't think of it before. I guess you try to forget those things. (*Flicks knife open.*) Anyone who's ever used a switch knife would never have stabbed downward. You don't handle a switch knife that way. You use it underhanded. (*Illustrates.*)

Eight. Then he couldn't have made the kind of wound that killed his father.

Five. I suppose it's conceivable that he could have made the wound, but it's not likely, not if he'd ever had any experience with switch knives, and we know that the kid had a lot of experience with switch knives.

Three. I don't believe it.

Ten. Neither do I. You're giving us a lot of mumbo-jumbo.

Eight (*to* **Twelve**). What do you think?

Twelve (*hesitantly*). Well—I don't know.

Eight (*to* **Seven**). What about you?

Seven. Listen, I'll tell you all something. I'm a little sick of this whole thing already. We're getting nowhere fast. Let's break it up and go home.

Eight. Before we decide anything more, I would like to try to pull this together.

Three. This should be good.

Four. He has a right. Let him go ahead.

Two. Do you want me to time this, too? (**Eight** *looks at* **Two.**)

Foreman. Let's hear him.

Twelve (*getting comfortable*). I'm in advertising. I'm used to the big shots pulling things together. Let's chip up a few shots to see if any of them land on the green.

Eight. I want you all to look at this logically and consistently.

Three. We have. Guilty.

Eight. I want to know—is the kid smart or is the kid dumb?

Four. What do you mean?

Eight (*moving* UC, *so that he is standing back of men at upstage side of table*). This is a kid who has gone to the reform school for knife fighting. The night of the murder he bought a knife, a switch knife. It would then take a very stupid kid to go and murder a man, his father, with an instrument that everyone would associate with the kid.

THREE. I quite agree, he's dumb.

EIGHT. However, if he were dumb, then why did he make the kind of wound that an inexperienced man would make with a knife?

FOREMAN. I'm not sure I understand.

EIGHT. To murder someone must take a great emotion, great hatred. (*Moves over to left of* FOREMAN.) And at that moment he would handle the knife as best he could, and a trained knife-fighter would handle it as he had been trained, underhand. . . . (*Makes underhanded motion.*) A man who had not been trained would go overhand. . . . (*Makes overhanded motion.*) But the kid is being very smart. Everyone knows that he is an experienced knife-fighter—so he is smart enough at that moment to make the wound that an amateur would make. That man is a smart man. Smart enough to wipe the fingerprints away, perhaps even smart enough to wait until an el train was going by in order to cover the noise. Now, is the kid smart, or is he dumb? (*Looks around.*)

THREE. Hey, now, wait a minute!

NINE. Well, the woman across the el tracks saw the murder through the el train, so someone in that el train could have seen the murder, too.

EIGHT. A possibility, but no one did that we know of.

NINE. It would take an awfully dumb man to take that chance, doing the murder as the train went by.

EIGHT. Exactly. A dumb man, a very stupid man, a man swept by emotion. Probably he heard nothing; he probably didn't even hear the train coming. And whoever did murder the father did it as well as he could.

FOUR. So?

EIGHT (*moving back to his place, at right end of table, not sitting*). The kid is dumb enough to do everything to associate himself with the switch knife—a switch knife murder —and then a moment after the murder he becomes smart. The kid is smart enough to make a kind of wound that would lead us to suspect someone else, and yet at the same instant he is dumb enough to do the killing as an el train is going by, and then a moment later he is smart enough to wipe fingerprints away. To make this boy guilty you have to say he is dumb from eight o'clock until about midnight and then about midnight he is smart one second, then dumb for a few seconds and then smart again and then once again he becomes stupid, so stupid that he does not think of a good alibi. Now is this kid smart or is he dumb? To say that he is guilty you have to toss his intelligence like a pancake. There is doubt, doubt, doubt. (*Beats table with fist as he emphasizes word "doubt."*)

FOUR. I hadn't thought of that.

EIGHT. And the old man downstairs. On the stand he swore that it was fifteen seconds; he insisted on fifteen seconds, but we all agree that it must have been almost forty seconds.

NINE. Does the old man lie half the time and then does he tell the truth the other half of the time?

EIGHT. For the kid to be guilty he must be stupid, then smart, then stupid and then smart and so on, and, also, for the kid to be guilty the old man downstairs must be a liar half of the time and the other half of the time he must tell the truth. You can reasonably doubt. (*Sits again. There is a moment of silence.*)

SEVEN (*breaking silence*). I'm sold on "reasonable doubt."

TWO. I think I am, too.

SIX. I wanted more talk, and now I've had it.

EIGHT (*fast*). I want another vote.

FOREMAN. Okay, there's another vote called for. I guess the quickest way is a show of hands. Anybody object? (*No one does.*) All right. All those voting not guilty raise your hands. (*Jurors* **TWO**, **FIVE**, **SIX**, **SEVEN**, **EIGHT**, **NINE**, **ELEVEN** *and* **TWELVE** *raise their hands immediately.* **FOREMAN** *looks around table carefully and then he, too, raises his hand. He looks around table, counting silently.*) Nine. (*Hands go down.*) All those voting guilty. (*Jurors* **THREE**, **FOUR** *and* **TEN** *raise their hands.*) Three. (*They lower their hands.*) The vote is nine to three in favor of acquittal.

TEN. I don't understand you people. How can you believe this kid is innocent? Look, you know how those people lie. I don't have to tell you. They don't know what the truth is. And let me tell you, they— (**FIVE** *gets up from table, turns his back to it and goes to window*)—

don't need any real big reason to kill someone, either. You know, they get drunk, and bang, someone's lying in the gutter. Nobody's blaming them. That's how they are. You know what I mean? Violent! (**NINE** *gets up and goes to window and looks out. He is followed by* **ELEVEN**.) Human life don't mean as much to them as it does to us. Hey, where are you all going? Look, these people're drinking and fighting all the time, and if somebody gets killed, so somebody gets killed. They don't care. Oh, sure, there are some good things about them, too. Look, I'm the first to say that. (**EIGHT** *gets up and then* **TWO** *and* **SIX** *follow him to window.*) I've known a few who were pretty decent, but that's the exception. Most of them, it's like they have no feelings. They can do anything. What's going on here? (**FOREMAN** *gets up and goes to window, followed by* **SEVEN** *and* **TWELVE**.) I'm speaking my piece, and you—listen to me! They're no good. There's not a one of 'em who's any good. We better watch out. Take it from me. This kid on trial . . . (**THREE** *sits at table toying with knife as* **FOUR** *gets up and starts toward* **TEN**. *All the other* **JURORS** *have their backs turned on* **TEN**.) Well, don't you know about them? Listen to me! What are you doing? I'm trying to tell you something. . . . (**FOUR** *stands over him as he trails off. There is a dead silence. Then* **FOUR** *speaks softly.*)

FOUR. I've had enough. If you open your mouth again I'm going to split your skull. (*Stands there and* *looks at him. No one moves or speaks.* TEN *looks at* FOUR *and then looks down at table.*)

TEN (*softly*). I'm only trying to tell you. . . . (*There is a long pause as* FOUR *stares down at* TEN.)

FOUR (*to* JURORS *at window*). All right. Sit down, everybody. (ALL *move back to their seats. When they are all seated* FOUR *takes a stand behind men on upstage side of table. He speaks quietly.*) I still believe the boy is guilty of murder. I'll tell you why. To me, the most damning evidence was given by the woman across the street who claimed she actually saw the murder committed.

THREE. That's right. As far as I'm concerned that's the most important testimony.

EIGHT. All right. Let's go over her testimony. What exactly did she say?

FOUR (*moving toward window*). I believe I can recount it accurately. She said that she went to bed at about eleven o'clock that night. Her bed was next to the open window and she could look out of the window while lying down and see directly into the window across the street. She tossed and turned for over an hour, unable to fall asleep. Finally she turned toward the window at about twelve-ten and, as she looked out, she saw the boy stab his father. As far as I can see, this is unshakable testimony.

THREE. That's what I mean. That's the whole case. (FOUR *takes off his eyeglasses and begins to polish them as they all sit silently watching him.*)

FOUR (*to all of them*). Frankly, in view of this, I don't see how you can vote for acquittal. (*To* TWELVE *as he sits again.*) What do you think about it?

TWELVE. Well—maybe. . . . There's so much evidence to sift. . . .

THREE. What do you mean, maybe? He's absolutely right. You can throw out all the other evidence.

FOUR. That was my feeling. I don't deny the validity of the points that he has made. (*Motions at* EIGHT.) Shall we say that on one side of the tracks there is doubt? But what can you say about the story of the woman? She saw it.) (**Two,** *while he is polishing his glasses, too, squints at clock.*)

Two. What time is it?

ELEVEN. Ten minutes of six.

SIX. You don't suppose they'd let us go home and finish it in the morning. I've got a kid with mumps. . . .

FIVE. Not a chance.

EIGHT (*to* TWO). Can't you see the clock without your glasses?

Two. Not clearly.

EIGHT. Oh.

FOUR. Glasses are a nuisance, aren't they?

EIGHT (*an edge of excitement in his tone*). Well, what do you all do when you wake up at night and want to know what time it is?

Two. I put my glasses on and look at the clock.

FOUR. I just lie in bed and wait for the clock to chime. My father gave it to me when we married, my wife and I. It was ten years before we had a place to put it.

Eight (*to* **Two**). Do you wear your glasses to bed?

Two. Of course not. No one wears eyeglasses to bed.

Eight. The woman who testified that she saw the killing wears glasses. What about her?

Four. Did she wear glasses?

Eleven (*excitedly*). Of course! The woman wore bifocals. I remember this very clearly. They looked quite strong.

Nine. That's right. Bifocals. She never took them off.

Four. Funny. I never thought of that.

Eight. I think it's logical to say that she was not wearing her glasses in bed, and I don't think she'd put them on to glance casually out the window. . . . She testified that the murder took place the instant she looked out, and that the lights went out a split second later. She couldn't have had time to put on her glasses then. Now perhaps this woman honestly thought she saw the boy kill his father. (*Rises.*) I say that she only saw a blur.

Three. How do you know what she saw? Maybe she's farsighted. . . . (*Looks around. No one answers. Loudly.*) How does he know all these things? (*There is silence.*)

Eight. Does anyone think there still is not a reasonable doubt? (*Looks around room, then squarely at* **Ten.** **Ten** *looks down at table for a moment; then he looks up at* **Eight.**)

Ten. I will always wonder. But there is a reasonable doubt.

Three (*loudly*). I think he's guilty!

Eight (*calmly*). Does anyone else?

Four (*quietly*). No. I'm convinced now. There is a reasonable doubt.

Eight (*to* **Three**). You're alone.

Foreman. Eleven votes, not guilty; one, guilty.

Three. I don't care whether I'm alone or not! I have a right. . . .

Eight. Yes, you have a right. (**All** *stare at* **Three.**)

Three. Well, I told you. I think the kid's guilty. What else do you want?

Eight. Your arguments. (**All** *look at* **Three** *after glancing at* **Eight.**)

Three. I gave you my arguments.

Eight. We're not convinced. We're waiting to hear them again. We have time. (*Sits down again.* **Three** *runs to* **Four** *and grabs his arm.*)

Three (*pleading*). Listen. What's the matter with you? You're the guy. You made all the arguments. You can't turn now. A guilty man's going to be walking the streets. A murderer! He's got to die! Stay with me! . . .

Four (*rising*). I'm sorry. I'm convinced. I don't think I'm wrong often, but I guess I was this once. (*Crosses* R.) There is a reasonable doubt in my mind.

Eight. We're waiting. . . . (**Three** *turns violently on him.*)

Three (*shouting*). You're not going to intimidate me! (*They are* **All** *staring at* **Three.**) I'm entitled to my opinion! (*No one answers him.*) It's gonna be a hung jury! (*Turns abruptly and sits in his chair again.*)

That's it!

Eight. There's nothing we can do about that except hope that some night, maybe in a few months, why, you might get some sleep.

Five. You're all alone.

Nine. It takes a great deal of courage to stand alone.

Four (*moving back to table, sitting*). If it is a hung jury there will be another trial and some of us will point these things out to the various lawyers. (**Three** *looks around table at all of them. As* **Three's** *glance goes from juror to juror each one of them shakes his head in his direction. Then, suddenly,* **Three's** *face contorts and he begins to pound on table with his fist. He seems about to cry.*)

Three (*thundering*). All right! (*Jumps up quickly and moves* DR, *his back to all of them as* **Foreman** *goes to door* L *and knocks. The other* **Jurors** *now rise.*)

(*The* **Guard** *opens the door* L *and looks in and sees them all standing. The* **Guard** *holds the door open for them as they all file past and out* L; *that is, all except* **Three** *and* **Eight**. *The* **Guard** *waits for them.* **Eight** *moves toward the door* L, *pausing at* LC.)

Eight (*to* **Three**). They're waiting. (**Three** *sees that he is alone. He moves to table and pulls switch knife out of table and walks over to* **Eight** *with it.* **Three** *is holding knife in approved knife-fighter fashion.* **Three** *looks long and hard at juror* **Eight** *and weaves a bit from side to side as he holds knife with point of it in direction of* **Eight's** *belly.* **Eight** *speaks quietly, firmly.*) Not guilty. (**Three** *turns knife around and* **Eight** *takes it by handle.* **Eight** *closes knife and puts it away.*)

Three. Not guilty! (**Three** *walks out of room.* **Eight** *glances around quickly, sighs, then turns and moves out through door.* **Guard** *goes out, closing door.*)

CURTAIN

Understanding Literature—Act III

1. What are the steps that lead toward the final agreement?
2. What is the significance of the last scene between Three and Eight?

Understanding Literature—The Whole Play

1. The playwright has helped the reader to understand what each character is like by providing, in the notes on the characters at the beginning of the play, a brief character sketch of each. Go back over the play to reread the speeches of one character at a time; then list the character traits that are indicated by these speeches. Compare your list of traits with the character sketch in the introductory notes. Do the speeches and actions of each of the jurors bear out the details of the character sketch?

2. At the beginning of the play, Eight is alone in voting "Not Guilty." At the end, Three is alone in voting "Guilty." What traits of character and what attitudes enable Eight to stand alone? On the other hand, why does Three give in?

3. Early in the play the reader learns of the circumstantial evidence of guilt. Explain the steps by which the jury realizes that this evidence is not truly a proof of guilt.

4. Each act builds toward a point of climax. Read again the last part of each act. How does the action in each act lead to the final decision or statement of the act? For example, what is the action in the first act that causes one juror to change his vote?

Further Activities

1. Several of the characters in this play hold ideas which are shown to be unreasonable in some way. People often *prejudge* a situation; that is, they *judge before* they have reasonably considered the situation, or they form an opinion on insufficient or inadequate evidence. Find and think about each of the following statements made by the jurors in the play. Discuss what is unreasonable in the attitude revealed by each of the statements. Can you think of similar unreasonable statements that you have heard or read?

    (*a*) "I never saw a guiltier man in my life."

    (*b*) "You can't believe a word they say."

    (*c*) "I just think he's guilty. I thought it was obvious."

    (*d*) "A liar is a liar, that's all there is to it."

    (*e*) "Bright! He's a common ignorant slob. He don't even speak good English!"

    (*f*) "What's the matter with you people? This kid is guilty! He's got to burn! We're letting him slip through our fingers."

REGINALD ROSE AND SHERMAN L. SERGEL

(g) "He comes over here running for his life, and before he can even take a big breath he's telling us how to run the show."

(h) "Look, you know how those people lie. . . . And let me tell you, they . . . don't need any real big reason to kill someone, either. You know, they get drunk, and bang, someone's lying in the gutter. Nobody's blaming them. That's how they are. . . . Human life don't mean as much to them as it does to us."

2. Notice that you, along with the jurors, never know for certain that the accused man is *not* guilty. Assume, for the sake of discussion, that the man on trial is guilty; then decide whether or not Eight acted rightly in persuading the other jurors to change their votes. Be sure to give reasons for your opinion.

Pyramus and Thisbe

William Shakespeare

as rehearsed and played by the mechanicals in
A Midsummer Night's Dream

THE STORY OF PYRAMUS AND THISBE: The tragic legend of Pyramus and Thisbe was a familiar one to Shakespeare's audience. In Babylon, an ancient city of Asia, the young lovers Pyramus and Thisbe lived next door to each other. Although their parents forbade the lovers to see each other again, they discovered a crack in the wall between their two houses and came there to talk, Pyramus on one side and Thisbe on the other. Talking thus, they decided to meet under a mulberry tree near the tomb of Ninus.

Thisbe was the first to arrive at the meeting place. As she waited, she saw coming toward her a lion that had just killed an ox. The lion's mouth was dripping with blood. Thisbe, terrified, ran, dropping her veil as she went.

Later, Pyramus arrived. Seeing Thisbe's bloody veil (for the lion had torn the veil), Pyramus thought that Thisbe had been devoured by the savage beast. In despair he thrust his dagger through his heart. Thisbe returned to the meeting place to find her loved one lying dead. She grasped his dagger and killed herself.

Since that time the mulberry tree near which Pyramus and Thisbe died has changed the color of its berries from white to red—stained red by the blood of Pyramus.

CHARACTERS in *A Midsummer Night's Dream*

The Duke and the Queen

The wedding of Theseus, the Duke of Athens, to Hippolyta, the Queen of the Amazons, is about to be celebrated. The play begins as the Duke says:
> "Now, fair Hippolyta, our nuptial hour
> Draws on apace."

The plays ends as the wedding ceremony ends.

The Lovers

There are two pairs of young lovers. At the beginning of the play, both Lysander and Demetrius are in love with Hermia, and Helena is in love with Demetrius. Their affairs become more and more confused when Puck, a mischievous fairy, squeezes a love potion on the eyes of the two young men and, as a consequence, they both fall in love with Helena. Things are cleared up before the end of the play, and the young lovers are married in a ceremony with the Duke and the Queen.

WILLIAM SHAKESPEARE

The Fairies

Because Oberon, King of the Fairies, is quarreling with Titania, Queen of the Fairies, he hits upon a mischievous scheme. He sends Puck to find the juice of a certain flower which, when squeezed upon the eyelids of someone sleeping, causes the person on waking to fall in love with the first person he sees.

Titania sees first one of the workingmen, or mechanicals, to whom Puck has given an ass's head. She falls in love with this unlovely creature—in a beautifully fairylike manner. She has all her fairies deck him with flowers and carry out his orders.

At last Oberon takes pity on his lovely wife and, as she sleeps again, he has Puck drop an antidote on her eyelids. When Titania awakes, she thinks she has been dreaming.

The Mechanicals

The workingmen, or mechanicals, have a genius for getting things mixed up. They are simple people—yokels. The scenes in which they appear are full of humor.

These men have decided to prepare a play to give at the Duke's wedding: "The most Lamentable Comedy and most Cruel Death of Pyramus and Thisbe." As you read what happened at their rehearsal and at the presentation of the play, remember that in Shakespeare's time, women's parts were played by men or boys.

The play has a dreamlike quality: during a night in a fairy forest, true lovers—of both the human and fairy realm—are united. Perhaps the very down-to-earth humor of the scenes with the mechanicals makes the rest of the play more fanciful, by contrast.

The language may at first seem a little strange to you. Remember, however, that the play was written at the end of the 16th century and that the English language has changed since then. In some cases words may have had a somewhat different meaning in Shakespeare's day. Most of them, however, have not changed in meaning.

THE REHEARSAL

(*from* Act III, Scene I)

In this scene the workingmen prepare to rehearse the play that they hope to give immediately after the Duke's wedding. This is their second meeting; the first one, for assigning parts, was held at the home of Quince. Now, the group is meeting in a wooded spot. These people are present:

QUINCE, a carpenter (the PROLOGUE in the mechanicals' play)
SNUG, a joiner—a cabinetmaker, or man who makes furniture
    (LION)
BOTTOM, a weaver (PYRAMUS)
FLUTE, a bellows-mender (THISBE)
SNOUT, a tinker—a person who mends pots and pans (WALL)
STARVELING, a tailor (MOONSHINE)

Although this scene is very humorous, the clowns are not trying to be funny. They take the rehearsal very seriously.

Enter the CLOWNS (QUINCE, SNUG, BOTTOM, FLUTE, SNOUT
    and STARVELING).

BOTTOM. Are we all met?

QUINCE. Pat,[1] pat; and here's a marvail's convenient place for our rehearsal. This green plot shall be our stage, this hawthorn brake[2] our tiring house,[3] and we will do it in action as we will do it before the Duke.

BOTTOM. Peter Quince!

QUINCE. What sayest thou, bully[4] Bottom?

BOTTOM. There are things in this Comedy of Pyramus and Thisbe that will never please. First, Pyramus must draw a sword to kill himself; which the ladies cannot abide. How answer you that?

SNOUT. By'r lakin,[5] a parlous[6] fear!

STARVELING. I believe we must leave the killing out, when all is done.

BOTTOM. Not a whit. I have a device to make all well. Write me a prologue; and let the prologue seem to say, we will do no harm with our swords, and that Pyramus is not killed indeed; and for the more better assurance, tell them that I Pyramus am not Pyramus, but Bottom the weaver. This will put them out of fear.

---

1 **Pat:** exactly.
2 **hawthorn brake:** hedge of hawthorn.
3 **tiring house:** dressing room.

4 **bully:** good fellow.
5 **By'r lakin:** a mild oath.
6 **parlous:** perilous; dangerous.

QUINCE. Well, we will have such a prologue, and it shall be written in eight and six.[7]

BOTTOM. No, make it two more; let it be written in eight and eight.

SNOUT. Will not the ladies be afeard of the lion?

STARVELING. I fear it, I promise you.

BOTTOM. Masters, you ought to consider with yourselves, to bring in (God shield us!) a lion among ladies is a most dreadful thing. For there is not a more fearful wild-fowl than your lion living; and we ought to look to't.

SNOUT. Therefore another prologue must tell he is not a lion.

BOTTOM. Nay, you must name his name, and half his face must be seen through the lion's neck, and he himself must speak through, saying thus, or to the same defect.[8] "Ladies,"—or "Fair ladies,—I would wish you"—or "I would request you"—or "I would entreat you—not to fear, not to tremble. My life for yours! If you think I come hither as a lion, it were pity of my life.[9] No! I am no such thing. I am a man as other men are." And there, indeed, let him name his name and tell them plainly he is Snug the joiner.

QUINCE. Well, it shall be so. But there is two hard things: that is, to bring the moonlight into a chamber; for, you know, Pyramus and Thisbe meet by moonlight.

SNOUT. Doth the moon shine that night we play our play?

BOTTOM. A calendar, a calendar! Look in the almanac. Find out moonshine, find out moonshine!

QUINCE. Yes, it doth shine that night.

BOTTOM. Why, then may you leave a casement of the great chamber window, where we play, open, and the moon may shine in at the casement.

QUINCE. Ay; or else one must come in with a bush of thorns and a lantern, and say he comes to disfigure,[10] or to present, the person of Moonshine. Then there is another thing. We must have a wall in the great chamber; for Pyramus and Thisbe, says the story, did talk through the chink of a wall.

SNOUT. You can never bring in a wall. What say you, Bottom?

BOTTOM. Some man or other must present[11] Wall; and let him have some plaster, or some loam, or some roughcast[12] about him,

---

7 **eight and six:** eight syllables in the first line, six in the second, and so on in alternate lines.
8 **defect:** Bottom means *effect*.
9 **it were . . . my life:** My own life would be in danger.
10 **disfigure:** Quince means *figure*, or represent.
11 **present:** represent.
12 **roughcast:** coarse plaster.

to signify wall; and let him hold his fingers thus; and through that cranny shall Pyramus and Thisbe whisper.

QUINCE. If that may be, then all is well. Come, sit down every mother's son, and rehearse your parts. Pyramus, you begin. When you have spoken your speech, enter into that brake; and so every one according to his cue.

Understanding Literature

1. Bottom is one of Shakespeare's funniest creations. He is the mechanical who, in another scene, has his head changed by Puck to an ass's head.
   (*a*) Find lines that indicate Bottom's notions about women.
   (*b*) Find lines showing that he feels he can solve any problem. Comment on the nature of his solutions.
   (*c*) Find several examples of Bottom's misuse of words.
2. Why does Bottom demand that a prologue be written for the play? Why is Snug (the lion) supposed to explain that he is really a man, not a lion?
3. How do the other mechanicals react to Bottom? What does their attitude toward him show you about them?
4. In discussing the setting of the play, the mechanicals show their lack of experience and also their lack of imagination. What two ridiculous arrangements for setting the stage do they make?

THE PRESENTATION OF THE PLAY

(*from* Act V, Scene I)

The setting of this scene is the splendid palace of the Duke.   The wedding has just taken place.   Now there is to be entertainment.   Several acts have been prepared, and the Duke is asked to choose which one he and his guests will see.   He selects the comical tragedy prepared by the mechanicals.

These three couples have just been married: the Duke Theseus and Queen Hippolyta; Demetrius and Helena; Lysander and Hermia.   Notice their comments about the play and the players.

Enter PYRAMUS *and* THISBE, *and* WALL *and* MOONSHINE *and*
LION.   PROLOGUE (QUINCE) *is already on stage.*

PROLOGUE.   Gentles,[1] perchance[2] you wonder at this show;
But wonder on, till truth make all things plain.
This man is Pyramus, if you would know;
This beauteous lady Thisbe is certain.
This man, with lime and roughcast, doth present
Wall, that vile Wall which did these lovers sunder;
And through Wall's chink, poor souls, they are content
To whisper.   At the which let no man wonder.
This man, with lantern, dog, and bush of thorn,
Presenteth Moonshine.[3]   For, if you will know,
By moonshine did these lovers think no scorn
To meet at Ninus' tomb, there, there to woo.
This grisly beast, which Lion hight[4] by name,
The trusty Thisbe, coming first by night,
Did scare away, or rather did affright;
And as she fled, her mantle she did fall,[5]
Which Lion vile with bloody mouth did stain.
Anon comes Pyramus, sweet youth and tall,
And finds his trusty Thisbe's mantle slain;
Whereat, with blade, with bloody blameful blade,
He bravely broached[6] his boiling bloody breast.
And Thisbe, tarrying in mulberry shade,
His dagger drew, and died.   For all the rest,
Let Lion, Moonshine, Wall, and lovers twain
At large discourse while here they do remain.

---

1 **Gentles:** gentlefolk—ladies and gentlemen.
2 **perchance:** perhaps; maybe.
3 **This man . . . Moonshine:** Remember the plans made during the rehearsal to represent moon-shine.
4 **hight:** is called.
5 **fall:** let fall.
6 **broached:** stabbed.

WILLIAM SHAKESPEARE

THESEUS. I wonder if the lion be to speak.

DEMETRIUS. No wonder, my lord. One lion may, when many asses do.

(*Exeunt* PROLOGUE, PYRAMUS, LION, THISBE, *and* MOONSHINE.)

WALL. In this same enterlude it doth befall
That I, one Snout by name, present a wall;
And such a wall, as I would have you think,
That had in it a crannied hole or chink;
Through which the lovers, Pyramus and Thisbe,
Did whisper often, very secretly.
This loam, this roughcast, and this stone doth show
That I am that same wall. The truth is so.
And this the cranny is, right and sinister,[7]
Through which the fearful lovers are to whisper.

THESEUS. Would you desire lime and hair[8] to speak better?

DEMETRIUS. It is the wittiest partition that ever I heard discourse, my lord.

Enter PYRAMUS.

THESEUS. Pyramus draws near the wall. Silence!

PYRAMUS. O grim-looked night! O night with hue so black!
O night, which ever art when day is not!
O night, O night! alack, alack, alack,[9]
I fear my Thisbe's promise is forgot!
And thou, O wall, O sweet, O lovely wall,
That stand'st between her father's ground and mine!
Thou wall, O wall, O sweet and lovely wall,
Show me thy chink, to blink through with mine eyne!

(WALL *holds up his fingers.*)

Thanks, courteous wall. Jove[10] shield thee well for this!
But what see I? No Thisbe do I see.
O wicked wall, through whom I see no bliss,
Cursed be thy stones for thus deceiving me!

THESEUS. The wall, methinks, being sensible,[11] should curse again.

PYRAMUS. No, in truth, sir, he should not. "Deceiving me" is Thisbe's cue. She is to enter now, and I am to spy her through the wall. You shall see it will fall pat as I told you. Yonder she comes.

---

7 **right and sinister:** right and left; that is, the crack runs horizontally.
8 **lime and hair:** a kind of plasterer's cement.
9 **alack:** alas.

10 **Jove:** Jupiter, the Roman king of the gods, identified with the Greek god Zeus.
11 **being sensible:** having feelings.

DRAMA

WILLIAM SHAKESPEARE

Enter THISBE.

THISBE. O Wall, full often hast thou heard my moans
For parting my fair Pyramus and me!
My cherry lips have often kissed thy stones,
Thy stones with lime and hair knit up in thee.
PYRAMUS. I see a voice. Now will I to the chink,
To spy an[12] I can hear my Thisbe's face.
Thisbe!
THISBE. My love! thou art my love, I think.
PYRAMUS. Think what thou wilt, I am thy lover's grace;[13]
And, like Limander,[14] am I trusty still.
THISBE. And I, like Helen,[15] till the Fates me kill.
PYRAMUS. Not Shafalus to Procrus[16] was so true.
THISBE. As Shafalus to Procrus, I to you.
PYRAMUS. O, kiss me through the hole of this vile wall!
THISBE. I kiss the wall's hole, not your lips at all.
PYRAMUS. Wilt thou at Ninny's[17] tomb meet me straightway?
THISBE. Tide life, tide death,[18] I come without delay.

(Exeunt PYRAMUS and THISBE.)

WALL. Thus have I, Wall, my part dischargèd so;
And, being done, thus Wall away doth go. (Exit.)

THESEUS. Now is the mural[19] down between the two neighbors.

DEMETRIUS. No remedy, my lord, when walls are so willful to hear without warning.

HIPPOLYTA. This is the silliest stuff that ever I heard.

THESEUS. The best in this kind[20] are but shadows; and the worst are no worse, if imagination amend[21] them.

HIPPOLYTA. It must be your imagination then, and not theirs.

THESEUS. If we imagine no worse of them than they of themselves, they may pass for excellent men. Here come two noble beasts in, a man and a lion.

Enter LION and MOONSHINE.

LION. You, ladies, you, whose gentle hearts do fear
The smallest monstrous mouse that creeps on floor,

---

12 an: if.
13 grace: gracious, or attractive, self.
14 Limander: He means Leander, who, according to Greek legend, proved his love for the maiden Hero by swimming the Hellespont, a narrow strait between Europe and Turkey, to visit her every night. One night he drowned; the grieving Hero then threw herself into the sea.
15 Helen: Here Flute, as Thisbe, is confused; he means Hero.

16 Shafalus . . . Procrus: He means the ill-fated lovers Cephalus and Procris of Greek mythology.
17 Ninny's: He means Ninus's.
18 Tide . . . death: whatever befalls, whether I live or die. *Tide* means "betide; happen."
19 mural: wall.
20 best . . . kind: the best of plays.
21 amend: correct.

May now perchance both quake and tremble here,
    When lion rough in wildest rage doth roar.
Then know that I one Snug the joiner am,
A lion fell,[22] nor else no lion's dam;
For, if I should as lion come in strife
Into this place, 'twere pity on my life.

THESEUS. A very gentle beast, and of a good conscience.

DEMETRIUS. The very best at a beast, my lord, that e'er I saw.

LYSANDER. This lion is a very fox for his valor.

THESEUS. True; and a goose for his discretion.

DEMETRIUS. Not so, my lord; for his valor cannot carry his discretion, and the fox carries the goose.

THESEUS. His discretion, I am sure, cannot carry his valor; for the goose carries not the fox. It is well. Leave it to his discretion, and let us listen to the moon.

MOONSHINE. This lanthorn doth the hornèd moon present—

DEMETRIUS. He should have worn the horns on his head.

THESEUS. He is no crescent, and his horns are invisible within the circumference.

MOONSHINE. This lanthorn doth the hornèd moon present.
Myself the man i' th' moon do seem to be.

THESEUS. This is the greatest error of all the rest. The man should be put into the lanthorn. How is it else the man i' th' moon?

DEMETRIUS. He dares not come there for the candle; for, you see, it is already in snuff.[23]

HIPPOLYTA. I am aweary of this moon. Would he would change!

THESEUS. It appears, by his small light of discretion, that he is in the wane; but yet, in courtesy, in all reason, we must stay the time.

LYSANDER. Proceed, Moon.

MOONSHINE. All that I have to say is to tell you that the lanthorn is the moon; I, the man i' th' moon; this thornbush, my thornbush; and this dog, my dog.

DEMETRIUS. Why, all these should be in the lanthorn; for all these are in the moon. But silence! Here comes Thisbe.

Enter **THISBE.**

THISBE. This is old Ninny's tomb. Where is my love?

---

22 **fell:** fierce. *Fell* also means "a skin."
23 **in snuff:** in need of snuffing, or having the burned wick (the snuff) removed; *in snuff* also means "in an angry or resentful mood."

LION. O!   (*The* LION *roars.* THISBE *runs off.*)
DEMETRIUS. Well roared, Lion!
THESEUS. Well run, Thisbe!
HIPPOLYTA. Well shone, Moon! Truly, the moon shines with a
good grace.   (*The* LION *tears* THISBE's *mantle, and exit.*)
THESEUS. Well moused,[24] Lion!
DEMETRIUS. And then came Pyramus.
LYSANDER. And so the Lion vanished.

Enter PYRAMUS.

PYRAMUS. Sweet moon, I thank thee for thy sunny beams;
I thank thee, moon, for shining now so bright;
For, by thy gracious, golden, glittering gleams,
I trust to take of truest Thisbe sight.

> But stay! O spite!
> But mark, poor knight!
What dreadful dole[25] is here?
> Eyes, do you see?
> How can it be?
O dainty duck! O dear!
> Thy mantle good,
> What, stained with blood?
Approach, ye Furies[26] fell!
> O Fates,[27] come, come!
> Cut thread and thrum;[28]
Quail,[29] crush, conclude, and quell![30]

THESEUS. This passion, and the death of a dear friend, would
go near to make a man look sad.
HIPPOLYTA. Beshrew[31] my heart but I pity the man.
PYRAMUS. O, wherefore, Nature, didst thou lions frame?
Since lion vile hath here deflowered my dear;
Which is—no, no!—which was the fairest dame
That lived, that loved, that liked, that looked with cheer.

> Come, tears, confound!
> Out, sword, and wound
> The pap of Pyramus!
> Ay, that left pap

---

24 **well moused:** The mantle has been treated by
the lion in the way a cat treats a mouse.
25 **dole:** sorrow.
26 **Furies:** The Furies were three goddesses, according to Greek myths, who avenged evil deeds.
27 **Fates:** These were, the Greeks believed, three
goddesses who controlled each person's life. One

spun the thread of life, another decided how long
it was to be, and the third cut it.
28 **thrum:** the unwoven end of thread in a woven
fabric.
29 **Quail:** overpower.
30 **quell:** destroy.
31 **Beshrew:** a very mild oath.

DRAMA

Where heart doth hop.   (*Stabs himself.*)
Thus die I, thus, thus, thus.
 Now am I dead,
 Now am I fled;
My soul is in the sky.
 Tongue, lose thy light;
 Moon, take thy flight.

                                        (*Exit* MOONSHINE.)
 Now die, die, die, die, die!   (*Dies.*)
DEMETRIUS. No die,[32] but an ace, for him! for he is but one.
LYSANDER. Less than an ace, man; for he is dead, he is nothing.
THESEUS. With the help of a surgeon he might yet recover, and
yet prove an ass.
HIPPOLYTA. How chance Moonshine is gone before Thisbe
comes back and finds her lover?

                        Enter THISBE.

THESEUS. She will find him by starlight. Here she comes; and
her passion ends the play.
HIPPOLYTA. Methinks she should not use a long one for such a
Pyramus. I hope she will be brief.
DEMETRIUS. A mote[33] will turn the balance, which Pyramus,
which Thisbe, is the better; he for a man, God warr'nd us!—she
for a woman, God bless us!
LYSANDER. She has spied him already with those sweet eyes.
DEMETRIUS. And thus she means, videlicet:[34]
THISBE.   Asleep, my love?
                  What, dead, my dove?
                O Pyramus, arise!
                  Speak, speak! Quite dumb?
                  Dead, dead? A tomb
                Must cover thy sweet eyes.
                  These lily lips,
                  This cherry nose,
                These yellow cowslip cheeks,
                  Are gone, are gone.
                  Lovers, make moan!
                His eyes were green as leeks.
                  O Sisters Three,[35]
                  Come, come to me,

---

32 **die:** a play on words. A die is one of a pair of
dice.
33 **mote:** small particle, such as a speck of dust.
34 **videlicet** (vĭ dĕl'ə sĭt): to wit; namely.
35 **Sisters Three:** the Fates.

WILLIAM SHAKESPEARE   585

With hands as pale as milk;
   Lay them in gore,
   Since you have shore
With shears his thread of silk.
   Tongue, not a word!
   Come, trusty sword;
Come, blade, my breast imbrue![36]

(Stabs herself.)

   And farewell, friends.
   Thus Thisbe ends.
Adieu, adieu, adieu!   *(Dies.)*

THESEUS. Moonshine and Lion are left to bury the dead.

DEMETRIUS. Ay, and Wall too.

BOTTOM *(starts up)*. No, I assure you; the wall is down that parted their fathers. Will it please you to see the Epilogue, or to hear a Bergomask dance between two of our company?

THESEUS. No epilogue, I pray you; for your play needs no excuse. Never excuse; for when the players are all dead, there need none to be blamèd. Marry, if he that writ it had playèd Pyramus and hanged himself in Thisbe's garter, it would have been a fine tragedy; and so it is truly, and very notably discharged. But, come, your Bergomask! Let your epilogue alone.

(A dance.)

---

36 **imbrue:** stain (with blood).

Understanding Literature

1. What is the purpose of the Prologue presented by Quince?
2. Explain each of the comments by the lords and ladies of the court. Try to imagine what tone of voice is used in each.
3. In what tone of voice do you suppose Bottom, as Pyramus, delivers his long speech after he discovers Thisbe's stained mantle?
4. In what speeches does Bottom forget his role as Pyramus and speak to the audience? What other mechanical speaks directly to the audience?

5. The speeches in the mechanicals' play are filled with exaggerations and absurdities.
   (*a*) One absurdity is the overuse of alliteration in the speeches of the mechanicals. (Alliteration is the repetition of an initial consonant sound.) Find examples of alliteration used to the point of absurdity. One example is, "Whereat, with blade, with bloody blameful blade,/ He bravely broached his boiling bloody breast."
   (*b*) Another absurdity is the exclamatory, highly emotional, exaggerated language in some of the speeches, such as Pyramus's speech beginning "O grim-looked night!" What other speeches in the play use such bombast—inflated, exclamatory, ranting language?
6. Which member of the court seems least appreciative of the players' efforts?
7. What are some of the expressions in Thisbe's last speech which make it comic instead of tragic?
8. How does the play of Pyramus and Thisbe end? What follows the play?

Further Activities

1. These scenes must be read aloud to be fully appreciated. The group reading them should understand each character and experiment until the right tone of voice and manner of speaking is found for each player.
2. Some members of the class will enjoy reading the whole play. Perhaps groups might present other scenes to the class.

WILLIAM SHAKESPEARE

Poetry

PROBABLY THE FIRST question you ask about poetry is, Why should I read it? This chapter opens with an essay by C. Day Lewis, a famous English poet, who tries to answer the question. He wrote this essay during the dark days of World War II when, in the minds of many people, the place of poetry in a man's life needed some justification.

The rest of the chapter shows you how to read poetry. If you know how to do something, you may become more interested in it. If you know the theory and care a painter puts into his picture, you may look at a painting more intelligently. If you know how a motor is put together, you may better appreciate a good engine. If you know how the poet works, you may better appreciate the poem.

What Is the Use of Poetry?

C. Day Lewis

A LOT of young people—and a lot of grownups, too, who ought to know better—ask this question. They are suspicious of poetry. When someone is suspicious of poetry, or painting or music, it is generally because he does not understand them, does not see the point of them. We are always suspicious and a little afraid of things we do not understand. But, instead of admitting this, we are apt to invent reasons for our dislikes which are more complimentary to ourselves. If you ask people who "have no use for poetry" why they don't like it, they'll probably answer, "poetry is daft,"[1] "poetry is soft and unmanly," or "poetry won't help you to get on in life, to get a job, to make money." Let's take these ideas one by one, and see what they amount to.

"Poetry is daft"

People who say poetry is daft are usually frightened of life, frightened of their own feelings and the mysteriousness of the world. Poetry is a special way of using words in order to create a special effect upon the reader and to light up the world for him. If you're afraid of having your feelings stirred in the way poetry can stir them, if you don't want to see more of the world than meets the eye, if you're afraid to see beyond your own nose, then you will certainly avoid poetry as you would avoid a lunatic. But that does not prove that poetry, or poets, are mad. In the old days, people used to think the prophets were mad and throw stones at them: but very often they found out in the long run that the prophets had been right and they themselves wrong. It was the same with the poets. In fact, when you read the Old Testament, you realize that many of the Hebrew prophets *were* poets. From the earliest times there had been a close connection between poetry and magic; and long after this connection ceased, there still survived a vague notion that the poet had supernatural powers. The ancient Greeks believed that poets were "possessed"

---

1 **daft:** silly or foolish.

by a god when they wrote poetry: our word *enthusiasm* comes from a Greek word meaning this very thing—the state of having a god inside you. And people still talk about the poet's "inspiration," which means a spirit breathed into him from somewhere outside.

But we must not assume, because of this, that poets are crazy. After all, you don't have to be a poet to feel "enthusiasm": each of you has moments when he feels a strange, unaccountable excitement welling up inside him, a kind of "inspiration"; but you don't go whizzing off to the doctor and ask him whether he doesn't think you ought to be put into a lunatic asylum. Some poets do go mad, of course—William Blake, William Cowper, John Clare, Christopher Smart did, and they were all fine poets. The wonder is that more poets don't get queer in the head; for poets carry about inside themselves, so to speak, a specially sensitive apparatus, which can be very easily damaged. But, even when a poet himself seems to be mad, his poetry is often sane—far saner and wiser than the talk of many men who boast that there is "no nonsense" about them.

"Poetry is soft"

Now that's a most extraordinary thing to say. There's nothing in the world less soft than poetry. A good poem is just about as hard as a diamond: it has to be, or it wouldn't last for centuries and continue to thrill men as keenly as it did when first it was written. Think of the things you know that have the longest lives—yew trees, tortoises, marble temples, ancient castles. Well, a good poem can live on for centuries longer than a tortoise or a yew tree; when the castle and the temple are no more than beautiful old ruins, a poem written in the same year as that in which they were built may still be as bright and new as ever.

"All right," perhaps you're saying, "I admit poetry isn't soft. But *poets* are. Everyone knows that." Well, if you think so, you're wrong again. The Elizabethan age was one of the great ages of English poetry: the Elizabethans were a very tough lot of people indeed, but *they* never called their poets soft. Sir Philip Sidney, who told them to give the drink of water to another soldier when he himself was dying, was one of the best Elizabethan poets. In the last war English poets fought gallantly and many of them died. There was one who used to creep into the enemy trenches at night, alone, armed only with a heavy stick, and lay out all the Germans he came across. Another was killed while leading his men across a heavily defended canal in France. Both of these got the Military Cross. In the present war,[2] many of our young poets are fighting, and some have been killed.

But that isn't really the point. The chief reason why it is silly to call poets soft is not because they can fight as bravely as anyone else: it is because, to go on writing poetry, you need such great patience and endurance. True poets will go through poverty, despair, the indifference or the flattery of the world, for years and years, in order to produce a good poem. They are never satisfied, always trying to write better. At an age when other men generally retire from work or business, the poet is still working as hard as ever, to wring the last drop of poetry out of himself before he dies.

"Poetry won't help you to get on in life"

This is the sort of thing superior persons say, or men who think the main object in life is to make money. Poetry, they imply, is all very well for highbrows and people with plenty of time to waste, but it's no use to the man-in-the-street. Now that's a very newfangled idea. The man-in-the-street in ancient Greece would never have said it: he flocked in crowds to watch poetic drama; and so did the Elizabethan man-in-the-street, to see the poetic plays of Shakespeare and other dramatists of the time. Then think of the medieval minstrels and ballad singers, who drew great audiences in village or castle to hear them recite poems. Think of the peasants in Russia, in Ireland, in Spain, in many other countries, still making up their own poems.

No, it's just untrue to say that poetry has nothing to do with ordinary men and women. And certainly the last thing any Englishman should despise is poetry. Poetry is the greatest glory of our nation, though you don't often find it mentioned in the history books. Your geography book tells you about our exports —iron, coal, woolen goods, etc.—but never mentions that one of our most famous exports is poetry. It *is*, though. Every civilized nation has recognized that poetry is the art in which England excels: our poets are as famous abroad as our sailors and our industrial craftsmen. So the fact that poetry does not help you to "get on" in life or to make money is no argument for not caring about it, or for being superior about it.

2 present war: This article was written during World War II.

"What's the use of a rainbow?"

We've got rid of some false ideas about poetry; but we still have to try and find out what *is* the use of it. Now, in a way, to ask what is the use of poetry should be as absurd as asking what is the use of a rainbow, or the sea, or a piece of toffee, or a game of football, or a nice dress. A rainbow is a natural phenomenon, the result of the refraction and reflection of the sun's rays in drops of rain. As far as mankind is concerned, it's a perfectly useless object: it certainly won't help anyone to make money. Yet the poet who said, "My heart leaps up when I behold a rainbow in the sky," only put into words the feeling of wonder and excitement we all have when we see a rainbow. It is something beautiful in its own right, just like a good poem. When you are given a piece of toffee, or a nice dress, you don't sit about wondering what is the use of it: you put the one into your mouth, or your head into the other. You enjoy bathing in the sea on a hot day, or playing a game of football, in just the same way.

Now poetry is, first and foremost, something to be enjoyed— a pleasant experience like bathing or wearing a new dress or eating toffee—and don't let anyone tell you anything else. But, just as bathing is more fun if you have learned how to swim and dive, just as a boy will enjoy football more when he knows the finer points of the game, and a girl will get more satisfaction out of a new frock if she has developed a good taste in dress, so you will find a keener pleasure in poetry if you understand what it is aiming at and how it works.

There are some people who are very fond of poetry but say that, as a form of entertainment, it is obsolete: it was all very well in the days when there were no cinemas,[3] no radio, no cheap books and papers to amuse us, they say, but nowadays competition is so strong that poetry will soon have to go out of business. First, let us look at the two chief uses of poetry, which no amount of modern inventions can ever affect.

"Bright is the ring of words"

If you are at the seaside, and you take an old, dull, brown penny and rub it hard for a minute or two with handfuls of wet sand (dry sand is no good), the penny will come out a bright gold color, looking as clean and new as the day it was minted. Now

---

3 cinemas: movies.

poetry has the same effect on words as wet sand on pennies. In what seems almost a miraculous way, it brightens up words that looked dull and ordinary. Thus, poetry is perpetually "re-creating language." It does this in several ways. It may coin new words: it may help to bring into common use words which, before, had only been used by experts—technical, scientific words, for instance: it may put common words into new contexts, introduce them to other ordinary words they had not met before, as a good hostess introduces strangers to each other at a party and makes them interest one another: it may enrich the value of words by giving them new associations—for instance, when Tennyson, writing a poem about an eagle looking down from a cliff, said, "The wrinkled sea beneath him crawls," he was able to give a most vivid picture of what the sea looks like from a great height by bringing into a new association two quite ordinary words, *crawled* and *wrinkled.*

To realize how important a job this perpetual re-creation of language is, you need only ask yourselves what words are *for.* They are the chief instruments by which human beings communicate with one another, get to know one another, carry on life with one another. We should still be merely animals if we were all dumb[4] or if mankind had not invented languages. But words, like any other instruments, must be kept clean and efficient if they are to do their job for civilization. People who treat words in a careless, sloppy way are not properly civilized. Poetry, on the other hand, is an art which has to treat words with care, respect and accuracy.

This does not mean that the language of poetry is something quite different from ordinary speech. Slang is often extremely poetical, because it uses words in a fresh, vigorous way, and makes pictures out of them.

(1) "I feel tired and limp."
(2) "I feel like a bit of chewed string."

(3) "I'm terribly depressed."
(4) "I feel so low I could crawl under a snake."

(5) "The tea is so strong, you could stand a spoon up in it."
(6) "It's lovely, strong tea—you could trot a mouse on it."

Look at these phrases. (2) and (4) are slang ways of saying (1) and (3). They convey the meaning of (1) and (3), but more for-

---

4 dumb: lacking the power of speech.

cibly because they illustrate it with pictures—of a chewed, limp piece of string and of a man crawling under a snake: (4) does it more effectively than (2) because it is less hackneyed; that is to say, (2) was a vigorous piece of language when first it was used, but it has been used too often and got stale. The same applies to (5); it was once a good, slang way of describing a cup of strong tea, but so many people used it that it has become worn out: (6), which I heard an old Irish countrywoman say, is a far stronger, more vivid expression. (2), (4), (5), and (6) are all slang, but they are also poetic ways of expressing a prose meaning.

I am not saying that poetry is just a glorified form of slang. But it *is* true to say that slang comes from the same source as poetry, from the imagination. And it is interesting to note that, when a nation is young, vigorous, self-confident, its common people generally have a vigorous slang: the Elizabethans had; the cockneys in Queen Victoria's time had; the Americans have today, and so have our men of the R.A.F.[5] Slang is good, then, when it shows that people are using their imagination, bad when it's a sign of mental laziness.

Two ways of looking at a daffodil

That word *imagination* brings me to the chief use of poetry, an even more important one than the re-creation of language. When we are very young, the world, nature, people are mysterious to us. Give a baby an orange. He stares at it, fingers it, dribbles on it, drops it, howls for you to pick it up again. To him, it is a beautiful, round, colored object, with a strange smell, which is heavy to hold and stays put on the floor when he drops it, instead of walking away like the cat. A baby uses all his senses to make such discoveries: he is like an explorer in a new world, full of wonder and surprise at the novelty of everything. In a way, a poet is a man who never grows out of that sense of wonder. It keeps his imagination constantly on the stretch and quivering at the mysteriousness and beauty of the world; and thus his poetry helps *us* to understand the world by sharpening our own senses, by making us more sensitive to life.

Now there are two ways of getting to understand the world—through our heads and through our hearts, our feelings. Science tells us a great deal about how the world works, what it is made

5 R.A.F.: Royal Air Force.

of, and so on. Science is the chief way of learning through our heads. But that's not the *only* way of learning about the world—perhaps not even the best way. Let's take a very ordinary object, the common wild daffodil. Here are two ways of describing it:

(1) Narcissus pseudo-narcissus: flower-stalk hollow, two-edged, bearing near its summit a membranous sheath and a single flower: nectary notched and curled at the margin, as long as the sepals and petals.

(2) I wandered lonely as a cloud
 That floats on high o'er vales and hills,
 When all at once I saw a crowd,
 A host of golden daffodils:
 Beside the lake, beneath the trees,
 Fluttering and dancing in the breeze.

Now, which do you think is the more satisfactory description of daffodils—the scientific one which I have taken from a text-book on botany, or the poetic one which comes from a poem by Wordsworth? Many of you would say "the poetic one," straight away: and that is, incidentally, a bit of a blow for those who argue that science has made poetry obsolete. Of course, it's not quite fair to compare a scientific description with a poetic one like this, as though they were competing against each other for a prize. Science is concerned with finding out and stating the facts: poetry's task is to give you the look, the smell, the taste, the "feel" of those facts. Each has its own purpose and reward. But, by contrasting these two descriptions, you can see how poetry and science differ in method. Description (1) is analytic: that is to say; it examines the daffodil as though it was a single object quite separate from every other object which presents itself to our senses, tells us how it is composed, and classifies it. Description (2) relates the daffodils with a number of other things—with trees, a lake, a breeze, and with the poet's feeling of loneliness (at least, he was "lonely as a cloud" until he met this "host of golden daffodils").

To make the world your friend

It is the inclusion of *feeling* that makes the difference between poetry and science. Science is not concerned merely with analyzing things: it also must try to relate them with each other and thus discover the natural laws at work behind them. But the scientist uses theory, observation and experiment to relate his facts with each other, whereas the poet uses his own feelings, his emotions. It would be all wrong for a scientist to get emotional when he describes a daffodil; and it would be all wrong for a poet *not* to.

There, then, is the great use of poetry. It tells us about the world through our feelings. It sharpens our senses, makes us more keenly and fully aware of life, exercises our imagination and stores up treasure in our memory: once we have seen that "host of golden daffodils" colored by the poet's feeling, they will continue for the rest of our lives to "flash upon that inward eye which is the bliss of solitude."

Imagine, for a moment, that you are trying to describe one of your friends. It wouldn't be difficult to give the sort of description you hear on the radio when someone has disappeared from his home or the police are after him. You could say he is five foot tall, has blue eyes, a mole on his left cheek, a wooden leg or a red nose. But that would only describe the *outside* of him. It wouldn't tell people what this friend of yours is really like—his habits, his feelings, all the little peculiarities that make him himself and different from everyone else. You would find it very difficult indeed to describe the *inside* of him, even though he is such a great friend that you feel you know him through and through. Now good poetry *does* describe life in that way; it tells you about its inside as well as its outside, and thus it helps you to know and love the world as intimately as you know and love a friend.

Narrative Poetry

THE EARLIEST FUNCTION of poetry was to tell a story. The earliest poets were those who made up stories based on great tales of heroism in their own lands. Wandering from town to town, they sang their songs to entertain the people. Some of the earliest of the British ballads or songs were those which recited the adventures of Robin Hood, an English legendary hero. Who he was no one knows. What is known about him has come from references to him in ballads and in other literary works. The earliest references to him go back at least to the 14th century.

A legend is a traditional story that is believed to be based on fact. The legend is usually handed down through many generations. At some time a man probably did live and act like the one called Robin Hood. As various people told his story, they imaginatively added to what really happened, in order to make the tales more exciting. In the ballad which follows, for example, it is quite unlikely that Robin Hood and Little John met in such a way, but the story is an interesting one. They did meet in some fashion: Little John is often referred to as a leading member of the band of outlaws who wandered in Sherwood Forest.

Reading "Robin Hood and Little John"

For hundreds of years men traveled around England singing ballads to the accompaniment of stringed instruments, long before there were printed books. The subjects of their songs were the great tales of the past: stories of heroes or of strange events. Their purpose was to entertain the people. Today people still sing some of these ballads, and some even create new ones.

The form of the *ballad* is a series of simple four-line stanzas which, when taken together, tell a story. The first and third lines tend to have four major beats, or heavily accented sounds. The second and fourth lines have three major beats. To hear these, however, because of changes in the sounds of language, you have to slur over certain syllables and often make two seem as one:

"Where-ever he cáme, they quak'd at his náme"

The slanted lines indicate the main accented sounds in the line. In this ballad each stanza is made up of one sentence.

Words You Need to Know. In reading poetry, the meanings of words are doubly important because a poet compresses so much meaning into a single word. Although the words in the following poem are simple, they have meanings here that you may not be used to. To read the poem well, watch for the following words as you read; if you cannot figure out their meanings, look them up in the glossary and decide which of the meanings suggested there fits into the context of the poem. Words you need to know: *tarry, mettle, accoutrements, transpose.*

You will observe that the scholarly collections from which this and other ballads in this book were taken have preserved the ballads in their original forms. The ballads were probably first written down at a time when spelling was not standardized.

Robin Hood and Little John

When Robin Hood was about twenty years old,
   He happened to meet Little John,
A jolly brisk blade,[1] right fit for the trade,
   For he was a lusty young man.

Tho he was calld Little, his limbs they were large,   5
   And his stature was seven foot high;
Where-ever he came, they quak'd at his name,
   For soon he would make them to fly.

How they came acquainted, I'll tell you in brief,
   If you will but listen a while;   10
For this very jest, amongst all the rest,
   I think it may cause you to smile.

Bold Robin Hood said to his jolly bowmen,
   "Pray tarry you here in this grove;
And see that you all observe well my call,   15
   While thorough the forest I rove.

"We have had no sport for these fourteen long days,
   Therefore now abroad will I go;
Now should I be beat, and cannot retreat,
   My horn I will presently blow."   20

Then did he shake hands with his merry men all,
   And bid them at present good b'w'ye;[2]
Then, as near a brook his journey he took,
   A stranger he chanced to espy.

They happened to meet on a long narrow bridge,   25
   And neither of them would give way;

---

1 blade: dashing young man; swordsman.

2 good b'w'ye: good-by. The early form of the word was *God be with ye.*

Quoth bold Robin Hood, and sturdily stood,
    "I'll show you right Nottingham play."

With that from his quiver an arrow he drew,
    A broad arrow with a goose-wing: 30
The stranger reply'd, "I'll liquor thy hide,[3]
    If thou offerst to touch the string."

Quoth bold Robin Hood, "Thou dost prate[4] like an ass,
    For were I to bend but my bow,
I could send a dart quite thro thy proud heart,   35
    Before thou couldst strike me one blow."

"Thou talkst like a coward," the stranger reply'd;
    "Well armd with a long bow you stand,
To shoot at my breast, while I, I protest,
    Have nought but a staff[5] in my hand."   40

"The name of a coward," quoth Robin, "I scorn,
    Wherefore my long bow I'll lay by;
And now, for thy sake, a staff will I take,
    The truth of thy manhood to try."

Then Robin Hood stept to a thicket of trees,   45
    And chose him a staff of ground-oak;
Now this being done, away he did run
    To the stranger, and merrily spoke:

"Lo! see my staff, it is lusty and tough,
    Now here on the bridge we will play;   50
Whoever falls in, the other shall win
    The battel, and so we'll away."

"With all my whole heart," the stranger reply'd;
    "I scorn in the least to give out";
This said, they fell to 't without more dispute,   55
    And their staffs they did flourish about.

And first Robin he gave the stranger a bang,
    So hard that it made his bones ring:

---

3 **liquor thy hide:** throw you in the water.

4 **prate:** talk foolishly.
5 **staff:** pole used as a weapon.

The stranger he said, "This must be repaid,
   I'll give you as good as you bring.

"So long as I'm able to handle my staff,
   To die in your debt, friend, I scorn":
Then to it each goes, and followd their blows,
   As if they had been threshing of corn.

The stranger gave Robin a crack on the crown,
   Which caused the blood to appear;
Then Robin, enrag'd, more fiercely engag'd,
   And followed his blows more severe.

So thick and so fast did he lay it on him,
   With a passionate fury and ire,
At every stroke, he made him to smoke,
   As if he had been all on fire.

O then into fury the stranger he grew,
   And gave him a damnable look,
And with it a blow that laid him full low,
   And tumbld him into the brook.

"I prithee, good fellow, O where art thou now?"
   The stranger, in laughter, he cry'd;
Quoth bold Robin Hood, "Good faith, in the flood,
   And floating along with the tide.

"I needs must acknowledge thou art a brave soul;
   With thee I'll no longer contend;
For needs must I say, thou hast got the day,
   Our battel shall be at an end."

Then unto the bank he did presently wade,
   And pulld himself out by a thorn;⁶
Which done, at the last, he blowd a loud blast
   Straitway on his fine bugle-horn.

The eccho of which through the vallies did fly,
   At which his stout bowmen appeard,
All cloathed in green, most gay to be seen;

⁶ thorn: thorn tree.

60

65

70

75

80

85

90

So up to their master they steerd.[7]

"O what's the matter?" quoth William Stutely;
  "Good master, you are wet to the skin":
"No matter," quoth he; "the lad which you see,   95
  In fighting, hath tumbld me in."

"He shall not go scot-free," the others reply'd;
  So strait they were seizing him there,
To duck him likewise; but Robin Hood cries,
  "He is a stout fellow, forbear.[8]   100

"There's no one shall wrong thee, friend, be not afraid;
  These bowmen upon me do wait;
There's threescore and nine; if thou wilt be mine,
  Thou shalt have my livery strait.[9]

"And other accoutrements fit for a man;   105
  Speak up, jolly blade, never fear;
I'll teach you also the use of the bow,
  To shoot at the fat fallow-deer."

"O here is my hand," the stranger reply'd,
  "I'll serve you with all my whole heart;   110
My name is John Little, a man of good mettle;
  Nere doubt me, for I'll play my part."

"His name shall be alterd," quoth William Stutely,
  "And I will his godfather be;
Prepare then a feast, and none of the least,   115
  For we will be merry," quoth he.

They presently fetchd in a brace of fat does,
  With humming strong liquor likewise;
They lovd what was good; so, in the greenwood,
  This pretty sweet babe they baptize.   120

He was, I must tell you, but seven foot high,
  And, may be, an ell[10] in the waste;

---

7 **steerd:** made their way through the trees.
8 **forbear:** hold back.
9 **livery strait:** The livery is the green costume of

Robin's band; *strait* means "right away."
10 **ell:** measure of length; in England about 45 inches.

A pretty sweet lad; much feasting they had;
    Bold Robin the christning grac'd,

With all his bowmen, which stood in a ring,   125
    And were of the Notti[n]gham breed;
Brave Stutely comes then, with seven yeomen,
    And did in this manner proceed.

"This infant was called John Little," quoth he,
    "Which name shall be changed anon;   130
The words we'll transpose, so where-ever he goes,
    His name shall be calld Little John."

They all with a shout made the elements ring,
    So soon as the office was ore;
To feasting they went, with true merriment,   135
    And tippld strong liquor gillore.

Then Robin he took the pretty sweet babe,
    And cloathd him from top to the toe
In garments of green, most gay to be seen,
    And gave him a curious long bow.   140

"Thou shalt be an archer as well as the best,
    And range in the greenwood with us;
Where we'll not want gold nor silver, behold,
    While bishops have ought in their purse.

"We live here like squires, or lords of renown,   145
    Without ere a foot of free land;
We feast on good cheer, with wine, ale, and beer,
    And evry thing at our command."

Then musick and dancing did finish the day;
    At length, when the sun waxed low,   150
Then all the whole train the grove did refrain,
    And unto their caves they did go.

And so ever after, as long as he livd,
    Altho he was proper and tall,
Yet nevertheless, the truth to express,   155
    Still Little John they did him call.

1. The first problem in reading a narrative poem is understanding what happens. Tell the story of this ballad in your own words.
2. The author says, in the third stanza, that he will tell us how "they came acquainted." What, then, do the first two stanzas add to the story?
3. Why does Robin go off by himself? What does the sound of his horn signal to his men?
4. Why does Robin challenge the stranger? How does the stranger persuade Robin to put down his bow and arrow?
5. The author tells much of the story by relating what the characters say. Find the places, and read them aloud, where characters are being quoted directly.
6. What are Little John and Robin like? Point out evidence for your conclusions.
7. In the third stanza the poet calls his tale a "jest," and says "it may cause you to smile." Did it? Why?

Reading "The Glove and the Lions"

In the following narrative poem, the story is told in only four stanzas. The first stanza sets the scene; the second sets up a contrasting scene. The last two stanzas create an incident between two people, De Lorge and his lady, "one for whom he sighed." The author, however, uses King Francis to interpret the incident, to show its meaning. Francis is an onlooker, but his remarks help you to understand the action.

IMPROVING YOUR READING. When a person performs an act in a literary work, the author usually shows you the *motivation* for the act; that is, the writer interprets the act by showing *why* it was done. Watch for the motivation for the main acts in this poem.

The Glove and the Lions

Leigh Hunt

King Francis was a hearty king, and loved a royal sport,
And one day as his lions fought, sat looking on the court;
The nobles filled the benches, and the ladies in their pride,
And 'mongst them sat the Count de Lorge, with one for
    whom he sighed:

And truly 'twas a gallant thing to see that crowning show,   5
Valor and love, and a king above, and the royal beasts below.

Ramped and roared the lions, with horrid laughing jaws;
They bit, they glared, gave blows like beams, a wind went
    with their paws;
With wallowing might and stifled roar they rolled on one
    another,
Till all the pit with sand and mane was in a thunderous
    smother;   10
The bloody foam above the bars came whisking through
    the air;
Said Francis then, "Faith, gentlemen, we're better here
    than there."

De Lorge's love o'erheard the King, a beauteous lively dame
With smiling lips and sharp bright eyes, which always
    seemed the same;
She thought, "The Count my lover is brave as brave can be;   15
He surely would do wondrous things to show his love of me;
King, ladies, lovers, all look on; the occasion is divine;
I'll drop my glove, to prove his love; great glory will be
    mine."

She dropped her glove, to prove his love, then looked at
    him and smiled;
He bowed, and in a moment leaped among the lions wild: 20
The leap was quick, return was quick, he has regained his
    place,
Then threw the glove, but not with love, right in the lady's
    face.
"By God!" said Francis, "rightly done!" and he rose from
    where he sat:
"No love," quoth he, "but vanity, sets love a task like that."

Understanding Literature

1. How is the picture in the first stanza contrasted with that of the
   second stanza?
2. Why is the description in the second stanza important to an
   understanding of the third stanza?

3. In the first two stanzas what do you learn about the setting and about the people?
4. Why does De Lorge's love drop her glove? Why does the poet keep saying "his love"? Why does he never refer to *her* love?
5. Why does De Lorge throw the glove in the lady's face? Why did he go after the glove in the first place?
6. What is the meaning of the last line?

Reading "The Charge of the Light Brigade"

The next narrative commemorates a famous charge by the British cavalry at Balaclava in 1854, during the Crimean War. Because of an error by one of their officers, the troops went up the hill to their slaughter. Tennyson tells their story with short, pounding lines in which the sound reflects the situation being described.

IMPROVING YOUR READING. You will find the poet here making use of *refrain,* the repetition of one or more lines, sometimes with slight changes in the wording. His purpose is to arouse appreciation in the British people for this act of patriotism. The use of refrain increases the rhythmic effect of the poem in the same way that a football cheer, with its constant repetition, works up its audience.

The Charge of the Light Brigade[1]

Alfred, Lord Tennyson

Half a league,[2] half a league,
Half a league onward,
All in the valley of Death
    Rode the six hundred.
"Forward the Light Brigade!   5
Charge for the guns!" he said.
Into the valley of Death
    Rode the six hundred.

---

1 Brigade: large unit of soldiers.   **2 league:** measure of distance, about 3 miles.

"Forward, the Light Brigade!"
Was there a man dismayed? 10
Not tho' the soldier knew
   Someone had blundered.
Theirs not to make reply,
Theirs not to reason why,
Theirs but to do and die. 15
Into the valley of Death
   Rode the six hundred.

Cannon to right of them,
Cannon to left of them,
Cannon in front of them 20
   Volleyed and thundered;
Stormed at with shot and shell,
Boldly they rode and well,
Into the jaws of Death,
Into the mouth of hell 25
   Rode the six hundred.

Flashed all their sabers bare,
Flashed as they turned in air
Sabring the gunners there,
Charging an army, while 30
   All the world wondered.
Plunged in the battery smoke
Right thro' the line they broke;
Cossack and Russian
Reeled from the saber-stroke 35
   Shattered and sundered.[3]
Then they rode back, but not,
   Not the six hundred.

Cannon to right of them,
Cannon to left of them, 40
Cannon behind them
   Volleyed and thundered;
Stormed at with shot and shell,
While horse and hero fell,
They that had fought so well 45
Came thro' the jaws of Death,

---

3 **sundered:** separated.

Back from the mouth of hell,
All that was left of them,
   Left of six hundred.

When can their glory fade?   50
O the wild charge they made!
   All the world wondered.
Honor the charge they made!
Honor the Light Brigade,
   Noble six hundred!   55

Understanding Literature

1. You may have had difficulty in reading this poem because the author leaves out so much. After you are able to answer the following questions, reread the poem.

    (*a*) Who were the "six hundred"?

    (*b*) Who said, "Forward the Light Brigade!/ Charge for the guns!"?

    (*c*) Who had "blundered"?

    (*d*) Who are "they" in line 37?

2. How does the author feel about the charge?

Reading "In School Days"

This narrative poem was written by John Greenleaf Whittier, who in the late 19th century was one of America's most popular poets. In all parts of the country, towns and streets are named for him. He wrote about what in his day were common occurrences, treating them with much feeling, or sentimentality. In this poem he remembers an incident in his school days. But the poet goes beyond just telling a story; he contrasts the incident with what life has been like since he left school. To understand the poem, you need to know how a spelling bee works.

IMPROVING YOUR READING. In this poem the author keeps shifting the scene. "Still sits the schoolhouse," he begins, showing how the school looks at the time the poem was written. In the fourth stanza, he moves back into the past, "Long years ago." Watch for similar phrases that indicate a shift in time.

In School Days

John Greenleaf Whittier

Still sits the schoolhouse by the road,
   A ragged beggar sleeping;
Around it still the sumacs[1] grow,
   And blackberry vines are creeping.

Within, the master's desk is seen,   5
   Deep scarred by raps official;
The warping floor, the battered seats,
   The jackknife's carved initial;

The charcoal frescos on its wall;
   Its door's worn sill, betraying   10
The feet that, creeping slow to school,
   Went storming out to playing!

Long years ago a winter sun
   Shone over it at setting;
Lit up its western windowpanes,   15
   And low eaves' icy fretting.

It touched the tangled golden curls,
   And brown eyes full of grieving,
Of one who still her steps delayed
   When all the school were leaving.   20

For near her stood the little boy
   Her childish favor singled:
His cap pulled low upon a face
   Where pride and shame were mingled.

Pushing with restless feet the snow   25
   To right and left, he lingered;—
As restlessly her tiny hands
   The blue-checked apron fingered.

---

1 sumacs (shoo′măks or soo′măks) : shrubs or small trees which become very brightly colored in the fall.

He saw her lift her eyes; he felt
    The soft hand's light caressing,   30
And heard the tremble of her voice,
    As if a fault confessing.

"I'm sorry that I spelt the word:
    I hate to go above you,
Because"—the brown eyes lower fell—   35
    "Because, you see, I love you!"

Still memory to a gray-haired man
    That sweet child-face is showing.
Dear girl! the grasses on her grave
    Have forty years been growing!   40

He lives to learn, in life's hard school,
    How few who pass above him
Lament their triumph and his loss,
    Like her—because they love him.

Understanding Literature

1. What are the main divisions of the poem? How many scenes are there?
2. What is the opening scene? Why is the school compared to "a ragged beggar"? What details are you given of what the school looks like?
3. What incident does the author recall? How old, would you guess, are the boy and the girl in this scene? Why are the girl's eyes "full of grieving"?
4. In line 20 what is meant by "all the school were leaving"?
5. Give the meaning of the last stanza in your own words. How is the last stanza related to the incident recalled in the poem?
6. How old, at least, is the speaker in the poem? How is he related to the boy in the poem?

In an earlier poem, you read of Robin Hood. In the following poem a modern poet looks back to the days when Robin and his band lived in Sherwood Forest and tries to recapture the past by imagining what it had been like in those long ago days.

IMPROVING YOUR READING. This poem, like all poems, needs to be heard; it is arranged largely for its musical effects. Not only does the author use rhyme, but he also makes use of *alliteration:* the repetition, within a line, of initial consonant sounds, as in "Gray . . . ghostly . . . gliding." He also makes use of *assonance:* the repetition of similar vowel sounds. Note the repeated *a* sounds in "faint and far away" and in "about the break of day." Can you find other examples of these two devices?

A Song of Sherwood

Alfred Noyes

Sherwood in the twilight, is Robin Hood awake?
Gray and ghostly shadows are gliding through the brake,[1]
Shadows of the dappled deer, dreaming of the morn,
Dreaming of a shadowy man that winds[2] a shadowy horn.

Robin Hood is here again: all his merry thieves 5
Hear a ghostly bugle note shivering through the leaves,
Calling as he used to call, faint and far away,
In Sherwood, in Sherwood, about the break of day.

All the gnarled old thorn trees are blossom-white for June.
All the elves that Marian[3] knew were here beneath the moon— 10
Younger than the wild thyme,[4] older than the trees,
Lob and Mab and Bramblescratch, on their unbridled bees.

Oaken-hearted England is waking as of old,
With eyes of blither[5] hazel and hair of brighter gold:
For Robin Hood is here again beneath the bursting spray[6] 15
In Sherwood, in Sherwood, about the break of day.

1 **brake:** area of bushes; thicket.
2 **winds:** blows.
3 **Marian:** Maid Marian, one of Robin's band. She and Robin were in love.
4 **wild thyme:** low, creeping, fragrant shrub.
5 **blither:** merrier; more cheerful.
6 **spray:** spread of branches or foliage.

Love is in the greenwood building him a house
Of wild rose and hawthorn and honeysuckle boughs:
Love is in the greenwood, dawn is in the skies.
And Marian is waiting with her laughter-loving eyes.   20

Hark!   The dazzled laverock⁷ climbs the golden steep!
Marian is waiting: is Robin Hood asleep?
Where the last dark arrow fell, the white scuts⁸ flash away,
In Sherwood, in Sherwood, about the break of day.

Oberon,⁹ Oberon, the hazel copses¹⁰ ring,   25
Time to hush the nightjar¹¹ and let the throstle¹² sing,
Time to let the blackbird lift a bonny head,
And wake Will Scarlet from his leafy forest bed.

Friar Tuck and Little John are riding down together
With quarterstaff and drinking can and gray goose feather.   30
The dead are coming back again, the years are rolled away
In Sherwood, in Sherwood, about the break of day.

Softly over Sherwood the south wind blows.
All the heart of England hid in every rose
Hears across the greenwood the sunny whisper leap,   35
Sherwood in the red dawn, is Robin Hood asleep?

Hark, the voice of England wakes him as of old
And, shattering the silence with a cry of brighter gold,
Bugles in the greenwood echo from the steep,
Sherwood in the red dawn, is Robin Hood asleep?   40

Where the deer are gliding, down the shadowy glen,¹³
All across the glades of fern he calls his merry men—
Doublets¹⁴ of the Lincoln green glancing through the may¹⁵
In Sherwood, in Sherwood, about the break of day—

Calls them and they answer: from aisles of oak and ash   45
Rings the *Follow!   Follow!* and the boughs begin to crash,

---

7 **laverock:** lark.
8 **scuts:** short tails of animals, such as rabbits' or hares' tails.
9 **Oberon:** King of Fairyland.
10 **copses:** thickets.

11 **nightjar:** a bird which sings in the night.
12 **throstle:** thrush.
13 **glen:** small, narrow valley.
14 **doublets:** close-fitting jackets.
15 **may:** hawthorn bush and its blossoms.

The ferns begin to flutter and the flowers begin to fly,
And through the crimson dawning the robber band goes by.

Robin! Robin! Robin! All his merry thieves
Answer as the bugle note shivers through the leaves,   50
Calling as he used to call, faint and far away,
In Sherwood, in Sherwood, about the break of day.

Understanding Literature

1. The poem opens with a description of twilight. At what time of day does the poem end?
2. What specific pictures does the poet show you in his description of the forest?
3. The poet imagines that he sees several of Robin's band. In what characteristic poses does he see them?
4. What colors are stated or suggested by the words used in this poem? Do they create a pleasant or an unpleasant picture?
5. In what lines do you find examples of alliteration and of assonance? How would you read those lines aloud? What connection do you see between the sound of the lines and their meanings?

Further Activity

Look back at the note on alliteration and assonance at the beginning of this poem to remind yourself of what the terms mean. Find five illustrations of either of these devices in advertising slogans. Often you will find both devices in the same slogan. Copy the slogans and bring them to class.

Reading "Opportunity"

Here in another narrative a poet not only tells a story, but also uses his story as a lesson about life. You should see this poem as a statement about the person who will not fight because he thinks he does not have the right sword. You should also see it as a poem about similar people: the person who cannot catch a ball because his glove is not good enough, the one who cannot hit a golf ball because he needs new clubs, or the football player who would be the best man on the team if only he had new shoes. What does this poet think about the excuse-giver?

Opportunity

Edward Rowland Sill

This I beheld, or dreamed it in a dream:
There spread a cloud of dust along a plain;
And underneath the cloud, or in it, raged
A furious battle, and men yelled, and swords
Shocked upon swords and shields.   A prince's banner   5
Wavered, then staggered backward, hemmed by foes.
A craven[1] hung along the battle's edge,
And thought, "Had I a sword of keener steel—
That blue blade that the king's son bears—but this
Blunt thing—!" he snapped and flung it from his hand,   10
And lowering[2] crept away and left the field.
Then came the king's son, wounded, sore bestead,[3]
And weaponless, and saw the broken sword,
Hilt-buried[4] in the dry and trodden sand,
And ran and snatched it, and with battle shout   15
Lifted afresh he hewed his enemy down,
And saved a great cause that heroic day.

1 **craven:** coward.
2 **lowering:** frowning; scowling.
3 **bestead:** situated.
4 **Hilt-buried:** buried up to the handle (of the sword).

Understanding Literature

1. With what details does the poet quickly suggest a battle?
2. Why does the poet say that the "prince's banner" was "hemmed by foes"?   Does he mean only the "banner," or does the word stand for a larger idea?
3. How is the craven contrasted to the prince?   Point out words used in describing each man which indicate the writer's attitude toward each.

Descriptive Poetry

Many people expect poetry to be very subtle; they hunt for hidden meanings. But the meanings are no more hidden than your own experiences. During a summer trip you often take photographs of places that interest you. These pictures later remind you of pleasant or unpleasant experiences. The photographs are meaningful to you because you were there. When you show your pictures to your friends, however, they may look at them politely, but they will not have the same experiences you had.

Poets, on the other hand, work very hard at putting their experiences into words that may help you to relive those experiences with them. You as a reader have to put your imagination to work; in this way your experiences become nearer to those of the poets.

The following six poems create pictures for you. The purpose of reading these is to see common experiences in a new way. You may become more observant yourself.

Reading "Velvet Shoes"

In the first poem the writer describes what it is like for her to walk in the snow.

Velvet Shoes

Elinor Wylie

Let us walk in the white snow
　　In a soundless space;
With footsteps quiet and slow,
　　At a tranquil pace,
　　　Under veils of white lace.　　　　5

I shall go shod in silk,
　　And you in wool,
White as a white cow's milk,
　　More beautiful
　　　Than the breast of a gull.　　　　10

We shall walk through the still town
  In a windless peace;
We shall step upon white down,[1]
  Upon silver fleece,
  Upon softer than these.   15

We shall walk in velvet shoes:
  Wherever we go
Silence will fall like dews
  On white silence below.
  We shall walk in the snow.   20

---

1 **down:** soft, delicate feathers.

Understanding Literature

1. What feeling about the snow is the author trying to convey here? What words contribute to the effect?
2. Is she describing the scene during or after a snowstorm?
3. Is she walking on "velvet shoes" or does it just seem that way? What other words in the poem name fabrics? How does each fit the meaning of the poem?

Further Activity

Write a paragraph in which you create a pleasant feeling about a walk in the woods, in a snowstorm, on a beach, or on a riverbank. Choose four or five images, things you see or hear in this case, and describe them in language that is new and fresh to you.

In the previous poem, Elinor Wylie describes a personal experience: how it feels to walk in the snow. In this poem, Jean Toomer looks at a scene and presents a series of pictures. Try to see what the poet saw.

Storm Ending

Jean Toomer

Thunder blossoms gorgeously above our heads,
Great, hollow, bell-like flowers
Rumbling in the wind,
Stretching clappers to strike our ears . . .
Full-lipped flowers   5
Bitten by the sun
Bleeding rain
Dripping rain like golden honey—
And the sweet earth flying from the thunder.

Understanding Literature

1. How can thunder "blossom"? Does the word "thunder" include the idea of lightning? of clouds? What do you think the poet means by "bell-like flowers"?
2. What is meant by the phrase "bitten by the sun"? How can rain be "bleeding"? like "golden honey"?
3. How can the earth be "flying from the thunder"?
4. What images in the poem are caused by thunder? by lightning? by the sun?
5. Would the title "Storm" be as appropriate for the poem as "Storm Ending"?

Often a poet presents in his poem a series of images. The effect is as though he held out to you a series of pictures. Then, as a reader, you say, "What do these images add up to? What feeling am I supposed to get from this poem?"

Silver

Walter de la Mare

Slowly, silently, now the moon
Walks the night in her silver shoon;[1]
This way, and that, she peers, and sees
Silver fruit upon silver trees;
One by one the casements[2] catch   5
Her beams beneath the silvery thatch;[3]
Couched in his kennel, like a log,
With paws of silver sleeps the dog;
From their shadowy cote[4] the white breasts peep
Of doves in a silver-feathered sleep;   10
A harvest mouse goes scampering by,
With silver claws and a silver eye;
And moveless fish in the water gleam,
By silver reeds in a silver stream.

1 **shoon:** shoes.
2 **casements:** windows.

3 **thatch:** roof of straw or rushes.
4 **cote:** small shelter for birds.

Understanding Literature

1. Why is *shoon* an appropriate word in the poem? To what is the author comparing the moon's shoes?
2. Except for the movement of the mouse, nothing moves in the poem except the moon and its light. Find the verbs in this poem and show how they give a sense of the movement suggested by the glittering of moonbeams.
3. What feeling does the author have toward this evening he is describing? Prove your answer by referring to images in the poem.

Further Activity

Make a list of five images which the poet might have chosen to describe a moonlit night. Try to get them down in as few words as possible.

In this brief poem, Carl Sandburg gives his impression of the fog. Have you ever watched a fog come in over water, envelop you, and then go on? The poet may help you to recapture the experience.

Fog

Carl Sandburg

The fog comes
on little cat feet.

It sits looking
over harbor and city
on silent haunches
and then moves on.

Understanding Literature

1. What does *haunches* mean here?
2. The verbs which describe the fog are *comes*, *sits*, and *moves*. How many lines are associated with each verb? How do these lines represent the movement of the fog?
3. The writer compares the fog to a cat. How are the two things alike?
4. How does the author feel about the fog? How do you know?

Reading "The Eagle"

This poem, like the others you just read, could be compared to a painting. Again, the author gives you the words; you have to project the picture for yourself. Unlike the other poems, this one focuses on one part of the picture—an eagle. The rest of the picture is sketched in quickly to put him in a setting.

IMPROVING YOUR READING. In much of your reading, the characters are operating in a *setting*, a time and place for the action. In poetry the setting is often only suggested; you fill in the answers to the questions: Where and when is the action taking place?

The Eagle

Alfred, Lord Tennyson

He clasps the crag with crooked hands;
Close to the sun in lonely lands,
Ringed with the azure world, he stands.

The wrinkled sea beneath him crawls;
He watches from his mountain walls,
And like a thunderbolt he falls.

Understanding Literature

1. Where is the eagle in the first stanza? What is the "azure world"?
2. Why does the sea seem wrinkled? Why does it seem to crawl?
3. For what is the eagle probably watching? How can his fall be like a thunderbolt?
4. What characteristics of the eagle are described in this poem?

Further Activity

Keeping the same form and rhythm as the above poem, write a similar one on some characteristics of a dog, a cat, a snake, or a child. Read your poem aloud to compare the stressed words or sounds with those of Tennyson's poem.

Reading "Sea-Fever"

John Masefield was appointed England's poet laureate in 1930; as such he has written poems to celebrate official occasions of the state. In "Sea-Fever" he expresses the Englishman's great love for the sea. Since the English live on an island, much of their life and history is connected with the ocean, and a recurring theme in their poetry deals with their attitude toward their ships and the men who sail them.

IMPROVING YOUR READING. Rather than directly stating his attitude, the poet sets forth a series of images which recall his experiences at sea. The reader's problem is to recapture the experience which the images suggest. This poem differs from some you have read because the *imagery* (all the words in the poem which appeal to any of your five senses) goes beyond things you can see. The author appeals to your senses of touch and of hearing. A good reader who has had some experience with sailing should even taste and smell the sea.

Sea-Fever

John Masefield

I must go down to the seas again, to the lonely sea and
   the sky,
And all I ask is a tall ship and a star to steer her by,
And the wheel's kick and the wind's song and the white
   sail's shaking,
And a gray mist on the sea's face and a gray dawn
   breaking.

I must go down to the seas again, for the call of the
   running tide   5
Is a wild call and a clear call that may not be denied;
And all I ask is a windy day with the white clouds flying,
And the flung spray and the blown spume[1] and the sea
   gulls crying.

I must go down to the seas again to the vagrant gypsy life,
To the gull's way and the whale's way where the wind's
   like a whetted[2] knife;   10
And all I ask is a merry yarn from a laughing fellow rover,
And quiet sleep and a sweet dream when the long trick's[3]
   over.

1 **spume:** foam; froth.   2 **whetted:** sharpened.   3 **trick:** turn on duty; for example, steering or standing watch.

Understanding Literature

1. The choice of words, the diction, must be looked at carefully in this poem. How can a sky be *lonely?* a ship be *tall?* a wheel *kick?* a sea have a *face?*

2. What does *call* mean in the second stanza?
3. Why are words like *gypsy* and *rover* appropriate to the meaning of the poem?
4. What do you understand the last line to mean? Could it have more than one meaning?
5. Why is the poem called "Sea-Fever"?

Reading "Mother to Son"

In this poem Langston Hughes, a contemporary Negro writer, creates an image of people climbing a stair. He is also comparing the act to the difficulties of living.

IMPROVING YOUR READING. An image can also be a metaphor; that is, climbing a stair in this poem is like a kind of life. When you read an image, you should ask: "Is the image being compared to a similar, unstated situation? How are the two situations (living and climbing stairs) alike?" Not all images are metaphors, but you should always ask the question.

Mother to Son

Langston Hughes

Well, son, I'll tell you:
Life for me ain't been no crystal stair.
It's had tacks in it,
And splinters,
And boards torn up,   5
And places with no carpet on the floor—
Bare.
But all the time
I'se been a-climbin' on,
And reachin' landin's,   10
And turnin' corners,
And sometimes goin' in the dark
Where there ain't been no light.
So, boy, don't you turn back.
Don't you set down on the steps   15

'Cause you finds it kinder hard.
Don't you fall now—
For I'se still goin', honey,
I'se still climbin',
And life for me ain't been no crystal stair.   20

Understanding Literature

1. What is meant here by a "crystal stair"? How would a crystal stair be different from the other stair being described here?
2. As metaphor, what do the specific characteristics of the stairs ("no carpet," "landin's," "dark," and any others) stand for?
3. What do the specific acts of climbing ("reachin' landin's," "turnin' corners," "set down," and others) stand for?
4. How would the idea be different if the author had used the metaphor of a road, "Life for me ain't been no crystal road," instead of that of a stair?
5. Why does the author so obviously repeat the word "And"? What does this device have to do with the meaning?
6. The basic metaphor in this poem suggests a particular kind of house. What kind? How does this suggestion relate to the meaning of the poem?

Further Activity

Write a similar poem beginning "Life for me ain't been no crystal road." Try to create the same mood by your choice of images. Remember that your images should be comparisons with life's difficulties.

Here the poet suggests an emotion through the mood of his poem. He is giving you his reaction to the fall of the year.

IMPROVING YOUR READING. The author's words in the poem should evoke pictures, or images, in your mind. Can you see those pictures here? What feeling, or *mood*, do they create?

A Vagabond Song

Bliss Carman

There is something in the autumn that is native to my blood—
Touch of manner, hint of mood;
And my heart is like a rhyme.
With the yellow and the purple and the crimson keeping time.

The scarlet of the maples can shake me like a cry   5
Of bugles going by.
And my lonely spirit thrills
To see the frosty asters like smoke upon the hills.

There is something in October sets the gypsy blood astir;
We must rise and follow her,   10
When from every hill of flame
She calls and calls each vagabond by name.

Understanding Literature

1. What effect does autumn have on the writer?
2. What, in autumn, might be yellow, purple, crimson?
3. What are two images suggested in the second stanza?
4. What is meant by "gypsy blood"? by "hill of flame"?
5. Who calls each vagabond by name? Why?
6. Why is the poem called "A Vagabond Song"?

The following poem is an exercise in sound. The author, Oliver LaGrone, is a poet, sculptor, and teacher of art. In this poem, he joins sound and sense. His subject, Lionel Hampton, was one of the great jazz drummers and orchestra leaders of the 1930's. The poet not only talks of the influence of the drummer, but also makes the lines of the poem sound like rhythms of a drum.

The repeated *s* in "sunshine comes again" might sound to you like the swishing of the drummer's brush. The harsh sounds and the repeated *r* in

> Unroll the thunder from
> The Gods of rain

imitate the rolling and falling sounds of the drum. Watch for further examples of sound/sense associations.

For Lionel Hampton

Oliver LaGrone

Bring down the elements
Into your snare.[1]
Unroll the thunder from
The Gods of rain.
Peal off flash lightning—   5
Sharps of laughter's break
Then broadens them, till
Sunshine comes again . . .

Beat out that sermon,
Old as those first men who   10
Talked across the reaches[2]
With the throb of
Tom-tom rhythms—
Deft to laugh and cry,
To shout and dance, or   15
Tell the grief-stricken sob . . .

1 **snare:** a drum.
2 **reaches:** spaces of time.

Unleash a dim but
Unforgotten past, from
Dormant chambers of
Man's modern mind,   20
To stir again the common
Kindred pulse—
To answer back this call
To all mankind.

Understanding Literature

1. What words in the poem remind you of sounds associated with drums?
2. The rhythm of the lines echoes the irregular sound of a jazz drummer. Find examples of irregular rhythm.
3. Each stanza demands that the drummer should do something. What are the three main things that he is asked to do?

Cabaret[1]

Langston Hughes

Does a jazz-band ever sob?
They say a jazz-band's gay.
Yet as the vulgar dancers whirled
And the wan[2] night wore away,
One said she heard the jazz-band sob
When the little dawn was grey.

1 **cabaret:** a night club.
2 **wan:** tired.

Understanding Literature

1. The mood of the first two lines is different from the lines beginning with "Yet . . ." What repeated sounds in the fourth line slow up the sound? What harsh sounds in the fifth line are difficult to say and bring in the rhythm of a sob?
2. How can a jazz band "sob"? How can a dawn be "little"?

Themes of Poetry

The main purpose of much poetry is not just to present pictures, but rather, by means of images, to say how the writer feels about some aspect of life. The poet may look at a scene or object: a barren desert, an autumn landscape, a broken statue. He or she then says, "This reminds me of something: that people can be lonely, that love may end, that fame does not last." The idea that the poet is expressing is called the *theme* of the poem. This theme may be stated directly or only implied.

In other words, the poet makes a comment on some idea that is important to him or her—and important to everyone. As you read these poems, and if you read enough poetry, you may look at life in a new way. Those poems which last through hundreds of years are those in which many, many people have found important statements about things that have mattered very much: loneliness, help in troubled times, love, patriotism, youth and age, death.

The following poems are *lyric poems*. The term meant to the Greeks a song accompanied by a lyre, a stringed instrument. Now the term has come to mean a short poem with a single speaker (not always the poet) who expresses some thought and feeling about a subject. In reading lyrics, your key questions in reading are always: Who is speaking? What is the speaker's main thought or observation about life? How does the speaker feel about the subject? How does the poet feel—that is, if the poet is not the speaker?

Reading "The Shell"

Poets aim at making you feel some emotion by their choice of words. What you are reminded of by the words will control how you feel about the idea or picture being offered to you by the poet. Your job as a reader is to let the words remind you of your past experiences with those words. The feelings or ideas that the reader associates with a word, apart from the dictionary definition of it, make up the *connotation* of the word. For example, words may remind you of cold, bleak scenes; the feeling aroused in you might then be one of sadness. If a poem is full of words that suggest light colors, sun, and warmth, the poet might be suggesting a happy feeling. In reading poetry, then, try to see and hear what the poet is suggesting; then you will get the appropriate feeling.

IMPROVING YOUR READING. Much of the meaning of the following poem is suggested by the *connotation* of words like *icy* and *desolate,* for example. Can you find other suggestive words?

The Shell

James Stephens

I

And then I pressed the shell
Close to my ear,
And listened well.

And straightway, like a bell,
Came low and clear   5
The slow, sad, murmur of far distant seas

Whipped by an icy breeze
Upon a shore
Wind-swept and desolate.

It was a sunless strand[1] that never bore   10
The footprint of a man.
Nor felt the weight

Since time began
Of any human quality or stir,
Save what the dreary winds and wave incur.   15

II

And in the hush of waters was the sound
Of pebbles, rolling round;
Forever rolling, with a hollow sound:

---

1 **strand:** shore of a river or sea.

And bubbling seaweeds, as the waters go,
Swish to and fro
Their long cold tentacles of slimy gray:

There was no day;
Nor ever came a night
Setting the stars alight

To wonder at the moon:
Was twilight only, and the frightened croon,[2]
Smitten[3] to whimpers, of the dreary wind

And waves that journeyed blind . . .
And then I loosed my ear—Oh, it was sweet
To hear a cart go jolting down the street.

20

25

30

2 croon: soft, murmuring singing.   **3 smitten:** struck forcefully.

Understanding Literature

1. The poet listens to the sea shell. Tell in your own words what scenes he imagines as he listens.
2. Many of the words used in the poem create a particular feeling. What is that feeling? Point out the words which arouse that feeling.
3. Where has the poet suggested sounds to you? What are the sounds? How do they contribute to the effect he is after?
4. Why does he feel glad to hear a cart go by?
5. What, would you say, is the poet's theme?

Reading "To a Waterfowl"

Here, again, a poet shows a natural scene, a duck or goose flying overhead. He wonders how the bird finds its way, a thought which leads the poet to the question of how he himself finds his own way through the problems of life. And that leads the reader to ask with the poet, How do people find guidance in life?

IMPROVING YOUR READING. The author here uses a comparison to convey his idea. He sees that his own life is in some ways like that of the waterfowl. As he makes this comparison, he is creating a *metaphor*, an implied comparison between two things which are basically unlike (such as a waterfowl and a man) but which have some similarities. In reading, you must see the comparison. How is the poet's life like that of the waterfowl?

To a Waterfowl

William Cullen Bryant

Whither, midst falling dew,
While glow the heavens with the last steps of day,
Far, through their rosy depths, dost thou pursue
    Thy solitary way?

Vainly the fowler's[1] eye   5
Might mark thy distant flight to do thee wrong,
As, darkly seen against the crimson sky,
    Thy figure floats along.

Seek'st thou the plashy brink[2]
Of weedy lake, or marge[3] of river wide,   10
Or where the rocking billows rise and sink
    On the chafed[4] oceanside?

There is a Power whose care
Teaches thy way along that pathless coast—
The desert and illimitable[5] air—   15
    Lone wandering, but not lost.

All day thy wings have fanned,
At that far height, the cold, thin atmosphere,
Yet stoop not, weary, to the welcome land,
    Though the dark night is near.   20

And soon that toil shall end;
Soon shalt thou find a summer home, and rest,
And scream among thy fellows; reeds shall bend,
    Soon, o'er thy sheltered nest.

Thou'rt gone, the abyss of heaven   25
Hath swallowed up thy form; yet, on my heart
Deeply has sunk the lesson thou hast given,
    And shall not soon depart.

---

1 **fowler's:** hunter's. A fowler is a hunter of wild birds.
2 **plashy brink:** wet shore line.
3 **marge:** margin or edge.
4 **chafed:** worn or irritated by rubbing.
5 **illimitable:** endless; without boundary.

He who, from zone to zone,
Guides through the boundless sky thy certain flight,   30
In the long way that I must tread alone,
    Will lead my steps aright.

Understanding Literature

1. What does *thou* mean in the third line?
2. What is the setting of the poem? What feeling do you get from the setting?
3. How might the fowler "do [the bird] wrong"?
4. How does the poet think the waterfowl finds its way? Where is the bird going?
5. As the bird disappears, the poet says that he has learned a lesson from the bird. What is that lesson?
6. How is the bird's flight like the man's life?
7. What statement of theme is made in the last stanza?

Reading "To a Wild Goose over Decoys"

The previous poem by Bryant was written about 150 years ago. The following is a contemporary poem based on a similar situation. Man is still involved with the idea of how he finds his way through life.

IMPROVING YOUR READING. Again a poet is using the language of *metaphor*. He keeps comparing his situation with others that are similar. At the end of the poem you will find an exercise on metaphor. As you comment on the exercise, you will be seeing how things are alike and how they are unlike. To learn to compare is to learn one of the most crucial types of thinking.

To a Wild Goose over Decoys[1]

Lew Sarett

O lonely trumpeter, coasting down the sky,
Like a winter leaf blown from the bur-oak tree
By whipping winds, and flapping silverly
Against the sun—I know your lonely cry.

---

1 **Decoys:** artificial or trained birds used by hunters to attract wild birds.

I know the worn wild heart that bends your flight   5
And circles you above this beckoning lake,
Eager of neck, to find the honking drake
Who speaks of reedy refuge for the night.

I know the sudden rapture that you fling
In answer to our friendly gander's call—   10
Halloo! Beware decoys!—or you will fall
With a silver bullet whistling in your wing!

Beat on your weary flight across the blue!
Beware, O traveler, of our gabbling geese!
Beware this weedy counterfeit of peace! . . .   15
Oh, I was once a passing bird like you.

Understanding Literature

The following comments may be *true, untrue,* or *partially true.*
Which of these words best describes each of the following statements about "To a Wild Goose over Decoys"?
1. The speaker in the poem is a bird.
2. The speaker is looking at a plane coming in for a landing.
3. The honking drake is a girl friend of the flier.
4. The honking drake is a hunter's decoy-horn, calling for the
   flier to land.
5. The silver bullet is a white feather in the duck's wing.
6. The silver bullet will be shot by the hunter.
7. "Our gabbling geese" are women who talk too much.
8. "Our gabbling geese" are a flock of duck-decoys.
9. "This weedy counterfeit of peace" is a pond where a hunter
   hides in a duck-shooting blind.
10. The author compares himself to the goose because he is re-
    minded of his past life as an aviator.
11. The last line means that the speaker was fooled once; the
    poem is warning the goose not to be fooled.

Further Activity

Compare and contrast "To a Wild Goose over Decoys" with
"To a Waterfowl." How are the two poems alike and how are
they unlike? Make one point at a time and then show evidence
in the poems that supports your answer. What does each flying
bird stand for? How do the hunters differ? What do they stand
for? What is the theme of each poem?

Poems of Love

You can now turn to the subject matter of poetry by looking at groups of poems about similar subjects. The subject of love has brought poets to write some lovely songs. Some of them, like the next two poems, deal with not very serious aspects of what happens to a boy or girl in love.

Rondeau

Leigh Hunt

Jenny kissed me when we met,
    Jumping from the chair she sat in;
Time, you thief, who love to get
    Sweets into your list, put that in:
Say I'm weary, say I'm sad,
    Say that health and wealth have missed me,
Say I'm growing old, but add,
    Jenny kissed me.

Understanding Literature

1. Who is the speaker in the poem? Who is Jenny?
2. What do you learn about the speaker?
3. Why is Time referred to as a thief? What does it steal? What can it not steal from the speaker?
4. What is the theme of the poem?

Reading "The Banks O' Doon"

One of Robert Burns's lyric poems tells of a time when his love has left him. The continuing popularity of such songs rests on the fact that a similar experience happens to almost everyone.

The Banks O' Doon

Robert Burns

Ye banks and braes[1] o' bonie Doon,
    How can ye bloom sae fresh and fair?
How can ye chant, ye little birds,
    And I sae weary fu' o' care!
Thou'll break my heart, thou warbling bird,   5
    That wantons thro' the flowering thorn!
Thou minds me o' departed joys,
    Departed never to return.

Aft hae I rov'd by bonie Doon
    To see the rose and woodbine twine,   10
And ilka[2] bird sang o' its luve,
    And fondly sae did I o' mine.
Wi' lightsome heart I pu'd[3] a rose,
    Fu' sweet upon its thorny tree!
And my fause[4] luver staw[5] my rose—   15
    But ah! he left the thorn wi' me.

---

1 braes: hillsides.
2 ilka: every.
3 pu'd: pulled.

4 fause: false.
5 staw: stole.

Understanding Literature

1. Who is the speaker? Why is the speaker weary and full of care?
2. With what does she contrast her own position?
3. In the first stanza, the speaker sees a bird playing in a flowering thorn tree. When she uses the word *thorn* in the last line of the poem, it has another meaning. What does it stand for at the end?
4. What does the repeated word *rose* stand for in the last four lines?
5. Give the main idea of the poem in your own words.

Poems of Patriotism

Another theme popular with poets deals with the idea of patriotism: one's duty to one's country must be put ahead of one's duty to oneself. The first two poems in this section deal with Americans: the first with Abraham Lincoln, who was assassinated at the end of one war; and the second with those American soldiers who died during World War I and were buried in the fields of Flanders. Walt Whitman compares Lincoln to Captain of the Ship of State; John McCrae speaks from the burial place of the soldiers and becomes, for purposes of the poem, one of them.

O Captain! My Captain!

Walt Whitman

O Captain! my Captain! our fearful trip is done,
The ship has weathered every rack, the prize we sought is
    won,
The port is near, the bells I hear, the people all exulting,
While follow eyes the steady keel, the vessel grim and
    daring;
        But O heart! heart! heart!   5
          O the bleeding drops of red,
            Where on the deck my Captain lies,
            Fallen cold and dead.

O Captain! my Captain! rise up and hear the bells;
Rise up—for you the flag is flung—for you the bugle trills,   10
For you bouquets and ribboned wreaths—for you the shores
    a-crowding,
For you they call, the swaying mass, their eager faces
    turning;
        Here Captain! dear father!
         The arm beneath your head!
           It is some dream that on the deck,   15
            You've fallen cold and dead.

My Captain does not answer, his lips are pale and still,
My father does not feel my arm, he has no pulse nor will,

The ship is anchored safe and sound, its voyage closed
  and done,
From fearful trip the victor ship comes in with object won: 20
        Exult O shores, and ring O bells!
          But I with mournful tread,
            Walk the deck my Captain lies,
              Fallen cold and dead.

Understanding Literature

1. How is the entrance of the ship into port like the close of war?
2. Where is the poet in the poem?
3. How does the poet use contrast in the poem?
4. State in your own words the theme of the poem.

In Flanders Fields

John McCrae

In Flanders fields the poppies blow
Between the crosses, row on row,
    That mark our place; and in the sky
    The larks, still bravely singing, fly
Scarce heard amid the guns below.   5

We are the Dead. Short days ago
We lived, felt dawn, saw sunset glow,
    Loved and were loved, and now we lie,
            In Flanders fields.

Take up our quarrel with the foe: 10
To you from failing hands we throw
    The torch; be yours to hold it high.
    If ye break faith with us who die
We shall not sleep, though poppies grow
            In Flanders fields.   15

Understanding Literature

1. Who is the speaker in the poem?
2. In the first stanza why does the author contrast poppies and

crosses, and larks and guns? What do these contrasts stand for or symbolize?
3. What other contrasts do you find in the poem?
4. In the last stanza, what does the torch symbolize? What does the poet mean by "failing hands"? by "We shall not sleep"?
5. What is the theme, or main idea, of the poem?

Reading "Border Song"

The next poem is a call to the men of Scotland to rally and fight "for the Queen and our old Scottish glory." Scott organizes his words and rhythmic beats so that the poem, properly read, sounds like a series of drumbeats.

Border Song

Sir Walter Scott

March, march, Ettrick and Teviotdale,[1]
 Why the deil[2] dinna ye march forward in order?
March, march, Eskdale and Liddesdale,
 All the Blue Bonnets[3] are bound for the Border.
  Many a banner spread,   5
  Flutters above your head,
 Many a crest[4] that is famous in story.
  Mount and make ready then,
  Sons of the mountain glen,
 Fight for the Queen and our old Scottish glory. 10
Come from the hills where your hirsels[5] are grazing,
 Come from the glen of the buck and the roe;
Come to the crag where the beacon is blazing,
 Come with the buckler,[6] the lance, and the bow.
  Trumpets are sounding,   15
  War-steeds are bounding,
 Stand to your arms then, and march in good order;
  England shall many a day
  Tell of the bloody fray,
 When the Blue Bonnets came over the Border. 20

---

1 The names in the poem refer to Scottish clans, groups of men each under one chieftain.
2 **deil:** devil.
3 **Blue Bonnets:** a reference to their hats, blue

tam-o'-shanters.
4 **crest:** coat of arms.
5 **hirsels:** sheep.
6 **buckler:** shield.

1. What kind of men are being called by the poet?
2. How does he suggest what the gathering of the army looks like? What images are in the poem?
3. How does the poet get the pounding effect of the drum? How does he use alliteration?

Reading **"Stanzas on Freedom"**

In this poem, James Russell Lowell, an American poet, does not use a series of images to present his idea, but rather asks a series of questions and then answers the questions with his definitions of freedom and slavery.

Stanzas on Freedom

James Russell Lowell

Men! whose boast it is that ye
Come of fathers brave and free,
If there breathe on earth a slave,
Are ye truly free and brave?
If ye do not feel the chain,   5
When it works a brother's pain,
Are ye not base slaves indeed,
Slaves unworthy to be freed?

Women! who shall one day bear
Sons to breathe New England air,   10
If ye hear, without a blush,
Deeds to make the roused blood rush
Like red lava through your veins,
For your sisters now in chains—
Answer! are ye fit to be   15
Mothers of the brave and free?

Is true Freedom but to break
Fetters for our own dear sake,
And, with leathern hearts, forget
That we owe mankind a debt?   20

No! true freedom is to share
All the chains our brothers wear,
And, with heart and hand, to be
Earnest to make others free!

They are slaves who fear to speak   25
For the fallen and the weak;
They are slaves who will not choose
Hatred, scoffing, and abuse,
Rather than in silence shrink
From the truth they needs must think;   30
They are slaves who dare not be
In the right with two or three.

Understanding Literature

1. What is Lowell's definition of a slave?
2. What is his definition, then, of a free man?
3. Are there more slaves or more free men, according to Lowell? Why?

Poems of Courage and Faith

The next group of poems deals with some troubles that poets feel keenly and with their persisting belief that all will be well. The first poem is one by Henry Wadsworth Longfellow. It was written shortly after his wife's death—at a time when he was searching for some meaning to his life. In the next two poems, Tennyson and Scott are sorrowing: each over the death of someone he cared about. Then Sir Walter Raleigh's statement of faith in God is followed by one of the greatest of all statements of faith, "The Twenty-third Psalm." These poems, when read together, show that although man does face troubles, he can carry on with great courage and faith.

A Psalm of Life

Henry Wadsworth Longfellow

Tell me not, in mournful numbers,
   Life is but an empty dream!—
For the soul is dead that slumbers,
   And things are not what they seem.

Life is real! Life is earnest!   5
   And the grave is not its goal;
Dust thou art, to dust returnest,
   Was not spoken of the soul.

Not enjoyment, and not sorrow,
   Is our destined end or way;   10
But to act, that each to-morrow
   Find us farther than to-day.

Art is long, and Time is fleeting,
   And our hearts, though stout and brave,
Still, like muffled drums, are beating   15
   Funeral marches to the grave.

In the world's broad field of battle,
   In the bivouac of Life,
Be not like dumb, driven cattle!
   Be a hero in the strife!   20

Trust no Future, howe'er pleasant!
   Let the dead Past bury its dead!
Act,—act in the living Present!
   Heart within, and God o'erhead!

Lives of great men all remind us   25
   We can make our lives sublime,
And, departing, leave behind us
   Footprints on the sands of time;

Footprints, that perhaps another,
    Sailing o'er life's solemn main,
A forlorn and shipwrecked brother,
    Seeing, shall take heart again.

30

Let us, then, be up and doing,
    With a heart for any fate;
Still achieving, still pursuing,
    Learn to labor and to wait.

35

Understanding Literature

1. Probably no other poem by Longfellow is quoted more often than is "A Psalm of Life." What do you think might account for the poem's lasting popularity?
2. What attitude toward life—what way of looking at life—does Longfellow reject? Which of his arguments for rejecting that point of view impressed you most?
3. What would you say is the central thought of the poem?
4. What does the seventh stanza (lines 25-28) mean to you?
5. Which lines of the poem seem to you to be particularly effective—perhaps worth remembering?

Reading "Break, Break, Break"

In describing settings, poets choose words that will affect their readers emotionally. If the poet paints the picture in bright greens, reds, and yellows, the reader should see a pleasant scene and feel in a happy mood. If the poet describes rain and darkness, he or she may be describing an unhappy feeling. In the following poem, the poet lets the scene reflect his sadness at the death of someone he has cared about.

Break, Break, Break

Alfred, Lord Tennyson

Break, break, break,
    On thy cold gray stones, O Sea!
And I would that my tongue could utter
    The thoughts that arise in me.

O, well for the fisherman's boy,
 That he shouts with his sister at play!
O, well for the sailor lad,
 That he sings in his boat on the bay!

5

And the stately ships go on
 To their haven under the hill;
But O for the touch of a vanished hand,
 And the sound of a voice that is still!

Break, break, break,
 At the foot of thy crags, O Sea!
But the tender grace of a day that is dead
 Will never come back to me.

Understanding Literature

1. Where is the speaker, the "I" in the poem? Describe the setting of the poem.
2. What is the dominant color in the setting? the dominant sound? What contrasting sounds are brought into the second stanza? Why?
3. Of all the things a poet may see, he selects those that have some bearing on what he is trying to say in his poem. What does the ship stand for? the haven?
4. What is meant by the last two lines of the third stanza? by "the tender grace of a day that is dead" in stanza 4?
5. How, in the first two lines, has the writer kept the sound and rhythm of his words like the sound of the breaking sea? Where has he put the letters that are difficult to read aloud? How does this affect the rhythm of the lines?

Dream Variation

Langston Hughes

To fling my arms wide
In some place of the sun,
To whirl and to dance
Till the white day is done.
Then rest at cool evening   5
Beneath a tall tree
While night comes on gently,
    Dark like me—
That is my dream!

To fling my arms wide   10
In the face of the sun,
Dance! Whirl! Whirl!
Till the quick day is done.
Rest at pale evening . . .
A tall, slim tree . . .   15
Night coming tenderly
    Black like me.

Understanding Literature

1. The "I" of the poem wants to "fling my arms wide" and "to whirl and to dance." The whirling and dancing are images that represent what attitude or feeling?
2. In the last lines of each stanza, what words suggest the kind of rest the speaker desires?
3. Why is the speaker dreaming? How might the dream become reality?

The sudden shock of catastrophe is reflected in this short metaphoric poem.

Earth-Quake

Waring Cuney

God was poring over[1] the world
the other day,
as a scholar pores over a book.

Then suddenly as a scholar
weary of his book
God shoved the world aside.

1 **poring over:** examining.

Understanding Literature

1. What two ideas are being compared in this poem?
2. How are they alike?

The Twenty-third Psalm

The Lord is my shepherd; I shall not want.[1]
He maketh me to lie down in green pastures:
He leadeth me beside the still waters.
He restoreth my soul:
He leadeth me in the paths of righteousness   5
For his name's sake.
Yea, though I walk through the valley of the shadow of death,
I will fear no evil: for thou art with me;
Thy rod and thy staff they comfort me.
Thou preparest a table before me   10
In the presence of mine enemies:
Thou anointest my head with oil;
My cup runneth over.
Surely goodness and mercy shall follow me
All the days of my life: 15
And I will dwell in the house of the Lord forever.

1 **want:** lack.

Understanding Literature

1. Why does the writer compare the Lord to a shepherd? To
   what is the writer comparing himself? How does he develop
   this idea in the first six lines?
2. What does he mean by "the valley of the shadow of death"?
3. What part of man's life, according to this psalm, is guided by
   the Lord?

Poems of Youth, Age, and Mortality

The last group of poems deals with two main ideas: first, the
conflicts between youth and age; and, second, the fact of death
and humankind's views of it. Robert Frost speaks of a boy who
wanted something which belonged to someone who was older.
The narrative is told by the older person. Oliver Wendell Holmes
tells his story of the loneliness of old age as seen through the eyes
of one who is still young.

In the final three poems we get a variety of views about death.
Frost is struck by the idea, as he finds an abandoned pile of wood,

that our human works may not live after us. In contrast, Countee
Cullen, in a poem about his grandmother, expresses the idea of
immortality. Langston Hughes sees death as a drum, summoning
not only all people but also all things in the universe.

To a Young Wretch

Robert Frost

As gay for you to take your father's ax
As take his gun—rod—to go hunting—fishing.
You nick my spruce until its fiber cracks,
It gives up standing straight and goes down swishing.
You link an arm in its arm, and you lean   5
Across the light snow homeward smelling green.

I could have bought you just as good a tree
To frizzle resin[1] in a candle flame,
And what a saving 'twould have meant to me.
But tree by charity[2] is not the same   10
As tree by enterprise and expedition.
I must not spoil your Christmas with contrition.[3]

It is your Christmases against my woods.
But even where thus opposing interests kill,
They are to be thought of as opposing goods   15
Oftener than as conflicting good and ill;
Which makes the war-god seem no special dunce
For always fighting on both sides at once.

And though in tinsel chain and popcorn rope,
My tree a captive in your window bay   20
Has lost its footing on my mountain slope
And lost the stars of heaven, may, oh, may
The symbol star it lifts against your ceiling
Help me accept its fate with Christmas feeling.

1 **frizzle resin:** The flame of a Christmas candle
would make the resin sputter. Real candles were
used in trees until the use of electricity became
widespread.
2 **by charity:** given free.
3 **contrition:** your sorrow for what you did.

Understanding Literature

1. About what incident, described in the first stanza, is the poet writing?
2. How much do you learn of the "you" in the poem? of the "I"?
3. One of the characteristics of poetry is its use of common words in an uncommon way. What is unusual about the manner in which the following words are used: *lean, smelling green, captive?* What two meanings are given to the word *arm?*
4. What does Frost mean in the line "It is your Christmases against my woods"?
5. In line 16 the poet speaks of "conflicting good and ill." What is the "good" and what is the "ill" in the poem?
6. How does the speaker feel about what happened to his tree?

The Last Leaf

Oliver Wendell Holmes

I saw him once before,
As he passed by the door,
  And again
The pavement stones resound,
As he totters o'er the ground   5
  With his cane.

They say that in his prime,
Ere the pruning-knife of Time
  Cut him down,
Not a better man was found   10
By the Crier[1] on his round
  Through the town.

But now he walks the streets,
And he looks at all he meets
  Sad and wan,   15
And he shakes his feeble head,
That it seems as if he said,
  "They are gone."

1 **Crier:** town crier.

The mossy marbles rest
On the lips that he has pressed
    In their bloom,
And the names he loved to hear
Have been carved for many a year
    On the tomb.

My grandmamma has said—
Poor old lady, she is dead
    Long ago—
That he had a Roman nose,
And his cheek was like a rose
    In the snow;

But now his nose is thin,
And it rests upon his chin
    Like a staff,
And a crook is in his back,
And a melancholy crack
    In his laugh.

I know it is a sin
For me to sit and grin
    At him here;
But the old three-cornered hat,
And the breeches, and all that,
    Are so queer!

And if I should live to be
The last leaf upon the tree
    In the spring,
Let them smile, as I do now,
At the old forsaken bough
    Where I cling.

Understanding Literature
1. What do you know about the speaker in this poem?
2. What details are you given in the poem of what the old man looks like? What was he like in his youth?

3. To what is the author comparing "the pruning-knife of Time"?
   "mossy marbles"? "The last leaf upon the tree"?
4. Which of the following answers (*a*, *b*, or *c*) best completes the
   sentence?
   The author is showing in this poem that:
   (*a*) the young man looks forward to old age.
   (*b*) old age is a time of loneliness.
   (*c*) old people are funny.

The Wood-Pile

Robert Frost

Out walking in the frozen swamp one gray day,
I paused and said, "I will turn back from here.
No, I will go on farther—and we shall see."
The hard snow held me, save where now and then
One foot went through. The view was all in lines   5
Straight up and down of tall slim trees
Too much alike to mark or name a place by
So as to say for certain I was here
Or somewhere else: I was just far from home.
A small bird flew before me. He was careful   10
To put a tree between us when he lighted,
And say no word to tell me who he was
Who was so foolish as to think what *he* thought.
He thought that I was after him for a feather—
The white one in his tail; like one who takes   15
Everything said as personal to himself.
One flight out sideways would have undeceived him.
And then there was a pile of wood for which
I forgot him and let his little fear
Carry him off the way I might have gone,   20
Without so much as wishing him good night.
He went behind it to make his last stand.
It was a cord of maple, cut and split
And piled—and measured, four by four by eight.
And not another like it could I see.   25

No runner tracks in this year's snow looped near it.
And it was older sure than this year's cutting,
Or even last year's or the year's before.
The wood was gray and the bark warping off it
And the pile somewhat sunken.   Clematis   30
Had wound strings round and round it like a bundle.
What held it though on one side was a tree
Still growing, and on one a stake and prop,
These latter about to fall.   I thought that only
Someone who lived in turning to fresh tasks   35
Could so forget his handiwork on which
He spent himself, the labor of his ax,
And leave it there far from a useful fireplace
To warm the frozen swamp as best it could
With the slow smokeless burning of decay.   40

Understanding Literature

1. What scene should you see as you read the opening lines of the poem?
2. The speaker says that a bird flew into the scene and "put a tree between us." What does this last phrase mean? The bird reminds the poet of what type of person? Why?
3. The bird then flies behind a pile of wood. What details does Frost use to show that the pile has been there a long time? What kind of person, does Frost think, piled the wood there?
4. How can the wood "warm the frozen swamp"? Does Frost approve of the person who cut and piled the wood?
5. What is the theme of the poem?

For My Grandmother

Countee Cullen

This lovely flower fell to seed;
Work gently sun and rain;
She held it as her dying creed
That she would grow again.

Understanding Literature

1. If we read the first line as metaphor, who is "This lovely flower"? What is meant by "fell to seed"?
2. The second line does not follow the natural word order. What is the subject of the verb "Work"?
3. Who is "She"? What is meant by "grow again"? Does it mean a return to life? Does it mean that her influence will live on? How do you know?
4. Is the metaphor of flower and seed better for carrying the intended idea than one of a tree dropping its leaves, grass turning brown, or a bear hibernating? Why?

Further Activity

Write a similar epitaph for an important person. Begin with "This lovely tree has lost its leaves" or with any line you can create. Your title should name or suggest the person.

Drum

Langston Hughes

Bear in mind
That death is a drum
Beating forever
Till the last worms come
To answer its call,   5
Till the last stars fall,
Until the last atom
Is no atom at all,
Until time is lost
And there is no air   10
And space itself
Is nothing nowhere,
Death is a drum,
A signal drum,
Calling life   15
To come!
Come!
Come!

Understanding Literature

1. What characteristics of death are being described here?
2. To emphasize the passing of time the author describes the breakup of the universe. By what order of events does he think it will decay?
3. Why does the poet say "Till the last worms come" instead of "Till the last person's done"? What different idea is suggested by the first quotation that is not in the second?
4. What is the purpose of the repetition of the word "Come" in the last three lines? How would the sound and meaning be different if the word was repeated in the same line, "To come, come, come!"?
5. In what way does the sound of this poem when read aloud suggest the passing of time?

Author Biographies

ANGELOU, MAYA (nee **Marguerite Johnson**, 1928-). Maya Angelou —dancer, actress, director, activist, screenwriter, poet, and journalist— was born in St. Louis, Missouri. She was a dancer in the federally sponsored touring production of *Porgy and Bess.* She has directed and acted in theater in New York City. At Dr. Martin Luther King, Jr.'s request, she worked for the Southern Christian Leadership Conference. Her books (mainly poetry and autobiography) include *I Know Why the Caged Bird Sings* and *Just Give Me a Cool Drink of Water 'fore I Diiie.*

ANNIXTER, PAUL (1894-). Born in Minneapolis, Minnesota, Paul Annixter (the pseudonym of Howard Allison Sturtzel) now lives in Pasadena, California. He left school at eighteen and for a time traveled over the country doing odd jobs. Later he took up a timber claim in Minnesota; there, living in solitude, he began to write stories about animals and nature. He and his wife have written several novels and over five hundred short stories. His best-known novel is *Swiftwater.*

BALDWIN, JAMES (1924-). The oldest of the nine children of a Harlem preacher James Baldwin himself was a boy preacher in Harlem's storefront churches. A gifted writer, after high school he left home and church in pursuit of a literary career.

When he was twenty-four, he went to France where he lived for the next ten years and wrote his first three books: *Go Tell It on the Mountain* and *Giovanni's Room*, both novels, and *Notes of a Native Son*, a collection of essays. His writing includes short stories and plays, as well as novels and essays, and he has received a number of literary awards. Mr. Baldwin lives in New York City when he is not traveling. He spends a great deal of time in Turkey.

BENÉT, ROSEMARY CARR (1898- Rosemary Benét was born in Chicago and graduated from the University of Chicago in 1918. She then went to Paris, attending school there for a year and writing for various publications. In 1921 she married Stephen Vincent Benét; they have three children. Since 1944, she has been a member of the Editorial Department of the Book-of-the-Month Club; she has also written articles for various magazines.

BRADBURY, RAY (1920-). Ray Bradbury was born in Waukegan, Illinois, but moved to California when he was in his teens. As a boy he was interested in stories of magic and fantasy. At the age of twelve he began to write stories of his own. Since then, he has written many short stories and radio and television dramas; he also writes for the motion pictures. He is best known for his science fiction, such as *The Mar-*

tian Chronicles, The Illustrated Man, and *The Golden Apples of the Sun.*

BRYANT, WILLIAM CULLEN (1794-1878.) Bryant, born in Cummington, Massachusetts, studied for the law at nearby Williams College. During his twenties he practiced law, but his real interest was in writing. He contributed poems to the *North American Review;* among these poems was his famous "Thanatopsis" (thoughts on death). In 1825 he went to New York to devote his full time to literature as an editor and a poet. He made several trips abroad, which he reported in *Letters of a Traveler* and in other works. His translations of Homer's *Iliad* and *Odyssey* are considered of high rank.

BUCKLEY, F. R. (1896-   ). An Englishman who lived in America for a time, F. R. Buckley has published most of his work in England. His adventurous, romantic books make good movies. He also has been an actor and a newspaperman and has written screenplays.

BURNS, ROBERT (1759-1796). Robert Burns was born in Alloway, Ayrshire, in Scotland. Because his father was a poor tenant farmer, the poet had little formal education. His mother, well-versed in the ballads and folk sayings of Scotland, influenced her son's poetry. Robert Burns worked hard on the farm, frequently without enough food. His first book, which he hoped would provide his passage money to Ja-

maica, attracted the attention of influential people who helped him to publish more poems. Today he is recognized as the best Scottish poet.

BYRD, RICHARD E. (1888-1957). Born in Winchester, Virginia, Richard E. Byrd was educated in his native state until he entered the U.S. Naval Academy, from which he graduated in 1912. In 1917 he ventured into aviation; he received his wings in 1918. In 1927, shortly after the famed Lindbergh solo flight to Paris, Byrd and three companions flew from New York to France with the first official trans-ocean air mail service, although fog forced abandonment of the plane just off the French coast. Byrd is world-renowned for his polar explorations. On May 29, 1926, he and Floyd Bennett made the first flight over the North Pole. Three and a half years later three men accompanied Byrd on a flight over the South Pole, as part of his first exploration of Antarctica in 1928-30. He returned to the Antarctic in 1933-35, 1939-40, 1946-47, and 1955-56. He described his adventures in *National Geographic* magazine and in several books: *Skyward, Little America, Discovery, Exploring with Byrd,* and *Alone.*

CAREY, ERNESTINE GILBRETH (1908-   ). A graduate of Smith College, Mrs. Carey worked for many years as a buyer for a New York City department store. After writing several books, the most famous being *Cheaper by the Dozen,* which she wrote with her brother, she retired from business to devote herself to her family, writing, and lecturing. (See **GILBRETH.**)

CARMAN, BLISS (1861-1929). The Canadian writer Bliss Carman also resided in the United States. While a student at Harvard, he began writing poetry, later combining writing with editorial work and lecturing. Among his works are *Pipes of Pan* and *A Winter Holiday* (both poetry) and *Talks on Poetry and Life.*

CONNELL, RICHARD (1893-1949). Born in Poughkeepsie, New York, Richard Connell worked, as a boy, on newspapers. After college he worked for advertising agencies, with time out to serve with the armed forces in World War I. Later, he became a free-lance writer of short stories, novels, and screen plays.

CULLEN, COUNTEE (1903-1946). Born in New York City, Countee Cullen won poetry prizes as well as scholastic honors when he was still in high school. While a student at New York University he published his first book of poetry, *Color.* Following his graduation from college he received his master's degree from Harvard. Until his death in 1946 Cullen taught French in the New York City public schools. In addition to one novel, *One Way to Heaven,* he published a number of collections of poetry. Prominent among these are *The Ballad of the Brown Girl, Copper Sun,* and *The Medea and Other Poems.* He edited *Caroling Dusk,* an anthology of Negro poetry, and collaborated with Arna Bontemps on the musical play, *St. Louis Woman.*

CUNEY, WARING (1906-   ). Waring Cuney was born in Washington, D. C., and was educated in the public schools there. He attended Howard University in Washington, the New England Conservatory of Music in Boston, and he studied voice in Rome. When he was twenty years old, his poem "No Images" won first prize in an *Opportunity* contest. Since then his lyrics have appeared in magazines and anthologies, and some of them have been set to music and recorded.

CURIE, EVE (1904-   ). The second daughter of Marie and Pierre Curie found her career not in science, but in writing. During World War II she was a correspondent, an officer in the Women's Auxiliary Forces, and an active worker (in the U.S.) for the French resistance. From 1945-1949 she was co-publisher of the *Paris-Presse,* and from 1952-1954 special adviser to the Secretary-General of NATO. Eve Curie married Henry R. Labouisse in 1954 and two years later became an American citizen. She lives in New York City.

DAY LEWIS, C. (1904-   ). Cecil Day Lewis, who was born in Ireland, began writing poetry when he was six years old. After graduation from Oxford he became a teacher, then a full-time writer. During World War II he worked for the Ministry of Information, and he now does university teaching as well as writing. He has written several books of poetry, as well as books about poetry and—under the pen name of Nicholas Blake—popular detective stories.

DE KRUIF, PAUL (1890-   ). Paul de Kruif was born in Zeeland, Michigan, of Dutch ancestry. His career has blended writing and science. Between 1916-1929, de Kruif taught at the University of Michigan (bacteriology) and the Rockefeller Institute (pathology). From 1923-1929 he worked with Sinclair Lewis to provide the necessary scientific and medical information for Lewis's novel *Arrowsmith*. In the thirties, de Kruif turned from scientific reporting to crusading for preventive medicine. His articles on behalf of this cause were collected and published as *Men Against Death*. Among de Kruif's other works are *Our Medicine Men* and *Microbe Hunters*.

DE LA MARE, WALTER (1873-1956). Walter de la Mare was born in a village in Kent, England, and was educated at Saint Paul's Cathedral School in London. For many years, before a government grant enabled him to devote his time to writing, he was a bookkeeper for an oil company. Best known among his writings are the poem, "The Listeners,"

a volume of poetry for children called *Peacock Pie*, and a novel, *Memoirs of a Midget*.

FINCH, ROBERT (1909-1959). Finch, a native of Montana, attended the University of North Carolina and, on a dramatic fellowship, Yale University. He began writing plays in his student days and later published a volume of one-act plays. His play "Whistler's Grandmother" appeared on Broadway, and he was also the author of television productions on national networks.

FINNEY, CHARLES G. (1905-   ). Charles Finney grew up in Sedalia, Missouri. After attending the University of Missouri for a year and a half, he enlisted in the Army and was assigned to a station in Tientsin, China. Some of his observations of Oriental culture are expressed in his first and best-known novel, *The Circus of Dr. Lao*. He is now a newspaperman in Tucson, Arizona.

FROST, ROBERT (1874-1963). One of the most famous of modern American poets, Robert Frost decided to become a poet when he was in high school in Lawrence, Massachusetts. He did not like college and did not attend long enough to get a degree. In 1912-1915 he lived in England, where the value of his poetry was first recognized. When he returned to America, he was famous. He received the Pulitzer Prize for poetry five times, as well as many other prizes and honorary degrees. Frost read one of his poems at the inauguration of President Kennedy in 1961.

FUTRELLE, JACQUES (1875-1912). Jacques Futrelle was born in Georgia. He worked on newspapers as a reporter while he wrote stories, many of which appeared in the papers for which he worked. His most popular stories are those dealing with Augustus S. F. X. Van Dusen, the hero of "The Problem of Cell 13." Futrelle died as a hero in the disaster of the ship *Titanic*.

GALLICO, PAUL (1897-1976). Born and educated in New York City, Paul Gallico became a reporter for the New York *Daily News* shortly after his graduation from Columbia University in 1921. He began work for this paper as a motion picture reviewer, but he was soon transferred to sports writing; in 1924 he was promoted to sports editor, a position he held until he left the newspaper in 1936 to become a free-lance writer. In order to gain extra insight into the contests and the players he wrote about, Gallico participated, at one time or another, in about three dozen different sports. Often he persuaded star performers to let him play against them. He has boxed with Jack Dempsey, golfed with Bobby Jones, swum with Johnny Weissmuller. Especially fond of Lou Gehrig, Gallico wrote a book-length biography, *The Pride of the Yankees*, which was adapted as a motion picture. In more recent years, Gallico

has become noted as a writer of fiction. *The Snow Goose*, a gentle love story, is a favorite of young adults.

GIBBS, WOLCOTT (1902-1960). Wolcott Gibbs was the great-grandson of Martin Van Buren, the eighth President of the United States. For many years he was a member of the staff of *The New Yorker* magazine, during his last years as drama critic. He wrote a play called *Season in the Sun*, which was presented on Broadway. Since he had been critical of the plays of others, he expected severe criticism of his own plays, but instead he received only praise. *More in Sorrow* (1958) contains his own selection of his writings on many subjects.

GILBRETH, FRANK B., JR. (1911-   ) and **ERNESTINE GILBRETH CAREY** (1908-   ). Frank and Ernestine Gilbreth were two of twelve children of Frank and Lillian Gilbreth, whose firm of Gilbreth, Inc., specialized in motion studies. The way in which the parents put their ideas into practice in rearing their large family is described in *Cheaper by the Dozen*. A later book, *Belles on Their Toes*, in which "Mother Was There First" appears, deals with the family after the death of the father. Frank B. Gilbreth, Jr., is now assistant publisher of two newspapers in South Carolina.

HALE, EDWARD EVERETT (1822-1909). Edward Everett Hale, born in Boston, Massachusetts, was a graduate of Harvard University. He taught school, wrote for newspapers, and later, became a minister. For the last few years of his life he served as chaplain of the United States Senate. He is remembered best for the short stories "My Double and How He Undid Me" and "The Man without a Country."

HENRY, O. (1862-1910). O. Henry, the pseudonym of William Sydney Porter, began to work for his uncle in a drugstore in North Carolina at the age of fifteen. Later he went to Texas where he worked in a bank and on a newspaper. He was tried for embezzling funds from the bank. Most people think now that he was not actually guilty, but he served a three-year prison sentence. In New York, after being released, he became acquainted with many different kinds of people and wrote many stories. Among his best-known collections are *Cabbages and Kings, The Four Million,* and *The Trimmed Lamp.*

HEYERT, MURRAY (1912-   ). Born in New York City, Murray Heyert grew up in the Bronx, attending public schools and then New York University. During World War II he was a civilian electronics specialist for the Air Force. He has taught electronics in vocational schools and has also done advertising and publicity work for electronics companies. Now he has his own business as a management consultant. In his spare time he writes for magazines.

HEYLIGER, WILLIAM (1884-1955). A native of Hoboken, New Jersey, William Heyliger began his writing career as a newspaper reporter, but he devoted most of his life to writing stories for boys. *Radio Patrol* and *Son of the Apple Valley* are among his best-known stories for adolescents.

HOLMES, OLIVER WENDELL (1809-1894). Oliver Wendell Holmes was a poet, an essayist, a novelist, and a physician. He attended Phillips Andover Academy and Harvard University, graduating in 1829. He had a successful career in medicine, practicing in Boston, serving as professor at Dartmouth College, and writing articles. He is well known, too, for his poetry—"Old Ironsides," "The Chambered Nautilus," and "The Deacon's Masterpiece, or The Wonderful One-Hoss Shay," for example—and for his essays, especially those in *The Autocrat of the Breakfast Table.*

HORGAN, PAUL (1903-   ). In addition to "Pages from a Rio Grande Notebook," Paul Horgan has written a two-volume history of the Rio Grande entitled *Great River.* The book was praised by critics both for its literary excellence and its historical accuracy, and it was awarded the 1954 Pulitzer Prize for history. Much of Paul Horgan's writing is set in New Mexico, where he has lived for much of his life. Born in Buffalo, New York, he went West during his eleventh year, when his family moved to Albuquerque. He attended New Mexico Military Institute in Roswell for three years. In 1922, his father died and the family returned to Buffalo. For the next three years he worked on the production staff of the Eastman Theater in Rochester, New York, where his experiences centered around music and drama. In 1926, he returned to Roswell as a member of the staff of New Mexico Military Institute. He resigned from the Institute in 1950 to devote full time to writing.

HUGHES, LANGSTON (1902-1967). Born in Joplin, Missouri, Langston Hughes attended the public schools of Lawrence, Kansas, and Cleveland, Ohio, where he began to write poetry. After graduation, he spent a year in Mexico, then returned to study at Columbia University. After a break with his father, Hughes left college, worked at several jobs in New York, then voyaged for about two years in Africa and Europe. While he was still in his twenties, his poetry began to attract attention, and he entered Lincoln University in Pennsylvania and graduated in 1929. For almost 40 years, Langston Hughes made his living from his writing, earning many awards and honors. He wrote novels, books of short stories, plays, news columns, children's books, history books, musical lyrics and librettos, and volumes of poetry. His first publication *The Weary Blues*, was a collection of poems which appeared in 1926. Other works include *Not Without*

Laughter, a novel (1930); *The Big Sea*, an autobiography (1940); *Selected Poems* (1958); and *The Langston Hughes Reader* (1958). His last book, *The Panther and the Lash*, a collection of poetry, was published soon after his death.

HUNT, LEIGH (1784-1859). Born near London, England, Leigh Hunt was sent at the age of six to Christ's Hospital School. At thirteen he began writing verses. In 1801 he had enough verses to make a book, and his father, who was a minister, persuaded enough of his congregation to subscribe funds to print the book. Hunt published other poems and edited several magazines and was a personal friend of many famous poets.

JEWETT, SARAH ORNE (1849-1909). Sarah Orne Jewett was born in South Berwick, Maine. Her father was a country doctor, and as a child she often rode with him on his visits to patients. Her father taught her to observe nature closely and to understand many things about human nature. She began to write stories and articles for *The Atlantic Monthly* magazine when she was nineteen years old. Of her several fine novels and short stories, her best-known work is *The Country of the Pointed Firs*, a collection of sketches about a seaport town in Maine.

KATKOV, NORMAN (1918-   ). Norman Katkov was born in Russia, grew up in St. Paul, Minnesota, and studied at the University of Minnesota. While serving in the United States Army, he worked on *Yank*, the Army newspaper. Later he was a newspaperman with the St. Paul *Pioneer-Press*. He moved East to work for the New York *World-Telegram*, for which he was a feature writer. He is especially interested in the problems of foreign-born Americans.

KELLER, HELEN (1880-1968). Helen Keller was born at Tuscumbia, Alabama. At the age of nineteen months she became blind and deaf. Through the help of Miss Anne Sullivan, her teacher, she learned to speak, to read and write by Braille, and to use a typewriter. She graduated from Radcliffe College with honors in 1904. She served on many committees for the blind and made many lecture tours throughout the world. The play *The Miracle Worker* tells the story of how Anne Sullivan helped her to come out of the lonely world of the blind and deaf. Helen Keller's principal writings include *The Story of My Life* and *The World I Live In*.

LaGRONE, OLIVER (19—-   ). Born in McAlester, Oklahoma, Oliver LaGrone attended Howard University and the University of New Mexico. In addition to writing poetry, he is a distinguished sculptor and a teacher of Afro-American history and culture. At present an art teacher in the Detroit Public Schools, he is a frequent lecturer and consultant-exhibitor. He has published a collection of his poems, entitled *Footfalls*.

LAPP, RALPH E. (1917-   ). Dr. Ralph E. Lapp is both an internationally renowned physicist and a writer of popular books and articles on modern physics and its impact on civilization. After graduating from the University of Chicago in 1940, he remained on the campus as an instructor and part-time student. He received his Ph.D. degree in 1946. At Chicago he became involved in the atomic energy experiments of the famous group of scientists who laid the groundwork for the development of the atomic bomb. In recent years Lapp's attention has shifted from the pursuit of pure science to the education of the public about the serious problems of living in the atomic age.

LAYCOCK, GEORGE E. (1921-   ). George Laycock, a free-lance writer and photographer, was born in Zanesville, Ohio. A former columnist on outdoor life for *Sports Age* and *Argosy*, Laycock has also written articles for such magazines as *Popular Science, Boy's Life, Field and Stream, Outdoor Life*, and *Sports Illustrated*. Popular books for young readers include *Never Pet a Porcupine; Big Nick: The Story of the Remarkable Black Bear; Whitetail;* and *Never Trust a Cowbird*. Laycock's most recent books include *Alaska: The Embattled Frontier* and *Death Valley* and emphasize conservation and the environment.

LOMAX, JOHN A. (1867-1948). Born in Mississippi, John Lomax became interested in cowboy songs when his family moved westward. He attended the University of Texas, but it was in New England, when he was doing graduate work at Harvard, that he found others sharing his enthusiasm for the ballads of the American Southwest. Two professors arranged for him to receive a traveling fellowship, which enabled him to spend three years collecting cowboy songs, ballads, Negro songs, and spirituals. His son Alan was co-editor and co-compiler of many of his books.

LONGFELLOW, HENRY WADSWORTH (1807-1882). Longfellow was born in Portland, Maine, of New England parents. He became professor of modern languages at Bowdoin College, the college from which he graduated, and later at Harvard. He traveled and studied in Europe at various times. The poet led, for the most part, a peaceful, happy life, being well loved both as a poet and a person. However, the tragic death of two wives affected him greatly. Longfellow has been called the poet of home, of serenity, of peace. His narrative poems *The Song of Hiawatha, The Courtship of Miles Standish,* "Paul Revere's Ride," and *Evangeline* have an American setting. He also wrote many lyric poems.

LOWELL, JAMES RUSSELL (1819-1891). James Russell Lowell was born in Cambridge, Massachusetts. He graduated from Harvard College and then, two years later, from Harvard Law School. After practicing law briefly, he became an editor and a poet. In 1844 he married a gifted woman who was interested in current reform movements; she inspired him to increased literary and anti-slavery activity. He was editor of the *Atlantic Monthly* and the *North American Review* and, as editor, encouraged several fine young authors. He later served as minister to Spain and to England. He was a brilliant man, successful as poet, scholar, critic, teacher, editor, and diplomat.

McCRAE, JOHN (1872-1818). John McCrae was a physician as well as a poet. Born in Canada, he obtained his medical degree from the University of Toronto. He was a university professor in medicine for a time. During World War I he fought at the front until he was placed in charge of a medical unit. His poem "In Flanders Fields" is one of the most famous of all war poems.

MARSHALL, PAULE (1929-   ). Born in Brooklyn, New York, of West Indian parents who had immigrated from Barbados shortly after World War I, Paule Marshall began to write sketches and poems before she was ten years old. After graduation from Brooklyn College, she worked as a feature writer for *Our World* magazaine and traveled on assignments to Brazil and the West Indies. She is the author of a novel,

Brown Girl, Brownstones (1959), which tells some of the problems of the Barbadian immigrant, and a volume of short novels, *Soul Clap Hands and Sing* (1961).

MASEFIELD, JOHN (1878-1967). John Masefield, born in Ledbury, England, trained to be a sailor. However, when he came to New York to join a ship's company, he changed his mind and stayed in New York for two years, working in a factory and doing much reading. He returned to England in 1897, and five years later published his first book, *Salt Water Ballads*, which contained "Sea-Fever." Author of long narrative poems and plays, Masefield served as poet laureate of England.

MERRICK, ELLIOTT (1905-   ). A native of New Jersey and a graduate of Yale University, Merrick has had a varied career in writing, farming, college teaching, and U.S. government service. He was also at one time a member of the Grenfell Mission in Labrador. *True North* and *Northern Nurse* are two of his books based on his stay there, and *Frost and Fire*, from which "Without Words" is taken, is a novel set in the far north.

NOYES, ALFRED (1880-1958). Alfred Noyes grew up in Staffordshire, England, and was educated at Oxford, where he excelled in athletics, and was also recognized as a promising poet. In addition to shorter poems, his best-known works are *Drake*,

Tales of the Mermaid Tavern, and *The Torch Bearers, an Epic Trilogy of Scientific Discovery*. His autobiography, published in 1953, was entitled *Two Worlds for Memory*, because he spent several years in the U.S. as professor and lecturer.

OLIVER, DIANE (1943-1966). The promising literary talent of Diane Oliver was brought to a tragic end when she died in an automobile accident at the age of twenty-three. After her graduation from the University of North Carolina in 1964, she was guest editor of *Mademoiselle* magazine and a student in the Writers' Workshop of the University of Iowa. Her short stories have been published in *Red Clay Reader, Negro Digest*, the *Sewanee Review*, and *New Writing of the Sixties*. The University of Iowa awarded the Master of Fine Arts degree to Diane Oliver posthumously, and her short story "Neighbors" was included in *Prize stories 1967: The O. Henry Awards*.

ROSE, REGINALD (1921-   ). Reginald Rose, a native New Yorker, is best known as a writer for television. His first play was "The Bus to Nowhere," which appeared in 1951. Since then, he has written adaptations for Studio One, has done a number of pilot films, and has written several hour-long originals (of which *Twelve Angry Men* is one). He has also written several episodes for the popular series *The Defenders*. Several of his plays are available in the book *Six Television Plays*, published in 1956. Rose's screenplays are in continual demand.

SANDBURG, CARL (1878-1967). Carl Sandburg was born in Galesburg, Illinois, and worked at various odd jobs after leaving school at thirteen. After serving in the Spanish-American War, he attended Lombard College, worked for newspapers, and wrote vigorous, free-verse poetry. His first poems did not attract attention until "Chicago" won a prize offered by *Poetry* magazine. In 1936 he published *The People, Yes,* which contains the selection "Paul Bunyan of the North Woods." He has also written books for children, as well as a novel, an autobiography, a collection of folk songs, and his master work—a six-volume biography of Abraham Lincoln.

SARETT, LEW (1888-1954). Born in Chicago, Lew Sarett lived part of his life in Michigan, where he spent as much time as possible in the woods, close to nature. For some years he taught English and public speaking at the University of Illinois; he began writing poetry while teaching there. He is the author of a book on speech as well as of books of poetry. In 1925 he won the Poetry Society Prize for the best volume of poetry (*Slow Smoke*) published in America during the year.

SCHRAMM, WILBUR (1907-   ). Wilbur Schramm is a university professor. He began his career as a newspaper reporter and an editor, then became a correspondent for the Associated Press and, later, a professor of English at the University of the Institute for Communication Research in 1957 and has written books on mass communication. He founded the Writers' Workshop at the University of Iowa and was its first director.

SCOTT, SIR WALTER (1771-1832). Sir Walter Scott was born in Edinburgh, Scotland. As a child he learned to love stories of the Scottish past, and he was more interested in literature than in law, the subject of his formal study. His poems were popular from the beginning, but when people lost interest in his poetry, he began to write novels. (*Ivanhoe* is the best known.) He acquired a manor house, called Abbottsford, and was made a baronet. In 1826, a bookselling business in which he was involved failed, and Sir Walter assumed the firm's debt of many thousands of pounds. He worked in law courts and wrote prolifically until he collapsed from overwork.

SHAKESPEARE, WILLIAM (1564-1616). William Shakespeare was born in Stratford-on-Avon, in Warwickshire, England. His father was a substantial citizen of the town and his mother's people were landowners. He went to grammar school in Stratford and at eighteen married Anne Hathaway. Nothing more is really known about his younger days, until 1592, when he was in London, writing plays and acting. The fact that he started his career as an actor may explain in part his ability to write plays that pleased both the actors and the audience. Shakespeare, at about the age of fifty, returned to Stratford and bought a fine house in which he lived during his last years.

SHARP, DALLAS LORE (1870-1929). Dallas Lore Sharp grew up in New Jersey and was graduated from the South Jersey Institute. He planned to become a surveyor but failed because his interest in nature took his attention away from his surveying duties. He enrolled at Brown University, partly because his nature study had already acquainted him with Professor J. W. P. Jenks of Brown, the Professor Jenks in "Turtle Eggs for Agassiz." In the decade after his graduation from Brown in 1895, Sharp completed a theological course at Boston University, served as pastor for several churches in Massachusetts and as a librarian and a professor of English at Boston University, worked on the editorial staff of *Youth's Companion,* and published his first three books about nature. Professor Sharp remained on the faculty of Boston University until 1922, when he gave up regular teaching to devote his time to lecturing and literary work.

SILL, EDWARD ROWLAND (1841-1887). Edward Rowland Sill was born in Windsor, Connecticut. After graduation from Yale University, he sailed around Cape Horn to California, hoping for better health. After trying various occupations he returned to the East to enter Harvard Divinity School. Instead of entering the ministry, however, he became a writer of articles and poetry and a professor of English at the University of California. His writings are lyrical; his best-known poems are "Opportunity" and "The Fool's Prayer."

STEELE, WILBUR DANIEL (1886-1970). Wilbur Daniel Steele was born in North Carolina; he was educated in Berlin and, later, at the University of Denver. At first he planned to be a painter and studied painting in Boston, Paris, and New York. His writing has won four O. Henry Committee awards for outstanding short stories.

STEFFENS, LINCOLN (1866-1936). After being expelled from a military school, Lincoln Steffens was tutored privately. A native of California, he graduated from the University of California in 1889, then studied in Europe for three years. He became a newspaper reporter, then an editor and a crusader for reform. His articles and his book *The Shame of the Cities* (1904) called the attention of the people to the dishonesty that was present in American public life at the turn of the century. His autobiography, published in 1931, makes interesting reading—both the early part, containing accounts of his boyhood, and the later part, picturing the civic reforms that took place over a period of thirty years.

STEPHENS, JAMES (1882-1950). Born in Dublin, Ireland, James Stephens was very poor as a boy. He was a struggling clerk when one of his first books, *The Crock of Gold*, was published. This is a novel told in the style of a fairy tale. He was interested in Irish mythology, art, and folk music and became a lecturer, as well as a writer, on these subjects.

STROTHER, ROBERT S. (1904-   ). A native of Winfield, Kansas, Robert Strother entered the publishing field when he was employed in the advertising department of the Winfield *Courier* during vacations from Southwestern College in Winfield and, later, the University of Kansas. After leaving college in 1925, he spent ten years as a reporter before becoming an Associated Press correspondent in Egypt, Palestine, Iraq, and Syria. During World War II he was an editor of *Yank*, the Army weekly, and later of the Middle East edition of the *Stars and Stripes,* another servicemen's newspaper. In 1949 he joined the staff of the *Reader's Digest*, and is now an editor.

SUCKOW, RUTH (1892-1960). Iowa-born Ruth Suckow studied at Grinnell College in Iowa and at the University of Denver. In order to have time for writing, she took up beekeeping, a seasonal occupation. Her first published short story appeared in a magazine in 1921; her first novel *Country People* describes the lives of a German-American family in Iowa. She is considered a specialist in stories and novels about people who live in small towns.

SYLVESTER, HARRY (1908-   ). A native of Brooklyn, New York, Harry Sylvester wrote for three New York City newspapers between his graduation from college in 1930 and his decision to become a free-lance writer in 1933. His short stories and articles have appeared in *Commonweal, Collier's, Esquire,* and many other magazines. His most successful novel, entitled *Moon Gaffney*, appeared in 1947. Recently, he has resumed writing for newspapers.

TENNYSON, ALFRED, LORD (1809-1892). Alfred Tennyson was the fourth of twelve children. He did much reading in his father's parsonage at Somersby, Lincolnshire, and began composing poems while a youth and later as a student at Cambridge University. After the death of his father, Tennyson assumed the responsibility of caring for his mother and sisters. He published a volume of poetry in 1832, but it was not until a second volume appeared (in 1842) that he was recognized as the leading poet of his day. He became poet laureate of England in 1850, and in 1884 received the title Lord (Baron) Tennyson. He is best remembered for his narrative poems, such as the *Idylls of the King*, and for many beautiful lyrics.

Thomas, Dana. See **Thomas, Henry.**

Thomas, Henry (1888-   ). Born in the Baltic region of Europe, Henry Thomas, a pseudonym of Henry Thomas Schnittkind, came to the United States with his parents when he was eight years old. Since receiving his formal education at Harvard University, he has been a writer, editor, publisher, and educator. From 1916 until 1932 he was editor of *Stratford Magazine*. For the past two decades he has devoted his time chiefly to writing, with biography his chief form. Recently he has written several books with his son, Dana Arnold Schnittkind, whose pseudonym is Dana Lee Thomas. His son was a war correspondent.

Toomer, Jean (1894-1967). Born in Washington, D.C., Jean Toomer was the son of a prominent New Orleans family. Racially, he was French, Welsh, Dutch, Negro, German, Jewish, and Indian. He was the grandson of P. B. S. Pinchback, a Negro who served for a short time as acting governor of Louisiana and was then elected to the United States Senate but denied his seat. Jean Toomer attended the University of Wisconsin and the City College of New York, but a search for self-identity prompted him to leave both schools. He began to write around 1920 and his work appeared in magazines. Some time around 1924, he went to France and became a disciple of a Russian yoga mystic.

About 10 years later, he "disappeared" from the literary scene; some reports state that he became a Quaker and settled in Bucks County, Pennsylvania. His principal work, *Cane* (1923), is a collection of stories and poems which only recently has received widespread acclaim.

Twain, Mark (1835-1910). Many of the literary works of Mark Twain (the pseudonym of Samuel Langhorne Clemens) are humorous accounts of his own experiences and travels. His experiences provided a good basis for his writing, because he traveled extensively and was involved in numerous interesting adventures. He spent his boyhood in Hannibal, Missouri. His early life included employment as a printer, as a writer for his brother's newspaper, as a Mississippi River steamboat pilot, and as a Confederate soldier. After a brief and discouraging service with the Confederate Army, he journeyed to the West, where he tried silver mining in Nevada with very little success. In 1862, while employed as a reporter for the *Enterprise* of Virginia City, Nevada, he first used the name "Mark Twain." Although the reader may visualize Mark Twain as a jovial humorist, much of his later writing was pessimistic and cynical. His later life included considerable unhappiness: the earnings from his writing and lecturing were absorbed by unwise business ventures and his wife died. Only one of four children survived him.

ULLMAN, JAMES RAMSEY (1907-   ). Mountains and mountain-climbing are the subjects of many of James Ramsey Ullman's principal writings. His literary interest in mountaineering is founded on personal experience, for he has climbed mountains in various parts of the world and is a member of the exclusive American Alpine Society, which enrolls only those who can prove that they have made certain difficult ascents. His writings about mountain climbing include *The Other Side of the Mountain* (1938), *High Conquest* (1941), and a novel, *The White Tower* (1945). In the 1930's, before he began his adventure-writing career, Ullman was first a newspaperman and later a producer of plays on the New York stage.

WHITE, E. B. (1899-   ). E. B. White was born and reared in Mt. Vernon, New York and was graduated from Cornell University in 1921. In 1926 he joined *The New Yorker*, and he is best known to adult readers for his contributions to this magazine. He has also written two excellent children's books: *Stuart Little* and *Charlotte's Web*. In 1960 he received a gold medal from the National Institute of Arts and Letters for his writings.

WHITMAN, WALT (1819-1892). Walt Whitman grew up and was educated in Brooklyn, New York. At an early age Whitman left school and became a printer's apprentice in a news-paper office. During the next few years he went from job to job, always reading extensively. In 1855 he published the first edition of *Leaves of Grass*, a book containing twelve of his poems. The book aroused severe criticism, but Whitman lived to see it accepted as a truly important work. His poems about Lincoln, "O Captain! My Captain!" and "When Lilacs Last in the Dooryard Bloomed," are among his finest works.

WHITTIER, JOHN GREENLEAF (1807-1892). John Greenleaf Whittier was born near Haverhill, Massachusetts, where he lived the life of the boy described in his poem, "The Barefoot Boy." He had little formal schooling, but he read widely and at the age of twenty-one became an editor. During the Civil War he was very much involved in writing in favor of abolition of slavery. After the war he turned more and more to the writing of poetry. *Snowbound* is perhaps his best-known work.

WYLIE, ELINOR (1885-1928). Elinor Wylie grew up in Pennsylvania and in Washington, D.C., where her father held a high position in the government. In 1921 she published *Nets to Catch the Wind*, a volume of poetry. This, and a later collection, *Black Armour*, established her literary reputation. Her poetry is rich in images that reflect her keen appreciation of physical beauty. She was also the author of four novels.

Literary Terms

Definitions for literary terms used in this book and also for certain fairly common terms not used in the text itself are given below. Page references in parentheses indicate that a term is further discussed on the pages listed. An asterisk after a word within a definition indicates that the word is defined under its own heading.

Abstract Words: Words naming ideas or qualities which cannot be known directly by the senses; for example, the words *happiness, freedom,* and *beauty* are abstract.

Act: A major division of a play.

Action: What happens in a narrative.* Action refers not only to physical happenings but also to all events in a narrative. Thus the dialogue,* the details of setting,* and character development, as well as physical movement, make up the action.

Allegory (ăl′ə gōr′ĭ): A narrative* in which characters, objects, and actions are equated with or represent ideas or qualities. In an allegory the author usually does not strive to make characters and events realistic.

Alliteration: See **Sound Devices.**

Anecdote: A brief, simple narrative* of a single incident.

Assonance: See **Sound Devices.**

Autobiography: A written account of someone's life written by the person himself. *The Autobiography of Lincoln Steffens,* Lomax's *Adventures of a Ballad Hunter,* Byrd's *Alone,* and Helen Keller's *The Story of My Life* are autobiographies.

Ballad: A narrative* poem, often meant for singing, characterized by simplicity of language. Ballads usually deal with basic subjects such as love, honor, or death. The action is brief and to the point; it is often developed by dialogue,* with a minimum of description* and characterization.* The device of repetition of a line or lines contributes to the musical effect. The ballad stanza* usually consists of four lines, with the second and fourth lines rhyming. A FOLK BALLAD, as its name suggests, comes from the people; it is passed down by word of mouth for generations. "Robin Hood and Little John" (p. 598) is a folk ballad celebrating the alliance of two folk heroes. A LITERARY BALLAD has the characteristics of a folk ballad, but it has a known author and is written down by its author. "Skipper Ireson's Ride," by John Greenleaf Whittier, is a literary ballad. (See p. 226.)

Biography: An account of someone's life written by another person. (See pp. 432-435.)

Characterization: The technique of showing what a person is like. An author characterizes a person by telling what the person says, thinks, or does; by telling what others say or think about him; and by providing details of his dress and appearance. In fiction* the author can tell the reader directly about a person's character. In drama or in a "dramatic" short story,* the author can reveal character only through a person's conversation and actions, and through others' comments about him. (See pp. 100-103.)

Character Sketch: An essay* devoted to characterizing an individual or a type of individual. A character sketch suggests, without great detail, the chief character traits of its subject.

Chronological Order: Arrangement of events according to the order in which they occurred in time.

Climax: The point of greatest emotional impact in a story or drama. The climax is also the turning point in the action,* the point at which the outcome of the conflict* is determined; it is the decisive action in the plot. The turning point in the action is also called the Crisis.

Colloquial (kə lō′kwĭ əl): Colloquial language is that which is appropriate to conversation. It includes usages such as slang and contractions and permits a certain relaxation in the niceties of grammar which are observed in more formal usage.

Comparison: The technique of showing the likenesses between two things. A comparison may be literal: "This fog is as dense as London fog." Or a comparison may be be-

tween two things in different classes, such as the fog and a cat in "The fog comes/On little cat feet."

Complication: See **Rising Action.**

Concrete Words: Words naming things which can be known directly by one of the five senses; the opposite of abstract words. Whereas the word *comfort* is abstract, the words *coat, hat, gloves, boots, snow* are concrete.

Conflict: A struggle of some kind, on which drama and fiction* are based. Conflict in literature may involve a struggle of man against man, man against nature, man against the universe; or it may be an inner conflict, in which a character attempts to understand a situation, to overcome a fear, or to make a crucial decision, for example. Literature may deal with physical, mental, or spiritual conflict. More than one level of conflict may be present in one single work of literature; for instance, in "The Most Dangerous Game," the conflict is both physical (as the two opponents match physical strength) and intellectual (as they match wits). (See p. 3.)

Connotation (kon′ə tā′shən): The emotional associations which one has with a word, apart from the dictionary meaning of the word. For example, the word *dead* in "We're having a dead chicken for dinner," although accurate enough, calls up an unpleasant connotation. A good writer chooses words which will produce the associations he desires in the reader's response. (See p. 626.)

LITERARY TERMS

Context: The words or passages surrounding a term or passage in speech or writing. The meaning of a word or passage should always be determined in its context. For example, the word *run* means something quite different in these two contexts: "He scored a run in the ninth inning" and "He had a run of bad luck."

Contrast: The technique of showing the differences between two things. A work of literature is often based on contrast of character, or of setting, or of ideas.

Crisis: See **Climax.**

Definition: An explanation of the meaning of a word or concept. The most common form of definition first determines the class of the term being defined and then distinguishes the term from other members of the same class. For example, a definition of *lion* is "an animal [class] that has four feet, a tawny coat, a mane, a loud roar, etc." [all the characteristics that distinguish it from other animals].

Denotation: The dictionary meaning of a word.

Description: Writing which describes something. Good description usually is a result of the use of many concrete words* and specific details.

Dialogue: Conversation between two or more characters.

Downstage: The front part of a stage; the part nearest the audience.

Epic: A long narrative* poem which tells of the adventures and achievements of a hero important to the history of his race or nation. The *Iliad* and the *Odyssey* are Greek epics believed to have been written by Homer; the *Aeneid,* by Virgil, tells of a Roman hero; *Beowulf,* an Old English epic, celebrates the achievements of a Germanic hero.

Epigraph (ep'ə grăf'): A motto at the beginning of a work of literature or of a section of a work of literature. The epigraph is related in some way to the meaning of the piece which follows it.

Epilogue (ep'ə lôg'): A final statement, usually at the end of a play. The epilogue often invites the reader's or audience's appreciation or calls attention to the meaning of the literary work.

Episode: An incident* in a piece of writing. A plot* is made up of a series of episodes, all closely related and each leading logically to the next.

Essay: A type of prose literature which discusses a particular subject. So many kinds of essays exist that a specific identification of the elements of an essay is impossible. An essay may deal with any subject; it may be descriptive, expository (explanatory), argumentative, narrative, or any combination of these; it may be humorous or serious. An essay is usually unified by a central idea, with all parts of the essay contributing to that idea.

Exposition: Writing which explains something. The beginning of the plot of a short story or drama is called the exposition. In this section of the plot, characters are introduced and information about their backgrounds and their present situations is given. In essays,* exposition is the explanation of an idea or thing.

Falling Action: The action following the climax* of a plot;* the outcome of a plot, also called the resolution. The falling action presents the solution to the problem raised, it answers the questions posed, and it resolves the conflict* in the story or play.

Fantasy: Literature which deals with the unreal world, such as Bradbury's "December 2001: The Green Morning." In fantasy, characters or events or setting may be unreal.

Fiction: Imaginative writing, as distinct from factual reporting. The term *fiction* ordinarily refers to novels or short stories, but it can refer to any narrative* in which characters, setting, or events are imaginatively created. For example, the biography* "Galileo, the Stargazer Who Defied the World," in recounting imaginary conversations and in creating some imaginary characters, contains fictional elements.

Flashback: An episode which suddenly interrupts the action of a story or play and shifts to an earlier time. The purpose of the flashback is usually to explain something; it supplies information necessary to understanding the characters or plot.

Folklore: Sayings, songs, poems, tales, legends, or any pieces of knowledge which have been handed down by word of mouth for generations until they have become a part of the common heritage of the people of a region. Folklore includes not only folk ballads,* poems, and stories, but also folk remedies, superstitions, beliefs, and customs. (See pp. 178-179.)

Image: A word or representation that appeals to one of the five senses. An image creates a picture or suggests a sensation of sound, smell, taste, or touch. An image is always concrete, never abstract. In "Silver" (p. 617), for example, the images appeal to the sense of sight.

Imagery (ĭm′ĭj rĭ): The collection of images* in a work of literature. In some literary works the imagery centers around a main image; for example, in "To a Waterfowl" (p. 629), the imagery is made up only of images associated with the flight of the bird and a hunter watching it.

Incident: An event. The plot* of a story or drama is made up of a series of incidents. An incident does not necessarily involve physical action: it can include anything—such as a character's reaction or an exchange of conversation—which furthers the plot.

Irony: The contrast between what appears to be so and what really is. Irony of statement occurs when a writer or speaker appears to be saying one thing but is really saying the opposite. For example, "What a beautiful day!" is an ironic statement to make when the day is actually a very unpleasant one. Irony of situation occurs when the outcome of a situation is opposite to what one would expect. For example, "The Ransom of Red Chief" is based on an ironic situation: one would expect a kidnaped child to be a victim of the kidnapers; but, ironically, the kidnapers are victimized by the child.

Legend: A narrative, sometimes based on historical people or events, handed down from the past. (See p. 178.)

Lyric: A poem with a single speaker who expresses personal thought or emotion about a subject. Most lyric poems are particularly melodic. (See p. 626.)

Metaphor: An implied comparison between two basically unlike things which are alike in some way. For example, in "The Fighting Soul" Theodore Roosevelt's body is compared to "the sturdy temple of a flaming, crusading spirit." The body and a temple are essentially unlike things; yet the writer suggests that likenesses exist between the two —for instance, both can endure shocks and withstand strain. (See p. 628.)

Mood: The feeling that an artistic work produces in the reader, viewer, or hearer.

Motivation: The reason or reasons underlying the behavior of a character. If an author has skillfully motivated a character, the reader will believe that the character's behavior is not only possible but probable.

Narration: Writing which tells a story.

Narrative: A story. A narrative may be very brief (see **Anecdote**) or very long, as a novel is. A narrative poem is a poem which tells a story, such as "Robin Hood and Little John" (p. 598) or "The Glove and the Lions" (p. 603).

Narrator: A person who tells a story. The author is the narrator of "The Most Dangerous Game"; one of the kidnapers, Sam, is the narrator of "The Ransom of Red Chief." See **Point of View.**

Objectivity: A term applied to an impersonal and unemotional attitude of a person toward a subject. A writer who is objective reveals no feelings and expresses no opinions for or against his subject.

Parable (păr′ə bəl): A brief story designed to teach some truth or moral lesson.

Personification: The device of giving qualities or objects characteristics of a human being, as in "A Vagabond Song" when the poet says of October, "She calls and calls each vagabond by name."

Plot: The arrangement of events in a story or play. Plot refers to what happens first, second, third, etc.—to the author's plan for presenting the action. In a good plot, there is a cause and effect relationship between the events depicted. (See pp. 2-4.)

Point of View: The vision through which a narrative is presented.

Point of view in fiction refers to the teller of the story, to the person through whose eyes the reader sees the action. An author may handle point of view in many ways. Some of the most common are:

THE OMNISCIENT ("all-knowing") AUTHOR'S POINT OF VIEW, in which the author, as narrator,* can supply any information about motivation,* character, theme,* etc., can move from one place or time in the action to another, and can reveal the thoughts of any character. Most of the stories in this book are told from the omniscient (omnĭsh'ənt) author's point of view.

THE FIRST PERSON POINT OF VIEW, in which the first person, "I," is narrator. The narrator may be a character in the story, as in "The Ransom of Red Chief," or a detached observer or recorder of the action, as in "The Man without a Country." What he tells is limited to what he would be able to observe.

THE THIRD PERSON LIMITED POINT OF VIEW, in which the story is told in the third person but is limited to what one person would be able to observe, as in "Without Words."

Preface: A brief opening statement at the beginning of a book. The preface explains the occasion and purpose of the book, and it usually acknowledges those who have helped with the book. (See p. 180.)

Prologue (prō'lôg): An opening statement, usually to a play. A prologue serves as a preface.* It sometimes describes the setting or explains the background of the characters or events.

Pun: A play on words depending on two words which sound alike or on one word with a double meaning.

Refrain: A line or lines repeated at certain intervals in a poem. (See p. 605.)

Resolution: See **Falling Action.**

Rising Action: That section of a plot in which the conflict is developed. The rising action, also called the complication, leads to the climax* of the story or play.

Rhyme: See **Sound Devices.**

Rhythm: The beat of prose or poetry.

Scene: A division within an act of a play. Scene also sometimes refers to an episode* in a story.

Script: The written version of a play, meant for use in production.

Selection of Detail: An author's choice of details to include in a work. Because a writer cannot possibly include every detail about his subject, he must choose which to include and decide which to exclude. The details he chooses are presumably only those which are especially necessary for revealing the theme.*

Setting: The time and the place of the action. Setting often contributes directly to the feelings aroused in a reader by a piece: a setting of a dark, rainy night creates in the reader a feeling different from that created by a setting of a bright, sunny day. Setting also may reveal

672

something about character, as in "A Start in Life."

Short Story: A brief work of fiction,* designed to produce a single effect. Short stories vary in length: a short story is longer than an anecdote* and shorter than a novel. A short story shows characters (usually only a few characters) in a setting* and in action; it develops a conflict* and reveals a theme* through its plot.*

Sonnet: A fourteen-line lyric* poem, using rhyme. Although there are many variations in sonnet form, a sonnet usually has a five-beat line and a definite rhyme scheme.

Sound Devices: Techniques for producing a musical or pleasing effect in literature, used especially in poetry. (See p. 624.) Some of the most common sound devices are the following:

ALLITERATION: The repetition of the same beginning sound in closely linked words or syllables, as "He clasps the crag with crooked hands; / Close to the sun in lonely lands," in "The Eagle." In these lines the c sound is alliterative; so too are the cl sound in clasps and Close, the cr sound in crag and crooked, and the l sound in lonely and lands.

ASSONANCE (ăs′ə nəns): The repetition of a similar vowel sound in two words in which the consonants are different, as close and lonely in the above lines.

RHYME: The repetition of similar or identical sounds in two words,

as *hands* and *lands* (see ALLITERATION).

Speaker: The person supposed to be speaking or thinking in a poem. The speaker is not always the poet himself. For example, a woman, not Robert Burns, is the supposed speaker of "The Banks O' Doon" (p. 633).

Stage Directions: Instructions in a play to a director or actor about the arrangement of the stage, the physical location of characters and their movements, and the manner in which speeches are to be delivered (as *loudly, angrily, teasingly,* etc.). (See pp. 483-484.)

Stanza: A division of a poem, often determined by repetitive units of lines, in which each unit is like the others in numbers of lines, rhyme scheme, and/or rhythm.*

Subjectivity: A term applied to an extremely personal attitude of a person toward a subject. A subjective writer expresses his own feelings toward, and opinions about, his subject. (See p. 283.)

Suspense: The curiosity aroused in a reader as to what will happen next. A skillful writer will try to introduce the element of suspense early in a story or drama, so that the reader will be eager to read on. The suspense is usually greatest at the climax* of the story or drama.

Symbol: Something which stands for, or represents, something else, as a school mascot represents the school or as the American eagle represents the United States.

Tall Tale: An exaggerated story, usually humorous. American frontier literature abounds in tall tales, such as the tales of Paul Bunyan or of Davy Crockett.

Theme: The major idea of a work of literature; what the literary work means. All parts of the piece should contribute to, develop, or relate to the theme in some way. The theme is often not stated directly, and usually any attempt to reduce the theme of a story or poem to a single statement vastly oversimplifies the meaning. However, some statement about the meaning of a particular piece may help the reader to formulate the idea illustrated by all the elements of the work of literature.

Tone: The expression of an author's attitude toward his subject and sometimes toward his readers. The tone is revealed partly through the details presented and the words chosen in a literary work. Tone in literature corresponds to the tone of voice a speaker uses: a work may have an indignant tone, a humorous tone, an objective tone, etc.

Topic Sentence: A sentence expressing the main idea of a paragraph.

Transition: A movement from one idea to another. Words and phrases, such as *of course* and *nevertheless*, often serve to bridge the ideas in two sentences or paragraphs. Any device which enables a writer to move smoothly from one idea or episode to another is a transitional device. Ordinarily a writer wishes to create smooth transitions, so that the reader can follow clearly the progress of ideas or events and see the connections between them.

Upstage: The rear of the stage; the part farthest from the audience.

Usage: What is customary. Language usage frequently varies in different parts of a country and in different social groups. What is considered appropriate usage in one region or in one group may differ from the accepted usage in another. Ordinarily, correct (or "preferred") usage is determined by the use of language by educated speakers or writers.

Verse: Generally, lines which employ rhythm and rhyme. A distinction is to be made between verse and poetry. Verse usually refers only to the technical aspects of a poem. Poetry expresses a meaningful experience of some kind; verse does not necessarily do so.

Word Choice: The words a writer chooses. A good writer uses only those words which express exactly the idea he wishes to convey to, as well as the feeling he wishes to create in, the reader.

Glossary

The glossary includes unfamiliar words used in this anthology. The words are always defined according to their use in the book; in addition, other commonly used meanings are frequently given. In most cases words that are footnoted in the text are not included here.

The order and kinds of information given in an entry are shown below:

1. The word that is defined, divided into syllables. Example: **a·bra·sive.**
2. Pronunciation. When there are two common pronunciations of a word, both are usually given. Example: (ăb′·străkt, ăb·străkt′).
3. The part of speech and, when useful, information about the singular or plural form.
4. Usage labels. Example: **chaise** . . . *Colloq.* **shay.**
5. Definition. The use of the word is illustrated (as for *decry*) when helpful.
6. Alternate spellings. Example: **ac·cou·ter·ments** . . . *Also,* **ac·cou·tre·ments.**
7. Derivative parts of speech. Other commonly used parts of speech derived from an entry are frequently given. The division of syllables and the accent marks for these derivative forms are always given. Pronunciation is noted wherever it might be unclear. Example: **co·ni·fer** . . . **—co·nif·er·ous** (kō nĭf′ər əs), *adj.*

The following abbreviations are used:

adj.	adjective	pl.	plural
adv.	adverb	prep.	preposition
Colloq.	colloquial	pron.	pronoun
Fr.	French	sing.	singular
Ger.	German	v.	verb
n.	noun		

Pronunciation Key*

ă, act; ā, able; â, air; ä, art; b, back; ch, chief; d, do; ĕ, ebb, ē, equal; f, fit; g, give; h, hit; ĭ, if; ī, ice; j, just; k, kept; l, low; m, my; n, now; ng, sing; ŏ, box; ō, over; ô, order; oi, oil; ŏŏ, book; ōō, ooze; ou, out; p, page; r, read; s, see; sh, shoe; t, ten; th, thin; th, that; ŭ, up; ū, use; û, urge; v, voice; w, west; y, yes; z, zeal; zh, vision; ə = a in *alone*, e in *system*, i in *easily*, o in *gallop*, u in *circus*;

à as in Fr. *ami*; KH as in Ger. *ach*; N as in Fr. *bon*; œ as in Ger. *schon*; Y as in Ger. *uber.*

*The pronunciation system of *The American College Dictionary,* © Copyright 1947, 1963, Random House, Inc., New York. Used by permission.

a·bra·sive (ə brā′sĭv, ə brā′zĭv), *adj.*, *n*
—*adj.* causing a wearing away or a wearing down by rubbing or scraping. —*n.* a substance used for grinding, polishing, or otherwise wearing down.

ab·stract (ăb′străkt, ăb străkt′), *adj.*, *n*.
—*adj.* 1. theoretical; not practical: as, *an abstract argument.* 2. difficult to understand; deep. 3. thought of in general rather than in connection with specific cases: as, *an abstract idea of truth.* 4. in art, the use of color and shape alone, as opposed to the representation of objects as they appear in physical reality. —*n.* a short statement of the contents of a book, speech, etc.

ac·cede (ăk sēd′), *v.* 1. to agree to, especially by giving in. 2. to enter into a position or office (followed by *to*).

ac·cou·ter·ments (ə kōō′tər mənts), *n.* 1. equipment. 2. a soldier's equipment other than clothing and weapons. Also, **accoutrements.**

a·cute (ə kūt′), *adj.* 1. sharp; with a pointed end. 2. mentally sharp or quick. 3. sensitive; keen: as, *acute eyesight.* 4. severe and sharp: as, *acute pain.*

ad·her·ent (ăd hĭr′ənt), *n.* one who supports a cause or a leader.

al·ien (āl′yən, ā′lĭ ən), *n.*, *adj.* —*n.* 1. one who is not a citizen because he belongs to a foreign country. 2. a foreigner; an outsider. —*adj.* 1. foreign, strange. 2. belonging to some other country. 3. not belonging to the given situation: as, *ideas alien to the American way of life.*

al·lude (ə lōod′), *v.* to mention indirectly.

al·ter·nate·ly (ôl′tər nĭt lĭ, ăl′tər nĭt lĭ), *adv.* by turns; one after the other in order.

a·lum·nus (ə lŭm′nəs), *n.* a male graduate or former student of a school or college. —*pl.*, **a·lum·ni** (ə lŭm′nī).

a·men·i·ty (ə měn′ə tĭ, ə mē′nə tĭ), *n.* 1. pleasantness, agreeableness. 2. *usually pl.*, attractive or desirable features or qualities (of a place, situation, climate). 3. courteous, kind act.

an·i·mate (*v.*, ăn′ə māt′; *adj.*, ăn′ə mĭt), *v.*, *adj.* —*v.* 1. to make alive; to give life. 2. to make active, lively, or vigorous. —*adj.* 1. having life; alive. 2. lively; active; spirited.

an·tag·o·nism (ăn tăg′ə nĭz′əm), *n.* 1. hostile activity; active opposition. 2. an opposing principle or force.

an·tic·i·pate (ăn tĭs′ə pāt′), *v.* 1. to look forward to; to expect. 2. to realize or do in advance. 3. to do (something) before someone else can act.

ap·pall·ing (ə pô′lĭng), *adj.* shocking; horrifying: as, *an appalling explosion.*

ap·pre·hen·sive (ăp′rĭ hĕn′sĭv), *adj.* 1. anxious; fearfully concerned; uneasy; worried about something that might happen. 2. quick to understand. —**ap′pre hen′sion,** *n.*

ar·dent (är′dənt), *adj.* eager; enthusiastic.

ar·du·ous (är′jōō əs), *adj.* 1. difficult; requiring great effort; laborious. 2. steep; hard to climb. 3. energetic.

ar·tic·u·late (*adj.* är tĭk′yə lĭt; *v.* är tĭk′yə-lāt′), *adj.*, *v.* —*adj.* 1. spoken clearly and distinctly. 2. able to speak. 3. well planned; clearly presented: as, *an articulate reply.* 4. having joints; jointed. —*v.* 1. to say distinctly; to pronounce with precision. 2. to express clearly and understandably. 3. to put together with or by joints.

at·trib·ute (*v.*, ə trĭb′ūt; *n.*, ăt′rə būt′), *v.*, *n.* —*v.* to assign a quality or cause to a person or thing. —*n.* a characteristic or quality of a person or thing.

at·tune (ə tūn′, ə tōōn′), *v.* to bring into agreement; to harmonize.

au·di·ble (ô′də bəl), *adj.* 1. capable of being heard. 2. actually heard.

aug·ment (ôg mĕnt′), *v.* to make larger; increase; enlarge.

au·gust (ô gŭst′), *adj.* 1. causing one to feel respect; noble. 2. dignified; majestic; magnificent.

ban·ter (băn′tər), *v.*, *n.* —*v.* to tease playfully; to make fun of in a good-natured

---

ăct, āble, dâre, ärt; ĕbb, ēqual; ĭf, īce; hŏt, ōver, ôrder, oil, bŏŏk, ōōze, out; ŭp, ūse, ûrge; ə = a
in *alone*; ch, chief; g, give; j, judge; ng, ring; sh, shoe; th, thin; t̷h, that; zh, vision. See the full
key at the beginning of this glossary.

way; to joke. —*n.* playful, good-natured teasing or ridicule.

bas·re·lief (bä′rĭ lēf′), *n.* sculpture in which the images project only slightly from the background.

Bed·lam (bĕd′ləm), *n.* **1.** an asylum in England for the mentally ill. **2.** any such asylum. **3.** any scene of noisy madness and confusion; a madhouse.

bel·lig·er·ent (bə lĭj′ər ənt), *adj.* **1.** warlike; ready to quarrel. **2.** engaged in war.

bleak (blēk), *adj.* **1.** bare and windswept. **2.** cold; harsh; gloomy.

blithe (blīth, blīth), *adj.* gay; lighthearted; joyful; cheerful.

bol·ster (bōl′stər), *v., n.* —*v.* to support, prop up, or strengthen; to keep (something) from falling or collapsing. —*n.* a long pillow or cushion.

boon (bōon), *n.* a benefit received; something to be thankful for.

broach (brōch), *v.* to mention or suggest for the first time; to bring up: as, *to broach the subject.*

buoy·ant (boi′ənt, bōō′yənt), *adj.* **1.** tending or having the ability to float in a fluid; lightness. **2.** able to keep a body afloat. **3.** cheerful; light-spirited; gay. **4.** cheering; uplifting.

cal·li·o·pe (kə lī′ə pē′, kăl′ĭ ōp′), *n.* a musical instrument made of a set of steam whistles and played like an organ, sometimes mounted on wheels and used in parades.

car·nage (kär′nĭj), *n.* **1.** bloodshed; bloody slaughter. **2.** dead bodies, as on a battleground.

chaise (shāz), *n.* a lightweight, horse-drawn carriage. *Colloq.* **shay.**

ci·pher (sī′fər), *n.* **1.** zero. **2.** a person or thing which amounts to nothing. **3.** any of the Arabic numbers. **4.** a system of secret writing; a code, or the key to a code.

cit·a·del (sĭt′ə dəl, sĭt′ə dĕl′), *n.* **1.** a fortress for the defense of a city. **2.** any fortified place. **3.** a refuge; a place to which one or many can retreat.

com·pla·cen·cy (kəm plā′sən sĭ), *n.* a state of satisfaction with one's situation.

con·cen·tric (kən sĕn′trĭk), *adj.* having the same center: as, *concentric circles.*

con·cep·tu·al (kən sĕp′chōō əl), *adj.* related to the forming of ideas or thoughts.

con·cert·ed (kən sûr′tĭd), *adj.* planned or agreed upon; planned together. —**con·cert** (kən sûrt′), *v.*

con·done (kən dōn′), *v.* to pardon or allow by overlooking an offense.

co·ni·fer (kō′nə fər, kŏn′ə fər), *n.* any of the trees or shrubs, mostly evergreens, which bear cones, such as the pine, spruce, or cedar. —**co·nif·er·ous** (kō nĭf′ər əs), *adj.*

con·sign (kən sīn′), *v.* **1.** to hand over; to deliver. **2.** to assign; to put (something) into someone's care; to entrust.

con·stric·tion (kən strĭk′shən), *n.* **1.** the act of drawing together or squeezing. **2.** state of being drawn together. **3.** a part that is drawn together.

con·tig·u·ous (kən tĭg′yōō əs), *adj.* **1.** bordering upon; touching; in contact. **2.** close by, but not actually in contact.

con·trive (kən trīv′), *v.* **1.** to devise, plan, or scheme. **2.** to design or invent: as, *to contrive a swinging bridge.* **3.** to manage; to bring about: as, *to contrive an escape.*

con·tro·ver·sy (kŏn′trə vûr′sĭ), *n.* **1.** an argument, quarrel, or dispute. **2.** a debate; a discussion which includes the clash of opposing views.

Cos·sack (kŏs′ăk, kŏs′ək), *n., adj.* —*n.* one of a group of people of the southern Soviet Union, well-known as horsemen and mounted soldiers. —*adj.* having the qualities of the Cossack.

coy (koi), *adj.* **1.** shy; retiring; bashful; modest. **2.** pretending to be shy and modest.

crass (krăs), *adj.* **1.** very stupid or dull. **2.** coarse; not refined.

crest·fall·en (krĕst′fô′lən), *adj.* **1.** with bowed head or drooping crest. **2.** in a state of defeated unhappiness or deep gloom; depressed.

crit·i·cal·ly (krĭt′ə kə lĭ), *adv.* with careful analysis or judgment about the worth of an object, idea, etc.

cur·ry (kûr'ĭ), *v.* **1.** to rub and clean; to clean by rubbing and combing. **2.** to beat; to thrash.

cyn·ic (sĭn'ĭk), *n.* a complaining fault-finder; one who doubts the general good intentions of others; one who thinks that people are basically selfish.

de·bil·i·tat·ed (dĭ bĭl'ə tāt'ĭd), *adj.* weakened; enfeebled.

de·cry (dĭ krī'), *v.* to speak out against; to describe as undesirable or worthless: as, *we decry careless driving.*

de·hy·dra·tion (dē'hī drā'shən), *n.* the process of removing the water from something; a thorough drying; a loss of water.

de·lib·er·ate (*adj.*, dĭ lĭb'ər ĭt; *v.*, dĭ lĭb'ə-rāt'), *adj.*, *v.* —*adj.* **1.** done on purpose; done after planning; intentional. **2.** careful, not hasty. —*v.* **1.** to consider thoughtfully. **2.** to weigh in thought.

de·mure (dĭ myo͞or'), *adj.* **1.** modest; shy; serious or pretending to be so. **2.** having a sober or settled appearance.

de·plet·ed (dĭ plēt'ĭd), *adj.* **1.** entirely or partly emptied. **2.** exhausted; used up.

dep·re·cate (dĕp'rə kāt'), *v.* **1.** to express strong disapproval of; to argue against; to protest. **2.** *Archaic.* to seek to avoid or escape by prayer.

de·ranged (dĭ rānjd'), *adj.* **1.** in a state of disorder. **2.** mentally disordered.

de·spond (dĭ spŏnd'), *v.* **1.** to lose courage or hope. **2.** to be disheartened or sad. —**de·spond'·ent,** *adj.*

de·vi·ate (dē'vĭ āt'), *v.* to turn aside from a course; to swerve; to depart (from a plan or procedure): as, *to deviate from the rules of a society.*

de·void (dĭ void'), *adj.* empty; completely without.

di·a·tribe (dī'ə trīb'), *n.* a bitter criticism; a violent spoken or written disapproval.

dif·fuse (*v.*, dĭ fūz'; *adj.*, dĭ fūs'), *v.*, *adj.* —*v.* to pour in all directions; to spread out; to scatter. —*adj.* **1.** scattered; not concentrated; widely spread. **2.** using more words than needed; long-winded; wordy.

dil·a·to·ry (dĭl'ə tōr'ĭ), *adj.* **1.** inclined to be late or to put things off; not prompt. **2.** causing delay; intending to gain time or postpone decision.

dire (dīr), *adj.* terrible; disastrous; awful; causing fear or suffering.

dis·arm·ing (dĭs är'mĭng), *adj.* removing fear, suspicion, or anger.

dis·cern (dĭ zûrn', dĭ sûrn'), *v.* **1.** to see or recognize clearly. **2.** to see mentally the difference (between two or more things).

dis·con·cert·ed (dĭs'kən sûr'tĭd), *adj.* confused; disturbed; ruffled; embarrassed.

dis·con·so·late (dĭs kŏn'sə lĭt), *adj.* unhappy; gloomy; without comfort.

dis·creet (dĭs krēt'), *adj.* careful not to say or do the wrong thing in a given situation; cautious. —**dis·creet'·ly,** *adv.*

dis·cre·tion (dĭs krĕsh'ən), *n.* **1.** the quality of being discreet, of using care and judgment in one's remarks and actions. **2.** freedom to make judgments and choices; power to judge or act.

dis·crim·i·nat·ing (dĭs krĭm'ə nā'tĭng), *adj.* **1.** able to notice small differences; able to make distinctions with care and exactness. **2.** showing favoritism; treating differently.

dis·mayed (dĭs mād'), *adj.* **1.** alarmed, frightened, or horrified. **2.** discouraged; downhearted.

dis·pir·it·ed (dĭs pĭr'ĭt ĭd), *adj.* depressed; discouraged; downhearted; sad.

dis·si·pate (dĭs'ə pāt'), *v.* **1.** to scatter, often wastefully. **2.** to waste one's time and energy through wild living.

dis·tend·ed (dĭs tĕn'dĭd), *adj.* **1.** stretched out; expanded, as by inflation. **2.** swollen.

dis·tort (dĭs tôrt'), *v.* **1.** to twist out of shape; to make crooked. **2.** to twist or misrepresent in the process of telling or reporting.

dis·tract·ed (dĭs trăk'tĭd), *adj.* **1.** mentally disturbed; emotionally upset. **2.** hav-

ăct, āble, dâre, ärt; ĕbb, ēqual; ĭf, īce; hŏt, ōver, ôrder, oil, bo͝ok, o͞oze, out; ŭp, ūse, ûrge; ə = a in *alone*; **ch**, chief; **g**, give; **j**, judge; **ng**, ring; **sh**, shoe; **th**, thin; **t̶h̶**, that; **zh**, vision. See the full key at the beginning of this glossary.

GLOSSARY

ing one's attention drawn aside or divided. —dis·tract′ing, *adj.*

di·vert (dĭ vûrt′, dī vûrt′), *v.* **1.** to turn (a person or thing) away from a path or course. **2.** to turn one's attention to a new subject of thought or conversation. **3.** to amuse or entertain.

di·ver·sion (dĭ vûr′zhən, dĭ vûr′shən), *n.* **1.** the act of turning aside, as from a course or a train of thought. **2.** anything that turns thought or attention away from its original course. **3.** the act of drawing one's mind away from problems or worries. **4.** entertainment; amusement.

doc·ile (dŏs′əl), *adj.* **1.** easily trained. **2.** easy to manage or control: as, *a docile servant.* —do·cil·i·ty (dō sĭl′ə tĭ), *n.*

dog·ma (dôg′mə, dŏg′mə), *n.* **1.** the official principles of a religion. **2.** a positive, settled opinion.

dole·ful (dōl′fəl), *adj.* sad; gloomy; sorrowful; full of grief.

du·bi·ous (dū′bĭ əs, dōō′bĭ əs), *adj.* **1.** doubtful; causing doubt: as, *a dubious statement.* **2.** of questionable quality or fitness: as, *a dubious compliment.*

ec·sta·sy (ĕk′stə sĭ), *n.* overpowering delight; intense joy; the peak of pleasant emotion that seems mentally to carry one away from his surroundings: as, *she was in ecstasy when she won the scholarship.* —ec·stat·ic (ĕk stăt′ĭk), *adj.*

e·go·tism (ē′gə tĭs′əm, ĕg′ə tĭz′əm), *n.* **1.** too much concern about oneself. **2.** talking about oneself excessively. **3.** selfishness.

e·gress (ē′grĕs), *n.* **1.** an exit; a way out. **2.** the act of going out of a place.

e·lu·sive (ĭ lōō′sĭv), *adj.* **1.** difficult to catch; continually escaping: as, *an elusive butterfly.* **2.** hard to grasp mentally; difficult to understand; puzzling.

em·a·nate (ĕm′ə nāt′), *v.* **1.** to come forth; to proceed from a source. **2.** to send out; emit.

em·bel·lish·ment (ĕm bĕl′ĭsh mənt), *n.* **1.** a decoration or ornament. **2.** a fancy touch added to a statement or story.

em·i·nent (ĕm′ə nənt), *adj.* **1.** rising above the surroundings; lofty: as, *an eminent*

tree *in a forest.* **2.** standing high among others in fame, worth, rank; outstanding. em′·i·nent·ly, *adv.*

en·gross·ing (ĕn grō′sĭng), *adj.* occupying one's attention completely; very interesting.

en·hance (ĕn hăns′, ĕn häns′), *v.* to make greater, as in value or beauty; to add to; to improve: as, *the cosmetics enhance her beauty.*

e·nig·ma (ĭ nĭg′mə), *n.* **1.** something puzzling or unexplainable. **2.** a question, picture, or expression with a hidden or puzzling meaning.

en·nui (än′wē), *n.* boredom; tiredness which comes from lack of interest.

e·on (ē′ən, ē′ŏn), *n.* a very long, indefinite period of time.

es·say (*v.*, ĕ sā′; *n.*, ĕs′ā), *v., n.* —*v.* **1.** to try; to attempt. **2.** to put to a test; to try out. —*n.* a brief prose discussion of a specific subject.

ex·e·crate (ĕk′sə krāt′), *v.* **1.** to hate strongly; to detest. **2.** to curse; to call down evil upon.

ex·hil·a·rat·ing (ĭg zĭl′ə rāt′ĭng), *adj.* making cheerfully lively; causing a lively joy or a vigorous gaiety.

ex·pi·ate (ĕks′pĭ āt′), *v.* to make up for wrongdoing; to pay the penalty for misdeeds.

ex·ploit (ĭk sploit′), *v.* **1.** to make use of; to get the full value from: as, *to exploit atomic energy for scientific purposes.* **2.** to use for one's selfish advantage: as, *to exploit a talented child.* —*n.* ex′·ploi·ta′·tion.

ex·trem·i·ty (ĭk strĕm′ə tĭ), *n.* **1.** the extreme limit or end of something. **2.** the end of a limb of the body, such as a hand or foot. **3.** a condition of utmost distress or danger.

ex·ult (ĭg zŭlt′), *v.* to rejoice; to feel triumphant.

fa·tal·ism (fā′ tə lĭz′əm), *n.* **1.** the doctrine that a person's destiny is decided by fate and that he can do nothing about it. **2.** the view that whatever will be will be.

fath·om·less (făth'əm lĭs), *adj.* **1.** too deep to be measured. **2.** too deep or complex to be understood.

fea·si·ble (fē'zə bəl), *adj.* **1.** possible to accomplish; able to be done: as, *a trip to Venus is not yet feasible.* **2.** likely; probable: as, *a feasible answer.*

fer·vent (fûr'vənt), *adj.* **1.** showing eager, warm, and enthusiastic feeling; earnest; ardent. **2.** hot, glowing.

fe·tish (fē'tĭsh, fĕt'ĭsh), *n.* **1.** an object believed to have magical power. **2.** anything to which a person is unreasonably devoted or which he considers much more important than it really is.

font (fŏnt), *n.* **1.** a stone bowl which contains the water used in certain church rites. **2.** a fountain; a spring. **3.** a source; an origin.

for·mi·da·ble (fôr'mĭ də bəl), *adj.* **1.** causing fear or dread, especially in dealings or encounters. **2.** difficult to deal with.

fraud (frôd), *n.* **1.** dishonesty in dealing; trickery; cheating. **2.** an instance of such dishonest practice. —**fraud'ful, fraud'u·lent,** *adj.*

frus·trate (frŭs'trāt), *v.* to cause to come to nothing; to baffle; to disappoint; to block or obstruct: as, *the weather may frustrate our plans for a hike.* —**frus·tra'tion,** *n.*

fur·tive (fûr'tĭv), *adj.* **1.** sly; shifty. **2.** done in a sly, hidden, or sneaky manner.

fu·tile (fū'təl, fū'tĭl), *adj.* **1.** useless; unsuccessful; not capable of producing an effect. **2.** unimportant. —**fu·til'i·ty,** *n.*

gamut (găm'ət), *n.* the entire range or scale of anything: as, *the gamut of emotion, from love to hate.*

gen·er·ate (jĕn'ə rāt'), *v.* **1.** to cause, produce, or originate; as, *to generate electricity* or *to generate hope.* **2.** to produce offspring.

gird (gûrd), *v.* **1.** to encircle or fasten with a belt or band. **2.** to surround;

to enclose. **3.** to equip; to clothe. **4.** to prepare (oneself) for action.

glib (glĭb), *adj.* **1.** done in a smooth, easy manner. **2.** spoken in such a smooth, fluent, offhand manner as to sound insincere and unconvincing. —**glib'ness,** *n.*

gra·ti·fy·ing (grăt'ə fī'ĭng), *adj.* satisfying; pleasing.

gri·mace (grĭ mās', grĭ'məs), *n., v.* —*n.* **1.** a twisting of the face. **2.** an ugly facial expression, sometimes intended to be amusing. —*v.* to make misshapen facial expressions.

gro·tesque (grō tĕsk'), *adj.* **1.** fantastically odd in form or character; having striking distortions in shape. **2.** ridiculous in appearance. —**gro·tesque'ly,** *adv.*

grov·el (grŭv'əl, grŏv'əl), *v.* **1.** to lie or crawl on the ground, especially face down. **2.** to act in a humble way.

har·ass (hăr'əs, hə răs'), *v.* **1.** to bother, torment, disturb or trouble, as with questions, gossip, etc. **2.** to provoke with frequent attacks or raids, as in war.

her·e·sy (hĕr'ə sĭ), *n.* **1.** an opinion in conflict with official views or doctrines. **2.** a religious belief which disagrees with the established doctrine of a church. **3.** the holding of such a belief.

hy·per·bo·le (hī pûr'bə lē', hī pûr'bə lĭ), *n.* an exaggeration for effect, not meant to be taken as stated.

id·i·om (ĭd'ĭ əm), *n.* **1.** the language usually employed by a people, class, or region. **2.** an accepted phrase or expression which violates the usual patterns of a language. **3.** a distinct style, as in music, art, drama, etc.

ig·no·min·y (ĭg'nə mĭn'ĭ), *n.* **1.** shame and dishonor. **2.** a cause of disgrace; a degrading act or quality.

im·me·mo·ri·al (ĭm'ə mōr'ĭ əl), *adj.* very old; extending back farther than recorded history.

ăct, āble, dâre, ärt; ĕbb, ēqual; ĭf, īce; hŏt, ōver, ôrder, oil, bŏŏk, ōōze, out; ŭp, ūse, ûrge; ə = a in *alone*; **ch**, chief; **g**, give; **j**, judge; **ng**, ring; **sh**, shoe; **th**, thin; **th**, that; **zh**, vision. See the full key at the beginning of this glossary.

im·mi·nence (ĭm′ə nəns), *n.* 1. state of being about to occur at any moment. 2. a threat of evil or danger.

im·pair (ĭm pâr′), *v.* 1. to make worse or weaker. 2. to reduce the value of.

im·pend·ing (ĭm pĕn′dĭng), *adj.* 1. about to happen. 2. hanging over.

im·per·a·tive (ĭm pĕr′ə tĭv), *adj.* 1. absolutely necessary; unavoidable. 2. showing authority; commanding.

im·per·vi·ous (ĭm pûr′vĭ əs), *adj.* 1. impossible to be penetrated or passed through. 2. not affected by; resistant to: as, *a person impervious to logic.*

im·pet·u·ous (ĭm pĕch′o͞o əs), *adj.* 1. moving with great impetus; having much force; rushing. 2. acting quickly without thinking; acting on impulse.

im·pi·ous (ĭm′pĭ əs), *adj.* 1. lacking respect for God. 2. lacking respect for ideas, practices, or institutions which many people hold in esteem.

im·plau·si·bil·i·ty (ĭm plô′zə bĭl′ə tĭ), *n.* a situation or observation which is difficult to believe, which does not appear possible or true.

im·pov·er·ished (ĭm pŏv′ər ĭsht), *adj.* 1. extremely poor. 2. made poor; reduced to having nothing.

in·car·cer·a·tion (ĭn kär′sə rā′shən), *n.* imprisonment; a state of being shut in.

in·ces·sant (ĭn sĕs′ənt), *adj.* never stopping; continuing without interruption. —**in·ces′sant·ly,** *adv.*

in·con·ti·nent (ĭn kŏn′tə nənt), *adj.* lacking in self-control; not restrained.

in·cred·u·lous (ĭn krĕj′ə ləs), *adj.* 1. not inclined to believe; doubting. 2. showing doubt. —**in·cred′u·lous·ly,** *adv.*

in·crus·ta·tion (ĭn′krŭs tā′shən), *n.* 1. a crust or hard layer of some substance on a surface. 2. the process of putting such a coating on a surface.

in·cur (ĭn kûr′), *v.* to bring upon oneself (usually something undesirable): as, *to incur your friend's anger.*

in·do·lent (ĭn′də lənt), *adj.* lazy; disliking work or other exertion.

in·dom·i·ta·ble (ĭn dŏm′ə tə bəl), *adj.* unconquerable; not yielding.

in·ef·fa·ble (ĭn ĕf′ə bəl), *adj.* not capable of being told or expressed in words.

in·ert (ĭn ûrt′), *adj.* 1. not having power to move or to resist other forces. 2. mentally or physically inactive; slow. 3. not having active properties. —**in·ert′ness,** *n.*

in·ev·i·ta·ble (ĭn ĕv′ə tə bəl), *adj.* not able to be avoided, prevented, or escaped; certain to occur, by the nature of things.

in·frac·tion (ĭn frăk′shən), *n.* the breaking of a law, rule, pact, or moral principle; violation.

in·her·ent (ĭn hĭr′ənt), *adj.* existing in something as a natural quality of that thing; inborn; basic: as, *the inherent ferocity of the grizzly bear.*

in·i·ti·ate (ĭ nĭsh′ĭ āt′), *v.* 1. to begin; to get started. 2. to do something for the first time and thus establish that act or process: as, *to initiate a safety campaign.*

in·or·di·nate (ĭn ôr′də nĭt), *adj.* 1. not properly controlled; disorderly. 2. not within accepted limits; unrestrained. —**in·or′di·nate·ly,** *adv.*

In·qui·si·tion (ĭn′kwə zĭsh′ən), *n.* in the Roman Catholic Church, a court (established in the 13th century and abolished in the 19th) to find and punish nonbelievers.

in·sen·sate (ĭn sĕn′sāt, ĭn sĕn′sĭt), *adj.* 1. without feeling; not having sensation. 2. without sense or reason; stupid.

in·ter·ject (ĭn′tər jĕkt′), *v.* to throw (something) in between other things; to interrupt with; to insert.

in·ter·mit·tent (ĭn′tər mĭt′ənt), *adj.* repeatedly stopping and starting; pausing now and then. —**in·ter·mit′tent·ly,** *adv.*

in·ter·ven·ing (ĭn′tər vēn′ĭng), *adj.* 1. coming or lying between: as, *the intervening referee separated the boxers.* 2. separating two points in time: as, *the intervening week between the first and second lesson.*

in·ti·mate (*adj., n.,* ĭn′tə mĭt; *v.,* ĭn′tə māt′), *adj., n., v.* —*adj.* 1. very private or closely personal: as, *an intimate friend.* 2. detailed; deep: as, *an intimate knowledge of a subject.* 3. innermost; deep within: as, *the intimate structure of the atom.* —*n.* a very close friend. —*v.* to hint or suggest. —**in′ti·ma′tion,** *n.*

in·tu·i·tive (ĭn tū′ə tĭv, ĭn tōō′ə tĭv), *adj.* **1.** having an instant, automatic understanding of something. **2.** known without study or reasoning; known instinctively.

in·var·i·a·ble (ĭn vâr′ĭ ə bəl), *adj.* **1.** not changing; always the same; without exception. **2.** with no possibility of changing or being changed. —**in·var′i·a·bly,** *adv.*

in·vest (ĭn vĕst′), *v.* **1.** to put money to use in something which offers a profit. **2.** to clothe, adorn, or cover. **3.** to surround with soldiers; to besiege. **4.** to endow: as, *to invest with confidence.*

ir·ra·tion·al (ĭ răsh′ən əl), *adj.* **1.** unreasonable; not logical. **2.** not having the ability to reason. **3.** not possessing sound judgment.

jeop·ar·dy (jĕp′ər dĭ), *n.* **1.** danger; hazard; risk of loss or injury. **2.** *in law,* exposure to being convicted of a crime; the situation of a person on trial.

lac·er·ate (lăs′ə rāt′), *v.* to tear, mangle, or cut jaggedly.

lan·guor (lăng′gər), *n.* **1.** weakness; lack of vigor and energy. **2.** lack of interest or enthusiasm. **3.** tenderness; emotional softness.

la·tent (lā′tənt), *adj.* hidden but present; existing, but not yet revealed or discovered.

leer (lĭr), *n., v.* —*n.* a sly or insulting glance; a look of bad will or intention. —*v.* to look with evil intention.

le·thar·gic (lĭ thär′jĭk), *adj.* **1.** unusually drowsy or sleepy; dull; sluggish. **2.** not interested; not caring; unresponsive.

lin·e·a·ment (lĭn′ĭ ə mənt), *n.* **1.** any of the features of the face or body, especially in outline. **2.** a distinctive or unusual feature.

list·less (lĭst′lĭs), *adj.* spiritless; lacking interest in what is going on around one

because of fatigue, sickness, or sadness. —**list′less·ly,** *adv.*

lit·er·al (lĭt′ər əl), *adj.* **1.** true to fact; not exaggerated or fanciful. **2.** giving words their direct, not implied, meaning. —**lit′er·al·ly,** *adv.*

mach·i·na·tions (măk′ə nā′shənz), *n.* evil plans; crafty schemes.

ma·lev·o·lent (mə lĕv′ə lənt), *adj.* having evil intentions; showing or wishing ill will to others.

ma·li·cious (mə lĭsh′əs), *adj.* **1.** having a desire to harm; having evil intentions. **2.** ill-willed: as, *malicious gossip.*

ma·lig·nance (mə lĭg′nəns), *n.* **1.** evil intention; spite. **2.** danger; deadliness.

mal·le·a·ble (măl′ĭ ə bəl), *adj.* **1.** able to be pounded or pressed into various shapes without breaking. **2.** adaptable; yielding; able to be formed or trained: as, *a malleable personality.*

man·i·fes·ta·tion (măn′ə fĕs tā′shən), *n.* **1.** the act of showing, of proving, or of making clear. **2.** the thing that shows or illustrates.

me·di·e·val (mē′dĭ ē′vəl, mĕd′ĭ ē′vəl), *adj.* **1.** of or pertaining to the period in history known as the Middle Ages, approximately 500 A.D.-1450 A.D. **2.** in the style of the Middle Ages. **3.** extremely out-of-date.

mel·an·chol·y (mĕl′ən kŏl′ĭ), *adj., n.* —*adj.* **1.** sad; gloomy. **2.** causing sadness: as, *a melancholy fog.* **3.** deeply thoughtful, especially about sad things. —*n.* a state of sadness or a tendency to be sad.

met·tle (mĕt′əl), *n.* **1.** spirit; courage. **2.** quality of character.

min·cing (mĭn′sĭng), *adj.* **1.** speaking, walking, or acting in an unnaturally delicate way. **2.** deliberately dainty.

miz·zle (mĭz′əl), *v.* to drizzle.

mod·i·fi·ca·tion ((mŏd′ə fə kā′shən), *n.* **1.** a partial or minor change. **2.** the process of making such a change. **3.** the result of such a change: as, *the piano is a modification of the harpsichord.*

ăct, āble, dâre, ärt; ĕbb, ēqual; ĭf, īce; hŏt, ōver, ôrder, oil, bŏŏk, ōōze, out; ŭp, ūse, ûrge; ə = *a* in *alone*; ch, chief; g, give; j, judge; ng, ring; sh, shoe; th, thin; ᵵʰ, that; zh, vision. See the full key at the beginning of this glossary.

682   GLOSSARY

mo·tif (mō tēf′), *n.* **1.** a main theme or subject in a work of art, music, or literature. **2.** a repeated or outstanding figure in a design, as of wallpaper.

mul·ti·tu·di·nous (mŭl′tə tū′də nəs, mŭl′tə tōō′də nəs), *adj.* **1.** existing or present in great numbers; very numerous. **2.** having many parts or pieces.

muse (mūz), *v.* **1.** to think quietly. **2.** to think seriously for a long time; to consider carefully.

mus·ter (mŭs′tər), *v., n.* —*v.* **1.** to assemble or gather together (usually soldiers or sailors) for battle, inspection, etc. **2.** to gather, collect, or summon: as, *he mustered up his courage.* —*n.* **1.** a gathering together or collecting, usually of troops, for any purpose. **2.** the body or list of people assembled.

na·ive (nä ēv′), *adj.* having a plain, simple nature; childlike; unsuspecting.

ob·liv·i·ous (ə blĭv′ĭ əs), *adj.* **1.** unaware; unmindful; not giving attention; not noticing (followed by *of* or *to*). **2.** forgetful or causing forgetfulness.

ob·scure (əb skyōōr′), *adj., v.* —*adj.* **1.** not easily seen; not easy to notice. **2.** difficult to understand; not clear. **3.** not well known; not of importance. —*v.* **1.** to make dim, indistinct, hard to see. **2.** to make difficult to understand. **3.** to hide or conceal.

om·i·nous (ŏm′ə nəs), *adj.* threatening; suggesting an approaching evil.

o·paque (ō pāk′), *adj.* **1.** not allowing light to pass through. **2.** difficult to understand.

o·pi·ate (ō′pĭ ĭt, ō′pĭ āt′), *n.* **1.** a drug which contains opium and thus tends to make one sleepy or dull. **2.** anything that causes mental dullness or that soothes the feelings.

op·tion (ŏp′shən), *n.* **1.** a choice. **2.** the right or freedom to choose.

op·u·lence (ŏp′yə ləns), *n.* **1.** wealth. **2.** abundance, especially of resources.

os·cil·la·tion (ŏs′ə lā′shən), *n.* **1.** act or process of moving to and fro. **2.** changeableness; lack of stability; variation in opinion or condition.

pae·an (pē′ən), *n.* a song of triumph, joy, or thanksgiving.

pal·at·a·ble (păl′ət ə bəl), *adj.* tasty; pleasant to taste.

pal·lid (păl′ĭd), *adj.* lacking in color; pale.

pal·lor (păl′ər), *n.* lack of color, especially in the face; paleness.

pal·pa·ble (păl′pə bəl), *adj.* **1.** easily or plainly seen or heard. **2.** capable of being felt, touched, or handled.

pal·pi·tate (păl′pə tāt′), *v.* **1.** to tremble or quiver. **2.** to throb or flutter; to beat rapidly (as the heart).

par·a·sit·ic (păr′ə sĭt′ĭk), *adj.* **1.** living at the expense of another without making any contribution. **2.** receiving food or protection from another: as, *a flea on a dog is parasitic.*

par·ry (păr′ĭ), *v.* **1.** to turn aside, as a blow in boxing or fencing. **2.** to avoid; to evade: as, *to parry a question by not answering or by ignoring it.*

pas·to·ral (păs′tə rəl, päs′tə rəl), *adj.* **1.** having to do with shepherds or their way of life. **2.** having the simple, peaceful quality of the country. **3.** portraying rural life.

pa·tri·arch (pā′trĭ ärk′), *n.* **1.** the father and ruler of a family or a tribe. **2.** a man who is the founder of a business, colony, church, etc. **3.** a man who is very old and respected.

pent (pĕnt), *adj.* shut in; confined; held back.

per·cep·ti·ble (pər sĕp′tə bəl), *adj.* **1.** able to be seen or heard. **2.** noticeable; observable. —**per·cep′ti·bly,** *adv.*

per·cep·tion (pər sĕp′shən), *n.* **1.** consciousness or awareness (of things) gained by means of the senses. **2.** knowledge or understanding gained in this manner. **3.** insight.

per·emp·to·ry (pə rĕmp′tə rĭ, pĕr′əmp tōr′ĭ), *adj.* **1.** not able to be refused, denied, or opposed. **2.** so positive and decisive (as a statement) that it can not be questioned or debated.

per·si·flage (pûr′sə fläzh), *n.* 1. a light, easy style of writing or speaking. 2. playful or joking talk.

per·tur·ba·tion (pûr′tər bā′shən), *n.* 1. state of being mentally upset or bothered. 2. agitation; alarm.

pet·tish (pĕt′ish), *adj.* peevish; ill-natured; cross. —**pet′tish·ly,** *adv.*

pic·tur·esque (pĭk′chə rĕsk′), *adj.* 1. picturelike; suggesting a picture; having natural beauty; colorful. 2. leaving a strong, lifelike visual impression.

plac·id (plăs′id), *adj.* quietly peaceful; pleasantly calm.

por·tal (pōr′təl), *n.* a door or any other entrance, especially a large, impressive one.

pre·car·i·ous (prĭ kâr′ĭ əs), *adj.* 1. uncertain; unreliable; dependent on changeable circumstances. 2. dangerous; risky.

pred·a·to·ry (prĕd′ə tōr′ĭ), *adj.* 1. pertaining to robbery or plunder. 2. habitually preying upon other animals. 3. living by taking advantage of others.

pre·cip·i·tate (*v.,* prĭ sĭp′ə tāt′; *n.,* prĭ sĭp′ə tāt′; *adj.,* prĭ sĭp′ə tĭt), *v., n., adj.* —*v.* 1. to cause to happen before desired or planned; to hasten an occurrence. 2. to cast or hurl down. 3. *in chemistry,* to separate out or settle something in a solution. —*n.* 1. moisture condensed, as rain, snow, etc. 2. any substance separated out of a solution. —*adj.* 1. falling abruptly; flowing steeply downward. 2. happening suddenly; very hasty.

pre·dom·i·nance (prĭ dŏm′ə nəns), *n.* 1. authority, power, control, or influence over others. 2. superiority because of numbers, size, position, etc.

pri·mal (prī′məl), *adj.* 1. original; first. 2. most important.

prime (prīm), *v.* 1. to prepare or make ready. 2. to prepare a gun for firing. 3. to start the action of a pump by pouring water into the cylinder.

pro·cliv·i·ty (prō klĭv′ə tĭ), *n.* 1. a natural tendency; an inborn inclination. 2. a habitual leaning toward something, especially something discreditable: as, *a proclivity to crime.*

pros·trate (prŏs′trāt), *v., adj.* —*v.* 1. to lay (something) flat on the ground. 2. to overcome by weakness, fatigue, or exhaustion. —*adj.* 1. lying face down on the ground. 2. in a condition of weakness or helplessness.

prov·i·dence (prŏv′ə dəns), *n.* 1. the care or guidance provided to man and the world by God or nature. 2. divine or supreme direction of events. —**prov′i·den′tial,** *adj.*

pro·vin·cial (prə vĭn′shəl), *adj.* 1. having to do with a province or small local area, as contrasted with a nation or other large area. 2. having qualities of people in the provinces; simple; countrified.

pum·mel (pŭm′əl), *v.* to strike or beat, as with the fists.

pun·gent (pŭn′jənt), *adj.* 1. producing a sharp, biting taste or smell. 2. *of language,* cutting; sarcastic; sometimes stimulating; expressive.

qua·ver (kwā′vər), *v.* 1. to shake or tremble. 2. to speak or sing with a shaky, quivering voice; as when one is afraid or very sad.

quiz·zi·cal (kwĭz′ə kəl), *adj.* 1. odd; queer. 2. ridiculing; teasing; making fun of others. 3. questioning.

ra·tion·al·ize (răsh′ən ə līz′), *v.* 1. to explain reasonably and logically. 2. to invent explanations for one's behavior.

re·cip·ro·cate (rĭ sĭp′rə kāt′), *v.* to give or do in return: as, *to reciprocate greetings.*

ăct, āble, dâre, ärt; ĕbb, ēqual; ĭf, īce; hŏt, ōver, ôrder, oil, bŏŏk, ōōze, out; ŭp, ūse, ûrge; ə = a in *alone;* ch, chief; g, give; j, judge; ng, ring; sh, shoe; th, thin; th, that; zh, vision. See the full key at the beginning of this glossary.

GLOSSARY

rec·on·cil·i·a·tion (rĕk'ən sĭl i ā'shən), *n.* **1.** act of bringing (opponents or differing statements) into agreement. **2.** act of bringing into harmony two things or ideas that had been at odds. **3.** state of being in harmony or agreement.

re·con·nais·sance (rĭ kŏn'ə səns), *n.* a survey or examination of an area, usually either to discover its physical features or to learn what an enemy is doing.

re·con·noi·ter (rē'kə noi'tər, rĕk'ə noi'tər), *v.* **1.** to inspect, examine, or survey an area, particularly to view an enemy's position. **2.** to study a region for scientific or commercial purposes.

re·crim·i·na·tion (rĭ krĭm'ə nā'shən), *n.* an accusation in reply to another's accusation.

re·cum·bent (rĭ kŭm'bənt), *adj.* **1.** lying down or leaning. **2.** inactive; at rest.

re·fec·tory (rĭ fĕk'tə rĭ), *n.* a dining hall in a religious institution or a college.

re·flec·tive (rĭ flĕk'tĭv), *adj.* **1.** reflecting; cast back by reflection; mirroring. **2.** thoughtful; given to serious thinking. —**re·flec'·tive·ly,** *adv.*

re·flex·ive (rĭ flĕk'sĭv), *adj.* done automatically without intention; responding in an unplanned way, as when sneezing or blinking the eyes.

re·it·er·ate (rē ĭt'ə rāt'), *v.* to say again; to repeat or do again and again.

re·join·der (rĭ join'dər), *n.* an answer to a reply.

rem·i·nis·cence (rĕm'ə nĭs'əns), *n.* the act of recalling things of the past.

re·mote (rĭ mōt'), *adj.* far away; distant in space, time, etc.

ren·der (rĕn'dər), *v.* **1.** to do; perform. **2.** to make or cause. **3.** to provide: as, *to render assistance.*

ren·di·tion (rĕn dĭsh'ən), *n.* a performance.

ren·e·gade (rĕn'ə gād'), *n.* a person who gives up or turns away from his religion, friends, principles, etc.; a deserter.

re·plen·ish (rĭ plĕn'ĭsh), *v.* **1.** to fill up again; to renew a supply. **2.** to supply with fresh or additional fuel.

re·press (rĭ prĕs'), *v.* **1.** to hold down; to keep back: as, *to repress a yawn.* **2.** to check or keep under control: as, *to repress anger.*

re·pug·nance (rĭ pŭg'nəns), *n.* **1.** extreme dislike or distaste. **2.** contradictoriness.

re·sil·i·ence (rĭ zĭl'ĭ əns), *n.* **1.** ability or tendency to return to original form after being bent, squeezed, etc.; elastic quality. **2.** ability to recover strength, happiness, or other traits which have been absent for a time.

ret·i·cent (rĕt'ə sənt), *adj.* not inclined to speak; not talkative; usually silent. —**ret'·i·cence,** *n.*

rev·er·ent (rĕv'ər ənt), *adj.* deeply respectful; showing or feeling great love and respect. —**rev'·er·ent·ly,** *adv.* —**rev'·er·en'·tial,** *adj.*

rev·er·ie (rĕv'ə rĭ), *n.* **1.** dreamy thinking, especially of pleasant things. **2.** a daydream.

re·viv·i·fy (rē vĭv'ə fĭ'), *v.* **1.** to put new life into; to make lively. **2.** to revive.

re·vul·sion (rĭ vŭl'shən), *n.* **1.** a sudden, complete change of feeling, as from love to hate. **2.** act of drawing back or away; withdrawal.

roist·er·ous (rois'tər əs), *adj.* acting, frolicking, or celebrating in a noisy, rowdy, or swaggering manner.

ruse (rōōz), *n.* a trick.

rus·tic (rŭs'tĭk), *adj., n.* —*adj.* **1.** of the country, as contrasted with cities or towns; rural. **2.** lacking refinement, culture, or polish; simple, plain, and natural. **3.** rough, crude, and socially awkward. —*n.* a country person, especially one who is rough and uncultured.

sal·low (săl'ō), *adj.* having a sickly, pale yellow color.

san·guine (săng'gwĭn), *adj.* **1.** cheerful and hopeful. **2.** having the color of blood; red.

sa·vor (sā'vər), *v., n.* —*v.* **1.** to give flavor or odor to. **2.** to enjoy a taste or smell. —*n.* **1.** a certain taste or odor. **2.** ability to arouse interest or excitement.

scru·ple (skrōō'pəl), *n.* hesitation or reluctance due to uncertainty as to whether a certain act is right, proper, or honest.

scru·ti·ny (skrōō'tə nǐ), *n.*   a careful examination; a detailed study or inspection.

se·cu·ri·ties (sǐ kyōōr'ə tǐz), *n. pl.*   stocks and bonds or other certificates of business ownership.

sed·en·tary (sĕd'ən tĕr'ǐ), *adj.*   1. involving much sitting rather than moving about.   2. not physically active.

se·duce (sǐ dūs', sǐ dōōs'), *v.*   to lead one to do something disloyal, illegal, immoral, or contrary to principles.

self-de·pre·ci·a·tion (sĕlf'dǐ prē'shǐ ā'shən), *n.*   act of representing oneself as being of little value; giving a low estimate of one's own worth or importance.

self-suf·fic·ing (self'sə fīs'ǐng), *adj.*   1. able to get along without help.   2. independent.

sen·su·ous (sĕn'shōō əs), *adj.*   1. of, based on, or appealing to the senses of sight, hearing, touch, etc.   2. enjoying the pleasures of the senses.

se·ques·tered (sǐ kwĕs'tərd), *adj.*   secluded; apart from others; out-of-the-way.

shod (shŏd), *adj.*   provided with shoes or other foot coverings.

shrew (shrōō), *n.*   an ill-tempered woman.

sim·u·late (sǐm'yə lāt'), *v.*   1. to look or act like; to imitate, deliberately or accidentally.   2. to pretend; to give a false indication of a feeling or a condition: as, *to simulate happiness.*

si·mul·ta·ne·ous (sī'məl tā'nǐ əs, sǐm'əl tā' nǐ-əs), *adj.*   existing or happening at the same time; occurring together.   —**si'·mul·ta'·ne·ous·ly,** *adv.*

sin·gu·lar (sǐng'gyə lər), *adj.*   1. unusual; strange.   2. individual; being the only one of a type; separate; single.

skep·ti·cism (skĕp'tə sǐz'əm), *n.*   1. a doubting or disbelieving attitude.   2. doubt or disbelief concerning religion.

sol·ace (sŏl'ĭs), *n.*   1. something that eases or relieves grief, sorrow, distress, or discomfort.   2. comfort which comes when one is in trouble or sorrow.

so·lic·it·ous (sə lĭs'ə təs), *adj.*   1. showing concern or attention: as, *he was solicitous for his passenger's comfort.*   2. showing eager desire, especially for the approval or friendship of other people.

som·ber (sŏm'bər), *adj.*   1. dark and gloomy; shadowy; dimly lit.   2. mentally gloomy or sad.

som·no·lent (sŏm'nə lənt), *adj.*   1. drowsy, sleepy.   2. causing drowsiness or sleep.

spawn (spôn), *v., n.*   —*v.* to give birth to; to bring forth.   —*n.* 1. the mass of eggs of fish or other sea life.   2. something produced, usually in great numbers, and often considered of little value.

spo·rad·ic (spō răd'ĭk), *adj.*   1. happening at uneven intervals; occasional.   2. occurring or appearing alone or in scattered instances: as, *sporadic tornadoes.*

squal·or (skwôl'ər), *n.*   filth, misery.

squeam·ish (shwē'mĭsh), *adj.*   1. easily shocked by things which are offensive to the senses.   2. excessively dainty, modest, or fussy.

stac·ca·to (stə kä'tô), *adj.*   disconnected, abrupt (said of sounds or musical tones).

stat·ic (stăt'ĭk), *adj.*   having a fixed or stationary condition; not moving or active.

stilt·ed (stĭl'tĭd), *adj.*   acting, speaking, or writing in a stiff, unnaturally formal manner.

stim·u·lus (stĭm'yə ləs), *n.*   something that rouses to action or increases action or thought: as, *the smell of food is a stimulus to a dog.*

sto·ic (stō'ĭk), *n.*   a person who shows very little emotion, who expresses neither grief nor joy; one who holds back his feelings.

stra·ta (strā'tə, străt'ə), *n.*   horizontal layers of something such as rock, usually with the layers lying one upon another.   *pl.* of **stratum.**

ăct, āble, dâre, ärt; ĕbb, ēqual; ǐf, īce; hŏt, ōver, ôrder, oil, bŏŏk, ōōze, out; ŭp, ūse, ûrge; ə = a in *alone*; ch, chief; g, give; j, judge; ng, ring; sh, shoe; th, thin; **th,** that; zh, vision. See the full key at the beginning of this glossary.

sub·ju·gate (sŭb′jə gāt′), **1.** to conquer or subdue; to bring under control. **2.** to assert mastery over; thus, to make (something or someone) inferior.

sub·se·quent (sŭb′sə kwənt), *adj.* coming later; following in time or sequence. —**sub′se·quent·ly**, *adv.*

sub·tle·ty (sŭt′əl tĭ), *n.* **1.** the ability to make fine judgments between things that are only slightly different. **2.** mental sharpness. **3.** a refinement or nicety of character, thought, or argument.

su·per·flu·ous (soo pûr′floo əs), *adj.* **1.** more than is needed or wanted; surplus. **2.** not necessary.

sur·ly (sûr′lĭ), *adj.* rude; bad-tempered.

sur·mise (sər mīz′), *v., n.* —*v.* to conclude or infer on the basis of incomplete evidence. —*n.* a thought or opinion arrived at on the basis of evidence that is not certain or complete; an educated guess.

sur·mount (sər mount′), **1.** to conquer or overcome. **2.** to get on top of or above.

sur·rep·ti·tious (sûr′əp tĭsh′əs), *adj.* **1.** done or made in secret or in a sneaky manner. **2.** acting in a secret, sneaky way.

swathe (swāth), *v.* to wrap in some material; to surround; to enclose.

syl·van (sĭl′vən), *adj., n.* —*adj.* **1.** of the woods or forests. **2.** wooded or woody. —*n.* a person who lives in a wooded area.

sym·bol·ize (sĭm′bə līz′), *v.* **1.** to represent or stand for; to be a symbol of. **2.** to represent by symbols. —**sym·bol·ic** (sĭm bŏl′ĭk), *adj.*

tac·i·turn (tăs′ə tûrn′), *adj.* not inclined to talk; usually silent.

tan·gi·ble (tăn′jə bəl), *adj.* **1.** capable of being touched. **2.** real; actual.

tarry (tăr′ĭ), *v.* **1.** to remain; to stay. **2.** to wait. **3.** to delay; to be tardy.

taut (tôt), *adj.* **1.** tightly drawn: as, *a taut wire.* **2.** tense: as, *taut nerves.* **3.** neat; tidy; orderly.

taw·dry (tô′drĭ), *adj.* cheap and gaudy; showy.

tax·i·der·my (tăk′sə dûr′mĭ), *n.* the art of preparing, stuffing, and mounting animal skins in lifelike form.

te·na·cious (tĭ nā′shəs), *adj.* **1.** clinging fast; holding tightly. **2.** able to hang on, keep, or retain: as, *a tenacious memory.* **3.** sticky; adhesive. **4.** stubborn; clinging tightly to an idea.

ten·dril (tĕn′drĭl), *n.* a leafless, threadlike part of a climbing plant, which coils around objects in order to hold up the plant.

ten·u·ous (tĕn′yoo əs), *adj.* **1.** thin or slender. **2.** not dense; rare, as air at high altitudes. **3.** not substantial; flimsy: as, *a tenuous excuse.*

tol·er·a·ble (tŏl′ər ə bəl), *adj.* **1.** bearable; endurable; capable of being tolerated or put up with. **2.** acceptable in quality.

tol·er·ant (tŏl′ər ənt), *adj.* able to put up with ideas or experiences that are displeasing.

tor·tu·ous (tôr′choo əs), *adj.* **1.** winding; crooked; full of twists and turns. **2.** not direct; deceiving; immoral.

tran·sient (trăn′shənt), *adj.* temporary; not permanent; passing away with time.

trans·pose (trăns pōz′), *v.* to change the order of.

trans·verse (trăns vûrs′, trănz vûrs′), *adj.* crosswise; lying across or placed across; crossing from one side to the other.

trea·tise (trē′tĭs), *n.* a formal book or other writing which treats a particular subject.

trep·i·da·tion (trĕp′ə dā′shən), *n.* **1.** fear; alarm. **2.** trembling movement.

trib·u·la·tion (trĭb′yə lā′shən), *n.* serious trouble or distress; great misery.

tu·mul·tu·ous (tū mŭl′choo əs, too mŭl′choo əs), *adj.* **1.** marked by uproar; noisy and confused. **2.** mentally upset or agitated.

un·couth (ŭn kooth′), *adj.* **1.** rude; uncultured; unmannerly. **2.** awkward and ungraceful in form or appearance.

un·du·late (un′dyə lāt′, un′də lāt′), *v.* **1.** to cause a wavy up and down movement or appearance. **2.** to move in a wavy manner. —**un′·du·la′·tion**, *n.*

un·flag·ging (ŭn flăg′ĭng), *adj.* not drooping; remaining strong, alert, and spirited: as, *his unflagging determination.*

un·im·ped·ed (ŭn′ĭm pēd′ĭd), *adj.* not hindered, obstructed, or limited in activity or progress.

un·let·tered (ŭn lĕt′ərd), *adj.* 1. ignorant; uneducated. 2. unable to read and write.

un·mit·i·gated (ŭn mĭt′ə gā′tĭd), *adj.* 1. not lessened, eased, or softened: as, *unmitigated pain.* 2. not modified; absolute: as, *an unmitigated scoundrel.*

un·par·al·leled (ŭn păr′ə leld′), *adj.* unmatched; having no equal.

un·re·quit·ed (ŭn′rĭ kwĭt′ĭd), *adj.* not returned; not given back in return: as, *unrequited love.*

un·swerv·ing (ŭn swûrv′ĭng), *adj.* not turning away from a course of action or an opinion, but remaining constant: as, *her unswerving faith sustained her.*

veg·e·tate (vĕj′ə tāt′), *v.* 1. to grow like a plant. 2. to lead an inactive life.

ve·he·ment (vē′ə mənt), *adj.* 1. full of intense, deep feeling. 2. characterized by eager or violent feeling, action, or effort. —**ve′he·ment·ly,** *adv.* —**ve′he·mence,** *n.*

ven·er·a·ble (vĕn′ər ə bəl), *adj.* 1. worthy of respect because of age, dignity, character, or office. 2. respected because of historic or religious importance.

ver·ba·tim (vər bā′tĭm), *adv.* word for word; using exactly the same words.

ver·i·fy (vĕr′ə fī′), *v.* to prove to be true; to confirm.

vex·a·tion (vĕks ā′shən), *n.* 1. state of annoyance, of being troubled, disturbed, or angry. 2. the cause of such annoyance or distress.

vi·al (vī′əl), *n.* a small container, often glass, for fluids.

vig·i·lance (vĭj′ə ləns), *n.* watchfulness; alertness to danger.

vir·ile (vĭr′əl), *adj.* 1. manly; masculine. 2. strong; vigorous; forceful.

vis·ta (vĭs′tə), *n.* 1. a view, especially one seen through a long passage or avenue of trees. 2. a long row of trees framing a view. 3. an extensive mental view.

vo·cif·er·ous (vō sĭf′ər əs), *adj.* shouting noisily; clamorous; crying out loudly.

vol·u·ble (vŏl′yə bəl), *adj.* characterized by a free flow of words; talking a great deal.

waft (wăft, wäft), *v., n.* —*v.* to move or carry lightly over the air or through the water, as a sound or an odor. —*n.* 1. an odor or sound carried on the air: as, *a waft of music.* 2. a puff of wind.

wan (wŏn), *adj.* 1. having a sickly pale color; nearly colorless. 2. suggesting poor health, weakness, or fatigue.

warp (wôrp), *v.* 1. to twist, bend, or curve. 2. to turn from the natural path. 3. to twist the facts or the truth.

wend (wĕnd), *v.* 1. to travel; to go. 2. to direct one's own way; to proceed.

wist·ful (wĭst′fəl), *adj.* showing a sad wishfulness; thoughtful longing.

ăct, āble, dâre, ärt; ĕbb, ēqual; ĭf, īce; hŏt, ōver, ôrder, oil, bŏŏk, ōōze, out; ŭp, ūse, ûrge; ə = a in *alone*; ch, chief; g, give; j, judge; ng, ring; sh, shoe; th, thin; th, that; zh, vision. See the full key at the beginning of this glossary.

GLOSSARY

Contents by Types

Narrative Poems

Plays

Stories

Index to Authors and Titles

Where there are two or more page references, the last one refers to a brief biographical sketch of the author.